A SAVAGE CONFLICT

A SAVAGE

CIVIL WAR AMERICA *Gary W. Gallagher, editor*

CONFLICT

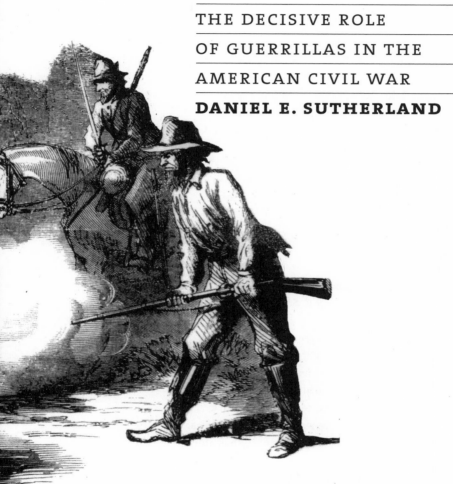

THE DECISIVE ROLE
OF GUERRILLAS IN THE
AMERICAN CIVIL WAR

DANIEL E. SUTHERLAND

The University of North Carolina Press *Chapel Hill*

Set in Miller, Madrone, and The Serif types
by Tseng Information Systems, Inc.
Manufactured in the United States of America

The paper in this book meets the guidelines for
permanence and durability of the Committee on
Production Guidelines for Book Longevity of the
Council on Library Resources.

The University of North Carolina Press has been a
member of the Green Press Initiative since 2003.

Library of Congress
Cataloging-in-Publication Data
Sutherland, Daniel E.
A savage conflict : the decisive role of guerrillas in the
American Civil War / Daniel E. Sutherland. — 1st ed.
    p. cm. — (Civil War America)
Includes bibliographical references and index.
ISBN 978-0-8078-3277-6 (cloth : alk. paper)
1. United States—History—Civil War, 1861–
1865—Underground movements. 2. Guerrilla
warfare—United States—History—19th century.
3. Guerrilla warfare—Confederate States of America.
4. Guerrillas—United States—History—19th century.
5. Guerrillas—Confederate States of America. I. Title.
E470.S89 2009
973.7'3013—dc22   2008050475

13 12 11 10 09   5 4 3 2 1

For the Wee One,
Lilith Eire Rain Sutherland

CONTENTS

Preface ix

Acknowledgments xv

Prologue: Baltimore 1

Part I: Beginnings *(Spring–Summer 1861)*

1. A People's War 9

2. A Border War 26

3. A Delayed War 41

Part II: Rules of the Game *(Fall 1861–Summer 1862)*

4. Stringent Orders 57

5. Sanctioning Barbarity 76

6. Not the West Point Way 99

Part III: Democracy Run Amok *(Fall 1862–Summer 1863)*

7. Communities of Bitter Memories 121

8. In Bad Repute 145

9. Some Definite Policy 171

Part IV: Day of the Outlaw *(Fall 1863–1864)*

10. So Tired of War 193

11. A Terror to the Citizens 220

12. One Vast Missouri 246

Epilogue: 1865 267

Notes 281

Bibliography 357

Index 421

ILLUSTRATIONS AND MAPS

Illustrations

Baltimore, April 19, 1861 3

Destroying a railroad 22

Meeting of Tennessee Unionists 36

Civilian refugees 62

John Hunt Morgan's raiders 79

Death of General Robert L. McCook 85

Policing blacks in Mississippi 112

Guerrillas hunting guerrillas 137

Protecting a railroad 148

Guerrillas versus a gunboat 150

A Unionist scout 176

The sack of Lawrence 195

Bush-Whackers, Beware! 207

Lynching the enemy 231

John Mosby's men in action 241

A destroyed home and lives ruined 255

Maps

1. The Trans-Mississippi 69

2. The Border South and Lower Midwest 88

3. The Deep South 108

Most people think of the American Civil War as a clash of mighty armies. The so-called guerrillas of the war, we have been told, barely qualified as a "sideshow." They certainly did not influence how the war was fought or decide its outcome. I believe that view of things may be wrong. This is not to deny the generals and battles their due, but it is also true that the great campaigns often obscure as much as they reveal. In point of fact, it is impossible to understand the Civil War without appreciating the scope and impact of the guerrilla conflict, although that is no easy thing to do. The guerrilla side of the war was intense and sprawling, born in controversy, and defined by all variety of contradictions, contours, and shadings. In the face of such complexity, wisdom dictates a sketch of the story to come.

Large numbers of Confederates wanted to fight as guerrillas in the spring of 1861. Southern history and culture drew them to this style of warfare, and they never questioned its value. Rebel leaders were not so sure. They knew the historical precedents for guerrilla warfare, not least of all in the American Revolution, but they also considered it slightly dishonorable. An extensive guerrilla war also seemed likely to undermine military discipline and cohesiveness, and it most certainly defied the wisdom of conventional military strategies. Even so, when forced to employ guerrillas in the early months of the war, Confederate leaders found them extremely useful. Guerrillas helped check invading armies at every turn. They distracted the Federals from their primary objectives, caused them to alter strategies, injured the morale of Union troops, and forced the reassignment of men and resources to counter threats to railroads, river traffic, and foraging parties. They shielded communities, stymied Union efforts to occupy the South, and spread panic throughout the lower Midwest. The politicians and generals could not have hoped for more, and so they vacillated, never fully endorsing their guerrillas but uncertain how best and how long to use them. History had shown that guerrillas could not win wars on their own, but rebel leaders knew not how to make them part of some broader plan.

This indecisiveness hurt the Confederates. Guerrillas grew increasingly independent and ungovernable, very nearly waging their own war. They also drew a devastating response from the enemy. Seeing the dangers posed by guerrillas to their own military operations, the Federals retaliated. They treated rebel guerrillas as brigands, not soldiers, and they punished rebel civilians who supported or encouraged guerrilla warfare. That was not all. As Union armies encountered an entire countryside arrayed against them—guerrillas in the bush, citizens cheering them on—U.S. military and political leaders realized that winning the conventional battles would not end the war. They must also crush rebellion on the southern home front. This revelation yielded profound changes in Union military policies and strategy. Those changes, in turn, produced a more brutal and destructive war that led to Confederate defeat.

This sketch summarizes the military story, but important social elements in the guerrilla war also caused disarray. First, southerners who opposed the Confederacy formed their own guerrilla bands and clashed with rebel neighbors in violent contests for political and economic control of their communities. These local struggles often caused people to lose sight of the national goals—union or independence—that had inspired the war. The need to maintain law and order reigned supreme. In places where Unionists gained the upper hand, or where rebel guerrillas could not ward off occupation by Union armies, the Confederate war effort splintered. Rebel citizens blamed their government for failing to protect them; winning distant battles became less important than preserving homes. Then the guerrilla war bred cancerous mutations. Violent bands of deserters, draft dodgers, and genuine outlaws operated as guerrillas to prey on loyal Confederates and defend themselves against rebel authorities. This broadened the South's internal war, and where deserters and draft dodgers made common cause with armed Unionists and slaves, anarchy prevailed.

By 1865, support for the Confederacy had eroded badly. People who had entered the war as loyal Confederates came to believe their government could not protect them. Surrounded by violence, all semblance of order—and with it civilization—seemed to collapse. People who originally looked to local guerrillas for defense blamed them for much of the ruin, but they also cursed the government. It was the government's inability to protect them that had led many communities to rely on guerrillas in the first place. Then, as Union armies retaliated, and mutant forms of the guerrilla war engulfed them, those same people saw that their leaders could not control the upheaval. They lost their stomach for war.

What follows is a narrative of that guerrilla war. It is best to proceed in this way—chronologically, rather than topically—because the unfolding of events over time is vital for understanding how, why, and when things happened. Besides, there are some clear chronological breaks in the guerrilla story. I have not described every guerrilla action or provided a history of every guerrilla band. Beyond the impossibility of the thing, such an approach contributes little to appreciating larger issues. The book, then, is divided into four sections, each with a loosely defined theme. Each section has three chapters, with one chapter in each section telling the story of a different geographical region, roughly the Trans-Mississippi, the upper South, and the Deep South, although the lower Midwest also makes an occasional appearance.

Now, a few words about definitions. It should be acknowledged from the start that the name *guerrilla*, used broadly here to describe the participants in this irregular war, is fraught with difficulties. To start with, rebel guerrillas frequently preferred the name *partisan*, and indeed, for at least the first year of the war, the two names were interchangeable. Then, in the spring of 1862, the Confederacy used the name "partisan," or "partisan ranger," to identify its "official," government-sanctioned guerrillas. Unlike regular guerrillas, who decided for themselves where, when, how, and against whom to fight, partisans were expected to obey army regulations and coordinate their movements with local military commanders. Generally mounted and organized in company- or battalion-sized units, they operated on "detached service" to provide reconnaissance, conduct raids, and attack small groups of enemy soldiers.

Yet, beyond this fairly clear distinction between independent and official guerrillas, Civil War irregulars came in a variety of shapes, sizes, and persuasions. I use the name *bushwhacker* to represent a third general and very amorphous category. Bushwhackers were, strictly speaking, lone gunmen who "whacked" their foes from the "bush." However, the name also became a pejorative term for anyone who apparently killed people or destroyed property for sport, out of meanness, or in a personal vendetta. It bore the taint of cowardly behavior. All of the outlaws, deserters, and ruffians who behaved like guerrillas fall into this category, but then many Union soldiers referred to all guerrillas as bushwhackers. And the list continues. Some guerrillas and partisans called themselves *scouts*, *raiders*, or *rangers*, and not a few home guards and militia companies operated as guerrillas. On the Union side, there were *Red Legs*, *buffaloes*, and *jayhawkers*, although jayhawker, like bushwhacker, gained more universal application. The Union army tried to define its wily rebel foes more precisely midway through the war, but the resulting list, which included *bandits* and *marauders*, did little to clarify matters. There was also much swapping of identities, with partisans often becoming mere guerrillas and guerrillas calling themselves partisans or behaving like bushwhackers.

It must be said, though, that at least two things defined nearly all "guerrillas," whatever they called themselves, whatever other people called them, or on whichever side they fought. First, there was the "irregular" way they attacked, harassed, and worried their foes, quite unlike the methods used by regular soldiers in conventional armies. Second, their principal responsibility, their very reason for being in most cases, was local defense, protection of their families or communities against both internal and external foes. Guerrillas often stretched and tested the second of these conditions, especially the rebels, and especially early in the war, when men volunteered from everywhere to halt the invasion of the upper South. Still, even then, they considered defense of the Confederacy's borders as tantamount to sparing their own states the enemy's presence. If this is a somewhat elusive, ungainly, and untidy definition, it only reflects the nature of the guerrilla war.

The same elusiveness confounds efforts to determine the number of guerrillas. We know approximately how many men served in the Union and Confederate armies, but few documents, such as muster rolls and pension applications, have survived to tell us the number of guerrillas. Some thirty-odd years ago, Albert Castel, one of the first scholarly authorities on Civil War irregulars, estimated that as many as 26,550 Union and Confederate guerrillas participated in the conflict, but that number is surely low, perhaps by as much as half. Castel excluded Confederate partisans from his tally, calculated a mere 600 guerrillas as the total for six states, and estimated no more than 300 rebel guerrillas (missing the Unionists entirely) in all of Alabama and Mississippi. In truth, we do not even know how many bands of guerrillas operated during the war, much less the number of individuals. The story to follow will show in a variety of ways that many, many guerrillas roamed the wartime South, but it is impossible to supply precise figures. Besides, it may well be argued that precise figures are irrelevant. The central story of the guerrilla war is not so much the number of participants as their impact on military operations, government policies, and public morale.

Finally, a word about historical comparisons. Despite the world's current—and understandable—interest in what has come to be known as *asymmetrical* or *compound* warfare, I have resisted using the nineteenth century to probe the twenty-first century. All guerrilla wars bear similarities, but time, geography, and circumstances cannot disguise their frequent differences. Insights and lessons may doubtless be drawn from the 1860s, but any systematic comparison to the present must necessarily diminish the message I want to convey. References are made to the guerrillas of the American Revolution and the Mexican War because they influenced the thinking of Americans during the Civil War era. Likewise, guerrilla resistance against Napoleon in Spain anticipated America's war in nearly every respect, from the organization and objectives of guerrilla fighters to the response of citizens and governments to their style of warfare. But all that is peripheral to my main interest, which is to show how the guerrilla conflict, especially as waged by the Confederates, helped decide the outcome of the Civil War.

ACKNOWLEDGMENTS

Thanking people in a project of this sort, which began fifteen years ago, is always a treacherous business. It is inevitable that someone will be forgotten, and so I apologize at the outset for any lapses of memory.

Naturally, and at the forefront, I am grateful to the scores of archivists and librarians who have placed the raw materials of history at my disposal. They include the entire staffs of the institutions listed in my bibliography, but I also recall the following people as having been particularly kind, generous, and obliging: Ann Evans Alley and Julia D. Rather of the Tennessee State Library and Archives, Gary Arnold and Connie Conners of the Ohio Historical Society, David Bartlett of the West Virginia and Regional History Collection at West Virginia University, John M. Coski of the Museum of the Confederacy, Elizabeth Dunn of Special Collections at Duke University, Richard Shrader of the Southern Historical Collection at the University of North Carolina at Chapel Hill, John Fowler of the Louisiana State Archives, Henry G. Fulmer of the South Caroliniana Library at the University of South Carolina, John C. Konzal and David F. Moore of the Western Historical Manuscript Collection at the University of Missouri, John T. Kneebone of the Library of Virginia, Michael Musik of the National Archives, Dennis Northcott of the Missouri Historical Society, Frances S. Pollard of the Virginia Historical Society, James M. Prichard of the Kentucky Department of Libraries and Archives, Cheryl Schnirring of the Illinois State Historical Library, Geoffrey W. Scott of the Indiana State Archives, Brandon Slone at the Kentucky Military History Museum, William B. Statzer III of the Wyllie Library at the University of Virginia's College at Wise, and Michael Veach of the Filson Club Historical Society.

More personal assistance has been given, either by way of advice, information, or research materials, by Anne J. Bailey, Terry L. Beckenbaugh, Keith Bohannon, Joseph G. Dawson III, William Furry, Bertil Haggman, Kevin Hasely, Leo E. Huff, James J. Johnston, Robert R. Mackey, Matt Matthews, Clay Mountcastle, the late Phillip S. Paludan, T. Michael Parrish, Jeffery S. Prushankin, George C. Rable, Troy J. Sacquety, Harold Selesky, Samuel Solberg, Emory M. Thomas, and Frank J. Wetta. Several generations of graduate research assistants have strained their eyes and contributed their energy to the cause. They include James Bird, James Finck, Michael Johnson, Michael McCoy, Jeremy Taylor, Monica Taylor, and Gary Zellar at the University of Arkansas, and Gardner Mundy at the University of Richmond. Stephen V. Ash, Joseph Fitzharris, Perry D. Jamieson, James M. McPherson, and Carol Reardon provided useful comments on essays or conference papers that became part of this larger work, and I have profited from the analysis of Gary W. Gallagher and Kenneth W. Noe, who read the completed manuscript for the University of North Carolina Press. I am especially grateful, profoundly so, to Michael Fellman, the dean of Civil War guerrilla studies, for reading a much earlier, much longer, and much less polished draft. And I must not forget the superb copyediting of Stevie Champion.

Research grants were offered at various stages of the project by the National Endowment for the Humanities, Andrew J. Mellon Foundation, Virginia Historical Society, and Fulbright College, University of Arkansas. A semester spent as the Douglas Southall Freeman Professor at the University of Richmond provided much needed time and support during the writing phase. Thank you especially to Hugh A. West, John L. Gordon, John D. Treadway, Earnest C. Bolt Jr., and Blues Brother Robert C. Kenzer. And thanks also to Jeannie M. Whayne, who encouraged me to write an essay about guerrillas in Civil War Arkansas all those years ago.

A SAVAGE CONFLICT

A frenzy of patriotic display greeted the 6th Massachusetts Infantry Regiment—700 men strong—as it marched through New York City on Thursday, April 18, 1861. Fort Sumter had surrendered just four days earlier. It had been only three days since President Abraham Lincoln asked for 75,000 volunteers to crush the southern rebellion. Yet here were the New Englanders, already parading proudly through the great American metropolis. New York had more than its share of rebel sympathizers, but on this day, U.S. flags, banners, and bunting festooned the old town. "Immense crowd; immense cheering," reported a local lawyer of the 5,000 and more people. "My eyes filled with tears, and I was half choked in sympathy with the contagious excitement. God be praised for the unity of feeling here! It is beyond, very far beyond, anything I hoped for. If it only last, we are safe."[1]

Safe? A curious choice of words, one would think. New York, safe? Well, surely so. Perhaps the gentleman meant that the nation was safe, that such fervor promised the Union would be preserved. Yet the day's newspapers had caused the lawyer to think not only of the war's outcome, but also of how it would be fought, and on that score, he believed no fouler gang of cutthroats than the so-called Confederate States had ever claimed the title "government." Their president, Jefferson Davis, had issued letters of marque to any sea captain who would attack northern shipping. This "'Algerine' Confederacy" advocated piracy, plain and simple, decided the lawyer.[2]

Other northerners shared the New Yorker's fears that the United States faced an unscrupulous foe prepared to wage a barbarous war. The next day justified those fears, not on the high seas, but in the streets of Baltimore, Maryland. By midmorning of April 19, the 6th Massachusetts had passed through New York to arrive by rail at the southern city. The regiment was bound for Washington, D.C., where President Lincoln needed men to defend his terribly vulnerable capital, surrounded, as it was, by the slave states of Maryland and Virginia. Maryland had not seceded, but Lincoln would feel more secure once the 6th Massachusetts arrived. Irritatingly, a local ordinance that prohibited locomotives from passing through Baltimore slowed the regiment's progress.

The cars would have to be horse-drawn one-and-a-half miles across town from one railroad depot to a second, where they would be coupled to a new locomotive. It sounded easy enough, if tedious, but civil authorities in Baltimore and Maryland generally feared trouble.

Rumor had it that "unlawful combinations of misguided citizens" would not allow federal troops to travel through Maryland. After neighboring Virginia seceded on April 17, the excitement in Baltimore rose visibly. The majority of citizens in Maryland had opposed secession before Fort Sumter, but Lincoln's call for troops caused much dissatisfaction. Unionist sentiment wavered. Confederate army recruiters operated openly in Baltimore, and some secessionists turned violent. An angry crowd jeered and threw stones at cars filled with unarmed Pennsylvania militia passing through town on April 18. Secessionists at an "immense spontaneous" meeting later that day vowed not to let the next train slip by so easily. Mayor George W. Brown and Maryland governor Thomas H. Hicks grew anxious. They begged Lincoln to summon no more troops through Baltimore. Their request surely resonated with the president. He would have recalled how, just two months earlier, he had been marked for assassination when traveling through the city en route to his inauguration. Nevertheless, Lincoln did not intervene.[3]

On April 19, as feared, hundreds of snarling, cursing citizens converged on the cars that carried seven companies of the 6th Massachusetts along the Pratt Street rail line. They were not all secessionists. Some of them, inspired by more abstract "republican" principles, simply resented the coercive central government that had forced them to participate in an unwanted military mobilization. Others in the crowd espoused neither secessionist nor republican views. They were "plug-uglies," plain and simple, general riffraff keen to join any violent recreation. Baltimore was notorious for political violence and mob action. It had a sinister reputation as the "mob town," where street gangs, unemployed workers, and common thugs set the tone. Whatever the crowd's motivation that day, it seemed to act in concert. People initially tossed taunts and jeers at the New England trespassers, but then someone hurled a paving stone and the crowd turned rabid. Rioters smashed windows in the cars and swarmed around the train all the way to the Camden Street station. They then turned their attention to the four remaining companies of soldiers still waiting to enter the gauntlet.[4]

The crowd piled sand on the tracks at the intersection of Gay and Pratt streets, about a third of the way between the two depots, and obstructed other portions of the line with cobblestones, bricks, even ship anchors from nearby wharves. Warned of the obstacles ahead, the

Baltimore rebels attack the 6th Massachusetts Infantry Regiment on April 19, 1861. The guerrilla war had begun. From *Harper's Weekly*, May 4, 1861.

regiment's officers ordered their remaining 220 men out of the cars and into two columns. They would march down Pratt Street. Take no notice of the mob, the officers cautioned, look straight ahead; but such resolve would have required hardened veterans. These were green recruits. The crowd engulfed the marching soldiers. They jostled them, knocked down a few, threw stones, wrenched muskets from sweaty hands, and fired shots over their heads. The New Englanders, still in columns, started to trot, but then they reached Gay Street. Unable to push through, they halted and, hopeful of dispersing the mob, fired a volley in the air. The citizens, though momentarily stunned, responded vehemently. Soldiers fell from gunfire, and the hail of stones, bricks, and bottles thickened.[5]

The troops pushed forward, many of them on the verge of panic. Mayor Brown arrived to plead for order. "They were firing wildly," the mayor later reported of the soldiers, "sometimes backward, over their shoulders. . . . The mob . . . was pursuing with shouts and stones, and, I think, an occasional pistol shot. The uproar was furious." The city's police force of fifty men rushed with drawn pistols to meet the approaching hoard. They saved lives on both sides by forming a cordon in the rear of the marching troops. That kept most of the crowd at bay. By 12:30 P.M., two hours after arriving in Baltimore, the entire regiment had boarded the train that would carry them out of the city and away from the first "battle" of the war. Most estimates placed the number of dead at 4 soldiers and 12 citizens, with another 36 soldiers and at least 49 citizens wounded.[6]

But the violence had not ended. Though thankful for the narrow escape, the Massachusetts volunteers were also irate by the time their train passed Robert W. Davis, a local merchant, standing along the tracks about a half mile from the station. Unaware of the men's ordeal, and clearly ignorant of their mood, the merchant taunted them with a cheer for Jefferson Davis. In defiance of orders, several soldiers fired their muskets at him. Davis fell dead. Meantime, back at the first depot, citizens attacked another set of railroad cars that had just delivered more northern militia. The terrified men, unarmed and lacking uniforms, leaped from their cars and rushed into town, protected to some extent by their civilian garb. The melee broadened when pro-Union citizens stepped in to assist the militia and confront their secessionist neighbors. The police arrived to separate all parties, but not before five more soldiers had been killed and nearly three times that number injured. Militiamen who had preferred the security of the cars to flight returned north on the train that had brought them.[7]

April 19 set the tone for the war to follow. "Anxiety, alarm, and rage have taken possession of the town," submitted a leading citizen on the following day. Hoping to avoid further violence, Mayor Brown and Governor Hicks authorized local police and militia to burn the railroad bridges north and east of Baltimore. Someone then tore up a section of track on the line leading to Washington and cut telegraph wires to the capital. Hundreds of armed men flocked to Baltimore over the next several days. Some of them came organized as companies of militia, but others arrived in hastily formed gangs. Contributing equally to the growing air of menace, outraged calls for vengeance came from the North. New Englanders were in a "white heat over the murder of Massachusetts soldiers." The president of the city's police commission feared an invasion by "the vilest and most reckless desperadoes" from the North. An alarmed citizen reported, "The treatment promised us is worse than any Chinese or Sepoy vengeance, and is enough to make one incredulous of the influence of civilization."[8]

Had the U.S. government not intervened to maintain order, crush rebel resistance, and keep Maryland in the Union, the situation might have deteriorated dreadfully. Federal troops arrived by ship at Annapolis to occupy the state. Unaccountably, the 6th Massachusetts was sent back to Baltimore in May. "Our men fairly itched to have a sett to with them," reported one of its soldiers. He and his comrades took particular pleasure in marching and drilling in the city's streets, a signal to the "Baltimore Mob" that their regiment would brook no opposition. President Lincoln suspended the writ of habeas corpus in Maryland and detained several Baltimore public officials, including Mayor Brown. Four months later, in September, he arrested pro-Confederate members of the Maryland legislature and other reportedly disloyal citizens in order to abort any threat of secession or military uprising in the state.[9]

While most Maryland secessionists went south to enlist in the Confederate army, not a few men remained to resist Union rule. They tried to poison the army's provisions, entered federal camps as spies, and plotted to kidnap public officials who aided the invaders. They struck at Unionist neighbors, too, by stoning, beating, and otherwise maltreating them, as well as by stealing their horses and cattle. They drilled clandestinely at night, and shadowy bands ranged the countryside between Baltimore and Annapolis to observe and, when possible, disrupt federal movements. Considerable numbers of Union soldiers worked to break up these irregular bands and guard the state's railroads against saboteurs. "Occurrences . . . suggestive of assassins behind the bushes" gave "a smack of the excitement of real war," reported an observer. Rebellious Marylanders sneered at the occupiers. "These Northern troops are not good soldiers," one man judged. "Whenever there is a battle they will be terribly defeated, and then, our time will come. As soon as they begin the retreat through Maryland the people will rise upon them. I know that many are only waiting for the opportunity."[10]

The pattern of events in Baltimore and across the state would be repeated throughout the South and in some portions of the North during the next four years. Violence in the streets, bushwhackers lying in wait, attacks on noncombatants, terrified communities: It had only begun. Equally important, this pattern grew not only in scope, but also in degree. Sabotage, assassination, fear and suspicion of one's neighbors, lynching of unarmed civilians, the use of terror to maintain law and order, the cover of war to settle old scores, retaliation against those who used violence, a subsequent escalation of violence against those who retaliated, and an apparent sanctioning of terror by governments became commonplace. A guerrilla war had been set in motion, and its influence would know few bounds.

BEGINNINGS

SPRING–SUMMER 1861

As news spread of the bloody events in Baltimore, Americans understood the symbolic importance of April 19. British troops and Massachusetts minutemen had tangled at Lexington and Concord on that date in 1775. Northern newspapers christened Baltimore the "Lexington of 1861" and hailed conflict with the South as "a continuation of the war that Lexington opened—a war of democracy against oligarchy." A British journalist even claimed that the first soldier killed in Baltimore was descended from the first patriot killed at Lexington. No one seemed to notice the awkwardness of the comparison. Massachusetts volunteers had been intruders at Baltimore, while the citizens they confronted behaved more like the New Englanders who had pursued British lobsterbacks to Boston. In another bit of topsy-turvy, Confederates boldly compared the "Baltimore Massacre" of 1861 to the Boston Massacre of 1770, when British soldiers had fired into a crowd of American patriots.[1]

Comparisons to the American Revolution came easily in 1861. Southerners even used it to justify secession. Northerners, they claimed, had abandoned the governing principles forged in the Revolution and the spirit of government defined by the U.S. Constitution. The Confederacy represented a return to those earlier, purer values; a new rebellion would challenge a tyrannical and despotic central government. Confederate editorialists, orators, and pamphleteers used these themes to rally the populace. "Who can resist a whole people, thoroughly aroused, brave to rashness, fighting for their existence?" asked a Virginian. "This revolution is not the work of leaders or politicians," elaborated a Tennessean. "It is the spontaneous uprising and upheaving of the people. It is as irresistible as the mighty tide of the ocean."[2]

Equally important—and going to the heart of things—many southern rebels imagined they had won that first war of independence as "partizans," the eighteenth-century name for guerrillas. Of course, George Washington and his Continental army deserved most of the credit for defeating Great Britain, and the "minutemen" tradition of the Revolution would send the vast majority of both northern and southern volunteers into the conventional armies of 1861. Yet even Washington had relied on ragtag militia to operate as irregulars in critical situations, and, revered though he was as a native son, Washington had done nothing personally to liberate the Deep South. And so, as southerners again braced for invasion by vastly superior numbers—as in 1776—an important part of their collective memory associated military victory with a romanticized brand of partisan resistance.[3]

In mobilizing to wage this new "People's War," as some enthusiasts soon called it, rebels had a slate of real and fictional heroes to document their selective version of the past. William Gilmore Simms, the foremost novelist and poet of the antebellum South, had exalted both types in a biography of Francis Marion—known as the "Swamp Fox"—and a series of historical romances that celebrated the South's Revolutionary partisans. Nathaniel Beverley Tucker went Simms one better. In 1836, he had published *The Partisan Leader: A Tale of the Future*, a remarkable novel that predicted the creation of a southern Confederacy and a war of independence against the North. Tellingly, he chose a Virginia guerrilla chief as the story's hero.[4]

Southerners in 1861 marveled at Tucker's prophetic powers. Publishers, knowing a good thing when they saw it, reprinted the book in both New York and Richmond soon after the war started. Tucker's vivid descriptions of partisan fighting in the mountains and valleys of northern Virginia forecast wonderfully the war to come. "Stooping from his mountain fastness," Tucker wrote of the novel's hero, Douglas Trevor, "he soon broke up all the military posts in the adjacent counties; so that in a few weeks, not a blue-coat was to be seen. . . . Freed from the presence of their enemy, the people were found ready to rise en masse." Federal troops entered Trevor's domain at their peril. He could scatter or rally his devoted followers within a matter of days to meet any threat. His men carried none of the drums, trumpets, or banners "deemed necessary in a regular army," but they possessed "stout hearts, and strong hands, and fleet limbs, and good rifles, and knives and tomahawks; and that system and harmony which spring from a sense of danger, a high purpose, and confidence in a leader."[5]

Rebels, then, did not think it strange that first blood had been shed spontaneously, chaotically, in the crowded, littered streets of Baltimore. If not duplicating the romantic parry and riposte of Tucker's partisan war, the incident had been, nonetheless, a natural response to danger. Indeed, *natural* was the key word. Europeans had associated the guerrilla style with "natural man" since the eighteenth century. Guerrilla fighting was basic, uncomplicated, primordial. Men need only grab muskets and squirrel rifles to defend their homes or form an army. Small wonder that irregular warfare sprang up from California to Florida in the early weeks and months of genuine fighting.[6]

Nowhere was the rebel response more immediate or intense than in Missouri, which makes that state a good place to understand what happened next. Missourians had contributed to a fierce political and paramilitary clash over the future of slavery in neighboring Kansas since 1855. Kansas jayhawkers meant to keep slavery out of the new state; Missouri slaveholders believed the expansion of slavery necessary for its survival. Ultimately, too, the struggle was a matter of law and order, of suppressing a rival faction that threatened violence to one's family and property. Even Kansans, as "northerners," shared that view of the bloody struggle. Many Americans west of the Mississippi River still lived in 1861 beyond the effective rule of courts and legislatures. They settled their own feuds, and they were not squeamish about employing vigilante justice. The Missouri-Kansas border war represented just one of many violent antebellum confrontations in the West.[7]

Missouri's new troubles began just a few weeks after Lincoln's election as president, even before South Carolina seceded. Some three hundred jayhawkers, led by a forty-nine-year-old abolitionist and former schoolteacher from Ohio named James Montgomery, rounded up and hanged several proslavery residents of Kansas Territory. Rumors said that Charles R. Jennison, the most famous jayhawker of them all, had also been involved. Scores of Kansans fled to Missouri. Many Missourians, fearful of imminent invasion, deserted homes near the Kansas line for the interior of their state, even as the state militia assembled to guard that boundary. Civil and military authorities in Kansas also mobilized and soon disbanded Montgomery's gang of "outlaws and marauders," but Kansans and Missourians kept an uneasy eye on one another through the spring. If the situation continued to deteriorate back East and war did come, both sides knew there would be hell to pay on the western border.[8]

Meanwhile, James H. Lane, chief political spokesman for the jayhawkers, exported western ways to the East. The lean, fifty-year-old Hoosier had moved to Kansas in 1855 and risen quickly to political prominence through his brilliant oratory. Unfortunately for antislavery Kansans, his reputation as a cynical, calculating, and unscrupulous demagogue somewhat tarnished their cause. Elected in April 1861 as a U.S. senator for the new state, he arrived in Washington five days before the 6th Massachusetts battled its way through the Baltimore gauntlet. When news of the attack reached the vulnerable capital, people panicked. God only knew what conspiracies were afoot. Lane rounded up about one hundred Kansans to form a "Frontier Guard." General Winfield Scott, commanding general of the U.S. Army, and Secretary of War Simon Cameron, both fearing for Lincoln's life, assigned Lane's men to protect the president. The Frontier Guard bivouacked in the East Room of the Executive Mansion until May 3 before being relieved of duty. That was long enough for word to spread through the South that Lincoln had resorted to recruiting "horse thieves & murderers."[9]

By then, U.S. troops had been pouring into St. Louis for several months. With the secession movement now at its zenith, the government pledged to keep Missouri in the Union. But Missouri was also a slave state, with a sizable prosecessionist population in its southern half. That spelled trouble.

The defining moment for Missourians came at St. Louis in an episode reminiscent of Baltimore. Despite being rebuffed by the state's secession convention in March, Claiborne Jackson, Missouri's prosecessionist governor, still hoped to deliver his state to the Confederacy. At worst, he intended to keep Missouri "neutral," even if that meant imposing his own brand of "armed neutrality." In May, Jackson assembled two regiments of the largely secessionist state militia at St. Louis. The independent "Minutemen," a quasimilitia organization that also favored secession, joined them. Standing in uneasy proximity to both groups was a growing body of U.S. troops, loyal "Home Guards," and the "Wide-Awakes," an antisecessionist equivalent of the Minutemen. General Nathaniel Lyon, a fiery forty-three-year-old West Point graduate and veteran of both the Seminole and Mexican wars, commanded the U.S. troops.[10]

After weeks of bluff and bluster by both sides, Lyon struck on May 10. Having learned that Governor Jackson had received a shipment of muskets and cannons from the Confederate government, he ordered 6,500 regular army troops and Home Guards to break up an encampment of 650 state militia and Minutemen. A U.S. flag flew over the camp—named Camp Jackson—where the militia claimed to have mustered legitimately under state law. They certainly posed no danger to Lyon's forces. However, Lyon saw Camp Jackson as a symbolic threat to the central government. He ordered his men to shut it down, and as word spread of his intentions, a large numbers of citizens followed the troops to Camp Jackson. Tensions rose when the anti-Union crowd heckled Lyon's minions, but the people were disappointed if they expected a dramatic showdown between federal troops and state militia. The militia prudently surrendered, and Lyon's men marched them toward the city arsenal.[11]

What happened next, and who precipitated events, is muddled. At some point, the crowd buttressed its taunts by throwing clods of earth and stones at Lyon's men. The regulars, who led the marching column, pressed on by driving back citizens at bayonet point. In their wake, the crowd moved in against the mostly German Home Guards. Scuffling ensued. Panicking Germans fired their muskets into the air, then into the menacing crowd. Pandemonium followed. Screaming people, "stupefied, bewildered" by the indiscriminate killing, ran in all directions. The Guards forged ahead, but pistol and musket fire soon struck their ranks. They returned fire. Former army captain William T. Sherman, retired from the military to direct a streetcar company in St. Louis, had been walking with his son near where the rioting began. "There must have been some provocation at the point where the Regulars charged bayonets," he reported to his brother, an Ohio congressman, "and when the militia began their fire—the rest was irregular & unnecessary—for the crowd, was back in the woods, a fence between them and the street."[12]

Twenty-eight civilians, including several women and children and some of the prisoners from Camp Jackson, died in the melee. At least forty people were wounded. As the rioting spread and other parts of the Union column came under attack, another eight civilians died before nightfall. Six soldiers fell dead during the day, another nine being wounded. Rioters controlled the city through the night, and on the next day, May 11, they attacked a column of 1,200 troops. The results were two more dead soldiers, ten more dead civilians, and thousands of converts to secession. Only staunch Unionists applauded the action. "While deploring the shooting and killing," explained one woman, "there was a feeling of satisfaction that at last the government was taking some action to protect its property from becoming a prey to the Confederacy."[13]

Governor Jackson used the riots to justify an emergency session of the legislature. He demanded, and got, an expansion of the state militia (now renamed the Missouri State Guard) and a military budget of $2.5 million for defense of the state. The next day, former Missouri governor and Mexican War veteran Sterling "Old Pap" Price accepted command of the State Guard. Negotiations to resolve the crisis continued over the next several weeks, but secessionist forces grew in size and seized stores of arms across Missouri and neighboring Arkansas. Jackson, Price, Lyon, and Frank Blair, a congressman who had recently been made colonel of the 1st Missouri Volunteers, met at St. Louis's Planter Hotel on June 10. After five hours of fruitless haggling, Lyon settled the issue. Speaking "deliberately, slowly, and with a peculiar emphasis," the general told Governor Jackson, "Better, sir, far better that the blood of every man, woman, and child within the limits of the State should flow, than that she should defy the federal government. *This means war.*"[14]

Missouri fell into chaos, which continued throughout the summer. Governor Jackson deserted the capital—Jefferson City—to form a rival Confederate state government in southern Missouri and appealed to Richmond for help. Jefferson Davis, convinced that Missouri's neutrality had been irrevocably violated, permitted troops in Mississippi and Arkansas to enter the state. Pap Price and his State Guard rallied to the governor and cooperated with the Confederate reinforcements. The season culminated with rebel victory at the battle of Wilson's Creek, near Springfield, Missouri, on August 10, but that paled alongside the real terror and destruction generated by a spontaneous guerrilla war. Meriwether Jeff Thompson, who would earn fame as the "Swamp Fox of the Confederacy," described the public mood: "Every Southern man in the State, from the Iowa line to Arkansas was picking his flint, cleaning his gun, and sharpening his knife to be ready for the coming storm." Thomas C. Reynolds, Claiborne Jackson's lieutenant governor, informed President Davis that the state's "Southern men" had vowed to throw Missouri "into a general revolution" and oppose the Federals in "a *guerilla* war" until a Confederate army arrived.[15]

Missouri Unionists then aggravated the situation. Desperate to prevent rebel control of the state, they formed their own partisan bands— often calling them "home guards"—to wage war against secessionists. Unionists resolved to defend their farms, towns, and neighborhoods while federal troops mobilized. Everyone spoke of "home protection." Some neighborhood divisions dated back to political and personal feuds that had begun years earlier. The violence unleashed by war only intensified the quarrels and gave people another excuse to torment or bully those whom they already disliked or distrusted. Julian Bates, a son of Lincoln's attorney general, confirmed the situation in the family's home state. "There will be hard fighting in Mo," he informed his father, "[but] not between the soldiers, & in many of the Counties there will be ugly neighborhood feuds, which may long outlast the general war." The senior Bates understood the potential dangers. "If things be allowed to go on in Mo as they are now," he warned the new pro-Union provisional governor, Hamilton R. Gamble, "we shall soon have a social war all over the State."[16]

The number of Missouri communities splintered by war multiplied. One woman wrote to tell her soldier-brother that he was safer in the army than at home. Rebel bushwhackers had already killed three of their neighbors, burned one home to the ground, and looted a nearby town. A resident of Shelbyville reported no fewer than five "gangs" of "desperadoes" operating in his vicinity. The community was in a continuous state of excitement over the "depredations of the Secessionists in robbing houses, Stealing whatever they could place their hands on and maltreating Union men in every conceivable way." A man from southwestern Missouri agonized, "We have civil war in our midst. We have union men & secessionists and there is a deadly hostility existing between them. . . . Men seem to have lost their reason and gone mad."[17]

An ethnic element further leavened Missouri's anarchy, as nativist animus against the "Dutch" Home Guards of St. Louis surfaced in other communities. Most Missouri Germans were Unionists and so became, for that reason alone, targets of secessionist violence. But they also suffered abuse because they were foreigners who, from the secessionist perspective, had no business poking their noses into a conflict they could not understand. German Home Guards and militia particularly incensed rebels, and even some Unionists saw German military service as a needless provocation. One Unionist protested to Governor Gamble in mid-August that German Home Guards had arrested and hanged suspected rebels with no legal authority and terrorized the entire state. Their actions, the man feared, would drive thousands of neutral people to side with the Confederacy.[18]

The deadly situation became even more perilous when Kansas jayhawkers rejoined the fray. It was a delicious moment for the Kansans. Most of their encounters with Missouri border ruffians in the 1850s had been on Kansas soil. Now, with a genuine Confederate presence in this adjacent slave state, Kansans could justify an incursion as necessary to protect themselves and preserve the Union. "They have a grudge against Missouri and the South," observed one Kansan of his neighbors, "that they will never forget until it is wiped out in blood." The raids began in late June, as jayhawkers stole, pillaged, and destroyed whatever secessionist property they could lay hands on.[19]

Slaves were among the stolen rebel "property," an important fact for understanding the jayhawkers. At a time when the broader war was about reunion, not slavery, westerners insisted on pushing abolition to the forefront. Kansas may have been the most rabidly abolitionist state west of Massachusetts, and stories about the horrible treatment accorded both slaves and Unionists in Missouri created a public mood in Kansas that sanctified the destruction of slavery. If nothing else, striking at slavery further injured Missouri "pukes," as they called them. Men like Doc Jennison and James Montgomery considered themselves "practical abolitionists." They knew how to rid the continent of slavery, and they would use all means necessary to accomplish that end.[20]

Ignoring the wishes of the state's cautious governor, Charles Robinson, Montgomery and Jennison organized their own army. "They have called on me to lead them," Montgomery proclaimed proudly in mid-June, "and I promised . . . to keep them [the rebels] from our doors, by giving them something to do at home." True to his word, the dark-complected, black-haired Montgomery, his piercing "black eyes . . . all ablaze with enthusiasm," directed a series of summer raids that freed dozens of slaves and reaped wagonloads of plunder. Other, lesser-known jayhawkers, including ex-convicts, murderers, and ruffians like John Stewart and Marshall Cleveland, also joined the fun. All the raiders, both leaders and followers, were "well-versed in guerrilla warfare."[21]

Kansans delighted in reports of the marauding, one newspaper going so far as to propose that Jennison replace Simon Cameron as U.S. secretary of war. That Jennison's men preyed on Unionists when rebel homes did not yield enough spoils was not so widely known. Some raiders disapproved of the practice, and at least one man returned to Kansas because he believed his companions were more interested in "stealing operations" than in quelling rebellion. Nor did he believe such men could be trusted in combat. "So many thieves as hangers on," he feared, "would in all probability run at the first approach of danger."[22]

James Lane joined the campaign in August 1861, fresh from his stint as Lincoln's bodyguard. Montgomery agreed to lead one of three regiments in Lane's new Kansas brigade. Jennison's independent Southern Kansas Jay-Hawkers, as his company was officially known, rode with Lane, too. But Lane exerted no more control over his men than did Jennison, and perhaps because of his political prominence, Missourians came to associate the jayhawker rampage most closely with him. When Lane did strike, he could be ruthless. "We found the country for 20 miles laid waste, the inhabitants plundered, several persons killed, & the people in much alarm for their safety," reported a Confederate officer of raids by Lane's "Jayhawkers & abolitionists" in early September.[23]

By that time, Iowans had also been drawn into the guerrilla war. Their initiation began with provocative oratory by rebel sympathizers who hoped to inspire rebellion, and threats of violence soon followed. Citizens warned Governor Samuel J. Kirkwood to beware. A "horde of traitorous abominations" threatened to "wage the most relentless warfare" against the families of men who had enlisted in the Union army. The governor must send troops to protect endangered communities. "In our county there is open & avowed expression [of] Secession sympathy & feeling," a loyal man informed Kirkwood. "Violence is threatened [against] our Citizens & towns."[24]

Graver yet came rumors of forays by rebel raiders. Just as Missourians feared an onslaught by Kansas jayhawkers, so the Hawkeye State grew increasingly uneasy about the guerrillas of northern Missouri. Unionist refugees from that state, who arrived in droves during the summer, told Governor Kirkwood what to expect. Reports of "armed bands" and "marauding bands" resounded along the border, most notably in southwestern Iowa. Residents demanded troops; the state must devise a plan, they wailed, "to hold the Border Ruffians in check." Confirmed reports and wild rumors alike warned of plans to steal horses, confiscate grain, rob banks, and "burn out 'every d——d abolitionist" in the state. Kirkwood organized home guards to protect his southern border, and his military aides set up a "secret organization" in Missouri to gather news about rebel intentions.[25]

Iowans decided that to avert disaster they must carry the fight to the enemy. Hundreds of men—some reports said thousands—not waiting for official permission, grabbed whatever weapons they could find, organized themselves into irregular bands, and headed south. With a scarcity of rifles and ammunition, they carried mostly "knives, hatchets, and clubs," but the important thing was to keep the guerrillas in Missouri. Better to fight them there, they agreed, than on their own farms and in their own towns. Better to join forces with Missouri Unionists than stand alone.[26]

The deteriorating situation in Missouri inspired other midwestern residents to volunteer for guerrilla service. They seldom described themselves as "guerrillas." More often, they stressed their experience as hunters and backwoodsmen, qualities, they believed, that suited them for tracking down elusive rebels. Offers of assistance arrived at the U.S. War Department from Indiana, Illinois, Wisconsin, Minnesota, and Nebraska Territory. Some men volunteered to fight anywhere as "sharp shooters," "skirmishers," and "rifle rangers," but many wanted to go specifically to Missouri, where they could "cut off those marauding bands" and protect vulnerable Unionists. The government needed mounted men of the "right stamp," a Wisconsin citizen told President Lincoln, men whose unique talents would be wasted in the conventional army.[27]

Meantime, Governor Gamble had a tough time controlling the passions of Missouri Unionists who meant to defend kith, kin, and fireside. Farmers and grocers retaliated against rebels with "knives, hatchets, shot guns or any thing they could get," and they urged Gamble to organize Unionists throughout the state "for self-protection." A resident of Hannibal wanted to raise a mounted battalion of four hundred men to "ride the Scoundrels down from one side of our state to the other." Then, when the rebel guerrillas had been cleared out of Missouri, he pledged that his men would "go thro Arkansas & eat green peas in New Orleans under the Stars & Stripes" by February. Such spirited determination got out of hand when people neglected to distinguish between friend and foe. Governor Gamble received daily complaints about the excesses of loyal state troops and "independent" companies, of unwarranted arrests, thefts, and violence that sullied the Union cause.[28]

National troops provided no balance wheel. "The Missourians believe very generally that we came here to steal their niggers, hang the men and ravish the women," judged a northern newspaper correspondent. Many Union troops lived up to expectations by treating all Missourians, whether friend or foe, as potential guerrillas. They made new "secessionists every day" by shooting down loyal men and searching private homes when there were "no grounds for suspicion." Gamble blamed some of these problems on the fact that many federal troops, hailing as they did from other states, did not understand the confused situation in Missouri. It is also worth remembering that the soldiers on both sides were amateurs at war. A few months earlier, these men had been farmers, clerks, blacksmiths, and shopkeepers. Some of them had fought in the Mexican War, a few may have drilled with local militia companies; but even these "veterans" had to adjust to the military discipline and special demands placed on soldiers fighting a war against their own countrymen. Many men also entered the war to punish the enemy rather than secure some abstract political principle. Confederate as well as Union officers wrestled with this problem.[29]

It was also true that some Union officers gave their men free rein. Lincoln's government had entered the war hoping to pursue a military policy of "conciliation." That is, southern noncombatants were to be spared confiscation, intimidation, and physical abuse in hopes of winning their confidence, converting them to Unionism, and causing the Confederate government to collapse for want of popular support. Yet, conciliation was never practiced universally, in Missouri perhaps least of all. Many generals came to consider the policy as "misguided," and judging by the large number of complaints by both Unionists and secessionists, soldiers and officers in the field often operated according to their own needs and local circumstances. "I am not ignorant of the fact that in all wars there are violations of private rights," Gamble complained to President Lincoln, "but it is seldom in modern times that such abuses have the express sanction of officers high in command."[30]

In truth, the average Union army officer was not so much concerned about a few excesses on the part of his men as about the army's inability to control rebel guerrillas. Officers newly appointed to Missouri were at a loss as to what to do, although they gradually recognized a dual problem. On the one hand, rebel guerrillas seldom endangered organized bodies of troops. To the contrary, Union soldiers complained that the rebels refused to stand up to a fair fight. "They are the bigest Set of cowards I Ever Saw," an Illinois soldier grumbled in mid-July. "If they would fight we would soon doo up the woork for them but they keep out of Gun Shot range." Having attacked supply trains, fired on pickets, or ambushed lone patrols, they slipped back to their homes to pose, from all outward appearances, as peaceful citizens. "It is too easily done," fumed a frustrated Union sergeant. "Shoot a few soldiers or Union men from behind a tree or a fence—gallop home—turn your horse loose in the woods—throw your rifle in the fence corner, & get lost in the tall corn, with a hoe in your hand."[31]

This war of "eternal vigilance" was annoying enough, but observant Union officers soon identified a second and larger problem. As rebel guerrillas moved furtively through the countryside, they forced the Federals to expend valuable time and resources on defense that should have been used to wage war. General Ulysses S. Grant, assigned to command troops at Ironton, Missouri, reported that the terror produced by local bushwhackers among Unionist civilians was his most formidable challenge. "Marauding parties are infesting the country, pillaging Union men, within 10 miles of here," he reported in early August. "At present I . . . have not suitable troops to drive these guerrillas out and afford to Union citizens of this place or neighborhood the protection I feel they should have."[32]

What was more, Union officers generally had no idea who confronted them. They reported fights with vaguely defined "hostile organizations," "marauders," "mounted rebels," "bands of armed secessionists," "irregular forces," "bands of rebels," and "rebel hordes." Because Sterling Price allowed "irregular" bands to operate with his State Guard, the actions of the Guard and the guerrillas became confused in public reports of battles, ambushes, sabotage, and intimidation of civilians. Appearances also made it hard to identify the enemy. Nearly everyone outside the Union army—jayhawkers, militia, home guards, and guerrillas—had the same "ragged and . . . scarecrow" look. They wore mismatched clothing, mostly civilian garb with here and there a uniform jacket or pair of trousers. They armed themselves with an equally odd assortment of muskets, pistols, shotguns, and rifles. A northern newspaper correspondent attributed the rebel penchant for homespun dress and unconventional tactics at least partly to tales of Revolutionary partisans. "These fellows have evidently read a good deal of yellow-covered literature," he decided, "in which, of course, they have learned all about Marion's horsemen."[33]

Further confusing things, some State Guard officers preferred guerrilla tactics to conventional warfare. Jeff Thompson, like Price, always had several companies of "partizans" working with him; he found the hit-and-run tactics of the guerrillas an effective way to strike at the Federals from his base in southeastern Missouri. "They cannot spare men to hunt me in the swamps," Thompson assured his superiors, "for they know that I will kill all that come." His location on the Mississippi River also made Thompson one of the first Confederate commanders to impede navigation on that mighty waterway, an objective that, in time, would gain equal importance to the destruction of railroads. Thompson himself boasted in August, "I stopped the navigation of the Mississippi River for ten days, by . . . firing four shots across into Illinois; and if I were only allowed to make my appearance at different and unexpected places, I could effectively stop all steamboats except the gunboats."[34]

By midsummer, the identity of their tormentors meant little to army commanders in danger of losing Missouri. John Pope, a no-nonsense West Point graduate from Kentucky who commanded Union troops in northern Missouri, made the first move to crush guerrilla resistance. The son of a federal judge and nephew of a U.S. senator, Pope was also related by marriage to Mary Todd Lincoln, the president's wife. He had served in the Mexican War and been promoted to captain five years before the Civil War, a not insignificant achievement in the antebellum army. Pope's brashness and conceit prevented him from being especially popular among his fellow officers, but he knew how to handle rebels.[35]

Pope announced in July that he would hold citizens living along the North Missouri Railroad responsible for "wanton destruction" of bridges, culverts, and track. Residents within a five-mile radius of guerrilla "outrages" would pay a "levy of money or property sufficient to cover the whole damage." Unable to distinguish among the bushwhackers, their supporters, and innocent citizens, he would treat all alike until the violence ended. Pope cautioned his men to treat noncombatants with respect, but he meant to arrest anyone engaged in "open acts of hostility" or "stimulating others to such acts."[36]

A week later, Pope toughened even these orders and extended them to all of northern Missouri. He now held citizens responsible for the "peace and quietude" of their communities and the safety of their own property. He was tired of trying to keep "lawless marauders" at bay, he explained, and the constant labor of "hunting out these guerrilla parties" was "demoralizing" his men. If he must send out troops in fruitless expeditions, they would be quartered and provisioned at the expense of the inhabitants.[37]

Pope tested his philosophy by dispatching General Stephen A. Hurlbut and six hundred men to occupy Marion County, where guerrillas had destroyed portions of the railroad and fired into passenger trains. The son of a South Carolina mother and Massachusetts father, Hurlbut had spent the first thirty years of his life in his mother's state, but he subsequently moved to Illinois, where he prospered for fifteen years prior to the war as a lawyer and later a Republican politician. His experience as an army officer in Missouri had led him to understand, like Pope, that rebel guerrillas could be controlled only by intimidating the general population. He drove out the guerrillas in ten days while living off the local inhabitants. Hurlbut informed Pope triumphantly, "The wealthy citizens of this county are very much sick of guerrilla warfare." Seeing the populace throughout his district fall into line, Pope predicted that the guerrilla war had been won. The citizenry's response only went to show that the "disturbances" in northern Missouri had been "purely local and personal," he decided. "The people in that region are merely fighting with each other," he explained with some insight, "in many cases to satisfy feelings of personal hostility of long standing."[38]

Pope celebrated too soon. A backlash occurred when his subordinates became overzealous. Some local commanders went beyond monetary penalties to hold guerrillas and their supporters "individually responsible, both in persons and property, for any outrage . . . committed on Union men." In Marion County, where Hurlbut had supposedly implemented the plan without a hitch, civilians complained of numerous irregularities. People had been arrested "without cause," their homes "opened and searched, for no good reason." Federal troops, far from maintaining "discipline and good order," had stolen livestock, foodstuffs, and personal items, and they had raped black women. One person protested to Governor Gamble that Pope's orders were "indiscreet & unwise," and that he, like all "petty commandants," was attempting to usurp the governor's own powers.[39]

One of the first—and always essential—roles for rebel guerrillas was to disrupt Union lines of supply and communication. From *Harper's Weekly*, October 24, 1863.

Nor had the situation in Missouri improved even marginally outside of Pope's jurisdiction. A federal colonel in the southeastern part of the state burned the warehouse and confiscated sixty mules and a quantity of corn from the family of a captain of "marauders." He then threatened to hang family members if the captain's men did not cease "killing stock, stealing horses, burning corn fields, destroying household property, robbing women and children of their wearing apparel, and . . . carrying off young girls to their camps." Confederates, including Jeff Thompson and Lieutenant Governor Reynolds, reacted swiftly and unambiguously to the colonel's actions and threats by vowing to hang federal prisoners. "I am content," Reynolds added, should such a step be forced on the Confederacy, "that impartial men should judge who is morally responsible for their melancholy fate."[40]

None of these particular threats or counterthreats materialized, but even so, an escalation of the violence and a general pattern of retaliation seemed inevitable. Rumors already circulated about rebel bushwhackers being unceremoniously executed. By late July, Unionists spoke openly of retaliation, and not a few Union soldiers voiced their approval. "Many are in favor of 'making a clean sweep' (as they express it) of secession," observed a northern journalist at Springfield, "which means, I suppose, *taking no more prisoners*." On the Confederate side, talk surfaced after the battle of Wilson's Creek of executing some German prisoners of war as repayment for the "innocent" civilians "butchered" by German militia in the St. Louis riots. James Lane's activities also continued to gall the rebels. Responding to Lane's pledge to kill all prisoners taken by his command, a Confederate officer swore, "Just let him try . . . and see how it will work. . . . Let him show his barbarism by having them shot. We will shoot ten for one."[41]

A new Union commander in Missouri, John C. Frémont, had seen and heard enough. Sent by President Lincoln to wrest the state from rebel hands, the famous explorer, soldier, and first Republican presidential candidate found that the Trans-Mississippi conflict defied all notions of "civilized warfare." It did not surprise him that benighted southerners should behave in this way, but the general judged the retaliatory measures of renegade Kansans—even though he sympathized with their ends—to be just as unacceptable, and he heard protests from all sides about Pope's capricious orders. More than that, the general found himself, as he sought solutions to these problems, enmeshed in local politics. From Kansas, Governor Robinson wanted Frémont to control his own political rival, James Lane. Unless Lane and his jayhawking friends stopped antagonizing Missourians with senseless raids, the governor insisted, Kansas would be invaded by rebel hordes. In Missouri, Hamilton Gamble wanted Frémont to prevent Unionists from joining the guerrilla war.[42]

From his headquarters at St. Louis, Frémont responded to the pressure on August 30 with a sweeping proclamation of martial law. He meant to eliminate the "bands of murderers and marauders" whose "daily-increasing crimes and outrages" were "driving off the inhabitants" of Missouri. The stunned populace watched as Frémont went beyond even what Pope had dared do. Anyone taking up arms against the United States would be court-martialed, he announced; people found guilty would be shot. The property of people taking up arms would be confiscated and their slaves freed. People guilty of sabotaging railroads, bridges, or telegraphs would "suffer the extreme penalty of the law." Anyone engaged in "treasonable correspondence," aiding enemies of the United States, or "fomenting tumults" would suffer "severe punishment."[43]

It was powerful stuff, and just what some people wanted to hear. "They should be *summarily shot by thousands*," declared a second son of Edward Bates, who urged that the orders be made national policy. "They have well earned the fate, and the example made of them may be of great value elsewhere in deterring . . . robbers, spies, and assassins." However, President Lincoln, who had not been consulted about the new policy, thought it went too far. That he had not been advised of the stringent orders was not necessarily strange. Everyone was improvising in these early months of the war. Pope had issued his orders without consulting anyone, and the national government had neither issued nor recommended any policy regarding the conduct of the war or of troops in the field. Be that as it may, Frémont had trod onto controversial political ground when he mentioned the emancipation of slaves. Whatever Lincoln's feelings on the subject, the president knew it was politically impossible to address the issue at a time when he needed desperately to keep slave border states like Missouri, Kentucky, and Maryland loyal to the Union. When he learned what Frémont had done, Lincoln asked him to "modify" that portion of his proclamation dealing with the confiscation of rebel property.[44]

Equally important, the president forbade Frémont to go around shooting people. The rebels would surely retaliate, Lincoln said, which would compel the United States to respond in kind, "and so, man for man indefinitely." Frémont brazenly, if politely, protested the president's interference. So did his spunky wife Jessie. People already chuckled that Jessie operated Frémont's headquarters, and she now traveled to Washington, D.C., to tell Lincoln how to run the war. Her husband would modify his emancipation plan, Jessie informed him, only if Lincoln so ordered it. As for dealing summarily with rebel guerrillas and their abettors, Frémont insisted in a letter presented by Jessie that he deserved the traditional freedom allowed commanders in the field to deal with the enemy as he saw fit. Jessie was taken aback when her considerable charms, more than ample to sway most men, failed to win over Lincoln. Indeed, the president was considerably put out by her husband, and he reminded her pointedly that the war was being waged to preserve the Union, not to advance the abolitionist cause.[45]

Being the president, Lincoln had the final word, or nearly so. He ordered Frémont to modify the emancipation policy, but he let stand the remaining provisions. Not that Lincoln condoned shooting captured rebels. He thought the policy "impolitic," at best, but the president also assumed such drastic action would be a rarity. He misunderstood the depth of the guerrilla problem. As soon as Jeff Thompson learned of the orders, he announced his intention to "'*hang, draw*, and quarter' a minion" of Lincoln's army for every Confederate "soldier" put to death by Frémont. "I intend to exceed General Frémont in his excesses," Thompson pledged. Rebels rejoiced as far away as Virginia. "If this does not extend the insurrection, & speedily free the state from the power of the Yankees & tories," one man commented, "I do not know what will."[46]

So as the summer wound down, Missouri's rebel guerrillas seemed to have the advantage. They had given General Price time to organize a sufficiently large conventional force to win the second major battle of the war at Wilson's Creek. They had given Claiborne Jackson opportunity to organize a rebel government in exile. They had terrorized Unionists, destroyed railroads, kept federal forces off guard, and generally thrown the state into chaos. Union soldiers and officers dismissed them as cowards and described them as more nuisance than threat, but the stark measure of the guerrillas' success could be seen in the harsh proscriptive response to their operations. The Federals had not anticipated this kind of war, and the military and civil officials responsible for rooting out guerrillas had only begun to understand the extent of the problem.

The Civil War remained ill-shaped everywhere through that first summer. Many people still found it hard to believe that war had come at all; most assumed it would not last long. What none doubted, given the widely publicized experiences of Maryland and Missouri, was that this people's war must now be played out "on the border." That is where the United States would try to muscle its way into the South, and where Confederate defenders must confront the invaders. The rebels knew they could not risk losing Virginia, Tennessee, or Kentucky. They also knew it could be fatal to wait until a Confederate army had been mustered, organized, equipped, and trained for combat.[1]

George Fitzhugh, a Virginia lawyer and polemicist who had achieved national fame in the 1850s for his inventive defense of slavery, had a plan. Writing in the July issue of *DeBow's Review*, the South's most influential political and commercial magazine, Fitzhugh urged fellow Confederates to embrace guerrilla warfare. Of course, he acknowledged, conventional armies must ultimately defend the nation, but the people should be prepared "on proper opportunities to pursue that desultory partisan method of warfare." If the war became protracted, with Union troops gaining the interior of the country, the Confederacy's "chief reliance," Fitzhugh declared, "must be on irregular troops and partisan warfare." He provided several examples from modern history of how smaller nations, fighting on the defensive, had triumphed in partisan wars. And no nation, he submitted, no citizenry in the world, was better suited by inclination and circumstances than the Confederacy to wage such warfare. Moreover, the mountainous terrain, scattered settlements, and poor roads of the border lands, while impeding an invading army, provided marked advantages for "irregular defensive warfare."[2]

It was as though Fitzhugh had been reading Tucker's *Partisan Leader* or Simms's biography of Francis Marion, but, then, the same could be said of many southerners. Even before Fitzhugh's manifesto circulated through the country, hundreds of men in every corner of the Confederacy had organized as "Marion Men," "Swamp Fox Rangers," or merely "partisans" and "guerrillas." Many did so to defend their own communities, but many also volunteered to fight in the upper South, to halt the Union invasion before it reached their homes. A South Carolinian informed Secretary of War Leroy Pope Walker that he had one hundred men eager to serve "as partisans . . . on the border." The Carolinian added, "We want to be destructive warriors." A Mississippian offered his "Guerrilla Company" directly to President Jefferson Davis. "It is my idea to assist the borders," he explained. Scores of similar offers came from across the South.[3]

As Virginia Confederates braced themselves for invasion by land and sea, they welcomed all assistance, and no one was more certain of how to defend the state than Edmund Ruffin. Like Fitzhugh, the sixty-seven-year-old fire-eater acknowledged that victory depended on conventional armies in open battle, but he also insisted that Virginians must defend their homes and communities independent of the armies. "Home guards" would be necessary, not only to repulse Union soldiers, but also to quell slave insurrections inspired by the presence of blue uniforms. Old men, boys, and all those unfit for regular service, even if armed only with ancient fowling pieces, must prepare "to act as a guerrilla force." Women could help, too. "I am trying to persuade all the ladies of my acquaintance in this neighborhood to learn to shoot," Ruffin explained, "& to become familiar with using guns & pistols."[4]

Whether influenced by Ruffin, Fitzhugh, Tucker, their own instincts, or the Richmond press, which also advocated a "partisan soldiery," Virginians responded. Governor John Letcher and the state's military commander, General Daniel Ruggles, received requests from across northern Virginia to organize guerrilla bands. Letcher, who had no military experience, exploited the public enthusiasm. He decided in early May to recruit conventional troops to meet the enemy's advance and a reliable militia reserve to defend the home front in case of "actual invasion." Guerrillas, he reasoned, could be used where these "organized forces" proved inadequate. Thus would he rely on "the bold hearts and strong arms of a united people, to make each house a citadel, and every rock and tree positions of defense."[5]

Letcher's tacit approval heartened potential guerrillas, many of whom seemed possessed by a ruthless, almost murderous, instinct to destroy the invader. "We will go with our knives and hatchets," one man proclaimed. Another citizen pledged that his "home guard" would use "Rifles, Dogs & Tooth Pickes & Revolvers." Sheer rage drove the Virginia and North Carolina Irrepressibles, recruited in Hanover County toward the end of July. They swore to avenge the death of two popular officers, one a Virginian, the other a North Carolinian, who had fallen in early fighting. The Irrepressibles would wear civilian clothing and furnish their own weapons, mostly Bowie knives, pistols, and shotguns. They would serve without pay until the invader had been driven from southern soil. A more calculated anger inspired an innovative fellow who wanted to bury "Bomb shells" in the roads used by invading Federals. It was a drastic, perhaps even barbaric, tactic the man acknowledged, but "Northern Vandals" must be exterminated, and he deemed any method to achieve that end "fair and honorable."[6]

References to the "savagery" and "barbarity" of the enemy became commonplace, and the words held interesting connotations. Popular imagination associated savagery and barbarity with Indian warfare, and the ties were twofold. First, Americans associated the *style* of guerrilla warfare with the Indian mode of fighting. This derived partly from impressions of Native Americans as stealthy, sly, and cunning, but decades of experience in fighting Indians had also taught whites many practical lessons. From the colonial wars to nineteenth-century confrontations in the Old Northwest, Florida, and Texas, Americans had become familiar with Indian raids, ambushes, and desultory fighting. Many of the men who organized guerrilla bands presented as credentials for such service their experience as Indian fighters. When advocating the use of Bowie knives or "creeping" upon the enemy, they spoke of lessons learned from their old adversaries. Here was "natural man" at his most formidable.[7]

Both northerners and southerners understood this imagery, as they did a second connection between guerrilla and Indian warfare: "savage" retaliation. Even before the war, northern abolitionists had invoked the equivalent of Indian "savagery" in their uncompromising "war" against slavery. Slaveholders, they had decreed, deserved no pity. Union soldiers reacted the same way to skulking guerrillas as did those same "wild" guerrillas when confronting their Yankee foes. Both sides learned the need for ruthlessness. "Well! let the Yankees invade our mountain region and burn a few houses," exclaimed *DeBow's Review* in its advocacy of guerrilla fighting, "and we predict that our mountain boys will become as savage as the Seminoles and twice as brave."[8]

William Gilmore Simms had never met a Native American in peace or war, but his historical romances defined the nature of Indian warfare as well as of "partizan" resistance for literate southerners. Speaking as yet another self-proclaimed expert on military strategy, he advocated the Indian style of combat. The Confederate army, he proclaimed, should assign ten men from every company to guerrilla operations. "Have them . . . painted and disguised as Indians," Simms urged the local Confederate commander, then arm them with "rifle, bowie knife & hatchet." Plenty of volunteers, he assumed, were familiar with Indian warfare. "If there be any thing which will inspire terror in the souls of the citizen soldiery of the North," reasoned the poet-strategist, "it will be the idea that scalps are to be taken by the redmen."[9]

These were strong words, and a bit too strong for southerners who remained squeamish about out-and-out barbarity, even against Yankees. They preferred to justify guerrilla warfare with another, quite different, image of Native Americans: the noble savage. No Confederate warriors better fit this pattern than the followers of Turner Ashby. The thirty-two-year-old Virginia farmer and his men epitomized old-school partisan warfare, the romanticized Marion school. Organized first as a company of "Mountain Rangers" and assigned to arrest Unionists and patrol the Potomac River, they eventually formed part of the 7th Virginia Cavalry. Even then, as members of an apparently conventional cavalry regiment, Ashby's men used guerrilla tactics, thought of themselves as partisans, and conducted themselves as honorable savages. In the notoriously brutal border war, they engaged in a war of chivalry. Born of the woods and fields, they acted as "natural man," imbued with inherent virtue and a pastoral innocence, as much a product of the natural world as Indian peoples.[10]

Not that nobility entirely balanced savage instincts. Given a choice of weapons, the 7th Virginia preferred the Bowie knife to the cavalry saber. It became the regiment's emblematic weapon, the white man's equivalent of the hatchet. Bowie knives were meant for hand-to-hand combat, primitive fighting, with no quarter asked or given. "At them with your knives, men!" Ashby would command in attacking Union soldiers. His men obeyed, and so with "bowie knifes and revolvers put the cowardly dogs to flight." One subordinate smiled contentedly, "We have . . . struck terror into the hearts of the abolitionists along the border."[11]

However it might be justified, the outcome delighted Edmund Ruffin. "Guerrilla fighting has been begun, & with great effect, near Alexandria & also near Hampton," he reported in late June. "Some of our people, acting alone, or in small parties, & at their own discretion, have crept upon & shot many of the sentinels & scouts. It is only necessary for the people generally to resort to these means to overcome any invading army, even if we were greatly inferior to it in regular military force." Some Confederate army officers, he knew, objected to this sort of warfare, and Ruffin admitted that he would not stoop to such tactics if the Confederacy faced "an honorable enemy, carrying on honorable &

legitimate warfare." Unfortunately, he declared, the Federals had given Virginians no more choice than they had proud Marylanders and Missourians.[12]

Nonetheless, northwestern Virginia, rather than Ruffin's eastern region, is where the border war first erupted in earnest. It was a vulnerable spot from the Confederate perspective. Besides facing the prospect of invasion from Ohio, Pennsylvania, and Union-occupied Maryland, these northwestern counties contained the largest block of antisecessionists in the state. They were small farmers and miners who had stronger economic ties to the Midwest and Northeast than to the South, even to the rest of Virginia. A goodly number of the people had been born in the North, and so had no loyalty to southern social and cultural traditions, including slavery. Many of them also resented the political power held by slave interests in central and eastern Virginia. They formed a separate pro-Union government in mid-June. By the end of 1863, they would enter the Union as the state of West Virginia.

Northwestern Virginia Unionists hoped the federal army would succor them, but, like Missourians, they took no chances. They formed "Guerrilla parties" to defend, as one man put it, "our respective regions . . . as well as . . . the Union." They would protect themselves first, assist the Union army when possible, and hang traitors wherever they found them. All of this, too, while carrying on with their normal lives, a seemingly impossible task but the very rationale for home protection. As one Union army officer recalled, "They worked their farms, but every man had his rifle hung upon his chimney-piece and by day or by night was ready to shoulder it, . . . and every neighborhood could muster its company or squad of home-guards to join in quelling seditious outbreaks."[13]

The swiftness of their revolt gave Unionists an early advantage, and a bad situation promised to grow worse for the Confederates when the army arrived. The Kanawha River valley offered the Federals a convenient invasion route into the rest of the state from its conjunction with the Ohio River. Strategic railroad heads at Wheeling, Charleston, and Harpers Ferry gave the Federals secure bases in western Virginia. Harpers Ferry also had an arsenal, the same one that had sparked John Brown's imagination two years earlier. A series of battles at Phillippi, Rich Mountain, Laurel Hill, and Carrick's Ford sent the rebel army reeling backward by mid-July. Then, too, the army's success further emboldened local Unionists and attracted "gangs of unorganized marauders" from Maryland and Ohio.[14]

Francis H. Pierpont, newly elected governor of the Reformed

State of Virginia, went so far as to invite Ohio home guards to lend a hand. The Buckeyes were natural allies. They, too, worried about pro-Confederates in their midst, traitors who might aid invading armies or raiding parties. Even if not in communication with Virginia rebels, these people, many of whom had emigrated before the war from Tennessee and Kentucky, were capable of threatening lives and destroying property in Ohio. They drilled openly in some places, flew rebel flags, and declared themselves for Jeff Davis. So loyal Buckeyes, who had hesitated to enter Virginia without proper authority, leaped at the opportunity to "chastise the rebels" on their own soil and in their own "manner of fighting."[15]

Not surprisingly, the rebels rallied. Taking to "the warpath," they vowed to "shoot and hang tories and put down rebellion in Western Virginia." The name "tory," which had once identified the American supporters of George III, was another remnant of the Revolutionary past. By whatever name, Unionists found themselves in a tussle the remainder of the summer. It was their turn to be intimidated by "armed bands," threatened with imprisonment and physical abuse, betrayed by spies and informers, driven out by "marauding parties," exposed to bushwhackers "lurking in the woods and brush," and stripped of their property. Intense, bloody, and bitter contests ensued. A terrible equilibrium gripped the region.[16]

Perry Connolly (or Conley) and Nancy Hart ranked among the earliest and best-known rebel leaders. Twenty-four-year-old Connolly, who stood well over six feet, led a guerrilla band known as the "Moccasin Rangers." The men formed originally as a home guard, but when some of them began to terrify defenseless Unionists, their officers—two gentlemanly county officials—resigned. The company then divided. One half, led by fifty-two-year-old farmer and justice of the peace Daniel Dusky (or Duskey), remained a fierce bunch, but the other half, led by Connolly, developed a genuinely murderous streak. Their vengeful attacks against Unionists in a cluster of counties north of Charleston were fueled more by a desire to settle old scores than to achieve any military end. When and where Connolly's sixteen-year-old girl friend, Nancy Hart, joined the band is uncertain, but she and Perry reportedly rode together at the head of the Moccasins.[17]

Challenging Moccasin supremacy were the Snake Hunters, one of western Virginia's most effective Unionist home guards. Organized by Captain John P. Baggs in August, the Snake Hunters sometimes operated as scouts or skirmishers for the Union army, but they devoted most of their energy to tracking Connolly's men. They came from the same mountain stock as the rebel guerrillas, knew how to handle knives and rifles, and enjoyed an intimate knowledge of the local terrain. They dressed as they pleased, and not even Baggs was very keen on drill. The six-foot-two-inch, hard-swearing captain customarily dismissed the men by declaring, "Put down them thar blasted old guns and d——d to you! . . . Now to your holes you ugly rats, and don't let me see you again till I want you!" But they knew their business. In one raid, Baggs's men killed five rebels and "severly" wounded nine others. In addition, they captured six horses and a yoke of oxen and burned down the house that had quartered the rebels.[18]

Local chieftains aside, Albert G. Jenkins became the region's most feared Confederate "guerrilla." Whether or not Jenkins and his men fairly deserved the name is hard to say. They fall into the same category as Jeff Thompson's Missouri command and Turner Ashby's Virginia partisans. A Harvard-educated, ex-congressman from Virginia, Jenkins entered the war as captain of the "Border Rangers," organized to defend Virginia against raids across the Ohio River. In July, the Rangers became part of the 8th Virginia Cavalry, with Jenkins as their colonel, but they enjoyed a license to strike the enemy where and when they chose to do it. The regiment also became a symbol of Confederate authority around which local guerrillas could rally. Jenkins the "desperado" proceeded to threaten Ohio communities along the border and terrorize Unionists in his own domain.[19]

With the Confederate army effectively driven out of northwestern Virginia, both Jenkins and local guerrilla chieftains focused equally on driving out the Federals. General George B. McClellan, who had led the Union advance, and General William S. Rosecrans, who took over when McClellan became the commanding general of all Union armies in July, assigned large numbers of troops — one estimate is 4,800 men — to guard vulnerable railroad bridges and tunnels, the Cheat River viaduct, and telegraph lines. Unionists complained that the army had abandoned them, but with a rebel army still within striking distance and a dozen strategic points vulnerable to raiders and saboteurs, the Federals could not protect many neighborhoods. Troops responded to emergency calls from communities when possible, but they accomplished little. Rebel guerrillas "dodge[d] off in the woods" as soon as the soldiers arrived, only to reappear when they had gone. A woman near Clarksburg vowed to defend her homestead with or without the army's help. "I sharpened my butchers knife," she reported calmly to her husband, who was absent with the Union army, "made a sheath for it, and hung it to my belt, and resolved I would not leave my home alive."[20]

Although outnumbered, the rebels did have the advantage of terrain. Winding, twisting roads—more nearly paths in many places—provided unmatched opportunities for ambush. Governor Letcher's military aides judged the area around Harpers Ferry "extremely suitable for guerrilla warfare," a region where "every species of arms" could be used "by resolute men with most decided effect." Local defenders could dart and weave, strike without warning to "cut down the enemy." Neither professional nor amateur soldiers could mistake the advantages. General Joseph E. Johnston, commanding conventional Confederate troops around Harpers Ferry, endorsed the use of guerrillas; a Methodist minister volunteered to organize a guerrilla company to roam western Virginia's mountains.[21]

General McClellan understood the problem at once. On June 23, he announced a policy similar to the one to be used by Pope and Frémont in Missouri. If the rebels continued "to carry on a system of hostilities prohibited by the laws of war," the normally conciliatory McClellan vowed to deal with "marauding parties" according to the "severest rules of military law." Rosecrans, on replacing McClellan, took even stronger action against this "species of warfare." Citizens must take "prompt and vigorous measures to put a stop to neighborhood and private wars," Rosecrans insisted, and so "prevent the country from being desolated by plunder and violence, whether committed in the name of secessionism or Unionism." Neighborhoods failing to suppress local violence would be treated "as accessaries to the crime."[22]

McClellan and Rosecrans also cautioned their own men to treat civilians with respect, but the troops paid scant attention to them. The guerrilla war, by turns, frightened and angered Union soldiers. They found it difficult to distinguish friend from foe. They could not predict which of these seemingly peaceful farmers might ambush them at the first opportunity. The mountain rebels were notorious for claiming to be loyal Union men, some of them even signing oaths of allegiance to the federal government, only to take to the bush and practice their deviltry. They were damned liars and not to be trusted. Consequently, while officers ordered restraint and spoke of occupying "the country of friends, not of enemies," Union soldiers scoffed at "talk of winning these people over with kindness."[23]

A Pennsylvania soldier, having seen the corpse of a friend who had been shot, stripped, and left lying in the road by bushwhackers, wanted blood. "Our boys have born with this damning mode of warfare and suffered their comrades picked off until forbearance has ceased to be a virtue," he informed friends at home. "We are fully able to cope with them at their own game. No more prisoners is the watch word." That, indeed, became the standard response, even, on occasion, with official sanction. The first credible results of the McClellan/Rosecrans policy came in mid-August with the execution of two Confederate guerrillas captured near Beverly, Virginia.[24]

Union soldiers hated this sort of war. They found no glory in tracking bushwhackers, and all knew that scouting through the mountains was "dangerous business." Wagon trains, foraging expeditions, and columns of troops were constantly harassed by guerrillas. The rebels posed little threat to a regiment or brigade, which counted thousands of men, but they routinely killed or wounded a half dozen or so Federals at a time. As the number of casualties grew, the psychological toll of fighting a phantom enemy wore on the soldiers. They dared not stray far from their tents, even though officers established picket lines three and four miles from camp. Some laughed at the futile efforts of a few hundred guerrillas to intimidate tens of thousands of men; they scoffed at the antique "squirrel guns" used by many bushwhackers. Yet, as one soldier admitted, squirrel guns were "often sufficient." A Pennsylvania soldier reported, "We have been learning our full share of the realities of this conflict rendered more terable in this section than any other from the savage and brutal mode in which it is waged by our enemies . . . who carry on a war more barborous than any waged by the savages who once inhabited this same country."[25]

Major Rutherford B. Hayes, future president of the United States, came to appreciate these perils while serving with the 23rd Ohio Infantry. Even though appalled by the "murder" of Union soldiers in ambushes near Weston, Virginia, Hayes was at first reluctant to retaliate against civilians. However, as the attacks continued and as more Unionists fell victim to "plundering" and "divers acts of violence," Hayes realized that the army faced "a general rising among the Rebels." The road between his camp and the next closest one, about one hundred miles away, was "so infested with 'bushwhackers'" that direct communication had been severed; officers regarded travel between the camps "unsafe." Daily expeditions of ten to one hundred men tracked elusive bands for dozens of miles, but they could not stem the persecution, robbery, and killings. Some rebel bands grew so large that Hayes did not know if they were guerrillas or part of a rebel army.[26]

Elsewhere on the border, Tennessee, which remained in the Union until June, did not seem to face imminent peril. With Kentucky buffering it to the north, immediate invasion looked unlikely, but scattered Unionist enclaves soon raised irregular bands, and northern newspapers encouraged them to wage a merciless war. So, even as thousands of Tennessee rebels joined the Confederate army and marched off to fight in Virginia, hundreds more embraced their "special" role as guerrilla fighters at home. "If the people are armed, and have powder, ball and caps *in their houses, ready for use,*" emphasized one advocate, "they will rise *en masse* and the whole country will be filled with armed men to repel the enemy at every point." They would silence Unionists, too, and invade Ohio, Indiana, and Illinois if given the opportunity. Confederate women, as in Ruffin's Virginia, also prepared for war. They purchased revolvers, vowed "to fight to the last," and practiced shooting. "We think and talk of little else here," confessed one woman.[27]

The gravest threat of upheaval came in the eastern third of the state. East Tennesseans had resisted the original secession movement, and when the rest of the state finally voted to join the Confederacy, they tried to secede from Confederate Tennessee. That scheme failed, but their opposition to the Confederacy never faltered. They professed a curious brand of Unionism, defined as much by social class, race, and political party as by national, sectional, and local ties. They would have preferred some form of "armed neutrality" for the border states, but that hope died when Confederate soldiers promptly occupied their region. As a result, some Unionists fled north, either to live out the war in peace or to join the army. Others, more "fierce and bloody minded," remained to contest control of the home front.[28]

East Tennessee Unionists showed how dangerous they could be when Governor Isham G. Harris and rebel military commanders tried to mollify them. General Felix K. Zollicoffer, a Whig politician in Tennessee before the war, took command of the army at Knoxville in July. He promised not to disturb Unionists if they acknowledged Confederate rule. Unionists repaid his forbearance by murdering secessionists, ambushing detachments of Confederate soldiers, and using the *Knoxville Whig*, edited by outspoken editor William G. "Parson" Brownlow, to support the Lincoln government. "We as Freeman are rubbing up our Riffles, and Muskets, and drilling for the purpose of defending ourselves, and protecting our liberties," insisted the people of one East Tennessee county. The rebels could not be trusted, they declared, and it would require "40,000 brave mountaineers [to] pour forth from the hill-top, and valley, mountain gorges, and creeks, and rivers, and avenge the wrongs that have already been too great!"[29]

The Confederates did not take long to respond. General Zollicoffer received orders from Richmond to arrest dissident leaders, break up disloyal home guards, and close refugee routes into Kentucky. By Sep-

Tennessee Unionists vow to defend their community in a clandestine meeting.
From *Harper's Weekly*, March 29, 1862.

tember, he was directing raids against Union supply lines, depots, and training camps in Kentucky. Governor Harris ordered hundreds of additional arrests. For the moment, at least, East Tennessee Unionists went to ground.[30]

Kentucky, that looming northern neighbor, was a different story altogether. Virginians referred to their own northern border counties as "the Flanders of America," a reference to that part of Europe devastated during the Thirty Years War; but Kentuckians could justly contest the title. After Missouri, no other southern state was so bent on remaining neutral, or had less chance of doing so. Control of the Bluegrass State, birthplace of both Abraham Lincoln and Jefferson Davis, became a point of personal pride for the rival presidents, and both men appreciated the state's strategic importance. With its northern border formed by the Ohio River, Kentucky provided a buffer against invasion in either direction. Federal occupation of Kentucky would leave Tennessee, arguably the most important manufacturing and food-producing state in the Confederacy, terribly exposed. Rebel control would put Confederate troops within striking distance of Cincinnati, Indianapolis, even Chicago. "I think to lose Kentucky is nearly the same as to lose the whole game," Lincoln declared. "Kentucky gone, we can not hold Missouri, nor as I think, Maryland."[31]

As Union and Confederate leaders maneuvered for military and political advantage, the people of Kentucky fell out among themselves. Whether believing that they must inevitably be engulfed by war or simply heeding the way in which Unionists and secessionists in other states had divided into armed factions, Kentuckians prepared for any eventuality. It was a schizophrenic mobilization, not at all neat or predictable, though somewhat akin to what happened in Missouri. "This State is not like Va & Tenn, divided into sections, East & West," Edmund Ruffin's daughter, a resident of Frankfort, explained to her father. "But there is division every-where throughout the State. There is scarcely a family that is not divided in sentiment, some for the North & others for the South."[32]

The fact that Governor Beriah Magoffin, like Claiborne Jackson in Missouri, favored the Confederate cause, made the situation even more tense and unpredictable. The state legislature, not trusting the governor, gave his military powers to a special board in late May. State inspector general Simon Buckner, another pro-Confederate, organized the Kentucky State Guards to maintain order and neutrality, but the Guards were so overwhelmingly secessionist in sympathy that Unionists formed a rival group. They also requested and promptly received five thousand "Lincoln guns" (rifles) from the federal government. Kentuckians spoke of the seeming inevitability of "civil war" within their borders, as jealousies, distrust, and bitterness grew daily.[33]

Community tensions did not produce blood as speedily as in Missouri and Virginia, but that was largely because Kentuckians, whatever their political persuasion, worried more about their state's northern and southern borders. They knew that Kentucky's ultimate fate depended on the forbearance of the U.S. and Confederate armies. Not surprisingly, rebel guerrillas caused the earliest fracture of neutrality when bands of Tennessee "plunderers" crossed the border in early May to sack the railroad depot at Paducah. The raiders were "wholly uncontrollable," people reported from the troubled town, "breaking the cars to pieces, fighting, etc." Tennessee officials apologized for the raid and assured Governor Magoffin that Confederate armies had no intention of invading the state, but independent military commanders routinely entered Kentucky in search of recruits, weapons, and supplies.[34]

Kentucky neutrality disappeared completely when General Leonidas Polk, a West Point classmate of Jefferson Davis, an Episcopal bishop, and commander of Confederate troops in western Tennessee, occupied Columbus on September 4. Polk's action followed Unionist victory in state elections that had given them a majority in the Kentucky legislature. Emboldened by their political success, Unionists had then established an army recruiting depot. These events killed any hope that Kentucky might secede. Polk entered the state as a self-proclaimed liberator, and a delegation of Columbus's leading citizens welcomed him as such. Two days later, on September 6, Ulysses S. Grant occupied Paducah. In response, more Confederate troops arrived in the state. The Kentucky legislature asked both sides to withdraw, but that had become impossible. Kentucky's guerrilla war grew apace, even as the legislature begged people "not to engage in . . . strife among themselves, on account of political differences."[35]

With the war firmly lodged in Kentucky, panic hit a broader portion of the Midwest, where two generations of southern migration had deposited thousands of potential rebels on northern soil. People in southern Illinois had already been worried about invasion by Confederate armies through Kentucky. Now, internal uprisings, "lawlessness," and "mob violence" within the state and guerrilla raids from without posed more immediate dangers. A heavily pro-Confederate population in the part of southern Illinois known as "Little Egypt" (centered on Cairo) boldly threatened Unionist neighbors. "Some of them say . . . they are going to hang cut throts & shoot every Republican in egypt," reported a resident to Governor Richard Yates. U.S. loyalists beseeched Yates to send troops to their communities, or at least provide them with weapons. If "bandit parties" of secessionists were not promptly broken up and "treason crushed out," loyalist "property [would be] stolen, houses burned, & union men murdered."[36]

Illinois men volunteered to enter Kentucky on "secret service" to learn rebel designs. Other people called for border patrols and scouts to guard river crossings and railroads. Citizens of Carbondale reported armed bands crossing the Ohio River. The state's current defenses could not "deter local rebels nor forbid invasion by Gorrillas," a worried man warned Governor Yates. A Unionist who had fled persecution in Tennessee believed that the pro-Confederates of Illinois were "worse" than the rebels he had left behind. Loyal citizens, daily expecting swarms of "plundering" guerrillas, slept with rifles near at hand.[37]

Neighboring Indiana had a shorter border to defend, but paranoia about guerrilla raids and internal enemies ran just as deep. In Madison, perched on the banks of the Ohio River, Unionists formed a home guard to patrol the streets at night, suppress riots, and "oppose any surprise from . . . Kentucky." Even citizens in Lebanon, in the middle of the state, believed that "many traitors" in their midst merited "close watching." Rebel sympathizers were suspected of trying to derail trains that carried Union troops to the front, and they reportedly threatened life and property everywhere. As in Illinois, loyal people wanted the state to arm them and beef up defenses on the Ohio River. Governor Oliver P. Morton summarized the mood of his people for the War Department. "They are in deadly fear that marauding parties from the other side of the river will plunder and burn their towns," he declared. With no means of defending themselves, they lived "in a state of intense alarm."[38]

One other theme, familiar in both northern and southern communities, echoed from the Midwest. With such threats looming, men hesitated to join the army and leave their families and property unprotected. Instead of enlisting, they formed companies of "rangers" and "guards" to fight at home. The captain of the Harmony Rangers made clear to Lew Wallace, Indiana's adjutant general, the expectations of his men. "The company is made up of chiefly young men & married men who have farms & families," he explained, "& whose expectation was that being within 15 mi[les] of the border their service would be required for home protection, & could be rendered without interfering much with the raising of a crop." Ohioans, though principally concerned with Virginia during the early months of war, also looked to defend their border with Kentucky. These midwestern loyalists rarely called themselves "partisans" or "guerrillas," as did southerners, but their instincts were the same.[39]

Edmund Ruffin could not have been happier with the state of rebellion in the upper South and Midwest by September. The two wavering states, Missouri and Kentucky, had been forced to confront the reality of "civil war" within their borders. They must now choose between North and South, and Ruffin had no doubt this meant "triumph for the southern side." Unionists—the "Submissionists"—on the border might outnumber secessionists in some places, but they were "the old, the timid, the cowardly, the imbecile & the mean-spirited," Ruffin declared. They could not possibly stand against "patriotic & public-spirited citizens."[40]

ar unfolded at a slower, more measured pace below the border. All seven original Confederate states plus Arkansas and North Carolina seemed secure against immediate hostilities. Many people believed the war would never reach them. At the very least, the Yankee invasion would be delayed. This largely explains why rebels in those states rushed to serve in the upper South. There loomed the immediate danger and, for the adventurous, the only chance of glory. Certainly, with fewer Unionists living among them, Confederates in the Deep South saw little evidence of the bitter, destructive social wars being waged elsewhere. Still, precautions were in order. Some army regiments being raised for the Richmond government would have to stay at home, and it would be foolish not to supplement them with "independent" companies of guerrillas, scouts, or home guards.

Coastal defense received the most attention through the first summer of the war. States along the Atlantic coast and Gulf of Mexico were vulnerable to invasion by sea. Port cities and towns as far west as Texas would be targeted by the federal naval blockade. What was more, hundreds of miles of coastline between these ports laid exposed.

North Carolinians believed their stout system of coastal defenses would keep any large landing force at bay, but they dreaded the thought of raiders penetrating the state by way of sounds and rivers. The object of such invaders, no one doubted, "would be for plunder and burning more than to fight any battle." Confronting this possibility, some eastern Carolina men decided to serve locally as guerrillas. "They are a hearty set," insisted an officer of a company at Beaufort, "inured to hardships, and . . . perfectly acquainted with every hill, skirt of woods, bay & creek and are withal excellent marksmen."[1]

Other states took like precautions. The southern parishes of Louisiana west of New Orleans looked exceedingly vulnerable. When the region's majority population of Creoles, Cajuns, free blacks, and Indians did not rush to bear arms for the Confederacy, "mounted men, on the guerilla order" volunteered from farther inland to patrol coastal swamps and lowlands. In Georgia, a "Guerrilla Corps" of forty-five men, armed with shotguns, prepared to "meet the enemy on the coast

... at a few hours notice." The Camden Chasseurs volunteered to patrol forty miles of coastline north of the Florida border, where the enemy could "land in small boats and be in our midst in a short time."[2]

Militiamen bore responsibility for defending Florida until midsummer, when the Confederate government organized the state into military districts and assigned army regiments to guard the coast. Even so, being exposed to the sea on virtually all sides, Florida's rebels grew anxious. "Insecurity and apprehension are predominant feelings now," declared the citizens of Apalachicola, as the approaches to their town by land and water remained "entirely unguarded." Many people still thought shore batteries and infantry could repel invaders, but a "large majority" of the state's men now volunteered as "scouts" and "mounted guerrillas." This passion for mounted service alarmed Governor John Milton. "Almost every man that has a pony wishes to mount him at the expense of the Confederate government," he complained to President Davis. The governor did not oppose guerrillas on philosophical grounds, but he knew that only "heavy caliber" guns and infantry regiments, not "independent" companies, could protect his state.[3]

Milton was correct about the inability of either guerrillas or cavalry to turn back a concerted invasion, yet some military men understood the valuable role these mobile units could play as supplemental forces. As ever more stretches of the South's coastline became threatened in the coming months, Confederate commanders needed scouts and rangers to link coastal garrisons, provide reconnaissance, warn of impending danger, and deploy to fight delaying actions until reinforcements arrived. They also prized horsemen armed with double-barreled shotguns and capable of making surprise attacks on coastal invaders. Guerrillas could not win the war, but they clearly had a role to fill.[4]

Mississippi and Alabama had the shortest coastlines, and the formidable Fort Morgan, guarding Mobile Bay, solved most of Alabama's problems. Still, partisan defenders, such as Mississippi's Swamp Rangers, made coastal defense a priority. On learning that Federals had landed at Mississippi City, just west of Biloxi, residents a hundred miles from the coast formed companies of mounted scouts "to cut off the Cow Stealing yankees," who might venture inland. At Pass Christian, east of St. Louis Bay, the Piney Woods Rangers mustered for "defense of the Sea Coast." All of these men, insisted their captain, could use a shotgun with effect and knew "every tree, ravine, and lagoon" in southern Mississippi.[5]

Confederates in the Deep South also looked northward. Less than two weeks after Fort Sumter surrendered, a resident of Atlanta formed a company of "mounted rifleman"—not mere "cavalry," he emphasized— to protect Georgia's "extensive frontier." He and his men hoped to ascertain enemy positions, defend "defenseless points," raid supply lines, and disperse "predatory Bands" that might assail their border. Mississippi Confederates similarly enlisted for "special service" and "ranger service" within the state. Georgia's Cherokee Rangers, a band of fifty men, vowed to rush anywhere in the state or to the border counties of North Carolina and Tennessee on five hours' notice. They meant to suppress rebellion and repel invasion by "vandal hordes of lawless men and unprincipled fanatics."[6]

Regardless of the direction from which danger might threaten, local defense, which became the theme and essence of the guerrilla war everywhere, remained the priority. Even the Cherokee Rangers preferred to serve in their own neighborhood. Collecting no pay, they asked only the freedom to operate independently of any larger military force. "Our object," explained their captain, "is to remain at home and attend to our crops and other domestic affairs." Georgia's Mounted Forest Rangers—sixty-five men armed with "country Rifles" and double-barreled shotguns—served on much the same terms. Otherwise, they said, their farms would fail. This need "to cultivate their farms" motivated many men who entered the irregular ranks. They simply could not afford to serve in distant places for months at a time. Many Floridians emphasized that they had formed bands strictly for "home service." As the Confederate government assigned army recruits outside the state, independent companies wanted assurances that they would remain in Florida for the "protection of the locality."[7]

Even before his state seceded, a South Carolinian who had battled jayhawkers and abolitionists for five years in Bleeding Kansas helped spread the gospel of local defense. He had seen the effectiveness of guerrilla warfare in the West, and being well-versed in the exploits of native son Francis Marion, he volunteered to raise a partisan company of forty to one hundred men. The company would, of course, operate according to the wishes of the governor, but he stressed that it must be "independent of all other military organizations." If allowed to serve "upon the principle adopted by the 'Swamp Fox,'" he told friends, his band could "do more effective service by hampering the enemy than could 1000 men by the usual mode."[8]

Internal enemies provided an equally strong justification for staying close to home. Aware of the trouble "traitors" had caused across the upper South, communities formed "home guards," "home companies," and "vigilance committees" to throttle dangerous malcontents. *Vigi-*

lance was the key word, and the vigilante tradition thrived as much in the Deep South as it did on the Kansas-Missouri border. Texas, for example, which happened to have a sizable concentration of Unionists in its northern counties, swore by it. In South Carolina, a tradition of armed "Vigilant" committees and "Minute Man" companies dated back to the nullification crisis of the 1830s. Every southern state, especially sparsely settled areas where courts and lawmen remained few, embraced the spirit.[9]

Arkansas faced perhaps the most unpredictable situation. The state was betwixt and between, not part of the Deep South but not currently threatened by the border war. Yet, Arkansans could but think of Missouri as an extension of their own state, which meant that if their northern neighbor fell to Union rule, the war must inevitably roll southward over them. The first call for guerrilla recruits went out in July, and even then, people equated "local" service with the salvation of Missouri. A resident of Helena, located on the Mississippi River, recruited a company of thirty men to wage a "guerrila campaign" in Missouri. Seeking legal protection for what might otherwise look like a piratical expedition, he requested a "Letter of Marque" from the Richmond government. "Our paramount object," he explained to the secretary of war, "is to act as an *independent* scout for the Confederate & State forces in Missouri."[10]

An Illinois schoolteacher who had been living in the South learned all about local watchdogs when he tried to escape the Confederacy through Arkansas. Some communities through which he passed, especially in mountainous, isolated parts of the thinly populated state, took no interest in politics. People went about their daily chores and rushed neither to defend nor to defy the Union. However, emotions ran high in other places, and as support for the Confederacy grew, Arkansans viewed strangers like himself with suspicion. Known Unionists risked death as armed bands of "guerrilla-looking" men, some "partly intoxicated," patrolled communities. This northerner's quick wits enabled him to pass through the state without injury, but he later learned that several resident Unionists had been hanged.[11]

Pockets of "Abolitionist and Lincolnite" citizens alarmed North Carolinians, too. The western half of their state seemed most vulnerable. Unionist "fiends" threatened the families of Confederate men who had gone to war, and reports of "outrages" circulated by mid-June. North Carolina rebels also suffered early on from raids by East Tennesseans. Even more alarming was the possibility that Tennessee and North Carolina tories would join forces, hide in the mountains that joined the two states, then swoop down on defenseless citizens in an orgy of "bloodshed, house burning & death." Communities asked that Confederate troops be posted in the western counties, and when the governor proved unequal to that task, they formed patrols to guard mountain passes.[12]

The perils grew for both North and South Carolina when Georgia Unionists reacted precipitously in the wake of secession. "We do not intend to submit to . . . secession, which has been taken out of the hands of the people and fallen into the hands of Dimegaugs," one of them wrote defiantly to Governor Joseph E. Brown from northern Georgia. Loyal Confederates warned the governor that traitors lurked everywhere in the northern mountains. "Some of our countys, just above us, are now making threats . . . to plunder and devastate our little county town," chimed in a citizen. As would occur from time to time through much of the South, this brand of northern Georgia Unionism was leavened in some instances by class antagonism. "No less than three of our citizens have been heard to say that they have all their lives been poor but if the war continued long they would be rich," the captain of the Mounted Rangers informed Governor Brown.[13]

Confused about the motives of the malcontents, and still adjusting to the reality of a "civil" war, Confederates remained uncertain at first about how to deal with these internal threats. Some home guards doubted their legal authority to take action against Unionists. Some even feared they would be "liable to the punishment of the laws" should they "molest" them. The issue of legality appears curious under the circumstances, yet one heard frequent concerns about it. Governor Hicks in Maryland had believed the solution to the guerrilla problem after April 19 was to arrest the rabble-rousers, with county sheriffs calling on the army for assistance "if necessary." Likewise, state authorities in Georgia now urged vigilance committees to bring suspicious characters before the "proper tribunal," lest local defenders become as lawless as the traitors and plotters with whom they contended.[14]

Alabama political leaders also preferred to deal with malcontents through legal strictures, although they faced a grave challenge in the state's northern hill country. Hard feelings between rebels and antisecessionists had substantial roots in the region, nourished by fierce political battles that went back to the 1830s. Reports of armed tories preparing to destroy secessionist communities alarmed Governor Andrew B. Moore, but he relied on county sheriffs to handle the problem. Moore understood that old political divisions and private feuds fueled most of the quarrels. To give secessionists free rein in suppressing dissent, he believed, would bring out the worst in both sides and lead to the social war that ravaged Missouri.[15]

Confederates in the Deep South also associated internal security with slave rebellion. Fear of black insurrection had been embedded in the southern psyche since the eighteenth century, but the anxiety became particularly acute with the rise of a passionate abolitionist movement in the early 1830s. Nat Turner and John Brown had demonstrated the potential dangers of abolitionist fervor, and civil war greatly increased the risks of insurrection. Confederates expressed less foreboding on the border, where the slave population had not swelled so enormously as it had in cotton-, rice-, and sugar-producing regions of the South. However, anyone who depended on the plantation economy knew slave unrest could be the most serious consequence of the national conflict.

Responsibility for preventing slave rebellion fell to guerrillas, scouts, and home guards. Outwardly, their duties resembled those of the traditional slave patrollers, but the heightened demands of wartime security required even keener vigilance and more formidable deterrents. On the surface, this dynamic between slavery and the guerrilla war looks paradoxical. On the one hand, guerrilla activity in a neighborhood seemingly would have diminished the ability of slaveholders to control their human property. The turmoil should have made it easier for slaves to escape or revolt. On the other hand, the principal task of guerrillas in all circumstances was to defend against potential enemies. Thus, irregulars policed the slave population as carefully as they did white Unionists, and roving bands of guerrillas often discouraged slave rebellion. They retaliated quickly and forcefully to signs of unrest, and their stealthy presence endangered slaves who wandered too far from home.[16]

Further joining guerrillas to the specter of slave rebellion was the well-nigh universal belief that tories intended to "incite slaves to mutiny." Many people worried about a possible alliance between Unionists and slaves, and whatever other dangers they posed, tories could inspire flight and rebellion. A band of Mississippians organized for the dual purpose of "repelling insurrection among the negroes" and "keeping down Toryism among the people." The citizens of Limestone County, Alabama, one of those unstable northern counties, formed a vigilance committee and enlarged its slave patrol. "It seems that the negroes have concluded that Lincoln is going to free them all, and they are everywhere making preparations to aid him when he makes his appearance," explained one resident. His observation cloaked a degree of scorn for the gullibility of the blacks, but everyone took rumors of plots seriously.

Should intrigue be discovered, retaliation came swiftly. Residents of Limestone hanged two slaves, whipped several others, and sentenced a free black to the penitentiary for plotting rebellion. The "base white men" who had aided them escaped. An Arkansas community killed a New England schoolteacher suspected of abolitionist activities.[17]

Beyond the dangers of home-grown agitators, most Confederates believed the biggest threat of slave unrest would arrive with the blue-clad armies. A Texan saw this as yet another peril of seaborne invasion. The Federals, he reasoned, could never defeat the South in a conventional war. Instead, their strategy must be one of "marauding upon the coast" and capturing ports like Galveston. "I think the war will finally dwindle down into a marauding and negro-stealing affair probably to be prolonged for some time," he observed. His solution was to loose a similar war upon the North. *"Forward to Philadelphia!"* he exclaimed. *"Sack and burn Black Republican cities!"* Similarly, Georgians formed home guards to protect themselves and their property against invaders from the coast or through Florida, but also "to suppress any insurrection of Slaves or other hostile movements against our citizens."[18]

Elsewhere, people thought slaves needed little encouragement or guidance; they could cause trouble all on their own. A Georgia militia colonel saw a crisis looming as early as June near Savannah. "Our country is infested with runaway slaves," he reported to Governor Brown, all of them armed. He had located three camps of runaways with up to forty slaves combined within six miles of the town. "Not a night passes," he swore, "that does not witness robbery from farms smoke-houses etc. The ladies are very much frightened, as runaway negroes have committed two rapes & two murders the last week." Ordinary militia patrols had failed to penetrate the dense swamps where the camps were located, let alone subdue the blacks. The colonel believed large forces of scouts were needed to kill, capture, or drive them out.[19]

Native Americans also influenced the evolution of guerrilla warfare in the Deep South, but in ways that contrasted with their roles on the border. While romance and historical memory shaped images of Indian savagery and nobility in the upper South, parts of the Deep South lived in the presence of potentially hostile tribes. Indian warfare there was less a symbol than an active ingredient of guerrilla operations. In Florida, reports of Seminole "outrages" against people and property sparked a call for local defense equal to fears of slave rebellion. Texans and Arkansans worried as much about Indian raids as they did about Yankee invaders, perhaps more so in the opening months of the war. Smaller bands of Indians—most notably the Cherokee of North

Carolina—would play a role in the border war, but the tribes of the Trans-Mississippi had a more profound impact.[20]

Hostile Comanche and Kiowa had attacked isolated ranchers and small settlements in western Texas since long before the war. In fact, Texans embraced secession at least partly because the U.S. government had failed to protect them against Indian raids. Ironically, the situation deteriorated after secession, as the United States surrendered or abandoned its western forts. The absence of any armed authority encouraged the tribes to escalate their raids. White settlers had been encroaching on their domain and disrupting their way of life for a generation. Now, with the white men squaring off with each other, the tribes struck back. They rustled horses, cattle, and sheep in Texas and the territories. They attacked small detachments of soldiers, supply trains, and mail couriers. Indeed, during the first few months of the war, southwestern Indians killed more Confederate troops in that region than did the Federals.[21]

Texans and Arkansans also worried about the "civilized" nations of Indian Territory. Settled in the decade since the Indian removal of the 1830s, these lands formed the northern border of Texas, across the Red River, and the northwestern border of Arkansas. The resident nations, far from being raiders or marauders, had adopted white ways. They had become farmers and herders, and many of them had embraced southern customs and culture, including black slavery. The Cherokee, alone, owned 4,000 slaves and had over 100,000 acres under cultivation. Still, the nations resided on U.S. lands, and the U.S. government held millions of dollars of their monies in trust. Should they be pressed to side with the North in the white man's war, these Indians would pose a danger. Even without them, Kansas jayhawkers and the Union army could use Indian Territory as a corridor into Texas and Arkansas.[22]

Opinion divided over how to handle this peril. Some Confederates, thinking the words "civilized" and "Indian" posed an inherent contradiction, wanted to drive them out. This was the plan of some Texas guerrillas who volunteered in June to attack Choctaw, Chickasaw, and Cherokee whom they believed had converted to abolitionism. More often, people saw the value of an alliance with Indian Territory. As early as April, Major Edmund Kirby Smith, a veteran of frontier service, pressed the urgency of the situation on the War Department. The Confederacy's relations with these thousands of potential warriors were of "utmost importance," he submitted. Win their allegiance, and the nation would have a "strong barrier on the north, forcing the line of operations of an invading army westward into a region impracticable to the passage of large bodies of troops."[23]

Some Confederates went even further than Smith. They argued that the tribes should be used to invade enemy territory. Confederates delighted in the prospect of "a few thousand Warriors" sweeping over the domain of Lane and Jennison. One ardent rebel, who had much of his personal property stolen or destroyed before being driven out of Kansas when the war started, offered to return with a mixed battalion of Texans and Indians. "It is time I obtained a little revenge," he explained. Confederates as far west as Arizona Territory advocated similar roles for friendly tribes. "One regiment of Cherokees or Choctaws, well mounted," insisted a man in Arizona, "would inspire more wholesome terror in the minds of our refractory Mexican population than a vast army of Americans from the States." At the very least, insisted another advocate, a regiment of Indians—he thought Creeks the best—could "Range between the Red River & Canses [Kansas] line."[24]

The Confederate government agreed, and so dispatched Albert Pike, a brilliant Arkansas lawyer and politician, to win the loyalty of Indian Territory. Pike, holding the title of "Indian Commissioner," signed treaties with nearly all of the nations by October and authorized the Cherokee to raise several brigades of troops. Some three hundred Cherokee enlisted as early as July under the command of Colonel Stand Watie, one of their tribal chiefs. They effectively guarded the northern border of their lands against Kansas jayhawkers and, consequently, protected Arkansas's western flank. While organized as conventional cavalry and used as such during much of the war, the Confederate tribes specialized in guerrilla tactics and operated as raiders.[25]

Northerners living west of the Mississippi understood the danger posed by the Confederacy's Indian alliance. After the Kansans, Nebraskans felt most at risk. "'*Something is up*' among the Aloe Indians," the territorial governor—borrowing a currently popular phrase from Charles Dickens—warned the U.S. War Department. Some Choctaw from Indian Territory had been in the area, and the governor feared they may have stirred up additional northern tribes, including the Kaw, Sac, and Fox. "Rebels exercise a great influence over the Indian Tribes located in this and adjoining Territories," he emphasized. Iowans saw trouble brewing in both Nebraska and Minnesota. The remedy, some people said, was to rally northern tribes to the Union cause. The Federals eventually won the loyalty of some Native Americans, but not in the numbers enjoyed by the Confederacy.[26]

Meanwhile, another feature of Texas history, the "ranger" tradition, helped to validate the guerrilla war. Using armed men to patrol or scout a region—to "range" over it—was not unique to Texas, or even the South, but Texas was the only state that had depended on rangers for security before the war. Companies patrolled the frontier and guarded against Indian attacks as early as 1823, well before Texas became an independent republic. Over the course of several decades, these Texas Rangers—sometimes called "minutemen"—adopted the "art of plains warfare" from their native foes. Even after Texas joined the Union, and so gained the protection of the U.S. Army on its borders, ranger companies remained the principal defenders of some communities. Consequently, Texas had hundreds of experienced guerrillas when war came.[27]

Reinforcing the ranger tradition was the Texas Revolution of 1836, the people's war against Mexico. The state's Confederate military leaders exploited this tradition with emotional appeals for recruits just days after Texas seceded from the Union. "Remember the days of yore," challenged a typical proclamation, "when your own red right hands achieved your independence." Texans must rally once again "to keep [their] soil free from the enemy's touch and to preserve unsullied the fame of the Texas ranger." Such words rang no less powerfully on the frontier than did the memory of eighteenth-century "partizans" among seaboard Confederates. Men volunteered to serve as "sort of Guerillas, like warriors, men of old times." Heirs of the Texas Revolution as well as rangers like Ben McCulloch, Benjamin F. Terry, and John S. "Rip" Ford rushed to Virginia, volunteered to invade Kansas, or prepared for "frontier defense" at home against hostile tribes, Kansas jayhawkers, and the Union army.[28]

The impact was immediate. Rangers initiated much of the early fighting in Texas, and could be said to have wrested control of the state from federal authority. General David E. Twiggs, commanding the U.S. Department of Texas from San Antonio in February 1861, surrendered all U.S. property in the state to Ben McCulloch's rangers. When Twiggs—a Georgian—joined the Confederacy soon thereafter, his replacement, Colonel Carlos A. Waite, evacuated all remaining troops. Waite informed the War Department that with U.S. garrisons so widely scattered in the state, resistance was "not practicable." His presence in Texas could lead to "a kind of guerilla war," his men exposed to relentless "partisan operations." The colonel had fought guerrillas during the war with Mexico and wanted nothing more to do with them. As jubilant rangers caroused in the streets of San Antonio, "recklessly shooting any one who happened to displease them," Unionists also fled. In the northern part of the state, rangers acted without any authorization to capture parties of U.S. troops and claim their horses. When ordered to report to the region's Confederate commander, they ignored the summons.[29]

This image of the dashing, aggressive Texas Ranger appealed to rebels east of the Mississippi River. Some irregular warriors in Kentucky and Tennessee modeled themselves on the rangers and insisted on invading Ohio, Indiana, and Illinois in the same way Texans spoke of sacking Kansas. The exploits of a band of Kentucky partisans known as the "Red Rangers" caused a Louisville newspaper to hail its captain as "another Ben McCulloch." A former Texas Ranger living in Georgia wanted to raise "that class of troops" to defend the region near Atlanta. A company of "picked men" could "do more harm to an invading army than any other force I could raise of the same size," he told the War Department. Similar voices called from Alabama, Louisiana, and Mississippi. Confederate guerrillas thought they could find no better model than the Texans.[30]

By the end of that first summer, many Confederates, in every part of the South, saw the practical benefits of a guerrilla defense. It satisfied southern instincts for survival, suited their heritage, complimented history and local traditions, and provided security for communities against a variety of foes, be they Yankee invaders, intransigent Unionists, rebellious slaves, or some combination of that unholy trinity. Yet, in all this, the system had a serious flaw, a paradox of sorts, that would weaken Confederate efforts to wage a successful guerrilla war.

The paradox grew from conflicting views of how the guerrilla war should be fought. Besides its other benefits, men frequently chose guerrilla service because it offered an escape from the regimentation, discipline, and endless drill required in the conventional army. Romantic images of Revolutionary "partizans" and Texas Rangers contrasted sharply with the dull routine of the uniformed ranks. The difference between the two types of warfare was particularly stark for men who had practiced the latter. "Most of these men," an Arkansan concluded of his fellow guerrillas, "preferred the free but more hazardous life of an independent soldier or scout, to the more irksome duties of the regularly organized forces of the Confederate Army." Likewise, a band of Louisiana "rangers," all of them with experience in Mexico and on the frontier, wished to be "unconnected" to the nation's armies.[31]

Rebel guerrillas prized their unfettered status, subject to the orders of no one *"save the Genl in Chief."* They relished their ability to go where and when they wanted, "to fight," a Georgian expressed it, "on our own responsibility." A Texan insisted on "fiting the Skermishing fite in my own way." "Give us our mountain Rifles and our own mode of fight," claimed another man, "and we are secure." An Alabamian wanted "the largest liberty in carrying on in Virginia or on the border a partisan or guerrilla warfare." This could not be done, he declared, if his band was "attached to any regiment." A group of "one hundred Gentlemen" from Alabama volunteered to go "Gurillaing," but they wished to do so on their "own hook." An Arkansan who soon deserted the conventional army to serve as a guerrilla explained, "That kind of warfare did not suit me. I wanted to get out where I could have it more lively; where I could fight if I wanted to, or run if I so desired; I wanted to be my own general."[32]

Irregular volunteers also believed they had special qualities and skills that qualified them for "this peculiar service." They stressed their marksmanship, familiarity with knives and hatchets, experience as woodsmen, fit and rugged constitutions, and horsemanship. Their captains touted them as elite fighters, "picked men," "stout and active," "young, athletic, and bold," "accustomed to a hardy frontier life," with "great powers of endurance." They were braver and more daring, they maintained, than the average soldier. They would accept any assignment, "however hazardous" it might be. A company of Florida "Scouts, Rangers & Spies," many of the men being "old and experienced Indian fighters," vowed to perform "any, the most desperate service." "We are the best of horsemen, good fighters, accostomed [sic] to camping out on hunting expeditions," testified a proud captain, and would fight like "warriors." Quite simply, boasted another man, his company represented "the flower of the frontier of Texas."[33]

Yet just here, amid all the talk of independent action, arose the paradox. Jefferson Davis and his state governors had welcomed partisan warfare on the border because it proved invaluable in thwarting invasion and occupation. Guerrillas effectively disrupted supply lines and communications, cowed or neutralized Unionists, forced redeployment of federal forces, distracted U.S. commanders, eroded the morale of invading troops, and generally created multiple military obstacles until rebel armies could be mustered and deployed. The guerrillas had then been valuable adjuncts to the armies, able to operate in ways, in places, and under circumstances not possible for regular soldiers. However, before many months had passed, the Confederate government came to realize the difficulty of controlling and coordinating this sprawling guerrilla war. Most dangerous was the inherent contradiction between independent action and the implementation of a coordinated military strategy.

The requirements of local defense revealed the contradiction most starkly. The government and its guerrillas had very different priorities. A band of Texans rebelled when the local Confederate commander assigned them to a conventional cavalry regiment, destined, no doubt, for service outside Texas. "This created a great deal of dissatisfaction amongst the boys," recalled one man, "for service in a local Partizan Regiment, for which they had enlisted, was very different from that in a regular corps." A company of South Carolina "rangers," led by Captain Alexander H. Boykin, faced two separate crises while serving in Virginia. First, the men heard rumors that they would be combined with a battalion of Virginia cavalry. They resisted. They had enlisted, the Carolinians declared, "with the express understanding" that their company would be "independent." To be combined with the Virginians, and to serve under officers not of their choosing, ignored "the laws which govern a corps of Rangers." Several weeks later, the men heard rumors that their home state might soon be threatened by invasion through North Carolina. "The Government will not be able to keep us here," Boykin assured his wife, if federal troops entered the Palmetto State.[34]

The Confederate government had not anticipated this conflict of interests. What if Confederate irregulars, posted far from home like Captain Boykin's South Carolinians, believed their towns, counties, and states faced greater perils than the places they had been assigned to defend? What if they balked, like the company of Texans, at being sent to distant parts? The Confederacy was pledged to state sovereignty, local defense, preservation of its territory, and maintenance of the geographical integrity of the South, but what if the Davis government could not provide the blanket of security implied by its rhetoric? What would happen when its priorities clashed with local needs? What would happen if citizens had to choose between the well-being of the nation and the security of their communities? What would happen when citizens had to fend for themselves?

The government's response to several of these questions was clear from the start. It discouraged guerrilla warfare where it provided only marginal benefits, as in the Deep South. It accepted companies for guerrilla service only if they mustered a minimum of sixty-four men, furnished their own weapons, and enlisted for twelve months. These requirements alone, especially the last one, caused many units to disband. The War Department limited recruitment still further by simply rejecting many independent companies from the Deep South. In mid-June, Jefferson Davis informed a hopeful Alabama guerrilla captain that his company could not be accepted if "the term guerrilla" implied "independent operations." Two weeks later, the secretary of war told an applicant, "The Department will not be likely to have any immediate use for mounted men organized at remote points from the scene of military operations." Other volunteers were simply told, "Independent Guerilla companies cannot be accepted in the Confederate service."[35]

In some instances, the War Department accepted men for service but insisted that they be "attached to a command deemed proper by the Government." It welcomed a regiment of Louisiana guerrillas eager to defend the vulnerable southern portion of their state, but told them the government could not promise the type of service they would perform or where their "field of operations" might be located. By August, seeking to curtail the flood of applications for guerrilla service and to bring order to this guerrilla mania, the Confederate Congress tried to legislate the problem. The act for "local defense and special service" authorized President Davis to limit the number and type of volunteers and to assign them where most needed. This gave cavalry regiments operating under men like Turner Ashby "large discretionary powers" without releasing them from government control. Davis and the War Department hoped this modified endorsement would define the limits of guerrilla warfare. They hoped to reap the benefits of partisan service without its messy complications.[36]

But Davis and the Congress had miscalculated if they thought this settled matters. The Confederate people had seized control of the war, and their passion for guerrilla fighting could not be easily slacked. Irregular operations continued to define large parts of the border region, and the rest of the South found them increasingly necessary. Guerrillas would flourish despite the government's needs or wishes.

RULES OF THE GAME

FALL 1861–SUMMER 1862

John Frémont may have preferred extreme measures, but he also understood the dangers of an unchecked guerrilla war. So did Sterling Price. So did most people who had witnessed its effects in Missouri. The morality of it quite aside, such unregulated conflict was too unpredictable, too hard either to direct or combat. Perceptive leaders on both sides knew the rules had to change, and Frémont and Price thought they had found a solution. Outnumbered better than two to one, Price had fallen back into southern Missouri by late October 1861. His force shrank still further when a majority of the men, lacking arms and loath to abandon their families, left the army when their enlistments expired. He and Frémont, worried about how irregulars on both sides would respond to the sudden absence of Confederate troops, agreed that future combat should be "confined exclusively to armies in the field." Arrests and intimidation "for the mere entertainment or expression of political opinion" should cease, and "all bodies of armed men acting without . . . authority or recognition" should disband. The implications of this pact were enormous. If implemented and mutually enforced, irregular warfare would be sharply reduced.[1]

But the agreement never had a chance. President Lincoln replaced Frémont with General David Hunter in November, and Hunter canceled it. "Black Dave," as he became known, had graduated from West Point nearly forty years earlier and was serving in Kansas when the war started. A volatile man of action, he caused a stir wherever he went. He expressed his opinions boldly and aggressively, and among his most decided views were a long-standing hatred of slavery and slaveholders. He attributed the chaos in Missouri more to Frémont's inept administration of the department than to the relentless nature of the guerrilla war. In any event, Hunter favored the jayhawker response to rebellion.[2]

Abraham Lincoln reinforced Hunter's assessment of the situation by leading him to believe that Price's army would retreat into Arkansas if pursued. The president also thought that Missourians were sick of the guerrilla war and would be in no mood to continue fighting with Price gone. The president's analysis was true enough in its way, but Lincoln still underestimated the volatility of the situation in Missouri and

Kansas. "Doubtless local uprisings will for a time continue to occur," Lincoln told Hunter, "but these can be met by detachments and local forces of our own, and will ere long tire of themselves." If Hunter required additional forces, Lincoln added fatefully, he could seek "judicious co-operation with [James] Lane on the Kansas border."[3]

An alliance with Lane would have been bad enough, but Hunter made matters worse by turning instead to Charles Jennison. In the Great Jayhawking Expedition that followed, Jennison entered Missouri from Kansas City in mid-November with his newly formed 7th Kansas Cavalry. John Brown Jr., son of the martyred abolitionist, commanded one company that included several blacks, an appropriate symbol, since the expedition intended to "stir up an insurrection" among Missouri slaves. "Playing war is played out," Jennison told Missourians. If "peaceful" farmers did not lay down their arms, they would forfeit both lives and property. But the jayhawkers had come to rob Missouri, not police it, and all rebel sympathizers, peaceful or otherwise, suffered. Some of Jennison's men regretted the wanton destruction, but they believed the Union army had shown itself incapable of cowing rebels. Governor Robinson and General Hunter voiced support for Jennison in the midst of the raid. Hunter went so far as to praise him as "one of those men peculiarly fitted for bringing [the] war to a successful termination."[4]

As it turned out, Hunter was reassigned to the Department of Kansas within the week, replaced by a quite different but ultimately no less controversial commander. Henry Wager Halleck had graduated from West Point nearly twenty years after Hunter. The bookish Halleck, known as "Old Brains," had published a series of lectures on military tactics and a treatise on international law before the war, but he was an insecure man who expressed his opinions cautiously. Sensitive to criticism, he anxiously avoided censure and blame. It was unsettling for him, then, on assuming command of the rechristened Department of the Missouri, to receive urgent complaints, advice, and appeals from citizens and soldiers about conditions in the state. Virtually everyone identified the guerrilla war as the root of all evil.[5]

More than that, said the consensus, rebels understood only brute force. The government was foolish to remain "bound by the rules," declared a son of Edward Bates. "You may depend upon it," Bates explained, "that there will be trouble in Mo until the Secesh are *subjugated*," noncombatants as well as soldiers and guerrillas. Halleck reached the same conclusion. Missouri had too many "very bad" men, "shrewd and crafty men," who scoffed even at martial law. Faced with hundreds, perhaps thousands, of guerrillas, their numbers swelled by

Price's disintegrated army, Halleck decided that Lincoln's conciliatory policy could not work.[6]

Halleck's soldiers also denounced the old rules of engagement. They were tired of being shot by supposedly peaceful farmers and exhausted by fruitless marches against phantom foes. It was not the danger often-times as much as the wear and tear of campaigning that frayed men's nerves. Extremes of weather, rocky terrain and swamps, insects and sickness all lowered the threshold of what men could endure. They wanted to punish the people responsible for their condition. "Nothing that I can see now short of extermination will save Mo," a Union sergeant confessed to his wife. "Here we are only playing second best at their *own chosen game*—while . . . the Union Men are under coercion such as the world has never seen except say in a French revolution." An Ohio soldier believed the patience of many men was nearly played out. "As I go through this traitor country," he allowed, "two impulses are struggling in my heart, one to lay waste as we go—like destroying angels, to kill & burn and make the way of the transgressors hard—the other is to wage a civilized warfare." Thus far, he judged, the army had chosen the latter course, but "in view of the atrocities of the rebels," he warned, "our boys only wait for the word, to make the land desolate."[7]

Some soldiers had already begun to retaliate. An Iowa infantryman, completely fagged after a fruitless sixty-mile pursuit of Jeff Thompson's men, admitted that part of his regiment was fed up. "I suppose the boys burnt one mill down after they ground what we wanted," he told his wife, "& busted into Stores & houses & took what they wanted & Sat some houses on fire & cut up verry bad. Our Colonel tried to kep our Soldiers from distroying them but could not." An embarrassed Illinois soldier revealed to his wife: "Our army is doing some very disrespectful and disgraceful things. A perfect reign of terror, starvation and hatred we leave behind us as we go. . . . We never can be successful in this mode of warfare I know, Nancy, for some of our army is perfect thieves. Annihilation and destruction seems to be their motto."[8]

Halleck saw only one solution. Having abused his government's "mild and indulgent course," he declared in December, rebel guerrillas would henceforth be liable to capital punishment. Persons "not commissioned or enlisted" in Confederate service but suspected of murder, robbery, theft, pillaging, or marauding would be arrested and tried as criminals. If found guilty, they would be shot or otherwise dealt with. A few weeks later, as guerrillas continued to burn bridges, destroy railroads, and cut telegraph lines in northern Missouri, Halleck dispensed with the niceties of arrests and trials. "These men are guilty of the highest crime known to the code of war. . . . Any one caught in the act will be immediately shot." The orders satisfied Halleck's desire as a legal scholar to abide by the law, but he intended to enforce them in the spirit of a hanging judge.[9]

Some people thought Halleck's "stringent orders" posed a difficult question. On the one hand, a northern journalist acknowledged, such "severe and prompt punishment" did not go far enough. "Something more than 'General Orders' must be applied," he feared, to curb the outrageous behavior of rebels. On the other hand, and quite paradoxically, he wondered if the orders went too far. Several St. Louis rebels had challenged the constitutionality even of monetary assessments, and the journalist thought the law might well be on their side. Did not retaliatory measures threaten to escalate, rather than alleviate, the bitterness of the conflict? he asked. Halleck believed he acted strictly within the code of military justice. He distinguished very carefully between the acts of "soldiers" and those of "banditti" and "marauders," but the journalist wondered if rebels would appreciate the difference.[10]

Halleck and his subordinates applied the same standards of behavior to their own men, partly because complaints about depredations by U.S. troops had grown too numerous to ignore. Governor Gamble told him that loyal citizens had applied for protection against the "outrages" of federal troops. Nothing like the scenes depicted in Francisco Goya's "Horrors of War" could be found in Missouri, although it might be argued that Napoleon Bonaparte's suppression of Spain's original *petite guerre* was part of a national, as opposed to a civil, war. Even so, Halleck ordered that federal troops caught in heinous acts be shot down like bushwhackers.[11]

This included Jennison's jayhawkers, who had continued their raids into Missouri. Curiously, Halleck did not order the Kansans out of the state until mid-January 1862. Even then, he did so largely because Jennison's men had attacked rebels and Unionists indiscriminately. As a consequence, he claimed, the raiders had driven eighty thousand more Missourians to the rebel cause. One Unionist told Halleck that the jayhawkers and home guards had sent hundreds of men directly into Price's army. Halleck agreed with the Kansans that conciliation and "playing war" were "played out," but their tactics threatened the rule of law. Even more appalling came rumors that Jennison would be promoted to general. What worse example of leadership could the army be given? When Sterling Price protested the jayhawker outrages, Halleck assured the Confederate general that Jennison's men did not belong to his command and that he had ordered General Pope to deal with them.[12]

Halleck may also have acted when he did because the jayhawker problem still threatened the stability of Iowa. Tensions on Missouri's northern border had not disappeared. Fear of guerrilla raids remained a constant of Iowa life. Whole communities begged Governor Kirkwood to protect them from Missouri raiders who threatened "to blow their brains out." The culprits were likely men from Price's disbanded army. What was more, a new danger had appeared. Some Missouri rebels, in an effort to save their lives and property from Kansans, had joined the Unionist migration northward. Iowans claimed that these unwanted newcomers endangered the "public peace." When bands of jayhawkers then pursued the Missourians across the border, Iowans anticipated "almost certain . . . collision and bloodshed."[13]

Collisions had already occurred. Jayhawkers paid as little heed to the distinction between loyal and disloyal citizens in Iowa as they did in Missouri. "These Marauders under the pretense of being armed in the cause of the Union have commenced a system of Midnight Robbery," wailed the people of Fremont County. They demanded arms from Kirkwood and authority to retaliate. As for the growing number of "Rebel Refugees," a "bitter feeling" had grown between them and their neighbors. Loyal Iowans were afraid that "but a word [would] . . . bring on a civil strife." Kirkwood feared a "border war" should these conditions continue, and even with Jennison's men ordered back to Kansas, the potential for conflict remained palpable through the spring.[14]

Despite these associated evils, the damage inflicted by rebel guerrillas on Union resources remained Halleck's chief concern. He estimated that attacks on Missouri railroads and bridges alone destroyed $150,000 worth of property in the last ten days of 1861, even though he had assigned ten thousand troops to guard those very same lines. Halleck reiterated his orders to arrest and execute guerrillas, and officers threatened to discipline soldiers who failed to comply. Judging by the reports and rumors of summary executions, most men required no such prompting. Rather than conduct two captured guerrillas to prison, a detachment of Ohio cavalrymen told them to "run for life." "One was making good his escape when one of the officers took after him and killed him with his revolver," reported a trooper. "The other man was shot down almost instantly with several balls." When a Missouri cavalryman learned that his brother had been shot by "a d——d bushwhacker," he vowed "to get revenge of them."[15]

Refugees, whether driven from their homes by soldiers or by guerrillas, were a common sight in all parts of the South and lower Midwest during the war. From *Leslie's Illustrated Newspaper*, as reproduced in *The Soldier in Our Civil War* (1894).

Captured guerrillas fortunate enough to escape drumhead convictions had their fates decided by military commissions. Unlike courts-martial, which passed legal judgments on soldiers, the United States used commissions to consider the cases of civilians accused of such crimes as treason, collaboration, and spying. By letting the commissions also decide the fates of rebel guerrillas, the government underscored its conviction that these men were not worthy of being called soldiers. And, indeed, the trials exposed the brutality and heartlessness of some guerrillas. One prisoner justified hanging a Unionist by saying he had wanted "to see one union man shit his last dieing turd." In another case, a gang of men had burst into the home of a "d——d Black Republican," plundered his dwelling, kidnaped and executed him, and left his body lying in the road. When the man's wife found the corpse, her husband's entire upper body had been riddled by bullets, "his head and face . . . all shot to pieces."[16]

Nonetheless, most guerrillas appear to have received fair trials. Even when convicted, they often escaped death. Conflicting testimony could result in a prison sentence rather than a hangman's noose. Prisoners able to convince trial boards that they had been operating as soldiers, not guerrillas, also received leniency. One commission found James E. Hicks guilty of being a guerrilla and stealing personal property but did not think he had been involved in the worst of his band's crimes, cattle rustling. He received a sentence of only five months at hard labor.[17]

Other men just got lucky. Joseph Hart was sentenced to hard labor with a ball and chain fixed to his leg for the duration of the war. However, so extensive were his crimes, and "so notoriously low" his reputation, that the district military commander expressed surprise that Hart had gotten off with "so mild a sentence." James Howard, who confessed to tearing up railroad tracks, burning depots, and cutting telegraph lines, claimed that peer pressure had made him a guerrilla. His brother-in-law, testifying in Howard's behalf, told the commission, "He like myself is a poor man. . . . I think he did not know what they were going to do when he joined." A sympathetic commission, while condemning Howard to death, recommended leniency due to his "apparent ignorance & credulity." Halleck reduced the sentence to imprisonment for the duration of the war.[18]

Even so, Sterling Price challenged Halleck's right to put Confederates on trial and blamed the entire guerrilla war on the Federals. In a January letter to the Union commander, he insisted that "peaceful" Missourians could not be blamed for defending themselves. He further protested the arrest and execution of men whom he had "specially appointed and instructed" to destroy enemy property—mostly railroads and bridges—in accordance with "the laws of warfare." Price maintained, "It is necessary that we understand each other and have some guiding knowledge of that character of warfare which is to be waged by our respective governments." Halleck could not have agreed more. There should indeed be an understanding, he responded. "You must be aware, general," he elaborated, "that no orders of yours can save from punishment spies, marauders, robbers, incendiaries, guerrilla bands, etc., who violate the laws of war. You cannot give immunity to crime."[19]

President Lincoln summoned Halleck to Washington to replace McClellan as commanding general of the Union armies in June 1862, but the new commander in Missouri followed Halleck's course. General John M. Schofield had served under Halleck since November, and he had been the ranking officer in the state since April, when Halleck's growing departmental responsibilities had forced him to delegate more authority. Once in full command, Schofield expanded the assessment program and persuaded Governor Gamble to create a second militia force, the Enrolled Missouri Militia, to serve primarily against guerrillas.[20]

Whatever the changes, Missouri continued to be a breeding ground for restless and disaffected rebels, and no man better fit that description than a slender, blue-eyed, twenty-four-year-old drifter from Ohio. William C. Quantrill had tried his hand at a number of occupations before settling in Kansas in 1859. He sided with the antislavery movement on arriving but switched sides within a year to become a proslavery border ruffian. The change appears to have been inspired by a combination of political sympathies and personal animosities, but motivations are always hard to determine where Quantrill is concerned. He was a restless spirit in search of the main chance and some modicum of fame. In Missouri, he kidnaped escaped slaves and rustled livestock from both slaveholders and antislavery settlers. When the war started, he enlisted with Sterling Price but, like many other men, remained in Missouri when Old Pap retreated to Arkansas.[21]

Quantrill joined a small "home guard" in Jackson County, located just below the Missouri River and squarely on the Kansas border, and vowed to kill jayhawkers and protect Confederate citizens. Charismatic, a good horseman, and a crack shot, he soon headed the little band of fifteen men. At first, they did not think of themselves as "guerrillas"; they even paroled captured Union soldiers. Not until they realized that Henry Halleck's orders to execute guerrillas applied to them did

Quantrill's men turn ruthless. By early 1862, their leader had become "the notorious Quantrill," his men a "gang of robbers." The band numbered one hundred by the end of March, two hundred by July. Most Union soldiers dismissed Quantrill as "more a jayhawker than a Warrior," but legend enveloped him early on. One Federal compared him to Dick Turpin, the romanticized eighteenth-century English highwayman. "With his Gallantry & Chivalry . . . & sometimes bloody deeds," the soldier considered, "[he] is . . . the Great Hero of this section."[22]

In truth, Quantrill's band represented a curious, though not atypical mixture. The majority came from prosperous, middle-class families, most of them owning slaves. A few men had opposed secession, and nearly all of them understood the political ramifications of the war. They believed that jayhawker raids, Union confiscation, assessments, and the departure of the Confederate army from Missouri made guerrilla warfare necessary to protect property, maintain order, and preserve their own social status. Survival became their priority in a society that had collapsed around them. Which is not to label all of Quantrill's followers southern patriots. Many of them were ornery men in search of adventure and a legal way to raise hell. Not a few were just meanspirited. George Todd, a Canadian-born stonemason who became Quantrill's chief lieutenant, was "hot tempered" and "callously brutal." William Anderson, known as "Bloody Bill," decorated his bridal and saddle with Yankee scalps.[23]

By the spring of 1862, the woes of Missouri had spread to Arkansas. General Samuel R. Curtis, a West Point–educated former congressman from Iowa, had led his 12,000-man Army of the Southwest out of Missouri to defeat General Earl Van Dorn at the battle of Pea Ridge, Arkansas, fought March 7–8, 1862. The Union victory had two far-reaching effects. First, it cleared Missouri of any serious threat by rebel armies for the remainder of the war. Second, it inadvertently brought guerrilla warfare to Arkansas.[24]

After retreating from Pea Ridge, Van Dorn, a dashing, vain, and impetuous cavalryman, took what remained of his army into his home state of Mississippi. He left only guerrilla bands and militia to defend Arkansas, and even his arrangements with those men were slipshod. Most of the guerrillas turned out to be deserters from his own army who refused to leave their homes. Van Dorn and Price, who now served under him, commissioned a few men to form partisan companies, but no central military authority coordinated them. They had ignored the suggestion of one officer that Stand Watie, the popular Cherokee leader, lead resistance in the western part of the state. "His thorough knowledge of the country renders him eminently suitable to direct the movements of guerrilla bands along the border of Cherokee country," the officer submitted, "and the Indians will make the very best guerrillas."[25]

With or without a commanding officer, and quite against the odds, Arkansas guerrillas created a swarming defense that caught the Federals unprepared. "I don't suppose it is expected our little company to fight them much, but to watch them close and occasionally get one or two," reasoned a Texan who had come to help the Arkansans. The advancing Federals, thinking that Van Dorn's departure meant they could easily occupy the state, were stunned. "We are going down to the Mo. and Arkansas line again," a Union cavalryman informed his family. "I was shot at the last time and this time I may not be so lucky, for we think out here we would rather be in a big fight than to be shot at when we are going along the road." An Illinois soldier who had assured his wife that the guerrillas posed no threat soon changed his mind. Unnerved when the rebels bushwhacked some twenty men from his regiment in a matter of weeks, he declared that he had "rather be killed in battle than to be shot from behind a tree by . . . marauding bands of desperadoes."[26]

More than a dangerous nuisance, Arkansas guerrillas threatened the entire Union advance. Curtis had fallen into another Missouri. By the time he reached Searcy, Arkansas, forty miles north of his ultimate target of Little Rock, guerrillas had smothered him. Armed bands lurked everywhere in the surrounding hills and timber. Union soldiers disappeared almost daily, their mutilated bodies later found lying in the woods or swamps. Farmers along the line of march professed to be "good Union men," but soldiers sensed "a bitter and malignant spirit." Some officers were uncertain how to handle the dangerously ambivalent situation. Not so an Iowa colonel. Having lost a "considerable number of men," all butchered "in cold blood," he advocated "retaliation." Curtis took his advice and ordered that no bushwhacker be taken alive.[27]

But the federal predicament only worsened in late May, when General Thomas C. Hindman arrived to reorganize Confederate defenses in Arkansas. He faced a daunting prospect. Because Van Dorn had taken not only the army but also every spare animal, gun, and wagon, Hindman would have to rebuild the state's defenses from scratch. He would also have to restore morale, for rebel citizens felt abandoned. Hindman had been sent to Arkansas because its governor, Henry M. Rector, threatened to secede from the Confederacy if Richmond did not send help. A concerned Jefferson Davis replied that he would forsake neither Arkansas nor the Trans-Mississippi. Hindman, he promised, would remedy the situation.[28]

Though a Tennessean by birth, Hindman felt a personal responsibility to rescue Arkansas. He had settled in the state six years earlier, following volunteer service in the Mexican War, to become a prominent attorney and politician in the Mississippi River town of Helena. A forceful man, as well known for his hard drinking and abrasive personality as for his legal and political acumen, he now declared martial law, ordered Texas troops passing through Arkansas to join his command, snatched non-Indian troops from Indian Territory, enforced the new national conscription act passed by the Confederate Congress in April 1862, set price controls, increased manufacturing and mining operations, and burned stored cotton likely to be captured. Most of what he did was legal, but Hindman was not shy about stretching the law to achieve his ends. Citizens and politicians protested his policies so loudly that he was replaced as district commander in mid-July, but by then, the Tennessean had saved Arkansas for the Confederacy.[29]

Most importantly, Hindman had organized Arkansas's guerrilla war, assisted, unexpectedly, by the Confederate Congress. The full and quite profound ramifications of the Partisan Ranger Act, passed by the legislature in April, will be explored in due course. Suffice it to say here that the law allowed Hindman to organize and regulate "independent companies" of ten to eighty men each. Volunteers armed themselves, were paid only for subsistence and forage, and had to abide "by the same regulations as other troops." But when added to the bands authorized by Van Dorn and the volunteer companies drifting in from Missouri and Texas, they gave Hindman a large irregular defense force.[30]

And the system worked. Hindman's irregulars ambushed Curtis's wagon trains, cut telegraph wires, and bushwhacked Union troops. Captain Alf Johnson, praised as a "brave and skilled partisan" by Hindman, "literally destroyed an entire Union company" with his men. Other guerrilla chieftains, including Jack Chrisman and George W. Rutherford, took similar tolls on men and resources, occasionally extending their operations northward into Missouri. "There has been more done and with fewer men than any other part [of the country]," one satisfied guerrilla informed his wife from northern Arkansas. "So it does not require many men to harass a considerable army. . . . It is very exciting to be in the enemy's country not knowing what moment we will be attacked. When we camp, we hunt for a swamp and then move before day." The Federals had to send additional men to northern Arkansas, but, even then, they abandoned their march on Little Rock in favor of an easier objective: Hindman's Arkansas home of Helena.[31]

The Union march across northeastern Arkansas, begun in June, became part ordeal, part retaliatory strike. Curtis's supply line from Rolla, Missouri, had been effectively cut. When guerrillas and Confederate troops then stopped a supply expedition from moving up the White River to rendezvous with him, Curtis became the first Union general reduced to living off the land. His men confiscated and destroyed huge amounts of provisions and other property. They also collected thousands of slaves, which Curtis eventually freed. "Fields all burned out, houses, barns, cotton gins, and fences burned, and the smoke mingling with the dust darkens the heavens," reported an Iowa soldier on the march. "No white man to be found. Women crying but makes little impression on us." Despite the sense of satisfaction, it was an exhausting march. One man predicted that history would record it as "one of the most perilous events of the war."[32]

The army reached Helena in mid-July but found itself nearly besieged by guerrillas. Union raiding parties into the surrounding territory could not relieve the pressure. Curtis had established a Union foothold in Arkansas, but it was a slippery one. Thankful just to be out of the woods, he was content to consolidate his base and use the Mississippi River to supply his army.[33]

Debate over the legality of the guerrilla war also followed Curtis into Arkansas. Colonel Graham N. Fitch's 46th Indiana Infantry had formed part of the failed relief expedition up the White River. A combination of low water, river obstructions, and heavy fire from Confederate troops and guerrillas forced the navy's gunboats and transports to turn back, but Fitch blamed the entire fiasco on guerrillas. He had been appalled by the way they fired from shore at the river transports, once even shooting at the crew of a sinking gunboat as the men struggled to swim ashore. Fitch responded to this "barbarity" by warning inhabitants that "firing on the boats . . . would not be permitted." When the harassment continued, he issued another proclamation three days later. Thereafter, rebel citizens would be accountable for the savagery of their partisans, to be punished by seizure or destruction of their property.[34]

Hindman responded in writing to what he regarded as Yankee arrogance. What right had Fitch to dictate the rules of engagement? It so happened, Hindman informed him, that his men belonged to legally formed independent companies. "They are recognized by me . . . as Confederate troops," he declared, then added, with a touch of sarcasm, "I assert as indisputable the right to dispose and use those troops along

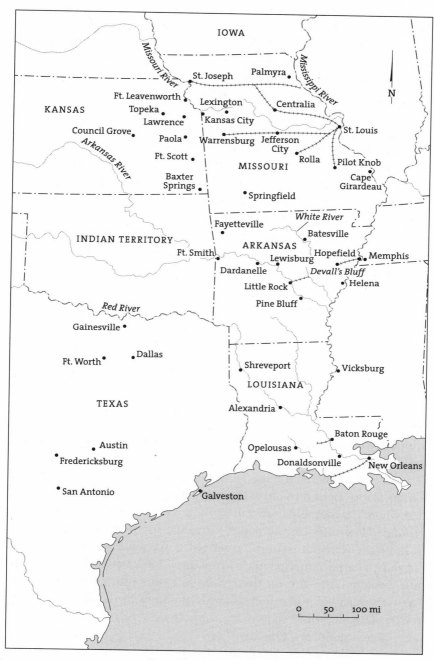

Map 1. The Trans-Mississippi

the banks of the White River, or wherever else I may deem proper, even should it prove annoying to you in your operations." To underscore his point, Hindman urged Arkansans in the next day's newspapers to resist the Federals by all means. "Attack him day and night," he directed, "kill his scouts and pickets, kill his pilots and his troops on transports, cut off his wagon trains, . . . shoot his mounted officers."[35]

Astonished by the "ill grace" of Hindman's response, Fitch asked if the rebel general did not understand the inevitable consequences of his policies. They encouraged "rapine and murder" and must surely lead his partisans to become "highway banditti, more terrible to citizens . . . than to soldiers and sailors of the United States." It was the same debate engaged in by Halleck and Price, and to be repeated many times by other Union and Confederate officers in the coming months. In this instance, the exchange resolved nothing. Confederate irregulars continued to hound Fitch, and he responded as he had vowed to do.[36]

Union and Confederate commanders in Louisiana were the next to square off over the guerrilla dilemma. Like other states of the Deep South, Louisiana had thus far been more observer than participant in the war. Defense of the coast had been the watchword in 1861. The state had busily recruited and trained troops to fight in the upper South, but Governor Thomas O. Moore had concluded that a well-structured and closely supervised militia would suffice for "home protection." People felt some unease in February, when the capture of Forts Henry and Donelson, in Tennessee, made possible a Union move down the Mississippi River, but the southern end of the river, opening into the Gulf, seemed safe enough. The situation changed inalterably when the Federals captured New Orleans in late April 1862.[37]

It looked at first as though New Orleans rebels might challenge the Union troops poised to enter their city. The Confederate garrison had fled when U.S. warships drew in sight, but defiant civilians stood their ground. "The mob on the wharf hurrahed for Davis and threatened to kill us if we came ashore," reported a marine aboard the flotilla's flagship. The potential people's army drew back when the ship's captain threatened to fire on the rebels, but they remained belligerent. "We were insulted and called all kinds of names by the filthy mob," the marine said. It would require martial law, severely enforced, to suppress rebellion in New Orleans.[38]

General Mansfield Lovell, the Confederate commander at New Orleans, had seen no choice but to order his outnumbered troops out of the city. However, he also realized that the Federals must not be allowed to occupy all of southeastern Louisiana and southwestern Mississippi.

With the backing of Governor Moore, he asked permission from Richmond to recruit five regiments under the new Partisan Ranger Act. Thus could he "contain the enemy in New Orleans and protect the state from his ravages." Moore hoped the rangers would also prevent possible slave rebellion. When no reply came from Richmond, the governor could wait no longer. He informed President Davis in early June that formation of a partisan corps had begun. "The urgent need of a defensive force admitted of no delay," he told Davis by way of apology.[39]

Richmond eventually approved the Lovell-Moore plan, and not a minute too soon. Having secured New Orleans, the Federals had moved quickly to capture the state capital of Baton Rouge, just eighty miles upriver, on May 9. From Baton Rouge, they could advance farther upriver to operate against Port Hudson and Vicksburg, and so close the lower Mississippi River. When the Federals captured Memphis on June 6 and Curtis moved into Helena a month later, the entire Mississippi valley seemed likely to be in Union hands by the end of the year. Governor Moore, having fled with his government to Opelousas, called on the citizenry to support the new partisan warriors until an army could be raised to drive out the invaders. "Let every possible assistance be rendered them in forming, arming, equipping, and mounting their companies and in giving them support and information," he declared. "Let every citizen be an armed sentinel to give warning of any approach of the insolent foe. Let all our river-banks swarm with armed patriots to teach the hated invader that the rifle will be his only welcome on his errands of plunder and destruction." Even without Moore's encouragement and Lovell's commitment, Louisianian Confederates understood their role. The first request from the state for a partisan ranger commission was sent to the War Department on the same day that New Orleans surrendered.[40]

Moore authorized nearly fifty partisan companies between mid-May and mid-June, although they were terribly slow to take the field. Richmond insisted on approving each of Moore's military decisions, and the uncertain communications between the capital and Louisiana delayed things considerably. Moreover, the Confederate Congress had determined by June that partisan rangers must be organized in battalions of no fewer than five companies. More than that, the War Department continued to siphon off conventional troops from Louisiana to reinforce Vicksburg. When Lovell, too, was sent to Mississippi in late May, Confederate Louisiana was left without a single general officer. Still, rebel guerrillas soon blanketed the swamps of southern Louisiana and the Mississippi delta. Moore also mobilized the state militia, which operated mostly as guerrillas. Without his irregulars, Moore's state, like Arkansas, would have been virtually undefended. It had, in any case, become part of an increasingly isolated Trans-Mississippi theater.[41]

Not that this eased the concerns of General Benjamin Butler, the Union commander at New Orleans. He had seen, while serving in Maryland, how quickly a guerrilla war could spread. The rebels in Louisiana appeared to be "poorly armed and worse organized," but Butler worried that their sheer numbers might pen him in New Orleans, demoralize his men, and expose Louisiana Unionists to danger. For those reasons, he ordered General Thomas Williams, his senior field commander, to "punish with the last severity every guerrilla attack and burn the property of every guerrilla found murdering your soldiers." Unionists at Baton Rouge, where Williams made his headquarters, demanded the same. "Many forbearing men on our side, Northern and Southern loyalists," he reported, "think leniency is all a mistake, but that the rebellionists must be chastized into loyalty."[42]

Butler's subordinates needed scant encouragement. As U.S. troops moved to control the railroads and protect telegraph lines connecting New Orleans to the outside world, they treated guerrillas as outlaws and confiscated or destroyed the private property of farmers suspected of being guerrillas or of assisting them. The navy had a tougher time. Concealed in underbrush that lined the river's banks, guerrillas fired at will into gunboats and transports that carried soldiers upriver. They captured slow-moving and lightly defended coal barges, and ambushed small parties that went ashore to acquire supplies or inspect the countryside. An exasperated Admiral David Farragut told the U.S. secretary of the navy, "The elements of destruction to the Navy in this river are beyond anything I ever encountered, and if the same destruction continues the whole Navy will be destroyed in twelve months." He ordered his gunboats to shell river banks where guerrillas had fired on his men, even in the vicinity of towns and villages.[43]

Striking at civilians often proved effective. Before Lovell took his army to Mississippi, citizens had begged him to use his partisans sparingly. The Federals always responded to guerrilla attacks with "outrages," they explained. Similarly, they asked Lovell not to destroy the railroad bridges, which he thought necessary to slow federal movements, because it would "bring down upon them Yankee vengeance." Disgusted by what he regarded as the self-interest of a well-to-do citizenry, the general nonetheless acquiesced, but he balked when planters asked him not to raise a partisan corps unless he could also provide conventional troops to protect them from the inevitable retaliation.[44]

Lovell would have been even more perplexed had he known how economic interests drove some planters into the Union camp. With the onset of U.S. occupation in Louisiana, rebel guerrillas received orders to burn cotton likely to fall into federal hands and hang any planter who resisted confiscation. Faced with financial ruin, some planters denounced the Confederacy and praised the northern occupiers for upholding the "principles of justice and civilization." Residents began to distance themselves from the rebels. "They represented these guerrillas as a lawless set," reported a Union naval officer, "whom the inhabitants of the country and small towns had a greater dread of than they had of the visits of our navy, or even of the army." A dozen wealthy citizens of Baton Rouge approached General Butler in late June to say they would do "everything possible to discountenance" the guerrillas. They would even swear allegiance to the United States if Butler wished it, although they suggested that this might not be for the best. "They thought they could do more good by abstaining from the oath at present," Butler explained, "because it would be impossible for them to have communication with these partisans if they took the oath and it should be publicly known."[45]

Other people felt genuinely caught in the middle. Two brothers living at Houma—a good twenty-five miles southwest of New Orleans—were accused of ambushing Union soldiers. They seem to have been innocent of the offense, but they were rebel sympathizers, and neighboring Unionists who bore them a grudge reported the men to the army. Learning what was up, the brothers fled the neighborhood with a group of genuine bushwhackers shortly before the 21st Indiana Infantry entered Houma. The Hoosiers swore to burn the town if the "murderers" were not handed over. Directed to one brother's home, they found neither fugitives nor evidence of their whereabouts, so contented themselves with driving off the family's livestock and leading away a dozen slaves. Soldiers kept the home under surveillance for several days and continued to hunt for the men. Finally, weary of the standoff, they burned the house to the ground. They never captured the brothers.[46]

Despite civilian fears and federal raids, rebel guerrillas succeeded in confining Union occupation to the areas around New Orleans and Baton Rouge. They had destroyed crucial railroad bridges and tracks, so that, unless the rivers and bayous ran high enough to allow the passage of gunboats, federal mobility was sharply restricted. Moore and Lovell also gained unexpected reinforcements when hundreds of Texans arrived, as they had done in Arkansas, to help defend southern Louisiana. One Louisiana Confederate believed that, despite federal retaliation, the state need not despair. "Even if we should have to have recourse to Guerilla Warfare," he declared, "we may sustain ourselves for several years."[47]

They had succeeded, too, with only tepid support from Richmond. The War Department, still reluctant to spread the guerrilla war farther than necessary, constantly reminded Moore that his partisans must be only a temporary remedy. Indeed, the partisan ranger program had been "greatly over done in Louisiana," warned Secretary of War George W. Randolph. Moderate numbers of partisans could "render effective service," he explained, but good partisan leaders were rare and the men they commanded "usually undisciplined." More than that, Randolph emphasized, an extensive partisan system diverted men and equipment from "troops in the line." Guerrillas and rangers could only "annoy the enemy"; they could not "materially aid in the conduct of the war." Moore knew that some ranger companies had proved ungovernable, but if the Confederate army could not guarantee the security of his state, what options remained? Many citizens, feeling isolated, abandoned, and vulnerable in scores of communities across the South, were asking the same question.[48]

None of that concerned Union generals in Louisiana. They only knew that the despicable rebel style of making war endangered their army. Although an attorney by profession, Benjamin Butler was not a legal scholar on a par with Henry Halleck, but he knew enough military law to spot an "uncivilized system of warfare" when he saw one. He also understood the precedents set by Halleck for punitive measures. Going Halleck one better, Butler offered bounties of one thousand dollars "for every guerrilla's head." Even more chillingly, being one of the first Union commanders to preside over a large slave population, Butler promised to emancipate any slave who brought in the head of a guerrilla.[49]

General Daniel Ruggles, commanding Confederates forces in eastern Louisiana, protested Butler's extreme measures. Confederate rangers had been sanctioned by their government, he reminded Butler, and even without such authorization, guerrillas represented the "first great law of nature, the right of self-defense." Every Confederate citizen, every community, Ruggles insisted, had the right to resist invasion. The Union army, by disregarding this right, which "no just law" could condemn, behaved like "the rudest savages." Proceeding to give Butler a history lesson, Ruggles reminded him that wars of independence, including the American Revolution, had "rarely been achieved by regular armies." Many other nations had employed partisans, and the right to make use of this "peculiar service" had been "universally conceded."

Certainly no nation other than the United States had ever denied an enemy the right to define its own military organization.[50]

Butler did not reply, but it hardly mattered. By August 1862, the war west of the Mississippi River had become almost exclusively a guerrilla conflict. There were no conventional Confederate forces at all in Missouri, and their presence in Kansas, Indian Territory, Arkansas, Louisiana, and Texas were either minimal or irrelevant. Federal commanders seemed to have the upper hand, yet they remained very much on the defensive. The stringent antiguerrilla measures of Halleck, Schofield, Curtis, and Butler betrayed concerns that "bands of desperate marauders" might dictate the course of the war. Any hope for a conciliatory policy was dead in the Trans-Mississippi, and its prospects east of the river looked dim.[51]

Edmund Ruffin had always known the Yankees were scoundrels, but by the autumn of 1861, he, like embattled generals in the Trans-Mississippi, was charging the enemy with "atrocious & systematic violations of the laws of civilized warfare." Their behavior only confirmed his instincts that the Confederacy must wage a guerrilla war of "retaliation." Of course, Ruffin may have been the most ardent rebel in the South, refusing even to recognize the legitimacy of the Lincoln government, but other people across the upper South also recoiled at the bitter and destructive war being waged against them. There would be no diminishment of guerrilla conflict in this region.[1]

One rebel took charge almost single-handedly on the middle border, the upper South between the Mississippi River and Virginia. John Hunt Morgan led officially recognized cavalry for much of the war, but as a master of guerrilla tactics, and generally leading independent commands within or behind enemy lines, he straddled an awkward divide between partisan and cavalry raider. More to the point, Morgan behaved more like a guerrilla chief than any other raider, including Alfred Jenkins. He looked the part, too. In his mid-thirties when the war started, the six-foot Morgan had broad, square shoulders and weighed an athletic 185 pounds. His well-groomed mustache and imperial beard, set against grayish-blue eyes, gave him a regal appearance. Like many of the best known irregular leaders, he was a prominent, well-educated member of his community. Unlike many of them, he had served in the Mexican War and, later, as a militia officer. Independent guerrilla bands looked to him for leadership, and desperate rebels everywhere hailed him as their Francis Marion.[2]

Morgan's most authoritative biographer believes he was drawn to a guerrilla's life by its inherent danger. He was a "pathological gambler" who thrilled at the excitement and high risks involved. Then, too, like many other guerrillas, he chaffed at the dull routine, discipline, and structure of the conventional army. He and his men relished their freedom as "detached" cavalry. "Morgan . . . is sort of an outsider," a Confederate soldier observed, "going when and where he pleases and most generally goes where he can do some damage." Revenge became another important stimulus. Creditors—apparently with Unionist leanings—seized his property when he entered rebel service. Thereafter, punishing Kentucky Unionists became a matter of personal pride. Morgan did not seek military glory as much as the destruction of his foes.[3]

Morgan's Civil War career began in late September 1861. Seeing the impossibility of Kentucky neutrality, Captain Morgan led his Lexington Rifles—a company of the Kentucky State Guard—on a month-long series of unauthorized attacks on Union pickets. The company mustered as conventional cavalry in late October but continued to operate independently, in partisan fashion. Their "deprivations," as the Federals called them, soon included attacks on railroads, bridges, ferry boats, telegraph lines, and Unionist homes.[4]

Morgan's fame grew rapidly in the early months of 1862, months of momentous change on the middle border. A rump Confederate state government had been formed at Bowling Green, Kentucky, to challenge the majority Union government, still in power at Frankfort; but Union victory at Mill Spring in January and the capture of Forts Henry and Donelson the following month gave the Federals control of eastern Kentucky and access to the Tennessee and Cumberland rivers. The swift strikes forced Albert Sidney Johnston to abandon Nashville, Tennessee, which the Federals entered unopposed in late February. The Confederacy's cordon defense of the upper South had begun to unravel, to be undone completely when Johnston was killed in early April at the battle of Shiloh. New Orleans surrendered at the end of April, as did Memphis in early June. The Confederacy had suffered its most costly five months of the war. The resulting occupation of western and central Tennessee, alone, deprived the rebels of crucial rivers, railroads, industry, natural resources, livestock, and grain.[5]

Morgan suddenly became the principal Confederate presence in Kentucky and a threat to the Union rear in Tennessee. The day after the Federals marched into Nashville, he slipped into the city to sink a steamboat. Using any trick to gain the upper hand, he dressed his men in Union uniforms and reportedly captured Federals by violating flags of truce. If themselves captured, and forced to swear allegiance to the United States, his men quickly returned to action. The noxious oath, they declared, was not binding. Small wonder Union soldiers and Kentucky Unionists called them vandals, scoundrels, plunderers, murderers, and all together a "desperate band." *Harper's Weekly* labeled their leader the "Bandit Morgan" and the "Highwayman of Kentucky."[6]

Strange to say, some northern newspapers, even a few Union soldiers, admired Morgan's boldness. The papers exaggerated his exploits and helped create a mystique around this "inscrutable guerrilla." Morgan's fame soon equaled that of Turner Ashby, and when the Virginian died that summer, Morgan stood alone as the premier Confederate partisan. Scores of young men flocked to him. "Morgan is now called the Marion of the War," reported a soldier in Johnston's army a week before Shiloh, "and he is doing most effective service and he is greatly dreaded by the Lincolnites."[7]

Morgan became the central figure in a network of "intrepid fellows," "enterprising scouts," "partisan soldiers," and detached cavalry throughout Kentucky and Tennessee. With their "characteristic craftiness," these rebels slowed and endangered the federal advance by tearing up railroad tracks, destroying tunnels and bridges, cutting telegraph wires, even fouling water wells. John S. Scott's 1st Louisiana Cavalry, Colonel James W. Starnes's 3rd Tennessee Cavalry, Colonel Jacob B. Biffle's independent (later, 19th Tennessee) cavalry regiment, and a battalion of Texas Rangers cooperated most frequently with Morgan. So did some independent guerrillas. Morgan's example resuscitated many local bands that had gone to ground. They collected weapons, ambushed patrols of Unionist home guards, and revived hopes of widespread resistance. Rebels even renewed their clandestine activities north of the Ohio River.[8]

Nathan Bedford Forrest played a similar role in rallying borderland rebels, but while the Federals would famously refer to him as "that devil Forrest," he maintained his identity as a cavalryman more successfully than did Morgan. The Tennessee planter, slave trader, and businessman recruited a battalion of mounted rangers early in the war, and he would always employ guerrilla tactics. However, unlike Morgan, Forrest worked more closely—if not always harmoniously—with conventional forces, and he eventually commanded an entire cavalry corps. His men, too, considered themselves cavalrymen. They neither sought nor earned reputations as marauders. Although Forrest led several devastating raids behind enemy lines, this could be said of many cavalry commanders on both sides. The role of cavalry had changed since the Napoleonic Wars. Reconnaissance and raids became their most frequent assignments. But, unlike Morgan, Forrest was just as ready to meet the enemy head on, and he did not use a "Union" state as his home base, as Morgan tried to do in Kentucky. Neither did he lead his raiders, as did Morgan, across the Ohio River, nor, most importantly, become synonymous with guerrilla resistance on the middle border.[9]

Meantime, Union soldiers had their hands full trying to decipher the loyalties of Kentucky and Tennessee civilians. They found the locals

"John Morgan's Highwaymen Sacking a Peaceful Village in the West" runs the caption in this northern newspaper. Most people, North and South, considered Morgan's men to be guerrillas, rather than raiders or partisans. From *Harper's Weekly*, August 30, 1862.

inscrutable. Rebel supporters, including people who fed and sheltered Morgan's men, sometimes welcomed Union officers into their homes and claimed to be Unionists. Only later did the officers learn that their hosts had cheered passing Confederates the preceding day. One historian has called this apparently devious behavior "survival lying." People, sometimes supporting neither side, would say anything to save their own skins. When faced by soldiers or guerrillas of any persuasion, they espoused the cause most likely to sit well with the armed men in their doorways. "There are to be [found] many persons calling themselves Union men," observed an Indiana officer, "but when you come to test the strength of their patriotism, it is invariably found that it is commensurate only with their interests."[10]

Confederate guerrillas seemingly knew whom to trust. "The citizens keep them informed . . . as to the location of our camps and picket posts," marveled a Union soldier in referring to Morgan's men, "and if need be are ready to serve them either as guides or spies." The support of the populace has always been necessary for the success of a guerrilla war. It had been true in the Spanish *petite guerre* against Napoleon, and it would be a guiding principle of twentieth-century guerrilla leaders from South Africa to the Middle East. Union leaders slowly recognized the warning signs, too. Spreading guerrilla resistance in Kentucky and Tennessee doomed any hope of conciliation or the resurgent Unionism Lincoln hoped would neutralize the border states. So-called noncombatants, Ulysses Grant told his wife Julia, were "worse rebels than the soldiers who fight against us."[11]

The situation made it harder for the Federals to trust genuine Unionists, who seemed unreliable under the best of circumstances. With a few notable exceptions, mostly in north-central Kentucky, not even the arrival of the army inspired very many of them to active resistance early in the war. Indeed, a goodly number, having taken refuge in Illinois, remained there, rather than return home. A colonel in central Kentucky believed tories only wanted a reunited nation if "it cost them nothing." They simply "disgusted" another soldier, who dismissed Kentucky Unionists as "a poor miserable, wretched looking and mean spirited class of men," mostly "cowards."[12]

His assessment was not entirely fair. Rebels posed a real danger, even to armed Unionists. A Union militia officer had difficulty recruiting in the region of Alexandria, Kentucky, because the community expected to be attacked nightly by guerrillas. Unionist families in eastern Kentucky lived "in fear & trembling." Late in 1861, a Captain Bails and twenty Red Rangers "bagged" nearly thirty "Lincolnites" in southwestern Kentucky. Confederates hailed Bails, who modeled his operations on the Texas Rangers, as a "terror" to Unionists. "If the *tories* capture a patriot, he immediately takes one of the tories," an admirer explained. "If they take a patriot's property, he will take a like amount from a tory." In this most recent action, Bails had responded to a Unionist leader who had vowed to cut out the heart of every Red Ranger and hang their collected carcasses from poles. Bails struck first.[13]

To their credit, the will to resist among both Kentucky and Tennessee Unionists generally rose in proportion to the advance of Union forces. Once certain they could rely on the army's protection, tories lost no time flogging rebel sympathizers "in payment for past treatment." Residents of two counties east of Memphis, having won resounding victories in recent political elections, asked the commander of a Union gunboat to help them finish off the rebels. "Send us arms and a sufficient force to protect us in organizing," they pledged, "and we will drive the secessionists out of Tennessee ourselves." Colonel John A. Garfield, future president of the United States, believed that Unionists in parts of eastern Kentucky were determined enough by March 1862 to resist the "small bands of reckless men" who still endangered them. Arm and organize them as militia, he thought, and they would speedily rid the region of Confederate "terrorism."[14]

As the seriousness of the guerrilla problem became clear, Union armies on the middle border also responded more resolutely. Their methods did not immediately mirror the radical remedies used in the Trans-Mississippi, but guerrillas and their fellow travelers, a "wild marauding set" altogether, received rough enough treatment. One rebel, guilty only of cutting telegraph wires south of Nashville, received ten years at hard labor. The new policy produced immediate controversy, too, just as it did in the Trans-Mississippi. When rumors surfaced in early March that General Don Carlos Buell had ordered the execution of four Morgan men as outlaws, their captain took action. Entering Union lines under a flag of truce, Morgan demanded a meeting with Buell. If his men were not released, Morgan said, he would hang thirty-six Union prisoners. The effrontery of the ultimatum—coming from a rebel captain of dubious legitimacy—enraged Buell, who generally endorsed conciliation and doubted the gravity of the guerrilla threat. He remained calm enough to assure Morgan that he never intended to hang the men, but he similarly refused to exchange prisoners. The matter ended there, with no apparent retaliation on either side, but danger clearly lay ahead.[15]

U.S. senator Andrew Johnson, appointed military governor of Tennessee by President Lincoln in March, changed things significantly on the middle border. Johnson, like Buell, had once endorsed conciliation, but the East Tennessee native was now prepared to battle rebel guerrillas. In his first public address as the civilian chief of his home state, Johnson warned that there would be a "terrible accountability" if rebel guerrillas did not cease their "depredations" against Unionists. He had been incensed by an instance the previous winter when Confederates hanged two Unionists accused of burning a bridge near Greenville, in East Tennessee. The bridge burning had been part of a Unionist plan to hasten the entrance of federal troops into the region by destroying rebel transportation. It was a legitimate guerrilla action, even by rebel rules. Yet, the new Confederate secretary of war, Judah P. Benjamin, had authorized executions "on the spot." Not only that, but the bodies hung for several days along the tracks so that passengers on passing trains could strike them with sticks. "Is there any outrage half so revolting in its magnitude?" Johnson thundered.[16]

The most murderous Confederate guerrilla in Tennessee and Kentucky by this time was Champ Ferguson. The forty-one-year-old Kentucky farmer was the only one of ten siblings not to support the Union. He joined Captain Scott Willis Bledsoe's independent company early in the war, apparently in exchange for having the Confederate courts drop a charge of murder against him in Tennessee. He then recruited his own outfit in late 1861. Ferguson ranged from north-central Tennessee all the way to the Ohio River, occasionally even into Alabama and Virginia; but he directed most of his operations against Unionists in his old neighborhood of Clinton County, Kentucky, and his new home of White County, Tennessee, southeast of Nashville. Ferguson shot his first Unionist in November 1861, apparently in cold blood. By the time he was captured and tried as a guerrilla at the end of the war, he would be charged with fifty-three murders. Eight of those murders came during a six-month spree between November 1861 and April 1862.[17]

Ferguson claimed to hold a captain's commission in the Confederate army and to have "only obeyed orders from superiors" in conducting his raids, but no evidence of a commission exists, and everyone knew Champ to be a hard man. Tall, slender, with sandy hair and blue eyes, Ferguson had a smiling countenance and easy manner. He insisted that every man he shot, tortured, or dismembered had first threatened him. One of Morgan's officers recalled of him, "The mountains of Kentucky and Tennessee were filled with such men, who murdered every prisoner they took, and they took part, as their politics inclined, with either side." Ferguson held no political views, only grudges.[18]

Andrew Johnson had been military governor of Tennessee barely a week when he first heard Ferguson's name. Reports from terrified and outraged citizens reached him at his headquarters in Nashville through the spring and summer. A rumor surfaced that Ferguson had been offered one thousand dollars to kill Johnson himself. Like most well-known guerrillas, he seemed to be omnipresent. His enemies attributed every assassination, every burned barn, every ambush to his band. Johnson set Unionist guerrillas and home guards on his trail, as well as to hunt down Bledsoe and Oliver P. Hamilton, another rebel guerrilla chief in the region.[19]

David C. Beaty, known as "Tinker Dave," led the deadliest of Johnson's Unionist guerrilla bands. Beaty formed his command in February 1862 in response to the "conscripting, killing, and shooting at Union men" in his home county of Fentress, Tennessee. He and Ferguson became bitter rivals who skirmished with each other regularly. Ferguson claimed that men like Beaty were his only enemies. "I haven't got no feeling agin these Yankee soldiers," he maintained, "except that they are wrong, and oughtn't to come down here and fight our people. I won't tech them; but when I catches any one of them hounds I've got good cause to kill, I'm goin' to kill em."[20]

Increasingly, "extermination" seemed the only way to eliminate rebel guerrillas. Newly promoted lieutenant colonel Joseph W. Keifer, a twenty-five-year-old graduate of Antioch College and a confirmed abolitionist, reached that conclusion earlier than some Federals. He had served in western Virginia before his Ohio regiment was transferred to Tennessee. Like Rutherford B. Hayes, he had seen how dangerous the Virginia guerrillas could be, but he did not appreciate the gravity of the guerrilla war until March 1862, when he learned that John Morgan's men had bushwhacked an Ohio cavalry officer. More shocking even than the devious act was the way local rebels openly rejoiced over it. When some "resident 'Sacesh'" who had acted as scouts for Morgan were captured a few days later, Keifer decided *"They should be shot."*[21]

His emphatic call for revenge marked a change of heart for Keifer. "When in W. Va I had great sympathy for the Rebels who remained at their homes," he explained to his wife. "I thought they were ignorant, and more objects of pity than of punishment." However, the death of a fellow officer taught Keifer that compassion would not work in Tennessee. Confederate guerrillas constituted a dangerous foe, and civilians who sheltered and encouraged them posed equal threats. These rebels, he believed, stood "ready at all times to stab us in the back." Buell had been too soft on them, Keifer decided. He hoped that Andy Johnson would respond "in a more *severe* and *summary manner.*" If not, Keifer warned his wife, the guerrilla war he had "long since predicted" would "be fully inaugurated."[22]

General Robert L. McCook, another son of Ohio, had also served in western Virginia, but his death in southern Tennessee cemented Union attitudes toward guerrillas on the middle border. McCook suffered so badly from dysentery that he was traveling by ambulance on August 5, 1862, when he encountered rebel horsemen between Winchester and Dechard. Precisely what happened on this journey is uncertain. Rebels said a cavalry patrol intercepted the ambulance and ordered McCook's driver to halt. The driver refused; pistols shots exploded. The mortally wounded McCook was taken to a nearby farmhouse, but a local doctor could not save his life. Not so, said the Federals: Guerrillas had attacked the ambulance and murdered McCook. The rebels may, in fact, have been partisan rangers, but that hardly mattered to northerners. *Harper's Weekly*, famous for its graphic depictions of the war, called them "miscreants" and "guerrillas," and published a drawing that showed McCook on his knees, apparently begging for mercy, as the rebels shot him in cold blood.[23]

More certain was the Union response. Blaming the incident on cowardly guerrillas, infuriated soldiers burned homes in the vicinity of the attack. They arrested nearly every male, regardless of age, for miles around and reportedly shot a Confederate officer home on sick leave. One soldier complained that the general's murder typified rebel behavior in Tennessee. Guerrillas nightly killed pickets, lone soldiers, and convalescing Union officers. "We are getting exasperated too now," he informed his sister, "and will soon balance matters if they don't stop."[24]

The same fate may have awaited McCook in western Virginia had he remained there. The guerrilla war had spread through that fretful region to a point where, by mid-1862, it hampered Union military operations and injured southern Unionist morale. The same thing had happened everywhere rebel guerrillas mobilized, but Virginia was different. Both the Lincoln and Davis governments were more acutely aware of the military situation in that theater and of the ways the war had been shaped there by irregulars. Both governments worried about the unchecked growth of guerrilla fighting. They worried for different reasons and to different degrees, but both sides recognized that a crisis was upon them and that definite military and political steps must be taken to deal with it. Their actions reverberated throughout the South and changed the nature and direction of the entire war.

Northerners accused rebel guerrillas of "murdering" General Robert L. McCook in August 1862. From *Harper's Weekly*, August 23, 1862.

The situation evolved this way. A series of military defeats and blunders had sent the Confederate army in western Virginia reeling all the way back to Staunton in mid-December 1861. However, even in the absence of supporting troops, Confederate guerrillas, as in Missouri, continued to bedevil the Union army and its civilian supporters. "There has been more Union men killed and more property stolen and destroyed within the last six weeks than at any previous time," asserted a western Virginia Unionist at the end of November. He estimated that at least one thousand rebel guerrillas, divided into companies of a dozen to one hundred men, operated in a seven-county area around his home. Even if he exaggerated the numbers, it must have seemed as though guerrillas prowled at will. Disruption of local government became one of their chief goals. By destroying post offices and county courthouses, waylaying sheriffs and tax collectors, and threatening the operation of law courts, they hoped to destroy Unionist morale.[25]

Something beyond political convictions divided many communities. Kinship and family ties produced a type of "clan" warfare that often intensified these tussles. The Civil War has often been called a "brothers' war," but sisters, spouses, and all variety of cousins could equally be at odds. This seems to have been especially true in the upper South, which had seceded reluctantly and maintained a large Unionist population. The same could be said of Missouri, but family clashes became even more likely "back east," with its older, more established communities. In any case, people understood the potential for grief. "Kindred will be divided by the sword. Ancient friendships changed to bloody feuds," predicted a northwestern Virginian who had opposed the "anarchy" of secession. "Organizing the neighborhood for local defense," protecting it against the chaos of rebellion, and maintaining law and order without endorsing either side seemed the wisest course to him.[26]

The intensity arose, too, from the middle-class status of many rebel guerrillas in western Virginia. Like their counterparts in Missouri and on the middle border, they included prosperous, educated, and respected leaders of their communities who had much at stake in the war. They may or may not have been slaveholders. They may or may not have been cruel men who relished blood sport, but they generally were not poor or landless people. Pennsylvania-born Daniel Dusky, a leader of the Moccasin Rangers, was a fifty-two-year-old farmer and justice of the peace. Forty-two-year-old Perregrine "Perry" Hays, another "notorious" Moccasin Ranger, was a man of property, former postmaster, and former state legislator. The leader of the combined Rightor and Curry clans, Peter B. Rightor, accused of murder and robbery by Unionist neighbors and described by the U.S. government as a "Bad Secesh & guerilla leader," was a "well-to-do farmer and grazier" in his mid-fifties. He had been an articulate leader of the secession movement, but when his handsome residence was burned in June 1861—whether by Unionists or the U.S. Army is unclear—he became a bushwhacker who lived only for "revenge." E. D. Thomison, who led a band of fifteen guerrillas in Fayette County, was only twenty-two, but at least four of his men were over forty, and over half of them came from landholding families. The young and the restless, like Perry Connolly, undoubtedly contributed many tough customers to these bands, and they often came to dominate as the war progressed, but it is not without significance that many sober-minded men with a good deal to lose in a local guerrilla war considered guerrilla operations the best means of resisting Union soldiers and combating tory neighbors.[27]

Whomever its opponents by early 1862, the Union army found it nearly impossible to control western Virginia without help from loyal citizens. These people, who had been angrily denouncing both the national and state governments for not protecting them, needed little coaxing. Unionists had been reluctant to join the volunteer army because that generally meant being assigned to duty outside western Virginia, but they were keen to form companies of "experienced woodmen and good shots" to defend their own and adjoining counties. The army played to this desire by allowing Unionist bands to round up rebel guerrillas, an assignment endorsed by local political leaders. The Mountain Marksmen and similarly named companies, knowing the haunts and habits of the men they pursued, captured many "thoroughbred guerilla secessionists." One Union army officer singled out an especially effective band, led by John Tucker in the area of Hardy County, for "striking terror" in the hearts of "rebel desperadoes."[28]

The antisecessionist Swamp Dragoons and rebel Dixie Boys of Pendleton County, located just northwest of Staunton in the Shenandoah Valley, understood this type of warfare. Both bands cooperated with respective companies of Union and Confederate "scouts" assigned to "special service" in the area, but they lived by their own rules. "We have caught and sent off over 100 [Unionists]," one of the Confederate scouts reported in early December, "but I can't see that it does much good. The union company have hoisted a black flag against our company." A month later, these scouts and the Dixie Boys, having learned of an impending raid by the "unionist pirates," launched a preemptive

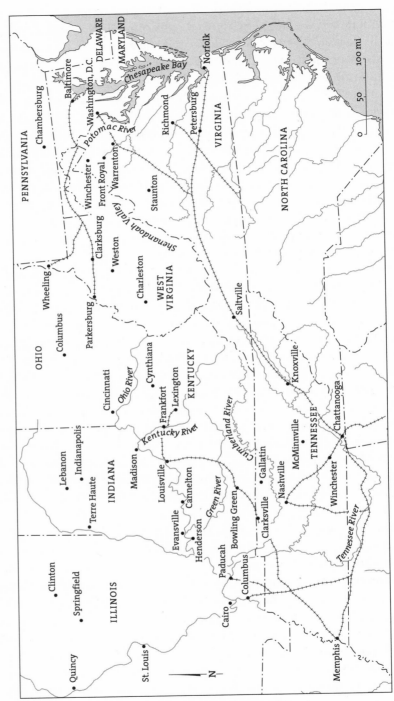

Map 2. The Border South and Lower Midwest

strike against the Swamp Dragoons. They killed eight, wounded two, and captured eight horses while suffering five casualties (two dead) of their own.[29]

The U.S. Army also assigned regiments of Virginia volunteers to track down and destroy guerrillas. Some recruits had already experienced the guerrilla war as home guards, and they all had a strong incentive to rid the region of bushwhackers. Company C, 11th [West] Virginia Infantry, recruited in the vicinity of Parkersburg, made the destruction of the Moccasin Rangers its priority. They fought the Moccasins on several occasions, and both sides aimed bold retaliatory raids at each other's strongholds. Company C finally got the better of this war of attrition in early 1862 by capturing a sizable number of rangers. They executed several leaders on the spot and delivered up the remainder for trial. Two men, Daniel Dusky and Jacob Varner, received lengthy prison terms.[30]

General Benjamin F. Kelley and the 1st [West] Virginia Infantry drew one of the toughest assignments in this antiguerrilla campaign: protecting the Baltimore and Ohio Railroad (B&O). Kelley made clear that guerrilla attacks on his troops, wagon trains, or the railroad would be punished severely. His soldiers tracked and wounded Perry Connolly, who had plagued the B&O for months, in an attack on Connolly's camp. They beat the guerrilla chief to death with gun butts, burned the house of the family on whose land he had encamped, and confiscated the family's livestock. Connolly's death had a chilling effect on many western Virginia guerrillas, who abandoned partisan ranks for the conventional army over the next few months. Nancy Hart, Connolly's lover, had not been in camp during the attack, and her subsequent activities may be traced only through rumors and local lore. She was apparently captured that summer but escaped and resumed her guerrilla career. In any event, she married another guerrilla, bore him a child, and survived the war.[31]

The gathering of so many reinforcements shows the U.S. Army's growing concern with the guerrilla problem, and virtually all Union soldiers, not just native Virginians, endorsed fierce retaliation by 1862. Their attitude was hardened further by scorn for the South's white population. The response was not unique to western Virginia, but it became apparent there early in the war, as seen by Colonel Keifer's condescending remarks. Regarding rebels—and many Unionists—as ignorant, duplicitous "crackers," northern soldiers could easily justify harsh treatment, not only of guerrillas but also of the general population. It was an understandable reaction, given long-held northern stereotypes of the South, but whether soldiers entered the South with preconceived notions of the white southern character or acquired them through personal experience, the result was the same: disdain for the enemy. They neither knew nor cared about Daniel Dusky's middle-class credentials. "What a good-for-nothing people the mass of these western Virginians are!" exclaimed Rutherford Hayes in mid-January. "Unenterprising, lazy, narrow, listless, and ignorant." Hayes respected the South's wealthy classes—the slaveowners—but he dismissed the rest as "serfs," inferior even to black slaves.[32]

Union soldiers also came to detest their government's policies and politicians—as well as some generals—that coddled southerners. The war would never end, and guerrillas would only be encouraged to resist further, unless executions and destruction of property replaced loyalty oaths and prison terms. They cursed the "sons of bitches" and "hell hounds" who tormented them, not only for the death and destruction the rebels wreaked, but also for the "privations and exposures" required to root them out. "Forbearance" had "ceased to be a virtue," they declared. "The more I see of this war in Western Virginia," a soldier testified, "the more thoroughly am I convinced that nothing short of extermination to all who are engaged in this rebellion will give peace to this section. But when will the *powers that be* realize the true state of affairs? I would to God that the Rebels *would* raise the *black flag*, and our government meet them under the same."[33]

Western Virginia soldiers and Unionists particularly hated the practice of releasing obviously guilty guerrillas who had taken the U.S. oath. Like Morgan's men, other rebels routinely broke their oath, and, once released, they encouraged "anarchy" and became a "terror to neighbors." Mary Jane Green, for example, had been arrested for cutting telegraph wires and providing information about Union troop movements to other guerrillas. The illiterate Green, known as much for profanity and hatred of Yankees as for sabotage, willingly took the oath in order to resume her activities. The captain of the Mountain Marksmen, seeing his own men bushwhacked by such duplicitous rebels, insisted, "It is not right, and I must either send my prisoners at once to the devil, where they belong, or to some more secure place." A western Virginia civilian reported, "Union sentiment has been most fearfully discouraged and in some instances destroyed from the fact of the release of some . . . notorious outlaws and cut-throats."[34]

As spring approached, federal soldiers and Unionists also worried about the large number of discharged and paroled Confederate soldiers who would be coming home. Even nature seemed to favor them. New foliage meant more camouflage to conceal their camps and movements and enhance their effectiveness as scouts and guides. Spring also made Unionist farmers more vulnerable. Returning to their fields to plant new crops, they ran the risk of being "shot down at the plow." After the capture of Peter Rightor, Unionists in his neighborhood anticipated that the remnants of his band would resume their murderous spree "as soon as the leaves cover[ed] the woods." A "general feeling of anxiety" gripped Unionists everywhere. Rumors spread that former soldiers would turn guerrilla and wage "a bloody and relentless war." Community petitions urged Governor Pierpont and army commanders to imprison discharged rebels for the duration of the war. An "impassable gulf" divided rebels and Unionists, they declared, "which forbids the idea of the two living together in harmony in the same community."[35]

It was precisely now, in the spring of 1862, as the attitude of Union soldiers unequivocally hardened, that Confederate leaders expressed their own concern about the guerrilla war by altering its structure and redefining its role. Rebel citizens, no less than southern Unionists, craved some dramatic action against the encroaching enemy, and if the army could not provide it, they said, then more guerrillas should be used. The authorities in Richmond were taking notice, both of the military situation and of the public mood, but the first politician to react was Governor John Letcher of Virginia.

On March 18, Letcher created the Virginia State Rangers, the first statewide system to regulate rebel guerrillas. Letcher's plan addressed two needs. Most importantly, it provided for local defense. At the same time, it offered a model for controlling Confederate guerrillas and refuting Union charges of barbarity. Letcher recruited most of his ten companies from existing guerrilla bands that operated in "districts overrun by the public enemy." They included George Downs's Moccasin Rangers and men led by John Spriggs, Ben Haymond, John Rightor, and George Dusky, a son of Daniel. However, in return for this legal protection, "rangers" must submit to the orders of Letcher and local Confederate commanders and "conform their operations to the usages of civilized warfare." They would be "rangers," not the "rebel scouts, 'bushwhackers,' and horse-thieves" the guerrilla movement had come to represent in Virginia.[36]

The new Virginia defensive system, which had been rumored for weeks before approved by the legislature, worried Unionists and Union soldiers. A western Virginia officer told Governor Pierpont that the prospect of facing a "regular system of Guerilla warfare" vexed him. "I have no fear of a general move by them [the Confederate army], *in force*," he explained, "but . . . then Guerilla operations . . . might do us much damage." Rebel sympathizers who had heretofore kept to their homes might "take up arms to aid them in committing any depredations either on Union citizens or troops." The officer recommended that rebels in western Virginia be disarmed immediately, Unionists formed into an organized militia, and more troops sent to areas of guerrilla activity. Even as he wrote, another of his own men was shot and several Unionists burned out of their homes by guerrillas.[37]

The officer was right about the rebel response. Confederate partisans swarmed through western Virginia during the spring and summer. Men who had previously stayed at home joined the rangers, and citizens who could not find a place among the sanctioned partisans formed still more independent bands. Whole communities of men, "their trusty rifles in hand," resolved to prowl the mountains and "bush whack" Yankees. The war suddenly grew even tougher for the Federals in Virginia. It would be enough that their grand conventional campaign of the spring and early summer—the Peninsula campaign to capture Richmond—would be turned back by Joseph E. Johnston and Robert E. Lee. The guerrillas now added to their woes by tying down large numbers of troops, forcing the Federals to scatter their commands, and frustrating efforts to mount larger operations "of a general character."[38]

But Virginia's new ranger system also worried some Confederates, including General Henry Heth, a thirty-seven-year-old West Point graduate who commanded troops in western Virginia. Heth complained twice in three days to Governor Letcher that the state's rangers were nothing more than "organized bands of robbers and plunderers, . . . notorious thieves and murderers, more ready to plunder friends than foes." Heth was especially critical of the Moccasin Rangers, which some local residents had begged him to disarm. The rangers also injured recruitment for the army by providing a "loophole" for men wishing to avoid regular service. Many of these volunteers doubtless relished the opportunity to fight "on their own responsibility," Heth said, but this too often meant "roaming over the country, taking what they want[ed], and doing nothing." Small bands of such men had their uses, Heth acknowledged, but they had to be well led and properly managed.[39]

The controversy brewed for several weeks. Charges against Letcher's rangers, insisted their friends, had been exaggerated. The companies had rescued western Virginia and nearly forced out the Federals. A few Moccasins may have abused tories unnecessarily, but their sins should not be allowed to damn the many. "I would not give Capt. George Downs for a Regt. of such commanders as Genl. Heth," declared an advocate of the rangers. Letcher consulted with his attorney general and General Robert E. Lee, who acted as President Davis's military adviser. Lee sided with Heth. He recommended that the rangers be disbanded, their arms placed in the hands of militia or volunteers, and the men made subject to Heth's command.[40]

In mid-May, Letcher and the General Assembly responded with a compromise: the Virginia State Line. This reorganization of the existing state militia was inspired by several military and political problems, not just the ranger controversy, but it led to the gradual death of Letcher's ranger system. Most ranger companies entered the State Line or became attached to conventional cavalry regiments. Coincidentally, around this time, the Federals captured some of the most controversial of the original ranger captains, including George Downs, Jack Chewning, John S. Spriggs, and Marshall Triplett.[41]

By then, the Confederate Congress had shown its concern by creating a nationwide partisan corps. With the first anniversary of the start of the people's war in Baltimore fast approaching, public calls for an expanded guerrilla war had grown. The government received requests from across the South to organize guerrilla companies. People pointed to the successes of Ashby in the Shenandoah Valley, Morgan on the middle border, and Jeff Thompson in Missouri. The resulting Partisan Ranger Act, approved in late April after spirited debate, thus met with popular approval. It saved the military crises in Arkansas and Louisiana, and for anyone still doubting the value of partisan warfare, *De-Bow's Review* offered a blunt endorsement. The nation faced a crisis, the journal declared. The time had come to relinquish "all fastidious notions of military etiquette." The enemy must be expelled "by any and every means."[42]

In all the excitement, however, few people appreciated one essential purpose of the Ranger Act. What the southern public and the Union government took to be an expanded commitment to guerrilla warfare was, in fact, an attempt to regulate it. The Confederate War Department stressed that district commanders would decide where, when, and to what extent partisan rangers would be used. There would be no "independent" fighting. The government freely admitted the reason for these limits, too. "The object of this rule," the War Department assured worried generals, "is both to restrict the number of such Corps within the actual wants of the service, and to ensure the selection of suitable persons for such commissions." Similarly, Secretary Randolph told a Virginia colonel, "The Partizan service is considered as subordinate to the general service. . . . To have two independent armies, conducting two independent systems of warfare in the same field, would lead to inevitable confusion and disaster."[43]

Ultimately, the Ranger Act did not spread irregular warfare geographically so much as intensify it and produce an ever more confusing system of guerrilla resistance. Dozens of new leaders emerged in Kentucky, Tennessee, and Virginia. Some of them, including Duncan Cooper and Lewis Kirk, tended to operate less like rangers than guerrillas, still independent of government direction. Other men, such as Adam Johnson, Ellis Harper, and T. Alonzo Napier, received ranger commissions and seemed more firmly in the fold.[44]

John D. Imboden, a Virginia lawyer and legislator before the war, emerged as one of the most visible new partisan leaders. As a captain of artillery in the conventional army, Imboden had long advocated an expanded guerrilla war. He had lobbied both Jefferson Davis and George Randolph for a commission as a guerrilla chief long before the Ranger Act was passed. "I shall expect to hunt Yankees as I would wild beasts," he promised Davis, "to live & fight like Indians." Davis replied that "special" organizations for "local defense" were indeed needed in northwestern Virginia, Imboden's proposed field of operations, but that Imboden could hardly be allowed to operate "to the full extent proposed." Whether by accident or design, Imboden's request became snarled in red tape for another two months. Only after passage of the Ranger Act did he receive his commission and permission to raise a regiment of partisans. He was assigned to the Shenandoah Valley, where, following the untimely death of Turner Ashby in early June, Imboden became the new partisan leader in Virginia.[45]

This new wave of energy swept across the entire upper South. Every community looked for another Morgan or Ashby to rise and defend it. The summer of 1862 marked the high point of public confidence in the guerrilla war. Rebels believed that the combination of conventional and irregular warfare would soon expel the invader. Edmund Ruffin even envisioned an invasion of the North. A force of 25,000 guerrillas, he believed, "might lay waste to Philadelphia with fire and sword, or lay Cincinnati & even Chicago in ashes." The "destitute population" of those cities, he fancied, would then join rebel invaders to plunder, sack, and burn. What better way, he asked, to retaliate against "their violations on our territory of the laws of war."[46]

Northerners had good reason to fear just such a scenario when, on July 4, 1862, John Hunt Morgan's brigade embarked on a 27-day, 1,000-mile raid northward from Knoxville. Driving as far as Cynthiana, Kentucky, just fifty miles from Cincinnati, Morgan captured and paroled more than 1,200 Union soldiers and thwarted a federal move toward Chattanooga. Across the river, the citizens of Ohio and Indiana went on heightened alert. Ohioans responded most forcefully. Unprecedented numbers of Buckeyes volunteered to raise "garilla" bands and companies of "rebel hunters." They vowed to "put a stop to the gurilla rebles" who were "committing sutch out rages in the border states."[47]

The Union army worried, too. Officers found their supply lines severed, their men "entirely powerless against the rapid movements of partisan cavalry," the situation "unsettled" and "ominous." General Buell, at the center of this storm, told the U.S. War Department in mid-May, "The warfare has already assumed a guerrilla character in Tennessee, and it is to be renewed in Kentucky by marauding bands organized in the State, assisted by a few rebel troops." Commanders who had reported their regions free of guerrillas a few months earlier found it "utterly impossible to beat them far back." A company of Ohio cavalry operating in Kentucky gained some satisfaction by breaking up one guerrilla band, capturing five horses, and rescuing two Unionist captives of the guerrillas. Yet the captain could only reflect that his men had been playing this same game for seven months with no end in sight. Whether in camp or on patrol, soldiers believed they could be bushwhacked or captured at any moment. Buell described the situation as a "general uprising" at the end of July.[48]

The guerrilla surge meant the end of conciliatory policies toward southern civilians on the border. The Confederate government's effort to dignify barbarity by calling bushwhackers "partisans" did not impress Union soldiers or politicians. They judged their enemy by its actions. One officer bitterly ridiculed the "chivalrous" Governor Letcher for enlisting "bands of robbers." The "chief delight" of Virginia's so-called rangers, he observed, was to "perpetuate atrocities that would bring the blush of conscious shame to the cheeks of a savage." They murdered citizens and soldiers alike, and demonstrated a particular talent for mutilating corpses. This officer had seen the remains of one victim. "His abdomen had been ripped open, his bowels extracted, his head severed from the trunk and placed all gashed and bleeding in the cavity," the officer reported in disgust. This, he said, was the type of warfare sanctioned by Letcher and practiced by his "honorable" rangers. When the U.S. government threatened to hang two captured ranger officers—John S. Spriggs and Marshall Triplett—everyone from Lee and McClellan, to Stanton and Randolph, to Letcher and Lincoln voiced an opinion. The Confederate government vowed to hang two

Union officers in retaliation. Both sides backed down, but the debate—and the futile use of retaliation to resolve it—went on.[49]

No one knew the liturgy better than John C. Frémont. The Pathmaker had been without a command since being replaced in Missouri, but he was too important a political figure to keep down for long. He had arrived at Wheeling, Virginia, in late March to direct the newly created Mountain Department, just in time to confront the new partisan ranger regime. It took only a few days for him to receive the first reports: telegraph lines cut, Unionist communities attacked, refugees seeking protection, railroads threatened, couriers shot. One of the wire cutters was Mary Jane Green, who had returned to her old ways.[50]

Frémont responded instinctively. He arrested anyone suspected of aiding the guerrillas. He sent expeditions against reported guerrilla strongholds, conducted, when possible, by western Virginia troops. He burned guerrilla rendezvous, including homes and entire villages. He encouraged drumhead courts-martial for "marauders" not killed outright. Immediate executions generally followed. The War Department discouraged the summary executions, but prompt hangings remained the fate of many rebel rangers. "The effect was to correct a mistaken belief in immunity for their crimes," a satisfied Frémont reported, "and to render more secure interior points and roads, as well as loyal inhabitants of the military districts."[51]

Frémont even had his own counterguerrilla company. He had first formed the Jessie Scouts, named for his indomitable wife, while in Missouri, where their efforts to gather intelligence had inevitably pitted them against rebel irregulars. Revived in Virginia, two dozen Kansans formed the core of the company. "They are perfect '*dare devils*,'" judged one admiring Union officer, "their principal business appears to be scouting the country for Guerillas." They fought the guerrillas on their own terms, too. Dressed in Confederate uniforms, they lulled unsuspecting rebels into divulging information that allowed them to "pounce down" on guerrilla camps. Confederates, while acknowledging their courage and horsemanship, despised them and hanged captured scouts as spies. The scouts eventually earned such a reputation as robbers—betraying their Kansas roots, some might say—that they had to be disbanded, although that did not deter their namesake Jessie from publishing a book in 1863 to glorify their exploits and defend her husband's brand of warfare.[52]

U.S. soldiers and civilians alike cheered Frémont's policies. Most people seemed convinced that punitive measures had become a necessity, and keenest of all to bloody guerrilla noses were western Virginian

Unionists. Whole communities signed solemn oaths to put down "Guerrillaism, in all its phases" or requested permission from the government to fight their foes with "guerrilla methods." With or without permission, they bushwhacked both traitorous neighbors and Confederate troops. "They are not amenable to reason," a western Virginia colonel said of the rebels. "Force must be applied."[53]

Defiant Unionist women played their part, too. Wat Cool's band of rebel bushwhackers had not counted on the resolve of Minerva Hyre when they sacked and robbed her mother's home. The guerrillas spared the women no indignity, even taking such personal items as hoop skirts, stockings, and garters; but when they demanded that Minerva surrender any valuables hidden "on her person," she refused in her "unflinching manner" to comply. The guerrillas, whether amused by her defiance or simply in a hurry, withdrew without harming her. However, when most of the band, including Cool, was captured several days later and put on trial, they found Minerva boldly testifying against them. Her calm recounting of the raid on her home did much to convict the men.[54]

Interestingly, too, much of this reaction against conciliation was fashioned and encouraged by veterans of the western guerrilla war. Besides Frémont, Ulysses Grant, who had served on both sides of the Mississippi River, struck at rebel pocketbooks as the commander in western Tennessee. He treated captured guerrillas as outlaws and used a system of reparation payments to discipline their noncombatant abettors. A Kansan whose regiment had been sent to fight in Tennessee thought such policies long overdue. It was time, he said, to transplant something of the "jayhawking" spirit east of the Mississippi. Many easterners agreed. A Pennsylvanian declared, "We have had enough of this child's play here. In the language of Jim Lane, I would 'lay waste devastate hurt somebody.'"[55]

More sweepingly, John Pope conveyed his Missouri experience to Virginia. Given command of the newly created Army of Virginia in July, Pope ordered his men to live off the civilian population of north-central Virginia, execute and destroy the property of bushwhackers, and force local residents to repair damaged railroads and telegraphs. Nor did he leave any doubt about the inspiration for these orders. "Let us understand each other," he told his new army. "I have come to you from the West, . . . from an army whose business it has been to seek out the adversary and to beat him where he is found." However, unlike his actions in Missouri, which had been taken on his own initiative, Henry Halleck, Edwin Stanton, and Lincoln now endorsed Pope's Virginia orders. Precedents for the Union response to guerrillas had been well and firmly set.[56]

By the end of the summer of 1862, guerrillas had shaped the war on the border every bit as much as they had done in the Trans-Mississippi. Whether played out in personal confrontations, community conflicts, or debates over military operations and strategy, the initial Confederate impulse to fight a people's war had produced a conflict very different from the one the warring governments had anticipated. The story was somewhat different in the Deep South, where the war developed more slowly. Yet there, too, similar patterns began to form.

The Confederate government's limited endorsement of guerrilla warfare came just as conflict reached the lower South, a region many southerners thought would never seriously be endangered. This ever-expanding conflict reminded rebel leaders—if, indeed, they needed reminding—that the difficulties of integrating their guerrillas with some larger strategy posed only one problem. Deeper even than that concern lurked philosophical doubts about the wisdom, not to say legality, of guerrilla warfare. In other words, the men in Richmond shared some of the same misgivings as the men in Washington, a paradox that became more evident in the second year of the war.

To begin with, Jefferson Davis and his chief military advisers had been educated in the nation's military academies, most notably West Point, where they had learned to think of wars in terms of grand, climactic, Napoleonic-style battles. They associated guerrilla combat not, as did the public, with romantic knights of the American Revolution, but with untutored, even uncivilized, peoples. Their experiences fighting Indians and Mexicans in the decades before the Civil War confirmed this prejudice. The Seminole of Florida and the Comanche and Kiowa of the Texas frontier may have been fierce and courageous, but whites also considered them heathen and barbaric. Nor were the "half-civilized" Catholic "greasers" encountered in the war with Mexico much better. Robert E. Lee had called Mexican "Guerilleros" thieves and cowards "who had not the courage to fight . . . lawfully." Jefferson Davis, himself a West Point graduate and battle-tested in Mexico, equated guerrilla warfare with "barbarism" and thought no soldier's reputation could be enhanced by that lowly form of combat. Some young Confederate officers had already begun to complain that fighting Unionist guerrillas brought no glory.[1]

Veterans of the campaigns in Mexico had also witnessed the debilitating effects of a guerrilla war. They had seen how Mexican noncombatants feared their own countrymen as much as they did the American invaders, the equivalent of the tussle between southerners who had taken opposite sides in the current war. More fearfully, these veterans could remember how, in fighting enemy *guerilleros*, U.S. soldiers had retaliated ruthlessly against Mexican peasants, whom they took to be allied with the irregulars. Despite the best efforts of American commanders to regulate both the guerrillas and their own men, the unsettling elements of this style of warfare had eroded discipline and morale in Mexico. Confederate leaders feared this dimension most of all. Union soldiers were already responding to Confederate citizens and irregulars as American soldiers had done to the Mexicans. If rebel guerrillas continued to antagonize U.S. troops, the result must be an ever-escalating cycle of gratuitous violence.[2]

The fact that armies are authoritarian by nature did not help matters. The bumptious, chaotically independent spirit that drove the guerrilla war concerned Confederate military leaders as much as it did the politicians. Army officers found it hard enough to discipline and direct men under their immediate control. The thought of loosing thousands of free-ranging guerrillas, however much they might contribute to military victory, struck them as madness. Good order and discipline, they insisted, were military necessities. Granted, some part of their unease was born of social prejudices against the plain folk they thought filled both army and guerrilla ranks. General Lee, for instance, had been as appalled by the implications of Jacksonian Democracy as by the military tactics of the Mexicans. If nothing else, the image of a Confederate military force that relied on scraggly guerrillas could not but tarnish southern ideals of honor and manhood, perhaps even damage efforts to woo European support for the war.[3]

And so, even while refusing to apologize for the excesses of their guerrillas, Confederate leaders privately expressed misgivings, often in the same language used by the Federals. In May 1861, Jefferson Davis had promised a British journalist that he need not fear any "guerrilla leader" while traveling through the South. "You are among a civilised, intelligent people," he had assured the reporter. A few months later, the Confederate War Department warned an Alabamian who wished to raise a partisan company that his men would have to "conform strictly to the laws and usages of civilized nations." Davis himself declared in early December 1861, before the controversy over rules of engagement had begun, that the war must henceforth be fought "on a scale of very different proportions than that of the partisan warfare witnessed during the past summer and fall." Confederate military forces, he implied, could not be seen to be in any way inferior to Union forces, which were led by "men of military education and experience in war."[4]

Thus the paradox of the Partisan Ranger Act, a law that endorsed guerrilla warfare while, at the same time, seeking to limit it. Popular confusion was inevitable. When hundreds of Confederate soldiers applied for transfers to the rangers, the War Department reminded applicants of the restrictive language of the Ranger Act, which forbade transfers from the volunteer forces. Albert T. Bledsoe, an assistant secretary of war, explained the government's reasoning to an entire company of Mississippi troops that wished to become partisans. "It is against the policy of the Department to make such transfers," Bledsoe said, "fearing that the Partizan service if too much entered will render it impossible to keep up the line." Mass transfers, he said, would also undermine the discipline of the army and severely test morale. More than a few men took exception to this rule, either refusing to reenlist or simply going home to become guerrillas. The army listed the latter as deserters. In truth, the men had only gone to fight the enemy as they had always wished to engage it.[5]

That the Confederate Congress passed the Ranger Act at the same time it established national conscription did not help matters. Untold numbers of southerners objected to the draft, as would northerners when the U.S. government introduced the same policy a year later. Conscription was not new to the war, but before the spring of 1862, levies had been issued by the states. *National* conscription, by comparison, was declared a "usurpation" of state sovereignty by both northerners and southerners. Long casualty lists, the geographical expansion of the fighting, and the pending expiration of tens of thousands of one-year enlistments made conscription necessary to the Confederacy; but so, too, oddly enough, had the guerrilla war, for without so many high-spirited men flocking to join "independent" companies, there would have been more soldiers in the ranks. Compounding this problem, potential conscripts thought the Ranger Act gave them the option of joining either the army or the rangers, and they, like men already in the army, preferred the latter. Such confusion forced the Congress to amend the original Ranger Act in July, when it made conscripts ineligible for partisan service and raised the minimum age for ranger service to thirty-five years.[6]

Union officers with any glimmer of this internal Confederate debate predicted where it must lead. Joseph Keifer observed that "dissatisfied" rebel soldiers from Kentucky and Tennessee were deserting in large numbers. They claimed, he said, to have "enlisted for the defense of their homes & for no other purpose." Seeing those homes endangered by the enemy's advance, they had decided it was time to defend their own neighborhoods, rather than be sent to distance places. "I predict the whole character of the war will be changed," Keifer told his wife.

"That in two months the Southern Army, instead of being concentrated, as in the past, will become divided into small & innumerable fragments, whose policy will be to annoy our Army by attacking our trains, and small bodies of our soldiers wherever they can find them."[7]

Keifer erred in thinking the entire Confederate army would fragment, but he hit the mark squarely in identifying the changed character of the war. By mid-1862, the romantic appeal of guerrilla service had been eclipsed by the practical need of local defense. The latter had always been the heart of the guerrilla equation, but it increasingly trumped all other considerations as more parts of the Confederacy faced Union occupation, especially in the Deep South. Gone were the days when impatient Alabamians dashed to Virginia to wage a guerrilla war. Less often would Carolinians feel the urge to lead partisan bands in the Trans-Mississippi. The change reflected no diminution of patriotism or sense of duty. Serve they would, and as guerrillas when they could, but the Confederacy, in their eyes, had shrunk to the size of their own states. Even soldiers who had been forced out of the army by wounds or sickness talked of returning to the war as partisan fighters in their own communities.[8]

Jefferson Davis felt trapped by the dilemma, as well as by an equally terrible fact. It was not just the guerrilla war that had spun out of control; the entire conflict had grown far more brutish than he could have imagined. "We find ourselves driven by our enemies by steady progress towards a practice we abhor and which we are vainly struggling to avoid," he told General Lee on the last day of July 1862. The United States seemed prepared to conduct a "savage war" of no quarter, to shatter all concepts of armed conflict between "civilized men in modern times." He loathed following Lincoln down that bloody path, the president said, but if the Federals continued their punitive policy of retaliation, the Confederacy would be compelled as a "last resort" to wage war "on the terms chosen by our foe."[9]

Sadly, had either Davis or Lincoln polled their respective peoples at that moment, they would have received impressive mandates to conduct savage war. Events of the past year in the Trans-Mississippi and upper South had clearly tilted the conflict in that direction, and the Deep South seemed poised to follow. The region's exposure to invasion had thus far been confined largely to its seacoasts. By the summer of 1862, northern portions of Mississippi, Alabama, Georgia, and the Carolinas had become the new border. Penetration of the region by Union armies remained slight, but the danger to life and property had increased markedly.[10]

Alabama and Mississippi saw the worst of it. The fighting in those states came as a mere extension of Tennessee's war, another illustration of how state boundaries counted for little in wartime. The South looked more and more like a single entity, a region under siege. Thus, more rebels devoted themselves to local defense at the same moment the component parts of their country became geographically less distinguishable.

Alabama became the first Deep South state to see large numbers of Union troops; the first, too, to mount a guerrilla defense. Two months after the Union victory at Shiloh, General Ormsby M. Mitchel entered Huntsville with a division of the Army of the Ohio. His men soon occupied other key Alabama towns north of the Tennessee River, including Decatur, Athens, and Tuscumbia. The state had been drained of manpower long before then, as most of its able-bodied men had been assigned to fight elsewhere. The state militia, inadequate under the best circumstances, had been sent to defend the Gulf coast in anticipation of an attack on Mobile. Mitchel faced only Confederate cavalry, a few Tennessee partisans who made dashes into the state, and four companies of partisan rangers hurriedly authorized by Governor John Gill Shorter.[11]

The timing could not have been worse for Alabama Confederates. With the Union conciliatory policy all but forsaken, and the Confederates determined to match federal retaliation, the stage was set for a bared-knuckles brawl. Both Unionist and Confederate noncombatants lived in terror through the summer. Union soldiers burned, plundered, and destroyed enormous amounts of rebel property, and an unprecedented number of personal crimes, including robbery, murder, and rape, marred the occupation. How much this spree reflected a predisposition to punish the rebels and how much came in response to rebel guerrilla attacks is difficult to judge. Mitchel, a native Kentuckian reared in Ohio, had opposed conciliation. As a West Point graduate, he also despised guerrilla warfare, even when waged by sanctioned partisans.[12]

Guerrillas, rangers, and defiant civilians gave Mitchel's men cause to retaliate. They nearly severed his supply lines, and hungry Union troops found the "intensely Secesh" region a difficult place to obtain food. Rebel men remained publicly passive, but the Union army had long since learned that counted for nothing. In any event, the wives and daughters of these seemingly peaceful farmers "spit out their venom." An Ohio colonel thought a military governor in the mold of Andy Johnson would suit Alabama. He also wanted to invite any member of the U.S. Congress who still doubted the need to punish rebels to visit the state. They would return to Washington "ready for vigorous measures," the colonel predicted.[13]

Colonel John Beatty, fresh from the guerrilla campaigns in Tennessee, wasted no time when rebels fired into a train and cut wires near the town of Paint Rock. "Hereafter every time the telegraph wire was cut we would burn a house," he said of his policy; "every time a train was fired upon we should hang a man; and we would continue to do this until every house was burned and every man hanged between Decatur and Bridgeport." To underline his seriousness of purpose, Beatty arrested three citizens—one of them a "notorious guerrilla"—and burned Paint Rock.[14]

Mitchel claimed to be "well pleased" with Beatty's actions, as did most Union soldiers in Alabama. This included Colonel Keifer, who served as Beatty's second in command. "It is the inauguration of the true policy," Beatty enthused, "and the only one that will preserve us from constant annoyance." Mitchel appointed Beatty provost marshal of Huntsville two weeks later, and endorsed extreme punishments for rebels who threatened his men, either directly as guerrillas or indirectly by aiding guerrillas. Colonel John B. Turchin, a former Russian army officer who commanded one of Mitchel's brigades, sacked Athens, Alabama, on May 2, the same day that Beatty torched Paint Rock. Turchin's action came in response to no specific guerrilla attack, but to express his displeasure with the menacing atmosphere.[15]

The violent acts stunned Alabama rebels. Even before the incidents at Paint Rock and Athens, one citizen noted that the occupation of his state "dispelled the illusion some were laboring under, that they [the Federals] would respect private property." Communities begged Governor Shorter either to send reinforcements or permit them to form partisan bands. Not that Mitchel approved of "lawless brigands and vagabonds" within his army. He issued frequent edicts against pillaging and asked permission from the War Department to hang men guilty of robbery, rape, and arson. Like any professional soldier, Mitchel did not want to see his division degenerate into a rabble, but neither would he relent against the enemy.[16]

And Mitchel left no doubt that the guerrilla war remained the crux of the matter. A resident of Athens reported of his arrival in that town: "He made them a speech denouncing & abusing the leaders in this rebellion, the guerilla mode of warfare, & the Southern Confederacy generally & citizens who take up arms particularly." He promised to protect the person and property of all "who remained quiet, neither aiding or abetting the rebellion," but no one believed him. The U.S. government endorsed his retaliatory policy, as well. When Mitchel sought permission to punish the lawless men in his army, Edwin Stanton granted it but also encouraged him to treat guerrillas the same way. He assured Mitchel, "Your spirited operations afford great satisfaction to the President."[17]

Alabama Confederates longed for some partisan chief to rescue them, and they soon had one. Tennessee-born John T. Morgan—no relation to John Hunt Morgan—had grown up in Alabama, where he practiced law before the war. Rising through the ranks from private soldier to colonel of an infantry regiment, he volunteered to lead a partisan command when Alabama was invaded and Governor Shorter called on the "people" to resist. "To repel these marauding expeditions we need a partisan cavalry force under the command of bold and discreet leaders who will . . . secure the homes and property of our people against depredations," Shorter announced. Alabamians flocked to enlist with the charismatic Morgan. A surgeon serving in Virginia even resigned from the Medical Department to join him as a private soldier. "I am fully determined to be with you in that service," he told Morgan.[18]

Morgan and other Alabama guerrillas operated against the Federals all summer, but not in sufficient numbers to drive them out. If anything, the guerrillas only made them angrier. Some Union soldiers merely scorned the "straggly guerillas" and "way-side Knights" who refused to fight face-to-face. Others expressed deep-seated hatred. "Boys are resolved to take no more prisoners," announced an Ohio cavalryman in early July, "but shoot every man they see in the woods." More officers adopted the hard line of Mitchel, Beatty, Keifer, and Turchin. General John J. Wood "vowed vengeance" against bushwhackers who killed his men.[19]

Mitchel and Turchin were gone by then, but their exits are not without interest. Both men had been relieved of command for mistreating noncombatants, although Mitchel's more complex case also involved cotton speculation and his failure to secure eastern Tennessee. Mitchel was simply reassigned to South Carolina. Turchin was court-martialed for allowing his men to run riot in Athens, but the board exonerated him. Luckily for the Russian, the trial came at the same time that retaliation became the accepted response to rebellion, just as George McClellan was stumbling on the Peninsula, John Hunt Morgan rampaging through Kentucky, and John Pope redefining occupation policy in Virginia. So while the excesses of Turchin's men were undeniable, his tough attitude reflected the government's new policy. His biggest sin, the court decided, had been in not dealing with the rebels "quietly enough." The court had to recommend that he be cashiered, but the majority also urged clemency. Stanton and Lincoln concurred, and the president promoted him to general.[20]

The broader implications of events in Alabama became evident that fall. Don Carlos Buell, as commander of the Department of the Ohio, had ordered Turchin's court-martial. Slower than most generals to abandon conciliatory policies, Buell had been appalled by the Russian's behavior. However, he lost his department in October, and the government ordered a military commission to investigate his direction of it. The nearly six-month-long hearings touched on numerous topics, but two of the most telling were Buell's earlier conciliatory philosophy and his inability to control the guerrilla war. The commission could not fault him for the former because, "whether good or bad in its effects, . . . it was at that time understood to be the policy of the Government." At least, the commissioners concluded, Buell "could violate no orders on the subject, because there were none." However, they also implied that, while Buell had not violated any stated policy, he clearly had not kept pace with the steadily hardening mood of the government, the public, or his own army.[21]

The Buell Commission, as it became known, also discovered just how seriously the irregular war had injured army operations and damaged Union strategy in Tennessee. One of the most serious charges against Buell had been his failure to capture Chattanooga. The commission decided that Buell had been hindered in his efforts by rebel cavalry and guerrillas, who repeatedly cut his supply lines. Henry Halleck and other officers disputed the commission's conclusion. They insisted that Buell had sufficient men to protect his lines and control the guerrillas. Yet the time spent debating such matters—perhaps even the very existence of the Buell inquiry—suggests the scale of the guerrilla problem.[22]

Meantime, Union occupation of northern Alabama exacerbated two other dimensions of the guerrilla war: Unionism and slavery. Like their rebels neighbors, Alabama Unionists defy easy classification. Geography defined some differences among them, for while they clustered most thickly in the state's northern hill country, large numbers also lived in the coastal southeast. Far from being poor, slaveless farmers, as stereotyped by Union soldiers and later historians, their number included planters and practitioners of every trade and profession. A variety of social and political factors, including family ties, friendships, neighbors, business relations, and community leadership, also shaped their loyalties.[23]

Rebel vigilance committees had temporarily suppressed Unionist sentiment in 1861, but when the federal invaders arrived from Tennessee, some Unionists gladly lent a hand. Of course, with "every public road . . . patrolled by guerrilla bands" and themselves still subject to arrest and conscription, they remained cautious. They especially feared retaliation by rebel guerrillas, their principal foes. "Many more would come in," predicted a Union officer, "were they protected from the bushwhackers in their immediate neighborhood." Still, by July 1862, men who had fled to the woods and mountains to avoid conscription began to return home. While many tories still hoped to avoid involvement in the war, others volunteered to act as couriers and guides for the Union army. They provided information about local roads and terrain, and they informed provost marshals about the loyalties of their neighbors.[24]

Equally intriguing was the new role played by Alabama slaves. Until the spring of 1862, the opportunities for slaves to flee masters or stage insurrections had remained greatest in the upper South. However, as Union troops penetrated the Gulf states, ever more slaves saw the possibilities of freedom. In Alabama, as elsewhere, blacks knew that guerrillas, partisan rangers, home guards, and state militias were the principal obstacles to freedom. Slaves, then, had a particular interest in rooting them out. Ormsby Mitchel, like most Union generals at this pre-emancipation stage of the war, did not encourage slave rebellion, but he did protect "watchful" plantation slaves who provided "valuable information" about rebel activities. Slaves seldom had knowledge of large troop movements not already known to the army, but guerrillas were another matter. Their operations would be a mystery to the army but widely known to local people. "Without their help," Mitchel confessed of his black informants, "it would be impossible for me to hold my position. I must abandon the line of railway, and Northern Alabama falls back in the hands of the enemy."[25]

Union officers, desperate to counter the guerrillas, even granted freedom for useful intelligence. Colonel Keifer thought it a fair exchange. Often the only witnesses to bushwhackings willing to tell what they had seen, slaves made "protection" from their masters the price for information. "I promised one his freedom, if he would tell me who fired into our train," Keifer admitted to his wife. "I have him now and if Genl Mitchel wont emancipate him *I will*." General Lovell H. Rousseau, who replaced Mitchel in Alabama, put less credence in the information provided by slaves, but he agreed that liberating them injured the rebels.[26]

Slaves interacted with Unionists in similarly complex ways. While most slaves were "Unionists" in sentiment, they formed no part of the

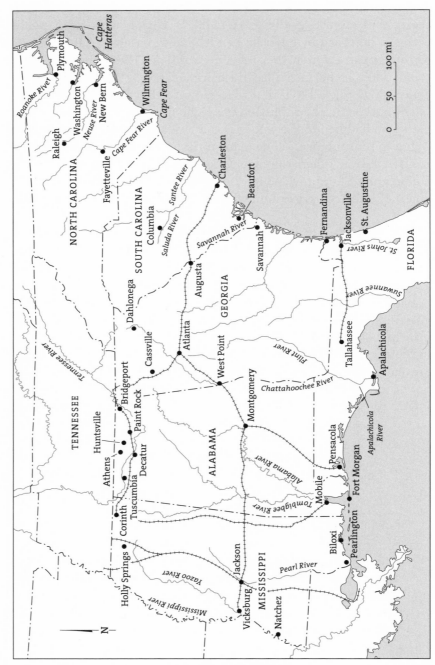

Map 3. The Deep South

political communities that defined "Unionism." Nor did many Unionists see blacks as natural allies, the relationship between slaveholding Unionists and blacks being especially delicate. No slaveholder, regardless of political persuasion, relished the idea of a mutinous slave population. That did not deter some nonslaveholding Unionists from encouraging servile rebellion, even when they remained devoted to white supremacy. Consequently, Alabama Unionists, like U.S. soldiers, used both enslaved and free blacks as spies and messengers to undermine rebel rule.[27]

How fully U.S. political leaders understood the value of the clandestine activities of slaves and Unionists is difficult to judge, but it is noteworthy that President Lincoln made emancipation an integral part of his new military policy as soon as he abandoned conciliation. At first, the pressure to do so was more political than military. Lincoln did not see, as did his soldiers in Alabama, the common thread running through slavery, a hostile southern population, and the guerrilla war. In truth, only a few soldiers could have articulated those connections quite so precisely at the time. It was also pure happenstance that the abolitionists in Lincoln's own party began a concerted push for emancipation at the same moment the president endorsed retaliatory military policies, but Lincoln quickly understood how it might all fit together. The results gratified his weary men in the field, who despised the "rose water" policy of conciliation. "The army will sustain Lincoln in a vigorous & rigid *policy*," Keifer decided toward the end of July. "The army may become demoralized unless such a policy is adopted at once."[28]

Much the same story unfolded in neighboring Mississippi, the next most important arena for guerrilla warfare that summer. The Union drive through western Tennessee and the victory at Shiloh positioned troops on the Mississippi border at the same time they entered Alabama. The soldiers strolled into Corinth, Mississippi, when the Confederates abandoned that crucial railroad depot at the end of May. It was another instance, increasingly obvious across the South, of a Confederate army being unable to protect every community within its sphere of operations. With northern Mississippi left badly exposed, the Ranger Act had not been passed a moment too soon.

Mississippians rushed to partisan service as the Confederate army receded toward the center of the state. They urged Governor John J. Pettus to form ranger companies and assign "minute men" to every county. Army officers who had been serving elsewhere resigned their commissions and returned home, determined to fight, as one man put it, "for my own State." Who better to defend Mississippi in this "mode of warfare" than men who had been reared among its hills, swamps, and rivers? Men who could have avoided service stepped forward now, so long as they did not have to "range far from home." "Our object is to repel or at least harass any Federal raid that may attempt to pass through our County," insisted a typical volunteer.[29]

The aggressive image of guerrilla warfare also appealed to Mississippians. Few men spoke any longer of limiting their service to scouting or reconnaissance. They wanted to deal "Death & Destruction" to the enemy. "Now is the time for bushwhacking and the black flag," announced the state's leading newspaper. This desire conflicted with Governor Pettus's broader plan to subordinate partisans to his state militia system. In fact, some confusion arose among partisans about whether they operated under state or national authority. Men expressed disappointment when, as the limit for ranger companies was exceeded, they were told they must serve as less glamorous militiamen.[30]

Mississippians knew they had to be aggressive, too. The refusal of the U.S. government to concede the legitimacy of the guerrilla war had become common knowledge. Not even partisan rangers could assume they would be treated "according to the usages of civilized war." So be it, they said. "We will neither ask nor give any favors if our country is to be over run, our wives & daughters insulted and beggared," one man insisted. Earl Van Dorn, who found himself commanding troops in his native state after retreating from Arkansas, proposed what he called a "Corps of Honor," an elite body of 1,200 rangers that would act exclusively on the offensive. "Members of the Corps will . . . rush side by side to the shock," explained Van Dorn in proposing the plan to General Pierre G. T. Beauregard, "not to flinch from the execution of any undertaking once begun." Nothing came of the scheme, but Van Dorn had divined the mood of his fellow Mississippians.[31]

William C. Falkner organized the best known band of Mississippi rangers, although he operated with mixed motives. At thirty-seven years of age, Falkner—great-grandfather of the future novelist—had already lived a full and colorful life. He had dabbled in politics; been successful in farming, business, and the law; served in the Mexican War; twice been acquitted of murder; and helped lead Mississippi's antebellum militia as a brigadier general. He commanded an infantry regiment during the first year of the war but lost his colonelcy when the regiment reorganized in April 1862. He sat in bitter retirement at his home in Tippah County, on the Tennessee border, until the Yankees came. The charismatic Falkner then saw an opportunity to regain his lost prestige by recruiting a regiment of partisan rangers. By the end of July, he had six hundred volunteers, most of them from Tippah County.[32]

Outside of northern Mississippi, the Mississippi River valley most needed defenders. Danger loomed in all directions, from invasion out of southeastern Louisiana, raids out of Tennessee, and gunboats converging from both ends of the river. Guerrillas and rangers helped communities from being picked clean of food, livestock, and cotton by Union troops. They also operated effectively along the river. Using the cover of the river banks, partisans and self-styled "bushwhackers" could "annoy the enemies' transports" and "sink or capture all not strongly guarded by Gunboats." More boldly, Jeff Thompson and his "swamp rats" arrived from Missouri to help man a flotilla of eight rebel gunboats, known somewhat laughingly as the "Confederate River Defense Service." Thompson worried the Federals initially. His bold and unexpected attacks on Union shipping around Memphis made Thompson "the nightmare of every post commander on the Mississippi." Alas, his career as a naval tactician proved short-lived. Union gunboats sank the last of his slow and aged vessels in barely a month. By the second week of June, Thompson had scurried onto dry land to muster new partisan ranger companies in Mississippi.[33]

Mississippi Unionists also caused trouble. While not as numerous as the tories of Alabama, they vowed to resist every symbol of Confederate rule. Like rebel guerrillas in parts of western Virginia, Unionist guerrillas made it impossible in some places to hold elections, collect taxes, or pursue any function of normal political life. Governor Pettus worried about their effect on Confederate morale. Only along the Gulf coast did tories flee more often than fight. Feeling more isolated and vulnerable than their brethren in northern Mississippi, both whites and free blacks went to the nearest Union haven, New Orleans, for protection.[34]

Nor did Mississippi slaves remain passive. Either witnessing or learning of the chaos caused by the advancing Federals, they ran away or challenged the authority of their masters. Communities called on vigilance committees and guerrilla bands to check "insubordination" and "keep the negroes in awe." Some companies devoted themselves entirely to the task; others divided their energies between community protection and military operations. Either way, the black rebellion stretched rebel defenses precariously thin.[35]

All that said, Halleck warned Union troops entering the state from Tennessee of the menace awaiting them in Mississippi. He worried most about resistance by Confederate soldiers, but he also understood the multiple problems posed by rebel irregulars. "To surrender any

Confederate guerrillas and home guards kept a close eye on the black population. Here, home guards check the passes of slaves near Vicksburg, Mississippi. From *Leslie's Illustrated Newspaper*, as reproduced in *The Soldier in Our Civil War* (1894).

territory we have acquired is certain death to all Union men in that territory," he warned Edwin Stanton. "Any loss on our part will be followed by insurrection in Tennessee and Kentucky, and we shall find still greater difficulty in the pacification of those States than we have encountered in Missouri."[36]

Accordingly, the Federals employed their own irregular tactics in Mississippi. Union "scouts," dressed in Confederate uniforms and claiming to be "sick" soldiers, stopped civilians on the road to ask seemingly innocent questions about local conditions. A more lethal variety of scout then arrived from Kansas. The 7th Kansas Cavalry had been transferred to Kentucky in mid-May, the first time these jayhawkers had operated as part of the army. Although they were no longer commanded by Charles Jennison, it took time for some of them to shed old habits. They behaved well enough on their first assignment, which was to protect the Mobile and Ohio Railroad against Confederate raiders, but when ordered into Tennessee, they raised a dozen kinds of hell. They plundered towns, stole horses and money from lone households, insulted women, even terrorized a funeral procession. Halleck, still in his final days commanding the department, groaned to see them in Mississippi. He restricted the Kansans to camp during the remainder of his tenure and sacked their colonel, an ardent abolitionist who had encouraged his men to bring fugitive slaves within Union lines. Not until Halleck left for Washington did the regiment resume operations in Mississippi.[37]

The rest of the Deep South, outside of Alabama and Mississippi, witnessed only slight increases in guerrilla activity but greeted the Partisan Ranger Act with enthusiasm. For some men, with their own states spared immediate invasion, the Confederacy's commitment to a limited guerrilla war briefly rekindled a desire to fight wherever needed. An artillery captain serving near Savannah volunteered to operate anywhere on the border as long as it was as a partisan ranger. Twenty-five men, all wishing to prove their "daring, bravery and quickness," had joined him. Similarly, a South Carolinian who had recovered from a wound received earlier in the war thought Virginia or Tennessee offered "fine fields" for partisan service, which, to his thinking, had been "more effective in driving back the invader than any other mode of warfare." An entire battalion of Georgia partisan rangers asked to join John Hunt Morgan. They would gladly "share the perils and the glory of 'Morgan's men,'" they told him, if only the guerrilla chief would lead them "to the Banks of the Ohio."[38]

More often, in light of recent federal advances, people had enough to do preparing for war on their own home fronts. In Georgia, Governor Joseph Brown followed Richmond's lead by discouraging the unchecked formation of partisan companies, but his people clamored for guerrillas to secure seacoasts, roads, and mountain passes. Lieutenant Charles C. Jones Jr. understood the situation. Coastal defense remained the priority in Georgia, he believed, but should Federals try to reach the interior, rebel citizens would make "every bush and swamp [a] . . . fortress." He admired the way Nathan Bedford Forrest and John Hunt Morgan had "gone to the rescue" and revived the "days of true chivalry" in their states. Georgians, he predicted, would do no less. "The scenes attendant upon the retreat of the British army from Concord and Lexington," he wrote on the approaching anniversary of those battles, "should be reenacted to the last degree; and every tree, every stone, should be clothed with a voice of thunder. Every man, woman, and child should rise in arms along the line of the retreating foe, and enforce . . . the vengeance of a people armed in the holy cause of liberty."[39]

Of all states in the Deep South, Florida most needed partisan defenders by 1862. Between March and May, Union troops had swooped into Fernandina, Jacksonville, St. Augustine, and Key West. Several old forts, including Pickens at Pensacola and Taylor and Jefferson in the Keys, were already in U.S. hands, and naval blockades had sealed off Tampa and Apalachicola. Incredibly, at this precise moment, the Confederate government seemed to abandon Florida by sending most of its troops to places deemed more strategically vital. Some men, preferring "death" to seeing their homes and families "at the mercy of the Enemy," threatened mutiny.[40]

The state's newly elected governor, John Milton, spotted others problems, too. He protested to Richmond that his state's population—smallest in the Confederacy—could not send volunteers to the national army and still field an effective militia. His adjutant general considered the existing militia system "defunct," incapable even of suppressing pockets of Unionists. What was more, Unionist sentiment was growing in some quarters, especially the northeast.[41]

One bright spot seemed to be the penchant of Florida rebels for guerrilla warfare. "Many of our people have formed their ideas of war," the adjutant general observed, "from experience derived from our Indian Wars." That could have an ill effect on discipline, he admitted to Milton, but "in a fight each man on his own hook, our people are invincible." Many men had already volunteered for guerrilla service "with enthusiasm." Milton turned this talent and inclination to his advantage. In March, he announced a new plan for "local defense" that drew ten

"Guerilla Companies" from the ten counties most endangered by Union troops. Milton mounted these companies on "good horses," that they might be more effective in "spying out the enemy and harassing him at every possible point." He also ordered them to check "any improper conduct of the slave population, to prevent their escape to the enemy, and prevent all communication between them and disloyal persons." In all this, Milton suppressed his own prejudices against "independent" companies and cavalry. Just five months earlier he had declared the latter "less requisite in Florida than perhaps any other State."[42]

Among Florida's most enthusiastic volunteers were John W. Pearson and his Oklawaha Rangers. Operating in cooperation with conventional cavalry forces prior to March, Pearson's independent company gained more freedom with the state seemingly near collapse. His followers, whom Pearson described as "mostly poor men" with "wives and children to look after," embraced their role as home defenders. "We are now a Guerilla Company in every sense of the word," Pearson rejoiced; "we dont tell where we stay or where we are going, nor when we return." Having operated mainly along the St. Johns River for the first year of the war, Pearson's men found themselves the lone defenders of Tampa by May 1862.[43]

Florida's partisans and guerrillas rarely encountered Union troops that spring and summer, but they expended considerable effort destroying railroad tracks, bridges, and trestles, enforcing conscription, and suppressing internal rebellion. The last assignment especially concerned Pearson. The eastern side of the St. Johns, within easy range of Union coastal patrols, was frightfully disloyal, and Pearson feared it would remain so without drastic action. His men scouted the region "nearly all the time" and arrested both white and black troublemakers. He had hanged one slave by April and had a few Unionists in mind for similar treatment. He drove whole communities of tories into the woods. He and other guerrillas became such a terror to Unionists living on one island in the St. Johns River that the Union navy had to destroy its lone bridge to the mainland in order to keep out the rebels.[44]

Both the Union navy and army realized it had a problem in John Milton's state. "There is a good deal of lawlessness in Florida," complained Flag Officer Samuel F. Du Pont, head of the Union's South Atlantic Blockading Squadron. He attributed this unhealthy situation mainly to rebel guerrillas. The Federals did manage to capture one fearsome guerrilla captain, George Huston, along the St. Johns that summer. Despite being surprised by a Union raiding party early one morning, Huston charged his foes with a double-barreled shotgun, two pistols, and a Bowie knife. He killed the lieutenant of the party, but sustained four wounds in the ensuing gunfight. Du Pont breathed more easily when he learned this "desperate character" had been captured, but he worried that too many like-minded rebels ran loose in Florida. General David Hunter, having been transferred from the Trans-Mississippi to command this part of the southeastern coast, ordered his officers to "take the most rigorous and prompt measures" in suppressing guerrillas. He wanted captured guerrillas sent to him in irons. "You will also threaten," he added with perhaps a hint of desperation, "to arm . . . all negroes and Indians who may be willing to enter the service."[45]

Fear of Unionist uprisings spurred the ranger movement in other Atlantic coast states. A citizen of West Point, Georgia, located on the Alabama border, reported a raid by a Unionist "cavalry company" that had been raised in his own and two adjoining Alabama counties. The ruffians, who had burst into his house with knives and pistols drawn, threatened to ride him on a rail and shoot him unless he gave them three hundred dollars. Confederates in parts of northern Georgia reported that Unionist majorities spoke openly against the government. These defiant tories often included "prominent, influential, and wealthy" citizens, including slaveowners, who cajoled or bullied neighbors onto their side. Confederate home guards assumed broad powers as irregular enforcers, but they had their hands full. They would execute or murder dozens of Unionists before the war ended.[46]

Southwestern Georgia and the adjoining corner of southeastern Alabama provided another breeding ground for discontent. Loyalists there were more likely small farmers and poor people than community leaders, but they worried Confederates no less. Many of these "spies and traitors" had no particular political grievances, but high prices for food and the threat of conscription led more of them daily to oppose the government. In any case, they were dangerously unpredictable. Where outnumbered or closely watched, they generally preferred flight to resistance. Yet, not a few went armed and became predators rather than the prey.[47]

North Carolina appeared to be in a particularly vulnerable position by the summer of 1862. The state's western border had been threatened by Tennessee Unionists and Union soldiers nearly from the start of the war, but eastern North Carolina had now become equally unsafe. Federals seized Roanoke Island in February and captured New Bern a month later. They proceeded to occupy the coastal towns of Washington and Plymouth over the next two months and send raiding parties inland and along the coast. With Confederate troops seemingly unable to halt the invasion, Governor Henry T. Clark increased the size of his militia and sanctioned guerrilla bands to operate against U.S. troops. Until then, guerrilla operations on the coast had been sporadic at best, the work of small groups of bushwhackers. But Clark understood the value of organized partisan resistance. "I like your plan of forming a company of Independent Rangers," he told one applicant as early as February, "and think they could render very efficient service." Recollecting his history of the American Revolution, Clark enthused that such a company could "fly around [and] harass an enemy when and where least expected." Some people thought it a grand notion, what with Missouri "ablaze with Guerillas" and Morgan "carrying all before him."[48]

Yet the situation in North Carolina also illustrates the complications that hindered the guerrilla movement by the summer of 1862. Clark, who had initiated his guerrilla war before the Confederate Congress passed the Partisan Ranger Act, reminded would-be guerrillas that their companies must not retard his efforts to strengthen the state-wide militia system. Guerrilla recruits must not be liable to conscription or existing service obligations, and they must, by all means, be led by "proper" officers who would instill discipline. Clark and his adjutant general ceased to sanction their own guerrilla companies when Congress passed the Ranger Act, but that did not matter to aspiring guerrillas. Self-constituted companies ignored the formalities of official recognition if they thought Union troops or Unionists endangered their homes, properties, or families.[49]

By July, large numbers of both authorized and unauthorized bands crowded the state. Even Governor Clark, while sympathizing with the need of his constituents to be defended, complained about the runaway growth. He was especially displeased that independent companies should claim authority under the Ranger Act. Neither the governor nor local military commanders wished to rely so heavily on guerrilla bands, which stymied efforts to enroll conscripts, hindered the growth of the militia system, and denied conventional troops needed horses and provisions. Most significantly, their apparent strength was concentrated outside the areas most threatened by the federal advance. Communities may have been better defended, but the strategically vital parts of the state were no better off.[50]

The gravest threat came in the western counties, adjacent to East Tennessee, where Unionists formed strong guerrilla bands. Confederate troops mounted occasional expeditions against their strongholds on both sides of the Tennessee–North Carolina line, but William Holland Thomas, a white man who had been raised by Cherokee Indians, enjoyed the most success. As an adult, Thomas worked as a merchant and U.S. government agent to the Cherokee before being elected to the North Carolina senate in the 1840s. When his senate term expired in 1862, the fifty-something Thomas organized two companies of Cherokee to serve as "a guerrilla force . . . for the local defense of the Carolinas, Virginia, and East Tennessee." Other men had proposed using the Cherokee in this role as much as a year earlier. Downplaying the image of the savage Indian warrior, they had emphasized the "nearly civilized" condition of the North Carolina Cherokee. But Thomas had the trust of the tribesmen, particularly after evading efforts by Jefferson Davis to assign them to the swamps of eastern North Carolina.[51]

And so the guerrilla war had reached a critical point across the entire South by midsummer 1862. Partly from desperation, partly from a recognition of its value, the Confederate government had decided to sanction a limited partisan war. It did so despite its own reservations and protests by the United States about the legality of guerrilla warfare. Guerrillas had cost the Federals dearly in lives and equipment, and the continued threat posed by irregulars to the security of the lower Midwest and the safety of southern Unionists could potentially erode support for the Lincoln administration. An expanded irregular contest might even force the United States to abandon important territorial gains. Guerrilla resistance must be crushed, U.S. authorities decided. For its part, the Confederate government was about to find it even harder to control the raw power it had unleashed.

DEMOCRACY RUN AMOK

FALL 1862–SUMMER 1863

"Y ou have all read of 'wars, & horrors of war,' among chris-
tianized civilized, & savages," a weary Confederate observed from western Missouri in August 1862, "but I
cannot convey to you the horrors of this one." Even with the rebel army
pushed out of Missouri, her town of Warrensburg remained a perfect
"thoroughfare" for Union soldiers, jayhawkers, bushwhackers, and
marauders of every stripe. First one side and then the other occupied
the place, its citizens caught in the middle. Trade was suspended; businesses collapsed. Civil law could not be enforced, and the flight of many
residents gave the appearance of abandonment and desolation.[1]

The woman's lament could be heard in nearly every part of the Trans-
Mississippi. A combination of hopelessness, uncertainty, and terror defined peoples' lives. By the end of 1862, with Henry Halleck directing
the Union armies from Washington and the retaliatory policy widely
adopted across the occupied South, people had hoped the guerrilla war
might be quashed. Instead, it grew. The Federals developed an even
broader antiguerrilla arsenal, but Confederates refused to be cowed.
Their guerrilla war suffered setbacks in the months to come, but most
of the reverses came from within. The Partisan Ranger Act failed to
discipline or channel the energy of rebel irregulars. Popular support for
them showed signs of weakening. So, too, in some parts of the Confederacy, did support for the war itself.

Even in a state supposedly controlled by the Union army, Missourians experienced "war in earnest." In September 1862, a band of two
hundred rebel guerrillas barged into the northeastern town of Palmyra.
Union troops had shot two of the band and captured six others in an
earlier skirmish, and the rebels wanted satisfaction. During the three
hours they occupied Palmyra, the raiders released fifty-one prisoners
from the town jail, plundered the provost marshal's office, rounded up
every breathing horse, confiscated weapons, and kidnaped an elderly
citizen. They scarcely bothered with a small number of Union troops
who barricaded themselves in some stout brick buildings.[2]

This seemingly minor incident of tit for tat did not end when the
rebels left, and its conclusion suggests the escalating ruin and vengeance of the war in Missouri. A few weeks after the raid, its leader,

Joseph C. Porter, received an ultimatum from the Federals. If Porter did not return the kidnaped citizen unharmed within ten days, ten of his men being held prisoner would be shot. Unfortunately, the old man was already dead. Porter ordered his release shortly after the raid, but his men had murdered him. With no prisoner to be returned, the ten rebels—only three of whom had ever served with Porter—met their promised fate on October 18. Confederates and Unionists in Missouri expressed horror as word of the "Palmyra massacre" spread. Apparently, too, one of the executed "guerrillas" was as elderly as the slain Unionist; another victim was a retarded boy.[3]

Governor Hamilton Gamble made no complaint. Desperate to rid his state of rebel guerrillas by any means, he even offered cash bounties for the capture of particularly nasty characters. Alfred Boland, who operated in the vicinity of Forsyth, was worth five thousand dollars, dead or alive. Two men, one of them a paroled Confederate soldier, went looking for Boland in December 1862. Tracking the "bloodthirsty villain" to his lair, they lured Boland into a trap and shot him, though some accounts say they struck the guerrilla from behind with a plowshare. Legend says the bounty hunters decided it would be easier to sever the guerrilla's head (all that was required for identification) than to lug his body halfway across the state to Jefferson City, where they would claim the reward. More reliable evidence has them carrying the whole corpse twelve miles to Forsyth and putting it on public display. Hundreds of people "gloated" over the remains of the man whose gang had "committed every [possible] atrocity." The corpse was then sent to the state capital. Besides collecting their five thousand dollars, the bounty hunters also received commissions as officers (captain and lieutenant, respectively) in the 11th Missouri Cavalry.[4]

Gamble's bounty system grew in part from his conviction that the "kind hearted" President Lincoln commuted or reduced the death sentences of too many convicted guerrillas. Gamble wanted the authority to endorse death sentences given either to him or to district military commanders. Lincoln refused to relinquish his prerogative, but the issue sparked debate in the president's cabinet. Sympathizing with Gamble, Attorney General Edward Bates told Lincoln, "We are habitually bullied by the enemy and constantly yield to his threats." The government, he argued, must act more forcefully against rebel guerrillas.[5]

Bates also made an astonishing—and frighteningly accurate—prediction. Should local authorities be denied more control over executions, Bates warned Lincoln, the government could expect to see fewer guerrilla trials, perhaps none. Fearful that guilty verdicts might be overturned, army commanders would embrace the Halleck doctrine of execution without trial. "I shrewdly suspect that your best officers are already acting upon that idea," the attorney general told Gamble. "And upon the whole, I am not sure that it is not for the best; for I am persuaded that *speed* is quite as necessary as the *fact* of the punishment of such marauders."[6]

One can imagine how swiftly word of the attorney general's view spread through the Union army. Senior commanders and junior officers alike chose their own means of stamping out rebellion. Even financial assessments, which had been used for more than a year in Missouri, became opportunities for physical intimidation and an excuse for outright plundering. General Lewis Merrill, the senior commander in northeastern Missouri, announced in September a dual program of reparation payments and public executions in his district. It is not clear if accused guerrillas received lawful trials, but Merrill, an 1855 graduate of West Point who had served earlier as Frémont's chief of staff, ordered their execution carried out with "due form and solemnity." He hoped a few such examples would end guerrilla resistance, but he vowed to continue the policy until achieving his ends.[7]

The state militia also felt free to act as judge and jury. "We captured a bushwhacker yesterday on the way coming here," a militia lieutenant confided in a private letter. "He had been tried by drumhead court marshall and condemned to death[;] he will be executed in about one hour[;] his grave [he] is now diging." The prisoner deserved no mercy, the lieutenant explained, as he was known to have helped "massacre" the teamsters of a supply train. Another scouting party shot two captured guerrillas without even a perfunctory trial, and this after forcing the men to lead them to the gang's camp. "We take no pleasure in putting to death any one in human shape," declared one militia captain, "but know of no other way of ridding our country of midnight assassins."[8]

When the *New York Times*, an avowed critic of Republican policies, accused General John McNeil of "butchery" in executing fifteen Missouri guerrillas after a perfunctory "trial," McNeil's provost marshal exploded in righteous anger. People back home did not understand the murderous conditions faced by soldiers and Unionists in this war, Colonel William R. Strachan said bitterly. "Had one half the severity practiced by rebels on the Union men of Tennessee, Arkansas, and Missouri been meted out in return to them, every trace of treason would ere this have been abolished from our land." Thousands of these scoundrels hounded honest folk, Strachan insisted, and their "long list of crimes . . .

would make even fiends in hell shudder." Besides, the colonel emphasized, the policies for dealing with guerrillas in Missouri, having been
initiated by Generals Halleck and Schofield, were long-standing.[9]

Frustration often spawned callous disregard for human life and suffering. A Pennsylvania-born soldier felt totally justified in shooting captured guerrillas in southeastern Missouri. "They are a set of murderers
and are not fit to live to encumber society," he told his wife plainly.
His attitude became even more ingrained one day in February 1863,
when he came across a woman crying beside the corpse of her guerrilla-
husband, who had been taken from their house and shot on the open
road. Any instinctive sympathy the scene might have aroused was
dashed by the woman's response to the soldiers. "She was no better than
he," the Pennsylvanian reported, "for she kept on swearing vengeance
against the Federals and said she would make them kiss his blood. . . . It
looks hard to me to see a man shot and his wife and children left alone,"
he admitted, "but these men are the ones that keep up the cruelties that
are continually being practiced in this part of Missouri."[10]

The Federals also continued to destroy rebel property as a form of
chastisement. The holdings of known bushwhackers had no chance of
surviving, and their supporters suffered if the guerrillas themselves
could not be hurt. It sometimes became a game of escalating revenge.
When army expeditions failed to capture their elusive prey, they contented themselves with burning rebel homes. If guerrillas burned a
Unionist home in response, the army burned two more rebel homes.
Rebel rendezvous became favorite targets. Insofar as rebels often
gathered at mills, taverns, or stores, their destruction, more than the
torching of a single home, could undermine the guerrilla network and
intimidate the neighboring populace. For a rural community to lose
a mill, for instance, could be a financial blow that caused people to
reconsider the price of disloyalty. Likewise, cavalry patrols sustained
themselves by demanding their meals and water for their mounts from
rebel households. Add to this the assessments and routine confiscation
of property, and it was reasonable to think that the Confederates would
eventually forsake their partisans.[11]

The army also used covert methods. Army commanders assigned
scouts in civilian dress to circulate through rebel neighborhoods, not
only to locate guerrilla camps, as was already being done, but also to
gather evidence against citizens who aided the irregulars. Provost marshals issued "detective" credentials with the same goal in mind. A team
of two detectives in western Missouri even "played off as bushwhackers" to incriminate one man. On visiting his home, they flashed a secret

sign known to be used by local guerrillas. The man responded and, as the detectives gained his confidence, he talked freely of having often sheltered rebels. "He fed us and our horses and told us which way to get out," they subsequently testified at the man's trial. "We pretended that we wanted to get over the river to find out where Quantrill was." He told them where to cross and gave them the names of two men on the other side who would further assist them.[12]

Banishment, while not widely applied, became another option. General Benjamin Loan used this threat to silence dissent around Lexington. He rounded up hundreds of men who spoke publicly against the United States in the latter part of 1862. "We do not know what minute we will be arrested and banished from the state," a Confederate citizen revealed in his diary. The "Tiranical" Loan had established "a perfect reign of terror." Unionists thought the policy long overdue. "If the government had adopted the plan . . . of banishing all rebel sympathizers . . . a year ago," judged one Missourian in June 1863, "the war would now be a great deal nearer a close than it is."[13]

U.S. military commissions continued to do a brisk business, as did some civil courts that claimed jurisdiction in guerrilla cases. The odds were getting longer for acquittal, but fair numbers of defendants still managed to escape the gallows. The fate of Jacob Fowler and ten members of his guerrilla band seemed certain. Found guilty of plundering Unionist property in Missouri and wounding several Union soldiers on an unarmed steamboat, all were sentenced to die. However, several of the men wiggled free of the hangman's noose when the district commander found technical irregularities in the commission's decision. Fowler's testimony saved two men when he acknowledged that they had not participated in the crimes. Almost shockingly, Fowler himself received a prison term rather than a death sentence. He swore that he had ordered his band of some fifty guerrillas not to fire on the steamboat. Two of his men, subsequently released, vouched for that statement. One of these men also testified that Fowler, while guilty of plundering, had refused to drive the Unionists from their homes, as some of his followers had wanted to do.[14]

Yet these efforts to dispense justice yielded two fearful realizations. First, hours of testimony in scores of trials confirmed the utter intransigence of rebel guerrillas. Second, and far worse, the evidence showed a distinctly new type of guerrilla emerging by the end of 1862. Common outlaws, deserters, and other misfits were exploiting the chaos of war for personal gain. Scattered complaints about "predatory bands," roaming gangs of "banditti," and other miscreants could be heard as early as the spring of 1861, but more of them, in larger numbers, were now operating. They sometimes claimed to be loyal Confederates or Unionists, but most of them had no allegiance other than to themselves. "It is an old saying . . . that the 'Devil is fond of fishing in muddy waters,'" an Arkansan observed in January 1862, "and as soon as *war* stired up the mud of confusion you see devils turn out in droves like avenging Wolves." He added, "I predict if the war lasts 12 months longer the country will be completely over run with vagabonds and [they] will have to be killed in some way."[15]

Curiously, this regrettable turn in the guerrilla war renewed Unionist hopes. It seemed likely, they reasoned, that even Confederate civilians would recoil from the excesses of these mutant guerrillas. The additional wave of violence and destruction could stir resentment against the rebel government for failing to protect its citizenry. The outlaws might tarnish the reputation of all rebel guerrillas and indisputably associate their cause with lawlessness. "I am sure the people here are tired—very tired—of the war," a Unionist reflected near Mexico, Missouri, center of some of the state's worst guerrilla violence. "I am confident the 'bushwhacker' will not have much aid or comfort in this part of the state again."[16]

Such complexity only made it more difficult for the two sides to agree on an acceptable definition of a "guerrilla," and this had begun to gnaw at Henry Halleck. He had been satisfied with his own handling of guerrillas in the Trans-Mississippi, but by August 1862, as general in chief, he came to understand both the scope of the guerrilla problem and the complex legal issues it entailed. Wishing to make sure the United States held the moral and legal high ground, he turned to Dr. Francis Lieber for advice. The German-born Lieber had taught history and political philosophy for twenty-one years at South Carolina College before moving to New York's Columbia College in 1856. The southern and northern residences produced a family with divided loyalties. One of Lieber's three sons had already died in Confederate service, and a son in the Union army had lost an arm. The professor, who felt passionately about the evil of both slavery and secession, had never wavered in his devotion to the Union or ceased to ridicule the "many hypocrasies or absurdidies" of the South. He also called the guerrilla war an affront to international law.[17]

Being personally acquainted with the professor, Halleck recognized a kindred spirit. "The rebel authorities claim the right to send men, in the garb of peaceful citizens, to waylay and attack our troops," he told Lieber, "to burn bridges and houses, and to destroy property and persons within our lines. They demand that such persons be treated as ordinary belligerents, . . . [with] the same rights as other prisoners of war." What did Lieber think of this reasoning? Halleck asked. Did it have any legal basis? Halleck had known how to deal with the problem as a department commander, but now, as head of all Union armies, he was proceeding with due caution.[18]

Lieber responded within weeks with an essay entitled "Guerrilla Parties Considered with Reference to the Laws and Usages of War." While filled with sometimes confusing qualifications and contradictions, Lieber's analysis reflected the elusive and controversial nature of the subject, addressed every issue plaguing Halleck, and countered any defense the Confederates might muster. He defined nearly a dozen types of irregular warfare but relegated most southerners to the general category of "war-rebel." These men posed the "greatest danger" to an occupying army, Lieber declared, and should be treated with the "utmost rigor of the military law." It mattered not if they organized and fought on their own initiative or had been "secretly called upon" by the government. Civilized governments should not employ or recognize them. Both the "bushwhacker" and "guerrillaman" qualified as war-rebels, and Lieber made little distinction between them. The bushwhacker acted more often alone, as an "armed prowler" or "simple assassin," but both were brigands. Neither one could claim legitimacy, even if their government had called upon "the people to infest the bushes and commit homicides."[19]

Lieber conceded that difficulties might arise when distinguishing partisans from guerrillas, which had been the thorniest issue facing Union soldiers in the field. Halleck had tended to lump both groups together. Not so Lieber. As long as suspected "guerrillamen" conducted themselves as partisans and were captured "in fair fight and open warfare," they should be treated as soldiers until proved guilty of some crime, such as murder or pillage. However, Lieber cautioned, the army should not tolerate "small bodies of armed country people" who resorted to "occasional fighting and the occasional assuming of peaceful habits, and to brigandage." No circumstances could justify their actions.[20]

Remarkably, in concluding his tour de force, Lieber claimed that he had not meant to suggest how these general "rules of action" should be applied to "evil-doers" in the present war. That must be decided by the government's leaders. He could only say, Lieber added with inspired coyness and profundity, that no society, either in peace or war, could allow "assassination, robbery, and devastation" to go unpunished. In wartime, such neglect could have "disastrous consequences which might change the very issue of the war."[21]

Halleck immediately distributed the work to his armies as a guide for identifying and treating rebel guerrillas, but Lieber was just warming up. Concerned that he had addressed only the most immediate questions raised by rebel guerrillas, he urged Halleck to issue another, broader "set of rules" to define the conduct of the general war. Halleck responded by appointing a five-man committee, including Lieber, to produce the recommended document. The resulting Lieber Code, as it became known, was issued to the army as General Orders No. 100 in August 1863. It has been rightly hailed as the first ethical guidelines for the conduct of war issued by a democratic state, but that should not obscure Lieber's more immediate and quite practical goals. He meant to enhance the Union army's legal authority and maximize its ability to crush the rebellion. "Military necessity" became the code's operating principle, and while Lieber was careful to emphasize the need for soldiers on both sides to treat combatants and noncombatants alike with compassion, his edicts defended the use of retaliation "to obtain great ends of state" and to battle "against wrong." Nations waging war in a "noble cause" must base their actions on "principles of justice, faith, and honor," but "the more vigorously" they pursued such wars, "the better . . . for humanity."[22]

The Confederates, quite naturally, denounced these "laws and usages of war" as Yankee propaganda, a "confused, unassorted and undiscriminating" mess. Secretary of War James A. Seddon dismissed Lieber as a foreigner who understood neither the American legal system nor American military traditions. He pointed, especially, to the principle of military necessity, which Seddon claimed was intended to defend the "acts of atrocity and violence" committed by U.S. troops. The Confederate States of America, he said, would not allow the United States to "frame mischief into a code."[23]

It is more difficult to judge the practical impact of Lieber's labors on the Union army. Neither officers nor men said much about the new orders. Lieber himself worried about the applicability of the section on guerrillas for soldiers in the field. Its usefulness must necessarily be "much diminished by the fact that the soldier generally decides these cases for himself," he admitted. As for the broader reaches of the Lieber Code, some Union officers dismissed it as a "defense of radical abolition principles." They called Lieber a "very learned" but dangerous "bookworm." His code, when combined with Lincoln's recently enacted emancipation program, "only served to unite the people of the rebel states, and to give strength to the rebellion."[24]

Certainly for the moment, codes, courts, and commissions would not resolve the guerrilla war in Missouri. Only relentless pressure, as even Lincoln had come to understand, could achieve that end. As rebel guerrillas emerged from winter hibernation in 1863, the internal threat to Missouri became unparalleled. It may as well have been the summer of 1861. In April 1863, a veteran Union cavalryman admitted, "Missouri since the commencement of the war never was so overrun with Guerrillas as it is at the present time." Worse still, no one knew how to slow the flood. "There is a terrible state of affairs here," a Union officer conceded, "the more I see of it the more complicated it seems."[25]

No part of that "state of affairs" had been more complicated than Missouri politics. Many Missourians had lost faith in the Lincoln administration's ability to manage the guerrilla problem. Some of them had also begun to question Governor Gamble's devotion to the Union. They suspected him of trying to conciliate "both Copperheads and conservative politicians" in order to win election to the U.S. Senate. Slavery further complicated matters. The slavery issue suddenly loomed large in all Union slave states by 1863. The Emancipation Proclamation, which took effect on January 1, excluded loyal states from its provisions, but the Lincoln administration pressured border state politicians to endorse gradual emancipation voluntarily. Loyal slaveholders in Missouri were livid. Here was the thanks they got for supporting the Union. Now, in this "abolition war," they stood to lose more than did many rebels. Advocates of emancipation feared that this "deep dissatisfaction" might swell the number of bushwhackers.[26]

Worse still for the state's stability, some Missouri slaves, trusting their fates to neither military victory nor legislative acts, turned renegade. Runaway slaves formed outlaw bands to plunder the countryside, then escape into Kansas. Indeed, white Kansans often joined the black gangs in their raids or led them to sanctuary. A few Missouri regiments tried to intervene. Colonel Odon Guitar, known as one of the state's premier "guerrilla hunters," ordered his 9th Missouri to arrest runaways in the vicinity of St. Joseph and return them to their masters. Another Missourian, General Richard C. Vaughn, who commanded the military district at Lexington, denounced the anarchy. "Hundreds of negroes every week," he estimated in May 1863, "run off from their masters. These negroes are all armed, and as the citizens are all disarmed, they take their horses, mules, oxen & wagons, by hundreds." Yet most Union troops ignored the crimes, Vaughn protested, knowing full well that his force of fifty militia was "powerless to protect . . . lives and property." A frightened citizen of the region reported, "Mob violence prevails."[27]

Speaking of Kansans, they had new troubles of their own. By 1863, with many state regiments assigned to duty east of the Mississippi River, in southern Missouri, or in northern Arkansas, Kansas had become more vulnerable to both internal and external enemies. A resurgent copperhead movement appeared, and bands of rebel sympathizers boldly engaged jayhawkers in pitched battles. In May, Missouri raiders penetrated the state as far as Council Grove, nearly one hundred miles from the border. That was unusual, as most raiders limited their rambles to thirty or forty miles. Yet here they were, destroying property and carrying away thousands of dollars in cash, horses, cattle, and "other plunder." They killed people, too. "The citizens . . . are becoming seriously alarmed at the threatening aspect of affairs upon our border," declared petitioners for protection in one county. Hundreds of Missouri bushwhackers threatened to descend on Kansas at any time. Elsewhere along the border, people simply deserted their farms and businesses. "Matters are going from bad to worse at a fearful rate," declared one man.[28]

A new, almost totally lawless element also surfaced in Kansas: the Red Legs. So named for their red-dyed leather leggings, these gangs first surfaced in the autumn of 1861 as another type of jayhawker. By 1863, they came in several forms. One group had served the Union army as volunteer scouts along the Missouri border in the winter of 1861–62. A second group, known as "Red-legged" or "Buckskin" Scouts, currently filled a similar but more official role, even drawing army pay. They first appeared in the spring of 1863 under the command of General James G. Blunt at Fort Leavenworth. When not serving the army as scouts, spies, or detectives, they freelanced as counterguerrilla fighters. The appropriately named William S. Tough became the best known of these hardened customers, who did not hesitate to cross the border into Missouri. A third—and seemingly the most numerous—type made criminal activity its chief occupation. Led by George H. Hoyt, these renegades held no political loyalties whatsoever. But, then, all Red Legs rode on the wrong side of the law when it suited them. Like the wildest of the rebel guerrillas, they used the war as an excuse to pillage and kill whom they pleased.[29]

Kansas officials responded to these several threats by expanding the militia, issuing decrees against Red Legs, authorizing new companies of home guards, and supplying communities with weapons. They even authorized independent companies "to arrest and detain any organized bands of guerrillas, or persons . . . contemplating robbery or violence." Military commanders tried to pacify the border by moving troops from Kansas into the southwestern tier of Missouri counties, where Quantrill tended to operate. They licensed their troops to deal summarily with all unauthorized bands of armed men, whether Red Legs or rebels. General Blunt, commanding the District of Kansas in April 1863, ordered the 9th Kansas Infantry to "exercise the utmost vigilance and promptness in discovering and destroying all bands of guerrillas and outlaws" along the Missouri border.[30]

Blunt also endorsed retaliation against civilians in Kansas and Missouri. Dismissing rebels and rebel sympathizers in both states as a "motley crew" of "insurgents and assassins," he ordered anyone who aided guerrillas to be "destroyed or expelled" from the district. "These instructions will not exempt females from the rule," he added pointedly. "Experience has taught that the bite of a she adder is as poisonous and productive of mischief as the bite of any other venomous reptile." The toll was particularly heavy in Missouri. With Kansas troops once more assigned to the state, unarmed farmers, accused of being "bushwhackers," fell dead in their fields. Marauding also resumed. The 11th Kansas Cavalry "effectively 'cleaned out'" whole neighborhoods in March. In June 1863, moving from Kansas City to Independence, the regiment left a line of burning buildings, mills, and homes in its rear.[31]

Iowans, too, remained snared in Missouri's sprawling guerrilla war. As in Kansas, Union military reverses and the political policies of the Lincoln administration had emboldened the state's copperheads. Both Governor Samuel Kirkwood and his adjutant general believed the dangerously subversive situation could worsen rapidly if rebel guerrillas and their sympathizers added violence to mounting political protests. They had established a special Border Brigade in September 1862 to keep out Missouri "jayhawkers." With people along the border clamoring for arms or protection, the governor also encouraged communities to organize for defense. In February 1863, he warned the U.S. government of the potential for anarchy. In March, he issued a statewide alert against the dangers posed by Missouri guerrillas.[32]

Iowans doubtless exaggerated the threats of both internal rebellion and invasion, but people living in such uncertain times could scarcely be blamed for seeing destruction at every turn. There were also enough incidents of bushwhacking, theft, and subversion to make even the most skeptical observer wary. A particularly insidious danger surfaced when Confederate sympathizers infiltrated several militia and independent companies. Meanwhile, guerrillas continued to drive Unionists out of northern Missouri and into Iowa. They secured munitions, provisions, and horses in Iowa, too, by taking them from defenseless citizens and receiving them from pro-Confederates. Officers of the Border Brigade reported that the most "desperate Set of Gurrillas that god ever made" engaged in a multitude of crimes. They also complained that they could not possibly protect the citizenry from such brigands without sufficient men to interdict contraband trade, ferret out deserters, and confiscate arms from "disloyal persons." The Emancipation Proclamation added to these woes when Iowans received threats from "Rebbles on Both sides of the line . . . of Raising and taking all of the darkes Back in to Missouria."[33]

Illinois had more to fear from guerrillas in Kentucky than in Missouri, but no part of the Midwest witnessed a more tangled pattern of irregular war than the Land of Lincoln. Hotly pursued Missouri guerrillas who found refuge in the state perpetrated brutal and senseless crimes. "Disloyal" citizens in the central river counties of Pike, Brown, Adams, and Schyler provided havens for many Missouri "ruffians" and "bushwhackers." The situation seemed to be under control by the summer of 1863, but not before the state's adjutant general formed a "permanent station" of cavalry in river towns like Quincy, in Adams County. Farther south, in the peninsula formed by the Mississippi and Tennessee rivers, the situation remained dicey. When Union troops from Missouri and Arkansas had to reinforce the region, one soldier marveled at the situation. "It is something new bushwhacking in Ill.," he informed his brother. "The country is full of deserters and Secesh. We have arrested a good many of both kinds. . . . It is easier to fight them in Arks."[34]

Not only did the Mississippi River fail to buffer Illinois from its western neighbor, but also, in a bizarre twist, Missouri became threatened by rebel sympathizers in Illinois. Union commanders on both sides of the river reported smugglers taking ammunition and other contraband into Missouri. In April 1863, General Thomas J. McKean, responsible for the security of northeastern Missouri, warned that rebel refugees and sympathizers in Illinois might stage a raid into his district. McKean had reliable information that smugglers in river towns like Quincy intended either to join the rebel army or form "bands of marauders" to "commit depredations" in Missouri. The rumored raid did not materialize, but the potential for such attacks remained real enough for additional militia and U.S. troops to be placed on the Illinois border during the spring and summer of 1863.[35]

Despite such problems, the biggest external threat to Missouri came from the south. Raids and rumors of raids out of Arkansas persisted through the winter of 1862–63 and into the spring. Semi-irregulars, such as John T. Coffee, Upton Hays, James Rains, Jeremiah V. Cockrell, and Sidney Jackman, caused most of the trouble, but conventional cavalry commanders, including Joseph O. Shelby, Gideon Thompson, and John Marmaduke, also made appearances in the state. None of their incursions did serious damage, but they encouraged Missouri-based guerrillas to remain active in the war, exposed the extremely weak hold Union troops had on northern Arkansas, and left open the possibility of an eventual Confederate resurgence in southern Missouri.[36]

As things stood, southern Missouri and northern Arkansas had become a vast no-man's-land. Union patrols burned houses and whole villages suspected of harboring guerrillas. The army even suspended an order prohibiting jayhawking for a time. The logical antidote would have been a campaign out of Helena to capture Little Rock and lay claim to all of Arkansas north of the Arkansas River. Instead, Samuel Curtis, still at Helena but now commanding the entire Department of the Missouri, ordered an invasion of northern Arkansas from Missouri. He hoped this would ensure the security of the border and provide a platform for a later advance on Little Rock, but the resulting winter campaign of 1862–63 was a disappointment. A combination of rebel cavalry and partisans made sure the army from Missouri never reached its destination of Batesville. The Federals had more success in northwestern Arkansas, where a separate army defeated the rebels at the battle of Prairie Grove in December; but calls for Curtis to be removed grew loud.[37]

Curtis would be replaced in May 1863, but not for his failure on the border alone. Curtis also failed to solve the guerrilla problem in the Mississippi River valley, and there he ran afoul of President Lincoln. Both the president and Henry Halleck placed a far higher premium on capturing Vicksburg than on securing the Missouri border. A necessary part of any such campaign involved clearing the valley of guerrillas. Curtis worked doggedly, despite being undermanned and undersupplied, to achieve that end. He sent river-borne expeditions along both the Arkansas and Mississippi shorelines. He sent gunboats up the Mississippi tributaries of both states. The meager results did not seem to justify such tiring and treacherous duty. Curtis's soldiers, already in a vile mood, cursed the swampy Arkansas delta unsparingly: the foulest place on earth, they called it. Flies, gnats, and mosquitoes tormented them. Bad drinking water bred sickness. Malaria, typhoid, and chronic diarrhea left no more than two-thirds of the army available for duty between August 1862 and February 1863. The population of Helena had grown to ten times its prewar size of two thousand people when refugee slaves crowded the town and its environs.[38]

The defiance of rebel citizens further riled the men. Alf Johnson, captain of a Texas "spy company," operated unimpeded between Little Rock and the Mississippi River. "He can now get this whole people to follow him," believed one of his admiring men. The Federals might call Johnson a "jayhawker," but the citizens praised him for "saving" them. Consequently, Johnson's men felt no qualms when operating close to Union garrisons and outposts. "They don't move a peg without our seeing them," a member of the company said proudly. "There is not a family east of White River but is willing to do anything for any of our company."[39]

It was small wonder, then, that once turned loose in eastern Arkansas, Union soldiers burned every house in every neighborhood where bushwhackers assailed them. Not even the plantations of supposedly "loyal" families escaped confiscation of food and livestock. One brigade, having failed to collar the guerrillas who ambushed its river convoy, burned nearly every plantation between Helena and Napoleon, a distance of over fifty miles. That evening, with the sky aglow from their day's work, at least one of the men realized that "military necessity" alone had not produced such "wanton destruction." Equally important was "a thirst for vengeance, and licentious desire to sack and burn," all a "natural consequence," he concluded, of the guerrilla war.[40]

Lightening could strike from afar, too. The nearly seventy-year-old town of Hopefield, Arkansas, the state's second oldest settlement, sat across the Mississippi River from Memphis. Its inhabitants had been obliged to take the U.S. loyalty oath in the summer of 1862, when Curtis's army tramped through on its way to Helena. That did not deter the town from offering safe haven to rebel guerrillas, but Hopefield paid dearly for its defiance. Guerrillas who rendezvoused there terrorized commercial shipping on the Mississippi. They captured or burned steamboats and flatboats; confiscated valuable cargoes, including livestock, ammunition, coal, and medicine; and destroyed cotton liable to fall into Union hands. By February 1863, General Stephen Hurlbut, the Union commander at Memphis, had seen enough. He ordered Hopefield burned to the ground. The town had become "a mere shelter for guerrillas," he explained to his superior, Ulysses S. Grant. Hurlbut warned his men not to harm the townspeople, but he allowed the inhabitants only one hour to leave with whatever property they could carry.[41]

Politicians in both Washington and Richmond ignored the chaos in Arkansas at their peril. In addition, poor harvests in 1861 and 1862, with armies claiming a large share of what crops remained, meant food shortages for all. So, too, did an epidemic of hog cholera. Local government disappeared in some places. As public officials fled the ravages of war, courts closed, jails were opened, and taxes went uncollected. Rebel citizens felt cut off from the "Eastern army," and perfectly innocent men lived in fear of being arrested as guerrillas. Otherwise loyal rebel guerrillas, desperate for food, stole from their own people. Neither the Union army's officers nor its provost guards seemed able to suppress crime, and many people regarded the latter as no better than "a band of thieves." More injuriously, some Confederate deserters, far from rushing to defend their families, abandoned the war entirely. They became outlaws and resisted any attempt to force them back into the army.[42]

Neither Federals nor Confederates could hope to benefit from such conditions, and the fortunes of noncombatants on each side shifted according to location and time. One moment rebel citizens felt secure; a month later, Unionists had cause to celebrate. People who had hoped to escape the war as "neutrals" found that option disappearing. No one was immune to violence and theft, either at the hands of guerrillas and outlaws or by the armies. People supported whichever side promised to restore order. When the Union army gained a foothold, many formerly loyal Confederates offered to help. They had become disenchanted by conscription and the failure of their own government to protect them. Other people, Unionists to the core, had only been waiting for the opportunity to retaliate. Then there were the opportunists, loyal to no side, who decided it was time to back an apparent winner. Consequently, hundreds of Arkansans rushed to take the U.S. loyalty oath. Hundreds of others, both rebels and Unionists, fled the state, usually to Missouri.[43]

Arkansans willing to counter rebel rule with violence responded in different ways. Some Unionists, still preferring to play cautious, formed secret societies. Clandestine resistance had been tried before in the state but unsuccessfully. The Peace Society, formed in northern Arkansas in 1861, had been neither strongly Unionist nor particularly peaceful. Rather, it was a network of local vigilance committees intent on protecting "homes, property, and family against Robbers and thieves." The rebel government had rooted out its members, placed them in chains, and marched them to Little Rock. The secret societies of 1863 were more clearly Unionist but no less endangered. They took up arms against Confederate troops and guerrillas, although, being outnumbered in most parts of the state, they maintained their secrecy. "There have been fights between the societies and Confederate troops, with various results," confirmed a sympathizer of the revolt in southern Arkansas. "Where the former have been defeated they have generally been hanged without trial."[44]

Bolder men organized home guards or joined the army. At first, Union officials, hoping to inspire a statewide militia in Arkansas, encouraged this option. "Mountain Federals" and "Union bushwhackers" soon struck ferociously in all parts of the state. "Our hills are filled with tories who resist the conscript law and plunder the loyal men," an alarmed citizen of Little Rock declared in February 1863. The situation looked "dark if not hopeless." Even in southern Arkansas, supposedly secure rebel ground, anti-Confederate bands formed, if for no other reason than to resist the draft. "Disaffected persons, and turblent characters" seemed to be everywhere.[45]

Martin D. Hart led the most notorious federal guerrilla band in Arkansas. A native of Indiana, Hart had established himself in Texas before the war as a businessman, lawyer, and politician. He began the war as a captain of Confederate cavalry but switched allegiances a year later. Finding his way to western Arkansas, he led several loosely coordinated guerrilla outfits that threatened rebel communications, preyed on Confederate patrols, and committed "numerous outrages" against rebel citizens between Fort Smith and Dardanelle, more than seventy rugged miles to the east. "Farmers are wanting to go to work," complained a man of Hart's activities, "but there will be but little done in regard to farming unless those thieving jayhawking villains are hunted down and hanged."[46]

Hart's career—and life—was cut short in late January 1863 by just such a fate. A battalion of Texas partisan rangers, apparently the only Confederate force capable of dealing with this "renegade," ran him and sixteen of his men to ground. A brief, efficient trial at Fort Smith found Hart and his chief lieutenant guilty of murder. Hart probably had not been the trigger man, but he bore responsibility for the killings. "Hart's party . . . killed a good old citizen of the town, in cold blood, right in his own yard & in the very presence of his family," reported a Confederate officer who had known Hart before the war, "& they killed him only because he was a good Southern man." Hart's lieutenant died alongside him on the gallows; the rest of the captured men went to prison.[47]

Rebel and Unionist guerrillas had been hunting each other since the war began.
Used by permission, State Historical Society of Missouri, Columbia
(*Harper's Weekly*, November 21, 1863).

Unionists and anti-Confederates had been slower to join the army, but that, too, changed in the spring and summer of 1863. Over eight thousand Arkansans chose to wear Union blue by the end of the war, not nearly as many as in Tennessee or Virginia, but more than in any other Confederate state. The Union army even sent recruiting expeditions into northern Arkansas, at great risk, it should be said, to both recruiters and volunteers. One of the first and most effective outfits recruited in the state, the 1st Arkansas Cavalry, operated in northwestern Arkansas. Being familiar with the terrain and the loyalties of people, it became a formidable adversary for such rebel chieftains as William Martin, Buck Brown, Peter Mankins, and James Ingrun. As more Unionist refugees sought protection at federal garrisons, they formed additional regiments, including the 1st Arkansas Infantry. Some home guard companies also joined these regiments.[48]

James Ingrun saw at once the danger presented by the 1st Arkansas Cavalry when it arrived at Fayetteville. Though born in Illinois, Ingrun had organized a rebel guerrilla band in Arkansas in the spring of 1862, when Earl Van Dorn abandoned the state. He had been a terror to Union troops in northwestern Arkansas ever since, but the 1st Arkansas posed a new type of challenge. Testing the resolve of his new opponent, the thirty-six-year-old, semi-illiterate guerrilla sent an improbable message to the regiment's lieutenant colonel, Albert W. Bishop. Writing boldly in red ink from his "hed quartyers," Ingrun told Bishop that his band had no desire to wage war against women and children and expressed hope that Bishop's men felt the same humane impulse. He would conduct an honorable war against the Federals and treat all prisoners with respect. The real danger to the region, Ingrun proposed, came from Union home guards, the "molisha." They had been merciless, he charged, as they burned homes and robbed and murdered innocent people. The guerrilla hoped Bishop would not follow their example. "If you carey out the plan of Burning and Robing I shal Be compeled to paternise your plan," he warned, "But it is a plan that I abhor. . . . We dont want it sed that the suthern people Brot familys to suffer."[49]

Bishop would not be drawn into that game, but the growing presence of Union regiments like his own caused more Arkansas rebels to enter the guerrilla war. George T. Maddox had served in the army for over a year, but when his regiment retreated from Prairie Grove, he decided to set an independent course. He returned home to join a band of seventy-five guerrillas and spent the rest of the war harassing Union troops, cowing Unionists, and being "*death* on the *militia*" in northern Arkansas. Captain James H. Love and his company did not have to desert the army. Having been assigned to Arkansas, they returned home to Searcy County, in north-central Arkansas, whenever lawlessness by either Unionists or rebel sympathizers endangered their families. Only when Confederate authorities expressly ordered Love's men elsewhere did they stray far from the neighborhood.[50]

Men like Maddox and Love underscore once again that the "Confederate cause" most often meant defense of home. They may have spoken of the Confederate "nation" and espoused Confederate "independence," especially in the first year of the war, but that was not what the conflict came to mean to them. Independence counted only if their homes were secure and their families safe. As Arkansas governor Harris Flanagin told Jefferson Davis in a marvelously succinct explanation of both the appeal and the corrosive effect of guerrilla warfare, "Soldiers do not enter the service to maintain the Southern Confederacy alone but also to protect their property and defend their homes and families." General Dandridge McRae, an Arkansas commander who often employed guerrillas and understood what motivated them, sympathized. Honorable soldiers became "desperate guerrillas," MaRae observed, because the "home they left had been given to the flames or a gray haired father shot upon his hearth stone." They became "harsh and vengeful, spared nothing clad in blue that could be captured." A familiar, once loving place became a "community of bitter memories."[51]

Louisiana saw its war intensify for similar reasons, especially in the parishes around New Orleans and along the Mississippi River between New Orleans and Port Hudson. This bayou country offered good terrain for war by stealth, and plenty of Louisianians remained keen to join the guerrilla ranks. "I can raise a company of Rangers I think and do good service not many miles from here," a schoolteacher insisted as Union occupation spread through the southern part of the state. "This is the finest country in the world for service of that kind," he reasoned, an assessment his Yankee foes could not gainsay.[52]

Confederate Louisiana had finally acquired some sense of direction, too, with the arrival in August 1862 of General Richard Taylor to command the District of Western Louisiana. Son of President Zachary Taylor and former brother-in-law of Jefferson Davis, Taylor was destined to become the highest-ranking non–West Pointer in the Confederate army. For the moment, though, he faced many of the same obstacles that had bedeviled Thomas Hindman in Arkansas, especially a paucity of troops. Like Hindman, Taylor made up the deficit with partisan rangers. Unlike Hindman, Taylor soon regretted his decision.[53]

Taylor arrived in the middle of yet another controversy involving

Louisiana's irregulars. Governor Moore, already pushing the Partisan Ranger Act to its limits, had caused uneasiness in Richmond. The War Department wanted him to use fewer rangers. At the same time, Union army and navy commanders at New Orleans had instituted a policy of retaliation against guerrillas. Not that it proved very successful. A Union officer, following a week-long guerilla-hunting expedition, admitted having "only dissolving views" of his elusive foe. A nervous lieutenant, following one "*dangerous* and *reckless wild goose chase*," claimed that his company might have been cut down at any moment by "three bold men . . . with shot guns." The Federals exalted over their few successes as though they had won major battles. They predicted that the apprehension of this or that guerrilla chief, or the scattering of a particularly large band, would seriously damage guerrilla resistance, but such results seldom materialized.[54]

A dramatic instance of U.S. retaliation in this frightful environment came shortly before Taylor arrived on the scene. Union warships and landing parties of marines partially destroyed the town of Donaldsonville, on the Mississippi River between New Orleans and Baton Rouge, and nearby plantations. Partisan rangers had been firing on river traffic for several weeks in the vicinity. When warnings from David Farragut failed to stop the deadly game, the admiral unleashed his flotilla. "Severity is the only thing that will bring this people to their senses," a Unionist in New Orleans said approvingly.[55]

Residents on that troubled part of the river asked Governor Moore to call off the rangers, commanded by Captain James A. McWaters. The attacks on Union shipping accomplished nothing, they claimed, other than to enrage the Federals, and civilians received the brunt of that rage. Elsewhere in the state, partisans seemed to be out of control. Citizens in southern Louisiana had complained recently that Captain Samuel M. Todd's Prairie Rangers, when seeking to arrest suspected Unionist collaborators, abused their authority to enter private households. One woman called them the "Prairie Banditti" and appealed to Governor Moore on behalf of all women in her community "for protection against the insults threats and outrages" of Todd's men. "We could not fare worse were we surrounded by a band of Lincoln's mercenary hirelings," she declared. Similar charges had been made against Captain W. A. Taylor's men in central Louisiana. It was precisely the kind of behavior the Richmond government feared a guerrilla war might generate.[56]

The root of such problems seemed obvious to Benjamin Butler, who still commanded at New Orleans. The gravest transgressions by guerrillas came when they operated outside their own neighborhoods, he noted. When "brought from a neighboring State into a community where they have neither interest nor restraint," Butler suggested, even supposedly disciplined partisan rangers could prove unmanageable. There was much in what he said. The Confederate government recruited rangers with the intention of assigning them where needed, but partisans who operated far from home saw their mission differently from local guerrillas, and they were not on such intimate terms with the population. Rebel bands had always represented a mixture of "home" guerrillas and outside volunteers, and partisan rangers represented just such "outsiders." Rather than defending their own home front, they were often deployed to fight or harass invading forces where military necessity, not individual preference, placed them.[57]

Pleas and arguments could not sway Governor Moore. He remained impressed by the way guerrillas had rushed to defend his state at a time when the Confederate government seemed to have deserted Louisiana. He never responded to War Department requests to limit the actions of McWaters's men. When the district militia commander, General R. C. Martin, tried to rein them in, Moore arrested him. Martin, like the citizens around Donaldsonville, had become frustrated by the "illegal, irregular, and derogatory" operations of independent companies. He announced that partisan leaders within his command would henceforth act only on his orders. Moore's adjutant general, to justify the shocking arrest of Martin, declared that the militia commander's directive had been "highly disrespectful to the Governor." Partisan rangers in Louisiana, he continued, served at the governor's request and would continue to operate according to the "special orders" issued by him.[58]

Richard Taylor, far less impressed by the rangers, responded to the controversy by rejecting new applicants for partisan service and placing existing companies in the army. Although forced to rely on some partisan companies to augment his forces, he integrated units that displeased him, including McWater's men, with conventional cavalry regiments. A Union gunboat captain noticed the difference. Accustomed to warding off attacks on river traffic, he found that rebel troops in the region, though still "exceedingly vigilant and active," were "not all composed of guerrillas, but [had] regulars and militia . . . combined with them."[59]

William H. Garig was one Louisiana partisan to escape Taylor's reforms. He was also precisely the sort of partisan Taylor thought needed reforming. Garig regarded the war as a lark, to be joined or ignored as it suited him. He spent much of his time between December 1862 and May 1863 visiting friends near home and wandering in and out of ranger camps to play baseball, race horses, gamble at cards, and drink large quantities of rum. Now and then he attended church. On the rare occasions when he saw action, Garig displayed a remarkably casual attitude. "We were ordered to Bayou Sarah," he recorded in his diary in late March 1863; "had a scrape there trying to arrest a man & killed him." Two days later, following a turn at sentry duty, he reported, "Drank some[,] had some fun of halting a good many fellows[,] than [sic] let them all pass." More typically, Garig returned to camp before getting "tight." Not infrequently, he was unfit for consecutive days of duty: "I was sick to day & layed in bed nearly all day[,] felt affull bad."[60]

Still, both Garig and General Taylor outlasted Ben Butler. The Massachusetts politician and general had confronted the guerrilla menace in no uncertain terms; but he had not pacified Louisiana, and his questionable financial affairs, heavy-handed dealings with citizens, and undiplomatic treatment of foreign consuls in New Orleans made him controversial. President Lincoln replaced him in late 1862 with General Nathaniel P. Banks, another Massachusetts politician-turned-general. Banks would become controversial in his own right, but he provided continuity in the guerrilla war by adopting Butler's antiguerrilla policies.[61]

By then, the guerrilla war had infected Texas. Despite the looming peril, menacing jayhawkers to the north and a seaborne threat from the Gulf, Texas saw few Union troops during the war. Consequently, Texans did not have to resort to guerrilla tactics to drive out invaders. If keen to fight as guerrillas, they generally had to serve in more troubled parts of the Confederacy. However, two exceptions appeared in the summer of 1862, when the prospect of conscription riled two very different sets of Unionists, one in northern Texas, settled mostly by emigrants from the Midwest and upper South, the other in the hill country of central Texas, which had a large German population. Only a combination of martial law, lynch law, home guards, militia, and partisan rangers could check the revolts.[62]

Hill-country Germans had formed a Union League early in the war, but they had not caused the rebels undue alarm. A sizable number of German families had moved to Mexico rather than resist the Confederate government. However, when the remaining Germans organized a home guard—ostensibly to ward off Comanche raids—local rebels grew nervous. Texas did not suffer the extreme ethnic animus that poisoned German-American relations in Missouri, but tensions were no less real. Confederate vigilance committees formed when rumors spread that

Germans were encouraging slave rebellion and attacking rebel families. Dead bodies from both sides—some shot, others hanged—soon littered the region.[63]

When partisan rangers arrived to arrest known Unionist leaders near Fredericksburg in July 1862, about sixty German men headed for Mexico. Their ultimate destination appears to have been New Orleans, where they could enlist in the Union army, but few of them completed the journey. A combined force of Confederate regular and irregular troops tracked them down a day's ride from the Rio Grande. Many of the Germans died in a pitched battle along the Nueces River. The rebels executed nine more wounded men who had surrendered, and they eventually tracked down and shot eight of the fugitives.[64]

The remaining Germans escaped, but back in the hill country, reprisals continued for several months after the "Nueces Massacre." Guerrilla war broke out in earnest. The Germans called rebel guerrillas *haengerbande*, or "hanging bands"; rebels accused German tories of being "bloodthirsty bushwhackers and villains." "The 'bushwhackers' or traitors are plentiful in this country," a Confederate cavalryman observed of the dissenters. "When *one* chances to fall into the hands of the C.S. soldiers he is dealt pretty roughly with and generally makes his last speech with a rope around his neck." The number of murders and lynchings multiplied. So did the arrests and executions of Unionists.[65]

The hill country remained unsettled until the end of the war, but an unusually accommodating policy toward the Germans brought relative calm by the spring of 1863. District military commander General John B. Magruder, after imposing martial law, convinced some Germans to accept conscription by allowing draftees to work as teamsters or to serve on the frontier against Indians. He also granted a generous number of exemptions to German farmers so they might make their land productive.[66]

The troubles in northern Texas, home of men like Martin Hart, required more force. The affected region included some two dozen counties between Dallas and the Red River. Its position adjacent to Indian Territory, where Unionists might cooperate with like-minded tribes and Kansans, magnified the dangers of dissent. Confederate home guards and vigilantes repressed any sign of Unionist mischief with arrests, lynchings, and brute intimidation. Outnumbered Unionists submitted, emigrated, took to the bush, or, like Martin Hart, carried the fight to the rebels.[67]

The most chilling instance of Confederate repression came with the "Great Hanging." Rebel fears of internal revolt peaked in Texas during the summer of 1862. The Federals had made another move to seize Indian Territory, and the rebels uncovered a Unionist plot to capture several militia arsenals. Confederates worried that "marauding parties composed of Yankee Guerrillas [and] . . . treacherous citizens" would soon overwhelm them. The specter of slave rebellion was never far from people's thoughts, either. Local "citizen courts" in northern Texas reacted initially by lynching a few Unionists. Then, in October 1862, the court in Cooke County ordered the arrest of more than two hundred men. Brought to the county seat of Gainesville for trial, several dozen of the prisoners were hanged. Before the month had ended, vigilantes rounded up and lynched dozens more men in Cooke and surrounding counties.[68]

The slaughter ended neither dissent nor violence in northern Texas. If anything, the violence increased. Unionists, having seen what fate awaited them, took to the bush and resisted Confederate rule even more ferociously. It became a war between "brush men" and vigilantes. By the summer of 1863, a portion of the state's Frontier Regiment— composed of Texas Rangers sworn into Confederate service—had to be reassigned from the western border, where they had guarded against Indian attacks, to northern Texas. Renamed the "Mounted Regiment of Texas State Troops," their new duties involved capturing draft evaders, deserters, and outlaws. Unluckily for the rebels, hostile Indian raids from the west also increased in 1863. Thereafter, guarding northern Texas would be no easy matter.[69]

No one understood the complexity of the guerrilla war better than William T. Sherman, and the longer he pondered it, the angrier he got. Garrison after garrison, patrol after patrol, supply train after supply train in Tennessee and Kentucky had been attacked, plundered, or destroyed by rebel guerrillas. "All the people are now guerrillas," he decided in August 1862. They were cowardly, too, assembling to attack small patrols but scattering when threatened by larger forces. Only stern retaliatory measures could save the Union. Sherman preferred to retaliate against slaveowners, whom, he believed, had the power to end the rebellion. Still, when no slaveowners were handy, the fiery Sherman trusted to collective punishment, and as the newly appointed district commander at Memphis, he had power to mete it out.[1]

Sherman's wrath finally broke on Randolph, Tennessee, twenty-five miles above Memphis. In September, guerrillas nearly captured the packet *Eugene* near Randolph. Unable to identify or apprehend the bushwhackers, Sherman struck at the rebel population by ordering the town destroyed. "Randolph is gone," he reported on the return of his avenging Ohio regiment. "It is no use tolerating such acts as firing on steamboats," he explained by way of justification. "Punishment must be speedy, sure, and exemplary." He opposed "wanton mischief or destruction," Sherman emphasized, but in this instance, the rules of war dictated action.[2]

When the rebels of western Tennessee ignored his message and continued their attacks on river traffic, Sherman leveled other guerrilla haunts. "All armed men must be destroyed or captured, their houses and property to be destroyed or brought away," he instructed his men. He also expelled ten families from every community where boats were endangered. Sherman never doubted the necessity of these actions. Confederates must suffer for the "barbarity" of their "fiendish" guerrillas until the rebel government "disavow[ed]" them. Who was the more "cruel and heartless?" he challenged a Confederate woman protesting his edicts. He, for sending away the families of men "engaged in such hellish deeds," or the "partisans," who endangered boats carrying women and children? He would order the "absolute destruction" of

Memphis, New Orleans, and "every other city, town, and hamlet of the South," he assured another woman, to maintain safe navigation of the Mississippi River. "Misplaced kindness to these guerrillas, their families, and adherents is cruelty to our people," Sherman insisted.[3]

That Sherman's actions came in response to guerrilla threats to his supply and communications lines is a point worth pursuing. Wagon trains, river traffic, and railroads were essential to the Union advance. Protecting railroads, the most important source of supplies, was a priority in all theaters of the war. Yet all of these conveyances remained terribly vulnerable, especially the railroads. Some Union officers estimated by 1863 that tens of thousands of men were needed to protect tracks, bridges, and tunnels. The line between Bowling Green and Nashville, alone, one general said, required no fewer than fifty thousand men. Having no such numbers to spare, the Federals in Kentucky and Tennessee relied on small permanent guards and roving patrols.[4]

Most soldiers hated this duty, either because of the danger or because of the boredom. The psychological stress wore them down, too. "We are kept almost constantly in suspense," one man explained, "not knowing when or where they may make a strike." Men sensed the danger of "being divided into small parties, liable at any time to an attack from Guerilla Bands." One soldier at first relished the independent duty of railroad guard but soon learned that it entailed "a great deal more danger" than people might suppose. "We were scattered in small squads," he explained to a sister, "where guerrilla bands were thick as hail and the citizens would aid them against us at any moment."[5]

Blockhouses and stockades afforded one means of protection. Constructed of logs and standing one to two stories high, most blockhouses held a full company. Wooden stockades, sometimes reinforced by earthworks, held up to two companies. Strategically positioned at bridges, these miniatures forts provided added security for the immediate vicinity and allowed relatively few men to protect long stretches of track. The idea of using a network of blockhouses and stockades apparently originated with General Grenville M. Dodge. Assigned to rebuild the Mobile and Ohio Railroad in northern Mississippi in the summer of 1862, the Massachusetts-born engineer used blockhouses to protect his workers. Ulysses S. Grant liked the idea so much that he ordered the same protection for all Union-controlled railroads in Kentucky and Tennessee. An army engineer in the Department of the Cumberland estimated that over 150 blockhouses were built along seven railroads (totaling more than 700 miles of track) between 1862 and 1864.[6]

Yet, despite their imposing presence, blockhouses provided only a static defense. This became most evident at posts manned solely by infantry, which was the norm. The 129th Illinois Infantry, a veteran of such service, had to be "constantly on the go." About 8:00 one evening in March 1863, the regiment was aroused by the crash of a falling locomotive and the discharge of musketry. Seventy guerrillas had derailed a train less than two miles from the 129th Illinois. Two companies arrived on the scene in just twelve minutes, but they only managed to wound one rebel and capture six others. Around the same time, part of the regiment surprised a gang of forty guerrillas tearing up tracks near Gallatin, Tennessee, but, again, the guerrillas, being mounted, eluded them.[7]

Both sides resorted to trickery. "They kept crying out to our boys that they was our boys," reported a Union guard of some rebels disguised in blue coats, "till they got close a nuff then they shot at our boys: skeared the horses and scattered the men." Wearing Union uniforms had been a common guerrilla dodge since early in the war. General William Rosecrans countered the subterfuge by telling his men to shoot all rebels "with arms in their hands and Uncle Sam's Clothes on." Federal troops at La Grange, Tennessee, had some tricks of their own. Learning that partisan leader Sol Street was waiting to ambush an army payroll train, they sent "an old wood train" ahead of it. Sure enough, the guerrillas revealed their position by derailing the worthless decoy. Unaccountably, they still risked an attack on the payroll train, even managing to burn a pair of cars and take prisoners, but without snatching the cash. Far from discouraged, Street's men derailed another train along the same line a week later and captured nearly forty men and officers.[8]

Sherman's experience at Memphis showed the urgency of protecting rivers, as well. Union armies depended on boats of every size, shape, and function (gunboats, troop transports, supply boats, mail boats, coal barges) to survive. Yet, slow-moving vessels made tempting targets. The navy's responsibility for safeguarding river traffic increased significantly in October 1862, when the army relinquished its authority over western gunboats. Uninitiated navy commanders soon learned that guerrillas had varied purposes and methods when attacking river traffic. If the rebels wanted only to cause injury or convey the threat of their presence, they shot at a boat's crew and passengers. If they wanted to capture or destroy a vessel, they used some pretext to lure unsuspecting captains toward shore or pounced at some narrow or restricted part of the river, where they could order a surrender. They could also fire into a boat's engines or wheels to disable it, and they were quick to move against a craft already in trouble, either run aground or disabled by

The Union army built stockades along vulnerable rail lines throughout the South.
From *Harper's Weekly*, August 30, 1862.

mechanical problems. They seldom took on gunboats, armed convoys, or heavily defended vessels, just as they rarely engaged large bodies of troops.[9]

When Admiral David D. Porter arrived to command the Mississippi Squadron in the autumn of 1862, he discounted no means for combating these dangers. An admirer of Grant and Sherman, he had "closely scrutinized their operations." Porter now copied their antiguerrilla policies. He arrested both known guerrillas and sympathizers in the area of attacks and seizures, assessed collaborators at ten times the value of plundered or destroyed property, and burned whole communities, including "buildings and fields." In reference to the last tactic, he told Secretary of the Navy Gideon Welles, "This is the only way of putting a stop to guerrilla warfare, and though the method is stringent, officers are instructed to put it down at all hazards."[10]

Navy lieutenant Le Roy Fitch borrowed Porter's methods while patrolling the Ohio, Cumberland, and Tennessee rivers in 1862–63. Sometimes commanding a single steamer with "two small guns," at other times directing a small flotilla, Fitch rarely passed a week without encountering rebel guerrillas or their handiwork. He shelled guerrillas, disembarked troops to pursue them, and collected reparations from their protectors. In October 1862, Fitch intended to burn the town of Caseyville, Kentucky, until he learned that most of the inhabitants were Unionists. Instead, he demanded $35,000 from the town's known rebels to pay for the damage recently done to a passing steamer. When the rebels proved slow in paying the assessment, he confiscated the amount in kind, including over 1,000 bags of wheat, 40 barrels of whiskey, and a dozen kegs of lard. He then arrested all disloyal men and sent them to Illinois as prisoners of war.[11]

That none of this significantly reduced the rebel presence frustrated Fitch mightily. He recommended that commercial shipping not be allowed to travel on the Tennessee River without convoys. Guerrillas would continue to harass river traffic, he pointed out, as long as they could capture lone steamers. Meantime, he worked to reduce those odds by seeking out the "most noted guerrilla haunts." In March 1863, he burned and destroyed stores and houses at Betsy Town, a notorious rendezvous spot on the Cumberland. He did similar work on the Tennessee River, where he confiscated livestock, provisions, and cotton and torched plantations known to harbor guerrillas. Swinging back to the Cumberland, he began the month of April by burning the town of Palmyra. "Not one house left," he reported to Admiral Porter. "A very

The Federals needed gunboats to protect river traffic against guerrilla attacks.
From *Leslie's Illustrated Newspaper*, as reproduced in *The Soldier in Our Civil War* (1894).

bad hole," he explained; "best to get rid of it and teach the rebels a les-son."[12]

Cotton also played a prominent role in the guerrilla war by the end of 1862. Cotton was the Confederacy's most valuable commodity, used to finance the war at home and wielded as a diplomatic tool abroad. Nec-essarily, then, cotton became important to the North. Every bale con-fiscated, purchased, or destroyed by Union soldiers injured the South. Confiscation and purchase were the preferred options. Salvaged cotton could be used to finance the Union war effort as readily as it did the Confederacy. Rather than let unprotected stockpiles of cotton fall into Union hands, the Confederate government ordered its armies to con-fiscate or destroy it. Rebel field commanders, who already had plenty to do in contending with enemy armies, often assigned this responsi-bility to partisan rangers and guerrillas. If too late to destroy cotton in gins and warehouses, rebel "cotton burners" intercepted north-bound steamers and cotton-laden wagons headed for Union-held towns.[13]

Another dimension of the cotton issue involved the black market. All variety of supplies, including food, medicine, and clothing, flowed down the Mississippi with the approval of U.S. Treasury agents at Mem-phis. The goods were to be exchanged for the cotton of loyal planters. However, it soon became clear that at least half of these valuable com-modities fell into rebel hands, with local guerrillas being the principal distributors. "They are as familiar with traders as if they had sent for their goods," a general complained in early 1863. "The guerrillas act as commissaries to the interior. . . . We are feeding them with one hand and fighting them with the other." Further complicating matters, some Union army officers engaged in the cotton trade for personal profit, either exchanging confiscated rebel cotton on the black market or sharing profits with loyal planters for the sale of their cotton. Guerril-las again intervened by driving black-market farmers from their homes. The problem perplexed the Federals throughout the war along the Mis-sissippi, from Memphis to New Orleans.[14]

Small wonder that anyone who doubted the need for stern policies on the border now fell in line. The remedies seemed hard to some men, "more like robbing than defending the laws and the constitution," one soldier said. Many of those who now burned homes and "jayhawked" had not done so a few months earlier. Yet, like their officers and the politicians, they believed that noncombatants who prolonged the war by aiding cowardly bushwhackers and saboteurs should suffer the con-sequences. A scouting party of Indiana troops retaliated against an entire neighborhood known to harbor guerrillas near Murfreesboro,

Tennessee. "We burnt houses and throud women and children out of dores and plaid hell generally," one of the party admitted. "This mode of warfare is quite the style now," observed a soldier of the middle border war by April 1863, "and I think it is the most effective and is rapidly telling." An Ohio soldier in Tennessee affirmed, "Put a little chunk of fire to thare houses, that is the way that we serve houses that harbors rebals."[15]

Soldiers could justify their actions by pointing to the consequences of inaction. Rebel "spies and bushwhackers," even "Gurrilla chiefs," could move freely in and out of army camps by dressing as "farmers, women, negroes, and the like." Besides stealing ammunition, supplies, weapons, and horses, they gathered information about Union troop strength and the army's future movements. Every citizen not in the rebel army seemed either to be a guerrilla or to be cooperating with them. "Things are in an awful state in this country and Ky," a soldier observed from Tennessee. "Armed bands over-run all the land." The South could never be subdued as long as such gangs flourished. "These raids," another man surmised, "will continue until a mortal blow is struck at the rebellion, and then the power of the guerrilla chief will be broken." Soldiers who believed that the general war had entered "its last stages" by the spring of 1863 often excluded the guerrilla war from their rosy calculations. *That* contest, they feared, might go on for years after the conventional fighting had ended.[16]

The "irregular" nature of guerrilla warfare most surprised Sergeant Eugene Marshall of the 5th Iowa Cavalry. Tennessee guerrillas seemed to slip in and out of the war as it suited them, he observed, and many of them carried only the most primitive weapons. Some men were not armed at all. The communities that spawned them also struck Marshall as irregular and primitive. The houses were crude, ramshackle affairs, with everything "in & about them" of "home manufacture." Few of the occupants could read or write, and, like most of Dixie, the region seemed mired in "ignorance, poverty & licentious drunkenness." Yet, these primordial people, in their scattered guerrilla bands, ran his regiment ragged. Ceaseless expeditions into the woods and mountains yielded meager results. The regiment caught only a few men at a time, and never enough to end the bushwhacking and ambushes. "It is getting to be any thing but pleasant to scout or do picket duty in this country," he decided.[17]

Even the satisfaction of a successful expedition had little lasting effect on Marshall's spirits. His regiment captured a few "notorious characters" and "noted Guerrillas." They uncovered caches of ammunition and recovered arms and equipment stolen by the guerrillas. They burned the "Secesh Hole" of Waverly, Tennessee, a rendezvous for local bushwhackers. "Firing part of the town will teach them to fire into our boys!" exalted one of Marshall's comrades. But it all seemed so fruitless and unending. Two months later, on learning of the spectacular Union victories at Gettysburg and Vicksburg, Marshall remained pessimistic. He dared hope that the rebellion might soon be broken, but he also believed the guerrilla war would only intensify, probably to continue for "a very long period."[18]

So desperate did the Federals become to crush the guerrillas that they mounted a few infantry regiments to join the hunt. An earlier attempt had been made to offset the immobility of infantrymen by transporting them in wagons—"wagon-mounted infantry," as one soldier scoffed—but the experiment failed. With few horses to waste on inexperienced riders, the best solution seemed to be mules. Endowed with mobility and endurance, those sturdy animals carried most of the newly mounted foot soldiers. A portion of the 7th Illinois Infantry became one of the first mule regiments in June 1863. Assigned to western Tennessee, the men boasted of how they would eclipse even the famous 7th Kansas Cavalry as guerrilla hunters and jayhawkers. They excelled more noticeably in the latter role. When a guerrilla leader named Horton slipped away from them, the men turned to raiding his corn pen, garden, and chicken coop. Other expeditions in Tennessee and Mississippi netted no guerrillas, but the regiment continued to eat well.[19]

The guerrilla danger also thrived because federal retaliatory policies tended to breed as many guerrillas as they stamped out. A western Tennessean named Jack Hinson kept quiet early in the war, but when his two sons were executed as bushwhackers in 1862, Hinson sought revenge. Turning bushwhacker himself, he would kill thirty-six Union soldiers and sailors by the end of the war. He knew the number precisely because he notched the worn stock of his rifle for every victim. In addition, he served as a guide and informant for Confederate cavalry. Acknowledging the existence of the many Jack Hinsons arrayed against them, one Union guerrilla hunter concluded, "A bitter feeling of hostility is naturally engendered, and we find the citizens ever willing to aid the armed rebels in all their designs against us."[20]

But if the guerrilla war looked to be going badly for the Federals, Confederates found themselves straddling a fault line on the middle border by mid-1863. Union raids and the retaliatory policy had not intimidated rebel guerrillas, but not all rebel citizens responded so resolutely to the demands of a guerrilla war. The harsh treatment they endured angered many people, stiffened their resolve, and strengthened their loyalty to the cause. However, other Confederates began to think the guerrilla war more burden than boon. "I dread guerrilla warfare more than the shock of vast armies in battle array," confessed a Kentuckian. This was nothing like the majority response in 1863, but there was evidence of a worrisome trend.[21]

Sherman spotted the first signs of dissolving Confederate loyalty shortly before leaving his post at Memphis. He told Grant that the army should allow noncombatants—rebels and Unionists alike—to trade their cotton and corn at Memphis for groceries and clothing. "Many of them are justly indignant at their own armies and partisans for burning their cotton," Sherman reasoned, "by the sales of which alone they can . . . maintain their suffering families." He acknowledged that some supplies taken from Memphis might go to the guerrillas, but he believed rebel citizens would eventually see the futility of the guerrilla war and welcome the protection of the Union army over that of rebel "bandits." Many farmers had grown "tired of the war, and especially of guerrillas."[22]

Yet, something more than weariness would decide southern loyalties on the middle border. The fact not fully appreciated by Sherman was how the unraveling of the war affected people's faith in the Confederate government. Rebel leaders had hoped guerrillas might satisfy the need for local defense, but even where the guerrillas succeeded, federal counterguerrilla operations had played hell with the citizenry. Rather than shielding noncombatants, the guerrilla war too often exposed them to suffering, financial loss, and danger. As a result, following the trend in the Trans-Mississippi, some communities denounced their guerrillas. That was bad enough, but the real danger would come if large numbers of communities believed their government, rather than the guerrillas, had failed to protect them. A Tennessee Unionist spotted the ultimate rebel nightmare. Some secesh neighbors seemed "worse scared than the union folks" by the turmoil of the guerrilla war. "It is strange they would run from their friends," she observed. "Much as they hate the Yankees, they feel protected under them."[23]

Clarksville, Tennessee, had been occupied at one time or another by Union soldiers, Confederate soldiers, and Confederate partisans since the summer of 1862. Community loyalties were mostly Confederate, but with the able-bodied men serving in the army, the remaining residents needed protection. The inevitable political struggle with Unionists ensued. Then, in October, the 5th Iowa Cavalry and 83rd Illinois Infantry came to town. They arrested people who had not taken the

U.S. oath, burned and destroyed private property and businesses, confiscated slaves, and threatened bodily harm to all, including women. The raid had been justified, the Federals said, by the suffering endured by Clarksville Unionists at the hands of rebel guerrillas. Their message was twofold: The citizenry could not rely on guerrillas to defend them, and their continued, misplaced trust in that "improper" form of warfare would produce only suffering.[24]

The rebels of Clarksville acknowledged the truth of these lessons. "We . . . have been visited by these men and treated in a savage and brutal manner," they informed the Confederate War Department, "and they daily threaten that they will return and utterly destroy the city and imprison all the citizens who do not take the oath of allegiance to the Federal Government." Without protection from the Confederate government, they warned, citizens would be "compelled to abandon their homes and seek protection in other sections." Secretary of War Randolph responded by ordering senior officers of the Union brigade "treated as felons" if captured, but it was an empty threat. The inability of the Confederacy to protect Clarksville had been exposed. The people felt their vulnerability. Their sense of security had been badly shaken.[25]

Contributing further to this trend, more Confederate guerrillas on the middle border mistreated their own wards. Henry Heth had warned of this danger: the independent spirit of partisan warfare could not be easily controlled. Loyal men and true, without proper restraint, discipline, and accountability, could still impose on the citizenry. Cotton burners fell into this category, but they were only following orders. More unsettling were complaints about unauthorized requisitions of private property, especially horses, food, and fodder. Of course, people engulfed by warring armies must expect something of the kind. Confederate soldiers as well as guerrillas stole chickens, knocked down fences, confiscated horses, carried away slaves, and generally rode roughshod over people; but irregular soldiers, operating under no clear authority, could be far more intimidating.[26]

Confederate soldiers resented the behavior of their irregular brethren. "Those guerrilla bands of ours that swarm around Memphis I think caused those people who live around there an immense deal of trouble," judged one rebel in March 1863, "whilst they are doing the cause scarcely any good at all." He thought guerrillas could do the nation "much more real service" if compelled to enter the army. As things stood, they did "just about as much harm as the enemy could possibly do." General Humphrey Marshall, who tried to incorporate guerrillas in his defense of eastern Kentucky, would have agreed. He believed even the heroic John Hunt Morgan fell short of expectations. Marshall called Morgan a "meteoric flash" who injured the Confederate cause more than he helped it. "He dazzled the public eye," Marshall noted, "but it was not a steady light which a prudent people would follow."[27]

The career of Colonel Robert V. Richardson, western Tennessee's leading partisan, shows how the people's war began to run amok. Richardson organized his command, the 1st Tennessee Partisan Rangers, in November 1862. Starting with only about fifty men, he had recruited or conscripted over one thousand rangers by March 1863. Additionally, he acted with several independent Tennessee guerrilla leaders, including Sol Street and Albert W. Cushman. Richardson's regiment made life miserable for Union troops and retaliated when Confederate citizens were abused. He looked after Confederate citizens in his domain, in one instance making the provost marshal in an especially beleaguered county responsible for indigent families. He also urged Union soldiers who were "tired of a war waged to free Negroes" to desert and seek "protection" within his command.[28]

Richardson caused so many problems that in March 1863 the Federals sent an expedition under Colonel Benjamin H. Grierson to destroy him. Leader of one of the Union army's most spectacular raids two months later in Mississippi, Grierson received orders on this occasion to proceed with 900 men and a battery of artillery against Richardson's rangers. He struck the partisan camp near Covington, Tennessee, although his men needed two hours of sharp fighting against only 150 guerrillas to capture it. Included in the haul were Richardson's muster rolls, lists of conscripts, official correspondence, "valuable maps," and lists of Memphis citizens who had smuggled arms, ammunition, and equipment to the partisans. Richardson admitted to losing as well an ammunition train (including 150 pounds of powder, 1,500 cartridges, and 70,000 percussion caps) valued at $4,000, although he had originally captured most of the munitions from the Federals.[29]

It appeared to be a staggering blow to the guerrillas, but Richardson had escaped with most of his men, and they continued to operate for another month in western Tennessee. He retreated seven miles before breaking his command into companies and squads "to harass and annoy the enemy on every hand." When Richardson learned from "Secret Sources" that Union troops planned to repair damage he had earlier inflicted on the Mobile and Ohio Railroad, he tore down several bridges and trestles on the same line. He also remained confident that even in this "isolated field of operations," his partisans could provide valuable service. He intended to recruit thousands more men, deny large amounts of supplies and livestock to the Union army, and worry the Federals within their own lines.[30]

Still, Richardson proved a mixed blessing for the Confederacy. One of his chief responsibilities, to police the cotton trade, made him extremely unpopular with farmers and planters desperate to sell their crops, just as Sherman had observed. Richardson allowed only a few bales to be smuggled into the city, with most of the profits used to furnish his men with arms and ammunition. Richardson also displeased the Confederate government. His men dressed and behaved more like "guerrillas" than rangers. They wore civilian clothing, extorted money from cotton buyers, committed violence against people who had taken the U.S. oath, and plundered the property of Unionists, mostly livestock and cotton. It was just the sort of image the government wanted to shed. Rather than conscripting men for the Confederate army—a common assignment for partisan rangers—he used his authority to increase the size of his own command. Following Grierson's raid on his camp, the government revoked Richardson's commission and tried to arrest him. It informed Confederate commanders that Richardson's men, if captured, should be treated as "robbers."[31]

Compounding Confederate problems in Tennessee and Kentucky, blacks and Unionists played more visible roles in the antiguerrilla campaign. For slaves, it was simply a matter of having more opportunity. The Second Confiscation Act, passed by the U.S. Congress in July 1862 as part of the new retaliatory military policy, meant that the armies could actively encourage slaves to desert their masters and offer them protection within Union lines. The result was a stream of information from within the Confederacy and a surplus of volunteers to serve as guides in locating guerrilla haunts. Some army officers found fugitive slaves to be even bolder, more willing to take risks, than white Unionists. "Two negroes led our cavalry," reported Grenville Dodge, as his men pursued guerrillas in western Tennessee. "No white man had the pluck to do it."[32]

Some soldiers ridiculed the "pomposity" of their black informants and questioned the validity of their reports, but perceptive men understood the value of winning blacks to the Union side. The army benefited more often than not from their information. Asking a runaway slave near Frankfort, Kentucky, if he knew the location of Morgan's men, one soldier seemed genuinely startled by the reply. "You see men riding around here every day in citizens clothes, don't you?" the black man asked by way of reply. "Well, when you see one of dem, you may say dar goes one of Morgan's men." Then, too, some soldiers understood that by undermining slavery, the army could weaken the entire Confederate war effort. "So long as the army leaves them their negroes & their cornfields," Eugene Marshall observed, "they can sustain this guerrilla warfare & . . . we can do nothing with them."[33]

Unionists, earlier denigrated by Union soldiers for their meekness, also stepped forward in larger numbers on the middle border. Kentuckians and Tennesseans who, for one reason or another, had not joined the initial rush to defend their communities, were tired of being targeted by the rebels. The attacks on them had also become even less restrained, nearly frenzied. Obed C. Crossland seethed with anger as he hunted Unionists on both sides of the Tennessee-Alabama state line. A resident of Jackson County, Alabama, he shot, lynched, and kidnaped Unionists without restraint as a member of William Gunter's guerrilla band. Crossland seemingly regarded none of these acts as crimes. Robert Gossett joined the Perkins band in Robertson County, Tennessee, solely to kill Unionists. "Prisoner's conduct . . . has been the cause of terror to his neighbors," concluded the judge advocate general at Gossett's trial, "and he has stained his hands with the blood of many an unoffending victim." Growing numbers of captured rebel guerrillas stood trial for such crimes as "helping hang a man" or of "hunting down," "threatening," "maltreating," or "oppressing" Unionists.[34]

Early evidence of this aroused Unionist spirit could be seen during General Braxton Bragg's invasion of Kentucky in the autumn of 1862. The invasion itself had been inspired by the successful operations of rebel cavalry and partisans in Kentucky and Tennessee, and Bragg assigned numerous partisans—"Mounted gunmen," he called them—to spearhead his advance. He trusted to their "peculiarly & specifically suited" skills to "break up rail roads, burn bridges, destroy depots, capture Hospitals & Guards, and harass him [the enemy] generally." All well and good, but Kentucky Unionists meant to match Bragg's guerrillas. "We were bushwhacked at every defile, and that too by old gray-haired men just tottering on the brink of this world," an Alabama cavalryman complained, "armed with the famous Kentucky rifle—skulking in the mountains and thick woods and blazing away at every poor rebel that passed." Bragg encountered similar resistance throughout the campaign, even after he had retreated back into Tennessee. He learned that this "people's war" worked both ways.[35]

Success against Confederate troops encouraged bolder attacks against rebel citizens, always the real war for southern Unionists. Confederates feared they would be "slaughter[ed]" when tories "band[ed] together" in East Tennessee to "carry on guerrilla warfare." At the other end of the state, a Captain Berry frightened even fellow Unionists, who described him as "cruel" and a "hard drinker." How much the drink affected his hatred of rebels is unknown, but Berry burned their homes and property mercilessly. In central Tennessee, swarms of bushwhackers descended from the hills in 1863 to sack the town of McMinnville. "I know whom to thank for this—the dear blessed Unionists of sweet McMinnville," declared one female rebel. The town's Unionist minority had apparently informed nearby friends of McMinnville's vulnerability and urged them to teach the haughty rebels a lesson.[36]

The sack of McMinnville also betrayed an element of class antagonism that could shape neighborhood political divisions. Hard on the heels of the raid came a swarm of "mountain people" to carry away rebel possessions. "Gaunt, ill-looking men and slatternly, rough barefooted women," one rebel called them, "famished as wolves for prey, hauling out furniture—tearing up matting and carpets—running to and fro . . . the women fully as full of avaricious thirst as the ruffianly men." The "reign of terror" reminded rebels of "the mob of Paris" during the French Revolution. No blood was shed at McMinnville, but that was only so, judged one resident, because no Confederate dared resist. "The masses had it all their own way in this memorable day," she testified, "and Democracy—Jacobinism—and Radicalism in their rudest forms reigned triumphant."[37]

Confronted by such chaos, both Federals and Confederates leaned more heavily on locally recruited regiments of volunteers to combat enemy guerrillas. Such regiments provided, in fact, a more reliable— meaning more easily controlled—type of partisan ranger. Unionist regiments seemed to make the better hunters. They appeared to be angrier than the rebels. No matter how much northern troops hated the guerrillas and worked to punish them, these home-grown guerrilla fighters had more incentive to drive out their foes. Some of them had tried to resist Confederate rule earlier as militia or home guards, only to be driven out themselves. Now they returned as well-armed, well-mounted Union soldiers, empowered to deal with the hostile population as they saw fit. Tennessee's military governor, Andrew Johnson, implored President Lincoln to reassign East Tennessee troops serving in Virginia to their home regions. "They are willing & more than anxious," he assured Lincoln, "to restore the government & at the same time protect their wives & children against insult[,] robbery[,] murder & inhumane oppression." Kentuckians serving outside the state petitioned to be sent home for similar reasons. Ninety members of the 14th

Kentucky Cavalry asked to be reassigned to the mountain counties of eastern Kentucky, where their defenseless families had been stripped of livestock, corn, hay, and clothing by the rebels.[38]

The Union's 5th Tennessee Cavalry ranked among the most ferocious of these federal regiments. Raised largely in central Tennessee during the summer and autumn of 1862 by Colonel William B. Stokes, many recruits came from neighborhoods "infested by guerillas and rebels of the most desperate and brutal character." They were uncompromising in their treatment of rebels, and although they were not as bad as outright guerrillas, rebel citizens called them "Bushwhackers." "They do as the Southern soldiers do a great many times," admitted one Unionist woman, "[and] take revenge on those who happen to be of the opposite party." The regiment did not pursue guerrillas exclusively, but the men were good at it.[39]

The Confederacy's 5th Tennessee Cavalry did the same work as Stokes's Union 5th, and it was equally severe. The men preferred to execute captured Unionist guerrillas on the spot, rather than marching them back to camp for mock trials. They also knew how to coerce information about Unionist plans and hideouts from suspicious looking "citizens." Apprehending a man they suspected of bushwhacking, the guerrilla hunters put "a halter round his neck" and extracted "a very humble confession." When they could not catch the "whackers," they consoled themselves by burning houses suspected of being guerrilla "lodges."[40]

In other words, neither side could gain the upper hand, and therein lies the essence of the unrelenting guerrilla contest. "The truth is each side when it gets a little the advantage and gets those of the opposite party trodden down a little, crows a little too big, and when the trodden down party gets a chance they retaliate rather severely sometimes," judged a resident of middle Tennessee. The situation was perhaps worse in Kentucky, where noncombatants on both sides had fewer conventional troops to keep order once the armies rumbled southward into Tennessee. The balance of power could shift over night. Neighbors distrusted one another, and arrests by one side or the other—depending on who held sway at a particular moment—became a "constant occurrence." "This war has become desperate," swore another Kentuckian, "& party feeling in the County alarming [with] . . . guerilla bands infesting the country, rendering life & property uncertain."[41]

The course of the guerrilla war ran along similar lines in Virginia, though with enough differences to bear comment. Western Virginia, as it moved ever closer to joining the Union, continued to see the most action. The region had ceased to play an important role in Union military thinking by 1863. Other than to protect the Baltimore and Ohio Railroad (B&O), which remained a major consideration, its control no longer seemed necessary for the invasion of Confederate Virginia. The situation heartened rebels, who believed this lax attitude gave them a chance to reclaim the region. Their confidence soared when the Emancipation Proclamation caused lukewarm Unionists to side with the Confederacy. Symbolic of the defiant tone and mounting confidence of the region's rebels, a new pro-Confederate newspaper began publication in Charleston in September 1862—its title, *The Guerilla*.[42]

Rebel designs became clear with a spectacularly successful raid in August 1862 by the "notorious" Albert Jenkins. Using a combination of regular cavalry, home guards, and guerrillas—a full brigade when assembled—Jenkins romped five hundred miles through northwestern Virginia and a portion of Ohio. He netted a large haul of prisoners and munitions and, more importantly, allowed the Confederate army to regain a foothold in northwestern Virginia. "Our condition is much worse than a year ago," estimated a Union man in September. From Wheeling to Grafton—indicating the most northern part of the state— citizens lived in fear of guerrilla raids, he said. Another man used almost identical words to describe the situation around Parkersburg, to the south. The effectiveness of such quick strikes was reaffirmed the following April, when another raid struck the B&O, captured several towns in western Virginia, and threatened Wheeling and Pittsburgh, Pennsylvania.[43]

Unionist militia and guerrillas resisted as best they could. John P. Baggs and his Snake Hunters still dueled with the Moccasin Rangers. Lone bushwhackers and "dangerous men" also harassed Confederate troops. Bartholomew Garvey, described as a "sort of king amongst the lo Irish" around Hunterville, had three sons in the Union army and a son-in-law whose outspoken Unionism had landed him in a Richmond prison. Garvey played his part by bushwhacking Confederate soldiers and citizens until captured in January 1863. John V. Young had organized a band of Unionist militia in Putnam County during the first year of the war, but he and his outnumbered men spent much of their time hiding from the rebels. In frustration, they joined the Union army, though not without warning rebel guerrillas in their old neighborhood that they would return and avenge any Unionist families that came to grief.[44]

The Federals had few effective answers. General Robert H. Milroy, a forty-six-year-old Indiana lawyer and Mexican War veteran, had served in western Virginia since the spring of 1861. He had seen the army's futile efforts to contend with rebel guerrillas. Northern troops were "useless" in that pursuit, Milroy decided. "They cannot catch guerrillas in these mountains any more than a cow can catch fleas," he told Governor Francis Pierpont. Now, as commander of the Cheat Mountain District, Milroy advised the governor to raise companies of "native mounted riflemen—rangers or gurillas or whatever you may choose to term them," and assign one or two companies to each "exposed" county. Many citizens, in fact, had been urging a similar plan on the governor.[45]

Nothing worked, and the Union antiguerrilla campaign in western Virginia faltered. "We might just as well quit," one exasperated soldier sputtered, "throw down our arms and make friends with the South." Lack of mobility, unfamiliar terrain, and a hostile civilian population hampered expeditions into the bush. When in camp, nervous pickets jumped at every sound in the night-shrouded forests, and midnight alarms roused entire regiments to confront vanished foes.[46]

John Imboden remained the most effective rebel partisan in the region. His battalion ripped into Union soldiers and Unionist civilians with untempered vengeance, and his energy and passion attracted other capable men to the partisan ranks. Imboden even stood up to General Milroy. Responding to Milroy's assessments, arrests, and executions, he threatened to seize every public official in the "pretended State" and execute two Union officers for every Confederate harmed by the Federals. Milroy dismissed Imboden as "the reble Gurilla Chief," but he took his threats seriously. A Unionist expressed his own fears in verse:

> I'm out to warn the neighbors, he isn't a mile behind,
> He seizes all the horses, every horse he can find.
> Imboden, Imboden the raider, and Imboden's terrible men,
> With Bowie knives and pistols are marching down the glen.[47]

Certainly the romantic *image* of guerrilla warfare maintained its allure for many Virginia Confederates. In December 1862, Richmond citizens flocked to see a new stage play about their intrepid heroes. Written by James Dabney McCabe Jr., *The Guerrillas* was the first original drama produced in the Confederacy. The plot features Arthur Douglas, the captain of a guerrilla band operating against General John C. Frémont in the mountains of western Virginia. Courageous and inventive, Douglas (the given name, incidentally, of Tucker's "partisan leader") outwits Frémont and a second, fictional, Union officer cast as the principal villain. Frémont and his "fierce hordes of the North" burn homes, hang defenseless civilians, and exhibit lecherous designs on Virginia's fair maidens. Of course, Douglas and his men eventually triumph, and the captain exalts as the curtain falls, "Our foes shall rue the hour they encounter the Guerrillas."[48]

Notwithstanding this resurgence in western Virginia, Confederates on the eastern border, no less than in Kentucky and Tennessee, wondered if guerrillas and partisans had outlived their usefulness. A farmer in western Virginia complained about the liberties two ranger companies had taken in pasturing their horses on his land and seizing his stocks of hay. "There must be a screw loose somewhere in the management of this Warr or otherwise private property would be respected," he told President Davis in an angry letter. He predicted that if "this reckless sistem of destroying property" continued much longer, the Confederacy would be "a great desert of woful waste."[49]

Complaints extended far beyond the destruction or confiscation of property. Dozens of partisan rangers had been arrested and court-martialed for misdeeds by early 1863, and many more would be added to the rolls before the summer had passed. Surviving records rarely specify the charges against these rangers, only their sentences. Some men were, in fact, acquitted or given such slight punishments as a reprimand or a few days' imprisonment. Most known offenses involved being absent without leave, which suggests a want of discipline rather than criminal intent. Nonetheless, some rangers felt the lash ("well laid on"), received prison terms at hard labor, or sat attached to a ball and chain in guard houses. Officers were cashiered, broken to the ranks, or assigned to dig entrenchments. At least three men were executed by musketry.[50]

The quantity of cases also provided ample ammunition for a Confederate War Department and president on the verge of curtailing the program. George Randolph had never been enthusiastic about the rangers, and James A. Seddon, who replaced him as secretary of war in November 1862, adopted his predecessor's views. Rangers were not reliable soldiers, he said. They lacked discipline and had "excited more odium and done more damage with friends than enemies." Shortly before Seddon assumed office, the Confederate Congress sought a precise count of the number of partisans. It was told that ninety-six companies had been mustered in eight states, but everyone knew that number to be low. For one thing, it did not credit a single company to Arkansas, Kentucky, Missouri, or Tennessee, where guerrilla warfare raged most intensely. The survey only reinforced claims that the system was out of control.

Seddon was reluctant to disband all partisan companies at once, but commissions became harder to obtain in 1863, and existing units, if allowed to continue at all, operated under "stricter regulations."[51]

An important transition had begun, as Imboden's command soon learned. His men had been less effective in several recent raids, and the colonel's personal duel with Milroy had alarmed important people, including General Lee. The War Department converted his partisan battalion into a brigade of conventional cavalry, assigned to screen troop movements, gather intelligence, and protect supply lines. Imboden's men might use their experience as partisans to slip behind enemy lines, but their tether had been significantly tightened. Other partisan chiefs soon joined them. Commanders like Elijah V. White, who led the "Comanches" in Virginia, continued to stress their "independent" status when recruiting, but they were now tied far more securely to the army.[52]

Strange to say, then, that the Confederate government allowed any partisan bands to operate, but Seddon left loopholes in the new regulations. First, he permitted communities to continue organizing "volunteer companies for local defense." These "volunteers" often operated as partisans but remained part of the "Provisional Army," received no pay or allowances, and could be disbanded at any time. Seddon thought it a useful way to wean the country from its attachment to partisans. Second, the secretary let a few reliable partisan bands continue. John McNeill's company, which did not join Imboden's brigade when it converted to conventional operations, survived the purge. So did William Thurmond, another Virginia partisan. Third, Seddon authorized the organization of partisan bands in areas already occupied by the Union army or exposed to Union raids. Even some critics of the rangers, such as Zebulon Vance, the new governor of North Carolina, encouraged this practice.[53]

The Confederates also added a new wrinkle to their irregular war: naval guerrillas. When the war started, northern merchants had worried more about piracy at sea than bushwhackers on land, and consternation spread when the Confederate government issued letters of marque to fifty-one vessels in 1861. However, many of those privateers never took a prize, and the Union blockade soon put an end to the more successful vessels. Thereafter, only navy cruisers, such as the CSS *Alabama* and the CSS *Shenandoah*, raided northern commerce at sea. Like partisan rangers, they were supposed to make the whole business more respectable. The rebels also developed a sophisticated "torpedo" program, but most of these "infernal machines" were only floating mines, used to blockade harbors and rivers. The Confederate navy did employ more deadly "spar" torpedoes to attack enemy ships, either by means of submarines or surface torpedo boats. The Federals denounced these weapons as barbarous and uncivilized. Yet torpedoes posed no serious threat to naval operations, any more so than the few rebel spies who managed to commandeer northern commercial vessels. None of this constituted a guerrilla war at sea.[54]

But the Confederates did find a way to use irregulars on the rivers and seacoast of Virginia and North Carolina. Thirty-two-year-old John Taylor Wood, a nephew of Jefferson Davis and an 1853 graduate of the U.S. Naval Academy, initiated the new twist in guerrilla strategy. Wood saw action as a navy lieutenant during the first year of the war, including service aboard the CSS *Virginia* in its famous duel with the USS *Monitor* at Hampton Roads. However, Wood could not ignore the more dramatic "War of Extermination" being waged ashore, and in September 1862 he joined it. He proposed that the Confederate navy adopt a guerrilla tactic used by Stephen Decatur sixty years earlier in the war with Tripoli. Known as "cutting-out," the object was to employ small, shallow-draft vessels carrying five to seven men to surprise and capture—generally at night—enemy gunboats, transports, and commercial shipping.[55]

Secretary of the Navy Stephen Mallory—one of the few men in the Davis cabinet not opposed to guerrilla warfare—approved Wood's scheme. He ordered the lieutenant to select fifteen to twenty "picked men" for "special duty" and construct three "cutters." The raiders first struck on October 7, 1862, by boarding and setting fire to a U.S. schooner loaded with hay on the Maryland side of the Potomac River. Following a second successful raid a week later, Mallory authorized additional cutter squadrons to destroy, disable, and capture enemy craft, burn lighthouses, and sever the Union's underwater telegraphic cable in Chesapeake Bay.[56]

Through another such loophole skipped the most famous of all Confederate partisans: John Singleton Mosby. The Gray Ghost, as he became known, had been operating behind Union lines as a "scout" for General James E. B. "Jeb" Stuart's cavalry. Both Stuart and General Lee had praised his efforts, but Mosby felt constrained. Like every guerrilla, he wanted more independence. He also wanted a ranger commission. He got both in March 1863, when, as reward for capturing a Union general, Seddon made him a captain of partisan rangers. A week later, he became Major Mosby.[57]

Jeb Stuart urged Mosby, whom he regarded as a protégé, to avoid calling himself a ranger, let alone a guerrilla. "It is in bad repute," he warned of the ranger label. "Call your command '*Mosby's Regulars.*'" Lee wanted Mosby to recruit no more than a battalion, which would then revert to conventional cavalry, but neither Mosby nor his men would consent to this arrangement. Recruited mostly from Fauquier, Loudoun, Fairfax, and Prince William counties, in northern Virginia, the men wanted to serve near home. They agreed to go farther afield on occasion, but, in the guerrilla tradition, their own turf came first. Rebels in northern Virginia hailed the "gallant band" as "our Bushwhackers." The region became known as "Mosby's Confederacy."[58]

Within weeks, the exploits of Mosby and his men surpassed those of the departed Turner Ashby and rivaled John Hunt Morgan's, although this did not please everyone. As Mosby's notoriety brought federal retaliatory raids, frightened citizens petitioned him to "discontinue" his brand of warfare. To their dismay, Mosby would not relent. "I unhesitatingly refuse to comply," he told them. "My attacks on scouts, patrols, & pickets, which have provoked this threat, are sanctioned both by the customs of war & the practice of the enemy."[59]

Elsewhere on the eastern border, Maryland waged a largely internal guerrilla war. Except for Robert E. Lee's sudden appearance during the Antietam campaign of September 1862 and the Gettysburg campaign of June–July 1863, no rebel army entered the state. Lee's two raids sparked flurries of activity among civilians on both sides, but they ultimately had only one another to fight. Most rebel men went south to enlist, but those who remained caused alarm among Maryland Unionists. "We have in our midst the elements of 19th Apl 61," warned one man, recalling how the guerrilla war had began, "with a large increase of numbers who have only been held at bay by the utmost vigilance who are now chafing like a chained lion." Lee's army may have been expelled from the state, reasoned another person, but the loyal people of his community remained vulnerable to "a party of outlaws." The gang had already burned churches and attacked "inoffensive negroes" along the Maryland-Delaware border. Now they were "swearing vengeance against Union men of the vicinity."[60]

Endangered Unionist communities formed "ranger" companies and "independent" battalions for both local defense and "border service." One man, seeking to raise a battalion of "Mounted Riflemen," told the U.S. War Department, "We want just such men, as the Rebels have, men raised in these counties and acquainted with the roads, and the people, to match the enemy." The residents of Lebanon, Maryland, fearing attacks even from southern sympathizers in eastern Pennsylvania, formed the Maryland Avengers. "We intend to arm ourselves giveing comfort and protection to our loyal friends but death to our foe," their leader informed Governor Augustus W. Bradford. "Do you wish us to kill the foe or deliver the oath of allegence which they have twice violated? . . . We'll kill the foe, hang the traitor, despise interference, and arm ourselves."[61]

Given such intensity along the entire border, it is not surprising that midwesterners remained vigilant. The Jenkins raid, which had swept through a twenty-mile stretch of southeastern Ohio, was evidence enough of that state's vulnerability. Earlier calls by Buckeye citizens to reinforce the militia with "independent" and "special cavalry" companies became more incessant. Military authorities acknowledged that they could not intercept every band of guerrillas, robbers, or horse thieves that might dash across the Ohio River. "The citizens living upon the border must aid in their own protection," asserted one general. "All the troops in the Dept if scattered along the line of the Ohio from Cairo to Wheeling could not entirely guard against small thieving bands."[62]

That "line" included Illinois, and while the citizens of Lincoln's state worried about their long western border with Missouri, they had more cause to fear raids out of Kentucky. Unquestionably, the state looked vulnerable in 1862–63. In some communities, men who aided the Union cause risked being hanged, beaten, or waylaid by mean men "with deadly weapons." People urged Governor Richard Yates to declare martial law across Illinois. A resident of Clinton, nestled in the center of the state, swore that people there were "afraid for their lives." Communities in southern Illinois felt insecure even when garrisoned by federal troops. The citizens of Shawneetown, convinced that nearby coal mines made them an especially tempting target, begged army officers around Henderson, Kentucky, known for their prowess as antiguerrilla fighters, to stay alert on their side of the river.[63]

By early 1863, citizens reported seeing rebel cavalry and guerrillas all along the Ohio River. Scouting parties of up to two dozen men were spotted as far north as Wayne County, dozens of miles from the river. "We feel ourselves in danger," one man wrote forthrightly. Union army commanders in Kentucky sympathized. In early May 1863, the colonel who had been approached by the citizens of Shawnee warned the commander of Illinois militia that his men would try to assist the community in an emergency, but that the state really ought to assign a company there. Pursuing that line of reasoning, one citizen believed every northern governor should enroll men beyond the legal military age of forty-five. Many older men, like himself, had fought in the Mexican War and against Indians. Every man in his part of the state owned a "good gun" which, if not always up to military standards, was still serviceable for warding off guerrillas.[64]

Of the northern border states, Indiana seemed the best prepared. It had a comprehensive and systematic militia organization, the Indiana Legion, which was supplemented in some places by locally recruited "Border Cavalry" and independent companies. Private railroad companies hired men to guard bridges and trestles against "ill disposed parties." Armchair strategists contributed grand defensive schemes. One Hoosier urged the government to recruit Sioux Indians for the war. Northern Indians, he reasoned, made superior fighters to the tribes of Indian Territory. In any case, Kentucky guerrillas had appeared infrequently in southern Indiana since a raid by Adam Johnson in the summer of 1862.[65]

Then, in June 1863, as talk about resisting the coming federal draft became shrill and worrisome in midwestern communities, the rebels struck. Captain Thomas H. Hines led about eighty of John Morgan's men across the river into Cannelton, Indiana. They stole only horses, but judging by how their presence galvanized the state, the rebels might have announced their intention to destroy Indianapolis. The Indiana Legion and numerous home guards, with Republicans and Democrats acting in concert, rushed to drive off or capture most of the band over the next two days. False rumors of a second raiding party circulated for a few days more, but when it failed to materialize, the Hoosiers breathed easy and congratulated themselves on thwarting the threat.[66]

They relaxed too soon. The Hines raid had been a mere probe; John Hunt Morgan was on the way. Whatever his transgressions, Morgan personified irregular warfare for Yankees and Confederates on the middle border. He, not prominent generals like Bragg or even Lee, buoyed rebel spirits and inspired terror north of the Ohio River. Southern boys dreamed of riding with his intrepid command and read florid novels about his daring exploits. Women sighed at the sound of his name. "Oh, how delighted I would be if I could go down to some of the places where Morgan goes," a teen-aged Kentucky belle confided to her diary, "& stay with some such families . . . who would have more full access to him." When Morgan rode into a community, women rushed to him. They touched him, called his name, snipped hairs from the mane of his horse.[67]

Fittingly, then, Morgan's July raid through Indiana and Ohio symbolized all that had gone right and wrong in the Confederacy's guerrilla war. He had definite orders to operate only in Kentucky, but Morgan, who had been planning the raid since May, was never one to let orders get in his way. He believed that recent setbacks had tarnished his honor and reputation. Rumors also said his recent marriage had made him soft. People whispered that he had lost his keen edge, his gambler's instinct. Morgan set out to prove them wrong.[68]

His scouts having reconnoitered the river crossings into Indiana, Morgan planned to ferry some two thousand men and horses across the Ohio River, dash through both Indiana and Ohio, and boldly reenter the South through the new state of West Virginia, which had officially joined the Union just weeks earlier. Despite its inherent risks, the venture started promisingly enough. Morgan's men weaved, dodged, and fought their way through scattered detachments of Union troops in Kentucky to reach the Ohio by July 8. "Wake up old Hoosiers," a confident raider wrote to his father the night before the river crossing. "We intend to live off the Yankees hereafter, and let them feel . . . some of the horrors of war."[69]

Morgan's men destroyed railroads, burned bridges, wrecked towns, looted, extorted money, and for nearly two weeks generally lived up to the Union image of rebel freebooters. However, they failed to produce the uprising among midwestern butternuts whom Morgan had hoped to inspire. Instead, every available army regiment, militia company, and home guard in Indiana and Ohio turned out to oppose him. Le Roy Fitch and his gunboats sealed off possible escape routes across the river and landed troops in advance of the raiders at vulnerable spots along the shore. That Morgan eluded them for as long as he did was an impressive feat, but in the end, the Federals captured him and over half of his "vile horde." Scores of his men had been killed or wounded, and only about four hundred of them escaped. Morgan surrendered on July 26 at West Point, Ohio, less than one hundred miles from Lake Erie.[70]

Oddly enough, nearly all parties gained some satisfaction from the raid. Having escaped disaster, midwesterners found a new resolve to wage war, and southern sympathy in the region declined. Indeed, more than a few Union soldiers thought it did the lethargic, copperhead Midwest good to see war at first hand. "It is the best thing for our cause that could happen," declared an Indiana soldier. "It will awaken the people of Indiana as it [Gettysburg] did those of Penn[sylvania]."[71]

Viewed another way, the raid underscored the vulnerability of northern soil more than two years into the war. It quickly dampened much of the euphoria over rebel defeats at Gettysburg and Vicksburg, and, despite his capture, the strike burnished Morgan's reputation in the public's eyes. He had destroyed millions of dollars in property and forced the redeployment of thousands of Union troops. The raid also came in the midst of violent protests against the draft in New York and other cities, further heightening speculation that the northern home front might soon disintegrate. "Look at New York," cried a Union staff officer while preparing to defend Cincinnati against Morgan. "What a spectacle for a civilized country—wars at home & abroad. If this country is not being chastised I dont know what to call it."[72]

In retrospect, the most disheartening aspect of Morgan's raid was what people failed to mention. No soldier on either side expressed shock at its destructiveness, and only its audacity surprised most civilians. Americans had come to expect war on these terms by mid-1863. A Kentucky Unionist serving with the Union army admitted that "Morgan was no worse than their [U.S.] cavalry. . . . They make raids through the South and burn every house they come across, just order the people out and set the house on fire, and not permit them to take one thing with them . . . and take the last horse or cow that a lone widow has and she holding to the animal pleading for it." Such scenes were not universal, but they had come to symbolize the war for many Americans, and they seemed likely to become more common, more widespread, and more destructive.[73]

E veryone knew what would happen next in the Deep South. If the Federals could capture Vicksburg, they would control the Mississippi River and isolate the Trans-Mississippi Confederacy. Lincoln had called this Mississippi citadel the "key" to victory. Federal intentions became clear when, beginning in August 1862, Union raiders fanned out to destroy Mississippi farms and businesses, wreck cotton gins and mills, round up fugitive slaves, and arrest suspicious-looking citizens. With only a token military force in the state, Mississippi needed help from its guerrillas. The only question was the extent to which the Confederate government should allow them to flourish.

Initially, only a few people in Mississippi lacked enthusiasm for a guerrilla war, although Earl Van Dorn and Sterling Price, who shared military command in the state, were among them. This may seem odd, given that Van Dorn and Price had inaugurated the guerrilla war in Arkansas. Yet, given the option of guerrillas or conventional cavalry, Van Dorn preferred the latter. His proposed "Corps of Honor," which never materialized, was to have functioned as a cavalry regiment. He ended the recruitment of partisan rangers in his district and mustered existing companies into the army as infantry. During his brief stay of four months in Mississippi, Van Dorn conducted his most successful operation—a raid against Ulysses S. Grant's supply base at Holly Springs—with mostly conventional cavalry.[1]

Price expressed more sympathy, but he, too, prescribed a limited role for partisans. Price assigned William Falkner to arrest dangerous Unionists and black market cotton traders in northern Mississippi. He also authorized an ultimately unsuccessful scheme by George L. Baxter, captain of an "independent company" in the state, to capture Grant. However, Price worried about the tendency of rangers to play rough, especially with Unionists. He cautioned Falkner to pursue a "kind and conciliatory policy" toward Union men not actively aiding the Federals.[2]

A few citizens cursed partisan rangers in the same ways heard elsewhere in the South. Too many rangers shirked their duty, people said. Men became partisan rangers only to "escape the deadly bullets of the enemy," one critic insisted, and they stayed well clear of Union raiding parties. "Rangers are totally inadequate to the protection of the country," he elaborated, "and are considered by most citizens . . . an injury instead of [a] benefit." A Mississippi newspaper dismissed the rangers as "notoriously more cunning than brave." Citizens also blamed the rangers for the ferocity of Union raids. When Union troops failed to capture or drive out the partisans, they explained, the Yankees took out their frustration on noncombatants. The Federals also retaliated against citizens when guerrillas or rangers fired at gunboats or commercial shipping.[3]

The military situation looked especially bright for the Federals in the late autumn of 1862. Battlefield victories at Iuka and Corinth in September and October chastened the Confederate army in Mississippi. Any thought of a coordinated campaign by soldiers and guerrillas then collapsed when Price's men insisted on returning to the Trans-Mississippi. At the same time, William Falkner's command disintegrated by running afoul of the conscription laws. In his enthusiasm to raise a guerrilla regiment, Falkner, like Richardson, had paid little attention to the stricture against enlisting men wanted for the army. Apparently, too, some of his followers abused loyal Confederates and confiscated private property. As one citizen put it, "There are some rough specimens among them." When Falkner finally received permission to reconstitute the regiment, he was told it must serve in the conventional army. Even so, northern Mississippi remained so unstable, and the government's authority so weak, that Falkner continued to operate until resigning his commission in July 1863.[4]

Regardless, Mississippians clung to their belief that rangers and independent guerrilla bands provided the only defense against invaders and the best hope for social order. Any attempt to disband or transfer them elicited anguished wails. Falkner's men, fiercely devoted to saving their state, vowed to fight invaders "to the death," and they inspired resistance by rallying rebel home guards, recruiting additional partisans, and retaliating against Union troops. Independent bands, seeking to imitate them, sprouted everywhere, though they grew thickest around Corinth, where the Union army was concentrated. Service was nearly universal in some communities.[5]

Defenders of the guerrilla system accused critics of being selfish and rapacious, interested only in selling cotton to the highest bidder, even to the enemy. They damned them as elitists opposed to the democratic guerrilla impulse. "Aristocracy & speculation," grieved an irregular leader who operated along the Gulf coast, would be the "down fall" of the Confederacy. "Give us a fair chance and we are as good Southerners and as good Soldiers as there is any where," he told Governor Pettus, "but we are neither dogs nor heathens to be drove and kicked about and forced to fight for gentlemans property[.] [G]ive us a white mans chance and we will defend Southern principles." In defending his own actions, Falkner condemned both independent companies and state militia as more "nuisance to the service" than were his men. "They are making fortunes for themselves," Falkner insisted in mid-March, "by taking property from what they call Tories." They, not his rangers, wanted discipline; they, not his men, should be conscripted into the army.[6]

Efforts to dissolve such resolute bands as Falkner led sometimes worsened a situation. When the government directed Steed's partisan rangers to report to the army, a couple of hundred of them organized smaller, independent bands and vowed to resist the order. A few of the men, it was rumored, went over to the enemy; the majority of the battalion, which was willing to obey the government, insisted on being able to join regiments of their choice. Until given that reassurance, they simply went home to "tend to their businesses."[7]

One of Steed's rangers, young Elers Koch, struggled with this dilemma of whether to go into the army or be labeled a deserter. The situation perplexed his family, too. His mother had always taught Elers to be "honest and upright," but the government's order, she decided, was unreasonable. "As he says Steeds batalion is not known in the confederacy, I dont think it would be much if he did come home." Ironically, one of the duties performed by Steed's men had been to round up conscripts. Now, as Koch and his mates contemplated deserting, they feared the independent guerrilla bands that made it their business to track down deserters. Koch's father urged his son to seek refuge "in the swamps."[8]

Chaos filled the vacuum caused by the disintegration of Steed's battalion, which shows that these men had, in fact, provided some semblance of order in the region. Pillaging increased, as did the number of runaway slaves, and some remaining slaves refused to work. Worse still were the "flagrant outrages of the Jay Hawkers and negro thieves." A member of the affected community around Pearlington told Governor Pettus that Steed's men would not have permitted such conditions. The government must understand, he went on, that desertion and draft dodging would continue unless loyal men who refused to leave their families "to the mercy of the Yankees" were allowed to "defend their homes & their country" simultaneously. Showing it was not oblivious to the crisis, the Richmond government temporarily suspended conscription in the state's ten northernmost counties so that men could volunteer for local defense.[9]

Neighborhood fights between rebels and gangs of tories multiplied with the presence of Union raiders. One particularly strong group, formed by Confederate deserters and draft dodgers in Choctaw County, managed to elect several Unionists to public office. The rebels appear to have restored order in the spring of 1863, when General James R. Chalmers took command of a special military district in northern Mississippi. His principal jobs were to serve as a buffer between Vicksburg and federally occupied western Tennessee and to break up the illicit trade—especially in cotton—between Mississippi and Tennessee. The fact that Chalmers had to depend heavily on partisan rangers and guerrillas to secure the district went largely unnoticed, or at least unappreciated.[10]

On balance, rebel rangers and guerrillas did good service through the spring and summer of 1863. Except for an area between Vicksburg and Jackson, occupied by General John C. Pemberton's command, Mississippi had no substantial number of Confederate troops. Independent bands led by W. W. Lowry, Sol Street, White Wilson, Funderburk Mooney, and hosts of others vowed to flummox Union raiders. Most citizens judged them "true as steel to the south, and good partisans." Local people considered partisan chiefs the ultimate authority in their neighborhoods, even to the point of seeking *their* permission, rather than that of political or military officials, to raise new companies of "independent scouts." Home guards aligned themselves with well-armed rangers like Falkner to suppress Unionists. Bands of "old men [and] boys" helped to drive off or capture Union soldiers bent on pillage or theft. One county revived talk of organizing Indians into a "force of Guerillas or Rangers."[11]

Desperate to break the resistance, the Union army made fewer distinctions between guerrillas and their accomplices. Following a skirmish with Falkner near Rienzi the previous summer, General Gordon Granger, commanding Union cavalry in Mississippi, had foreseen a situation where any man who owned a gun might turn guerrilla. He urged his superiors to devise "some definite and fixed policy . . . to combat and break up this most infernal guerrilla system." Make no mistake, Granger warned, "It is bound soon to waste our entire army away for no equivalent. We must push every man, woman, and child before us or put every man to death found in our line." To control the situation, he required four times his current force, armed "to the teeth." The war must ultimately become "a war of subjugation, and the sooner the better," the general concluded. By spring 1863, it was turning in that direction. "'Confiscation and extermination' is our motto," declared an Illinois soldier.[12]

Grant ordered Grenville Dodge to create a "secret service" network of spies, scouts, and agents to discern rebel intentions and break up the guerrilla network. Other Union generals, including Frémont, Rosecrans, and Sherman, had used agents to gather information, but none could match the Grant/Dodge system for scope or tenacity. From his headquarters at Corinth, Dodge selected the operatives, assigned their missions, and paid them from a special fund. Between November 1862 and August 1863, he paid scores of agents in Tennessee, Mississippi, Alabama, and Georgia the staggering sum of $21,000. Many of his agents came from the army, but the majority were southern Unionists, both men and women, who wanted nothing more than to root out people who had done "damage to the union men." One of Dodge's staff officers declared the system an essential part of the U.S. Army's anti-guerrilla campaign.[13]

Sol Street's men were the most active and elusive of Dodge's targets. Operating from a secure base in the creek bottoms of Tippah County, also Falkner's home base, Street coordinated the activities of several independent guerrilla bands with those of his own sanctioned company of rangers. The Federals used Unionist troops to counter Street and tried to infiltrate his band and network of supporters. None of these stratagems yielded marked success, and Street countered by dressing his men in blue uniforms to infiltrate federal lines. The information so gained allowed him to orchestrate ambushes and derail several heavily guarded Union trains.[14]

Street's most formidable opposition came not from the Federals, Mississippi Unionists, or Dodge's scouts but from one of his Unionist counterparts out of Tennessee, Colonel Fielding Hurst. Officially commanding the 6th Tennessee Cavalry, Hurst and his tory troops operated very much like Confederate rangers. Known to rebels as the "notorious" Hurst, many of his raids through Tennessee and Mississippi turned into horse-stealing and cotton-burning expeditions. Murder was always an option, too, as when he shot a Presbyterian minister known to be recruiting guerrillas in Mississippi. That instance may have been in retaliation for the torture and near execution of one of his own recruiters in Tennessee a few months earlier. Hurst and Street collided directly

Unionist scouts helped the Union army locate guerrilla camps and rendezvous across the South. From *Harper's Weekly*, May 7, 1864.

on more than one occasion. Neither man could soundly best the other, although Hurst captured a sizable number of Street's men during the first half of 1863.[15]

Yet, the stubborn devotion of rebel partisans to their independent status handicapped as much as it helped Confederate defense of Mississippi. They rarely communicated with Confederate commanders in the state. Partisan leader Lowry kept "out of the way" so his men would not be assigned to parts of Mississippi that were far from home. Street, likewise, insisted on operating on his own hook, either fearful of or philosophically opposed to acting under any central authority. For the same reason, he resisted the efforts of Governor Pettus to increase the number of state troops and partisans. He simply believed, like Falkner and most other guerrilla chiefs, that the governor's military system would limit his own ability to recruit. The only occasions when Street willingly acknowledged the authority of Richmond came when he needed the government to intervene and save captured men whom the Federals had condemned to death as outlaws.[16]

Not a few homes and communities went unprotected in this patchwork system of defense. The guerrillas could not, any more than the army, be everywhere at once. Twenty-year-old Cordelia Scales, living on her father's farm near Holly Springs, could attest to that fact. No shrinking southern violet, Scales knew how to handle a pistol, and she brandished one when Union soldiers descended on her family in early 1863. Nevertheless, she stood helpless as the Federals destroyed most of the homestead's outbuildings and fences and confiscated every horse, mule, wagon, and bushel of crops they could lay hands on. Her family fared no better when the 7th Kansas Cavalry swept through the neighborhood. "It makes my blood boil to think of the outrages they committed," she declared. "They tore the ear rings out of ladie's ears, pulled their rings & brest pins off, took them by the hair, threw them down & knocked them about." She rejoiced briefly when rebel guerrillas responded by capturing some Union troops who had been pillaging homes in the neighborhood, but such moments of retribution came far too seldom.[17]

The same pattern shaped the contest to control Mississippi rivers, especially the mighty waterway that formed the state's western boundary. Few weeks passed without a Union vessel being run aground or forced to shore to be scuttled, disabled, or burned, its cargo stolen, destroyed, or spoiled. A "successful partisan warfare," a Memphis newspaper observed, could be waged at "hundreds of points" along the river.

The attacks forced the Federals to invest additional men and resources to protect supply ships, troop transports, and commerce.[18]

Military gunboats and heavily armed commercial vessels provided the first line of Union defense. Their captains responded by firing into the vicinity of the attackers or landing troops to give chase. "Worming" expeditions dispatched from Helena and Memphis probed the banks of the Mississippi and its principal tributaries: the Yazoo, Tallahatchie, and Coldwater. Seldom able to catch their prey, landing parties destroyed any dwellings, outbuildings, or mills that may have concealed the guerrillas. One Union division, having debarked from transports fifteen miles above Vicksburg, marched twenty-five grueling miles without encountering any "detestable, roaming yellow-legged secesh bushwhackers," but then came what one man called the "real business of the expedition." The soldiers turned a string of plantations into a "sea of fire." More than merely destroying rebel "nests," they meant to injure the entire community. "Coton gin after coton gin was laid in ashes," reported one of the arsonists. "Large cribs of corn shared the same fate, and thus the flames did their work faithfully, destroying all personal property that we could not bring with us." The flames consumed millions of dollars in property, and the men led away many hundreds of mules and horses, flocks of "fat sheep," herds of cattle, untold numbers of chickens and geese, and wagonloads of hams.[19]

Admiral Porter was pleased. He had told subordinates, "There is no impropriety in destroying houses supposed to be affording shelter to rebels. . . . Should innocent persons suffer, it will be their own fault, and teach others that it will be to their advantage to inform the Government authorities when guerrillas are about certain localities." The relish with which Porter's gunboat sailors adhered to his proclamation produced another flurry of correspondence about definitions of "civilized" warfare. This time, Porter, Grant, John Pemberton, Union general Carter L. Stevenson, U.S. Navy captain Edwin W. Sutherland, and Confederate president Jefferson Davis participated in the debate. Davis, who generally distanced himself from the actions of rebel irregulars, spoke forcefully in this instance. Porter had been facing authorized "partisans," not "guerrillas," the president insisted. These men had operated well within the definition of "fit service" for a "partisan corps," and no amount of Yankee bluster could "deprive them of the rights of prisoners of war if captured."[20]

Unfazed, Porter replaced his occasional landing parties with a more destructive, specialized brigade of guerrilla hunters. Assigned to patrol the river on light, steam-powered craft, Porter's strike force could land "wherever they heard of guerrillas [and] . . . hunt them down." He selected General Alfred W. Ellet, who had long advocated such a response, to command the brigade. Subsequent wrangling between the War and Navy departments over who would control Ellet's men delayed organization. The army, though recently giving the navy command of the gunboats on which Porter's "marines" would operate, insisted the men were still soldiers. President Lincoln, who liked Porter's idea, settled the dispute with a compromise. Ellet's Marine Brigade would remain under the auspices of the army, but Porter would dictate its day-to-day operations.[21]

Ellet had recruited 1,035 men—about two-thirds of the desired number—by February 1863. More a legion than a brigade, the self-sufficient unit included infantry, cavalry, and artillery. It would be transported on seven converted civilian packet boats, which provided ample space for men, horses, artillery, and whatever spoils and prisoners might be captured. Recruits were drawn to the novel strike force by Ellet's sunny sales pitch. He portrayed service in his brigade as "Soldiering Made Easy! No Hard Marching! No Carrying Knapsacks!" Nor would his men have to dig trenches, sleep in the mud, or suffer short rations. The general's working relationship with Porter was not as bright or carefree. Porter resented not having received *absolute* control over the independent-minded Ellet, whose men showed early signs of being as ill-disciplined as any guerrilla band.[22]

The Marine Brigade did not operate exclusively against guerrillas, but the men became as frustrated as any group of guerrilla hunters by their inability to crush the rebels. They also resorted to retaliation against suspected guerrilla supporters. They burned the Mississippi towns of Eastport (in April) and Austin (in May), as well as Simmsport, Louisiana (in June). Some officers and men objected to the destruction of Austin, where the town's women had begged Ellet to spare their homes; but he insisted it was a center for contraband trade and a supply depot for guerrillas. More often, his men burned mills and confiscated cotton and livestock. Some of them also turned to theft, intimidation, and wanton destruction, all of which verified Porter's concerns about discipline. Ellet had a penchant for running afoul of most of the army and navy officers with whom he was supposed to cooperate, including Hurlbut, Dodge, and Fitch.[23]

To counter the Marine Brigade, General Chalmers consolidated all "roving bands" in northern Mississippi in April 1863. A few leaders, such as Sol Street, predictably ignored the summons, but others, including Falkner and Green L. Blythe, rendezvoused. So did Robert

Richardson's partisan rangers, who having overstayed their welcome in Tennessee, arrived to bolster defenses. Richardson's men, in fact, regained some respectability in Mississippi that spring and summer. Most notably, they obtained a measure of revenge against Benjamin Grierson by hounding him on his otherwise brilliant raid through the state in April and May. Richardson estimated that Grierson's men would have destroyed additional railroads, telegraphs, and Confederate property had he not harassed their eastern flank.[24]

Still and all, the combined efforts of regular and irregular Confederate troops in Mississippi could not halt one of the major Union successes of the war: the capture of Vicksburg on July 4, 1863. "The people of this State, like those of Kentucky . . . and those of Tennessee . . . are now much depressed," reported Chalmers in mid-July. Richardson had been ordered back to Tennessee, and Chalmers had barely enough men to repel "small parties." By August, William Sherman believed that no significant resistance could be revived in the state. He advised the people of Hinds County, home of the state capital at Jackson, to organize a loyal government "capable of protecting them[selves] against the bands of scouts and guerrillas that infest[ed] the land." Rebel guerrillas, as he had long since predicted, had become a greater danger to their own people than to the Union army.[25]

Alabamians did not suffer the dramatic military setbacks of Mississippians in 1862–63. Ormsby Mitchel's troops had continued to inflict a *"terrible retribution* upon the *Citizen Bushwhackers"* and their abettors through the summer, but when, in early September, they suddenly pulled out, rebel guerrillas pounced on them. The Confederates knew something was up when a "dense cloud" of smoke curling above Huntsville showed that the Federals were burning supplies they would be unable to carry away. As the five-mile-long Union column then snaked northward into Tennessee, bushwhackers crowded the flanks. The Federals deployed skirmishers to keep the rebels at bay, but the retreating army remained vulnerable and proceeded at a crawl. Further slowing Union progress, "great swarms" of slaves, desperate to reach free soil, joined the column. The army turned away most of these poor souls, who watched "hopelessly" as the troops marched on. Many blacks tried to rejoin the column after dark, but they were again turned back, often to be apprehended by their masters. It was a miserable affair all around.[26]

Rebel citizens, giddy with delight, proclaimed victory. Hundreds of Federals had been "bushwhacked" during the occupation, they boasted, and the Union army had met no more formidable opposition in all the South. True, they acknowledged, northern Alabama had paid a heavy price in destroyed and stolen property. Hundreds of slaves had success-fully run off. Some plantations had been "turned into barren wastes," and much of their railroad's rolling stock and machinery had been de-molished. The entire countryside between Huntsville and Stevenson—the path of the railroad—had been "deserted." Still, the rebels had sur-vived, and they believed they had seen the last of the Yankees.[27]

Of course, they had not done, and as Union raiding parties out of Tennessee returned to inflict damage into the new year, Governor Shorter turned to his guerrillas for defense. Captain Nelson Fennell led the state's most active and effective partisan company. Alabama rangers serving outside the state returned to help until new companies and bat-talions formed. Alabama soldiers urged family and friends to resist the enemy. "I appeal to you, as well as all other loyal people, to dissuade not those who would raise an avenging hand against the invasion," a soldier wrote to his father from Georgia, "for sooner or later the 'black flag,' with its awful inspiration, will have to close this war." He only regretted that he could not lead a dozen picked men to "teach them [the Federals] that death stood behind every bush or shade."[28]

With or without large numbers of Union soldiers to combat, guer-rilla defenders had to maintain "public order" amid growing white and black resistance to Confederate rule. Governor Shorter ordered par-tisan rangers in northern Alabama to police both groups by enforc-ing conscription and intimidating blacks who might otherwise be "demoralized" by contact with Union troops. By then, tory ranks also included people who had only recently turned against the Confeder-acy, mostly when threatened by rebel conscription. If pressed to fight, they reasoned, it would be in blue uniforms. (By the end of the war, 2,500 white Alabamians and nearly twice that number of blacks had joined the Union army.) Or, they might fight as guerrillas, and there lay a more immediate concern. Armed Unionists threatened and abused rebel neighbors, stole horses and money, and vowed to hang every rebel boy and man between fifteen and forty-five years of age. "This is what I have long feared," one woman responded to her topsy-turvy world, "that a tory party would be formed which will be more dreadful to us than the Yankees."[29]

By December, rangers also spent an increasing amount of time and energy dueling with gangs of "outliers." Shorter called for additional "volunteer companies" to supplement the rangers and state militia in this battle. The gangs included both draft dodgers and deserters, and by August 1863, one Confederate general estimated that they numbered eight thousand to ten thousand in northern Alabama. He probably exaggerated the numbers, but the impression of doom remained very real for defenseless citizens. More than just evading the law, the bands, often "composed of outlaws," were also "committing outrages." When the rangers proved unable to control the situation, Shorter asked the army to help.[30]

These tremors did not immediately strike southern Alabama, but that seemed only a matter of time. The bulk of the slave population labored there, and with so much of the Confederacy's attention fixed on the more vulnerable central and northern counties, the southern part of the state looked like a safe haven for outliers. The same danger also lurked in the Florida panhandle, which, geographically, was only an extension of Alabama. The panhandle's pine barrens provided perfect hideaways for deserters and Unionists, and by 1863, Alabama rebels expected ruthless bands to "sally out" at any time to "rob, & lay waste the country."[31]

Elsewhere in the Southeast, the guerrilla war had yet to sink deep roots. The Union army and navy put significant pressure on the region in the winter of 1862–63 but without creating the sense of crisis that infected many other parts of the South. Nor, with the exception of North Carolina, did large numbers of Unionists live in these coastal states.

Florida still looked the most vulnerable. Union warships blockading both its Gulf and Atlantic coasts acted like magnets for runaway slaves and Unionists in the interior of the state. The Gulf was the quieter side. Blockaders there sent occasional expeditions ashore, most often to capture or destroy saltworks, but these incursions were intended as much to break the monotony of blockade duty as to advance any strategic plan. On the more volatile Atlantic coast, the Federals held several towns, from which they launched destructive raids overland and along rivers. Raiders sent rebels scurrying for the safety of the interior as they wrecked abandoned plantations.[32]

In the face of such anarchy, Florida rebels felt abandoned by the national government. If not abandoned, they had certainly been slighted by Richmond. Still largely an unsettled frontier, with the smallest population of any Confederate state, Florida did not seem sufficiently threatened to rate much concern from the Davis government, even by the summer of 1863. Forced to rely on his own resources, Governor Milton patched together a defense force. Whether from lack of faith in the reliability of guerrilla defenders, or simply taking his cue from the War Department, Milton kept his partisans on a short leash. He had plenty of volunteers for a "Guerilla corps" and, as enlistments for the army had nearly ceased, men voiced a strong preference to serve in their home counties. Milton used this desire to resurrect the state's defunct militia system, but he had to rely equally on partisans and independent guerrilla bands.[33]

Florida rangers, operating in swamps and piney woods as far west as Pensacola, caused problems for both blockading Union ships and Unionist citizens. Major Theodore W. Brevard led the only recognized battalion of rangers in the state. Formed in October 1862, Brevard's command worked harmoniously with the state's conventional troops, if only from necessity. Only 2,500 Confederate soldiers remained in Florida by late 1862. In addition, Captain John J. Dickison, the state's most famous, "irregular," commanded a company of the 2nd Florida Cavalry. While attached to a regular army regiment, Dickison became known as a "partizan" for his successful guerrilla tactics. His men intercepted enemy supplies, disrupted communications, confronted Union landing parties, and removed slaves and free blacks from areas controlled by the Federals. Both his military superiors and grateful citizens praised Dickison's efforts. They lamented only that he had so few men.[34]

Florida Unionists remained an easy target for rebel guerrillas. "They rob, murder, and steal indiscriminately if reports of the refugees are to be credited," noted a Union naval officer of the Unionist plight. "Union men they threaten to hang, and do shoot, as we have lamentable proof." John Westcott led the largest independent guerrilla band—around 120 men—along the St. Johns River. This remained the region most heavily populated by tories, including the families of several black pilots on Union gunboats. Only constant patrolling by these gunboats could effectively limit guerrilla depredations and intimidate rebel citizens along the river. The navy also destroyed small boats the guerrillas might use to conduct illicit trade or stage raids. By early 1863, Union sailors had smashed over one thousand craft.[35]

Despite their effectiveness, Florida partisans suffered from the determination in Richmond to integrate rangers with conventional regiments. Brevard got the bad news in November and lodged his protest immediately. His men had enlisted "in good faith," he argued. To force them into the army would "destroy the organization of every Company in the Battalion" and leave citizens undefended. Brevard managed to keep his battalion functioning through the spring of 1863, but in June his partisan rangers were forced to become infantrymen.[36]

South Carolina found itself in a similar situation. The state had remained largely unscathed by war except for its seacoast. Not much of a guerrilla war developed until the spring of 1863, when some of the

Union's first black regiments, recruited mostly from fugitive slaves, took the field. General David Hunter, recently assigned to duty on one of Carolina's sea islands, played a role. Hunter had tried a year earlier, while in Georgia, to emulate John Frémont by freeing the slaves within his command. Lincoln, as he did with Frémont, reversed the order. However, by the time Hunter arrived in South Carolina, the Emancipation Proclamation was in force, and blacks could be accepted into the U.S. Army. Hunter acted at once to form the army's first black regiment. More than that, he told Lincoln that he would accept no officers—all of whom would be white men—who opposed "a vigorous prosecution of the war or any of its necessary measures."[37]

Hunter had been replaced by early June, but black and white troops continued for several months to destroy private property and free slaves in raids along the Carolina coast. In the thick of things was James Montgomery. Commanding one of South Carolina's black regiments, he applied his old jayhawker methods by torching the towns of Darien and Bluffton. "We are outlawed," he said, in reference to the Confederacy's refusal to recognize the legitimacy of black troops, "and therefore not bound by the rules of regular warfare." Rebels must learn that this was "real war," Montgomery told his officers, even to being "swept away by the hand of God." One of his subordinates, Colonel Robert Gould Shaw, though just as enthusiastic an abolitionist as his leader, condemned Montgomery's methods as "mere guerrilla warfare."[38]

South Carolinian William Gilmore Simms had seen and heard enough of Union retaliation. An advocate of unrestrained warfare from the beginning of the conflict, he tried both privately and publicly to rally the Confederacy's guerrilla defenders. Simms had already captured his countrymen's enthusiasm for the guerrilla war in his poem, "The Border Ranger":

My rifle, pouch, and knife!
My steed! And then we part!
One loving kiss, dear wife,
One press of heart to heart!

. . . .

Then for the deadliest strife,
For freedom I depart!
I were of little worth,
Were these Yankee wolves left free
To ravage 'round the hearth,
And bring one grief to thee!

Published in a Charleston newspaper early in the war, the poem, Simms said, had been inspired "by the Muse of Patriotism," its theme no doubt coming from the actions of guerrilla defenders on the border. The poem reached a national audience when republished in the March 1862 issue of the *Southern Literary Messenger*, just as the Confederate Congress was debating the merits of the guerrilla war and the Partisan Ranger Act.[39]

In the summer of 1863, following Montgomery's raids, Simms republished under a new title another poem, this one written more than thirty years earlier. Originally entitled "In Memory of Italian Patriots," Simms had penned it to protest the harsh repression of a liberation movement in Italy (and likely as a veiled comment on his own state's nullification crisis). Reappearing in the *Charleston Mercury* as "The Guerrilla Martyrs," the words remained apt for the Confederate predicament:

But to be cruel and brutal, does not make
Ye conquerors; and the vulture yet shall prey
On living hearts; and vengeance fiercely slake
The unappeasable appetite ye wake,
In the hot blood of victims, that have been
Most eager, binding freemen to the stake,——
Most greedy in the orgies of this sin![40]

South Carolina governor Milledge L. Bonham and General Pierre G. T. Beauregard, the latter responsible for the defense of both the Carolina and Georgia coasts, also protested the Union raids. Beauregard had been denied a ready pool of partisans by his predecessor, John C. Pemberton, who regarded partisans as "comparatively useless." By the time Beauregard took charge, only one company of rangers and one company of "scouts" remained in the state. Seeking to fill the void, he and Governor Bonham called on South Carolinians to resist the "vandal foe." Bonham urged citizens to defend neighborhoods with whatever weapons they possessed. He suggested attacks from ambush as an effective tactic. "Many a deadly volley may be successfully delivered at the raiders," he reminded the populace.[41]

Georgia and North Carolina presented more portentous problems. With their vulnerable seacoasts, both states still anticipated invasion by "robbers, plunderers, violators of virtue, and outlaws of humanity," but they feared equally an internal rebellion. Unionism had been vibrant in North Carolina and northern Georgia from the start of the war, and resistance to Confederate rule increased with the onset of conscription.

Governors Joe Brown and Zebulon Vance sympathized, for they also opposed national conscription. However, they could not condone violent resistance to Confederate law, which is what they got from Unionists. Making the situation especially treacherous, hundreds of army deserters had joined the tories in armed bands by late 1862 to spread fear and desolation through both states, just as they were doing in Alabama. The deserters were not necessarily opposed to the Confederacy, only to the Davis government, but they would no longer support it. They had also tired of war and wanted to escape its danger and hardships. Unfortunately, this meant supporting themselves as outlaws.[42]

Georgia rebels, still largely shielded from the war, were appalled by the unprecedented violence. "Armed insurgents," "scoundrels," "desperadoes," and "treacherous parties" set upon them, some in gangs two hundred and three hundred strong. Unionist bands appeared to be particularly numerous and dangerous in the state's northern hill country, where something of a crisis developed by the end of the summer. "We must have arms and ammunition," insisted a desperate rebel, "or this Town will be burned and the country over run and perhaps many citizens massacred."[43]

Confederate defense companies arrested troublemakers or chased them out of their communities, but the rebel crackdown caused as many problems as it remedied. In Dahlongea, Georgia, a roundup of deserters by the home guard only produced "disaffected families" who were "incensed" by the guard's action. Neighbors who had tolerated or even supported one another became "unnatural enemies." Exasperated by the punishment of relatives and friends, they sought "revenge." Some outliers let it be known that they would come out of the bush if local home guards—often as not including their friends or relatives— granted them immunity and allowed them to join in "home defense" against their common enemy, the Federals. However, they still refused to rejoin the general war effort. "They swear they will die before they will return to the army," one observer said.[44]

Perhaps the most unlikely scenario of all involved Confederate deserters who continued to claim sympathy with the rebel cause. John P. Gatewood, who deserted a Tennessee cavalry regiment in the autumn of 1862, operated on those terms in East Tennessee and northwestern Georgia. This "longhaired, red-bearded beast from Georgia," as he was described, put together a gang of fifty to one hundred deserters, bushwhackers, and "irresponsibles" that spent two years "pillaging, ravaging, plundering and killing" every Unionist within reach. Many of the murders were gruesome affairs. Yet the motives and operations of Gatewood were decidedly different from those of Confederate soldiers who deserted to return home and defend their neighborhoods. Gatewood's men, despite their claim to "Southern . . . sympathies," were outlaws at heart.[45]

Governor Brown responded to the chaos by creating the most inclusive militia organization in the Confederacy. Brown thought his system of universal service a more reliable means than partisans to mobilize defenders. Too many partisan rangers, once enrolled, he complained, scarcely budged. Whole companies sat idle for months on end, usually because of internal squabbles over who should command them. They devoted their energies to confiscating horses and requisitioning corn. Things had reached such a low point in some communities that rebel residents formed home guards to protect their property against these so-called defenders. Brown hoped that his new model for service would remedy these defects.[46]

North Carolina faced an even bigger challenge. The Union army occupied only a few towns on the seacoast, but its raids inland grew more frequent in the first half of 1863. So did the number of escaped or rebellious slaves and the resistance of North Carolina Unionists. There had always been rumblings of discontent in the state, but conscription and other infringements of personal liberties played less well in North Carolina than perhaps anywhere else in the South. Evidence of the divide could be seen politically at the polls, as support for progovernment candidates declined in 1863. When North Carolina deserters began to filter back home, circumstances were ripe for one of the most bitter internal wars in the Confederacy.[47]

Federals who occupied towns like Plymouth, Elizabeth City, and New Bern did not feel nearly the duress experienced by Union troops in states like Arkansas, Tennessee, or West Virginia. But not for lack of effort by the rebels. Guerrillas harassed their pickets and fought sharp skirmishes with Union raiders. The state mustered six regiments of partisan rangers and counted twice that number of companies and battalions. Tar Heels also organized such romantic-sounding bands as the "Scottish Chiefs" to serve as "sort of Partisan Ranger" companies. Yet few of the state's units had entered service by the spring of 1863, and the remaining forces could not seriously threaten the Federals. "There are no rebels in this vicinity except gurilla bands," verified a New York soldier from Plymouth, "[and] we are well prepared to meet them." This particular soldier complained more about the coastal mosquitoes, which he found "very troublesome." In any event, with the arrival of Confederate troops under General Daniel H. Hill in March 1863, the army assumed responsibility for driving the Federals from their eastern strongholds in North Carolina.[48]

The essence of North Carolina's guerrilla war, then, lay in the clash between rebel and Unionist guerrillas. Some four thousand Unionists (plus five thousand blacks) joined the Union army, but at least that many men stayed home to fight an irregular war. Called "buffaloes" in the eastern part of the state, they mounted a stiff challenge to rebel guerrillas. Their name, like "jayhawker," is of uncertain derivation. It has been traced to state political battles of the 1850s, but during the war, Confederates also complained of Unionists who prowled "in gangs like herds of buffaloes." The wartime species included some tough and violent customers. The first bands formed in August 1862 in Hertford County, where a hard-drinking Confederate deserter named John A. "Jack" Fairless pulled together a disparate crowd of deserters, fugitive slaves, draft dodgers, and "lawless white men" to resist the rebel government. Any number of puns might be fashioned from Jack's surname, for he was far from being "fair" or an ideal leader for a band of conscientious Confederate dissenters. Both the federal authorities and his own men became disgusted with his violent excesses and drunken behavior. Growing numbers of men refused to follow him, and one of the band finally shot and killed Fairless in October 1862. However, there remained plenty of other buffaloes to make life a misery for rebel citizens.[49]

Confederates feared these "deep dyed tories" more than they did the Union army. One Confederate general, unwilling to think that southerners would voluntarily turn against the Confederacy, attributed the violence and intimidation to Union soldiers rather than southern Unionists. Yet, he could not ignore the fact that many Tar Heels had become as dangerous to the rebel cause "as though they were regular traitors." One loyal rebel prayed, "Oh God grant us a Morgan, Jackson, Ashby or some such spirit . . . to free us of such mean, vile & abandoned creatures." The same man clipped two poems from his newspaper: "En Revanche," by North Carolina poet Paul Hamilton Hayne, and "The Guerillas," by S. Teacle Wallis, of Maryland. Commenting on the opening words of the latter poem—"Awake! and to horse, my brother!"—he confided to his diary, "I heartily commend these lines to every soul from 10 to 100 years old in the South."[50]

Despite eastern buffaloes, North Carolina's westernmost counties suffered the greatest trauma, as they had from the start of the war. Unionists and deserters formed several bands of one hundred or more men by joining forces with their counterparts in East Tennessee. Together they raided and found refuge on both sides of the border. Rebels slept "with their rifles at their side." They strayed from home only on the most urgent business, for they feared not only being attacked on the road, but also returning to find that "tory Bushwhackers" had sacked their homes and accosted their families. In one such instance, a man learned that his wife had been ordered into the kitchen while a gang destroyed or carried away nearly all of their possessions, including her clothes. Conditions reminded people of the violent days of the American Revolution, "when the Tories and Indians were so mischievous."[51]

In such circumstances, independent bands of defenders proved relatively useless. Unionist bushwhackers murdered people, forced families from their homes, and challenged local militia without fear of retribution. Even a veteran of the guerrilla war like William Thomas, who now commanded an entire legion of both Cherokees and whites, acknowledged that the western counties of North Carolina were "in danger of being over run by deserters and renegades." The boldest bands attacked small patrols of militia or Confederate troops that ventured too near their haunts. Lone county sheriffs, conscript officers, and army recruiters simply stayed clear. "If yo ever hunt for us a gin I will put lead in you[,] god dam your hell fired soll," three fugitives warned a local conscript officer. "Yo have give the people orders to shoot us down when they find us and if yo dont take your orders back i will shoot yo. . . . We have never done yo any harms for yo to hunt for us [but] we will give yo something to hunt us for here after." That was fair enough warning.[52]

The Davis government eventually ordered troops into the troubled region, but they failed to cure the ill. In fact, they occasionally made things worse. Ferocious skirmishes ensued, as strong Unionist gangs ambushed the encroaching soldiers. Stung and eager to retaliate, rebel soldiers sometimes overreacted when they finally did corner a band of anti-Confederates. Such was the case when the 64th North Carolina Infantry captured and summarily executed thirteen deserters in the Shelton Laurel valley of Madison County early in 1863. It was purely an act of revenge. Some of the murdered men had recently participated in a destructive raid through the county, which happened to be home to many men of the 64th Regiment. The killings embarrassed Confederate authorities. It was just the sort of crime they accused the Federals of perpetrating. Unhappily, too, such incidents—for Shelton Laurel was not an isolated case—only made Unionists more determined to seek vengeance in return.[53]

Zebulon Vance, elected governor of North Carolina in the summer of 1862, recommended full pardons for deserters who returned to their regiments and a moratorium on conscription in the western counties. That, at least, he and others fancied, would bring some guerrillas out of the mountains. Forcing men into service would only cause more problems. Vance saw a second advantage to relaxing conscription laws. He understood that in places inclined to revolt, the draft hurt the Confederacy doubly. It made enemies of men who "would dye at home before they would be forced off" to the army. At the same time, sending loyal men away from home deprived neighborhoods of their last defenders. "Unless an armed force is kept," citizens of one county told Vance, "we will have the worst of plunderers committing depredations among the families of soldiers in the service." The governor preferred to use men who would otherwise be stripped from their communities to form "a vigilant system of general police" to arrest local deserters who did not take advantage of his pardons.[54]

The breakdown of North Carolina's home front confirmed a growing impression that the partisan ranger system could not restore order. Vance, like most other southern governors, used rangers as best he could manage, but the Richmond government, by reducing their numbers and restricting their actions, had effectively eliminated them as a reliable means of defense. Vance tried to invigorate the ranger system by asking John Pool, a former gubernatorial candidate and known opponent of secession, to command a new battalion of partisans for "local defense" in the eastern counties. Pool politely declined. He admitted the rangers might well accomplish their mission as "a sort of police force," but he thought them generally unreliable, likely to scatter at the approach of any sizable Union force. "The Rangers will succeed in limiting the depredations & outrages of the few miserable 'Buffaloes' who infest that section," Pool elaborated, "but no military enterprize, that would reflect credit on a commander, is possible." The governor continued to commission companies of state rangers, but he relied principally on a reorganized militia system, called the "Guard for Home Defense."[55]

So, throughout the lower South, guerrillas caused more problems for the rebels by mid-1863 than even their opponents had foreseen. Earlier supporters of a people's war expressed second thoughts about its wisdom. With no end to the war in sight, the guerrilla war threatened to implode. And who knew how that might alter both Confederate and Union strategy.

IV

DAY OF THE OUTLAW

FALL 1863–1864

At dawn on August 21, 1863, William C. Quantrill and 450 hardened rebel guerrillas galloped four abreast into Lawrence, Kansas. By midmorning, they had burned and looted most of the town, the destruction estimated at two million dollars. They also murdered at least 150 men and boys. Some guerrillas had used the raid to settle personal scores, but the general motive was retaliation for three years of theft, murder, and destruction by Kansans in Missouri. Quantrill had hoped to capture James Lane, who resided at Lawrence, but the wily jayhawker escaped. Nothing so chillingly brutal had yet marred the war, but the Lawrence raid was no aberration. By August 1863, a cycle of retaliation and counterretaliation had deadened human sympathies and heightened tolerance for death and rapine. Lawrence represented a tipping point. Efforts to explain or apologize for the brutality came less often, and where the guerrilla war was concerned, an unsettling degree of outlawry came to dominate. Recent Union victories at Gettysburg and Vicksburg looked less decisive. The national conflict would not end soon.[1]

The raid threw Kansans into a panic. Even though columns of Union cavalry drove the guerrillas back into Missouri, rumors circulated for several days that Quantrill's men remained on the loose. New raiding parties, people heard, had set out from Missouri. Citizens hid their valuables or fled their homes. Formerly indolent men armed themselves and organized militia companies. But how to proceed? Should they pursue Quantrill, prepare for an attack, take their families and run? "Commotion, confusion, terror, and vengeance, all blended into one indescribable feeling," said one man.[2]

The "vengeance" part scared Missourians as Kansans screamed for justice. James Lane incited the town of Leavenworth, where he had found safety, with a frenzied, "wild speech." He demanded "devastation for safety," "plunder for profit," and the "indiscriminate murder of all border Missourians." A member of his audience, infused by the rage of the moment, decreed, "Hanging, disemboweling and quartering are not half severe enough to satisfy the righteous vengeance of the people." The town of Paola called upon Lane, Charles Jennison, George Hoyt, and other prominent jayhawkers to invade Missouri. "Make it a desert and call it peace!" they cried. Governor Thomas Carney, who opposed anything that might aggrandize Lane, warned General John Schofield, once more commanding the Department of the Missouri, that only stiff legal action could forestall a bloody day of reckoning. A Missouri Unionist who had seen enough of this war of retaliation blamed both sides for the "burning and killing." With three "southern men" and four "Union men" recently gunned down in her neighborhood, she lamented, "Oh I am so tired of war."[3]

Most people blamed thirty-four-year-old General Thomas Ewing Jr., who commanded Union troops on the Missouri-Kansas border, for the raid. Son of a prominent Ohio politician, brother-in-law of William T. Sherman, and a lawyer by profession, Ewing had settled in Kansas Territory before the war. He considered himself a "radical" when it came to mollycoddling rebels, and he understood the intricate machinations of Kansas politics. His problems arose from growing rebel guerrilla strength on the Missouri border. Paroled Missouri soldiers had been returning home in droves since the fall of Vicksburg, and many of them had "at once go[ne] to the bush." Three days before the Lawrence raid, Ewing issued General Orders No. 10, approved by Schofield, to address the situation. The order exiled rebels from Missouri's western counties to Arkansas. "While the families are here the men will prowl about, & the country is so well adapted by nature for bushwhackers that it is next to impossible to kill the scoundrels," he explained to his father. Ewing naively believed the guerrillas would follow their families rather than continue to fight. If Missouri politicians would then abolish slavery and allow the formation of black regiments, Ewing hoped to end the guerrilla war.[4]

Then came the Lawrence raid. Forced to take stronger measures, Ewing issued General Orders No. 11 on August 25. The new directive expelled nearly *all* inhabitants—loyal as well as disloyal—from their homes in three counties and part of a fourth. The most repressive U.S. military measure of the war against civilians, it uprooted many thousands of people at the heart of Quantrill's domain. Ewing knew it was harsh but hoped this action would placate Kansans and spare Missouri a potentially ruthless invasion. He also hoped it would answer the blistering personal attacks on him as the man responsible for the Lawrence "massacre." Those critics included James Lane, with whom Ewing met privately three days before issuing the order. Although he distrusted Lane, Ewing recognized the senator's political clout and wanted his approval.[5]

Order 11 saved Ewing. He had feared a court of inquiry over the

The August 1863 raid on Lawrence, Kansas, the most infamous guerrilla action
of the Civil War. From *Harper's Weekly*, September 5, 1863.

Lawrence affair, but his swift action satisfied everyone. Schofield felt relief. He needed Ewing, who understood the "shoals and quicksands" of Kansas politics. Besides, Schofield, who had favored a more drastic response to the raid than Order 11, blamed the inadequate antiguerrilla policies of his predecessor, Samuel Curtis, for what happened at Lawrence. Better still, neither Stanton nor Halleck blamed Ewing, and Lincoln approved of his action. Order 11 also satisfied Carney and most Kansas radicals. Missouri Unionists, glad to see that they would no longer be "the only sufferers," thought the step long overdue.[6]

Oddly enough, John Schofield lost the most from Quantrill's raid. Being closely associated with the "moderate" Governor Gamble, who was also under fire, he could not shake an undeserved reputation for being soft on guerrillas. Neither Missourians nor Kansans appreciated—or simply did not care—that Schofield was responsible not only for the security of their states, but also for the military campaign in Arkansas, where the war had picked up considerably since the surrender of Vicksburg. Unfortunately for the general, a few weeks after the Quantrill raid, Jo Shelby led a devastating, month-long raid into Missouri from Arkansas. That was enough for the Missourians. A joint delegation of Kansas *and* Missouri politicians visited Washington in early October to insist that Lincoln remove Schofield from command. The president, understanding Schofield's difficult military and political position, initially defended his embattled general. Still, Schofield would be gone by January, as would Gamble. The governor, who had been ailing physically for some time, died at the end of that month.[7]

Meantime, the effects of General Orders No. 11 met the fondest hopes of its supporters and the worst fears of its foes. The "removals" of disloyal people to Arkansas, unaccountably entrusted to Kansas troops, produced widespread robbery, destruction, and bullying. Houses went up in flames before the refugees were out of sight. Bands of jayhawkers, who had resumed their "chastising" raids in Missouri, attacked the exposed and forlorn columns of exiles as they wound their way southward. Not that enforcement by Missouri troops would likely have caused fewer problems. Colonel Bazel Lazear, the veteran guerrilla hunter of the 1st Missouri Cavalry, called Order 11 "one of the best orders" of the war. It might work a hardship on "some few" Unionists, he acknowledged, but he thought Ewing's plan so brilliant that he applied it to two guerrilla-infested counties—Lafayette and Johnson—under his own jurisdiction.[8]

The tragedy became fodder for rebel propaganda, although the most well-known protest came from an unexpected source. Missouri artist George Caleb Bingham had earned much fame for his paintings of western life in the decade before the war. Although a true Union man—he had even served in the army—Bingham had always condemned the treatment of Missourians by Kansas troops. Seeing the Kansans in action now, he responded with an overly dramatic rendition of the removal. The painting caused a sensation, its images of burning homesteads, slain farmers, and weeping women the epitome of what the Missouri-Kansas border war had become. Few people noticed when Ewing allowed "loyal persons" who had been forced from their homes to return in November. In January, when several of the affected counties were transferred to the command of Egbert B. Brown, a militia general decidedly hostile to Ewing, Brown allowed *all* people displaced by order 11 to return.[9]

Missouri's rebel guerrillas remained defiant as another unrelenting season of tit for tat ensued. Entering a deserted guerrilla camp in early October 1863, the 11th Kansas Cavalry found a Union soldier hanging from a rope around his neck. A note pinned to his shirt told the story: "This man was hung last evening, in revenge for the death of Ab Haller. He says his name is Thomas, and that he belongs to the Kansas 9th."[10]

Jo Shelby's raid inspired much of this stout resistance. Thirty-three-year-old Shelby had been born in Kentucky, but he made his name and fortune as a Missouri businessman and planter. He became a "border ruffian" in the 1850s and, in his words, entered Kansas "to kill Free State men." When the real war started in 1861, Shelby joined the cavalry of Sterling Price's Missouri State Guard, but as he rose to command his own regiment and brigade, he operated as a semipartisan. Federals called him the "notorious Shelby." By the time his "Iron Brigade" left Missouri in October 1863, it had covered 1,500 miles, destroyed two million dollars in public and private property, captured or executed scores of Union guerrillas and Confederate deserters, and rallied Missouri guerrillas. Incredibly, with Shelby safely returned to Arkansas, General Schofield informed Lincoln that he had "completely broken" rebel power in Missouri.[11]

More ominously, plain robbery and other crimes, bearing no connection to the war or its participants, had become daily affairs. "Our country is desolate, indeed almost entirely a wilderness," stammered a resident of western Missouri in early 1864. "Our farms are all burned up, fences gone, crops destroyed, and no one escapes the ravages of one party or the other." Though a Confederate, this woman disapproved of robbery and "bushwhacking in any shape," and she had come to recognize the "gross and fearful faults on both sides." Warfare in these "enlightened" times, she believed, ought to be "conducted upon honorable principles," yet she could think of "no age of barbarism" that had produced "such scenes of cruelty and plunder." Her family had been robbed five times and three times threatened "to be burned out." She had endured enough. She decided to leave her home in the spring. She knew not where to go but longed for peace "upon almost any terms."[12]

Willard Mendenhall, a carriage maker and farmer, lived in a neighboring county. A native of New Jersey, Mendenhall had moved to Missouri a decade before the war and married a local girl. He tried to remain neutral during the war, to "make no public enemies" and tend to his family and business. Yet, like many similarly disposed people, he suffered attacks and threats from both sides. Some neighbors were dragged from their homes and murdered by "midnight assassins," men who only wished to "gratify a malicious feeling . . . in thare bosom." More often, "robbers" brazenly entered their homes to demand money. "The country is full of them," Mendenhall decided, and the evidence was everywhere. More Missourians captured as bushwhackers faced charges of robbery, larceny, or theft. They were deemed "outlaws *and* guerrillas." The Union army had long denounced rebel irregulars as outlaws and brigands, but these labels could be taken more literally by 1864 and applied with increasing accuracy.[13]

The chief brigand, William Quantrill, provided the best example of this decline in the Trans-Mississippi. He remained relatively quiet for several weeks after the Lawrence raid. Then, on October 6, 1863, just one day after President Lincoln had defended Schofield's handling of the guerrilla war to the Kansas-Missouri delegation, Quantrill directed another "massacre," this time of Union soldiers. General James Blunt, a political ally of Lane and a terror to rebel guerrillas in Missouri, Arkansas, and Indian Territory, was traveling from his headquarters at Fort Scott, Kansas, to Fort Smith, Arkansas, which had recently been wrested from rebel hands. Purely by chance, Quantrill and four hundred of his men were headed for Texas on a converging route.[14]

The rebels had attacked and nearly captured a Union outpost near Baxter Springs, in the southeastern corner of Kansas, when they caught sight of Blunt's undermanned column about a mile away. In the assault that followed, they killed or grievously wounded ninety of the one hundred poorly armed men, many of them only musicians in Blunt's band. Not content with this, the rebels stripped and mutilated most of the soldiers. They incinerated many of the bodies by burning the wagon train. Among the slain were a twelve-year-old drummer and Major Henry Z. Curtis, son of General Samuel Curtis. Blunt escaped with the other survivors, but Quantrill captured many of the general's personal effects and all of his military correspondence.[15]

Baxter Springs confirmed the reputation of Quantrill's men as "fiends incarnate," "demons," and "devils from hell." Even many Confederates recoiled at their cruelty. An impressionable young Confederate officer who met Quantrill a week after the attack hailed him as a "celebrated Chieftain" and gushed over his "brilliant achievements," but wiser heads had grown wary of Quantrill's "mode of warfare." General Henry McCulloch, younger brother of Ben and commander of Confederate troops in northern Texas, stood with the latter group. When Quantrill's men arrived in his district, McCulloch voiced his concern to Kirby Smith, commanding the Trans-Mississippi Department. "I appreciate his services, and am anxious to have them," McCulloch said tactfully, "but certainly we cannot, as a Christian people, sanction a savage, inhuman warfare, in which men are shot down like dogs."[16]

The Missourians wintered in northern Texas, where they spent most of their time drinking, carousing, and terrifying loyal Confederates. Meantime, however, the command began to break up. The collapse of discipline had been troubling many original or early members for several months. Rivalries had emerged. Men quarreled and threatened one another. They lacked "individual devotion and mutual trust," said a man who had begun to question the entire purpose of the war. The excesses at Lawrence and Baxter Springs disgusted some men. In March, William "Bloody Bill" Anderson, one of his more mercurial lieutenants, turned Judas by telling Confederate authorities that Quantrill was responsible for several reported crimes in northern Texas. Bloody Bill wanted to break away with some of the rougher elements, and, come the spring, they cast their lot with him.[17]

Seeking to salvage his splintered band, Quantrill asked Thomas Reynolds, Missouri's Confederate governor in exile, for help. He appealed to the wrong man. Reynolds had endorsed guerrilla warfare when he believed it offered the only means of reclaiming his state, but he had decided months earlier that it now "damaged" the Confederate cause. Reynolds advised Quantrill to quit. "A man of your ability should look forward to a higher future," he told him. "You must see that guerrilla warfare, as an honorable pursuit, is pretty nearly 'played out.'" The time had come when every leader of an "undisciplined" band must either become a "slave of his men" or be put down. Reynolds urged Quantrill and his guerrillas to enter "the regular Confederate service" and engage in "ordinary warfare."[18]

Reynolds had told the War Department as much, and a few days after counseling Quantrill, he warned Kirby Smith that the guerrilla conflict could cost the Confederacy the war. Its gravest danger, Reynolds believed, came from the numerous deserters, "idlers," and "bullies," all of them in search of "lawless plunder," who exploited the guerrilla contest for personal gain. This new clientele "banded together under a semblance of authority," he told Smith, but they had no loyalty to the Confederacy. Their unchecked pillaging drove rebel citizens "to desire the presence of the enemy in the hope of safety from anarchy." Getting to the heart of the matter, Reynolds concluded: "These bands are *utterly* useless as military organizations. They war not on the enemy, but on our own people. The enemy makes little, if any, effort to put them down, because the U.S. authorities are shrewd enough to know that their excesses increase Unionism among the inhabitants and diminishes our real strength." Reynolds may have overestimated the shrewdness of Union strategists, but he did identify the same consequences of the guerrilla war predicted by Sherman almost two years earlier.[19]

The spring and summer of 1864 proved Reynolds's point in Missouri. Neither side seemed to hope any longer that the enemy would conduct anything like a "civilized" war. Leaven this attitude with increased brutality and banditry, and the future looked bleak. There was "no more forbearing" in this war, lamented a St. Louis rebel. "People of every political opinion and all ages, fleeing from their homes," he observed in early August. "The guerrillas prowling into the country and the Federals ravaging towns. Murder, arson of daily occurrence. Fights rendered horrible by their ferocity. No quarter being given, no mercy shown. It is horrible." Willard Mendenhall described the poor old state as "groaning from her center to circumference." Worst of all, while noncombatants knew perfectly well what to expect, they still had no idea how much longer these conditions—which is to say the war—would continue.[20]

Both the legitimate and illegitimate guerrilla wars exceeded all controls in the always troubled western and northern parts of the state, but no section was immune. To the southeast, a largely illiterate farmer named Sam Hildebrand had already shot or hanged a dozen men by 1864, and the most infamous part of his wartime career had only begun. In central eastern Missouri, around Rolla, an entirely different social class—outwardly respectable farmers—either rode with or supported the bushwhackers. Seventeen of these men owned between them 2,580 acres, an average of 152 acres per man, with all of the land valued at a minimum of two dollars per acre. Two of the men also operated mills, and two of them were preachers. Likewise, in the central part of the state, some men whose property had been seized by Unionist-controlled courts for payment of debts took to the bush. As for business in the region, it was *dead, dead,* asserted one merchant. "Every thing excepting *death* seems suspended," confirmed another man, "and almost every business except the coffin maker has closed."[21]

Reinforcing for many people the depths of the crisis, an unprecedented number of "she rebels" played ever bolder and more assertive roles. Some of them, like Sarah "Kate" King, who claimed to be Quantrill's wife and sometimes rode with his band, were genuinely deadly characters, known killers on "intimate terms with thieves and desperadoes." Other women were embittered "war widows," described by one Unionist as "ignorant and entirely uneducated, . . . entirely controlled by passion." Such "home-bushwhacker[s]," living alone and in "destitute circumstances," aided and abetted "all the depredations" of their "warring accomplices." More often, these girls and women reminded one of the boys and men whose romantic notions of "partisans" drew them into the guerrilla war. It was a game to them, and they seldom understood the dangers involved. Then, too, some women believed that their sex shielded them, that they would not be held accountable for their actions. That tactic worked for some of them, but federal authorities arrested and punished hundreds of southern women during the war on a variety of charges. Their most frequent crime, if not participating in murderous gangs, was "harboring and feeding" guerrillas.[22]

Some women, though, may have been as naive as the fox. Sarah Jane Smith never considered that she would be sentenced to death (later commuted to imprisonment) for cutting telegraph wires and chopping down telegraph poles in southern Missouri. A native of Arkansas whose father had fought with Sterling Price, the eighteen-year-old Smith refuged to Missouri midway through the war. There, she lived in the woods with two male guerrilla cousins. When standing trial for her crimes, she claimed to have been promised payment by a local rebel to cut wires and never considered that she had done wrong. Yet Smith steadfastly refused to divulge the names of her comrades. Similarly, the Mayfield sisters—Ella, Sallie, and Jennie—took to the bush when their two guerrilla brothers were killed. Ella was the eldest and best known of the sisters, but Sallie and Jennie made their own headlines when, having been captured in July 1864, they escaped from a St. Louis prison. This prompted the city's provost marshal to order "additional precautions" for the growing number of women prisoners, many of them of dubious "character."[23]

One of the most daring women never cut a telegraph wire or shot a man, but the Federals considered her a terror. Twenty-two-year-old Julia Martin denied having any knowledge of bushwhackers when she and three other women were arrested in September 1864. The evidence said otherwise. Martin had fed, harbored, and passed on information to rebel guerrillas for more than two years. The provost marshal charged her with being "a violent Rebel" who had guided guerrillas to Unionist homes in order to rob them. She had also threatened to have Unionist women kidnaped and "taken to the brush." She could be seen riding "day and night" to deliver messages, standing guard outside guerrilla camps, and keeping company with "armed men." The captain of the local home guard said of her, "She hoped to see a bushwhacker for every bush and that they might kill every militia man who could be caught." Martin spent the remainder of the war in an Iowa prison.[24]

Sterling Price also nurtured Missouri's guerrilla resurgence. The former governor had never lost hope of claiming his state for the Confederacy. In the summer of 1864, believing "the people" ready for a "general uprising," he sent agents into the state to recruit supporters and alert guerrilla chiefs to his coming. He gathered every Confederate soldier and guerrilla he could find in Arkansas. Many of them had no weapons, but Price assured his 12,000-man Army of Missouri that it would secure plenty of guns across the border. Price and his troops entered southeastern Missouri on September 19, one year after Jo Shelby had begun his momentous raid, and headed for St. Louis. Old Pap predicted that another 30,000 rebels, mostly "large guerrilla parties," would flock to him.[25]

Price, in timing the raid, was also mindful of the approaching U.S. presidential election. Just as William Sherman hoped to secure Lincoln's reelection by capturing Atlanta, so rebels across the South sought ways to frighten northern voters. The Democrats had selected a "peace" candidate, former general George B. McClellan, to challenge Lincoln. If Confederates could intensify the war in the weeks before the election and turn war-weary northerners against the administration, southern independence might well be in the offing. Confederate guerrillas in Arkansas had stepped up their attacks on Union patrols, riverboats, and communication lines during the summer. Price wanted to transfer that momentum to Missouri, where yet another electoral prize might be won: the election of a pro-Confederate governor and legislature.[26]

Unionists need not have worried. While many "men of the Bush," including the splintered parts of Quantrill's command, rallied to Price, the ex-governor did not get anything close to the 30,000 men he expected. A combination of Union troops, state militia, and home guards forced Price back into Arkansas by the end of October. Most discouraging for Price was the way the guerrilla bands wasted their potential strength by operating independently from his main force. There had been a time when these men might have understood the crucial strategic potential of the raid, and so cooperated more fully. By 1864, however, personal vendettas and marauding trumped any united goal.[27]

Bloody Bill Anderson led mostly "young men and youths" that autumn. One of his young admirers insisted that the band included only "a few" genuine marauders, but he admitted that "revenge and revenge alone, permeated and took possession of every fibre of Bill Anderson's body." That may explain what happened at Centralia, Missouri, in the midst of Price's raid. With only a couple of shops and hotels, Centralia was not much of a town. Nothing like Lawrence. Anderson had no firm plan in mind when he appeared on its streets at midmorning on September 27 with about eighty men, including Jesse and Frank James. He began by robbing and terrorizing the residents and the unlucky passengers of a stage coach that had pulled into town. The guerrillas then stopped a train as it approached the depot and robbed its passengers. Unhappily, the cars held about two dozen unarmed Union soldiers going home on furlough. The guerrillas ordered the troops off the train, stripped them of their uniforms, and executed all but one man.[28]

That might have ended things had not a Union cavalry patrol happened on the scene shortly after Anderson's men had left town. Struck dumb by the slaughter, the bulk of the patrol—about 115 men—pursued them. Unknown to the cavalrymen, Anderson had paused to rendezvous outside of town with several other guerrilla bands, a combined force of some 400 men. They set a trap for the cavalrymen. Any Federals not killed in the ensuing slaughter were shot down when they tried to surrender. The rebels mutilated most of the bodies and scalped about a dozen of them. Frank James felt no remorse. Years later, he swore that the Federals had carried a hastily made black flag. They would have killed every one of Anderson's men if given the chance. "What is war for," James challenged, "if it isn't to kill people for a principle?" The guerrillas then returned to Centralia to murder whatever remaining troopers did not flee their arrival. The death count on that day was 146 Union soldiers and 3 civilians.[29]

Although no one dared hope it at the time, the Centralia raid ended the worst of Missouri's war. One month later, shortly before Price's much-depleted column slipped back into Arkansas, Missouri militia gunned down Bloody Bill Anderson. A week earlier, a Union sharpshooter had killed George Todd, another former Quantrill lieutenant who had fallen out with his chief. Ironically, Todd had been killed while doing a legitimate bit of scouting for Price. Quantrill derived some satisfaction from the two deaths, but he had already decided Missouri was a lost cause and far too dangerous a place for his diminished portion of the old band. In early December, he moved his operations to Kentucky. "We now consider that all further attempts of the Confederates to invade Missouri or Kansas, are at an end," rejoiced a Wisconsin cavalryman after fighting guerrillas all that summer and fall. He acknowledged that "small bands of Gerrillas" would continue to operate, but he guessed they would devote themselves to robbing civilians.[30]

As the ferocity of Missouri's guerrilla war receded, so, too, did rebel threats to neighboring Union states. Kansas, of course, had to remain on the alert, but Iowa and Illinois appeared to breathe easier by the end of 1864. The latter two states deserved some respite, for they had shared in the tumult of the summer and fall. Any time northern Missouri rumbled, Iowa felt the tremors, and so the Hawkeyes had been on edge all during the rebel resurgence. One Iowan preferred a "Guerrilla Invasion" to the "insecurity" of living among armed rebel sympathizers. An out-and-out fight, winner take all, seemed the best solution to him. "Missouri is full of guerrillas and people are getting scared, for fear they will come up in Iowa," a woman told her soldier-husband in Georgia. The anxious husband advised her to stay at home and not betray fear if any guerrillas did appear. Should she suffer "any indignity" at their hands, he would leave the army and pursue them "to the end of the world."[31]

Serious trouble came to Iowa only once in 1864, but it rocked the state. On October 12, in the midst of Price's Missouri raid, a dozen blue-clad rebel guerrillas entered Davis County, in southeastern Iowa. Jim Jackson, a veteran Texas Ranger who had fought with John Hunt Morgan in Kentucky and Clifton Holtzclaw's guerrillas in Missouri, led them. Jackson's men enjoyed a twelve-hour spree before slipping out of the state untouched. They kidnapped several people (eventually releasing them), murdered three men, and robbed scores of homes. A wave of theft and intimidation lasting several weeks swept across all of southern Iowa, accompanied by real and imagined sightings of rebel raiders. Confederate recruiters also roamed the southern counties for several days, but the crisis had passed by December.[32]

More widespread panic struck Illinois. Most rebel activity in the state during the past year had been confined to illicit trade, but much of that trade was known to support the guerrilla war in Missouri and Arkansas. And there remained the constant fear that a major guerrilla force would cross either the Mississippi or the Ohio River to join with pro-Confederate citizens and terrorize the state. A strong militia presence prevented "invasion and domestic brawls" on its borders until late 1863, but then Illinois endured a full year of guerrilla-related crime and violence.[33]

In November 1863, the adjutant general of Illinois called on the 113th Illinois Infantry and the 7th Minnesota Infantry to help quell a disturbance in Scott County, one county removed from the Mississippi River in central Illinois. A band of three hundred mounted, well-armed "lawless men" had organized there to protect rebel and Union deserters and resist the provost marshal. The band scattered on the army's arrival, and a week-long expedition through the hills and thick timber of four counties netted only seventeen "bushwhackers." A serious gunfight occurred when the U.S. troops tried to arrest one of the ringleaders. Another fifteen men surrendered voluntarily when the colonel of the Union expedition promised them immunity. The captured men were charged with kidnaping, violence toward Unionists, and ripping up railroad tracks.[34]

Evidence of other disloyal bands, poorly armed but being drilled by Confederate deserters and recruiting officers, then surfaced. "I have good reason to believe," reported the colonel of the Scott County expedition, "that the real object is to bring upon the Southern & Central portions of this state, the same system of Guerilla warfare lately prevailing in Mo Ky & Tenn." Indeed, Governor Richard Yates and local provost marshals received numerous reports of intimidation and depredations by gangs of deserters, copperheads, and guerrillas, some of them home grown, others from Missouri. Yates had to rely on local militia to deal with most of the threats, his full military powers being restricted to "cases of actual insurrection."[35]

Insurrection, as such, never occurred in Illinois, but unrest continued, much of it attributed to the Clingman gang. The shadowy Thomas L. Clingman—sometimes identified as a Confederate officer—had assembled 200 to 300 "desperate characters" in Fayette and Montgomery counties, in the south-central part of the state. The gang tore up railroad tracks, stole horses, committed robberies, forced people to swear allegiance to the Confederacy, and generally terrorized the populace throughout the summer of 1864. Estimates put the number of veteran Missouri guerrillas in Clingman's gang at about 25, the rest being copperheads and "refugees." Some home guards stood up to them, though usually with disastrous consequences. Governor Yates finally asked General William Rosecrans, the new commander at St. Louis, for

150 Union soldiers to break up the gang. Rosecrans replied that he had no men to spare from Missouri, but that he would release the necessary numbers from guard duty at the Alton military prison, in southwestern Illinois.[36]

The mounting pressure forced Clingman's men to scatter. Smaller gangs ranged across the state through the remainder of the year, but a combination of home guards, militia, and Union troops gradually put them down. Except for a final brief flareup in early November, seemingly inspired by the presidential election, most of the unrest in Illinois ended when Price retreated from Missouri.[37]

By that time, the rebel war in Arkansas had largely floundered, too, but only after a brutal struggle. The Federals made impressive gains in the closing months of 1863 by capturing Fort Smith, Pine Bluff, and the state capital of Little Rock. An ever more desperate effort was required of the rebels just to hang on, and desperate it became. As in Missouri, 1864 was the most deadly year of the war for Arkansans.[38]

The rebels struck back in northwestern Arkansas by trying to recapture Fort Smith. The Confederacy's Indian allies played an important role in that operation. Stand Watie's Cherokee and Colonel Sampson N. Folsom's Choctaw operated officially as conventional regiments, but they specialized in raids and ambushes. As one Creek Confederate acknowledged, "It was a kind of warfare that was suited to the Indian character." Intent on isolating the fort, they cut telegraph lines to St. Louis and Little Rock and attacked all but the strongest supply trains sent south to Fort Smith from Fort Scott or out of Missouri through Fayetteville. Overland columns, steamboats dispatched up the Arkansas River from Little Rock, and a string of Union outposts along the river also became targets. The Indians wiped out foraging and haying parties from Fort Smith, and the general upheaval they created allowed independent guerrilla bands and bushwhackers to operate openly in the region.[39]

The level of Union consternation could be measured by the steps taken to halt these outrages. General John McNeil, who now directed the District of the Frontier from Fort Smith, issued a public warning in November 1863: "Bush-Whackers, BEWARE!" All "organized" and legitimate rebel resistance had been eliminated in the region, McNeil proclaimed. What remained was the "common foe of mankind—the guerrilla and bush-whacker." For every telegraph line cut, he warned, a "bush-whacking prisoner" would be hanged at that pole. Mindful of the civilians who shielded these rogues, he also vowed to burn the nearest "disloyal" house to where a wire had been cut. Jefferson Davis, in

BUSH-WHACKERS,
BEWARE!

HEAD QUARTERS DIST. OF THE FRONTIER,
Fort Smith, Ark., Nov. 17, 1863.

The organized forces of the enemy having been driven out of the country in our rear, and there being none on our lines of Telegraphic and Mail Communications, except that common foe of mankind—the guerrilla and bush-whacker—and the cutting of telegraph wires being now the act of these men alone—men who have no claim to be treated as soldiers, and are entitled to none of the rights accorded by the laws of war to honorable belligerents, it is hereby ordered that, hereafter, in every instance, the cutting of the telegraph wire shall be considered the deed of bush-whackers, and for every such act some bush-whacking prisoner shall have withdrawn from him, that mercy which induced the holding of him as a prisoner, and he shall be hung at the post where the wire is cut; and as many bush-whackers shall be so hung as there are places where the wire is cut.

The nearest house to the place where the wire is cut, if the property of a disloyal man, and within ten miles, shall be burned.

BY COMMAND OF BRIG. GEN'L JOHN McNEIL.

JOS. T. TATUM,
Act'g Ass't Adj't General.

General John McNeil gave fair warning to rebel guerrillas in the vicinity of Fort Smith, Arkansas. Courtesy The Littlejohn Collection at Wofford College.

his annual message to the Confederate Congress that December, used McNeil's proclamation, along with the actions of Benjamin Butler and John B. Turchin, as examples of the "terrible barbarities" practiced by the Union army.[40]

Barbarous or not, similar steps became necessary throughout the area of occupation. The Union commander at Little Rock fumed over the inability of 230 troops to protect the telegraph lines and loyal citizens around Clarksville, located midway between Fort Smith and Little Rock. "I want those guerrillas captured, killed, or dispersed," he exclaimed in April 1864 to the local commander. "Where do 300 or 400 guerillas come from? . . . You done well in capturing 23. You will do better by killing or capturing the rest." To the east, he had to protect the short but crucial Memphis and Little Rock Railroad, which connected the capital to the White River. It required a regiment of cavalry posted at every bridge "to prevent the Guerillas from burning them." Altogether, 9,000 Union cavalry at Little Rock patrolled the line, with another 2,500 cavalry and two regiments of mounted infantry at Pine Bluff, located to the south of Little Rock, available if needed. People said the Federals held the towns while rebel guerrillas ruled the countryside. A Union officer at Little Rock observed in June: "The country seems to have degenerated into bushwhackers. It is hardly safe to go out of our lines a mile."[41]

Not content to harass the Federals on the periphery of the occupied area, other guerrilla bands operated well within Union lines. Colonel Robert R. Livingston and his 1st Nebraska Cavalry patrolled a crucial part of the Missouri border north of Little Rock. The colonel knew what was expected of him. "My business here is to put down rebellion and exterminate guerrillas," he proclaimed early in 1864. He eliminated several hundred guerrillas by offering amnesty to all "bushwhackers"— whether "armed citizens, furloughed soldiers, or deserters from either army"—who surrendered and took the Union oath. All who remained in arms, especially if devoting themselves to "murder and pillage," could expect harsh treatment.[42]

Around Fayetteville, Buck Brown's band continued to cause mischief for Colonel Marcus LaRue Harrison's 1st Arkansas Cavalry. Indeed, Harrison had time for little else through 1864 than to defend his post and protect local Unionists. Much of Fayetteville had been leveled during two years of war. Many homes and buildings had been burned, and breastworks dominated the center of town. Not that Harrison could afford to sit comfortably behind his fortifications. He had orders from

General McNeil to hunt guerrillas in the bush. Even so, the regiment had no realistic chance of crushing the rebels. Having narrowly missed capturing Brown at a known rendezvous point, the soldiers vented their frustration by burning his home.[43]

George W. Rutherford, William Tucker "Tuck" Smith, Pleasant W. Buchanan, and at least a dozen other guerrilla chiefs prowled northern Arkansas counties. These men could not hope to dislodge the Federals on their own, but they tied down many Union troops and extracted a high financial price. On the broadest strategic level, they significantly confounded Federal plans, including hopes of controlling the Arkansas River. They also thwarted more limited Union intentions, sometimes in the most startling ways. Colonel Harrison, having already burned Buck Brown's home, decided in the summer of 1864 to destroy the gristmills in northwestern Arkansas, well-known rendezvous points and sources of supplies for the guerrillas. "The disabling of the mills," Harrison explained, "causes more writhing among bushwhackers than any other mode of attack." This was doubtless true, but the action ran counter to one of Harrison's chief responsibilities, which was to protect and maintain the mills.[44]

Colonel Harrison employed a more original idea for protecting Unionists in his district. He established self-contained communities of fifty families each on abandoned or confiscated rebel lands. This allowed Unionists to live within range of the army's protection, but Harrison also armed the settlers, helped them to fortify their "farm colonies," and authorized them to serve as home guards. In other times and other places, such settlements would be called "kibbutzim" and "strategic hamlets." Harrison's armed farmers occasionally took the field as adjuncts in his guerrilla hunts. The experiment was tried elsewhere in northern Arkansas, but Harrison's colonies enjoyed the most success. He authorized seventeen different settlements, although it is unclear how many were established.[45]

President Lincoln tried to mobilize Arkansas Unionists as a political force by establishing a loyal government in Little Rock. Although its influence was confined almost entirely to the northern half of the state, the new government inspired enough confidence for additional Unionists to enlist in the army, serve as scouts and guides, and form guerrilla companies. The Williams "clan" of Conway County became central Arkansas's most active Unionist band. A shadowy figure named Fenton led a company of men in the mountains between Little Rock and Russellville, to the west of the capital. A Union officer noted that

Fenton's band "sallied forth to deal justice to those who misused their families." Old-fashioned vigilantes also continued to capture and execute rebel bushwhackers, often with federal approval. Some Union officers, while admiring the pluck of these citizens, feared they were no match for hardened rebel guerrillas.[46]

Yet the defining element for Arkansas in 1864 became the surge of violence and banditry. "Bushwhackers, murderers and thieves" ruled the land in a "reign of terror." One rebel guerrilla lamented: "It was not a matter of principle that they were in the war; they did not care for either side, it was only for the purpose of robbing and plundering. That class of men were found on both sides." The scale, randomness, and gratuitous nature of the violence startled people even after three years of war. Granted, it is difficult to measure such things, and to say that a murder committed in 1864 was more heinous than a murder committed in 1861 defies logic. Yet, the people who experienced or witnessed guerrilla violence noted the difference. Some sort of ethical dam, if leaking before 1864, seemed to burst after the Lawrence raid. Whereas the earlier guerrilla war had often been inspired by a desire for "supremacy and revenge," later enmities became fueled by "heartless cruelty" and "intense bitterness." An Arkansas guerrilla looked back on 1863–64 as the "dark days" of the war, "when protection of the law . . . was in abeyance."[47]

Growing desertion rates in both armies partly explain the tone. Although Confederates continued to leave the army to defend homes and families against the "barbarous cruelty" of Union soldiers and Unionist guerrillas, deserters more often sought only plunder. The problem was already apparent by the summer of 1863. A band of nearly fifty rebel deserters—believed to be cooperating with the Federals—made "dayly and nightly" raids in the vicinity of Dardenelle, east of Fort Smith, to steal horses, saddles, guns, ammunition, and provisions. In nearby Clarksville, a band of two hundred deserters threatened to destroy the entire region. "Men who were original secessionists, the first to volunteer in the Confederate service," a citizen marveled, "are now to be found in the ranks of the enemy, and prowling through robbing and occasionally murdering their neighbors." Elsewhere, deserters became "perfect desperadoes," prepared to "kill a man for his horse or mule, rob & insult ladies" whose husbands were in the army. Arkansans asked the government to discharge or grant amnesty to these men. Thus freed of possible punishment, they reasoned, "disloyal" men might "quit the Jayhawkers" and engage in peaceful pursuits.[48]

More disturbing than this exploitation of the guerrilla war by armed thugs was the larger number of rebel guerrillas who crossed over to the dark side. The crimes of these men had less and less to do with the war, and more to do with acquiring riches or inflicting pain. They did not even pretend to be fighting for any "cause." A military commission at Batesville sentenced Gideon D. Bruce, a blacksmith by occupation, to hard labor for being a guerrilla, but his crimes had nothing to do with military operations. After serving with the Confederate cavalry earlier in the war, Bruce became a horse thief, plunderer, and worse. He and a "very bad man" named Ben Guess tortured and brazenly extorted money from a Unionist near Batesville. Dressed in Union uniforms, they aroused Wilford Baskett and his wife from their beds, accused Baskett of being a "d——d old Secesh," and demanded $750 from him. When he denied possessing any such sum, they called him a liar, dragged him outside to a rail fence, placed his neck between two rails, and "kicked and spurred" him. When Baskett continued to insist that he had no money, Bruce and Guess ransacked the house and frightened Mrs. Baskett into surrendering what money she had: $17.20. They then returned to Baskett, dragged him across the yard, and hung him from the limb of a peach tree. Twice they strung him up before releasing the pressure on his neck. They finally left him on the ground gasping for breath.[49]

The declining age of rebel guerrillas did not help matters. Like the followers of Bill Anderson, they joined the war for very different reasons than the more mature defenders of 1861. A Union chaplain at Fort Smith, summoned to comfort four Confederate bushwhackers who had been sentenced to death, was stunned both by the ages and the attitude of the criminals. The lads were graybeards compared to many Arkansas guerrillas in 1864, their average age being nineteen, but a military court had found them guilty of murdering a citizen and eight soldiers. They displayed no remorse for the crimes until shortly before their execution. Only then, Reverend Francis Springer reported, did they acknowledge having been "pretty bad boys." Even so, the youngest of them, who had killed twenty-one men "in search of adventure and fun," remained proud that "he had been deemed 'smart' in his tricks of mischief and merrymaking." All four lads, Springer realized, had, by the time of their capture, "become outlaws."[50]

Staunch rebels worried that such renegades tarnished the reputation of legitimate guerrillas and, by extension, the Confederate cause. One colonel called them "pirates" who "rob[bed] indiscriminately friend and foe." He complained to Jefferson Davis, "I do not wish to belong to a mob, or an army which, by its conduct, cannot be distinguished from one." A junior officer who had "opposed . . . the bush whacking policy from the start," urged friends inclined to the bush to join the army, where "they could serve their Country to profit."[51]

Other guerrillas condemned such unrestrained men as Joseph Harris. The Washington County farmer had been a Union man before federal troops confiscated his slaves and much other property in late 1862. He then resolved "to rob and jayhawk until he got his property all back again." He joined Buck Brown's company, but finding himself subject to discipline and restraint there, Harris began an independent career of looting and intimidating Unionists. He became so notorious for abusing women and children that Brown several times sent men in search of him with orders to hang the renegade. Another patriotic partisan captain, outraged when citizens falsely accused his men of stealing horses, declared, "There has been men in the country committing crimes on my credit, and if I find them the weather is two hot to Ride horses to headquarters with any such caracters."[52]

By contrast, law-abiding guerrillas took pride in their own restraint. Joe Bailey and about a dozen comrades rode into southern Missouri in the fall of 1864 looking for James M. Moore, who had led several "houseburning and murderous raids" into Arkansas. Not finding Moore at home, the rebels evicted his wife and two children from the house before torching it. Bailey later said he regretted burning the Moore home, not for Moore's sake, but because of his innocent family. Unfortunately, he explained in a remarkably honest statement of his motivation, "that was war," and he and his comrades had shown far more compassion than tories who attacked Confederate families. "We could have burned many more homes had we chosen to do so," he insisted, "but we were content with the burning of one."[53]

Most people did not appreciate such fine gradations of mercy; they only wanted the guerrilla war, in all of its manifestations, to end. One Arkansan had nearly left the army to fight as a guerrilla when he thought better of it. He heard that Union soldiers had ordered his wife and other women in his neighborhood out of their homes, but he feared that a guerrilla response would only elicit "worse" behavior from the Federals. "I believe that bushwhacking has been the main cause of all the killing and burning that has been done," he told his wife. He wished that all deserters, even men who had turned bushwhacker to defend their homes, would return to the ranks. Another Arkansan in similar circumstances asserted, "The least a soldier is about his house the better his family comes off with the enemy. They then have no excuse that he is bushwhacking or doing any mischief."[54]

Unprecedented numbers of Arkansans left the state in 1864. The majority fled not, as in the past, because they feared the general destructiveness of war, but because of crime and lawlessness. Unionists bore the brunt of it, though "bushwhackers and thieves" rode roughshod over defenseless people of all political persuasions. A hapless Confederate concluded that noncombatants were caught between the "Hawk & Buzzard."[55]

More fatefully, Arkansas Confederates began to think Union occupation might be preferable to unchecked violence. A resident of southern Arkansas said he would have felt "more safe" under federal rule. A woman in the northern part of the state agreed. "The whole country is full of robbers and murderers," she reported in late February 1864. Roaming bands of deserters from both armies preyed on both sides, regardless of loyalties. "Some of our citizens have been robbed and then hung off in the woods, where the family would not find them for days," she wrote; "others hung till almost dead and some burned nearly to death and then released." Conditions had deteriorated to the point that she, too, welcomed Union occupation—"anything for Peace and established Laws again." Both the local Union and Confederate commanders had executed several "jayhawkers" and were endeavoring to scatter the rest of them, but she feared that Arkansas was too "full of bad men to burn, plunder, and rob."[56]

Northern Arkansas got some relief when Price's raid failed. The region slowly returned to Union control, and this time, the Federals did not relinquish it. They resumed antiguerrilla operations, and while things went slowly at first in the western half of the state, the number of guerrillas around Little Rock had declined noticeably by the end of 1864. A resumption of summary executions speeded the process. "You don't often see an account in the newspapers of the punishment of Bushwhackers," an Iowa soldier informed his father, *but that is no sign that it is not done.*" The Iowan wished the army would follow Sherman's example at Atlanta and burn Little Rock. He wanted "the torch in one hand and the sword in the other." The Union had been "playing" with the rebels long enough. It was time to make *"war in earnest."*[57]

Louisiana could have been a different story. Arkansas suffered because of its proximity to Missouri and the inability of the Union army to establish a secure center of occupation. By contrast, federal troops in the Bayou State allowed a manageable military situation to lurch out of control. With Lincoln hoping in the fall of 1863 to expand his experiment in southern reconstruction by establishing a loyal government in Louisiana, the army thought to demonstrate federal might with a series of raids that extended into 1864. Military commanders assumed the rebel populace would crack with increased pressure and support the new state government, but they miscalculated. Much of the resulting meanness and destruction seemed senseless, as when soldiers drove children from a schoolhouse in eastern Louisiana and burned their books and slates. Rather than buckle under, Louisiana rebels and their guerrillas resisted.[58]

Admiral David Porter, who tended, if anything, toward optimism, confessed to Gideon Welles in October 1863, "If I were to remove a single vessel from their stations the passage of transports [on the lower Mississippi] would be stopped." Porter blamed the situation on the army's failure "to break the guerrillas up," but both army and navy had their hands full. Besides their usual destructive operations, irregulars had also begun to attack "leased" plantations. The U.S. government had unintentionally provided these targets by allowing northern investors to work confiscated rebel land along the Mississippi River with refugee slaves. The Union army protected the workers—often with black troops—but the system proved largely unworkable in a war zone. Most northern investors pulled out after a few months, and many workers and black guards were killed or kidnaped in guerrilla raids. The refugee camps, themselves, became rebel targets.[59]

With as many as seven thousand white Louisianians serving in the Union army, lots of Unionist families also remained vulnerable. Homeless refugees wandered everywhere, and the sight of so many women and children—often widows and orphans—led Union soldiers to give thanks that "the horrors of war" were confined to the South. "The husband of one of the women," reported an Ohio soldier of a group of refugees, "was taken from his own house by a band of rebel guerrillas and hanged a few rods from the house . . . and left him hang[ing] in the presence of his wife and children. [Two] sons of another woman . . . were shot at the same time. They were robbed of everything."[60]

Nevertheless, through the remainder of 1863, most Union troops regarded guerrillas as more nuisance than danger. They acknowledged the elusiveness of their shadowy foe but fancied that one good sweep of southern Louisiana's swamps would "put an end to their doing mischief." Soldiers and sailors on gunboats denied that the attacks on them did any damage. If anything, they injured the Confederate cause by turning businessmen who depended on river traffic against the government. In the end, it only amounted to tedious scouting duty and "a great deal of skirmishing." "The rebellion is almost *played out* [in Louisiana]," rejoiced a Union soldier the day after Christmas.[61]

A reduction in the number of partisan ranger battalions in Louisiana also took some zip out of rebel resistance. Two of Jefferson Davis's nephews found difficulty getting commissions as rangers in the state. When Jefferson Davis Bradford resigned from the army to raise a partisan band in Louisiana, the president approved his request but regretted that he had not chosen a "path more likely to lead to professional distinction and future promise." When Patrick F. Keary, the second nephew, asked to raise a ranger battalion, he had to settle for a battalion of "sharpshooters," and even that unit was dissolved at the end of 1863. By the time Colonel James H. Wingfield's famous 9th Partisan Ranger Battalion, containing the most effective rangers in the state, was designated the 3rd Louisiana Cavalry in mid-1864, few units of any consequence remained. Only a few consolidated cavalry regiments operating on detached service under Colonel John S. Scott showed occasional flashes of spirit and daring.[62]

Kirby Smith went so far as to solicit help from Quantrill's command, before it left Texas, to police the cotton trade in northeastern Louisiana. The guerrillas enjoyed some success arresting cotton thieves and speculators, with time left over to raid leased plantations and attack Union patrols. They also hanged an unknown number of "spies" and speculators. However, typical of the growing fashion, they made few distinctions between friends and foes. They apparently plundered several rebel farms in search of food and hanged at least one prominent Confederate citizen. The Federals sent Ellet's Marine Brigade to deal with them, but the marines failed to corral the Missourians. Indeed, the guerrillas eventually drove out Ellet's men and recaptured much cotton and livestock confiscated by the marines. In both cases, citizens suffered the most. Kirby Smith responded to complaints about the "serious depredations" by telling the Missourians to go home.[63]

Louisiana's gravest problems began when both sides attempted to enforce conscription. The Federals stumbled by wedding their draft to the U.S. loyalty oath: Men who swore their loyalty became eligible for the draft. This policy, initiated in 1863, became one of the most hated parts of Union occupation. It gave antigovernment Confederates another reason to resist the Federals, and even some Unionists complained. Many Louisianians had taken the Union oath as a matter of expediency to protect their property and businesses. The threat of conscription turned some of them back to the Confederacy.[64]

Rebel conscription caused more alarm. It seldom drove men to the

Federals, where they would only become fodder for a different army. Rather, it produced an internal, self-styled "jayhawker" movement across the state. The problem first surfaced in early 1863, when Unionists fleeing rebel conscription joined together in the swamps of southern Louisiana. By early 1864, what began as a nuisance had become a crisis, especially where draft dodgers and outlaws joined forces with deserters. It marked one of the most dangerous instances of guerrilla outlawry in the South, and if the legitimate guerrilla war had not directly inspired the proliferation of these gangs, it certainly suggested a means of survival. Richard Taylor redeployed whole battalions and regiments of troops to control the uprising, with orders to shoot "every man found with arms in hands."[65]

The resulting turmoil touched all parts of the state. In central and northern Louisiana, General Henry W. Allen, soon to be governor, reported the country around Alexandria "full of deserters and runaway conscripts." As early as October 1863, rumors put the number at eight thousand. What portion of these men formed guerrilla resistance bands is unclear, but they certainly did so in the northeastern parishes. The Confederate army used all means to rid the region of these southern jayhawkers, including loosing dogs to track them, as they would runaway slaves. General St. John Richardson Liddell, finding "demoralization on every side," allowed men who had deserted regiments in Virginia and Tennessee to join his cavalry. He knew the main interest of many of them was "legalized plunder, with the smallest possible amount of service or danger to themselves," but he hoped to limit, if not eliminate, their excesses by keeping a close eye on them. Liddell succeeded in running the chief jayhawker captain, Bob Taliaferro, into the swamps.[66]

Rebellion proved harder to contain in southern Louisiana. Some of the first calls for guerrilla defenders came from that area, where as early as 1861 men of "ungovernable tempers ready for the blackest deeds" refused to support the Confederacy. By 1864, mixed bands of draft dodgers, hard-core desperadoes, deserters, and runaway slaves roamed a vast no-man's-land between the Mississippi River and the Texas border. Both the Union and Confederate governments proclaimed them a threat to law and order. "We have been and still are much alarmed about the Jay-hawkers, who are very bad," a resident of southeastern Louisiana declared. "They commit all kinds of outrages upon men, women and children, rob, murder and rape. Oh, it is dreadful!" This woman knew of twelve people who had been killed at Lafayette, to the west of her. A self-described "Jayhawker killer" of the 4th Louisiana Cavalry boasted that his regiment was busy "exterminating the race" in that very region, but the danger continued. Communities had to be "strongly guarded all night" against attack.[67]

Ozème Carrière, a Creole deserter from the Confederate army, led the largest and toughest of the gangs. He operated out of St. Landry Parish in a region that had been a haven for rustlers and "scoundrels" of every description well before the war. By early 1864, Carrière reportedly had one thousand men. "It is no longer the case of a few isolated desperadoes," the Confederate conscription officer for that area warned; "the entire community . . . is implicated in these organizations. . . . Carrière is daily becoming more and more popular with the masses, and that every day serves to increase his gang."[68]

At first, Carrière's raids were bloodless, undertaken with caution and intended to secure only weapons and food from Confederate foes. This made him popular with the "masses." However, both targets and objectives changed with his growing power. Bold daylight raids and plain banditry became commonplace; murder and arson joined the repertoire. Hoping to harness this potential fifth column as "scouts," the Union army tried to enlist Carrière, but he rebuffed them. Meanwhile, the Confederate army directed a major offensive against his and like bands. By March 1864, it had succeeded in "capturing and killing . . . [and] hanging" many outlaws. Much of the populace, by now disabused of early perceptions of Carrière as a Robin Hood, also turned against him. Thus injured in numbers and repute, his band gradually withered, although it remained a source of trouble through the remainder of the year.[69]

If any amusement could be found in this bitter contest, it would have to come from William Garig's enduring talent for avoiding the war. Still serving in southern Louisiana—mostly around Baton Rouge—Garig continued to participate in the conflict only when it suited him. He began 1864 by joining several scouting expeditions but managed to sneak off long enough on January 5 to enjoy a party at the home of a local doctor. On January 14, he arrested a draft dodger but then slipped out of camp with two friends to spend the night at "a house away out in the woods." It is unclear if he slept with one of the "three young Ladys" who lived there, but he was awakened by one of his hostesses early in the morning to be told Yankees were approaching the house. The three men quickly dressed, but with no time to escape, they scrambled to conceal themselves until the Federals left. Garig climbed up the chimney. So it went for the remainder of the year: brief spurts of military or constabulary activity with plenty of time devoted to playing cards, drinking, attending parties, selling or swapping mules and cotton, and, of course, visiting the ladies. "I fooled with her nearly all night," he re-corded of one evening's tryst. "I kissed her as much as I wanted & she is a right sweet little thing. I stayed all night."[70]

The situation did not unravel completely for the Federals until the Red River campaign of March–May 1864. This attempt to extend the destruction and plundering northward to Shreveport concentrated on the confiscation and burning of cotton, but all variety of deviltry re-sulted. Had the campaign succeeded, the overall Union policy might have worked, too. Its failure—indeed, the campaign itself—only stirred guerrilla defenders.[71]

Following this fiasco, Unionists warned General Nathaniel Banks that the rebels meant to "burn all the cotton gins and sugar houses in Louisiana and along the Mississippi River," and that guerrilla warfare would be "organized on a large scale and encouraged in every possible way." They were right. Rebel resistance revived in the lower Mississippi valley, where Colonel Scott directed military operations for the remain-der of the year. Unable fully to defend the region with his cavalry, he sanctioned new militia bands and allowed self-styled partisans to take independent action. The war became more "ruthless" on both sides. The Federals renewed their raids, put a bounty of ten thousand dollars on Scott's head, hanged captured guerrillas, and assigned additional troops to "get shet of Bush Whackers," but they failed to contain the situation.[72]

By contrast, the war in Texas seemed tame, although the potential for "tory" uprisings and lawlessness continued through 1864. "Every body is either in the militia, or bush-whacking, or engaged in Govt employ," a Confederate marveled from the hill country around Austin. Far too many people fit the bushwhacker category. Unionists probably suffered most from random violence, but this only raised fears of retaliation among rebels and the prospect that the "barbarity" of the Missouri and Arkansas wars would inflame the state. Should that happen, Confeder-ates meant to be ready. "Let Anarchy come," roared one rebel. "To hoist the black flag suits my complaint." Texas had an image as a rough-and-tumble place, even for people who had never been there.[73]

The gravest concerns surfaced among disenchanted antigovern-ment Confederates in northern Texas. No sooner had the early signs of Unionism been suppressed by the Gainesville hangings than other Unionists joined with Confederate outcasts to form outlaw bands in the region. They included the usual draft evaders, deserters, and outlaws, and by the fall of 1863, their numbers had grown to dangerous levels. What made the threat particularly worrisome was that it came precisely in that part of the state most vulnerable to Indian attack and northern invasion, either by jayhawkers out of Kansas or Union soldiers out of Arkansas and Louisiana.[74]

Texans called them "brush men," and their presence became a difficult military problem for the rebels. As early as October 1863, Henry McCulloch estimated that three principal gangs, totaling as many as nine hundred men, caused most of the trouble. This number equaled nearly half of his own force. McCulloch had no way to tabulate the number of smaller bands scattered across the great expanse of northern Texas. The combined force very likely outnumbered him. The veteran Indian fighter knew something about war in the bush, but he had not bargained on anything like this situation.[75]

McCulloch tried every tactic available to him. He negotiated with the guerrilla leaders, most notably Henry Boren, a "desperate character" who led as many as five hundred "deserters, skulkers and bad men" in Collins County. McCulloch offered amnesty to deserters who would rejoin the army and guaranteed the safety of their families and property. The appeal brought hundreds of men in from the bush, though not the distrustful Boren. McCulloch organized a special, five hundred–man "Brush Battalion" to break up the remaining gangs, but it proved ineffective. He recruited much of the battalion from among his repentant deserters, which should have worked to his advantage. Unfortunately for the peace of the region, many of the men, while glad to leave the bush, had not lost their lust for booty. When disciplined for theft, the former deserters deserted again. By mid-March 1864, with fewer than two-fifths of the Brush Battalion still in service, McCulloch abandoned the experiment.[76]

McCulloch's misadventures with Quantrill ended at about the same time, which doubtless brought some relief. Still, the inability of McCulloch's troops to remedy the root problems increased war weariness among Confederates in northern Texas. Outlawry remained more manageable elsewhere in the state, but even without the complicating elements of a full-blown guerrilla war, the situation remained precarious. The district military commander reported the murder of some twenty men over a period of a few months near Fredericksburg. "Some had been waylaid and shot," he detailed in September 1864; "others taken from their homes at the dead hour of midnight and hung, and their houses robbed; and some had been mobbed and murdered in jail and in irons. No man felt secure—even at home."[77]

Thomas E. Bramlette meant to save Kentucky for the Union, but by late 1863, the state lay so far behind the Union advance that rebel guerrillas "infested" or had "complete possession" of many communities. The instability threatened Union control of the entire middle border, even the army's advance into Alabama and Georgia. Bramlette, the newly elected governor, acted decisively by enlarging his state militia to combat the menace. He decreed that five rebel citizens be arrested and held hostage for every loyal citizen taken by the guerrillas. He collected reparations from rebel citizens for damage done to Unionist property. Additionally, any citizen who encouraged or assisted rebel guerrillas or who failed to report their presence in a neighborhood would be fined up to ten thousand dollars and imprisoned for six to twelve months. The severe sanctions pleased Ulysses S. Grant, who had issued identical orders to his Military Division of the Mississippi, which included Kentucky. Grant rewarded the tough-minded governor by letting "civil law" determine economic sanctions in the state.[1]

However, just when it looked like Bramlette would succeed, John Hunt Morgan escaped from the Ohio penitentiary. Imagine the uproar. "The Pride of Kentucky is free once again!" his admirers exalted. Journalists and poets celebrated the escape of their Count of Monte Cristo and predicted a new dawn for Confederate hopes in Kentucky: "Then woe to the Northerner who crosses our path; For Morgan's avengers still cherish their wrath!" The majority of his old brigade remained imprisoned, but thousands more rebels volunteered to be "Morgan men." Soldiers, sailors, and entire companies tried, as in the past, to transfer to partisan service. With most requests still being denied by the government, men risked becoming "deserters" to serve with the "Great Raider." Former partisan rangers whose companies had been disbanded or thrown into the army also turned up, as did home guards and men who had been sidelined by wounds, discharges, or paroles.[2]

In June 1864, barely six months after his escape, Morgan led a raid into Kentucky from his Virginia camp. The foray disintegrated into pillage and looting. Many of the new officers and men lacked even the tenuous discipline of the old brigade. Morgan acknowledged their "disgraceful" behavior, although he insisted that a few men had tarnished the image of the many. The Confederate government, which had discouraged Morgan from taking the field in the first place, suspended him from command. "He is nothing . . . but a Robber," decided a relation of Edmund Ruffin, "wholly unfit for his present position—or any other of honour or responsibility." By the time Morgan died in an ambush three months later, he had come to symbolize the deterioration of the guerrilla war. "Am perfectly disgusted with Morganism. Am ashamed to be caught in such company," admitted one of his men. "There is honor for his bravery, love for his devotion to a good cause, admiration for his honorable exploits, & censure for his misdeeds!"[3]

The raid only convinced Kentucky Unionists that they required large numbers of federal soldiers to maintain peace and order. Otherwise, they could do no more than hunker down, ward off attacks, and hold on until Confederate armies elsewhere had been defeated. This also appeared to be Governor Bramlette's thinking when he made each county responsible for its own defense. In places already overrun by guerrillas, people doubted the wisdom of this approach. Capable men, qualified to raise or lead local companies, held back for fear of retaliation. Farmers dared not plow their fields without hanging a pistol on the horse's harness. And Morgan's raid had not been the only one that spring and early summer. In March and April, General Nathan Forrest's cavalry rampaged through western Tennessee and Kentucky. The Kentucky leg of his raid, which reached as far north as Paducah, was largely a diversion for the more important operation in Tennessee, but it inspired a surge in guerrilla activity.[4]

Recent federal policies also discouraged, not to say antagonized, white Kentuckians. First, the U.S. Congress made Kentucky blacks—both slaves and free—eligible for military conscription. Quite aside from the discontent this stirred among slaveholders—many of whom also feared slave rebellions—Unionists knew that no act would more surely rally Kentucky rebels. It also caused defections from Unionist ranks when, in June, black troops entered western Kentucky to draft other blacks into the army. Were that not incitement enough, the soldiers also "entered private homes, broke open the doors, . . . insulted women, and plundered and searched generally." When the U.S. government then tried to conscript white men, many Kentuckians joined rebel guerrilla bands. "Most of the guerrilla parties now up the Cumberland are composed of men who were drafted for our service," Le Roy Fitch acknowledged. "They . . . say if they must fight at all they will fight for Jeff Davis."[5]

Into this atmosphere of discontent and desperation strode General Stephen G. Burbridge. A native Kentuckian, the thirty-two-year-old farmer and lawyer had fought at Shiloh and Vicksburg, but when given command of the District of Kentucky in February, he still had no experience against guerrillas. He received credit for turning back Morgan's June raid but seemed inclined to steer a conservative course in his treatment of rebels. A blistering letter from his department commander, William T. Sherman, ten days after Morgan withdrew, shook him from his reverie. Burbridge must take sterner measures to bring the "so-called partisans or guerrillas" under control. Sherman had earlier urged Bramlette to arrest suspected or potential guerrillas, but the governor had apparently considered such a "sweeping exhibition of power . . . rather arbitrary." Kentuckians were now paying the price, Sherman said, and the state appeared headed for "anarchy." Deep into his drive toward Atlanta, the general blanched at the thought of Morgan running loose in his rear. He outlined a plan of action for Burbridge and reminded him that guerrillas were "not soldiers but wild beasts unknown to the usages of war." Burbridge must arrest any man or woman suspected of encouraging or harboring guerrillas. The civil authorities should have done so long since, Sherman said. Now, the army would do it.[6]

Sherman's directives changed the course of the war in Kentucky. The next day, Burbridge issued orders to "break up entirely . . . bands of thieving guerillas" and arrest all citizens complicit in their operations. Four days later, on June 30, 1864, he asked Washington to give him control of the economic sanctions against guerrillas that Grant had ceded to civil authorities. That same day, he received further encouragement from Sherman. "Clear out the guerrillas, root, and branch, and banish vagabonds that, under the pretense of being Confederates, commit murder and highway robbery," Sherman urged. By then, Burbridge had also heard from President Lincoln, who gave him the broad military powers he desired. He should act "promptly and energetically" to arrest all "aiders and abettors of rebellion and treason," regardless, the message stated pointedly, of "rank or sex." On July 5, Lincoln backed Burbridge publicly with a proclamation that suspended the right of habeas corpus and imposed martial law in Kentucky.[7]

With Kentucky still "full of guerillas and alarm," Burbridge issued a more comprehensive antiguerrilla policy in mid-July. Four guerrilla prisoners would be shot for every Union man killed. Rebel sympathizers within five miles of any guerrilla action would be banished from their homes. Rebel property would be seized as "necessary" when guerrillas stole or destroyed government or private property. The government in Washington gave Burbridge broader latitude when, a few days after he issued his orders, Joseph Holt, a Kentucky native, judge advocate general of the army, and a close political ally of Lincoln, arrived as the president's personal envoy to survey the situation. On Holt's recommendation, Burbridge was allowed to arm employees of the Louisville and Nashville Railroad—the state's main artery—with repeating rifles to ward off guerrillas attacks. The president's recently announced amnesty program, designed to establish a loyal political base in rebellious states, was suspended in Kentucky. Holt reasoned that loyalty oaths, to which nine-tenths of Kentucky's known guerrillas had sworn, meant nothing to rebels. Holt had also recommended using two black regiments as guerrilla hunters, but his government thought that proposal too controversial.[8]

Burbridge acted briefly in partnership with another Union general who relished his suppression policy. Eleazer A. Paine commanded the westernmost part of Kentucky, beyond the Cumberland River. A strong abolitionist and a man of "nervous temperament" in his late forties, Paine had gained significant experience battling guerrillas in Missouri and Tennessee before his transfer to Kentucky. The West Pointer reportedly executed over two hundred guerrillas while commanding his post at Gallatin, Tennessee, but he enraged even local Unionists by arming black refugees to help repel guerrilla attacks and ordering whites to pay wages to fugitive slaves who worked for them. Rumors of shady financial dealings also circulated. The complaints about Paine grew so numerous that Grant tried to transfer him in early 1864, but no district commander would take him. Besides that, Paine counted President Lincoln as a personal friend. Consequently, half a year passed before he could be sent to Kentucky. He swiftly executed forty-three guerrillas in fifty-one days. No one in Washington objected, but public complaints followed when Paine allowed his men to confiscate property indiscriminately from loyal and disloyal citizens. So loud did the outcry become from both sides that Paine was removed from his Kentucky command in September.[9]

Burbridge, meanwhile, recognized no restraint. In October, he decided not to bother imprisoning or indicting guerrillas: All were to be shot when captured. He may have issued the order to protect officers who already followed this practice. Even Paine had gone through the motions of drumhead proceedings, but as early as May, one of Burbridge's division commanders had executed guerrillas for robbing and murdering two Union women. Going still further, this general had told his subordinates, "I would prefer, and will insist, that no regular guerrillas be sent in as prisoners; direct your command to deal with characters in a speedy and summary manner." Interestingly, Burbridge's mentor, William T. Sherman, for all his tough talk and action against guerrillas, believed that "the veriest demon" should be given a fair hearing, but he did not interfere in this instance.[10]

Not by chance, the October order came at the height of the presidential election season. Burbridge intended that nothing should hinder Lincoln's reelection in Kentucky. "I have used every means in my power to accomplish this end," he informed Joseph Holt, who served as Lincoln's political liaison to the state. Those "means" included the arrest of people who spoke against the Lincoln administration. With many of his regiments transferred to Georgia for the necessity of capturing Atlanta before election day, Burbridge took no chances. Governor Bramlette, bruised in any event by the controversy over black conscription and the renewed authority of the army in his state, protested Burbridge's overzealous policies. Confederate citizens spoke of his "atrocious crimes" and dubbed him "Bloody Burbridge."[11]

Despite the suppression policy, rebel guerrillas flourished in Kentucky. George M. Jessee, Jacob Bennett, and Tom Henry led the most prominent bands, but dozens of more obscure "captains" and "chiefs" made life miserable for the Federals. Newspaper reports and military records frequently mentioned Moses Webster, Samuel O. Berry, Jack Allen, Tom Morrow, and Green Sexton, while other men—Moore, Bowling, Marion, Alexander, Colvin, Ingram, Tucker, Cushman, Hickman— were known only by their surnames. Many of the smallest bands—generally eight to ten men—had no apparent leader, although, if captured, their members claimed to have operated at some time under Morgan or Adam Johnson. Guerrillas and raiders based primarily in Tennessee or Mississippi, such as Sol Street and Champ Ferguson, also made occasional appearances in the state. Forrest led another raid through southwestern Kentucky in October, his principal targets being river traffic and supply depots on the Tennessee River. A Forrest protégé, Kentucky native General Hylon B. Lyon, led a smaller raid in November and December to destroy county legal records and courthouses.[12]

That these men waged a violent and embittered war against Federals and Unionists goes without saying, but, as in the Trans-Mississippi, the war had also become increasingly confusing. It was more difficult to distinguish merciless thugs from legitimate guerrillas. People complained of "thieves and murderers," men of "villainous" character, but such words conveyed little meaning by 1864. Townspeople had been reporting a rise in "housebreaking," shoplifting, and common theft for more than a year. Blacks in town and country had become "unmanageable," and murder and robbery occurred everywhere. "Organized bands of thieves" belonging "to no army," they complained, had placed the countryside in a "most lawless state." Deserters from both armies swelled the ranks of roving gangs, which, Kentuckians quickly learned, made "no distinction between friend & foe." Perplexed local sheriffs and judges wondered if they or the army had ultimate responsibility for apprehending thieves and desperadoes. Some of them, harkening back to the early days of the war, when guerrillas were treated as a local law enforcement problem, offered cash rewards for the "arrest and apprehension" of the worst characters.[13]

One Unionist, commenting on how a string of robberies by guerrillas had ruined local businesses, identified the attackers as "mere marauders banded together, willing to rob and murder on either side." From the mountains of southeastern Kentucky came this report: "There's a great many Deserters from both armies, and have banded to gether for mutual protection and defies the civial authority and they are stealing and robing from helpless women and children." A petition for state protection from Harrodsburg claimed, "Our Banks are in danger. . . . [The Isiah] Coulters gang have sworn they will burn our town. . . . *These gangs* are enemies of all mankind—have no principles, fight for no cause & they ought to be exterminated." Civilians reeled in the face of such violent acts, committed "so far . . . from the seat of *public* war."[14]

The most renowned rebel guerrillas in Kentucky's 1864 war were Jerome Clark—better known as Sue Mundy—and Henry C. Magruder. They often operated together, and both men cooperated with Quantrill when he arrived in 1865. Both also mixed outlawry with genuine partisan operations. Mundy gained nearly legendary status through newspaper accounts of his exploits. The name "Sue" apparently came from a combination of twenty-year-old Clark's feminine features and stories about two disreputable women, both named Sue Mundy. One of the women, a well-known prostitute in Nelson County, occasionally served Morgan as a spy. The other, a black washerwoman in Louisville, was "notorious for her cruelty." George D. Prentice, editor of the *Louisville Daily Journal*, affixed their name to Clark for political reasons. Displeased with Burbridge's initially tepid response to the guerrilla crisis, he thought he could pressure the general to restore order by suggesting that a mere woman terrified the Union army.[15]

Jerome Clark came of good family in Simpson County, Kentucky. His father was a prosperous farmer, former postmaster, and state militia general. An uncle had been a congressman and diplomat, and Clark was related by marriage to John Mosby. He entered the war as a Confederate soldier but turned guerrilla when a friend, also a soldier, was shot and nearly killed after surrendering to the Federals. Or so the story went. Clark claimed to have joined Morgan's regiment to escape duty as an infantryman in Mississippi. Whatever the case, he became infamous for robbing trains, terrorizing Unionists, and murdering U.S. soldiers. Clark said the newspapers exaggerated his misdeeds, and it is certain that many unidentified guerrillas and outlaws committed crimes under the name "Sue Mundy." For all his alleged deviltry—committed mostly in Nelson, Marion, Henry, and Woodford counties—the only charges against him when captured in March 1865 were for wounding three soldiers of the 30th Wisconsin Infantry in an ambush. Still, that was enough to hang him, given his reputation, and Clark knew it. "He said there was enough published against him to kill him and he knew he would be killed," testified one of his captors.[16]

Clark seemed a choir boy next to Henry Magruder, both in manner and deed. They were captured at the same time, along with many of their men. Magruder had been severely wounded in the fight that brought them to heel, and so was not tried for another six months. The government charged him with seventeen murders, mostly of captured Union soldiers, but that was not half of his shameful ledger. In addition to the usual "robbing and plundering," he had reportedly raped the wife of a Union soldier and six "Young Ladies," the latter in their schoolhouse. There was also evidence that he had burned alive a black man. At the same time, there is no doubting Magruder's hatred for the Yankee invaders. He called more than one northerner a "G-d D——d yankee S-n of a b——h" as he snapped his revolver in their faces, and he vowed to "kill every G-d D——d blue coat" he encountered.[17]

Kentucky's woes also meant another season of suspense for the Midwest. Activity along the Ohio River from Cairo eastward threatened raids into both Illinois and Indiana, particularly Indiana. Having survived Morgan's 1863 raid, Hoosiers were understandably unnerved by his resurrection in 1864. Nor was their confidence bolstered when General Burbridge persistently asked Indiana to send troops to reinforce him. As it turned out, Indiana had seen the last of Morgan, but small incursions and incidents within the state reminded midwesterners that, while they might be spared the tramp of large rebel armies, they remained vulnerable to the guerrilla war.[18]

"We are experiencing serious apprehension of danger along our Southern border from the guerrilla operations," Indiana's adjutant general told Governor Bramlette in early July. The Hoosier wanted Bramlette to position *his* militia along the Ohio River to prevent Kentucky guerrillas from going north. Some citizens had sought permission to invade Kentucky and wipe out "marauding parties." One militia officer thought eastern Kentucky should be made part of the military District of Indiana so that Hoosiers could deal directly with the rebels. Navy gunboats patrolled the Ohio River, both to discourage guerrilla crossings into the north and to protect civilian river traffic. Commander Fitch described the Kentucky shore across from Evansville, near where rebels captured three steamers loaded with hundreds of "fat cattle" in the summer of 1864, as "swarming" with guerrillas. "They are getting in such large squads that I am afraid to leave this part of the river . . . for fear they will do serious damage," reported the veteran guerrilla fighter.[19]

Although it was hard to verify all sightings of rebel guerrillas in Indiana, reports of "strangers" passing through communities increased during the summer. Large numbers of them claimed to be "refugees" fleeing rebel conscription, but Hoosiers believed they were "mostly disloyal" people who hoped to spread rebellion. In fact, Adam Johnson acknowledged that, prior to Morgan's raid, "secret emissaries" had been "sent into the disaffected portions of Indiana and Illinois to aid uprisings of citizens who were favorable to the South or sick of the war." Violence at the hands of home-grown rebels continued as well. An "organized band of butternuts and thieves" in Washington County was thought responsible for the robbery and murder of "respected citizens" in southern Indiana. A band of 250 "mounted men," seemingly residents of southwestern Indiana, robbed Union men of money and weapons as far north as Terre Haute.[20]

The same mixture of legitimate and illegitimate guerrilla activity afflicted Tennessee, although the conventional war played a larger role in shaping its contours. With the great siege at Chattanooga ended in late November 1863, the most serious campaigning occurred around Knoxville, where General James Longstreet spent several months trying to recapture the city. Elsewhere, the Federals clung to what they had gained and guarded Tennessee's extensive network of rivers and railroads. Between October and December 1864, the Confederates launched several cavalry raids into the state, including modestly successful forays by Forrest, Philip D. Roddey, and Joseph Wheeler. Otherwise, guerrillas bore the brunt of the war.[21]

The fact that the Union held fast to Tennessee revealed the limitations of the rebel guerrilla war, but the Federals did not have an easy time of it. From Memphis to Knoxville, they enjoyed few respites. Block-houses along the railroads, guards on trains and river craft, patrols into the bush, retaliation against civilians—nothing could thwart the rebel menace. The elaborate defenses occupied the time of thousands of Union troops and wore them out physically and emotionally. Men occasionally depreciated the danger from "miserable sneaking Gurrillas" or confidently predicted that the guerrillas would soon be whipped, but most of them remained wary. "Tennessee is . . . & will be for some time full of Guerrillas & to this war I see no speedy end," judged a Minnesota volunteer in mid-September 1863. "Bushwhackers rule the day," acknowledged another soldier.[22]

Rebel guerrillas intimidated veterans and greenhorns alike. An Illinois soldier who had seen nearly a year of campaigning in Kentucky, Georgia, and Tennessee, and knew how dangerous guerrillas could be, momentarily froze when confronted by two "stalwart, hale, hearty bushwhackers." On mounted picket duty near his camp in central Tennessee, he spotted the two rebels riding casually toward him at dusk. "I was astonished at their bold appearance," he recalled. The picket raised his Spencer carbine to fire and ordered the rebels to halt. They responded, seemingly no more than fifty yards away, by brazenly turning their horses into the timber and trotting away. The picket shouted again for them to halt, but they rode on until disappearing below the brow of a hill. "I felt cheap enough," the soldier admitted. "Two bushwhackers had ridden in close gunshot of me, had refused to halt, and I had not shot at them even."[23]

A pious Iowa schoolteacher who had enlisted as one of the "100 Day" volunteers recruited by the Union army in early 1864 was offended by the profanity and vice of army life, but that was nothing compared to his brief exposure to the guerrilla war. First came the physical devastation it produced. Traveling down the Mississippi River to Memphis, he saw the wrecked hulks of several steamboats, victims of "rebel marauders," rotting along the banks. Assigned to chase guerrillas and guard the railroad line running eastward out of Memphis, he saw further evidence of the guerrilla war. "Houses burned or torn down, fences demolished, plantations laid waste," he noted in his diary. "One or two little villages where a few residents yet remained but altogether the country was either a waste or a wilderness." He preferred service in an army of a hundred thousand men to the "perilous" assignment of "picket duty among the bushwhackers."[24]

The situation in Tennessee worsened as more Union troops left that state for the Virginia and Georgia campaigns of early 1864. What was more, larger numbers of guerrillas than in Kentucky remained mindful of the war's purpose. The "infamous" Dunbar and Hawkins gangs relished stealing horses and intimidating Unionists, but they also captured steamboats and fired into Union transport boats on the Cumberland River. One of Dunbar's young followers, twenty-two-year-old Oscar Scarborough, even had a Confederate flag tattooed on his right arm. A group of twenty spirited "young men" from Hickman and Humphreys counties, west of Nashville, occasionally stole horses, and one of them had murdered a man. However, when finally captured and tried as guerrillas, the boys insisted they were not "bush riders." The principal charge against them was the destruction of three circular saws and an enormous stockpile of wood, the whole worth $2,500. They explained their actions by saying, "It would be a loss to the Federal Government and . . . prevent the supply of wood on the [rail]road."[25]

Tennessee rebels considered the political ramifications of their actions, too. Guerrillas could not claim all of the credit for Andrew Johnson's failure to install a loyal government in Tennessee by mid-1864, but they certainly contributed to the air of insecurity that plagued his efforts. A resident of western Tennessee told Johnson as early as October 1863 that it was "idle to talk about . . . reestablishing civil authority" until people could be protected from "the depredations of Guerilla bands." Such elementary acts as disrupting local elections, burning courthouse records, and threatening public officials profoundly affected public morale. Unionists anticipated a rise in the violence as the presidential election of 1864 approached, an election in which Johnson would be Abraham Lincoln's running mate. When Johnson tried to create a statewide militia to suppress "marauding bands" in September, many local officials charged with enrolling men—usually justices of the peace—begged to be relieved of the duty. They feared being kidnaped or assassinated.[26]

Guerrilla reprisals against blacks might also be regarded as political statements. Much of the brutality resulted from the guerrillas' responsibilities as enforcers of law and order, a growing role for them as roaming and "straggling negroes" offered ever more "insolence and threats" to white people. Such violence rose noticeably, as it had in Kentucky, when the Union army enlisted black soldiers. Several thousand black troops served in Tennessee by 1864, and they became special targets of both conventional and irregular rebel forces. The most atrocious act involving Tennessee guerrillas occurred at Saltville, Virginia. Champ Ferguson's company happened to be in the southwestern Virginia town when Union troops tried to capture its vital saltworks in October 1864.

After driving off the attacking force, which contained parts of two black regiments, the Confederates, including Ferguson, stalked the battlefield and executed the wounded. They shot both blacks and whites, but they made particular targets of the former. At least forty-six black soldiers died at their hands.[27]

Yet, the epicenter of Tennessee's guerrilla war remained the entrenched struggle between rebels and Unionists. There, also, appeared the surest signs of moral deterioration. Unlike Kentucky, where Unionists tended to rely on the army and organized militia to protect them, Tennesseans had offered stout resistance from the start of the war. Consequently, the sad pattern of retaliation that gave the lie to any pretense of nobility in guerrilla warfare convulsed the Volunteer State. Champ Ferguson, for one, claimed to kill only those men who wanted to kill him, but his name froze every Unionist heart. People plucky enough to defy him generally suffered for it. The family of John B. Rodgers weathered robbery and persecution throughout the war, but the heaviest blow landed in the latter part of 1863. While Rodgers was away from home, a portion of Ferguson's band "assaulted" his wife and seventeen-year-old daughter "with guns and pistols." They apparently did not rape the women, but they stripped them of their clothing while some twenty to thirty other men ransacked the house. Rebel neighbors rarely showed sympathy for such victims. Rather, they "delighted at the destruction of the property of a union man."[28]

Unionist guerrillas and home guards who "vowed eternal vengeance" against former neighbors made sure the majority rebel population remained equally demoralized. Some people thought self-appointed "home guards" the toughest customers. Union army officers often denounced their crimes and violent methods of enforcing Union rule, but they seldom disbanded them. A Confederate cavalryman assigned to break them up insisted, "The worst enemies by all odds, and the ones for whom the people have the greatest dread, are those who call themselves 'home guards,' but who are simply organized bands of bushwhackers and robbers." A Confederate surgeon in Georgia worried about his wife's safety at their western Tennessee home. She had to survive not only pillaging by the Union army, but also "the outrages of the Robbers and Bushwhackers who were committing their depredations through the country."[29]

A Captain Brixey, operating west of Tullahoma, had once scouted for the Union army, but by early 1864, he led a "rough, blood thirsty set of desperadoes," including some Confederate deserters. The men cooperated with the Union army when it suited them, but "their motto

In this scene, Confederate guerrillas celebrate the lynching of Unionists, but the roles were often reversed. From *Thrilling Adventures of Daniel Ellis* (1867).

was 'death,'" said a midwesterner who had seen them in action. "They never spared an enemy (or friend either, I should think, judging from their conduct)," he concluded. On one occasion, Brixey's men stole two horses and two slave boys from an elderly Confederate. The old man was a former judge and respected by Union troops in the region for his "good humor." When the judge protested the theft to the Union officer under whom Brixey operated, the Federal ordered Brixey to return the horses, though not the two boys. The angry scout complied but sent some of his men after the old man. The judge was found lying dead the next day in a wooded ravine.[30]

Other veteran Union guerrillas, such as Tinker Dave Beaty, had relented not a whit after three years of war. Beaty worried only about his ability to keep fighting. "I have held this county [Fentress] with a small band, without the aid of state or government," he told Andrew Johnson in the spring of 1864, and now his men needed help. "Our stock is gon, ... & we have no where to go to obtain any thing," Beaty lamented. He wanted Johnson to send them food: "corn, flour, *crackers*, or anything that will sustain life." Whatever his resources, Tinker Dave remained a "terror" to the rebels in north-central Tennessee. "He is a whole souled fellow," a Union officer testified. "If he had a Regiment, instead of a Company, he would do wonders." This officer conceded that Beaty was a "rough man," but he credited the guerrilla with being the "Savior of the Union" in his region.[31]

The Unionists of East Tennessee, persecuted for much of the war, had their revenge when the Federals captured Knoxville in September 1863. Rebel bushwhackers like Bill Owens—"the most ferocious looking man I ever saw," admitted one Confederate—continued to operate in the region, but from the moment Union soldiers arrived in force, Confederate families fled "before large and numerous bands of marauding bushwhackers and tories." Union officers tried to organize a single Tennessee "National Guard," but they could no more convince independent bands to submit to military discipline than could the Confederate authorities. Dividing their time between bushwhacking rebel soldiers and robbing rebel civilians, East Tennessee tories wanted to savor the reversal of fortunes. Guerrillas and bandits from across the border in North Carolina, who continued to roam freely through the mountains and across state lines, frequently joined them.[32]

Most dangerous for the rebels were Unionists who operated as guerrilla hunters for the U.S. Army. Fielding Hurst, William B. Stokes, and George W. Kirk continued their pursuit of rebels through Tennessee and neighboring states while living freely off secessionist communities.

They engaged in some epic struggles with their quarry, and both sides racked up victories. The clashes between Champ Ferguson and Stokes probably attracted the most public attention, but plenty of lesser-known duels added to the bloodshed. Most of these guerrilla hunters were East Tennesseans who "had their property destroyed and their friends shot by the Rebels." If not for the blue uniforms, their "ruffianly and lawless appearance" would have made it difficult to distinguish between them and the guerrillas themselves. "They fight pretty well," admitted a Union general, "but rob, plunder and steal like a band of robbers." They seldom took prisoners.[33]

Rebel civilians took a beating from such men. "Fielding Hurst made his appearance in our county with his band of robbers," reported a woman from western Tennessee, "and visited almost every nook and corner in the county, taking stock, plundering houses, burning and every other species of meanness you could imagine." Nathan Forrest did what could be done to break up bands of tory "guerrillas, horse thieves and robbers," and he particularly disliked Hurst. Following a binge of house burning, extortion, and murder by Hurst's men in early 1864, Forrest demanded restitution and the surrender of Hurst for trial by the Confederate government. Elsewhere, in middle Tennessee, "Stokes' men" struck terror. "They always do more mischief than any others," insisted a woman. "They killed several men, one after they had taken him." Confederates in East Tennessee regarded George Kirk a "cruel commander of . . . bushwhackers and outlaws," a man of "reprehensible character."[34]

The unchecked violence bred further outlawry, as deserters and parole breakers made robbery and theft their new professions. As early as January 1863, an East Tennessean had warned the Confederate War Department that a new "species of warfare" had struck his region. "All mountain gorges, caves, [and] caverns . . . are filled with the dross of God's creation," he declared. Gangs of "yankees, renegades, deserters, and fugitive slaves" posed a "terror to honest mankind." By the end of the year, a Union cavalryman guarding railroads in southwestern Tennessee claimed that "a heep" of the guerrillas in that region were Confederate deserters "tring to keep a way from both armeys." A Wisconsin soldier realized, "Their object is not to fight but to rob and plunder. They are generally deserters from the Rebel army with now and then one from our own."[35]

In peacetime, it would have been a crime wave; in wartime, it appeared more like social collapse. "No one living ever will be able to give a full picture of its consequences & distress," a county sheriff in middle

Tennessee said of this "wicked war." Robberies occurred daily in his jurisdiction. Illegal trafficking in mules and horses seemed "the order of the day." Most frightening was the violence that accompanied theft, with ruffians "partially hanging & choking" their victims. Murders were not unknown.[36]

More Confederates also blamed their own guerrillas for needlessly drawing the ire of the Federals and tories. As the Federals burned rebel homes in central Tennessee in response to Champ Ferguson's raids, citizens saw Ferguson as a danger to their own security. A resident of Warren County, located precisely in the middle of the state, confessed, "The whole country is so demoralized we cannot tell what may happen." A woman in a neighboring county echoed his sentiments: "[I] do wish that the leaders of this war were as tired of this war as we are." Their remarks came in the latter part of 1863. Much worse was to follow, but they and their neighbors had already seen enough "Bushwhacking" on both sides. More Tennessee Confederates began to take the Union oath in hopes of escaping total destruction. The final collapse came only with the defeat of John Bell Hood's army at Nashville in December 1864, but by that time, the guerrilla war had already severely damaged public morale in Tennessee.[37]

A Union policy of retaliation in Tennessee had speeded the rebel collapse. By mid-1864, that policy mirrored the one in Kentucky, and for good reason. With the security of his men and swift advance of the Union cause paramount, Sherman had repeated his orders for Burbridge to district commanders in Tennessee. Even humble privates assigned to guard railroads knew by now that "Judge Lynch" was the favored means of ending the guerrilla war.[38]

Robert Milroy became the instrument of Sherman's will in Tennessee. Following his stint of duty against guerrillas in western Virginia, Milroy commanded a division at the start of the Gettysburg campaign. To his misfortune, he had allowed half of his division and twenty-three pieces of artillery to be captured. Although exonerated by a court of inquiry, the U.S. War Department thought it prudent to put him in charge of the militia and railroad guards at Tullahoma, Tennessee, rather than returning him to a field command. Arriving in Tennessee in May 1864, Milroy served briefly under Eleazer Paine, whose dislike of both West Pointers and slavery Milroy shared. Both men hated bushwhackers, too, and Milroy quickly adopted Paine's method of dealing with them.[39]

As guerrillas besieged his post the remainder of that year, Milroy imposed Paine's antiguerrilla and refugee policies. He used a brigade of "wild, half civilized" Tennessee cavalry as his prime "gurilla hunters" and favored loyal "home guards" for "putting down guerrillaism" in contested communities. He issued orders to shoot bushwhackers, confiscate their property, and burn their homes. Milroy made exceptions if the destruction of a home caused "too much suffering" for a guerrilla's widow and children, but he did not shy away from punishing dangerous women. In adding Cynthia McCallum to a list of "disloyal persons," he instructed his men, "Shoot if you can by accident." Of Charlotte McCallum, apparently Cynthia's daughter, he noted, "Almost as bad as her mother. Burn Everything."[40]

Beyond the reach of Sherman's eye and Milroy's vengeance, Federals elsewhere in Tennessee followed a similarly hard line. When a military commission at Tullahoma ordered five guerrillas hanged, the president of the court defended the penalty as a matter of justice and "necessity." Only by executing guerrillas and outlaws, he elaborated, could the army "restore peace and order." A commission at Murfreesboro sentenced a "pretty wild boy" named James Johnson to hang for "bushwhacking" a Union soldier. The evidence against Johnson was largely circumstantial, and given his youth, he might have escaped death had he been tried earlier in the war. However, his defiant defense of guerrilla warfare left the court few options. Johnson denounced common bushwhacking because it recoiled upon the citizenry, but he insisted that "Guerilla warfare," when authorized by the Confederate government, "ought to be tolerated." Going further still, and sounding every bit like Jefferson Davis, Johnson added, "It is certainly unfair for one Belligerent to govern the organization of the forces of the other or dictate the methods of fighting for the other." These were scarcely sentiments to earn sympathy from the commission.[41]

Such stubbornness characterized both sides in the Virginias. West Virginia was officially invited to join the Union in December 1863, but statehood did not guarantee security. With Confederate sympathizers constituting the majority population in at least half of its counties, intense local wars continued. Petitioners appealed to the new governor, Arthur I. Boreman, for help. "The County has been in a state of Anarchy since the Federal Troops have been withdrawn," protested the citizens of Gilmer County, in the center of the state. "Guerrilla bands have been prowling through the country, greatly annoying the union Citizens, and we are now in a more defenseless condition than we were two years ago." The condition was nothing new for this particular county, which had made a similar plea to Governor Pierpont. Either the number of federal troops must be increased or communities must be allowed to protect themselves. If the latter, men with military experience must be allowed to organize "independent companies" and companies of "scouts."[42]

Most West Virginia Unionists managed to hold their own, but peace remained impossible under any circumstances. The most remote of mountain homes could not escape violence, if not from outside intruders, than from the enemy within. Rebel and Unionist bands stole horses from each other, took hostages, searched homes, and did "some bushwhacking." People lived in "almost constant excitement." By May 1864, the Federals had reestablished a strong presence in some areas, and army patrols executed known guerrillas and burned their property. A Union soldier thought this cycle of retaliation had "long since ceased to be a wonder," but a less blasé citizen worried, "Unless it is stopped, I awfully fear another Lawrence massacre."[43]

Unionists in old Virginia enjoyed little more security. Living in the midst of a Union encampment helped, but just because a region had been "restored" did not make it safe. If the Confederate army lacked sufficient men to protect every community, the Union army also found it impossible to secure conquered territory. Wherever the Federals tried to restore pro-Union county governments, "rebel banditti"—meaning everyone from Mosby's men to genuine outlaws—set upon the loyal citizenry. Loyal men still sought shelter in the woods "to avoid capture or death." Independent resistance movements proved futile. In southwestern Virginia, a secret protective organization, known variously as the "Heroes of America" and the "Red Strings," had entrenched itself by 1864. Yet, incessant bushwhacking and thievery replaced any hope of effective protection with a leaden feeling of war weariness.[44]

Nothing so oppressed peoples' spirits as the sense of being trapped by the violence. No relief short of flight seemed possible. Bands of stragglers and deserters, called "scouters" in some parts of Virginia, appeared from nowhere. Wandering free of interference through isolated and largely inaccessible mountain regions, they "robbed and plundered" as they went. Elsewhere, community rivalries made life uncertain. Defined as much by family as by politics, the bitterness of these feuds deepened as the war progressed. As new grievances exacerbated old ones, days of reckoning multiplied. Justice seemed overdue, men quicker to settle accounts. "Just one thing after another seemed to fan the flame of war spirit," explained a resident of southwestern Virginia. A man from the same region declared, "People had grudges against some neighbor. So they got together to steal and destroy the property of absent soldiers, and even to kill those whom they particularly hated."[45]

The waterborne guerrilla war spread fear along Virginia's eastern shore. Neither the problems nor the responsibilities facing the Union navy there were as extensive as on western rivers, but sailors still had to protect their own craft, commercial vessels, shore installations, and Unionist communities near rivers and the seacoast. Like the guerrilla hunters of the mountains and valleys, sailors wearied of these numerous and often fruitless assignments. Frequently failing to capture their prey, they inevitably resorted to punishing the citizenry and destroying known guerrilla places of rendezvous.[46]

John Wood and John Y. Beall caused the most trouble. Wood, who had initiated this brand of guerrilla warfare the preceding year, still reigned as the most effective raider. His typically bold operations on the lower Rappahannock River and Chesapeake Bay captured or destroyed dozens of Union gunboats and commercial vessels. John Beall could be equally destructive but proved less lucky. Beall learned the partisan's trade by riding with Turner Ashby early in the war. Transferring those talents to the water, he captured gunboats and commercial vessels in Chesapeake Bay and destroyed lighthouses on the coast. He was captured and imprisoned in November 1863 but exchanged in March 1864. He then played an even more daring game by shifting his operations to the North, although, except for one instance when he captured a pair of steamers on Lake Erie, he acted more as spy than guerrilla. On capturing Beall a second time, the Federals hanged him on both counts in February 1865.[47]

Determined to match the Confederacy's naval partisans, the Federals turned loose Lieutenant Commander William B. Cushing. A nineteen-year-old midshipman when the war began, Cushing resigned from the U.S. Naval Academy to enter active service as a common seaman. A lieutenant by 1864, he made the coastal rivers around Cape Fear, North Carolina, his playground. Operating as "Lincoln's commando," he and his small contingent of men gathered intelligence on Confederate movements. They nearly captured a Confederate general in February 1864. The most dramatic moment in Cushing's career came in October, when he and his raiders sank the formidable Confederate ironclad *Albermarle* with a torpedo. Its destruction opened the way for the Federals to recapture Plymouth, North Carolina.[48]

Human targets of the mushrooming guerrilla war would have taken heart had they known how close the Confederate government now was to severing all ties to its guerrillas. The politicians had been hemming and hawing on this issue for two years, but by 1864, some influential army officers in Virginia had seen enough. General Thomas Rosser, a swaggering and only moderately competent cavalry officer, started the movement by blasting the ill effects of the partisan ranger system on public morale and military discipline in the Shenandoah Valley. Rangers had become mostly "a band of thieves," Rosser told General Lee in January 1864. Their "stealing, pillaging, plundering, and doing every manner of mischief and crime" made them "a terror to the citizens and an injury to the cause." Rosser went on to list the familiar catalog of the system's defects and implied that other senior officers, including Jubal Early and Lee's own nephew, Fitzhugh Lee, shared his opinions.[49]

Rosser found his biggest ally in Robert E. Lee. Although the Confederacy's leading general acknowledged the usefulness of some rangers—mostly Mosby—he had complained to Jefferson Davis just a few months earlier about the continued desertion of soldiers to partisan ranks. Nor had Lee changed his opinion that guerrilla warfare by any name tarnished the nation's image. Both he and Jeb Stuart, who defied common wisdom in their high regard for Rosser, endorsed the cavalryman's letter and urged the government to abolish the partisan system. As though this action and the growing body of complaints against rangers did not stack the odds sufficiently against them, some men from Major Harry W. Gilmor's 2nd Maryland Battalion robbed civilian passengers on a Baltimore and Ohio (B&O) train in March, just as the Confederate Congress debated the issue. Five days after the B&O incident, the lawmakers voted to transfer all partisan rangers to the army, although they allowed Secretary of War Seddon to make exceptions. Seddon, after consulting Lee, spared the battalions of John Mosby and John McNeill in Virginia.[50]

Not that this settled matters. Congress failed entirely to deal with the larger guerrilla problems. Local community wars, swarming gangs of outlaws, and desperate bands of deserters—all products of the irregular war—went untouched. Neither did congressional action faze the scores of guerrilla bands that had always operated outside the partisan system. The edict certainly did not alter the U.S. government's perception of Confederate guerrillas. The Confederates also had to endure a final rush by soldiers and former partisans to join the last two legal battalions. John McNeill accepted large numbers of these "deserters" into his command. When court-martialed for ignoring orders to dismiss them, a sympathetic board, headed by John Imboden, under whom McNeill served, acquitted him.[51]

Not surprisingly, then, the spring and summer of 1864 witnessed some of the most bitter partisan conflict of the war on the eastern border. Union commanders, under growing military and political pressure, approved new companies for "independent" and "scout" service against bushwhacking bands. They also relied more heavily than ever on the army's self-styled guerrilla hunters. The campaign produced epic confrontations. Portions of Elihu V. White's "Comanches" (officially the 35th Virginia Cavalry Battalion) dueled with the Loudoun Rangers. McNeill found a special nemesis in the Swamp Dragons. Mosby had any number of Union commands pursuing him, but Major Henry A. Cole's Home Brigade of Maryland Cavalry and Captain Richard S. Blazer's Independent Union Scouts made him their special mission.[52]

One of the most intriguing matchups came between the Loudoun Rangers and John W. Mobberly, who commanded a detachment from White's battalion. White had learned the art of partisan warfare in Bleeding Kansas before the war and honed those skills under Turner Ashby in the Shenandoah Valley. When the Confederate government converted his original battalion of "scouts" into volunteer cavalry early in 1863, some of White's men, recruited from Maryland and northern Virginia, mutinied. They had enlisted, they said, to engage in "independent service" near their homes. They would not remain in a unit that might be ordered out of northern Virginia. White only managed to keep their allegiance by detaching part of the battalion under nineteen-year-old Mobberly to serve in Loudoun County, where the majority of his men lived. Mobberly, White pledged, would protect their homes and families from Unionists and federal soldiers while the rest of the battalion served where needed.[53]

The White-Mobberly arrangement was unofficial, unique, and quite irregular. Mobberly's men operated without government sanction, and so, like all independent commands, earned a reputation among the Federals as "notorious" brigands. Union reports often mentioned Mobberly as serving under Mosby, but he only happened to operate in a part of northern Virginia called "Mosby's Confederacy." Union soldiers fighting against Mobberly knew he had no connection to Mosby, although one man did see a similarity between the two rebels: "Its hard telling which has the most impudence, they are both Desperate." Mobberly's men naturally became the target of Loudoun's principal band of Union guerrilla hunters, the Loudoun Rangers. What was more, the rival bands had similar histories. When Edwin Stanton tried to consolidate the rangers with a regiment of conventional cavalry in March 1864, a revolt similar to the one staged by White's men ensued. These Federals had no intention of leaving northern Virginia to the mercy of rebel guerrillas. Their captain, Samuel C. Means, led the protest, even to the point of resigning his commission. That proved unfortunate for the rangers.

Stanton eventually backed down, and the Loudoun Rangers continued to serve as an independent company, but they did so without Means, whose resignation Stanton accepted.[54]

Virginia's guerrilla war came to a head in the autumn of 1864 with a destructive, often murderous, orgy of retaliation and counter-retaliation. It had begun several months earlier, when General Franz Sigel failed to sweep aside Jubal Early's smaller Confederate army in the Shenandoah Valley. Ulysses S. Grant, made commanding general of all Union armies in March, had assigned Sigel the task of capturing the valley, the Confederacy's largest remaining source of grain and livestock, as part of his multifront spring offensive. Grant's grand design was the culmination of all he had learned in the war, much of it shaped by his understanding of the guerrilla conflict. Sherman's Georgia campaign was also part of the plan, as was Grant's own movement against Lee's army in what became known as the "Overland campaign." Each part was designed to stretch rebel armies and resources to the breaking point and destroy Confederate morale. But unlike Sherman and Grant, who successfully completed their assignments, Sigel failed utterly, thanks in no small part to constant harassment and destruction of supply lines by Mosby, McNeill, and former partisans-turned-cavalrymen Imboden, White, and Gilmor.[55]

Enter David Hunter to replace Sigel and contribute once more to the ferocity of the war. Though less important than men like Halleck, Grant, and Sherman in shaping the Union's antiguerrilla policy, Hunter kept popping up at critical moments. He appeared first in Missouri, then surfaced in South Carolina, and now he played his part in Virginia. Black Dave had been in the valley less than a week when, toward the end of May, guerrillas fired on one of his wagon trains near Newtown. It was a minor incident; only one Union soldier was wounded, but Hunter issued a list of reprisals to be taken against the citizens for future guerrilla actions. They ranged in severity from financial assessments of 500 percent to destruction of private property. When Mosby burned twelve Union supply wagons a week later near where the first ambush had occurred, Hunter ordered Newtown and every home for several miles to its south destroyed. A tearful appeal by the citizenry caused him to modify the orders: Only three houses were burned, one of them a known guerrilla rendezvous.[56]

Hunter's restraint dissolved rapidly. With orders to live off the land and destroy anything of value to the Confederate war effort, Union soldiers sought satisfaction for the hardships of the campaign and revenge for the guerrilla attacks. They huzzahed Hunter. "He is going to put an

John Mosby's men enjoy the rewards of a successful attack.
From *Harper's Weekly*, September 5, 1863.

end to this bushwhacking I hope," one soldier declared. Hunter, they believed, would kill guerrillas and demoralize their supporters: "That is the plan to . . . get rid of the cusses." Hunter erased any lingering doubts about the limits of his severity when, having forced Early as far south as Lexington by mid-June, he destroyed the home of former governor John Letcher and part of the Virginia Military Institute. Reports of the damage brought nods of approval from northerners. Southern civilians in his path cursed Hunter.[57]

Jubal Early, seeing that he was powerless to stop the onslaught, made a bold tactical and strategic move. He abandoned the Shenandoah Valley, slipped around Hunter, and headed for Washington, D.C. Hunter had to pursue, but he moved too slowly. The rebels, having taken the initiative, spent the month of July rampaging through West Virginia and Maryland and threatening the outer defenses of the U.S. capital. Mosby accompanied the army with about 200 rangers, who appear to have caused as much consternation as Early's 14,000 soldiers. McNeill's rangers added to the hysteria. While not operating directly under Early, they assisted his movements with a series of raids. Their most successful strikes came against the B&O Railroad, as they tore up track and burned several bridges. On July 2, 1864, the day Early reached the northern edge of the Shenandoah Valley at Winchester, President Lincoln hurriedly signed a bill that Congress had been debating for nearly a month: "An act to provide for the more speedy Punishment of Guerrilla Marauders."[58]

The most destructive episode in Early's raids came in Pennsylvania. A portion of his cavalry—not guerrillas—entered the town of Chambersburg on July 30. Early's men demanded $100,000 in gold or $500,000 in greenbacks from the town as compensation for the homes of three prominent rebels destroyed by Hunter in West Virginia. While waiting for the town to meet their demand, the cavalrymen looted homes and businesses. When the populace refused to pay the impossible sum demanded of it, the rebels proceeded "to lay the town in ashes." By the end of the day, hundreds of buildings had been destroyed, and more than half of six thousand townspeople were homeless. No citizen was injured, but the physical destruction—three times the cost of the extortion demand—exceeded the raid on Lawrence.[59]

Back in the Shenandoah Valley, General Philip H. Sheridan replaced Hunter. Sheridan received the same orders to confiscate or destroy all food, livestock, and property of military value, but this time Grant added ominously, "We want the Shenandoah Valley to remain a barren waste." It was early August, and after a bloody summer of fighting, the commanding general had finally forced Lee's army into the defenses of Richmond and Petersburg. Sherman had besieged but not yet captured Atlanta. The presidential election loomed, and President Lincoln doubted he would be reelected. Grant had to finish off the Confederacy, and fast.[60]

So when Mosby's "cutthroats and robbers" threatened his advance into the valley, Sheridan reacted. The diminutive "Little Phil" (5 feet 5 inches, 135 pounds) had been in command only a few days when he ordered the army "to exterminate as many of Mosby's gang" as possible. This included the execution of captured guerrillas. Some of them were hanged, others shot. Sheridan did not care about the method; he meant to win the war. His duel with Mosby—quite aside from the need still to defeat Early in the open field—extended beyond the valley by September to embrace all of northern Virginia. He hunted Mosby's men wherever they threatened his army or Unionist civilians. Sheridan's rage boiled over on October 3, when a personal friend, twenty-two-year-old Lieutenant John R. Meigs, son of Quartermaster General Montgomery C. Meigs, was reportedly killed in a gunfight with partisans well within Union lines.[61]

The killing of young Meigs not only increased the blood lust against guerrillas, but it also hardened attitudes toward the civilian population. Some men said the worst treatment of noncombatants and the most senseless destruction of property came in response to the Meigs affair. A New England soldier thought it entirely justified, an opinion solidified on learning that two men from his own state had been executed by guerrillas. "His throat [was] cut from ear to ear," he said of one of the victims. "Another was found lifeless hanging from a tree by his feet head downwards." What were a few burned homes or a little looting set beside such barbarism? he asked. "I think you can hardly call us very bad names in view of the atrocities by these infernal traitors," he told his wife.[62]

The violence reached a crescendo in November. First, Mosby concluded a personal duel of several months' duration with General George A. Custer. Custer's cavalry, following Sheridan's orders, had executed several captured rangers. In one instance alone, six of Mosby's men had been hanged at Front Royal. Instinctively, Mosby selected seven of Custer's men for execution, an action approved by General Lee and Secretary Seddon. Mosby picked the seven by lots from among twenty prisoners. Only four of the men died in the end, but Mosby was satisfied that he had made his point. Moreover, perhaps fearful of where such cold-blooded retaliation might lead, he sent Sheridan an explanation of his action. Mosby emphasized that, henceforth, he would treat all Union prisoners "with the kindness due their condition," unless, he added cautiously, Sheridan's men responded with "some new act of barbarity."[63]

Whether or not Sheridan believed Mosby, he soon received orders to finish off Virginia's biggest guerrilla threat. Sheridan had accomplished his two chief assignments—deplete the Shenandoah Valley's resources and defeat Early—by mid-November. Jubal Early, after a succession of military defeats that culminated at Cedar Creek, had retreated toward Richmond. The valley may not yet have been a barren waste, but Grant and Halleck now deemed it more important to end the nagging guerrilla threat to operations in northern Virginia. Specifically, they wanted Sheridan to destroy Mosby's home turf in Loudoun County. Sheridan understood.[64]

"It was a terrible retribution on the country that had for three years supported and lodged the guerrilla bands and sent them out to plunder and murder," judged a Union officer as he surveyed the smoke from hundreds of burning buildings and a thousand haystacks. The U.S. Army seized hundreds of horses and cattle in less than a week. Sheridan said he wanted no homes burned and he forbade "personal violence" against civilians, but everything else was fair game. The campaign delighted men who had fought against Mosby or seen his handiwork. They had no time for discretion, either. All citizens of Loudoun and its environs, including a considerable number of Unionists and neutrals, suffered the onslaught. "The task was not a pleasant one," confessed a cavalry captain, "for many innocents were made to suffer with the guilty, but something was necessary to clear the country of those bands of Guerillas that were becoming so formidable."[65]

Sheridan hoped his work in northern Virginia and the Shenandoah Valley would turn people against the guerrillas and "the authorities in Richmond," but it did not always work that way. Many Confederates did not see the Union's valley campaign, not even its excesses, as an antiguerrilla campaign. It looked more like plain meanness to them. Some northern Virginians had always regarded Mosby's men as more curse than blessing, but Mosby's heroics had won over others. As often as not, citizens blamed the Federals for the spirit of vendetta that had poisoned the war and excused Mosby's men because of "the wrong" they had endured at Yankee hands. When Mosby was wounded and nearly captured just before Christmas, people thanked a "kind Providence" for protecting him.[66]

So the end of 1864 did not see the last of rebel guerrillas on the eastern border. In West Virginia, Governor Boreman, weary of trying to regulate a system of home guards, called on all loyal citizens to rise up, like the rebels, and form vigilante bands. Denouncing the rebels as "outlaws" and "banditti," he told his people to hunt them down, capture and kill them "wherever they may be found." It was the only way, Boreman concluded, to restore "peace, order and security." In old Virginia, the Union army continued to exterminate guerrillas. A middle-aged soldier from New York rather liked Mosby. "He is smart. He is something like the Swamp Fox (Marion) in the Revolution," he told his sister. Yet, the New Yorker also understood the danger posed by men like Mosby. "There is no stopping this Infernal Guerilla Warfare," he concluded, "unless destroying [it] Root & Branch." [67]

G eneral Edward R. Wild abandoned his Massachusetts medical practice to join the Union army in 1861 because he hated slavery and rebels. A year later, he sacrificed an arm for his beliefs in the Antietam campaign. Seven months after that, he recruited a regiment of black troops from the refugee camps at New Bern, North Carolina. On December 3, 1863, Wild led his African Brigade out of Norfolk, Virginia, on a raid into northeastern North Carolina. In less than three weeks, he freed 2,500 slaves, destroyed four guerrilla camps, burned over a dozen homes, captured or killed "a number" of guerrillas, executed at least one of his prisoners, and took four hostages, three of them women. The fourth hostage was a seventy-three-year-old man.[1]

Wild's expedition ranks as the most intense antiguerrilla raid of the war. It also foretold the fate of the Deep South in 1864. As the rebels "crept" upon his men, "pestered" and bushwhacked them, Wild realized that "ordinary measures" of retaliation would not do. "I adopted a more rigorous style of warfare," he informed General Butler, his superior officer. A Confederate colonel phrased it differently. No expedition in the war, he charged, had shown "more bitter disregard for the long established usages of civilization or the dictates of humanity." A Union officer in northern Virginia, where the woods "looked rather guerillary!" thought Wild had "gone insane through fanaticism."[2]

Although not displeased with the results, even Benjamin Butler was taken aback. "General Wild . . . appears to have done his work with great thoroughness, but perhaps with too much stringency," he told the secretary of war. Butler's chief of staff spoke more bluntly. He said Wild had "no common sense." Wild's most controversial act was to take the female hostages, who were relatives of three guerrillas, in order to obtain the safe release of black soldiers captured by the rebels. Confederates had already hanged one of his men in retaliation for a guerrilla hanged by Wild. No sooner had Wild returned to Norfolk than he asked to lead a second expedition into the same region. His men had found the muster rolls of the principal guerrilla bands. He could cripple those self-styled "North Carolina Defenders" with "two weeks of stern warfare," he assured Butler. Given two months, he would "exterminate" them.[3]

The repercussions in North Carolina were twofold. First came indignation and protest. "Such men as this Wild are a disgrace to the manhood of the age," Governor Vance informed the U.S. government, "not being able to capture soldiers they war upon defenceless women! Great God! What an outrage." That the Union troops had been black only deepened his alarm, and news of these circumstances angered the entire Confederacy. The resulting protests had some effect. Almost at once, the Federals exchanged two of the women for a pair of captured Union soldiers (although Butler had wanted their guerrilla husbands instead); the seventy-three-year-old man was released when the last black soldier thought captured found his way back to Union lines. Wild insisted on keeping the third woman—the daughter of a guerrilla chief—as a witness in Butler's investigation of the hostage controversy, but she, too, was eventually freed. Governor Vance also protested the treatment of North Carolina "soldiers" and "state rangers" as guerrillas, but this claim fell on deaf ears. Wild called them all "bandits" and "pirates" whom Vance had "hired" to spread terror. Neither Vance nor Jefferson Davis could "legalize such a style of warfare," Wild maintained.[4]

The second, more telling, reaction came among the citizens who had endured Wild's raid. Butler believed the majority was "reasonably neutral," which is to say that while "sympathizing with the South, they were tired of the war, or weary of their own distress and privations." He also judged that many of them feared to speak their minds "on account of guerrillas." He judged correctly. Following the army's withdrawal, several communities in the region asked Vance to "denounce" the contraband trade and, more significantly, to "disband" his partisan rangers. "We believe that these rangers cannot be of any service to us," said the citizens of one county, "but that their further presence here will bring upon us speedy and inevitable ruin." This reaction differed markedly from the one in Loudoun County.[5]

So here, on the edge of the Deep South, the guerrilla war seemed to be doing more harm than good. North Carolina had been a reluctant partner in the Confederacy, and rebels elsewhere argued that Tar Heels lacked spunk. The state certainly seemed more vulnerable after the Wild raid, and internal dissent flourished to an alarming degree. Judge Thomas Ruffin, kinsman and friend of firebrand Edmund, had been one of those Carolinians slow to embrace secession. He lived far to the west of Wild's exploits, but he agreed with Confederates who had become disillusioned with the conduct of the war and the leadership of Jefferson Davis. The prospects for independence were fading. Victory, if still possible, might only come through "a protracted guerrilla war," and such a victory, a like-minded kinsman told Thomas Ruffin, could only "make one vast Missouri" of their country.[6]

Of all the states south of the border region, North Carolina seemed the most likely by 1864 to dissolve into the anarchy that defined Missouri. It was the home of Unionist "buffaloes" and site of the Shelton Laurel incident. Western North Carolina, especially, remained "*dangerously* infested with marauding bands of Tories & Bushwhackers," but across the state, violent enemies of the Confederacy arose "more mischievous *than ever before* . . . more daring & dangerous than ever." Besides its tories, North Carolina reportedly had more army deserters than any other state. As these men returned home, the same mountains that harbored Unionist guerrillas sheltered them. In coastal areas, swamps made safe havens. In central North Carolina, outlaws and deserters disappeared into caves, a mode of concealment they learned from runaway slaves.[7]

Deserters had been a problem since the spring of 1862, when national conscription commenced, but conscription was no longer the only impetus for leaving the army. The hardships of campaigning, discouragement over the course of the war, and difficult times at home triggered subsequent desertion. At first, deserters, like the draft dodgers, had been content to "lay out" and avoid Confederate authorities. However, as the government increased efforts to round them up, militancy replaced passivity. Thereafter, "herds of disloyal citizens and gangs of deserters from the Confederate army" threatened the "safety and security of . . . homes and property." Bands of several hundred men appeared, the boldest of which "assumed a sort of military occupation" of their neighborhoods.[8]

The number of combined deserters, tories, and outlaws defied all means of control. "Deserters are thick and heavy," reported a North Carolina conscript officer in the summer of 1864. "They have been holding meetings and planning for the winter Campaign." Other people complained about men "skulking about." Bands of "Robbers & outlaws" killed livestock and broke into smokehouses. Then came the "lively times . . . with rogues & tories" joining forces. "Deserters, Tories & bad spirits are banding themselves together," warned a man from eastern North Carolina, where "acts of violence[,] murder[,] plunder & defiance" marked the "degradation" of society. Meantime, a "state of anarchy" existed in the western end of the state. Deserters and Unionists had become "insolent & dangerous" and supported themselves as "outlaws" by pillage and plunder. "If something is not done for this country by the government," a man warned in November 1864, "our settlement will soon follow the sad fate of the French Rev[olution]."[9]

Anarchy and revolution are not easily contained, and in North Carolina, the cure made things worse. Determined to restore order, the Confederates executed deserters, but this only made the outliers more desperate. The security of outlaw guerrilla bands gained appeal. What had started as a military problem became a social crisis. Governor Vance assigned his Guard for Home Defense to round up "skulkers & deserters" and any gangs engaged in "depredations," but this dragnet caused more discontent. The hunters often treated communities like enemy territory. They confiscated food and forage and obliged citizens to support them. Vance became so determined to crush the deserter gangs that he allowed his home guards to seize the property of deserters and confine their families until the outlaws surrendered. "No efforts [will] be spared to apprehend or destroy the band," came the instructions to home guards in March 1864; "use every means in [your] . . . power to the accomplishment of this end."[10]

Vance's state troops saw nothing wrong with knocking heads. Accused of permitting "depredations" by his men as they rounded up "Deserters & Marauders," one officer defended their actions. His soldiers had only taken the horses, wagons, and forage of known deserters, he maintained, which they then used solely for the pursuit of the outlaws. "Certainly those who have been so lawless and those also who have harboured them," he reasoned, "are not entitled to expect that we shall observe every nicety in our dealings with them." Vance, though concerned at first about the rule of law, gradually came to embrace the officer's view of a critical situation. Assuming that any contrite or peace-loving man would have responded to his earlier offers to pardon deserters who returned to their regiments, Vance believed the time for reasonable solutions had passed.[11]

The violence escalated. Disloyal bands bushwhacked or executed home guards, conscript officers, guerrillas, and soldiers sent after them. Lone conscript officers dared not enter their domains, and local companies generally found themselves outnumbered or outclassed. "These undrilled and unequipped men are gone to cope with drilled men, armed to the teeth," protested the distressed wife of one home guard. "Six Bush Whackers of the kind can kill and disperse the whole Regt." Not robbed entirely of wit or humor, she concluded her complaint to

Governor Vance on a lighter note, but her concern showed through: "Now while I will give up my husband cheerfully as any other woman to serve his country, I do protest against his being taken in the woods to be shot down like a deer." Even when soldiers reinforced home guards, it was not uncommon "to hear of a man's having his brans shot out" by the gangs.[12]

Nearly lost in this confusion was the fact that the original guerrilla wars, pitting rebels against the Union army and southern Unionists, roiled on. The Confederate army could not contend with the widespread menace. North Carolina needed partisan rangers, or something very much like them, but the hardening prejudice against irregular warfare in Richmond meant that more states were thrown on their own resources. Vance commissioned independent companies for "special service" against raiders out of East Tennessee, the most formidable tory gangs, and uprisings by "troublesome" blacks. Unionists accused him of "military terrorism." Confederates saw the rangers as a matter of survival.[13]

William Thomas's legion remained the state's most adaptable partisan force. Moving continuously between East Tennessee and western North Carolina, the legion battled both Unionists and federal troops. Thomas's chief nemesis became George W. Kirk, who coordinated Union irregulars in the region. A native of Tennessee, the twenty-four-year-old carpenter operated mostly in his native state before John Schofield, newly assigned to command this border region, gave Kirk license to range into North Carolina and enlist "all straggling soldiers . . . and such efficient loyal citizens" as he pleased. Ostensibly commanding two regiments—the 2nd and the 3rd North Carolina Mounted Infantry—Kirk rarely led more than three hundred troops. He used them as either partisans or conventional cavalrymen, whichever the situation demanded. All of Kirk's men carried a Spencer repeating rifle and a brace of pistols. The raids of this "notorious tory and traitor, vagabond and scoundrel" played the "very devil" with Confederate citizens. They called his men "bushwhackers," and they knew his presence encouraged ever more Unionists to defy the government.[14]

Kirk's recruiting practices affected Thomas's own attitudes toward the region's deserter bands and nearly ended his service to the Confederacy. Appreciating Kirk's ability to recruit deserters and disgruntled Confederates, Thomas tried to reduce their numbers, as had John McNeill in Virginia, by placing captured deserters in his own command. "If they do not join us they will be compelled to join the enemy," reasoned Thomas. The philosophy, let alone the act, angered Vance. In October

1864, he ordered the "worse than useless" Thomas court-martialed for insubordination and "harboring" deserters. The court found Thomas guilty of all charges. His military career seemed over when, astonishingly, the never predictable Jefferson Davis intervened. Davis overturned the court's decision, ordered Thomas to return to the Tennessee–North Carolina border, and directed him to rebuild his legion by recruiting "within the enemies line."[15]

Try as they might, though, Confederate leaders could not prevent the guerrilla war from shredding the social fabric of North Carolina. "The warfare between scattering bodies of irregular troops is conducted on both sides without any regard whatever to the rules of civilized warfare or the dictates of humanity," admitted a stunned Governor Vance. "The murder of prisoners and non-combatants in cold blood has, I learn, become quite common." And this appraisal did not consider the many individual acts of bushwhacking sparked solely by the family feuds and personal vendettas that continued to punctuate the war. By now, such homicides seemed almost quaint. People had become immune to scattered incidents of thievery and lynching. Nothing shocked them any longer.[16]

Of the South's remaining Atlantic coast states, only Georgia could match the level of guerrilla activity in North Carolina. In northern Georgia, where rebels and Unionists already tussled, deserters and draft dodgers merely added to the instability and violence. Confederate and state troops sometimes entered this mountainous region to subdue them, but not enough men could be found to do a proper job. Good horses, a necessary requirement for chasing bushwhackers through thick forests and "deep and dark ravines," also grew fewer. Undisciplined militia tried to suppress Unionism by looting and pillage, but this only intensified anti-Confederate feeling.[17]

The danger to rebels increased when William Sherman invaded Georgia in May 1864. A Confederate militia officer had spotted the Union army's influence as early as March. "The most of the bushwhackers are known to be men who had deserted our own armies, and are now taking protection under the enemy," he explained, "dressed in yankee uniforms, raiding our country allmost weekly stealing, Robing and murdering all persons whom they have any spite or ambition at." It is hard to discern the precise composition of these gangs. Described variously by their victims as "deserters and union men," "bushwhackers and Tories," or just plain "ruffians," they doubtless contain elements of all groups. It all culminated in October 1864 with a coordinated and far-ranging Unionist raid to steal horses, plunder, and repay "past injuries." Some bands also carried away slaves, although whether for the purpose of freeing them or selling them is a mystery.[18]

With the Confederate army concentrating on Sherman, frightened communities mobilized against the gangs. The militia of Lumpkin County shot three "bushwhackers" thought to have been involved in the October raid. Militia in neighboring Gilmor County rounded up twelve more tories. The region's civil court system having long since broken down, the militia commander presided at a perfunctory hearing and ordered all twelve men hanged. John Gatewood played a hand, too. The "red-bearded beast" was still terrorizing tories along the Georgia-Tennessee border, and it took his band of fifty men barely a month to track down and execute two dozen suspected raiders. He caught some of them in East Tennessee as they fled Georgia to join the Union army. Gatewood personally executed six men by lining them up and shooting them in the face or head.[19]

Revolt was not confined to Georgia's northern counties. Surveying the state as a whole, one Confederate newspaper despaired in November 1863: "We are fighting each other harder than we ever fought the enemy." The pine barrens and cypress swamps of central and southern Georgia made as an inviting an environment for fugitives as the northern mountains. Deserters, rather than Unionists, remained the more frequent foe, but there were lots of them. By the end of 1863, some 1,500 deserters supposedly populated the Okefenokee Swamp. They did "much mischief—bush whacking, murdering & stealing" near the Florida border, and militia officers complained that they lacked sufficient strength to root out these former soldiers. Having butchered a conscription officer who ventured into the area, deserters left his remains lying in the woods "for the vultures" and tossed his severed head "some distance from his body."[20]

Slaves compounded the deserter problem in the southern half of the state. Georgia had the second largest slave population in the Confederacy, and reports of "organized" bands of "pilfering and plundering" blacks became frequent once Sherman's army arrived. With the partisan ranger system defunct, the state's adjutant general told militia companies to suppress "any disturbance" on the plantations. In addition, Governor Brown recruited men for "special service" in policing the slave population. They had orders to keep blacks away from the "corrupting influence of bad men," namely deserters and skulkers, who might "use the negroes for their own wicked purposes." Occasional violence still occurred, but Brown's men thwarted any general insurrection. A white man named John Vickery, whose motives are not entirely clear, planned an uprising that would have put slaves, deserters, and perhaps even Union troops in control of Brooks County, on the Florida border. The plot was discovered, and Vickery and his three chief slaves were hanged.[21]

Georgians waged a less successful guerrilla campaign against the Union army. Their best chance came as Sherman advanced from Chattanooga to Atlanta in the spring and summer of 1864. A combination of Confederate raiders and independent guerrilla bands tried to disrupt the extended Union supply line, but Sherman had anticipated their interference and planned accordingly. First, he stockpiled tons of equipment at Nashville and Chattanooga. He then assigned tens of thousands of troops to protect depots and the railroad lines that would carry the supplies to his advancing army. Sherman also worried about the rail lines farther north, through Kentucky, which explains why he roared at Burbridge for not containing the guerrilla menace in that state; but he had so arranged things that the supplies in Tennessee alone would support a four-month campaign.[22]

Sherman's army still ran a "gauntlet of Guerillas" during its five-month campaign to capture Atlanta. "Rebel scouts, bushwhackers, spies, and deserters," reported an Illinois infantryman, "were prowling around the country, all . . . ready to pounce upon and ditch a train any moment." Not only trains, but also foraging expeditions. "Some sections of the country is full of Bushes and under growth that a Bushwhacker can sit within six inches of the Road and shoot a traveler without being seen," a weary cavalryman reported. In mid-July, when it looked as though his rear guard might falter, Sherman increased the number of patrols and expeditions assigned to shield the railroad and protect telegraph lines. He warned against straggling, lest men be "picked up in detail." He ordered all "suspicious persons and families" imprisoned. "Show no mercy to guerrillas or persons threatening our roads or telegraph," he warned. The army must not be "imperiled by any citizens."[23]

Sherman's men, who had long subscribed to the "Jim Lane theory of pacification," hanged citizens who "betrayed" Union soldiers "into the guerrillas' hands." They arrested a woman—"an abandoned character," as one soldier described her—who had "harbored guerrillas" and burned her house. People who aided the guerrillas surely knew, from what they had heard of the conduct of the war elsewhere, what to expect. Yet, they often expressed shock at the reprisals. One man could not believe that a bushwhacking friend had been charged with murder simply because he had opposed "a devastating foe." Other rebels were more surprised by the inability of their guerrillas to halt the Union advance.[24]

Sherman stuck to his July orders during the remainder of the Georgia campaign. Even after capturing Atlanta, on September 2, he had to watch his rear. His men confiscated everything of value from one "sick old Bushwhacker" and left his house "in a blaze of fire." Other troops burned the town of Cassville "on account of its being a guerrilla haunt." The results pleased everyone on the Union side. "Your mode of conducting war is just the thing we now want," Halleck assured Sherman from Washington. "We have tried the kid-glove policy long enough." Both Halleck and Sherman, veterans of the guerrilla war since 1861, understood the "character" of the conflict. They believed the Union armies could do little that "the conduct of the enemy, and especially of non-combatants and women of the territory" did not justify. "I do not approve of General Hunter's course in burning private houses," Halleck added, in reference to the Virginia campaign, "or uselessly destroying private property—that is barbarous." Yet, he also conceded that the "safety" of the army required "severe rules of war." During the famously destructive march eastward to Savannah, meant to duplicate Union operations in the Shenandoah Valley, Sherman's men continued to target the homes and haunts of known guerrillas. Unionist scouts employed to lead the army through this unfamiliar territory took captured bushwhackers into the woods and shot them.[25]

Two of Georgia's neighbors, South Carolina and Florida, escaped disruption on this scale. South Carolina, the state that had caused the national schism, continued to lead a charmed life. While besieging the coastline, the Federals had failed to penetrate the state's interior. The slave population had yet to realize white fears, and the state had no significant numbers of Unionists or deserters. Complaints surfaced about "bold, defiant and threatening" deserter bands in the second half of 1863, but most of the gangs remained something less than marauders. Content to dodge the law, they mostly stole livestock and grain. Sherman's invasion of Georgia made South Carolinians anxious. When Atlanta fell, Governor Milledge L. Bonham created a "mounted force" to defend against the expected invasion. But Sherman headed for Savannah rather than Columbia, and the Carolinians breathed easy.[26]

The most serious threat to South Carolina by mid-1864 came from southern-bred "raiders" who descended on the state from Tennessee and North Carolina. Most of these gangs had only a few dozen men, but they were well organized and often cooperated with one another.

The ultimate tragedy of the guerrilla war, whether the work of guerrillas
or armies, left people with neither homes nor providers.
From *Thrilling Adventures of Daniel Ellis* (1867).

The largest band, numbering about three hundred men, operated on the border of Pickens County, where the residents requested an entire regiment of cavalry to "capture or kill" them. The "desperadoes" preyed on unprotected women and children by stealing horses and demanding money. They murdered any man who dared defy them. The band reportedly fueled itself with liquor made in a mountain retreat.[27]

Floridians had a much tougher time. Guerrillas and partisan rangers remained the principal defenders against Union soldiers and sailors, and in 1864, they faced a series of new challenges. First came repeal of the Partisan Ranger Act, which hurt Florida perhaps more than any other state. The inventive Governor John Milton, who relied heavily on rangers and cavalry raiders to protect his citizens, worked around repeal by retaining the services of several of his most redoubtable partisans and pressing Richmond to let his state troops operate as rangers. He also asked that the "gallant" John Dickison be promoted to colonel and given command of troops on the Florida peninsula. Richmond granted the promotion, but not until April 1865.[28]

Meanwhile, the Federals had expanded their antiguerrilla campaign. They began by forming a Unionist cavalry regiment, initially called the "Florida Rangers" but rechristened the 2nd Florida Cavalry in early 1864. Many of the men had been driven from their homes by the rebels and so relished the chance to operate as partisan raiders. Their principal mission was to steal Confederate cattle, but they also redressed "personal wrongs" by plundering Confederate property. Then, in February 1864, the 2nd Infantry Regiment, U.S. Colored Troops, arrived in Florida. Few whites, even among the Unionists, welcomed the black soldiers, but the newcomers complimented the 2nd Florida perfectly. Garrisoned at Fort Myers, they accompanied the cavalrymen on cattle raids and doubled the army's prospects of recruiting loyal Floridians. The "refugee rangers," as one general called the cavalrymen, urged whites to enlist, while the sight of blue-uniformed blacks inspired slaves to join the army.[29]

Deserters presented another problem for Florida rebels. Milton had worried as long as a year earlier about destructive raids by deserters and other "fugitives," but not even he foresaw the eventual gravity of the situation. The consequences proved most serious along the St. Johns River, the Atlantic coast, and the northern tiers of counties that bordered Georgia and Alabama—all rich areas of Unionism. Deserter bands prospered in large part because the U.S. Navy's blockading squadron supported their efforts, even to the point of supplying them weapons. The three strongest groups, led by William W. Strickland, James Cocker, and William White, operated in northern Florida. They were mostly deserters, although Strickland's band, organized in the summer of 1863 as the Independent Union Rangers, also included disgruntled men who had received discharges from the Confederate army.[30]

Strickland most worried rebel authorities. Few of his men appear to have had any strong ideological commitment to the Union, but all were weary of the war. Colonel Henry D. Capers had responsibility for breaking them up, and he took extreme measures. In the spring of 1864, he burned their homes and herded sixteen of their wives and children into a makeshift prison camp near Tallahassee. Thinking this would crush the will of Strickland's men, Capers then offered pardons to all who returned to the army. The Union Rangers, who by now called themselves the "Florida Royals," had no intention of bowing to Capers, no more than did Quantrill's men when faced by General Orders No. 11. "I ain't accountable for what they do now," Strickland warned him. "As for myself, I will do anything that any half white man ever done, only to go into the Confederate war any more." Milton, seeing the folly of Capers's action, ordered the release of the women and children, although, fearing more than ever retaliation against Confederate citizens, he also insisted that pursuit of the Royals continue.[31]

In proportion to the size of its population, Florida's guerrilla war may have been the most intense in the Confederacy, but a sense of impending doom also pervaded neighboring Alabama. The capture of Chattanooga opened the northern half of the state to invasion. The fall of Vicksburg made invasion from the west, out of Mississippi, inevitable. Add tories and deserters to the mix, and the lone Confederate garrisons at Selma and Mobile were woefully inadequate to meet the crisis. Although the state had several prominent cavalry raiders, including Philip D. Roddey and John T. Morgan, the Confederate government lessened their effectiveness by frequently detailing these regiments outside of Alabama. Likewise, most of the state's partisan rangers found themselves assigned to conventional regiments—often Roddey's or Morgan's—and sent to fight far from home.[32]

The situation perplexed Governors John Gill Shorter and Thomas H. Watts, who succeeded Shorter in December 1863. Both men tried to increase the number and mobility of state troops, but the national government's conscription policies had already stripped the state of too many able-bodied men. Small wonder the Union army moved at will through northern Alabama and met much diminished opposition in the southern half of the state after the summer of 1864. Pockets of resistance remained, but efforts to disrupt Union occupation looked increasingly feeble. Having gained the initiative in Alabama, and growing stronger every day, Union soldiers had no intention of relinquishing their advantage.[33]

The Union army's determination to break the spirit of largely defenseless communities spelled particular trouble for noncombatants. "The war is now conducted against us with feelings of *personal hatred*," a resident of Greensboro emphasized as early as November 1863, "and with all the cruelty of savages. There is no honour, justice, right or *principle* claimed by our enemies. It is with them a matter of passion & might. They would exterminate our race if they could. They will make it a war to annihilation if they can." The situation had grown worse a year later, with every Union soldier seemingly acting as "a law unto himself" and whole communities "ravaged" by Union occupation. "They call their victims out of their houses, accuse them of feeding bushwhackers or some such pretense, and then shoot them down," testified a rebel in Huntsville. Union raiders who swept through the nearby town of Athens knew its reputation as a guerrilla haunt and treated citizens accordingly. "[They] brutally assailed my mothers house[,] sacked it and drove the family from home," a member of the Hawkins Battalion learned while serving with Roddey's cavalry. When his sister tried hopelessly to smother a fire set by a Union soldier, an officer "*bravely* seized her by the arm and with a hissing '*damn you*' between his teeth he violently thrust her from the house."[34]

Yet, Union operations would not have been so fierce had not many soldiers still feared the enemy. "Four miles out of Huntsville Andy Church of Co. H killed by a bushwhacker," an Illinois infantryman recorded in his diary. "I saw him in a minute after the ball had passed through his head. He died without uttering a word." A year later, the same neighborhood remained a dangerous place. "The bushwhackers wont fight anything like their own Nos," complained an Indiana cavalryman. "As it was we burned 6 houses took all the men we caught on the road and sent them North 40 in No. and ordered all the inhabitants to leave & go South or North within five days." Burning houses and rounding up guerrilla supporters had become routine for the Hoosier's regiment, which had been guarding the railroad and chasing guerrillas in nearby mountains for four months. They also knew how to treat captured guerrillas. "Our Col[onel] has no mercy on these murderers and says he will arrest an officer that even brings him a prisoner," the cavalryman informed his father. "This is the only way to get rid of these fellows—

shoot them down like dogs when they are taken—of course we can expect no better treatment if any of us ever fall into their hands."[35]

Even a veteran like Eugene Marshall dreaded them. By late 1863, he had spent two years fighting guerrillas in Kentucky and Tennessee, only to face them again in northern Alabama. When bushwhackers captured and executed three new recruits from his brigade, Marshall's commanding officer, George Crook, ordered the region cleared of guerrillas, with no prisoners to be taken. The orders pleased Marshall, but he expected few results. Rebel guerrillas could never defeat the Union army, but they could deal out random death by hanging around the army's camps, shadowing it on the march, and picking off stragglers. No number of counterguerrilla expeditions would change the situation. A year later, reassigned to put down the Sioux rebellion in Dakota Territory, Marshall rejoiced to be out of the white man's war and fighting Indians. "The Guerrillas of the south," he maintained, "are far more formidable."[36]

Still, Alabama rebels were on their heels in 1864, and they began to reel even more unsteadily from attacks by armed bands of deserters and Unionists. The tory uprising of 1862 in northern Alabama spread and derived nourishment from the growing deserter population. Men who had not enlisted in Union regiments like the 1st Alabama Cavalry remained at home to war with rebel neighbors. Winston County earned a reputation as the most rebellious Alabama county, but that was only a matter of degree. Dangerous coalitions of tories and deserters appeared in many northern Alabama communities after the fall of Vicksburg. Rebel citizens fled their homes as "lawless bands," bent on "harassing, and intimidating the families of loyal citizens and soldiers," embarked on campaigns of pillage and robbery. Governor Shorter called them "bandits" and reorganized the militia to cope with local rebellions. The problem simply overwhelmed Governor Watts, as the need to suppress insurgents consumed his administration.[37]

The Confederate army did what it could to help control the situation, but military commanders usually had more pressing concerns. General Leonidas Polk, responsible for the security of Mississippi and Alabama in the spring of 1864, and knowing that his troops were as liable as Union soldiers to be bushwhacked in some parts of the district, tried both the carrot and the stick to round up deserters. He first followed the widespread practice of offering an amnesty period for deserters to rejoin their regiments. Enjoying little success with that approach, he then ordered the arrest of all deserters, conscripts, and armed Unionists.

Anyone who resisted, especially if "banded together," should be executed "upon the spot." Portions of Alabama regiments were reassigned to the state to break up "robber bands," as were the toughest soldiers Polk could find for such duty: Texas Rangers.[38]

More often, defense against armed bands fell to the state militia, local companies, and guerrillas. Being terribly undisciplined, however, all three groups could tread as heavily on friends as on foes. Governor Watts worried that many county militiamen were mere boys, under eighteen years, who did "little good and, frequently, great harm" in trying to catch deserters. "They commit trespasses on the property & persons of private individuals," Watts explained, "& thus arouse a spirit of opposition to the cause." Guerrillas could behave even more capriciously. John Gatewood, for example, began to roam as freely through Alabama as he did Tennessee and Georgia looking to throttle Yankees and Yankee sympathizers. He routinely shot deserters, rather than transporting them to the nearest provost marshal.[39]

By the summer of 1864, thanks partly to the infiltration of deserter/outlaw bands from Mississippi and Florida, much of southern Alabama—even without large pockets of Unionists—resembled the northern half of the state. Companies of deserters, claiming to be on furlough, and grey-clad gangs of six to eight men serving as "scouts," roamed the countryside. "Stealing . . . horses, driving off cows & calves, robbing, burning & stealing whatever they find valuable," they claimed to be impressing supplies needed by the government, said one victim. They also confiscated slaves from men they judged "disloyal," although the measure of loyalty depended on whether a man looked able to defend himself. "These are trashes . . . not soldiers," a woman declared bitterly.[40]

If anyone still doubted what course the war had taken in the Deep South, they need only have considered the condition of Mississippi. A rapid disintegration of civil government and legal authority reduced most of the state to chaos. The Federals sent raiding expeditions to all parts of Mississippi from their strongholds at Vicksburg, Jackson, and Memphis. Union gunboats tightened their grip on the Mississippi River and its tributaries. The Confederates lost their ability to collect taxes, hold courts, or enforce the law. Rival sets of guerrillas and an explosion of deserter/outlaw bands endangered lives and property. Mississippi Confederates forgot about the war outside their state. People might be fighting for southern independence somewhere, but that war was lost on individuals faced with the destruction of their communities. Citizens discovered corpses hanging from tree limbs, submerged in swamps with stones strapped to their chest, or "shot through the head" and lying in the road. "It is not known who did the dastardly deed" became an all-too-familiar refrain.[41]

Deserters, the newest peril, appeared to be strictly a procedural issue at first: How best could disaffected or discouraged soldiers be returned to the ranks? But disaffection ran deep in some men. "They are abolitionists, spies, deserters, liars, thieves, murderers, and every thing foul & damnable," railed a judge in condemning the gangs in an especially rebellious part of the state northeast of Jackson. By early 1864, these violent bands, sometimes hundreds of men, assumed a "formidable character." They so intimidated the citizenry that few dared speak against them. Some people even gave them "aid and comfort" in hopes of saving "themselves and their property." As in Georgia and Alabama, the northern half of Mississippi endured the worst travail, but in southern counties, too, deserter bands threatened vengeance against all who betrayed them. By autumn, the judge near Jackson warned Governor Charles Clark, "Deserters . . . are daily increasing in number and outrages, and constitute by far the greatest common & public nuisance in the land—hardly inferior to so many yankee troops in the country."[42]

But while armed deserters might weaken the Confederacy, militant Unionism could sink it. Deserters would oppose the government if necessary, but Unionists strove to destroy it. Open opposition, which had grown steadily since the Federals first occupied several northern border counties in the summer of 1862, swelled after Vicksburg. "Union or Peace meetings are boldly held and Union speeches made," declared a county sheriff who had been forced to flee his home. "No man's life is safe who dares to speak out against them." Not all Mississippi Unionists preached violence, but enough of them did so to require attention. Their strongholds were in the central and northern portions of the state, where, not incidentally, most deserters found refuge. Unionists became so destructive and unrestrained in some northern counties that the Union army had to disarm them. In more orderly fashion, the tories of Choctow County, toward the center of the state, formed the 1st Battalion of Mississippi Mounted Rifles in 1864. It was the only official Mississippi military unit in the Union army.[43]

The Koch family understood the complexity and uncertainty of the situation. Robbers, deserters, Unionists, and refugees of all stripes overran their part of southwestern Mississippi in 1864. Elers Koch was one of the "deserters." His partisan ranger battalion broke up completely after Vicksburg surrendered, the men believing that the Confederacy had gone up the spout. Elers had no intention of returning to the army, but neither did he plan to "lay out" or join the Federals. He wished only to be left alone. Elers spent much of the following year avoiding both Confederate and Union cavalry patrols. He planted corn and mowed hay on the family farm when able and took to the swamps when necessary.[44]

Life on the Koch farm became more precarious when robber bands targeted the family's home county—Hancock—in mid-1864. Elers called the raiders "jayhawkers," but at least some of them must have been Confederate deserters. They claimed "to be acting under Federal authority" when robbing people, which genuine Unionists would not do. Some Confederate cavalry arrived "to help the citizens," and Elers joined a local company raised to "put down" the raiders. By executing the men they captured, soldiers and citizens suppressed the worst of the gangs by November.[45]

The most unnerving part of Hancock County's war was the discovery that some local men—all thought to be loyal Confederates—had either assisted or joined the principal gang. "You cant believe how bad the people have got to be," lamented Elers's mother. "Persons that we thought were good and honest before the war have turned out to be the worst kind of men." They had stolen livestock mostly, but one man confessed to a bigger scheme. He had been part of a "plot" to rob every family thought to have more than a hundred dollars. When the men had "got enough to make them selves rich," he said, they planned to "clear out." The community shot the entire gang without a trial, which saddened Mother Koch. She believed the men deserved their punishment, but she also deplored the "dreadful way" it was done. The experience convinced her son to abandon all ties to the Confederate cause. He fled to New Orleans.[46]

The Mississippi community most celebrated for its opposition to the Confederacy was Jones County, in the southeastern part of the state. The county had few purely ideological Unionists, but the dangers and hardships of army life, economic suffering on the home front, and Confederate military defeats convinced many Jones County soldiers to quit the war. Once at home, some deserters converted to Unionism, but most of them sought only to survive. Confederate expeditions sent into the county to arrest them produced several bloody fights in 1863 and 1864. Confederate tax collectors and conscription officers learned to avoid the place after several of them were murdered. Local constables and judges turned a blind eye for the sake of their own lives. Worst of all, deadly feuds pitted family against family.[47]

Mississippi Confederates also had to contend with a swelling population of liberated and fugitive slaves. Harvey's Scouts gained a repu-tation for minimizing that danger. They captured several dozen slaves who had escaped from the Jefferson Davis plantation. In another, bloodier incident, they battled a "party of armed negroes" that had am-bushed them. The scouts captured twenty-eight of the blacks and killed several more. When some of the prisoners tried to escape, Harvey re-stored order by hanging one man "as an example." A year later, a force of some thirty slaves stole horses and weapons from their masters in southwestern Mississippi. A "squad of scouts" intercepted the gang as it headed for Union-occupied Natchez, killed most of them, and captured the rest.[48]

The largest concentration of fugitive slaves in Mississippi worked on the leased plantations. These field hands, most living as families, posed little physical threat to the citizenry, but Confederates regarded their very presence an affront to the nation. As in Louisiana, guerril-las targeted both whites and blacks, soldiers and civilians, who occu-pied what the rebels regarded as stolen property. A northern lessee named Isaac Shoemaker learned this at great cost. He had inspected confiscated plantations in Louisiana and Mississippi before leasing lands near Vicksburg in early 1864. Shoemaker settled in Mississippi because he had been told Louisiana was a more dangerous place, but he found conditions no better in Mississippi. "Guerrillas were roaming the neighborhood, driving off blacks, mules, & planters," Shoemaker reported. He had been in the state only a few weeks when the Union officer responsible for hiring out laborers told him the neighborhood was "no longer safe." When guerrillas kidnaped sixteen of his workers a few days later, Shoemaker sold out. The government, he decided, had "entirely underrated the ability and energy, and perseverance of the South to do mischief."[49]

Though overwhelmed by the forces of anarchy, the state's remaining irregular fighters did what was possible to stave off defeat. Their num-bers, though, had been reduced by death, capture, consolidation, and repeal of the Partisan Ranger Act. Funderburk Mooney, one of northern Mississippi's most colorful and popular guerrillas, died early in 1864 when he attempted to halt a shipment of cotton to the Federals. One of the smugglers split open Mooney's head with an ax. A few companies and battalions survived, but far more of them had been reduced to a dozen or so men. Sol Street, William Falkner, and Robert Richardson were gone. Some people said good riddance, for at times the trio had caused more trouble than they were worth.[50]

Captain William E. Montgomery survived as Mississippi's most effective rebel partisan. Operating as "scouts" under state authority, his disciplined Herndon Rangers had Clark's full confidence. The governor authorized Montgomery to impress needed provisions and gave him "full power" to apprehend spies, disrupt Union efforts to cultivate abandoned plantations, capture fugitive slaves, apprehend "troublesome or dangerous" deserters, and break up illicit trade. That he should also bedevil the Union army whenever possible went without saying.[51]

Montgomery operated primarily in Bolivar County, a crucial point on the Mississippi River midway between Vicksburg and Memphis. His rangers captured and burned river traffic and cotton. They fired into troop transports and captured both Union soldiers and civilian boat captains. They broke up a small but dangerous band of armed fugitive slaves that operated from an island in the river. The rangers delighted in arresting or punishing troublesome Unionists, especially men who had originally supported the Confederacy. "It looks hard to me," Montgomery confessed, "to see people taking the oath & placing themselves under the protection of the Yankees & living in plenty, when those who are true to the country have to be burned out & their families to suffer." Loyal citizens fully supported the Herndon Rangers and appreciated their handling of "disloyal people." Governor Clark showed his pleasure by promoting Montgomery to major, doubling the size of his command, and telling him to expand his operations to neighboring counties.[52]

Montgomery's success made him a special target of Union forces in northern Mississippi. As early as November 1863, when Montgomery first started to make a name for himself, the Mississippi Marine Brigade burned his plantation. Colonel George E. Currie allowed the family to remove some furniture and bed clothing before setting fire to the house, but his soldiers and Montgomery's slaves then took at least half of the salvaged articles. "He acted brutally & cowardly," charged an incensed Montgomery, who then redoubled his efforts against the Federals. They, in turn, responded by putting more pressure on the partisan chief. "The Yankees have made their boasts that they . . . intend to capture me at all hazards," he informed Clark, "[and] failing in that they threaten to take my family & hold them as *hostages* for my *good behavior*." It became more than a threat when a Union raiding party dragged Montgomery's father from his home and talked of hanging him. Seeing that not even this action would intimidate the son, they released the older man.[53]

Montgomery and his men outlasted the Marine Brigade, too. The Herndon Rangers remained in tact until the end of the war, but the Marine Brigade's mixed record had doomed it by August 1864. Operating primarily in Louisiana and Mississippi, General Alfred Ellet's men had destroyed guerrilla haunts, captured and killed guerrillas, and confiscated much livestock and cotton. Unfortunately for their reputation, not all of these raids had been authorized, and a good deal of looting had accompanied the legal confiscation. Then there had been episodes like the destruction of Montgomery's plantation, including, even more dramatically, the burning of the village of Austin, Mississippi. Admiral Porter, who had never warmed to the marines, believed that the brigade added to his problems. Like most army and navy commanders, Porter walked a fine line between retaliating against guerrillas and their supporters while, at the same time, discouraging the general mistreatment of southern civilians. His own sailors gave him enough trouble; he did not need the marines to make things worse. He wanted the navy—and his own squadron especially—to be "considered a protection to the people who wish to be peaceful."[54]

Yet, in some ways, the Marine Brigade became the scapegoat for deeper failures in the Union navy's counterguerrilla strategy. Whatever the brigade's record, the fact remained that rebel guerrillas continued to endanger naval and commercial vessels on the principal western rivers. As with their operations on land, the rebels no longer had a legitimate chance to defeat the navy or run the Federals out of the Mississippi River valley, but they continued to exact a toll in lives and property. Admiral Porter downplayed the threat. "Stories . . . about guerrillas are half fabrications," he insisted. True enough, but Porter well knew what trouble the other half brewed. Some of the continuing problems stemmed from a failure to coordinate the operations of the army and navy, but deeper, more systemic problems remained, most notably, illicit trade. Small wonder Porter leaped at an opportunity to escape the guerrilla mire by accepting command of the North Atlantic Blockading Squadron.[55]

Surveying the course of the war from his Virginia home, Edmund Ruffin remained optimistic as 1864 drew to a close. As he saw it, his guerrilla war still promised to win southern independence. Quantrill in Missouri and Mosby in Virginia should be models for the entire country, he declared. He knew guerrillas had their critics; he acknowledged that men like William Quantrill sometimes went too far. But had Quantrill in sacking Lawrence done anything that James Lane or Doc Jennison had not bragged of doing in Missouri? "It is truly a horrible & deplorable mode of warfare," the Virginian conceded. "But as the Yankee government & army have deliberately chosen to inaugurate & persist in it, I earnestly hope that numerous bands, like this of Quantrill's, even though actuated only by the love of plunder & thirst for vengeance, may thus rush into the Yankee territory, & burn & plunder the towns & devastate the country."[56]

Irregular operations had inspired the most significant rebel achievements of the past year, Ruffin maintained. Price's raid into Missouri, the burning of Chambersburg, the shooting of Meigs, Mosby's elusive strikes, harassment of federal river traffic, and a resurrected defense in Kentucky had buoyed spirits that might easily have been crushed by the sight of Lee's army trapped in Richmond and Hood's army destroyed in Tennessee. Ruffin was not convinced of the strategic value of all these operations, particularly not Price's ill-advised Missouri raid, but he admired the boldness of the undertakings. All, too, had been either much warranted retaliatory strikes or admirable efforts to resist ruthless invaders. He grieved to see so many places, especially on the border, "prey to lawless men" who had taken advantage of unsettled conditions, but he predicted that "strong guerrilla movements" across the South would eventually thwart the Federals.[57]

What bothered Ruffin—indeed, infuriated him—was the failure of Jefferson Davis to wage a more ruthless war and exploit the nation's guerrilla advantage. Time and again the Confederate president threatened more forceful retaliation against Yankee treatment of citizens and soldiers, only to shrink back. Davis would do well to follow Quantrill's example, Ruffin insisted. How could he allow the actions of Halleck, Sherman, Sheridan, Paine, Burbridge, Milroy, Butler, Wild, and countless others go unchallenged? The Federals ignored the clear legal status of the Confederacy's partisan warriors while dictating their own rules of engagement. They had murdered Confederate "soldiers" and burned entire communities, but still Davis did nothing. Why did such a "merciful & scrupulous president" even bother to wage war? Ruffin asked sarcastically. The Virginian longed to see again the fiery defiance, the unflappable resolve Confederates had shown at the start of the contest. He yearned for the grand people's war, even if it led to the often predicted "war of extermination."[58]

The Confederacy's "merciful & scrupulous" president got a jolt on April 2, 1865, when he learned in the midst of Sunday worship at St. Paul's Episcopal Church that Lee's lines had been broken at Petersburg. The general was preparing to escape Richmond with his army. Jefferson Davis, Lee advised, should also leave the city. As he exited the church, some worshipers thought the half-blind, physically frail chief executive looked alarmed. Other people saw no emotion. Most certainly, his still agile mind was racing, considering what to do next. He harbored no doubt that his government and the war must continue, but by what means? He left Richmond by train that night, bound for Danville, Virginia, near the North Carolina border.[1]

On April 4, from Danville, Davis issued his last proclamation to the Confederate people. A Union army had violated Richmond, he announced, but the war for independence would go on. The struggle had only entered "a new phase." Davis portrayed the loss of Richmond as a blessing in disguise. Confederate armies, freed from the necessity of "guarding cities and particular points," he explained, could move at will and "strike in detail the detachments and garrisons of the enemy." The principal armies remained in the field, and Lee would soon join forces with General Joseph E. Johnston in North Carolina. "Nothing is now needed to render our triumph certain," Davis emphasized, "but the exhibition of our own unquenchable resolve." By capturing Richmond, the Federals merely gained a few more acres of southern soil; they could never crush "unconquered and unconquerable hearts."[2]

It almost sounded as though the president, in these desperate days, hoped a people's war might yet save the country, but he thought nothing of the sort. Davis knew better. He had never seen guerrillas as anything more than an adjunct to his armies. They could not win the war single-handedly, or even prolong it for any significant time. Only the combined forces of Lee and Johnson, not scattered partisan bands, could halt the enemy's advance. Davis had said as much to Braxton Bragg, his new chief of staff, the day before receiving the fateful message at St. Paul's. He repeated his belief in a message to Lee on April 9, before learning of the general's surrender that same day.[3]

Lee agreed, even in surrender. He urged Davis on April 20 to end the war. The nation east of the Mississippi River was unable "morally or physically" to continue fighting, Lee wrote. No new armies could be raised. "A partisan war may be continued, and hostilities protracted," the general admitted, but that would only cause further suffering and devastate the country. "I see no prospect by that means," concluded the president's most trusted military adviser, "of achieving a separate independence." The president's cabinet endorsed this position two days later. Following nearly a week of negotiations and discussions, Generals Sherman and Johnston had reached tentative terms of surrender for the Army of Tennessee. Before approving the generous conditions, Davis asked the members of his cabinet if they saw any reasonable way or reason to continue the war. They recommended unanimously to end the fighting.[4]

Most cabinet members went a step further. Appreciating the prominent role that guerrilla warfare had played in the life of the Confederacy, and knowing the president's past efforts to find a workable partisan system, they urged him not to treat guerrilla warfare as an option. John C. Breckinridge, who had replaced James Seddon as secretary of war, said that many people might be willing to continue fighting as bushwhackers, but such a struggle would "lose entirely the dignity of regular warfare." Secretary of State Judah P. Benjamin, the president's longest serving and most trusted cabinet member, also rejected it. "Guerrilla or partisan warfare," he told Davis, "would entail far more suffering on our own people than it would cause damage to the enemy." Benjamin doubted, too, that most citizens had the stomach for protracting the contest in that way.[5]

The cabinet may have been so emphatic because they knew that many men wanted to fight on by any means. "We will fight a guerrilla war & be victorious in the end," predicted a North Carolina soldier who had sensed impending defeat several months earlier. "I hardly think it will come to this," he continued hopefully, "but if it must, let it come. I would rather fight them that way than any other." In Louisiana, a cavalry officer favored retreating to Texas to reconstitute the army as a guerrilla force. "From present prospects," he informed his wife, "I can see no hope but in the guerillas mode of defending our country. In a short time, perhaps in a few months, our armies will be so much reduced from divers causes, that we will not be able to face the enemy in the field. Then . . . we shall have to go to bushwhacking. I'll be one for the balance of my life rather than listen to propositions of reconstruction." Amazingly, General Rosser, so instrumental in having the Partisan Ranger Act repealed, wanted "to keep up a sort of Guerrilla warfare on the other side of Jas [James] River," reported a friend.[6]

Some civilians also saw hope in the country's partisan warriors. Diehards like Edmund Ruffin scoffed at capitulation. He willed President Davis to carry on the fight. Many people thought Mosby could reverse the Confederacy's fortunes single-handedly. Prior to the assassination of Abraham Lincoln, rumors circulated that he had captured the federal president. Another report had his men dashing into Richmond. "He tore down the enemies flag," rejoiced a North Carolinian, "planted ours in its stead & killed many Contrabands etc & made his way out without injury." Informed that Mosby's battalion refused to surrender with the rest of Lee's army, a Virginia woman gushed of their leader, "God bless his *noble, brave unyielding Southern heart.* . . . Oh! Mosby must we give thee up?" Equally telling, a rumor that Mosby had been wounded and captured sparked rejoicing in Union ranks.[7]

On the whole, though, Davis, Lee, and the others had read the mood of the country correctly. However unconquered their hearts, most people had long since given up hope of victory. Some folks had done so as early as 1863, and many more reached that conclusion in the final months of the war. The chaos of the guerrilla conflict influenced more than a few decisions. "Everybody is down on them," a Mississippian declared of the partisans in her state. Guerrillas would needlessly prolong the war's suffering.[8]

An Alabama clergyman hoped people would forsake both bushwhacking and organized guerrilla resistance. "These are wrong in principle and practice," he said, "and whatever apology men may have for them during the war, there can be none now." A South Carolinian who had gloried in the exploits of men like John Hunt Morgan, decided after talking to returning soldiers that it simply made no sense to ask "a handful of men to oppose the whole power of the victory flushed North." Many former guerrillas agreed. Like the president's cabinet, they thought it "would not only be fruitless of any good, but be a source of serious injury to the people by inviting retaliatory measures." A Louisiana guerrilla moaned when Richard Taylor surrendered his army in early May, "We are whiped, whiped, whiped."[9]

As obvious as all this seemed to be, it remained a difficult decision for some Confederates to make. An Arkansas guerrilla who came in quietly from the bush found it hard, nonetheless, to give up the struggle. "For eighteen months after the war," he recalled, "I never saw a scout of yankees but what I felt like fighting, and was uneasy every time I met them." A South Carolinian knew that guerrilla resistance must cause the South "to suffer," but the man so dreaded life "under Yankee rule" that he could not help calculating the odds of a continuing guerrilla war. "It will be a desperate game," he admitted, "but . . . if the Yankees attempt to drive us to the wall this is bound to be the result. There are too many men at home who know the use of arms ever to sit down quietly and submit." He could not endorse such action, but he was willing to let "God . . . work this thing in his own time and way."[10]

The soul-searching reflected a historical pattern. Guerrilla movements are born of the people they serve. Irregulars must have the active support of the civilian population to survive. When the people turn against them or grow weary of war, guerrillas cannot continue to fight as representatives of the people. Their end rarely comes in a grand capitulation, as it does for conventional armies. Rather, guerrillas gradually read the situation, lay down their arms, and return to peaceful pursuits. Men who refuse to recognize defeat become outlaws, condemned by the people.[11]

The Confederacy's guerrillas followed this pattern in most respects, yet America's guerrilla war had become so intense and confused that it could not fail to pose contradictions. By the summer of 1865, much of the Confederacy's guerrilla struggle had been divorced from the goals and purposes of the government for some time. Neither surrender nor decree could turn off the spigot of guerrilla violence. While the conventional fighting had been winding down, guerrillas and raiders carried on as usual. Deserter bands grew in size and boldness. The safety of citizens and security of communities was never more endangered. Not even the surrender of armies fazed them. Surrender, as they saw it, meant betrayal. They would become outlaws, if necessary, to settle accounts and continue their private wars. They feared, too, how the Federals would treat them if they came in from the bush.

Union soldiers and sailors had no reason to think rebel guerrillas would retire quietly. "There is more or less of our men found dead every day," reported a dispirited Union cavalryman only weeks before the armies began to surrender. "They are killed in various ways, some of them are shot, some hung, some have their throats cut." Eleven men had been found with their hearts cut out. Rumors circulated from Missouri to Virginia that bushwhackers had targeted leading Union officers, including Ulysses Grant. Someone shot at Grenville Dodge, recently installed as commander of the Department of the Missouri, in downtown St. Louis after he announced a new list of retaliatory measures against guerrillas. McNeill's rangers did not kill any generals, but in February they snatched Generals George Crook and Benjamin Kelley, no strangers to the guerrilla war, during a dawn raid on Crook's head-quarters at Cumberland, Maryland. They paroled them a few weeks later, and people on both sides laughed about the incident. An embarrassed Crook called it "the most brilliant exploit of the war!" although he later blamed it on skulduggery and an "ignorant" picket from whom the rebels had wangled the Union countersign.[12]

Confederates, for their part, were just as concerned about rampaging deserters and Unionists. "We are killing some of these fellows," a Confederate colonel reported from Virginia, "and as soon as the weather moderates sufficiently and my horses are in proper fix I intend to do my utmost to clear the country of them." Another officer used nearly identical language to summarize the situation in southern Louisiana, where rebel guerrillas supposedly held "almost undisputed possession" of the region. He reported the swamps "infested with Jay-hawkers" who were "robbing & murdering" the citizens. In North Carolina, expeditions continued to search the swamps for "deserters & Niggers." Even northern civilians were aware of the ongoing threats to rebel security. A New Yorker, on learning that Jefferson Davis had fled Richmond, considered, "The best disposition destiny can make of the scoundrel would be to let him be grabbed by some of the organized bands of deserters and refugees who hold the hill country of North Carolina and Virginia. They would award him a high gallows and a short shrift, and so dispose of a troublesome question."[13]

South Carolina finally experienced the guerrilla war in earnest, which was perhaps fitting. Not only had South Carolina been the first state to secede, but its Revolutionary War heritage of guerrilla resistance, founded by Francis Marion and Thomas Sumter, had done much to shape southern perceptions of war. Likewise, native son William Gilmore Simms had promoted and sanctified partisan warfare, and many South Carolinians had rushed to fight as guerrillas on the border. Yet, except for a few deserter bands, the state had remained largely untroubled by either guerrilla fighting or the conventional war before February 1865.

When Sherman's army, fresh from its subjugation of Georgia, entered the state, the heirs of Francis Marion accomplished little against the onslaught. The destruction of South Carolina towns and plantations exceeded the swath carved through Georgia. Even some Union soldiers expressed shock at the extent of the "awful punishment" so delivered. The most rebel guerrillas could do—although they accomplished it with uncommon flair—was to pick off stragglers and foragers. Lone Union soldiers did not stand a chance. The impotence felt by the rebels against the general advance made them all the more ferocious when given a chance to retaliate. They hanged, shot, or slashed the throats of over a hundred Federals, twice as many as guerrillas had killed between Atlanta and Savannah.[14]

South Carolina governor Andrew G. Magrath did not call on the citizenry to rise up in a people's war, as had most other governors when faced with Union invasion. Magrath, who served as a judge for most of the war, had only taken office in late December 1864. He preferred an organized militia system to partisan defenders, even proposing to Zebulon Vance and Joe Brown, the governors of neighboring North Carolina and Georgia, that they combine their militias for mutual defense. He hoped, in time, to bring Alabama, Mississippi, and Florida into the coalition. It was a radical, unprecedented plan, and a telling one. Magrath had clearly given up on the Confederate army for protection. Yet, even as the "savage violence" of Sherman's advance forced him to abandon his capital of Columbia, Magrath made only two concessions to independent operations. First, just prior to Sherman's invasion, he endorsed a new battalion of cavalry to serve along the Savannah River. Then, as the storm passed over his state and into North Carolina, he authorized three companies of independent cavalry "for the protection of persons and property from more lawless persons."[15]

As Magrath had anticipated, the most intense guerrilla fighting in South Carolina came in the wake of Sherman's departure. Bands of independent "scouts," having no apparent links to the government, organized to protect property. Some companies formed from army and militia commands that had been bypassed and cut off by the Union advance. Elsewhere, still loyal deserters, discharged soldiers, and citizens joined together. In either case, operating as "guerillas except in name," they pitted themselves against deserters, pillagers, and fugitive slaves. The blacks became their principal concern, especially where gangs of slaves plundered plantations and evaded capture. Brutal pitched battles occurred in some places, one of the biggest coming in late March near Pineville. Neighborhood rebels killed many of the band of thirty armed fugitives, including their leader.[16]

So dangerous did the situation appear at first that South Carolina scouts thought only of killing fugitive slaves, not of capturing them. Their desperate measures reflected the deepest fears of white South Carolinians, the most profound type of social breakdown imaginable. They trembled at the thought of complete anarchy and racial war, and it was now those fears that justified guerrilla action as a last defense. The same fear of racial upheaval spread to North Carolina when Sherman entered that state. Even though he was not bent on punishing the Tar Heels, destruction by an invading army now seemed the least of rebel concerns.[17]

Across the broader South, the surrender of Confederate armies made a difference, but only slowly and quite unevenly. In Virginia, last refuge of the partisan rangers, John Mosby gave the Federals a few uneasy days when he refused to surrender with Lee's army. He did not wish to spill more blood, Mosby claimed, but no one had ordered him to capitulate, and Joe Johnston was still in the field. Even when Mosby acknowledged the end—less than a week before Johnston did so—he could not bring himself to "surrender" his men. Instead, he told them, "I am no longer your commander," and asked them to "disband." It came as a relief to the Federals when nearly all of Mosby's battalion sought paroles over the next few days. In Arkansas, Jeff Thompson was no longer a "partisan," but the many guerrillas who attached themselves to his command followed his lead when he surrendered in early June. He waited that long, Thompson maintained, because, like Mosby, no one had ordered him to surrender, even though—again, like Mosby—he regretted "exceedingly the necessity of sacrificing more 'brave men.'"[18]

Other guerrillas, both the notable and the obscure, met harder ends. Sue Mundy had already been hanged in March, and his compatriot, Henry Magruder, followed him to the gallows in October. Buck Brown, in Arkansas, died in a skirmish with Union troops at nearly the same time Mundy met his fate. John Mobberly was assassinated in early April by Union rangers after being lured into a trap by three civilians. The civilians shared a $1,000 reward for their role. Authorities displayed the guerrilla's corpse at Harpers Ferry, where souvenir hunters cut off pieces of his clothing and hair. The remainder of Mobberly's men surrendered two weeks later. Most guerrillas received paroles if they surrendered voluntarily, but "notorious" characters, or men wanted for civil crimes, still faced legal proceedings. Champ Ferguson fell into that category. Tried and convicted on fifty-three counts of murder when captured in May, Ferguson was hanged in October. Tinker Dave Beaty enjoyed the opportunity to testify against his nemesis, but Ferguson remained unrepentant. "I . . . will die a Rebel," he told the court. "I believe I was right in all I did."[19]

As the guerrilla war flourished beyond these diehards and holdouts, northerners realized that added "inducements" might be required. For some people, this meant further retaliation, especially in the wake of the assassination of President Lincoln. Northerners who had thought the secessionists "conquered, crushed, subjugated, and under our feet" demanded "vindictive justice" for rebels who still refused to surrender after that dark deed. "Up with the Black Flag now!" shouted a New Yorker. More reasonably, if just as resolutely, the Union's military leaders followed a less provocative course. Ulysses S. Grant decided in early May that a two-week amnesty would be a "cheap way to get clear of guerrillas." He encouraged district commanders to offer paroles to guerrillas east of the Mississippi River who laid down their arms by May 20. Armed rebels found after that date would be treated as "outlaws." A week later, he extended the grace period to June 1.[20]

Grant's offer of paroles settled the matter for men who had hesitated to surrender only because they feared retribution. It appears to have inspired McNeill's rangers, the last of the active partisan rangers in Virginia, to lay down arms a few days later. However, other men either did not trust the Federals or simply refused to admit defeat. General Milroy asked Grant almost facetiously how he should treat a gang of Tennessee guerrillas who had murdered two of his scouts, robbed and shot several Unionists, gang-raped a Unionist woman, and attempted to rape a sixteen-year-old girl "in the same room with the corpse of her cousin," whom they had killed. Should such "demons incarnate," Milroy queried, be allowed to surrender under Grant's terms? No, came the reply, and as similar gangs operated through the summer and into the fall, they either went down fighting or, if captured, faced military courts. Quantrill, as one might suspect, went down fighting. He died on June 6, after being wounded and captured a month earlier near Louisville. A bullet lodged against his spine had left him paralyzed below the shoulders.[21]

The situation proved more dicey west of the Mississippi River. Communications were poor, and the Confederate command structure had dissolved rapidly. This explains Jeff Thompson's hesitancy to surrender, and the very last rebel general to wave the white flag was Cherokee partisan Stand Watie, on June 23. Then, too, some of the most ruthless and determined guerrillas roamed the Trans-Mississippi. Many of Quantrill's old band never gave up. In Louisiana, a few small bands thwarted the Federals well into October. Many of these men had fought as conventional troops through the entire war, usually far from Louisiana, but as their commands dissolved, they cast their lot with the irregulars. Operating along the Mississippi and in impenetrable swamps, H. U. M. C. Brown and Omer Boudreaux led the most elusive gangs. Brown, having been wounded in May, appears to have returned to his home in Arkansas. In any event, the Federals never apprehended him. Boudreaux, a native Arcadian, felt right at home in the swamps of the Lafourche region. Captured in October and sentenced to hang in November, he was suddenly and mysteriously released from custody. Then, like Brown, he quietly disappeared.[22]

But the rebels were not the sole engines of conflict. Southern Unionists also hindered efforts to wind down the violence. On the positive side, the army could mobilize them to help end the last vestiges of guerrilla resistance. In North Carolina, General Schofield distributed arms to newly formed local companies "for the defense of the state against guerrillas." In Missouri, Union officers depended on the "co-operation of the people . . . to hunt down bushwhackers and enforce the law." Recognizing that local wars had to end before the larger conflict could be concluded, they looked to southern sheriffs and judges to reconstitute civil authority and treat guerrillas as common criminals. "We are garded by our own county men," reported a Missouri Unionist. "We raised two companys of malatia in our Township yeastady to keep out Booshwhackers thieves & marawers of every kind."[23]

However, many Unionists had mixed motives. The dark passions of revenge raged stronger than ever in some communities; men embraced the opportunity to strike again at rebel neighbors, whether or not they posed a danger. Four years of persecution and retaliation had strengthened old quarrels, created new feuds, and instilled deeper bitterness. A Union general commanding at Talladega, Alabama, reported in early June that several Unionists "in disguise" hanged two ex-rebels who had helped arrest deserters during the war. The general sent a patrol in pursuit of the vigilantes, who had taken refuge in the mountains, but he sympathized with their motives. "The mob may have been actuated by a desire to retaliate," he surmised.[24]

The legal system satisfied the desire of many people for justice. Military commissions operated through the remainder of 1865, and civil courts heard cases for murder, arson, and theft against former guerrillas and partisans. Judges generally assumed guilt, and few people escaped punishment, but executions became rarer once the armies surrendered. When a military commission at Louisville sentenced a youthful guerrilla to death in June, Joseph Holt reduced the sentence to ten years' imprisonment. On further appeals, which made much of the culprit's age, he was eventually released after only a year of incarceration.[25]

This is not to say that summary executions ceased. "Nothing new is happening," reported a Union soldier from Little Rock on the last day of May, "except for the occasional rebel or rebel sympathizer who gets shot, or a few Guelleras who get hanged." In Unionist strongholds like northern Alabama and East Tennessee, local wars barely skipped a beat. Some Unionists believed their security was no less at stake than it had been in 1862, especially in communities beyond the reach of U.S. authority. Deserter bands continued to operate on this premise, too, unwilling to disband until they knew the rebels had been crushed. Just as often, though, tories wanted either to punish ex-rebels or drive them out of their communities completely, as rebels had done to them during the war. They waited expectantly for Confederate guerrillas to return home, that they might "send the ruffians without judge & jury to their long home."[26]

Some soldiers and guerrillas feared to return home even with parole in hand, and many former rebels recalled the early months of "peace" as the most dangerous time of the war. Walking in open country, deprived of their weapons, the men felt utterly exposed. While many victims were clearly targeted for assassination, much of the violence remained random, which was even more unnerving. Northern journalists who descended on the South to report conditions were appalled by the violence, but they little understood how or why the situation had evolved. Southerners had become almost inured to death, and far too many of them, having become accustomed to retaliating against enemies and threatening circumstances with deadly force, regarded punishment and revenge as ways of life. "Another man shot," noted a resident of Knoxville matter-of-factly in August. "This morning a man (southern) named Cox was in Tooles store when a Lincolnite named Foster came in shook hands with him, inquired after his health & just as Cox turned round shot him in the back first[,] then in three other places."[27]

A final source of continuing violence came from renegades, marauders, and outlaws who respected neither side. More bent on stealing horses and property than injuring people, they, nonetheless, did not hesitate to kill. Many gangs had operated during the war. Seeing that peace generated nearly as much confusion and brought few legal consequences, they saw no reason to end their spree. Some raiders were bitter ex-Confederate soldiers who believed they had a right to take what they wanted as payment for their wartime service. Union soldiers also continued to exploit and mistreat southern civilians when they thought they could escape detection. It was an all-too-familiar routine for many communities. "The citizens are out on guard every night," an Arkansan reported. "I listen every night to hear of a collision with some of the bands of robbers. . . . We are now experiencing a state of perfect anarchy."[28]

Nor would the South soon escape the legacy of violence, vigilantism, and outlawry spawned by the guerrilla war. The political battles of Reconstruction followed the military struggle of 1861–65. Union troops continued to occupy the South. Former rebels and wartime Unionists continued to fight each other. The struggle ostensibly played itself out at the ballot box, but in purpose and prosecution, it differed little from the war years. Community control and home rule remained the objectives, and, as in the guerrilla contests of the war years, postwar political battles often turned bloody. Revenge and retaliation remained important ingredients, too, with their roots often anchored in wartime collisions. New guerrilla bands formed to intimidate wrong-headed neighbors and outsiders alike. No one called them guerrillas any more, and they did not try to adopt the "partizan" label. Postwar irregulars took colorful names, such Ku Klux Klan or Knights of the White Camelia, but their methods were unaltered. The rifle, knife, and rope remained their weapons; the isolated, vulnerable, and weak were still their victims. One might label postwar enforcers the final mutation of the people's war. And to complete the wartime picture, former Unionist guerrillas and raiders, including Tennessee's George W. Kirk and Arkansas's Thomas Jefferson Williams, came out of retirement to oppose them.[29]

The worst wartime mutation—outlawry—survived quite literally. Whether fighting to resist northern Republican rule or only to gather additional spoils, some guerrillas embarked on careers of lawlessness after the war. The James and Younger brothers of Missouri achieved the most notoriety, but other, similarly hardened characters refused to forsake their bushwhacker lives. Some of them, doubtless, would have chosen the outlaw's path even without a war, but there is no dodging the fact that their wartime careers increased the chances of it. They became, in the end, victims of the violence they had spawned.[30]

Yet, the majority of ex-guerrillas retired, if grudgingly, to peaceful pursuits, some of them to contemplate their legacy. That legacy is worth considering. There are two of them, really: the collective and the personal. The collective legacy, meaning how guerrillas helped shape the war, can scarcely be overstated. The guerrilla conflict in all its guises— Unionist and rebel guerrillas, partisan rangers, lone bushwhackers, guerrilla hunters, deserter bands, and outlaw gangs—made the war a far bloodier affair than the armies alone could have done. They prolonged the war by months at least, and Confederate guerrillas influenced the military policies of both sides. Rebel irregulars also helped their nation lose the war. The Confederates may well have lost anyway, outnumbered and overmatched materially as they were, but the guerrilla war injured their efforts in two dramatic ways. First, they forced Union commanders to alter their military strategies and occupation policies. Both rebounded on the Confederates. Second, the guerrilla war contributed to the erosion of Confederate morale and unity. This resulted partly from the destruction wrought by Union strategy and policy on southern communities, but it came also from weaknesses the guerrilla war exposed in the Confederate government. The inability of political and military leaders to exploit the benefits of guerrilla warfare splintered a national bid for independence into a hundred local wars for survival and shook public confidence in the ability of the government to protect its citizens.

The personal legacy is a bit tricker. Union guerrillas and guerrilla hunters might well be satisfied with their wartime roles, for they had won. But what of the rebels, the losers? Historians, tending to endorse the nobility of the Union cause, have not been complimentary, but then neither, for that matter, were many ex-Confederates. The guerrilla war had exposed too many fissures in southern life. The community and family divisions that defined such a large part of the guerrilla war, not to mention its unbridled savagery, could only embarrass people who wished to have their rebellion remembered as a noble and united enterprise. Yet, rebel guerrillas had always thought of themselves as "soldiers," a conceit they continued to embrace for the rest of their lives. Believing they had fought honorably in a just cause, they seemed not to have understood the damage they often did to the image of the Confederacy and to the morale of its people. In truth, they could easily counter that much of the damage so done should not be attributed to them directly. The worst destruction in the South came from the track of anarchy bred by inconsistent government policies, the retaliation elicited from Union foes, and the outlaw bands that exploited their methods. Many ex-Confederate guerrillas tried to distance themselves from these consequences by joining Confederate veteran organizations, thus buttressing their identity as legitimate soldiers. Other, bolder men refused to hide or apologize. They emphasized their unique wartime roles by forming their own veterans groups. Quantrill's and Mosby's men, most notably, held reunions well into the twentieth century.[31]

In private correspondence and published memoirs, former guerrillas also justified their war. "I never understood guerillas as a 'debasing epithet," insisted John Mosby in 1899. As the Confederacy's most famous "partisan," the Virginian might well have denied any connection to guerrillaism. Instead, he declared, "I have often seen the term — Guerilla Chief — applied to me in Southern papers. I never regarded it as an insult." Nor did lesser-known men. "We had some bad men in our command who got to be almost as bad as the Kansas jayhawkers," admitted an Arkansas guerrilla in 1897. He could not excuse the repulsive actions of some guerrillas, and he insisted that no good southerner should try to do so. Yet, the Arkansan defended his chosen style of warfare. Unlike the marauders of both armies, whether soldiers or guerrillas, the war for him had been "a matter of principle." Of course, principle, like patriotism, can be the last refuge of a scoundrel. Frank James had excused the Centralia massacre in nearly identical language. The truth is, these men, caught in the snares of a violent world, did not give much thought to their actions at the time. They only did what seemed necessary to survive. Honest men who later understood the enormity of their violent deeds felt compelled to justify them. Either that or put them out of mind. John Mosby understood this impulse, too. Near the end of his life, the Gray Ghost confessed, "The bloody part of the War I like to keep in the background."[32]

NOTES

The full titles of both published works and manuscript sources, shortened in these notes, can be found in the bibliography. The only abbreviations used are the standard *OR* and *ORN*, for the *Official Records* of the Union and Confederate armies and navies; the full titles appear in the bibliography under "Published Primary Sources," U.S. War Department (*OR*) and U.S. Navy Department (*ORN*).

PROLOGUE

1. *New York Times*, April 19, 1861; Nevins and Thomas, *Diary of . . . Strong*, 3:124.

2. Nevins and Thomas, *Diary of . . . Strong*, 3:124.

3. Ellenberger, "Whigs in the Streets?" 27; Evitts, *Matter of Allegiance*, 168–79; Towers, "Vociferous Army." The latter is the best brief description of the April 19 episode; for the broader background, see Towers, *Urban South*, 159–66. See also Clark, "Baltimore and the Attack on the Sixth Massachusetts," and Baldwin, "First Blood in Baltimore."

4. Ellenberger, "Whigs in the Streets?"; Evitts, *Matter of Allegiance*, 97–98, 102–4, 108–17, 184; Grimsted, *American Mobbing*, 234–38; Towers, *Urban South*, 166–70.

5. Evitts, *Matter of Allegiance*, 179–80.

6. G. W. Brown, *Baltimore*, 49; Towers, "Vociferous Army," 25.

7. G. W. Brown, *Baltimore*, 52–53; *OR*, I:2:16–17; Towers, "Vociferous Army," 25; George M. Brown to Thomas L. Hicks, April 20, 1861, Letterbook, 1854–65, Maryland Governor Papers.

8. Evitts, *Matter of Allegiance*, 180–82; Nevins and Thomas, *Diary of . . . Strong*, 3:129; *OR*, I:2:11, 15; Agle and Wanzer, "Dearest Braddie," 83. Freehling, *South vs. the South*, 51, also notes the guerrilla dimensions of the events in Baltimore, although he does not recognize the significance of the pattern they established.

9. Evitts, *Matter of Allegiance*, 182–83, 185–90; J. H. Baker, *Politics of Continuity*, 54–58; Charles P. Lord to sister, June 17, 1861, Lord Papers.

10. J. H. Baker, *Politics of Continuity*, 55; Thomas H. Hicks to Edward M. Mobley, July 29, 1861, Letterbook, 1854–65, Maryland Governor Papers; Charles Henry Richardson to Lois Richardson Davis, July 2, 12, 1861, Lois (Wright) Richardson Davis Papers; James Francis to Augustus W. Bradford, February 2, 1862, Letters to Governor, Civil War Executive Papers, Maryland Adjutant General Records; Curl, "Report from Baltimore," 281; Agle and Wanzer, "Dearest Braddie," 84, 86.

CHAPTER 1

1. Nevins and Thomas, *Diary of . . . Strong*, 3:126; M. W. Summers, "'Freedom and Law Must Die Ere They Sever,'" 187; W. H. Russell, *My Diary*, 123; J. Baklin to wife, April 19, 1861, Lord Papers; G. F. Williams, "Under the Despot's Heel," 25. Even poets celebrated the event, as in Brownell, *War-Lyrics*, 69–70.

2. E. Thomas, *Confederacy as a Revolutionary Experience*, 44–46; Durden, "American Revolution as Seen by Southerners in 1861"; Rable, *Confederate Republic*, 44–48; W. C. Davis, *"Government of Our Own,"* 83; *Richmond Dispatch*, April 15, 1861; Wakelyn, *Southern Pamphlets*, 114, 177, 327; Dumond, *Southern Editorials*, 505, 507, 515.

3. Cooling, *Fort Donelson's Legacy*, 65–69. For some of the historical literature that highlights similarities between the partisan warfare of colonial America and the Civil War, see Sutherland, "Guerrilla Warfare," 267–68.

4. J. B. Jones, *Rebel War Clerk's Diary*, 1:87; Simms, *Life of Francis Marion* and *The Partisan*; Busick, *Sober Desire*; Edgar, *Partisans and Redcoats*, 90, 124–25, 132, 134–35; N. B. Tucker, *Partisan Leader*, vii–xix.

5. Marszalek, *Diary of . . . Holmes*, 231–32; N. B. Tucker, *Partisan Leader*, xix–xxiii, 268–71.

6. For the "natural" and "democratic" character of the Confederacy's guerrilla war, see Sutherland, "Guerrilla Warfare," 259–60. For guerrilla outbreaks far removed from the South, see D. A. Smith, "Confederate Cause in the Colorado Territory," 71–75; Conner, *Confederate in the Colorado Gold Fields*, 162–63; M. F. Taylor, "Confederate Guerrillas in Southern Colorado"; Josephy, *Civil War in the West*, 233–39; Kibby, "California's Military Problems," 253–57; *OR*, I:50(1):590.

7. Etcheson, *Bleeding Kansas*; J. Neely, *Border between Them*, 7–95; Mullis, *Peacekeeping on the Plains*; R. M. Brown, *Strain of Violence*, 98–103, and "Western Violence," 6–7; Cheatham, "'Desperate Characters'"; Castel, *Civil War Kansas*, 37–64; Tegtmeier, "Ladies of Lawrence."

8. Viles, "Documents Illustrating Troubles . . . , 1860," 67, 70–74; Cheatham, "Divided Loyalties," 99–102; Starr, *Jennison's Jayhawkers*, 30–35. See also Charles R. Jennison to George L. Stearns, November 28, 1860, Stearns Papers; Adams, *William S. Harney*, 219–22; John S. Bowen to Claiborne Jackson, March 10, 1861, Missouri Volunteer Militia Papers; Gall to Mary A. Gash, May 16, 1861, Mary A. Gash Papers.

9. Starr, *Jennison's Jayhawkers*, 11–14, 43–44; Langsdorf, "Lane and the Frontier Guard"; William B. Gulich to John W. Ellis, April 21, 1861, John W. Ellis Papers; Marszalek, *Diary of . . . Holmes*, 37–38.

10. C. Phillips, *Missouri's Confederate*, 248–49.

11. R. E. Miller, "Daniel Marsh Frost"; Gerteis, *Civil War St. Louis*, 84–87, 98–100.

12. Gerteis, *Civil War St. Louis*, 100–109; C. Phillips, *Missouri's Confederate*,

250–51; Fusz Diary, May 10, 1862; Simpson and Berlin, *Sherman's Civil War*, 81–82.

13. Sarah Jane Full Hill Reminiscences, pt. 1, p. 4.

14. Gerteis, *Civil War St. Louis*, 108–10, 114, 120–25; Adams, *William S. Harney*, 231–39; *OR*, I:1:640–41, 650–51, 655; C. Phillips, *Missouri's Confederate*, 251–61.

15. C. Phillips, *Missouri's Confederate*, 259–60; Crist et al., *Papers of . . . Davis*, 7:188–89.

16. John D. Macfarlane and Walter Lovelace to James O. Broadhead, May 10, 1861, Broadhead Papers; Julian Bates to Edward Bates, July 15, 1861, Bates Family Papers; Edward Bates to Hamilton R. Gamble, July 16, 1861, Gamble Papers. For a useful explanation of the variety of home guard and other local defense organizations, see Newton, "Confederate Home Guard," 44–45.

17. Sophia H. Burlingame to Asa Burlingame, July 31, 1861, Burlingame Family Papers; John F. Benjamin to Frankie, September 1, 1861, Benjamin Letters; Sarah Jane Full Hill Reminiscences, pt. 1, p. 5; Charles Gibson to Hamilton R. Gamble, August 2, 1861, Gamble Papers; Lowndes H. Davis to Mary Davis, June 28, 1861, Lowndes Henry Davis Papers.

18. Fellman, *Inside War*, 39–40; Frizzell, "'Killed by Rebels,'" 369–78; Robert N. Smith to Hamilton R. Gamble, August 13, 1861, Gamble Papers.

19. Murray and Rodney, "Letters of Peter Bryant," 348.

20. Castel, *Civil War Kansas*, 39–41; Starr, *Jennison's Jayhawkers*, 46–47; Sheridan, "From Slavery in Missouri," 31–36; Dirck, "By the Hand of God."

21. Castel, *Civil War Kansas*, 42–47, 50, 58, and "Kansas Jayhawking Raids," 1–4; James Montgomery to George L. Stearns, June 21, July 5, 1861, Stearns Papers; Banasik, *Missouri in 1861*, 227.

22. Starr, *Jennison's Jayhawkers*, 38–42; Trego Diary, June 27, 1861.

23. Starr, *Jennison's Jayhawkers*, 44–64; Gall to sister, May 16, 1861, Mary A. Gash Papers; John T. Hughes to R. H. Miller, September 4, 1861, Parsons Papers.

24. George C. Heberling to Samuel J. Kirkwood, April 24, 1861, War Matters, 1858–97, Iowa Governor Papers; B. T. Roberts to Samuel J. Kirkwood, July 31, 1861, James Mathews to Kirkwood, August 15, 1861, Kirkwood Papers.

25. Richard Chamberlain to Samuel J. Kirkwood, April 25, 1861, W. R. Laughlin to Kirkwood, May 24, 1861, Jesse Evans to Kirkwood, May 27, June 18, 1861, H. M. Hoxie to Kirkwood, June 19, 1861, Thomas M. Bowen to Kirkwood, May 23, 1861, J. C. Huges to Kirkwood, July 21, 1861, Iowa Governor Papers; Cyrus Bussey to Samuel J. Kirkwood, July 27, August 6, 1861, Kirkwood Papers; L. Cox, "Hawkeye Heroes," 5–6.

26. *OR*, I:3:413; John Edwards to Samuel J. Kirkwood, August 9, 1861, Box 68, Correspondence: Southern Border Brigade, Iowa Adjutant General Records;

Mahan, "Over the Border," 204–7, and "Marching as to War"; L. Cox, "Hawkeye Heroes," 10, 16.

27. Francis Deteler to Simon Cameron, July 9, 1861, John T. Croft to Cameron, July 30, 1861, and Albert Hadley to Abraham Lincoln, August 24, 1861, U.S. War Department, Letters Received by U.S. Secretary of War: Irregular Series; T. C. Anking to Abraham Lincoln, August 30, 1861, U.S. War Department, Letters Received by U.S. Secretary of War: Main Series.

28. Cudworth, "Memoirs of Fifty Years Ago," 227–28; J. P. Lancaster to James O. Broadhead, July 3, 1861, Broadhead Papers; C. D. Drake to Hamilton R. Gamble, August 3, 1861, D. K. Pitman to Gamble, August 5, 1861, George Brown to Gamble, August 10, 1861, E. B. Dobyns to Gamble, August 18, 1861, James T. Matson to Gamble, September 13, 1861, Gamble to Abraham Lincoln, August 26, 1861, Gamble Papers. See also letters of William R. Strachan to Simon Cameron, July 17, 1861, U.S. War Department, Letters Received by U.S. Secretary of War: Irregular Series. For one community's remedy for the violence, see *OR*, I:3:412–13, and "Compromise between Missouri Forces," July 24, 1861, Iowa Governor Papers.

29. Banasik, *Missouri in 1861*, 72; L. W. Burns to Hamilton R. Gamble, August 8, 1861, Gamble to Abraham Lincoln, August 26, 1861, Gamble Papers. For the Confederate perspective, see Missouri State Guard, *Letter and Order Book*, 13–14; McGhee, *Voices of the Swamp Fox Brigade*, 7.

30. *OR*, I:3:407; Grimsley, *Hard Hand of War*, 2–3, 35–46; "Lights and Shadows of Life," 143, in Grierson Papers; Hamilton R. Gamble to Abraham Lincoln, August 26, 1861, Gamble Papers.

31. William L. Broaddus to wife, July 12, 1861, Broaddus Papers; James E. Love to Molly, July 9, 20, 23, 1861, Love Papers.

32. *OR*, I:3:432, 438–39.

33. Castel, *Sterling Price*, 34–35, 48; Cudworth, "Memories of Fifty Years Ago," 228–29; *OR*, I:3:11, 130–31, 135, 159, 163, 166, 422, 449, 473, 495; Banasik, *Missouri in 1861*, 69, 71, 80–81, 118, 175, 179.

34. *OR*, I:3:139, 153–54, 658; M. Jeff Thompson to Gideon J. Pillow, August 19, 1861, Pillow Papers. Although dated, the most complete biography of Thompson is Monaghan, *Swamp Fox of the Confederacy*.

35. Schutz and Trenerry, *Abandoned by Lincoln*, 3–6, 57–63, 66–69.

36. *OR*, I:3:403–4, 415–16. See also *OR*, II:1:187, 189–93.

37. *OR*, I:3:417–18, 421–24, 427, II:1:195–203.

38. Cozzens, *General John Pope*, 36–40; *OR*, I:3:134, 456–57, II:1:185–88, 194, 203, 206–8, 210–13; William L. Broaddus to wife, July 26, 1861, Broaddus Papers.

39. *OR*, I:3:133, 458–59;, II:1:204–6, 214–15, 218–19; Charles Gibson to Hamilton R. Gamble, August 8, 1861, Robert N. Smith to Gamble, August 12, 1861, Gamble Papers.

40. *OR*, I:3:449–51.

41. Banasik, *Missouri in 1861*, 104 n.167, 129; John T. Hughes to R. H. Miller, August 29, September 4, 1861, Parsons Papers.

42. Starr, *Jennison's Jayhawkers*, 47; W. W. Smith, "Experiment in Counterinsurgency," 361–63; *OR*, I:3:433–35, 459.

43. *OR*, I:3:466–67.

44. Barton Bates to Edward Bates, September 8, 1861, Bates Family Papers; *OR*, I:3:469.

45. *OR*, I:3:469, 477–78; Gerteis, *Civil War St. Louis*, 149–52. For an earlier attempt by Jessie to intervene with the president over military policy, see Herr and Spence, *Letters of Jessie Benton Frémont*, 262.

46. *OR*, I:3:485, 693; Basler, *Works of Abraham Lincoln*, 4:532; Gerteis, *Civil War St. Louis*, 153–59; Scarborough, *Diary of Edmund Ruffin*, 2:125.

CHAPTER 2

1. Freehling, *South vs. the South*, 47–64, correctly stresses the role of the border states during the first year of the war as a determining factor in the eventual Union victory, although he does not appreciate the full extent or influence of the guerrilla fighting.

2. Fitzhugh, "The Times and the War."

3. *Memphis Daily Appeal*, September 20, 1861; D. M. Washington to Jefferson Davis, May 19, 1861, W. D. Covington to Davis, May 24, 1861, Ben W. Anderson to Davis, May 30, 1861, Stephen H. Rushing to Leroy Pope Walker, May 30, 1861, William James Smith to Walker, June 3, 1861, G. B. Lartique to Walker, June 21, 1861, E. E. Kidd to Walker, June 1, 1861, H. V. Keep to Walker, July 15, 1861, A. H. Canedo to Walker, April 30, 1861, F. F. Foscue to Walker, May 18, 1861, W. T. Harris to Walker, June 27, 1861, U.S. War Department, Letters Received by Confederate Secretary of War.

4. Richard H. Bagby to father, May 29, 1861, Bagby Papers; N. G. Harrison, "'Atop an Anvil,'" 133–47; Scarborough, *Diary of Edmund Ruffin*, 2:18–19, 23–24, 38, 42, 61.

5. J. W. Ware to Jefferson Davis, June 4, 1861, U.S. War Department, Letters Received by Confederate Secretary of War; P. C. Anderson, *Blood Image*, 125–26; Julian J. Mason et al. to Daniel Ruggles, May 29, 1861, Samuel P. Holt to John Letcher, May 7, 1861, Samuel C. Shelton to Letcher, May 6, 1861, Henry Bryan to Letcher, May 7, 1861, H. Duval to Letcher, April 28, 1861, F. W. Pendleton to Letcher, May 16, 1861, T. T. Sawyer to Letcher, April 25, 1861, Virginia Governor Executive Papers: Letcher; *OR*, I:2:833–34.

6. P. C. Anderson, *Blood Image*, 27; John J. Coleman to John Letcher, April 25, 1861, Charles B. Brown to Letcher, May 28, 1861, Virginia Governor Executive Papers: Letcher; Virginia and North Carolina Irrepressibles recruiting poster, Ruffin, Roulhac, and Hamilton Papers, Box 13, folder 158.

7. Carroll, "Lewis Wetzel," 85–87; McQueen McIntosh to Leroy P. Walker, June 26, 1861, J. M. Baker to Walker, September 7, 1861, U.S. War Department, Letters to Confederate Secretary of War.

8. Stauffer, "Advent among the Indians"; Fitzhugh, "The Times and the War," 4.

9. Oliphant et al., *Letters of . . . Simms*, 4:364. For Simms's understanding of the frontier past, see Busick, *Sober Desire*.

10. P. C. Anderson, *Blood Image*, 124, 143–48. Ellington, *Myth of the Noble Savage*, offers a detailed examination of the origins of this ideal, which he defines as "a mythic personification of natural goodness by a romantic glorification of savage life" (p. 1).

11. P. C. Anderson, *Blood Image*, 85–86, 160–65; W. N. McDonald, *Laurel Brigade*, 22–23; John Q. Winfield to wife, June 27, 30, 1861, Winfield Letters.

12. Scarborough, *Diary of Edmund Ruffin*, 2:52. See also Ex-cadet Moncure to Jefferson Davis, July 1, 1861, U.S. War Department, Letters Received by Confederate Secretary of War.

13. Henry H. Withers to W. C. Tavenner, June 22, 1861, Tavenner and Withers Papers; E. C. Smith, *Lewis County*, 306; R. F. Bowers et al. to Simon Cameron, June 4, 1861, U.S. War Department, Letters Received by U.S. Secretary of War: Irregular Series; Richardson, "Raleigh County," 227–29.

14. Allen C. Hammond to John Letcher, April 26, 1861, Jonathan C. Beckwith to Letcher, April 26, 1861, James M. H. Beales to Letcher, April 29, 1861, J. M. McGinis to Letcher, May 1, 1861, James T. Jackson to Letcher, May 1, 1861, J. J. Moorman to Letcher, June 2, 1861, Jonathan Newcomb to Letcher, June 17, 1861, William H. Morrow to Letcher, June 18, 1861, Virginia Governor Executive Papers: Letcher; L. D. Morrall to Samuel Woods, June 29, 1861, Woods Family Papers; D. S. Nicholson to Simon Cameron, May 3, 1861, William A. Hogarth to Cameron, May 13, 1861, Oliver G. Kidd to Cameron, May 17, 1861, U.S. War Department, Letters Received by U.S. Secretary of War: Irregular Series; F. P. Summers, *Baltimore and Ohio*, 80–89.

15. Larkin Pierpont to Francis H. Pierpont, June 19, 1861, George T. Walton to Jonathan S. Carlisle, June 21, 1861, B. D. McGinnis to F. H. Pierpont, July 1, 1861, F. H. Pierpont to McGinnis, July 4, 1861, Virginia Governor Executive Papers: Pierpont (Series I); S. G. Harnsberger to John Letcher, June 7, 1861, James H. Conklyn to Letcher, June 21, 1861, Virginia Governor Executive Papers: Letcher; Byron H. Robb to C. P. Buckingham, July 13, 1861, July 25, [1861] (2:8, 198), Wiley R. Johnston to William Dennison, July 16, 1861 (2:32), William O. Collins to Dennison, July 27, 1861 (3:152), R. G. Andrews to Dennison, August 17, 1861 (5:149), C. D. Brooks to C. P. Buckingham, July 31, 1861 (3:120), Samuel H. Cooke et al. to Dennison, July 10, 1861 (2:48), John Stone to Dennison, July 11, 1861 (2:51), Edward Archibald et al. to Dennison, July 22, 1861 (2:170), Series 147, Correspondence to Governor and Adjutant General, Ohio Adjutant General

Records. For a similar if less serious threat to Pennsylvanians, see W. E. Frazer to Simon Cameron, May 24, 1861, F. D. Hoffman to Cameron, August 16, 1861, U.S. War Department, Letters Received by U.S. Secretary of War: Irregular Series.

16. B. D. McGinnis to Francis H. Pierpont, July 1, 1861, A. I. Boreman to Pierpont, July 26, 1861, Jonathan O. Watson to Pierpont, August 28, 1861, George T. Walton to Jonathan S. Carlisle, June 21, 1861, Virginia Governor Executive Papers: Pierpont (Series I); West Virginia Historical Records Survey, *Calendar of the . . . Pierpont Letters*, 18; G. E. Moore, *Banner in the Hills*, 75–76; Matheny, *Wood County*, 44–46; Athey, "Loyalty and Civil War Liberty," 3–6, 12–13; Citizens of Gilmer County to Francis H. Pierpont, August 27, 1861, No. 420, Pierpont Papers: Small Collection.

17. Matheny, *Wood County*, 47–52; Stutler, *West Virginia*, 141; Curry and Ham, "Bushwhackers' War," 420–21.

18. Curry and Ham, "Bushwhackers' War," 420–21; "The Snake Hunters of Western Virginia," 1–3, Bound Vol. 28 (No. 561), Roy Bird Cook Collection; Phillips and Hill, *War Stories*, 413–14; *OR*, I:5:468.

19. Sedinger, "Border Rangers," 1–3 (No. 1561), Roy Bird Cook Collection; F. S. Sweeny et al. to ——, July 12, 1861 (2:164), J. M. Wisehart to Dear Sirs, August 1, 1861 (3:107), Series 147, Correspondence to Governor and Adjutant General, Ohio Adjutant General Records.

20. Noe, "Exterminating Savages," 106; R. D. Seaman and J. W. Gray to John Letcher, June 11, 1861, Virginia Governor Executive Papers: Letcher; F. P. Summers, *Baltimore and Ohio*, 80; Benson, *With the Army of West Virginia*, 8; Jonathan O. Watson to Francis H. Pierpont, August 28, 1861, Jasper S. Sprague to Pierpont, August 30, 1861, A. Rogers to Pierpont, September 7, 1861, Virginia Governor Executive Papers: Pierpont; Marcia Phillips Journal, June 27, 1861.

21. Charles W. Andrews to Anna Robinson, June 23, 1861, Charles Andrews Papers; W. Skeen to Leroy Pope Walker, June 19, 1861, U.S. War Department, Letters Received by Confederate Secretary of War; Henry Bryan to John Letcher, May 7, 1861, James H. Conklyn to Letcher, June 21, 1861, Jeremiah Morton and H. A. Edmundson to Letcher, June 4, 1861, William B. Mason and William G. Miller to Letcher, June 7, 1861, Virginia Governor Executive Papers: Letcher.

22. Noe, "Exterminating Savages," 107–9; Rafuse, *McClellan's War*, 111; *OR*, I:2:195–96, 5:575–77.

23. Noe, "Exterminating Savages," 107–11; *OR*, I:2:196; Benson, *With the Army of West Virginia*, 65.

24. Benson, *With the Army of West Virginia*, 65–66; Crist et al., *Papers of . . . Davis*, 7:301.

25. John B. Pendleton to wife, July 7, 1861, Pendleton Family Papers; R. C. Carter, *For Honor, Glory, and Union*, 78–79; W. M. McKinney to cousin, July 25, 1861 (No. 858), Roy Bird Cook Collection; C. R. Williams, *Diary and Letters of . . . Hayes*, 2:64; Benson, *With the Army of West Virginia*, 65.

26. C. R. Williams, *Diary and Letters of . . . Hayes*, 2:60, 63–70.

27. Daniel, "Special Warfare," 35–37, 40–43, 52–53; To Dear Sir [William B. Campbell], 1861, Campbell Family Papers; *Memphis Daily Appeal*, June 13, 19, 1861; Thomas B. Eastland to Leroy Pope Walker, July 23, 1861, U.S. War Department, Letters Received by Confederate Secretary of War; Theodore Harris to Isham G. Harris, June 12, 1861, A. O. W. Lattern to I. G. Harris, June 14, 1861, T. M. Carden to I. G. Harris, June 16, 1861, I. G. Harris Papers; Crist et al., *Papers of . . . Davis*, 7:171; Liz to Sallie, April 15, 1861, Lenoir Family Papers.

28. McKenzie, "Contesting Secession," 298; F. H. Gordon to William B. Campbell, April 21, May 24, 1861, Campbell Family Papers; William G. McAdoo to mother, June 7, 1861, McAdoo Papers; Fisher, *War at Every Door*, 37–42; Groce, *Mountain Rebels*, 68–87.

29. Fisher, *War at Every Door*, 42–43, 45–48; D. H. Young et al. to William B. Campbell, June 3, 1861, Campbell Family Papers.

30. Fisher, *War at Every Door*, 42–44, 48–49; Daniel, "Special Warfare," 50–51; Madden, "Unionist Resistance," 23–26.

31. David H. Conrad to brother, [Summer 1861], Conrad Papers; Cooling, *Fort Donelson's Legacy*, 1–7; Basler, *Works of Abraham Lincoln*, 4:532.

32. Mildred C. Sayre to Edmund Ruffin, August 13, 1861, Edmund Ruffin Papers.

33. L. H. Harrison, *Civil War in Kentucky*, 9–10; Coulter, *Civil War and Readjustments*, 226–27; Perret, *Lincoln's War*, 85, 253–54; Lemuel C. Porter Diary, August 17, 1861; J. J. Schovefield to Beriah Magoffin, June 6, 1861, V. Finnell to Magoffin, June 10, 1861, H. M. Price to Magoffin, May 28, 1861, B. F. Butler to Magoffin, July 4, 1861, General Correspondence, Kentucky Governor Papers: Magoffin; J. M. Alexander to Beriah Magoffin, May 23, 1861, Military Correspondence, Kentucky Governor Papers: Magoffin; Josiah A. Jackson to Phil Smigert, July 17, 23, 1861, Kentucky Adjutant General Records; James A. Holbrook to Simon Cameron, May 5, 1861, U.S. War Department, Letters Received by U.S. Secretary of War: Irregular Series; W. L. Coate to George W. Parker, June 5, 1861, George Washington Parker Papers.

34. Mrs. Gus Jones to Lizzie, July 1861, Winston-Jones Family Papers; Maria B. Holyoke to mother and sister, August 16, 1861, Holyoke Family Papers; Alfred Pirtle Journal, August 21, 30, September 1, 1861, Pirtle Papers; Jonathan M. Johnson to Beriah Magoffin, May 31, 1861, Jonathan A. Gardner to Jonathan M. Johnson, June 1, 1861, V. Finnell to Magoffin, June 10, 1861, T. E. Moore to Magoffin, July 13, 1861, General Correspondence, Kentucky Governor Papers: Magoffin; Wills, *Confederacy's Greatest Cavalryman*, 46–48; C. Wickliffe to Scott Brown, June 6, 1861, M. H. Wright to Beriah Magoffin, June 7, 1861, Military Correspondence, Kentucky Governor Papers: Magoffin; *OR*, I:4:182–83, 381.

35. L. H. Harrison, *Civil War in Kentucky*, 11–12; *OR*, I:4:181–82, 185, 193–94; Cooling, *Fort Donelson's Legacy*, 11–16; Maria B. Holyoke to sister, September

8, [1861], Holyoke Family Papers; R. R. Bolling to J. T. Boyle, August 29, 1861, Sherman Papers; Ansel Bement to parents, September 24, 1861, Bement Letter; Coulter, *Civil War and Readjustments*, 227.

36. Lucina Moss to Richard Yates, May 21, 1861, —— to Yates, [April 1861], Parker Earle and Charles Colby to Yates, April 21, 1861, Joshua Teague to Yates, May 13, 1861, Griffin Garland to Yates, May 29, 1861, Yates Family Collection.

37. T. B. Lawson to Richard Yates, April 23, 1861, Lambert Noland to Yates, May 4, 1861, Henry M. McAfee to Yates, May 16, 1861, William Geilhausen to Yates, June 4, 1861, J. M. Kelly to Yates, July 22, 1861, John Gilbert to Yates, July 29, 1861, Ada Earheart to Yates, August 12, 1861, William A. Ginshan to Yates, September 2, 1861, Yates Family Collection.

38. Jacob P. Dunn to Oliver Perry Aiken, May 6, 1861, Aiken Papers; E. Morehouse to Oliver P. Morton, April 1861 (L513, Drawer 106), T. J. Carson to Lazarus Noble, June 15, 1861 (A4017, Drawer 106), Civil War Miscellany, Indiana Adjutant General Records; Robert J. Price to father, October 16, 1861, Robert J. Price Letters; J. S. Power to Oliver P. Morton, June 9, 1861, William W. Slaughter to Morton, June 10, 1861, R. R. Roberts to Morton, September 11, 1861, Morton Correspondence; John Anderson to Oliver P. Morton, August 9, 1861 (L504, Box 28), M. C. Kin to Lew Wallace, April 22, 1861 (L507, Box 5), Morton to Simon Cameron, April 28, 1861 (L514, Drawer 107), Indiana Legion Papers, Indiana Adjutant General Records.

39. John S. G. Woodfill to Oliver P. Morton, May 14, 1861 (L508, Box 13), H. C. Sanray to Morton, May 14, 1861 (L508, Box 13), William W. Tully to Morton, September 21, 1861 (L507, Box 7), Richard Owen to Lew Wallace, April 27, 1861 (L510, Box 22), Indiana Legion Papers, Indiana Adjutant General Records; M. Jarvis to C. P. Buckingham, August 5, 1861 (4:87), Arthur J. Buckner to William Dennison, July 2, 1861 (1:103), R. W. McFarland to Dennison, July 16, 1861 (2:21), J. M. Cooke to Buckingham, July 16, 1861 (2:23), Series 147, Correspondence to Governor and Adjutant General, Ohio Adjutant General Records.

40. Scarborough, *Diary of Edmund Ruffin*, 2:121–22, 132.

CHAPTER 3

1. Barrett, *Civil War in North Carolina*, 32–47; Docton W. Bagley Diary, April 19, 1861, Bagley Papers; William E. Mann to Henry Toole Clark, July 29, 1861, Henry Toole Clark Papers; Benjamin Leecraft to John W. Ellis, June 29, 1861, John W. Ellis Papers.

2. Lathrop, "Lafourche District in 1861–1862: . . . Local Defense," 99–101, 107–10; *OR*, IV:1:475; H. D. C. Edmundson to Joseph E. Brown, October 18, 1861, R. F. Curry to Brown, September 19, 1861, George Lang to Brown, August 23, 1861, Georgia Governor Correspondence: Brown.

3. Bittle, "Florida Prepares for War," 145–49; Mother to Edmund Kirby Smith, July 19, 1871, Edmund Kirby Smith Papers; Waters, "Florida's Confederate Guer-

rillas," 136; A. T. Bledsoe to McQueen McIntosh, July 3, 1861, U.S. War Department, Letters Sent by Confederate Secretary of War; *OR*, I:1:347–48, 470–71; Marsh Middleton et al. to Madison Perry, August 15, 1861, William B. Davis to Perry, August 28, 1861, Incoming Correspondence, Florida Governor Papers; *OR*, I:6:7, 287, 290.

4. *OR*, I:6:280–81.

5. Paul Ravines to Leroy Pope Walker, June 6, 1861, U.S. War Department, Letters Received by Confederate Secretary of War; Oliver to John J. Pettus, May 2, 1861, F. R. Wittes to Pettus, July 23, 1861, Isaac White to Pettus, July 12, 1861, James Huddleston to Pettus, July 29, 1861, Pettus Papers; James Huddleston to Charles Clark, May 22, 1861, Charles Clark and Family Papers.

6. E. M. Seago to Joseph E. Brown, April 24, 1861, James Stewart to Brown, April 26, 1861, Joseph J. Bradford to Brown, May 30, 1861, Thomas J. Bacon to Brown, May 30, 1861, J. Rufus Felder to Brown, June 26, 1861, William A. McDonald to Brown, September 10, 1861, Georgia Governor Correspondence: Brown; J. W. S. McNeil to John J. Pettus, May 1, 1861, D. N. Conyer to Pettus, May 6, 1861, Robert Muldrow to Pettus, June 22, 1861, Pettus Papers.

7. J. C. Spurlin to Joseph E. Brown, June 17, 1861, William A. McDonald to Brown, September 10, 1861, A. M. Barrett to Brown, September 23, 1861, H. D. C. Edmundson to Brown, October 18, 1861, Georgia Governor Correspondence: Brown; Jonathan H. Brooks to John H. Reagan, July 19, 1861, U.S. War Department, Letters Received by Confederate Secretary of War; Nathaniel Wilds et al. to Madison Perry, April 29, 1861, Incoming Correspondence, Florida Governor Papers.

8. W. W. Herbert to Messrs. Woodrow, Boylston and McCants, December 3, 1860, McCants Family Papers.

9. Pickering and Falls, *Brush Men*, 11–24, 40–49; West, "Minute Men."

10. *Arkansas True Democrat*, July 18, 1861; W. R. Rightor to Leroy Pope Walker, July 15, 1861, U.S. War Department, Letters Received by Confederate Secretary of War.

11. Mathews, *Interesting Narrative*, 26–31.

12. John L. Fayleman et al. to John W. Ellis, June 22, 1861, L. J. Bicknell to Ellis, June 15, 1861, John W. Ellis Papers; John D. Whitford to Henry Toole Clark, September 19, 1861, J. M. Miller to Clark, July 30, 1861, Henry Toole Clark Papers; Inscoe and McKinney, *Heart of Confederate Appalachia*, 79–81.

13. Sarris, "Anatomy of an Atrocity," 687; Isaac M. David to Joseph E. Brown, May 10, 1861, William Moore to Brown, April 28, 1861, B. J. Rivers to Brown, May 24, 1861, Georgia Governor Correspondence: Brown.

14. John L. Fayleman et al. to John W. Ellis, June 22, 1861, John W. Ellis Papers; Thomas H. Hicks to Edward M. Mobley, July 29, 1861, Letterbook, 1854–65, Maryland Governor Papers; Bohannon, "They Had Determined to Root Us Out," 102–3; Francis B. Drake to Joseph E. Brown, May 28, 1861, Walter Kelley

to Brown, June 8, 1861, George A. Wright to Brown, June 26, 1861, B. T. Harris to Brown, July 22, 1861, Henry R. Fort to Brown, August 3, 1861, J. B. Patterson et al. to Brown, May 29, 1861, Georgia Governor Correspondence: Brown; H. H. Waters to William Lark, May 28, 1861, Executive Secretary Letterbook, Georgia Governor Correspondence: Brown.

15. Dodd and Dodd, *Winston*, 81–83.

16. Sutherland, "Guerrilla Warfare," 280–81 n.38; James L. Sandler to Madison Perry, May 4, 1861, Nathaniel Wilds et al. to Perry, April 29, 1861, Incoming Correspondence, Florida Governor Papers; *OR*, I:1:686; Mathews, *Interesting Narrative*, 27–28, 31.

17. Isaac M. David to Joseph E. Brown, May 10, 1861, B. J. Pinson to Brown, May 24, 1861, Georgia Governor Correspondence: Brown; *OR*, IV:1:475; B. A Terry to John J. Pettus, April 30, 1861, Pettus Papers; Daniel R. Hundley Diary, May–June 1861; *Memphis Daily Appeal*, May 14, 1861.

18. J. D. McAdoo to brother, September 25, 1861, McAdoo Papers; William Chester to Joseph E. Brown, September 10, 1861, Georgia Governor Correspondence: Brown.

19. William H. Phillips to Joseph E. Brown, June 2, 1861, Georgia Governor Correspondence: Brown. See similar concerns from A. Hood to Brown, May 6, 1861, and Robert Sandifur to Brown, July 4, 1861, ibid.

20. James L. Sandler to Madison Perry, May 4, 1861, Incoming Correspondence, Florida Governor Papers.

21. D. P. Smith, *Frontier Defense*, 19–20; Jewett, *Texas in the Confederacy*, 79–112; *OR*, I:1:618–19.

22. John William Brown Diary, May 7, 1861; Hauptman, *Between Two Fires*, 45, 47. See generally Confer, *Cherokee Nation*.

23. W. T. Harris to Leroy Pope Walker, June 27, 1861, U.S. War Department, Letters Received by Confederate Secretary of War; *OR*, I:1:628.

24. A. G. Mayers to Leroy Pope Walker, May 3, 1861, W. T. Harris to Walker, June 27, 1861, F. F. Foscue to Walker, May 18, 1861, George W. Gwin to Walker, May 10, 1861, Charles A. Hamilton to A. R. Wright, July 7, 1861, R. W. Stevenson to A. H. Garland, May 14, 1861, M. H. McWillie to Jefferson Davis, June 30, 1861, Owen L. Davis to William B. Ogletree, July 21, 1861, U.S. War Department, Letters Received by Confederate Secretary of War.

25. Hauptman, *Between Two Fires*, 46–48; *OR*, I:3:692.

26. A. S. Paddock to Simon Cameron, June 24, 1861, U.S. War Department, Letters Received by U.S. Secretary of War: Main Series; Jesse Bowen to Simon Cameron, July 5, 1861, M. M. Samuels to Abraham Lincoln, April 17, 1861, U.S. War Department, Letters Received by U.S. Secretary of War: Irregular Series.

27. D. P. Smith, *Frontier Defense*, 3–20. The best history of the Texas Rangers before the war is included in Utley, *Lone Star Justice*.

28. *OR*, I:4:115–16; W. T. Harris to Leroy Pope Walker, July 9, 1861, Robert

Butler Young to A. B. Wright, August 2, 1861, B. F. Terry to P. G. T. Beauregard, July 2, 1861, U.S. War Department, Letters Received by Confederate Secretary of War; Scarborough, *Diary of Edmund Ruffin*, 2:59–60, 62–65; D. P. Smith, *Frontier Defense*, 21–40, 57–58; Cutrer, *Ben McCulloch*, 185–89, 205–6, 257–58.

29. Cutrer, *Ben McCulloch*, 177–86; *OR*, I:1:521–23, 594–96; Darrow, "Recollections of Twiggs Surrender," 1:36.

30. Crist et al., *Papers of . . . Davis*, 7:171; M. J. Solomons Scrapbook, p. 60; E. M. Seago to Leroy Pope Walker, April 17, 1861, Lewis M. Stone to Walker, June 17, 1861, William O'Daniel to Jefferson Davis, June 17, 1861, S. Thorn Seawell to Walker, May 27, 1861, Amos McLemore to Davis, May 27, 1861, U.S. War Department, Letters Received by Confederate Secretary of War.

31. T. L. Baker, *Confederate Guerrilla*, 39–40; Thomas F. Fisher to Leroy Pope Walker, May 1, 1861, U.S. War Department, Letters Received by Confederate Secretary of War.

32. H. T. Harrison to Leroy Pope Walker, April 19, 1861, I. W. Garrott to Walker, June 5, 1861, T. L. Faulkner to Walker, June 26, 1861, Owen L. Davis to William B. Ogletree, July 12, 1861, A. L. Pridemore to John Letcher, July 30, 1861, U.S. War Department, Letters Received by Confederate Secretary of War; J. Rufus Felder to Joseph E. Brown, June 26, 1861, James Stewart to Brown, April 26, 1861, Georgia Governor Correspondence: Brown; Maddox, *Hard Trials*, 11–12. Michael Fellman, *Inside War*, vi, refers to this as "self-organized combat."

33. A. H. McLaws to Leroy Pope Walker, April 16, 1861, R. W. Stevenson to Walker, May 14, 1861, E. M. Seago to Walker, April 17, 1861, Henry E. Colton to Jefferson Davis, April 17, 1861, Burwell J. Curry to Walker, June 20, 1861, McQueen McIntosh to Walker, June 26, 1861, Samuel Matthews to Walker, July 1, 1861, W. T. Harris to Walker, July 9, 1861, H. V. Keep to Walker, July 15, August 2, 1861, U.S. War Department, Letters Received by Confederate Secretary of War.

34. R. H. Williams, *With the Border Ruffians*, 303; Jewett, *Texas in the Confederacy*, 123–24; William Burdell et al. to Alexander H. Boykin, July 28, 1861, Boykin to wife, September 6, 1861, Boykin Family Papers.

35. Crist et al., *Papers of . . . Davis*, 7:201; John Tyler to A. H. Canedo, May 11, 1861, A. T. Bledsoe to Levi W. Lawler, June 28, 1861, Bledsoe to Burwell G. Curry, July 1, 1861, Bledsoe to P. Van Rhyn Lee, July 31, 1861, U.S. War Department, Letters Sent by Confederate Secretary of War.

36. A. T. Bledsoe to A. D. Prentiss, August 10, 1861, U.S. War Department, Letters Sent by Confederate Secretary of War; *OR*, IV:1:475, 491, 579; John Q. Winfield to wife, June 30, 1861, Winfield Letters.

CHAPTER 4

1. Castel, *Sterling Price*, 50–64; Cutrer, *Ben McCulloch*, 259–65; *OR*, I:3:56–64; Banasik, *Missouri in 1861*, 230.

2. E. A. Miller, *Lincoln's Abolitionist General*, 75–77; Lowndes H. Davis to Mary

Davis, June 10, 1861, Lowndes Henry Davis Papers; Alfred Warner to Stephen, September 15, 1861, Warner Papers; Henry P. Andrews to wife and family, December 29, [1861], Henry P. Andrews Papers; Edward F. Noyes to R. H. Stephenson, October 5, 1861, Wright Family Papers; George H. Fifer to brother, October 9, 1861, Fifer Papers; J. B. Henderson to Hamilton R. Gamble, October 21, 1861, William M. McPherson to Gamble, September 28, 1861, James R. Birch to father, September 29, 1861, Gamble Papers; Charles B. Tomkins to Mollie Tompkins, November 11, 1861, Tompkins Papers; James E. Love to Molly, October 10, 1861, Love Papers; William Bishop to Mary A. Bishop, October 5, December 12, 20, 1861, Bishop Papers.

3. *OR*, I:3:553–54, 561–62, 565.

4. Allen T. Ward to sister, October 27, 1861, Ward Family Correspondence; Starr, *Jennison's Jayhawkers*, 84–118; F. Moore, *Rebellion Record*, 3(2):376–77, 431–32; Patrick, "This Regiment Will Make a Mark," 52–54; Margaret J. Hays to mother, November 21, 1861, Hays Family Papers (partially in Doerschuk, "Extracts from War-Time Letters," 100–102); Samuel Ayres to Lyman Langdon, November 15, 1861, Ayres Correspondence; Joseph H. Trego to wife, November 12, December 18, 1861, Trego Correspondence; Herklotz, "Jayhawkers in Missouri," 77–86.

5. *OR*, I:3:568, II:1:228–31.

6. Statement of J. D. Foster, [November 1861], James S. Rollins to Foster, November 9, 1861, U.S. War Department, Union Provost Marshal Files . . . Two or More Citizens; *OR*, II:1:233; Barton Bates to Edward Bates, September 8, October 10, 1861, Bates Family Papers; Simpson and Berlin, *Sherman's Civil War*, 165.

7. Case of Langston T. Goode (KK818), U.S. War Department, Court-Martial Cases; Hicken, *Illinois in the Civil War*, 15–16; David T. Stathem to father, September 3, 1861, Stathem to sister, April 20, 1862, Stathem Papers; James E. Love to Molly, October 10, 1861, Love Papers; Edward F. Noyes to R. H. Stephenson, September 21, 1861, Wright Family Papers.

8. Elisha Leaming to wife, November 11, 1861, Leaming Letters; John A. Higgins to Nancy Higgins, October 19, 1861, Higgins Papers.

9. Marszalek, *Commander of All Lincoln's Armies*, 110–11; Gerteis, *Civil War St. Louis*, 172–76; W. W. Smith, "Experiment in Counterinsurgency," 363–68; William L. Broaddus to wife, January 31, 1862, Broaddus Papers; *OR*, II:1:233–35, 237, 240–43. Grimsley, *Hard Hand of War*, 49–51, believes Halleck initially straddled the line between "conciliation" and a more "pragmatic" policy. Mountcastle, "The Guerrilla Problem," 1–15, calls it a "punitive" policy.

10. Banasik, *Missouri in 1861*, 273–74, 276–77; *OR*, II:1:242–43.

11. Hamilton R. Gamble to Henry Halleck, December 24, 1861, Gamble Papers; *OR*, II:1:233, 255, 261, 269–70.

12. Herklotz, "Jayhawkers in Missouri," 77–86; *OR*, II:1:266–67; Castel, "Kansas Jayhawking Raids," 8–11; Patrick, "This Regiment Will Make a Mark,"

54–57; Langsdorf and Richmond, "Letters of . . . Anthony . . .—Continued," 359; H. Miles Moore to John Sherman, January 16, 1862, Sherman Papers; *OR*, I:8:507, II:1:161–62, 255–56, 258–59.

13. J. B. Henderson to Hamilton R. Gamble, October 21–22, 1861, Gamble Papers; cases of Richard B. Crowder (KK820), William R. Roach (KK820), Farmer Moore (MM451), U.S. War Department, Court-Martial Cases; N. Chipman to General Baker, September 2, 1861, Box 6, Southern Border Brigade, Iowa Adjutant General Records; Frank M. Davis to Samuel J. Kirkwood, September 5, 1861, Citizens of Ringgold County to Kirkwood, [1861], Citizens of Appanoose County to Kirkwood, December 3, 1861, E. H. Spears to Kirkwood, January 14, 1862, C. Baldwin to Kirkwood, January 24, 1862, Correspondence: War Matters, Iowa Governor Papers; Samuel J. Kirkwood to Abraham Lincoln, October 4, 1861, Kirkwood Papers.

14. *OR*, I:8:518–23, 530–34; Fremont County Board of Supervisors to Samuel J. Kirkwood, January 10, 1862, William Baden and Charles Thorp to Kirkwood, April 15, 1862, John W. Jones to Kirkwood, May 3, 1862, John M. Schofield to Kirkwood, May 10, 1862, Correspondence: War Matters, Iowa Governor Papers.

15. Citizens of Southeast Missouri to Henry W. Halleck, March 15, 1862, Citizens of Bollinger County to Halleck, April 16, 1862, U.S. War Department, Union Provost Marshal Files . . . Two or More Citizens; *OR*, II:1:247; Special Order No. 47, April 21, 1862, Stevenson Papers; Lucy to Dear Friend, April 28, 1862, Draper-McClurg Papers; William Crede to Herman Crede, May 20, 1862, Crede Family Papers; Robert T. McMahan Diary, April 26, May 10, 1862. See *OR*, II:1:251–80, for a variety of reports on guerrilla activity.

16. Cases of Ephraim D. Harris (NN3833), Israel Young (LL716), U.S. War Department, Court-Martial Cases. See also James M. Freeman (MM451), Robert Dubrees and Lewis M. Lloyd (LL550).

17. *OR*, II:1:284–504; case of Benjamin S. Tucker, April 22, 1862, U.S. War Department, Union Provost Marshal Files . . . Two or More Citizens; cases of John P. Thistle (LL2634), Samuel Bryant (MM451), James E. Hicks (MM451), U.S. War Department, Court-Martial Cases.

18. Cases of Joseph Hart (MM453) and James Howard (KK817), U.S. War Department, Court-Martial Cases. Curiously, federal reports show another guerrilla named Joe Hart operating in the same part of Missouri a year later. See *OR*, I:22(1):335–36.

19. *OR*, II:1:255–56, 258–59.

20. D. B. Connelly, *John M. Schofield*, 40–54; W. W. Smith, "Experiment in Counterinsurgency," 368–72; Citizens of Texas County to John M. Schofield, July 9, 1862, J. D. Dadson to Colonel Lippscomb, July 12, 1862, U.S. War Department, Union Provost Marshal Files . . . Two or More Citizens; John M. Schofield to Henry W. Halleck, July 23, 1862 (telegram), Schofield to Edwin M. Stanton, July

26, 1862 (telegram), Schofield Papers; *OR*, II:1:270–71; Francis F. Audsley to wife, July 31, 1862, Audsley Letters.

21. Leslie, *Devil Knows How to Ride*, 66–96; Fellman, *Inside War*, 140–42. For an excellent review of the extensive literature on Quantrill, see Crouch, "Fiend in Human Shape?"

22. L. C. Miller Memoir, pp. 7–9; Leslie, *Devil Knows How to Ride*, 96–98, 104–6, 112–28; Castel, *Quantrill*, 70–72, 94; *OR*, II:1:273; Goodrich, *Black Flag*, 29–40; Guyer, "Journal and Letters of Gulick" (July 1930), 394–435; McMahan Diary, February 22–25, 1862; Elvira A. (Weir) Scott Diary, July 21, 1862; James E. Love to Molly, March 26, 1862, Love Papers.

23. Leslie, *Devil Knows How to Ride*, 97, 103; Bowen, "Guerrilla War in Western Missouri," "Quantrill, James, Younger," 42–48, and "Counterrevolutionary Guerrilla War."

24. Shea, "1862," 21–37. Interestingly, one of Price's last orders before exiting Missouri authorized the formation of guerrilla companies in the state to disarm home guards, protect Confederate sympathizers, and harass Curtis. *OR*, I:8:188.

25. Shea, "1862," 37–41; *OR*, I:13:823–24, 827–28.

26. Drury Connally to Anne Kilgore Connally, May 5, 1862, May 7, 1862, War Letters of Connally; Samuel C. Trescott to cousin, May 1, 1862, Trescott Correspondence; S. S. Marrett to wife, May 31, 1862, Marrett Papers.

27. Shea, "1862," 41–42; J. A. Williamson to Grenville Dodge, May 22, 26, 1862, Dodge Papers; *OR*, I:13:392, 396. See also Samuel McKinney Stafford to Abby S. Stafford, April 26, May 17, 18, 1862, Stafford Papers; John A. Higgins to Nancy Higgins, May 23, 1862, Higgins Papers.

28. Shea, "1862," 37–41; *OR*, I:13:827–28; Suite, "Federal Military Policy," 73; Crist et al., *Papers of . . . Davis*, 8:193–94.

29. B. L. Roberts, "General T. C. Hindman"; Neal and Kremm, *Lion of the South*, 113–27, 132–35; *OR*, I:13:29–44; Skinner, *Autobiography of Henry Merrell*, 299–301.

30. Neal and Kremm, *Lion of the South*, 127–28; *OR*, I:13:36, 835.

31. Belser, "Military Operations in Missouri and Arkansas," 362–74, 398–403; Neal and Kremm, *Lion of the South*, 128, 134; *OR*, I:13:35; List of Rutherford's Band, July 1862, U.S. War Department, Union Provost Marshal Files ∴ . . Two or More Persons; Drury Connally to wife, June 28, 1862, War Letters of Connally; Beckenbaugh, "War of Politics," 29.

32. Bearss, "White River Expedition"; Beckenbaugh, "War of Politics," 30–31; George E. Flanders to brother, June 7, 1862, Flanders Civil War Letters; Simon, *Papers of . . . Grant*, 5:202–3; Andrew J. Huntoon to wife, July 15, 1862, Huntoon Papers; Crist et al., *Papers of . . . Davis*, 8:360–63.

33. Shea, "1862," 42–44, and "Semi-Savage State," 92–97; Suite, "Federal Military Policy," 73–76; *OR*, I:13:12.

34. Voorhis, *Life and Times*, 57; *ORN*, I:23:176; *OR*, I:13:104–7, 119; Simon, *Papers of . . . Grant*, 5:197–98.

35. Neal and Kremm, *Lion of the South*, 131–32; *OR*, I:13:108.

36. *OR*, I:13:107–9.

37. Louis A. Bringier to Stella Bringier, March 4, 1862, Bringier and Family Papers; Lathrop, "Lafourche District in 1861–62: . . . Local Defense," 110–15; Sutherland, "Mansfield Lovell's Quest."

38. Oscar Smith Diary, April 26, 1862; Frank H. Peck to mother, May [5], 1862, Montgomery Family Papers.

39. Hyde, *Pistols and Politics*, 110–11: *OR*, I:6:653–54, 885–90, 15:747–49, 53:805–7.

40. *OR*, I:15:508–9; Q. A. Hargis to C. R. Marshall, April 25, 1862, U.S. War Department, Letters Received by Confederate Secretary of War.

41. *OR*, I:15:747–48, 767–69, 773–74, 53:813–14; Thomas O. Moore to Jefferson Davis, June 3, 1862, George W. Randolph to Moore, July 3, 1862, U.S. War Department, Letters Received by Executive, 1860–63, Records of Louisiana; Winters, *Civil War in Louisiana*, 103–5, 149–51; Hyde, *Pistols and Politics*, 112.

42. Hyde, *Pistols and Politics*, 112–13; *OR*, I:15:24–25; G. M. Williams, "Letters of General Thomas Williams," 321–22.

43. Oscar Smith Diary, May 28, 1862; Lathrop, "Lafourche District in 1861–62: . . . Local Defense," 118–25; G. M. Williams, "Letters of General Thomas Williams," 321–22; Frank H. Peck to David, May 31, 1862, Montgomery Family Papers; *ORN*, I:18:516, 520–21, 534.

44. Lathrop, "Lafourche District in 1861–1862: . . . Local Defense," 123–25; *ORN*, II:1:701–2.

45. *ORN*, I:18:125–27, 520–21, 532–35, 556–57; *OR*, I:15:502.

46. Lathrop, "Lafourche District in 1861–1862: . . . Local Defense," 120–23; Priscilla M. Bond Diary, May 12, June 29, 1862, P. M. Bond Papers. See also Stella Bringier to Mede Bringier, July 28, 1862, Bringier and Family Papers.

47. Lathrop, "Lafourche District in 1861–1862: . . . Local Defense," 125–29; Mrs. B. W. Bagby to sister, June 10, 1862, B. W. Bagby to brother, June 11, 1862, Bagby Papers.

48. *OR*, I:15:740–41, 768, 773–74, 824, 53:813; Lathrop, "Lafourche District in 1862: Militia and Partisan Rangers," 230–44; George W. Randolph to Thomas O. Moore, July 3, 1862, U.S. War Department, Letters Received by Executive, 1860–63, Records of Louisiana; Thomas W. Blount to L. D. Sandridge, July 4, 1862, Ruggles Papers; James H. Wingfield, "Position of Troops," July 6, 1862, plus rosters, Wingfield Papers; Hyde, *Pistols and Politics*, 112–16; Sutherland, "Guerrilla Warfare," 270–71.

49. *Harper's Weekly*, August 16, 1862; *OR*, I:15:504.

50. *OR*, I:15:519–21.

51. *Memphis Daily Appeal*, May 30, July 28, 1862.

CHAPTER 5

1. Scarborough, *Diary of Edmund Ruffin*, 2:109, 157–58.

2. Ramage, *Rebel Raider*, 1–2, 18–39; George J. Reed to wife, December 15, 1861, Reed Family Papers.

3. Ramage, *Rebel Raider*, 45–60; Robert Patrick to sister, April 1, 1862, Patrick Letters. See also Matthews, *Basil Wilson Duke*, 39–44.

4. Ramage, *Rebel Raider*, 43–51; Alfred Pirtle Journal, December 19, 1861, Pirtle Papers; George J. Reed to wife, December 15, 1861, Reed Family Papers.

5. L. H. Harrison, *Civil War in Kentucky*, 14–23; Cooling, *Fort Donelson's Legacy*, 26–33.

6. Ramage, *Rebel Raider*, 52–55, 60–62; *Harper's Weekly*, August 16, 30, 1862; *OR*, I:10(1):6.

7. Ramage, *Rebel Raider*, 52–55, 60–62; Cooling, *Fort Donelson's Legacy*, 49; Beatty, *Citizen-Soldier*, 114–15; McCutchan, *Dearest Lizzie*, 189; Robert Patrick to sister, April 1, 1862, Patrick Letters.

8. *Memphis Daily Appeal*, April 16, 20, 1862; Solomons Scrapbook, 80, 166, 213–14, 216, 231, 244, 317–20, 376; Angus Waddle to Eleanor W. McCoy, February 16, 1862, McCoy Papers; Elisha A. Peterson to cousin, March 9, 1862, Peterson Papers; Graf et al., *Papers of Andrew Johnson*, 5:293, 370; Cooling, *Fort Donelson's Legacy*, 14, 49, 54–56, 70–73; George K. Miller to Dear Friend, February 7, 1862, George Knox Miller Papers; *OR*, I:10(1):81, (2):30; Marshall Diaries, March 6, 13, 1862, Eugene Marshall Papers; J. G. Landrum to Jeremiah T. Boyle, July 7, 1862, H. C. Gassaway to Boyle, July 20, 1862, U.S. War Department, Union Provost Marshal Files . . . Two or More Citizens; G. Thomas Hanser to Julian Kennett, March 21, 1862, Kennett Family Papers; Edward P. Stanfield to father, March 13, 1862, Stanfield Correspondence.

9. William R. Stuckey to Helen Stuckey, December 29, 1861, Stuckey Papers; Theodore Harris to Isham G. Harris, June 12, 1861, Isham G. Harris Papers; Wills, *Confederacy's Greatest Cavalryman*, 45–56; Ramage, *Rebel Raider*, 83, 107. See Mackey, *Uncivil War*, 123–54, for the difficulty in distinguishing between partisans, raiders, and guerrillas.

10. Cooling, *Fort Donelson's Legacy*, 50–51, 53; Robert Winn to sister, August 17, 1862, Winn-Cook Family Papers; Fellman, *Inside War*, 48–52; Hyman, "Deceit in Dixie"; George J. Reed to wife, March 29, 1862, Reed Family Papers; McCutchan, *Dearest Lizzie*, 190–91; Marshall Diaries, March 10, 1862, Eugene Marshall Papers.

11. Cooling, *Fort Donelson's Legacy*, 44–45, 49–50; Simon, *Papers of . . . Grant*, 5:45–47; *OR*, I:7:498, 10(1):80–81. See Esdaile, *Fighting Napoleon*, for similarities between the Spanish and American experiences, including the reactions of the French and U.S. governments.

12. *OR*, I:7:523; Moses B. Walker to William Dennison, November 18, 1861 (18:140), Series 147, Correspondence to Adjutant General and Governor, Ohio

Adjutant General Records; Wilberforce Nevin to sister, December 22, 1861, Sayre Papers. See *Memphis Daily Appeal*, November 17, 27, 1861, for exceptions to the general timidity of Unionists.

13. James B. Fry to John W. Finnell, November 30, 1861, Kentucky Adjutant General Records; George W. Carvill to sister, September 10, 1861, Carvill Letters; Solomons Scrapbook, 60.

14. Joseph W. Keifer to wife, April 4, 5, 1862, Keifer Papers; *OR*, I:10(2):8, 13.

15. Cooling, *Fort Donelson's Legacy*, 44–45, 49; *OR*, I:10(2):30; case of John Cartwright (KK195), U.S. War Department, Court-Martial Cases; Ramage, *Rebel Raider*, 60–61; Engle, *Don Carlos Buell*, 191.

16. Graf et al., *Papers of Andrew Johnson*, 5:237, 241 n.52–53; Madden, "Unionist Resistance," 27–37; *OR*, I:7:701.

17. T. D. Smith, "Don't You Beg," 42–45; case of Champ Ferguson (MM2997), U.S. War Department, Court-Martial Cases. Sensing, *Champ Ferguson*, perpetuated many myths about Ferguson that have been corrected by Mays, *Cumberland Blood*.

18. Statement by Josephus C. Gould in Ferguson case file (MM2997), U.S. War Department, Court-Martial Cases; Duke, *History of Morgan's Cavalry*, 183.

19. Graf et al., *Papers of Andrew Johnson*, 5:257–59, 286–87, 312–13, 434, 478–79.

20. T. D. Smith, "Don't You Beg," 44; Ramage, *Rebel Raider*, 101. See also G. D. Norris, *Beaty's Independent Scouts*.

21. Marshall Diaries, April 4, 1862, Eugene Marshall Papers; Joe Dudley to brother, January 11, 1862, Dudley Family Papers; Isaac H. Rowland to father, April 9, 1862, Rowland-Shilliday Papers; McCutchan, *Dearest Lizzie*, 168; *OR*, I:7:375–76; Joseph W. Keifer to wife, March 4, 8, 9, 1862, Keifer Papers. For Keifer generally, see Pope, *The Weary Boys*.

22. Joseph W. Keifer to wife, March 4, 10, 14, 16, April 12, 1862, Keifer Papers.

23. O'Brien, *Mountain Partisans*, 101–10; Steenburn, "Wanted for Murder," 57–62; *OR*, I:16(1):838–41; *Harper's Weekly*, August 23, 1862.

24. Steenburn, "Wanted for Murder," 58–59; Beatty, *Citizen-Soldier*, 169; Wilberforce Nevin to sister, August 15, 1862, Sayre Papers.

25. Curry and Ham, "Bushwhackers' War," 418–19; E. C. Smith, *Lewis County*, 306–7; Bell N. Woods to Samuel Woods, February 19, 1862, Woods Family Papers; George Loomis to Francis H. Pierpont, December 24, 1861, A. Delany to Pierpont, March 22, 1862, A. I. Boreman to Pierpont, March 31, 1862, Virginia Governor Papers: Pierpont (Series I).

26. Jessie Sturn to Francis H. Pierpont, January 9, 1862, Henry R. McCord to Pierpont, February 18, 1862, Virginia Governor Papers: Pierpont (Series 1); Osborne and Weaver, *Virginia State Rangers*, 251; Berkey, "Fighting the Devil with Fire," 21–23.

27. Noe, "Who Were the Bushwhackers?" 9–31; Curry and Ham, "Bushwhackers' War," 427–28; Osborne and Weaver, *Virginia State Rangers*, 180, 202, 251; Phillips Journal, September 17, 1862; Henry R. McCord to Francis H. Pierpont, February 18, 1862, Virginia Governor Papers: Pierpont (Series 1).

28. Statement of James H. Evans, October 31, 1862, statement of James Hall, November 8, 1861, Theo Jones to Joseph Darr, October 6, 1861, William Dwight to [S. Williams], October 4, 1861, L. S. Elliott to T. Poschner, October 16, 1861, U.S. War Department, Union Provost Marshal Files . . . Two or More Citizens; Barr Journal, February 20, 1862; Castel, *Tom Taylor's Civil War*, 20–24; Leib, *Nine Months*, 95–96; Athey, "Loyalty and Civil War Liberty," 16–19; Curry and Ham, "Bushwhackers' War," 422–23; Osborne and Weaver, *Virginia State Rangers*, 7–10; Clayburn Pierson to Francis H. Pierpont, October 15, 1861, Jonathan C. Vance to Pierpont, September 18, 1861, P. G. Van Winkle to Pierpont, October 14, 18, 1861, Weston Rowland to Pierpont, October 30, 1861, Will Tomlinson to T. M. Harris, November 3, 1861, I. S. Hill to Pierpont, November 4, 1861, Dudley S. Montague to Pierpont, November 4, 1861, D. H. Smith to Pierpont, November 4, 1861, George D. Latham to Pierpont, December 18, 1861, George C. Davis et al. to Pierpont, January 11, 1862, D. D. Johnson to Pierpont, February 19, 1862, Virginia Governor Papers: Pierpont (Series 1); Susan Frances Young Diary, September 3, October 5–6, 1861, Bound Vol. 3, Roy Bird Cook Collection.

29. Jonathan E. Wright to William H. Richardson, February 15, 1862, Virginia Governor Papers: Letcher (Series I); Joseph H. Wilson to mother, December 7, 1861, January 10, 15, 1862, Joseph Hubbard Wilson Papers.

30. Richardson, "Raleigh County," 243–53; Matheny, *Wood County*, 211–22; Stutler, *West Virginia*, 131–35, 141–44; Noe, "Who Were the Bushwhackers?" 7.

31. *OR*, I:5:638–39, 702; Matheny, *Wood County*, 232–40.

32. Noe, "Exterminating Savages," 109–12; C. R. Williams, *Diary and Letters of . . . Hayes*, 2:188. See McWhiney, *Cracker Culture*, for the antebellum roots of these prejudices.

33. Oliver Parker to brother, April 22, 1862, Bound Vol. 26, Roy Bird Cook Collection; Frederick A. Wildman to Sam, March 11, 1862, Wildman Family Papers; Castel, *Tom Taylor's Civil War*, 32; Benson, *With the Army of West Virginia*, 69, 76.

34. Matheny, *Wood County*, 182–87; Phillips Journal, October 20, 1861; Henry Dwight to Francis H. Pierpont, January 13, 1862, Thomas M. Harris to Pierpont, January 8, March 3, 1862, Alex C. Moore to Pierpont, October 14, 1862, Will Tomlinson to Thomas M. Harris, November 3, 1861, George Loomis to Pierpont, January 12, 1862, Virginia Governor Papers: Pierpont (Series 1).

35. Robertson, *Soldier of Southwestern Virginia*, 93; George R. Latham to Francis H. Pierpont, January 20, 1862, Henry R. McCord to Pierpont, February 18, 1862, Thomas M. Harris to Pierpont, March 3, 1862, Ephraim Bee to Pierpont, March 31, 1862, Virginia Governor Papers: Pierpont (Series 1); Citizens of

Clarksburg to Benjamin F. Kelley, n.d., Thomas L. Moore et al. to Francis H. Pierpont, [Winter 1861–62], Pierpont Papers: Small Collection; Jacob M. Campbell to Francis H. Pierpont, April 7, 1862, Box 1, Jacob M. Campbell Papers.

36. *Richmond Dispatch*, March 18, 1862; Osborne and Weaver, *Virginia State Rangers*, 4, 7; Virginia Assembly, *Acts*, 51–52; Stutler, *West Virginia*, 173–74; Curry and Ham, "Bushwhackers' War," 427–28; Henry Solomon White Diary, April 22, May 27, 1862; muster rolls for Hampshire, Hardy, and Morgan counties, Box 21, f. 4, Virginia Governor Papers: Letcher; J. D. Hines to J. D. Cox, March 3, 1862, Charges against Prisoners Captured by George Webster, April 2–4, 1862, U.S. War Department, Union Provost Marshal Files . . . Two or More Citizens. The best known independent company operating in Virginia prior to this legislation was Boykin's Independent Company of Mounted Rangers. See Boykin Family Papers.

37. Jonathan W. Younger to John Letcher, February 2, 1862, A. J. Hoback to Letcher, February 19, 1862, Virginia Governor Papers: Letcher; George R. Latham to Francis H. Pierpont, January 20, 1862, Virginia Governor Papers: Pierpont.

38. Annie to Helen Robinson, April 16, [1862], Robinson Family Papers; Louisa Thompson to Gordon Thompson, April 20, 1862, Gordon Thompson Papers; *OR*, I:12(1):5.

39. Osborne and Weaver, *Virginia State Rangers*, 10–14; Henry Heth to John Letcher, April 2, 4, 1862, William Skeen to Henry Heth, [April 4, 1862], Virginia Governor Papers: Letcher. Also in *OR*, I:51:526, 531–32.

40. J. H. Deshons to John Letcher, April 16, 1862, Robert E. Lee to Letcher, April 9, 1862, J. R. Tucker to Letcher, April 11, 1862, including endorsements by Letcher and William H. Taylor, Virginia Governor Papers: Letcher; T. J. Haymond to George W. Randolph, April 10, 14, 1862, U.S. War Department, Letters Received by Confederate Secretary of War.

41. Osborne and Weaver, *Virginia State Rangers*, 4–6, 14–15, 24–27.

42. Sutherland, "Guerrilla Warfare," 281–83; Confederate Congress, "Proceedings of the First . . . Congress," 122, 128–29, 153, 160–61; *OR*, IV:1:1094–95; F. Moore, *Rebellion Record*, 6(3):5–6, 24, 32; Scarborough, *Diary of Edmund Ruffin*, 2:165–66, 238; C. D. Barham to Jefferson Davis, [February 1862], J. F. Johnson to George W. Randolph, April 2, 1862, E. O. Jones to Randolph, April 3, 1862, J. A. Cross to Randolph, April 8, 1862, Samuel L. Graham to Randolph, April 20, 1862, James F. Crocker to Randolph, April 23, 1862, Frederick Holmes to A. F. Bledsoe, April 26, 1862, U.S. War Department, Letters Received by Confederate Secretary of War; Crist et al., *Papers of . . . Davis*, 8:76–77, 125; *Memphis Daily Appeal*, March 4, 13, 14, 23, 26, 29, April 16, 22, June 1, 18, 23, 26, July 7, 10, 25, August 7, 1862; *Richmond Dispatch*, May 1, 7, 8, 14, 15, 16, 17, 24, 28, 1862; Thornwell, "Our Danger and Our Duty," 45, 47–48.

43. George W. Randolph to R. J. Breckenridge, April 29, 1862, R. G. H. Kean to Thomas Brooks, May 2, 1862, Randolph to R. J. Johnson, May 6, 1862, A. T.

Bledsoe to James W. Greene, May 19, 1862, Bledsoe to Richard S. Ewell, April 30, 1862, Randolph to Ivermont Ward, May 15, 1862, U.S. War Department, Letters Sent by Confederate Secretary of War.

44. Cooling, *Fort Donelson's Legacy*, 70–73, 86–89; case of Hugh Lawson Bell (NN1126), U.S. War Department, Court-Martial Cases; Buck, *Sad Earth*, 47, 50.

45. Crist et al., *Papers of . . . Davis*, 8:76; John D. Imboden to William Frazier, March 14, 1862, Imboden to George W. Randolph, March 26, 1862, Imboden to Thomas J. Jackson, March 29, 1862, U.S. War Department, Letters Received by Confederate Secretary of War; Randolph to Imboden, May 7, 1862, U.S. War Department, Letters Sent by Confederate Secretary of War; S. C. Tucker, *John D. Imboden*, 69–72, 76–93; F. Moore, *Rebellion Record*, 1(Supplement):757; G. E. Moore, *Banner in the Hills*, 165–66; *OR*, I:51(2):578–79; Phillips and Hill, *War Stories*, 419–21; Curry and Ham, "Bushwhackers' War," 424–25.

46. Scarborough, *Diary of Edmund Ruffin*, 2:258, 260, 278–79, 289, 307, 348–49, 381.

47. Ramage, *Rebel Raider*, 93–106; Oliver P. Morton to Edwin Stanton, April 28, 1862, A. M. Jackson to Lazarus Noble, June 27, 1862, Civil War Miscellany (A4017), Indiana Adjutant General Records; C. P. Buckingham to W. A. Collins, May 23, 1862 (50:2), Series 146, Correspondence from Adjutant General, Ohio Adjutant General Records; E. H. Heaglin to David Tod, July 15, 1862 (41:4) Mark Fowler to Tod, July 28, 1862 (45:2), E. S. Heisler to Tod, August 5, 1862 (46:2), A. W. Jones to Tod, August 12, 1862 (47:4), Nezekiah Campbell to Tod, August 21, 1862 (50:4), Series 147, Correspondence to Adjutant General and Governor, Ohio Adjutant General Records.

48. Barr Journal, May 20, July 23–24, 1862; Cooling, *Fort Donelson's Legacy*, 85–90; Ben S. Weller to William B. Campbell, June 7, 1862, Campbell Family Papers; Simon, *Papers of . . . Grant*, 5:236–37, 246–47; Samuel T. Wells to Lizzie, July 17, 1862, Samuel T. Wells Papers; *OR*, I:10(2):182–83, 16(2):110, 178, 194, 197, 228, 233, 252; Henry H. Withers to sister, June 27, 1862, Tavenner and Withers Papers; Wilberforce Nevin to mother, June 6, 1862, Sayre Papers; Castel, *Tom Taylor's Civil War*, 35–37; G. McFall to John Sherman, July 17, 1862, Sherman Papers; Ash, "Sharks in an Angry Sea," 220–21; Marshall Diaries, June 4, July 27–28, 1862, Eugene Marshall Papers.

49. Curry and Ham, "Bushwhackers' War," 419–23; *OR*, I:12(1):423, (3):75, II:4:43–46, 55, 58, 63; John Letcher to George W. Randolph, May 27, 1862, Virginia Governor Papers: Letcher; Osborne and Weaver, *Virginia State Rangers*, 14–17; V. C. Jones, *Gray Ghosts*, 90–93. For the treatment of prisoners by two of Letcher's ranger officers, see A. C. Kennedy to John Letcher, September 18, 1862, Virginia Governor Papers: Letcher. For another instance of retaliation to resolve the debate, see *Memphis Daily Appeal*, July 25, 1862.

50. *OR*, I:12(3):34, 41, 53, 55; V. C. Jones, *Gray Ghosts*, 84–85.

51. *OR*, I:12(1):4–5, 423, 496, (3):53, 58–60, 62, 78–79, 91, 95–97, 120; Fred-

erick A. Wildman to wife, May 18, 1862, Wildman Family Papers; Osborne and Weaver, *Virginia State Rangers*, 166; Castel, *Tom Taylor's Civil War*, 36; Curry and Ham, "Bushwhackers' War," 428–29.

52. Feis, *Grant's Secret Service*, 15, 57–58, 89–90; V. C. Jones, *Gray Ghosts*, 81–82; Frederick A. Wildman to wife, May 11, 1862, Wildman Family Papers; Hunter, *Women of the Debatable Land*, 28–29, 67–88; N. C. Baird, *Journals of . . . Edmonds*, 147; Gwin, *Woman's Civil War*, 137; Elder, *Love amid the Turmoil*, 237, 359–60 nn.13–14. See L. P. Stone, "I Was Completely Surrounded," for an account by one scout.

53. Anna Starr to mother, May 11, 1862, Starr Papers; Oliver Parker to father, July 29, 1862, Oliver Parker Letters; Phillips Diary, April 13, 15, 1862; West Virginia Historical Records Survey, *Calendar of the . . . Pierpont Letters*, 109–10, 118, 125, 132, 146; Frederick A. Wildman to wife, May 22, 1862, Wildman Family Papers; C. R. Williams, *Diary and Letters of . . . Hayes*, 2:190–91, 209–10, 212–13, 215, 219, 240–42, 320; C. B. Guthrie to John Sherman, May 20, 1862, Sherman Papers; Samuel T. Wells to Lizzie, April 21, 1862, Samuel T. Wells Papers; *OR*, I:12(1):15, (3):34, 85; Curry and Ham, "Bushwhackers' War," 425–26; Phillips Journal, April 26, 1862; Robertson, *Soldier of Southwestern Virginia*, 94–95, 130–31, 133, 135; V. C. Jones, *Gray Ghosts*, 78–80; F. B. Long to Jacob M. Campbell, July 31, 1862, Jacob M. Campbell Papers; "Guerrilla Oath" (Box 7, f. 3), Hiram Lewis to Francis H. Pierpont, March 9, 1862, George R. Latham to Pierpont, April 28, 1862, James H. Harris to Pierpont, May 1862, Silas Pettit to Pierpont, May 5, 1862, John G. Smith to Pierpont, May 16, 1862, T. A. Roberts to Pierpont, May 28, 1862, William R. Moore to Pierpont, May 30, 1862, William Bennett to Pierpont, June 18, 1862, William B. Halbert to Pierpont, July 22, 1862, Thomas M. Harris to Pierpont, June 10, July 1, 1862, Virginia Governor Papers: Pierpont.

54. Phillips Journal, May 17, 22, 24, 25, 1862. See also J. D. Todd to brother, June 5, 1862, Civil War Soldier Letters.

55. *OR*, I:10(1):874–76, 17(2):69; Wilberforce Nevin to father, May 8, 1862, Sayre Papers; Hicken, *Illinois in the Civil War*, 79–80; Samuel Ayres to Lyman Langdon, June 10, 1862, Ayres Correspondence; Benson, *With the Army of West Virginia*, 76; Frederick A. Wildman to wife, May 18, 1862, Wildman Family Papers.

56. Sutherland, *Seasons of War*, 117–20.

CHAPTER 6

1. This analysis is documented more fully in Sutherland, "Guerrilla Warfare," 273–78, but see Skelton, *American Profession of Arms*, 167–72, 306–12, 318–25, 345–46; Gates, "Indians and Insurrectos"; Gallagher, "'We Are Our Own Trumpeters,'" 369, 371–74; McWhiney, "Jefferson Davis and the Art of War," 105–6, 108–9, 111–12; Crist et al., *Papers of . . . Davis*, 3:203, 278; and Robert Coles to John Rutherfoord, September 7, 1861, Rutherfoord Papers.

2. Levinson, *War within War*, xiii–xviii; Foos, *Short, Offhand, Killing Affair*, 110–37.

3. Sutherland, "Guerrilla Warfare," 277–78.

4. Grant, "Partisan Warfare," 42; W. H. Russell, *My Diary*, 129; *OR*, IV:1:532; Crist et al., *Papers of . . . Davis*, 7:434; Castel, "Guerrilla War," 9.

5. J. L. Johnston to George W. Randolph, April 11, 1862, William R. Reasons to Randolph, April 22, 1862, J. W. Robinson to Randolph, May 1, 1862, J. M. Hines to Randolph, May 24, 1862, H. Hughes to Randolph, June 4, 1862, David Hudnall et al. to Randolph, [ca. June 6, 1862], T. G. Calvert to A. T. Bledsoe, June 8, 1862, William W. Harris to Randolph, July 6, 1862, John Holland and William Harvel to Randolph, July 19, 1862, D. W. Holman to Randolph, May 1, 1862, B. W. Childs to Randolph, June 16, 1862, endorsement on T. G. Calvert to A. T. Bledsoe, June 8, 1862, U.S. War Department, Letters Received by Confederate Secretary of War; A. T. Bledsoe to Richard S. Ewell, April 30, 1862, George W. Randolph to Ivermont Ward, May 15, 1862, Randolph to R. S. McKean, April 26, 1862, Bledsoe to Joseph G. Lockhart, April 29, 1862, Bledsoe to W. A. Singleton, April 30, 1862, R. G. H. Kean to W. M. Merritt, May 3, 1862, Randolph to Charles T. Goode, May 5, 1862, Randolph to W. C. Claiborne, May 9, 1862, Randolph to John R. Baylor, May 16, 1862, Randolph to C. M. Laurin, May 17, 1862, Randolph to Benjamin J. West, May 19, 1862, Randolph to A. R. Lawton, May 19, 1862, U.S. War Department, Letters Sent by Confederate Secretary of War; *OR*, I:5:1090, IV:1:1151; Ash, *When the Yankees Came*, 48; Castel, *Sterling Price*, 92. For Confederate comments on the desertion problem, see *OR*, IV:2:5–7. Interestingly, attempts by federal officials to conscript men in the upper South could have the same effect. See *ORN*, I:26:384.

6. Jefferson Davis anticipated many of these problems. See Crist et al., *Papers of . . . Davis*, 8:60; *OR*, IV:1:1151–52, 2:4–5, 26, 31, 71–72, 82–83, 1003.

7. Joseph W. Keifer to wife, March 7, 1862, Keifer Papers. For a similar Confederate perspective, see Crist et al., *Papers of . . . Davis*, 8:83.

8. C. H. Exall to Cousin William, July 8, 1862, Baxter Papers; J. P. Carter to John J. McRae, June 18, 1862, John J. McRae Papers; *Memphis Daily Appeal*, August 19, 1862; J. A. Cross to George W. Randolph, April 8, 1862, J. L. Johnston to Judah P. Benjamin, April 11, 1862, Alfred S. Cowand to Randolph, April 14, 1862, J. S. Coles to Randolph, April 17, 1862, J. H. Taylor to Randolph, April 21, 1862, Alexander Jordan to Randolph, April 25, 1862, U.S. War Department, Letters Received by Confederate Secretary of War.

9. Crist et al., *Papers of . . . Davis*, 8:292, 309–11.

10. For examples, see reactions to John Pope's Virginia orders in Sutherland, *Seasons of War*, 117–21; Marszalek, *Diary of . . . Holmes*, 187; Crabtree and Patton, *"Journal of a Secesh Lady,"* 222, 224, 230, 232–33.

11. M. C. McMillan, *Disintegration of a Confederate State*, 34–35, 63–64; Dodd and Dodd, *Winston*, 86–87, 91–92; *OR*, I:10(1):876–79.

12. Dodd and Dodd, *Winston*, 92–93; Engle, *Don Carlos Buell*, 245–47.

13. Timothy R. Stanley to John Sherman, May 21, 1862, Sherman Papers.

14. Beatty, *Citizen-Soldier*, 138–40; *Harper's Weekly*, August 16, 1862.

15. Beatty, *Citizen-Soldier*, 139, 142–43; Joseph W. Keifer to wife, May 3, 7, 8, 9, 1862, Keifer Papers; *OR*, I:10(2):167, 174; Mary Fielding Diary, May 4, 1862; Grimsley, *Hard Hand of War*, 79–81. See Keifer, *Slavery and Four Years of War*, 1:273–85, for the entire campaign in northern Alabama. For a biography of Turchin, born Ivan Vasilevitch Turchininoff, see Chicoine, *John Basil Turchin*; for circumstances surrounding the sack of Athens, see Bradley and Dahlen, *From Conciliation to Conquest*.

16. Joshua Burns Moore Diary, April 19, 26, 30, 1862; Rohr, *Incidents of the War*, 37–45; James Lamar to John Gill Shorter, May 14, 1862, Alabama Governor Papers: Shorter; *OR*, I:10(2):290–95, 16(1):350; Grimsley, *Hard Hand of War*, 81–82.

17. Mary Fielding Diary, May 19, 1862; *OR*, I:10(2):156, 162–63, 204, 209.

18. Mary Fielding Diary, April 27, 1862; John G. Shorter address of April 24, 1862, Alabama Governor Papers: Shorter; William M. Francis to father, May 12, 1862, Francis to John T. Morgan, May 12, 1862, Francis Family Papers.

19. Rohr, *Incidents of the War*, 61–62; Wilberforce Nevin to Dear ——, June 4, 1862, Sayre Papers; John W. Large to father, July 7, 1862, Large Letter; Lorenzo P. Myers to John Sherman, July 4, 1862, Sherman Papers.

20. *OR*, I:10(2):290–95; Shaw, *Crete and James*, 143–46; Beatty, *Citizen-Soldier*, 152–53, 156; Engle, *Don Carlos Buell*, 248–50, 264–69; Grimsley, *Hard Hand of War*, 81–85.

21. Engle, *Don Carlos Buell*, 247–49, 326–36; *OR*, I:16(1):8–9. For Buell's own statement regarding his policy toward the hostile population, see *OR*, I:16(1):59–60.

22. *OR*, I:16(1):9, 12–13, 31–37, 40, 254–58, 628.

23. Storey, "Civil War Unionists," 75–80, 92–100. More comprehensively, see Storey, *Loyalty and Loss*.

24. *OR*, I:7:155–56, 16(1):785–91; Dodd and Dodd, *Winston*, 84–91; Mary Fielding Diary, May 5, 1862; Wilberforce Nevin to Dear ——, June 4, 1862, Sayre Papers.

25. William G. Shorter address of May 12, 1862, Alabama Governor Papers: Shorter; Joshua Burns Moore Diary, April 19, 30, 1862; *OR*, I:10(2):162–63.

26. Joseph W. Keifer to wife, May 3, 5, June 25, 1862, Keifer Papers; Beatty, *Citizen-Soldier*, 140; *OR*, I:16(1):351.

27. Storey, "Civil War Unionists," 102–6.

28. Sutherland, "Lincoln, John Pope, and . . . Total War," 574–76; Joseph W. Keifer to wife, July 22, 1862, Keifer Papers.

29. *OR*, I:15:768; *Memphis Daily Appeal*, June 26, July 26, 1862; Burton N. Harrison to John J. Pettus, May 17, 1862, J. W. Clapp to Pettus, June 2, 1862,

Samuel N. Delany to Pettus, July 29, 1862, Richard Winter to Pettus, June 6, 1862, A. A. Trumbo to Pettus, July 4, 1862, Stephen P. Eggleston to Pettus, June 15, 1862, R. S. Bowles to Pettus, July 28, 1862, James A. Grovey to Pettus, May 25, 1862, Pettus Papers; Robert Hudson to Jefferson Davis, May 12, 1862, U.S. War Department, Letters Received by Confederate Secretary of War.

30. A. J. Sullivan to John J. Pettus, June 29, 1862, Richard Davis to Pettus, June 14, 1862, H. C. Tyler to Pettus, July 2, 1862, Lawrence Johnson to Pettus, July 3, 1862, W. H. Garland to Pettus, July 21, 1862, Pettus Papers; F. Moore, *Rebellion Record*, 6(3):24.

31. Stephen P. Eggleston to John J. Pettus, June 15, 1862, Pettus Papers; Earl Van Dorn to P. G. T. Beauregard, May 25, 1862, in private hands, copy provided by Kevin Hasely to author, January 26, 2001.

32. A. Brown, "First Mississippi Partisan Rangers," 371–76; Hoar, "Colonel William C. Falkner," 50–53.

33. *Memphis Daily Appeal*, June 17, 20, 24, 1862; Jonathan C. Casey to George W. Randolph, May 26, 1862, U.S. War Department, Letters Received by Confederate Secretary of War; Burton N. Harrison to John J. Pettus, May 17, 1862, John M. Grant to Pettus, June 28, 1862, R. S. Bowles to Pettus, July 28, 1862, Samuel N. Delany to Pettus, July 29, 1862, Pettus Papers; *ORN*, I:23:26, 54–55, 58, 139–40; Monaghan, *Swamp Fox of the Confederacy*, 51–57.

34. Bettersworth, *Confederate Mississippi*, 213–17, 222–23, 241–44, 252–54.

35. Ibid., 162–63, 252; Robinson, *Bitter Fruits of Bondage*, 180–81; Isaac Applewhite to John J. Pettus, June 6, 1862, A. A. Longstreet to Pettus, June 7, 1862, C. L. Buck to Pettus, June 7, 1862, Pettus Papers.

36. David D. Porter to David G. Farragut, June 23, 1862, David Dixon Porter Papers; *OR*, I:17(2):59.

37. Agnew Diary, June 6, 1862; *OR*, I:17(2):35, 44, 49, 53–54, 77; Starr, *Jennison's Jayhawkers*, 52–57, 156–57, 161–94; James J. Dollins to J. C. Kellow, July 7, 1862, U.S. War Department, Union Provost Marshal Files . . . Two or More Citizens.

38. Horatio N. Hollifield to George W. Randolph, May 30, 1862, W. P. Robuck to Randolph, May 11, 20, 1862, U.S. War Department, Letters Received by Confederate Secretary of War. See also W. W. Worley to Joseph E. Brown, March 29, 1862, Georgia Governor Papers: Brown; C. T. Goode to John Hunt Morgan, August 24, 1862, John Hunt Morgan Papers.

39. H. H. Waters to James Stewart, April 3, 1862, Waters to W. W. Morely, April 4, 1862, Waters to A. W. Wilson, April 11, 1862, Waters to James G. Hill, April 11, 1862, Executive Secretary Letterbook, Georgia Governor Papers: Brown; John H. Fitten to Joseph E. Brown, February 28, 1862, W. M. Sharpe to Brown, March 31, 1862, George A. Wright to Brown, April 4, 1862, James Stewart to Brown, April 10, 1862, John T. Ault to Brown, June 6, 1862, Georgia Governor Papers: Brown; John Brallie to W. G. McAdoo Jr., July 31, 1862, McAdoo Papers; J. L. Johnston

to Judah P. Benjamin, April 11, 1862, Johnston to Jefferson Davis, May 1862, A. M. Jones to George W. Randolph, May 21, 1862, U.S. War Department, Letters Received by Confederate Secretary of War; F. Moore, *Rebellion Record*, 1(Supplement):753; R. M. Myers, *Children of Pride*, 798, 849, 872, 938. See also Solomons Scrapbook, 60, 80, 85, 132, 188, 266, 360, 385, for clippings kept by a Savannah woman during the war that record guerrilla actions and stories about partisan heroes like Morgan and Mosby.

40. Johns, *Florida during the Civil War*, 64–71; R. A. Martin, "Defeat in Victory"; John Milton to John Darling, October 16, 1861, W. A. Hull to Milton, March 14, 1862, Milton to Hull, March 17, 1862, Milton to Jefferson Davis, April 7, 1862, Letterbooks, Vol. 6, Florida Governor Papers.

41. John Milton to Stephen R. Mallory, November 2, 1861, F. S. Dancer to Milton, November 24, 1861, Richard F. Floyd to Milton, April 11, 1862, Incoming Correspondence, Florida Governor Papers.

42. F. C. Dancer to John Milton, November 24, 1861, Incoming Correspondence, Florida Governor Papers; *OR*, I:53:224–25, 230–31; John Milton to Jefferson Davis, October 18, 1861, Milton to Judah P. Benjamin, October 28, 1861, Milton to John C. Pelot, March 13, 1862, John C. McGehee to Milton, March 15, 1862, Milton to McGehee, March 24, 1862, David S. Walker to Milton, March 18, 1862, Milton to George W. Randolph, April 15, 1862, Letterbooks, Vol. 6, Florida Governor Papers.

43. John Milton to John W. Pearson, February 20, 1862, Pearson to Milton, March 2, 1862, Letterbooks, Vol. 6, Florida Governor Papers; John W. Pearson to John Milton, April 8, 1862, Incoming Correspondence, Florida Governor Papers; Waters, "Florida's Confederate Guerrillas," 136–43.

44. Johns, *Florida during the Civil War*, 156–59; Waters, "Florida's Confederate Guerrillas," 139–43; *OR*, I:53:225, 233–34; Joseph Taylor to Richard F. Floyd, April 3, 1862, Floyd to John Milton, April 11, 1862, C. F. McCory to Broward, W. H. Hilton to Milton, April 21, 1862, Letterbooks, Vol. 6, Florida Governor Papers; *ORN*, I:13:245.

45. Hayes, *Du Pont: . . . Letters*, 1:410, 2:99–100, 111, 120–23, 196; *ORN*, I:13:64, 83–84; *OR*, I:14:356–57.

46. Abram Kauffman to Joseph E. Brown, March 31, 1862, Georgia Governor Papers: Brown; Sarris, "Anatomy of an Atrocity," 688–90; W. S. Adams to Henry C. Wayne, November 27, 1861, Georgia Adjutant General Records; R. S. Davis, "Memoir of a Partisan War," 107–12.

47. D. Williams, "'Rich Man's War,'" 14–36.

48. Martin Emmons to brother, February 14, 1862, Southworth Papers; Barrett, *Civil War in North Carolina*, 66–130; William Thigpen to Henry T. Clark, March 24, 1862, R. Boyd to Clark, February 21, March 7, 1862, Correspondence, Henry Toole Clark Papers; Henry T. Clark to R. Boyd, February 23, 1862, Letter-

books, Henry Toole Clark Papers; Crabtree and Patton, *"Journal of a Secesh Lady,"* 225, 239.

49. Henry T. Clark to R. Boyd, February 23, March 11, 1862, Clark to R. M. Sherrill, May 1, 1862, Letterbooks, Henry Toole Clark Papers; James G. Martin to Samuel J. Neal, April 30, 1862 (AG44), Martin to James W. Hinton, May 7, 1862 (AG54), Martin to W. J. Carman, May 8, 1862 (AG54), Martin to J. C. Moses, May 13, 1862 (AG44), Martin to M. C. Moore, May 21, 1862 (AG54), Martin to D. P. McEachen, May 24, 1862 (AG54), North Carolina Adjutant General Records; Manarin et al., *North Carolina Troops*, 2:xii, 263, 367, 584, 718, 722; Kenneth Haynes to Henry T. Clark, May 6, 1862, Correspondence, Henry Toole Clark Papers.

50. *OR*, IV:2:4–5, 31. For one man's difficulties in raising a guerrilla battalion, see Crabtree and Patton, *"Journal of a Secesh Lady,"* 122, 124, 164, 166, 184, 242.

51. Inscoe and McKinney, *Heart of Confederate Appalachia*, 108–10; Martin Crawford, *Ashe County's Civil War*, 86–87; *OR*, I:10(1):628; Godbold and Russell, *Confederate Colonel*, 90–103; Crow, *Storm in the Mountains*, 2–10; Thomsen, *Rebel Chief*, 168–83; G. N. Holt to Henry T. Clark, July 27, 1861, William H. Thomas to Clark, April 13, 1862, Marcus Erwin to Clark, April 17, 1862, Henry Toole Clark Papers.

CHAPTER 7

1. Editors, "A Warrensburg Family," 452–53; Robert W. Wells to daughter, August 17, September 7, 1862, Robert W. Wells Letters; James Peckam to General Davidson, September 19, 1862, U.S. War Department, Union Provost Marshal Files . . . Two or More Citizens; Alfred Warner to wife, August 17, 1862, Warner Papers; McMahan Diary, October 24, 1862; Connelley, "Diary of . . . Kitts," 322.

2. James L. Campbell to cousin, September 17, 1862, James L. Campbell Papers.

3. *OR*, I:13:719; John D. Crawford to Annie M. Baker, October 24, 1862, John D. Crawford Letters. See also Leslie, *Devil Knows How to Ride*, 150–51, and F. Moore, *Rebellion Record*, 6(2):27–29. For longer and contrasting descriptions of the events at Palmyra, see Speer, *War of Vengeance*, 29–41, and M. E. Neely, *Limits of Destruction*, 42–49.

4. Wellington Allen Reminiscences, December 28, 1885; Tilley, *Federals on the Frontier*, 107–8. Some sources give Boland's name as "Bowline" or "Bolin."

5. Hamilton R. Gamble to Edward Bates, July 14, 1862, Bates to Gamble, July 24, 1862, Bates Family Papers.

6. Edward Bates to Hamilton R. Gamble, July 24, 1862, ibid.

7. W. W. Smith, "Experiment in Counterinsurgency," 372–75; *OR*, I:13:611–12, 660–61, 700–702; G. W. Ballow to Mr. Frodsham, August 21, 1862, Ballow Letter. For an example of the terms and formulation of one assessment, see William E.

Mobberly to James D. Pierce, November 26, 1862, Benecke Family Papers. The War Department abolished financial assessments in January 1863, but some officers continued to apply them well into the spring.

8. William C. Long to children, December 23, 1862, Long Papers; M. M. Frazier, *Missouri Ordeal*, 61. See also Benjamin F. Loan to Hamilton R. Gamble, September 28, 1862, Gamble Papers; Sophia H. Burlingame to Lizzie Burlingame, April 19, 1863, Burlingame Family Papers; F. Moore, *Rebellion Record*, 6(2):250.

9. *OR*, I:22(1):860–66. For the Confederate response to this episode, see Crist et al., *Papers of . . . Davis*, 8:482, 496, 524–25.

10. Kiper, *Dear Catharine, Dear Taylor*, 80.

11. Frank J. White to Hamilton R. Gamble, September 27, 1862, Gamble Papers; William H. Crawford to family, June 19, 1863, Henry C. and William H. Crawford Letters; Vaught, "Diary of an Unknown Soldier," 75–76; George Wolz to John Wolz, June 19, 1863, Wolz Papers; Diana Benjamin to sister and niece, August 25, 28, 1862, John F. Benjamin to Frank, March 30, 1863, Benjamin Letters.

12. Matthews and Lindberg, "'Better Off in Hell,'" 23–25; G. O. Gesier to Lewis Merrill, September 20, 1862, report of M. R. Bruce, May 31, 1862, U.S. War Department, Union Provost Marshal Files . . . Two or More Citizens; case of James M. Lafoon (NN1793), U.S. War Department, Court-Martial Cases.

13. M. M. Frazier, *Missouri Ordeal*, 79, 83, 85; James Draper to sister, June 7, 1863, Draper-McClurg Family Papers.

14. M. M. Frazier, *Missouri Ordeal*, 61, 127; *OR*, I:22(1):245–46, (2):183, 195. See also Arthur Draper to sister, August 28, 1862, Draper-McClurg Family Papers; cases of Jacob A. Fowler, Thomas P. Connor, and George M. Anderson (LL875), U.S. War Department, Court-Martial Cases. For a variety of extenuating circumstances, see cases of William Willis (KK339), Jacob Snowden and William Marley (LL549), James Creiger and Robert Ward (LL563), William N. Darnell (LL1882), William Moore, Henry Garner, and Robert Oaks (MM451), William S. McGinnis (MM1300), Ephraim Huff (NN1445), U.S. War Department, Court-Martial Cases; Oath by Citizens of Rockport, Missouri, September 28, 1862, Petition from Citizens of Lincoln County, Missouri, September 1862, U.S. War Department, Union Provost Marshals Files . . . Two or More Citizens.

15. Cases of Andrew J. Alexander and James S. Blacketon (NN1237) and William H. Owsley (NN1147), U.S. War Department, Court-Martial Cases; Ben Loan to Hamilton R. Gamble, October 13, 1862, J. P. Mathews to Gamble, April 9, 1863, Gamble Papers; McLarty, "Letters of . . . Lazear: Part I," 268–69, 272; Henry C. Lay to Leroy Pope Walker, May 11, 1861, U.S. War Department, Letters Received by Confederate Secretary of War; Baxter, *Pea Ridge and Prairie Grove*, 59–68; James W. Peel to Lizzie, January 21, 1862, Peel Papers.

16. W. D. Kerr to William McCoy, November 29, 1862, McCoy Papers.

17. Sutherland, "Lincoln, John Pope, and . . . Total War," 584–85; Grimsley,

Hard Hand of War, 148; *OR*, III:2:301; Francis Lieber to Dear Sir, July 26, 1862, Lieber to Norman Lieber, February 8, 1863, Lieber Papers. For Lieber's life and family, see Friedel, *Francis Lieber*, and Breeden, "Oscar Lieber."

18. *OR*, III:2:301; Marszalek, *Commander of All Lincoln's Armies*, 167.

19. *OR*, III:2:301–9. See also Lieber, *Miscellaneous Writings*, 2:277–92.

20. *OR*, III:2:305, 308.

21. *OR*, III:2:307, 309.

22. Francis Lieber to Henry Halleck, November 13, 1862, Lieber Papers; U.S. Adjutant General, *General Orders*, 64–87; Grimsley, *Hard Hand of War*, 149–51; Marszalek, *Commander of All Lincoln's Armies*, 167–68; Carnahan, "Lincoln, Lieber and the Laws of War"; *OR*, III:3:148–64.

23. Grimsley, *Hard Hand of War*, 150–51; *OR*, II:6:46, III:3:164; Carnahan, "Lincoln, Lieber and the Laws of War," 217–18.

24. Marszalek, *Commander of All Lincoln's Armies*, 178–79, 218; *OR*, III:2:307; Nevins, *Diary of Battle*, 184.

25. 25. Rowland S. H. Mantor to father, April 22, 1863, Mantor Papers; Francis F. Audsley to wife, June 9, July 14, 1863, Audsley Letters; Edward Russell to Thomas Carney, June 9, 1863, Militia: 1861–1900, Kansas Adjutant General Records; McLarty, "Letters of . . . Lazear: Part I," 271–72.

26. Col. Benjamin to Frank, March 30, 1863, Benjamin Letters; McLarty, "Letters of . . . Lazear: Part I," 255, 257–58; Special Order No. 86, May 31, 1862, George M. Houston to Odon Guitar, August 17, 1862, Ephraim J. Wilson to Guitar, July 27, 1863, J. H. Ellis to Guitar, February 24, 1863, Guitar Collection; Canan, "Milton Burch," 223–30; Henry C. and William H. Crawford to Dear friends, August 8, [1862], Henry C. and William H. Crawford Letters; A. J. McRoberts to Mollie, August 10, 14, September 6, 12, 16, 1862, July 5, 1863, McRoberts Family Letters; Daniel M. Draper to sister, June 3, 1863, Draper to father, August 15, 1862, Draper-McClurg Family Papers; W. E. Parrish, *History of Missouri*, 55–58, 94–99; Boman, *Lincoln's Resolute Unionist*, 142–86, 207–18; Lowndes H. Davis to Mary, March 2, 1863, Lowndes Henry Davis Papers; F. T. Russell to Odon Guitar, February 3, 1863, Guitar Collection.

27. Richard C. Vaughn to James O. Broadhead, May 8, 1863, Broadhead Papers; N. J. Robertson to Francis S. Burlingame, July 3, 1863, Burlingame Family Papers; E. A. Christy to Dear Pa, February 24, 1863, Christy Letter; Herklotz, "Jayhawkers in Missouri," 89–93; J. H. Ellis to Colonel, February 24, 1863, Guitar Papers; M. M. Frazier, *Missouri Ordeal*, 127, 132–33, 137–38.

28. Cheatham, "Divided Loyalties" and "'Desperate Characters'"; Castel, "Jayhawkers and Copperheads"; Starr, *Jennison's Jayhawkers*, 214–15, 245–53; Samuel Ayres to Friend Langdon, June 1, 1863, Ayres Correspondence; Leslie, *Devil Knows How to Ride*, 164–67; Goodrich, *Black Flag*, 60–63; Malin, "Letters of . . . Lovejoy: . . . Part Five," 182–90; J. Broadhead et al. to Thomas Carney, May 5, 1863, Citizens of Douglas and Franklin Counties to Carney, May 9, 1863,

Militia: 1861–1900, Kansas Adjutant General Records; J. R. Parr to Carney, May 17, 1863, H. W. Farnsworth to Carney, May 18, 1863, O. C. Beach and W. H. M. Fishback to Carney, May 18, 1863, Box 2.1, f. 18, Kansas Governor Papers.

29. Starr, *Jennison's Jayhawkers*, 214–15; L. Barnes, "An Editor Looks at Early-Day Kansas," 121–23; Matthews and Lindberg, "'Better Off in Hell,'" 23–30; Samuel Ayres to Friend Langdon, June 1, 1863, Ayres Correspondence; M. M. Frazier, *Missouri Ordeal*, 129–31; Goodrich, *Black Flag*, 67–70.

30. A. T. Howard to Thomas Carney, May 20, 1863, Guilford Dudley to S. N. Wood, May 20, 1863, Carney to W. H. M. Fishback, May 22, 1863, General Correspondence: 1861–65, Kansas Adjutant General Records; J. C. Bunch to Thomas Carney, May 11, 1863, William Means to Carney, May 21, 1863, Edward Russell to Carney, June 9, 1863, Militia: 1861–1900, Kansas Adjutant General Records; Castel, "Jayhawkers and Copperheads," 290–93; *OR*, I:22(2):222–23.

31. Goodrich, *Black Flag*, 63–65, 69; *OR*, I:22(1):844–51; Bodwell Diaries, March 23, June 19, 1863. See Bodwell Diaries, June–July 1863, for "jayhawker" attitudes toward Missourians.

32. Wubben, "Internal Security in Iowa," 405–7; Jacob Geiger to Samuel J. Kirkwood, August 21, 1862, Kirkwood to W. W. Thomas et al., September 11, 1862, J. H. Summers to J. M. Hiatt, March 9, 1863, Jesse Evans to N. B. Baker, May 9, 1863, Box 68, Correspondence: Southern Border Brigade, Iowa Adjutant General Records; John R. Morlidge to Samuel J. Kirkwood, August 28, 1862, J. S. Beall et al. to Kirkwood, August 29, 1862, Samuel R. Curtis to Kirkwood, September 15, 1862, Correspondence: War Matters, 1858–97, Iowa Governor Papers; R. D. Kellogg to Samuel J. Kirkwood, August 14, 1862, Kirkwood Papers; Thomas G. Taylor to N. B. Taylor, August 7, 1862, Correspondence: Militia, 1839–75, Iowa Governor Papers; Wubben, *Civil War Iowa*, 117–25.

33. L. Cox, "Hawkeye Heroes," 21–32; A. M. Felton to Samuel J. Kirkwood, July 23, July 1862, J. H. White to Kirkwood, August 7, 1862, J. M. Humphrey to Kirkwood, August 11, 1862, Correspondence: War Matters, Iowa Governor Papers; H. C. Glendeming et al. to Samuel J. Kirkwood, September 10, 1862, Kirkwood Papers; Wubben, *Civil War Iowa*, 123; Joseph Ferris to P. Hall, April 25, June 19, 1863, Joseph Dickey to N. B. Baker, June 19, July 16, 1863, Box 68, Correspondence: Southern Border Brigade, Iowa Adjutant General Papers.

34. *OR*, I:22(1):865; Jacob Ammen to Thomas J. McKean, April 23, 1863, Thomas Schambeck to Ammen, June 22, July 8, 1863, Ammen Papers; J. B. Moore to Richard Yates, May 4, 1863, Yates Family Collection; Henry P. Andrews to wife and children, September 1, 1862, Henry P. Andrews Papers; Gallaher, "Peter Wilson . . . , 1863–1865," 363–65.

35. James J. Langdon to Ambrose E. Burnside, March 26, 1863, Thomas J. McKean to Henry Z. Curtis, April 8, 1863, D. P. Dyer to Samuel R. Curtis, May 8, 1863, Ammen Papers. For an instance of the general breakdown of law and order in Missouri, see Kronenberg, *Lives and Letters*, 163.

36. Hulston and Goodrich, "John Trousdale Coffee," 279–92; Leslie, *Devil Knows How to Ride*, 130–37; Edward Bates to Abraham Lincoln, September 19, 1862, Bates Family Papers. For the tenacity of some Missouri-based guerrillas, see Moss, "A Missouri Confederate," 18–27.

37. Tilley, *Federals on the Frontier*, 34, 36, 39, 42–43, 50, 56–57; Shea, "1862," 46–58; DeBlack, *With Fire and Sword*, 62–73; Bradbury, "This War Is Managed Mighty Strange"; Beckenbaugh, "War of Politics," 29–31; Edward Bates to Edwin V. Sumner, March 14, 1863, Bates Papers. See A. J. Bailey, "Texans Invade Missouri," for the type of raid Curtis feared.

38. DeBlack, *With Fire and Sword*, 74–87; Kohl, "This Godforsaken Town," 109–44; Gallaher, "Peter Wilson . . . , 1863–65," 370–71; J. A. Williamson to Grenville M. Dodge, September 20, 1862, Dodge Papers; Joseph Crider to brother, May 31, July 21, October 2, 1862, Crider Letters; Nathan J. Rhodes to wife, October 31, November 11, December 26, 1862, Rhodes Letters; Edward H. Ingraham to sister, September 10, 11–12, 1862, Ingraham Letters; Lew B. Jessup to Richard E. Blair, January 26, 1863, Blair Letters; Amasa O. Allen to wife, November 1, 11, December 24, 1862, Allen Correspondence; A. F. O'Neil to father, August 5, 1862, John F. O'Neil Papers; Anthony Francis O'Neil Diary, July 25, 27–28, August 1, 1863, Charles O'Neil Papers; Elder, *Love amid the Turmoil*, 40–41, 46, 114; Throne, "Diary of W. H. Turner," 270–71, 282; *Memphis Daily Appeal*, October 20, 1862; John F. Youngs to sister, August 26, 1862, Youngs to Thomas, September 29, October 4, 16, 1862, John F. Youngs Correspondence; McMahan Diary, February 27, March 16, 22, April 10, 1863; Popchock, *Soldier Boy*, 50–51, 53–54, 56–57; Minos Miller to mother, July 14, 1863, Minos Miller Papers. For examples of continuing trouble after Curtis left, see Harlan, "Pearson's War Diary, Pt. 2," 201–3; Robert Edwin Jameson Diary, June 16, 1863, and Robert E. Jameson to sister, June 17, 1863, Jameson Papers; J. T. Greene, *Ewing Family Civil War Letters*, 78–79.

39. Drury Connally to Anne Kilgore Connally, July 14, December 16, 1862, War Letters of Drury Connally.

40. George E. Flanders to brother, August 2, 17, November 25, December 14, 1862, January 9, 1863, Flanders to mother, October 16, 1862, Flanders Civil War Letters; *ORN*, I:25:172–74; Edward Paul Reichhelm Diary, pp. 1–3 (December 20–23, 1862), Reichhelm Collection. For the desperate measures of one Union naval officer to avoid guerrillas, see Hammond, "Arkansas Atlantis," 214–15.

41. Demuth, "Burning of Hopefield"; *OR*, I:22(1):230–33.

42. Shea, "1862," 58; DeBlack, *With Fire and Sword*, 72–74; Carrie to sister, May 13, 1863, McGee and Charles Family Papers; Quesenberry Diary, October 11, 18, 1862.

43. William G. Thompson to Harriet Jane Thompson, October 20, November 3, 1862, William G. Thompson Correspondence; Henry C. Lay to wife, January 4, 11, 28, 1863, Lay Papers. The Thompson letters may also be found in Bearss, *Letters of . . . Thompson*; Tilley, *Federals on the Frontier*, 96, 100, 114–15, 118,

120, 122–23, 127, 133, 136–37; James Loughing to John Sherman, May 25, 1863, Sherman Papers.

44. Worley, "Arkansas Peace Society of 1861: A Study," and "Documents Relating to the Arkansas Peace Society"; Charles A. Dana to Edwin Stanton, July 4, 1863, James Harrison Wilson Papers.

45. *OR*, I:22(2):8; DeBlack, *With Fire and Sword*, 75–79; J. Q. Anderson, *Campaigning with Parsons' Texas Cavalry*, 96, 100; House, "James R. Vanderpool," 2–4; Henry C. Lay to wife, January 11, 28, 1863, Lay to Mrs. John Perkins, February 28, 1863, Lay Papers; John William Brown Diary, February 26, March 19, 1863.

46. Sutherland, "Guerrillas: The Real War," 149–50; Pickering and Falls, *Brush Men*, 69–80; John H. Carson Diary, January 15, 1863, John H. Carson Papers; Jordan, "Martin Hart's Date," 40–46; Prier, "Under the Black Flag," 121–36.

47. *OR*, I:22(2):272–75; George W. Guess to Sarah Cockrell, January 17, 1863, Cockrell Papers.

48. L. G. Bennett, "Recruiting in Dixie" (Summer, Fall, Winter 1990, Spring 1991); Rowland Mantor to father, May 17, 1863, Mantor to family, September 6, 1863, Mantor Papers; J. J. Johnston, "Summer of 1863"; Current, *Lincoln's Loyalists*, 73–79, 213; Beall, "Wildwood Skirmishers"; Bishop, *Loyalty on the Frontier*, xi–xvi.

49. Prier, "Under the Black Flag," 47–54; Bishop, *Loyalty on the Frontier*, 156–57.

50. Maddox, *Hard Trials*, 11–12; McMahan Diary, March 22, 1863; Sutherland, "Guerrillas: The Real War," 136–37. See also Crouch and Brice, *Cullen Montgomery Baker*, 44–52. For the more controversial Arkansas guerrilla who may also fall into this category, see Davis, "Legend of Bill Dark."

51. Crist et al., *Papers of . . . Davis*, 9:10; "Discussion of Jayhawkers," Dandridge McRae Papers. For another rebel soldier turned guerrilla, see M. A. Davis, "Legend of Bill Dark." For contrasting positions on the contentious issue of Confederate "nationalism," see Beringer et al., *Why the South Lost*, 64–81, and Rubin, *Shattered Nation*, 1–6.

52. Bennette W. Bagby to brother, August 12, 1862, Bagby Papers; *ORN*, I:19:175, 181, 186, 215, 244–45, 437, 762, 765; B. Burnham to family, May 23, 1863, Burnham Letters.

53. T. M. Parrish, *Richard Taylor*, 245–306.

54. Crist et al., *Papers of . . . Davis*, 8:444; *OR*, I:15:124–26, 567; Frank H. Peck to brother, August 10, 1862, Peck to mother, October 20, 1862, Newton W. Perkins to brother, September 9, 1862, Montgomery Family Papers; C. H. Richardson to Lois Davis, August 4, 1862, Lois (Wright) Richardson Davis Papers; B. Butler, *Correspondence*, 2:199–200, 231–32, 278–79.

55. Hyde, *Pistols and Politics*, 114–16; Lathrop, "Lafourche District in 1862:

Confederate Revival," 301–2; Winters, *Civil War in Louisiana,* 152–53; Oscar Smith Diary, August 9, 1862; *ORN,* I:19:191; B. Butler, *Correspondence,* 2:232.

56. Lathrop, "Lafourche District in 1862: Confederate Revival," 303–5; E. Taylor, "Discontent in Confederate Louisiana," 425; A Soldier's Sister to Thomas O. Moore, August 9, 1862, Thomas O. Moore Papers; *OR,* I:15:753, 773–74.

57. *OR,* I:15:565–66.

58. Lathrop, "Lafourche District in 1862: Confederate Revival," 305–8; *OR,* I:15:798.

59. Winters, *Civil War in Louisiana,* 153–54, 172–73; *OR,* I:15:175–76; Lathrop, "Lafourche District in 1862: Confederate Revival," 316–17; *ORN,* I:19:215.

60. William H. Garig Diary, March 30, April 1, 27, 28, 1863, Garig Family Papers. Garig never clearly identifies his unit. Hewett, *Roster of Confederate Soldiers,* 6:215, says he belonged to the 1st Special Battalion (Rightor's) of the Louisiana Infantry, but that battalion disbanded in May 1862. See Bergeron, *Guide to Louisiana Confederate Military Units,* 148–49.

61. Nathaniel P. Banks to General Bowen, July 25, 1863, U.S. War Department, Letters Received by Provost Marshal, Department of the Gulf and Louisiana.

62. Lincecum et al., *Gideon Lincecum's Sword,* 179, 209; B. Warner Stone to George W. Randolph, September 4, 5, 1862, U.S. War Department, Letters Received by Confederate Secretary of War; Pickering and Falls, *Brush Men,* 3–27, A. J. Bailey, "Defiant Unionists," 208–12.

63. A. J. Bailey, "Defiant Unionists," 208–16. For a Texas German who enlisted as a *Confederate* irregular, see Editors, "German Partisan Ranger."

64. Crosby, "Wrong Side of the River," 48–54; A. J. Bailey, "Defiant Unionists," 212–18; *OR,* I:9:614–15.

65. A. J. Bailey, "Defiant Unionists," 218–20; T. C. Smith, *Here's Yer Mule,* 19–20.

66. A. J. Bailey, "Defiant Unionists," 220–21.

67. Pickering and Falls, *Brush Men,* 28–101; McCaslin, *Tainted Breeze,* 1–8, 35–59.

68. D. P. Smith, *Frontier Defense,* 61–65; McCaslin, *Tainted Breeze,* 60–107.

69. McCaslin, *Tainted Breeze,* 108–29; D. P. Smith, *Frontier Defense,* 41–51, 57–66.

CHAPTER 8

1. *OR,* I:17(1):23; Simpson and Berlin, *Sherman's Civil War,* 260–63, 265–66, 273, 279–88, 292, 295–97; Cooling, *Fort Donelson's Legacy,* 110–11; Royster, *Destructive War,* 107–9; Fisher, "Prepare Them for My Coming."

2. Cooling, *Fort Donelson's Legacy,* 110; Simpson and Berlin, *Sherman's Civil War,* 305–10; *OR,* I:17(1):144–45, (2):235–36.

3. *OR,* I:17(2):261, 279–81, 285, 287–89, 860; D. C. Anthony to S. T. Bankhead, October 20, 1862, Box 2, f. 10, Civil War Collection; Garrett, *Diary of . . .*

Campbell, 89. See also William T. Sherman to Grenville M. Dodge, October 21, 1862, Dodge Papers.

4. *OR*, I:16(1):265–71, 23(2):20–21.

5. Culp P. Johnson Diary, September 15, 1862; Reyburn and Wilson, "*Jottings from Dixie*," 88–89, 111–13; John Harper to father and mother, January 8, 1863, John and Alexander Harper Papers; Lysander Wheeler to family, February 4, June 28, July 5, 1863, Wheeler Letters; George Angle to wife, April 12, 1863, Angle Papers; Helium H. Dunn to parents, April 11, 1863, Helium H. Dunn Letters; Smith and Cooper, *Union Woman*, 113, 122, 137; E. Martin Gebbart to brother and sister, January 6, 1863, Gebbart Papers; E. P. Sturges to Folks, August 29, 1862, Sturges Papers; Throne, *Diary of Cyrus F. Boyd*, 103; Samuel T. Wells to Lizzie, December 5, 1862, July 9, 1863, Samuel T. Wells Papers; Oliver L. Spaulding Diary, December 20, 24–26, 1862, March 20, April 11, June 14, July 7, 9, 1863, Spaulding Family Papers; David W. Poak to sister, September 10, October 4, 1862, Poak Letters; Angus Waddle to sister, August 18, 1862, McCoy Papers; Sylvester, "'Gone for a Soldier,'" 42, 48, 51.

6. Reyburn and Wilson, "*Jottings from Dixie*," 121; "Use of Block-Houses during the Civil War," pp. 1–3, Box 38, vol. 87, file 7, Dodge Papers; J. R. Perkins, *Trails, Rails, and War*, 88–91; Merrill, "Block-houses."

7. William H. Bradbury to wife, January 1, March 3, 6, April 12, June 13, Bradbury Papers; *OR*, I:23(1):148–50, (2):33, 155, 157; Levi A. Ross Diary, April 11, 1863, Ross Papers. For the activities of the rest of the 129th Illinois brigade, see Romeyn, "Scouting in Tennessee," 241–62.

8. Henry to parents, August 25, 1862, Henry Letters; John W. Garriott to sister, March 19, June 24, July 24, 1863, Garriott Letters; James E. Love to Molly, April 25, 1863, Love Papers; John A. Boon to friends, [January 12, 1863], Boon Papers; William J. Helsley to wife, December 24, 1862, Helsley Papers.

9. E. P. Sturges to Folks, January 27, 1863, Sturges Papers; Bela T. St. John Diaries, May 15, 1863, St. John Papers; Milton T. Carey to Cornelia Carey, October 23, 1862, January 20, [1863], Carey Papers. A good synopsis of the U.S. Navy's river war against rebel guerrillas is provided in M. J. Bennett, *Union Jacks*, 87–95.

10. Cooling, *Fort Donelson's Legacy*, 115–16; *ORN*, I:23:451–52; Ballard, *Vicksburg*, 157, 160, 170; General Orders No. 2 and 4, in "Orders," (Lord Division) Eltinge-Lord Family Papers; Hearn, *David Dixon Porter*, 144–52; "Journal of Occurrences during the War of the Rebellion," 424–25, 433–34, David Dixon Porter Papers.

11. *ORN*, I:23:309–16, 322. See M. J. Smith, *Le Roy Fitch*, for a biography.

12. *ORN*, I:23:316–18, 24:39, 59, 62–65, 71–72, 75, 84, 86–87, 25:159–60, 204–5.

13. David W. Poak to sister, August 24, 1862, February 11, 1863, Poak Letters; David H. Thomas to parents, August 5, 1862, David Harrison Thomas Papers; *Memphis Daily Appeal*, August 1, 15, October 24, 1862.

14. *OR*, I:22(2):15–16; Beckenbaugh, "War of Politics," 34–42; Bennett and Tillery, *Struggle for the Life*, 59–60; Abbey E. Stafford to sister, [September] 1862, Stafford Papers; *ORN*, I:26:340–51, 376–77; Ned C. Ellis to mother, October 4, 1864, Edmund Curtis Ellis Papers; Hearn, *David Dixon Porter*, 268–71; L. H. Johnson, *Red River Campaign*, 49–78; Lash, "'Federal Tyrant at Memphis,'" 15–28. See also Lash's full biography of Hurlbut, *Politician Turned General*.

15. Isaac H. Rowland to father, January 15, 1863, Rowland-Shilliday Papers; Bela St. John to brother, February 10, 1863, St. John Papers; Robert J. Price to father, June 6, 1863, Elias Winans Price Papers; Wilberforce Nevin to brother, December 2, 1862, Nevin to father, April 29, 1863, Sayre Papers; William J. Helsley to wife, July 4, 1863, Helsley Papers; George Healey to mother, sisters, and brother, September 25, October 14, 1862, Healey Civil War Letters; E. P. Sturges to Folks, August 9, 1862, Sturges Papers; Reyburn and Wilson, *"Jottings from Dixie,"* 89; William R. Stuckey to Helen, April 27, 1863, Stuckey Papers; Murray and Rodney, "Letters of Peter Bryant . . . Concluded," 474–75; Thomas S. Hawley to parents, January 11, 1863, Hawley Papers; Elias Brady to wife, November 23, 24, December 12, 1862, Brady Papers; Arthur Vanhorn to wife, February 9, 1863, Vanhorn Papers.

16. Swedberg, *Three Years with the 92nd Illinois*, 52; Samuel W. Pruitt to Bettie Pruitt, April 20, 1863, Pruitt Papers; Thomas S. Hawley to parents, March 22, 1863, Hawley Papers; Edward P. Stanfield to father, [February 1863], Stanfield Correspondence; Wilberforce Nevin to brother, December 1, 1862, Sayre Papers; Reyburn and Wilson, *"Jottings from Dixie,"* 89; William J. Helsley to wife, July 25, 1863, Helsley Papers; Samuel W. Pruitt to Martha Pruitt, April 20, 1863, Pruitt Papers; Milton T. Carey to Cornelia Carey, November 2, 1862, Carey Papers; James E. Love to Molly, August 10, 28, November 19, December 6, 1862, January 15, February 15, April 10, 12, June 10, 1863, Love Papers; Murray and Rodney, "Letters of Peter Bryant . . . Concluded," 477; Samuel T. Wells to Lizzie, May 2, 1863, Samuel T. Wells Papers; Morse, *Diaries and Letters*, 46; L. P Deatherage Proclamation to the People of Kentucky, August 13, 1862, Edward Henry Hobson Papers.

17. Eugene Marshall Diaries, September 16, October 2, 26, November 18, 1862, January 15, 29, March 14, May 8, 22–23, 1863, Eugene Marshall Papers. Marshall's assessment of the situation is confirmed by the letters of another member of the regiment in Healey Civil War Letters. See Cooling, *Fort Donelson's Legacy*, 104, for a photograph of Marshall.

18. George Healey to mother, June 4, 1863, Healey Civil War Letters; Eugene Marshall to sister, May 27, 1863, and Eugene Marshall Diaries, May 8, July 15, 23, 1863, Eugene Marshall Papers. See also Reyburn and Wilson, *"Jottings from Dixie,"* 132.

19. Reyburn and Wilson, *"Jottings from Dixie,"* 58–59; D. L. Ambrose, *From Shiloh to Savannah*, 122–30; Edward S. Johnson to J. W. Barnes, August 31, 1863,

Box 2, vol. 5, f. 2, Dodge Papers; Wilberforce Nevin to father, April 29, 1863, Sayre Papers. See also the experiences of the 20th Ohio Infantry in David H. Thomas to parents, December 26, 30, 1862, February 1, 1863, David Harrison Thomas Papers, and requests from another regiment for mounts in William B. Jones to John W. Finnell, July 16, 1863, Kentucky Adjutant General Records.

20. Whitesell, "Military Operations," 166–67; Ridley, *Battles and Sketches*, 596–98.

21. T. E. Pickett to Bon Ami, July 25, 1862, Trimble Family Papers; Charles H. Sowle to mother, May 12, 1862, Sowle Papers.

22. *OR*, I:17(2):261, 273, 861.

23. Davis and Swentor, *Bluegrass Confederate*, 220, 245, 251–52; Lowndes H. Davis to Mary Davis, March 2, 1863, Lowndes H. Davis Papers; Mary E. Cooper to Sally Cooper, July 17, [1863], Cooper Papers.

24. Cooling, *Fort Donelson's Legacy*, 103–10.

25. *OR*, I:17(2):730–32; *ORN*, I:25:339; Ash, "Sharks in an Angry Sea," 227–29; Gildrie, "Guerrilla Warfare," 164–65.

26. For the experiences of one sheriff, see Nimrod Porter Diary, January–May 1863, esp. February 26, July 18, 23.

27. John W. Harris to mother, March 27, 1863, John W. Harris Letters; Crist et al., *Papers of . . . Davis*, 8:328. Also for Marshall, see McKnight, *Contested Borderland*, 106; Perry, *Jack May's War*. A Louisiana soldier called guerrillas "obnoxious to the peaceful country people" (W. Watson, *Life in the Confederate Army*, 388–89).

28. Wiggenton et al., *Tennesseans in the Civil War*, 1:80–82; Robert V. Richardson to John C. Pemberton, April 26, 1863, Richardson proclamations of January 25, February 5, 1863, U.S. War Department, Letters Received by Confederate Secretary of War; cases of J. E. Boyd (LL777), John B. Scarborough and Thomas W. Bass (LL3248), U.S. War Department, Court-Martial Cases; Will Kennedy to sister, February 17, 1863, Will Kennedy Papers.

29. *OR*, I:24(1):423–26; Robert V. Richardson to John C. Pemberton, April 26, 1863, U.S. War Department, Letters Received by Confederate Secretary of War.

30. *OR*, I:24(1):426; Robert V. Richardson to John C. Pemberton, April 26, 1863, U.S. War Department, Letters Received by Confederate Secretary of War.

31. Cases of Boyd, Scarborough, and Bass from n. 28 above; *OR*, I:24(3):111, 176–78, 654, 656, 658, 696–97, 757.

32. Grimsley, *Hard Hand of War*, 68–70, 75–78; Eugene Marshall Diaries, September 8, 1862, Eugene Marshall Papers; *OR*, I:17(1):30.

33. Culp P. Johnson Diary, September 11, 1862; Reyburn and Wilson, *"Jottings from Dixie,"* 81; Eugene Marshall Diaries, September 17, 25–26, 30, 1862, Eugene Marshall Papers.

34. Lysander Wheeler to family, November 5, 1862, Wheeler Letters; C. H.

Spilman to James T. Robinson, August 18, 1862, Frederick T. Walker to Robinson, August 21, 1862, William R. Fleming to Robinson, August 21, 1862, Robert Morris and S. W. Hunt to Robinson, September 9, 1862, Bennett Spears to D. E. Downing, August 8, 1862, Military Correspondence, Kentucky Governor Papers: Robinson; Graf et al., *Papers of Andrew Johnson*, 6:137, 299, 300n; Bennett Spears to D. E. Downing, August 14, 1862, Military Correspondence, Kentucky Governor Papers: Magoffin; Edward S. Johnson to J. W. Barnes, August 31, 1863, Box 2, vol. 5, f. 2, Dodge Papers; W. F. Camden to James T. Robinson, November 13, 1862, J. A. Morrison to John W. Finnell, December 3, 1862, R. R. Jones to Finnell, December 18, 1862, F. J. Ewing to Robinson, May 1, 1863, Daniel A. Brooks to Finnell, October 30, 1862, Ira H. Stout to Finnell, August 7, 1862, S. N. Marshall to Robinson, September 20, 1862, R. A. Buckner to Robinson, November 3, 1862, Samuel D. McCullough, November 4, 1862, Kentucky Adjutant General Records; cases of Obed C. Crossland (NN1477), Robert Gossett (NN1476), and John Jennings (NN2751), U.S. War Department, Court-Martial Cases; U.S. War Department, Register of Civilian Prisoners, McLean Barracks, Cincinnati, Ohio, April 1863–July 1865, Records Relating to Confederate Prisoners of War.

35. Cooling, *Fort Donelson's Legacy*, 78–81, 93–98; McDonough, *War in Kentucky*, 30–60; McKnight, *Contested Borderland*, 123–24, 141–45, 156–58; Crist et al., *Papers of . . . Davis*, 8:509–10; *OR*, I:20(2):421–23; Bolling Hall Jr. to father, August 11, 1862, Hall Family Papers; Davis and Swentor, *Bluegrass Confederate*, 153, 245, 247, 251–54, 257, 305; Lowery Diary, August 29, 1862; Edmund Kirby Smith to wife, August 29, 1862, September 16, 1862, Kirby Smith Papers; James T. Tucker to John Hunt Morgan, September 21, 1862, J. Chenault to Morgan, September 21, 1862, John Hunt Morgan Papers; McCreary Diary, October 12, November 14, 1862, January 20, 22, 24, 1863; George Knox Miller to Dear Friend, November 2, 1862, George Knox Miller Papers; J. W. Gash to Mary Patton, October 30, 1862, Mary A. Gash Papers; Martin D. Gash to sister, February 8, 1863, Gash Family Papers; Stephen Whitacker to father, July 23, 1863, Stephen Whitacker Papers; Smith and Cooper, *Union Woman*, 45; John M. Porter Memoirs, 45, 59–60. See also Prichard, "'A Grim Warning.'"

36. Charles G. McAdoo Diary, September 18, 29, 1862, Henry Elliot to William G. McAdoo, September 15, 1862, Floyd-McAdoo Family Papers; "Capture of Capt. Berry," Box 4, f. 5, Civil War Collection: Confederate; Wilberforce Nevin to mother, April 29, 1863, Sayre Papers; French Diaries, July 12, 19, 21, 25–27, 1863.

37. French Diaries, July 26–27, 1863. See also Trimble, "Behind the Lines," 60–61.

38. John Wesley Marshall Diary, July 18, 1863, John Wesley Marshall Papers; Graf et al., *Papers of Andrew Johnson*, 6:48–49, 626–27; Bentley, "Memoirs of . . . Speed," 238–39, 242; Anderson Memoir, 125–28; Robert E. Jameson to brother, June 21, 1863, Jameson Papers; J. C. Eversole to James T. Robinson, [January 1863], Kentucky Adjutant General Papers.

39. Wiggenton et al., *Tennesseans in the Civil War*, 1:329–33; Graf et al., *Papers of Andrew Johnson*, 6:111n; Amanda McDowell Diary, July 24, 25, 1863, Curtis McDowell Papers.

40. William E. Sloan Diary, September 28, 1862, January 26, 31, February 6, 7, March 9, 14, 18, 1863. For other Unionist perils, see Lysander Wheeler to family, November 5, 1862, Wheeler Letters; Garrett, "Guerrillas and Bushwhackers in Middle Tennessee," p. 47, Garrett Collection; Rainey Memoir, 11–12; Ash, "Sharks in an Angry Sea," 224; Graf et al., *Papers of Andrew Johnson*, 6:88–89, 243; Dunn, *Cades Cove*, 127–33.

41. Amanda McDowell Diary, July 25, 1863, Curtis McDowell Papers; Elisha to Mrs. Holyoke, August 17, 1762, Holyoke Family Papers; Haycroft Journal, October 10, 20, December 27, 1862; Davis and Swentor, *Bluegrass Confederate*, 220, 245, 251–52. For the shifting fortunes of Brandenburg and Lexington, Kentucky, see Letticia to George W. Parker, October 2, 1862, George Washington Parker Papers; Smith and Cooper, *Union Woman*, generally.

42. G. E. Moore, *Banner in the Hills*, 175–80; Matheny, *Wood County*, 351–69; *The Guerilla*, September 27, 1862, copy in Museum of the Confederacy, Richmond.

43. Cheeks, "Border Rangers"; Samuel Hatton to Francis H. Pierpont, August 11, 1862, J. M. Gorral to Pierpont, September 7, 1862, S. Parsons to Pierpont, September 1, 1862, A. I. Borman to Pierpont, September 20, 1862, Pierpont Papers; Nancy Hunt to Mr. and Mrs. J. H. Hoppings, December 7, 1862, Nancy Hunt Letters; Longacre, *Mounted Raids*, 123–47.

44. Buck, *Sad Earth*, 136; Jacob W. Marshall to Col. Swann, January 3, 1863, Paul McNeel to Cols. Jones and Swann, January 2, 1863, McNeel to John Letcher, January 2, 1863, Virginia Governor Papers: Letcher (Series I); Robertson, *Soldier of Southwestern Virginia*, 131–35; T. M. Harris to Francis H. Pierpont, August 12, September 10, 1862, Citizens of Braxton County to Pierpont, March 1863, Pierpont Papers; Curry and Ham, "Bushwhackers' War," 430–31; Horace Kellogg to Rufus Maxwell, November 28, 1862, Civil War Letters (#648); John V. Young to Dear Captain, April 5, 1863, Young to J. T. Bowyer, June 26, 1863, Young to Paulina, July 6, 1863, Young to Emma, July 10, 1863, John V. Young Letters. See also the diary of Sarah Frances Young, a daughter of John Young, for a good account of his militia activities.

45. West Virginia Historical Records Survey, *Calendar of the . . . Pierpont Letters*, 176; H. Chapman et al. to Francis H. Pierpont, August 2, 1862, D. Quinn Guthrie to Pierpont, August 29, 862, S. M. Harper et al. to Pierpont, April 4, 1863, W. D. Rolyson to Pierpont (telegram), September 8, 1862, A. I. Borman to Pierpont, September 20, 1862, Abram F. Gibbins to Pierpont, October 1, 1862, Andrew Wylie to Pierpont, September 16, 1862, Robert H. Milroy to Pierpont, October 27, 1862, Pierpont Papers; Matheny, *Wood County*, 370–74. For more on Milroy's handling of the rebels, see Noyalas, "Most Hated Man in Winchester."

See also J. D. Cox, *Military Reminiscences*, 1:420–25, for another general's understanding of the problems in West Virginia.

46. Edward W. Whitacker to Sister Ada, May 9, June 6, 1863, Edward W. Whitacker Letters; John H. Hite to Jacob M. Campbell, August 8, 1862, Jacob M. Campbell Papers; John J. Polsley to wife, September 16, 1862, April 5, May 15, 1863, Polsley Papers; Henry Solomon White Diary, August 5, 18, 23, October 15, December 1, 1862, May 25, June 23, 1863; Martin Oviatt Diary, May 12, 14, July 28, 1863, Oviatt Papers; David V. Porter to grandmother, June 1863, David Dixon Porter Papers; Elias W. Price to sister, December 22, 1862, Elias Winans Price Papers.

47. S. C. Tucker, *John D. Imboden*, 94–108; Philip P. Dandridge to sister, October 18, 1862, Robert M. T. Hunter Papers; Frank M. Imboden War Diary, December 1862, January 9, 1863, vol. 27, Roy Bird Cook Collection; Bright, "McNeill Rangers," 338–48; Delauter, *McNeill's Rangers*, 18–29; *OR*, II:4:739; John D. Imboden to Robert H. Milroy, January 20, 1863, Milroy to Imboden, January 27, 1863, Pierpont Papers. See also Governor Letcher's handling of the Imboden-Milroy clash in D. B. Stewart to John Letcher, September 19, 1862, William Harris to Letcher, September 22, 1862, Virginia Governor Papers: Letcher; Stutler, *West Virginia*, 144–46.

48. William Spotswood Fontaine to James A. Seddon, May 29, 1863, William S. Fowler to Seddon, June 15, [1863], U.S. War Department, Letters Received by Confederate Secretary of War; Waal, "First Original Confederate Drama," 459–61, 465–66.

49. Jonathan N. Fox to George W. Randolph, September 13, 1862, J. M. Jones to James Seddon, April 7, 1863, U.S. War Department, Letters Received by Confederate Secretary of War; Crist et al., *Papers of . . . Davis*, 8:508.

50. U.S. War Department, Records of Courts-Martial, 1861–62 (Chap. 1, Vol. 194), p. 194, November 1862–July 1863 (Chap. 1, Vol. 195), pp. 15, 33, 101, 142, 176, 219, 290–91, 307, 320, 365, 435, War Department Collection of Confederate Records.

51. *OR*, IV:1:1151, 2:26, 48, 71, 289, 585. Examples of negative War Department responses to hopeful rangers are A. M. Millard to James A. Seddon, January 30, 1863, W. H. Worthington to Jefferson Davis, February 16, 1863, B. S. Whitten to Seddon, April 18, 1863, Howard W. Wilkerson to Seddon, June 24, 1863, James W. Wood Jr. to Seddon, July 7, 1863, James W. A. Ford to Seddon, July 20, 1863, U.S. War Department, Letters Received by Confederate Secretary of War; James A. Seddon to Thomas Ball, June 15, 1863, Seddon to William C. Windley, September 2, 1863, U.S. War Department, Letters Sent by Confederate Secretary of War. On the vexing questions of the numbers of guerrillas, see Castel, "Guerrilla War," 50, although his estimates are low.

52. S. C. Tucker, *John D. Imboden*, 103–10; V. C. Jones, *Gray Ghosts*, 136–37; Robert White to W. S. Pilcher, February 23, 1863, R. Henry Glenn to Pilcher, Feb-

ruary 25, 1863, John D. Imboden to Pilcher, March 14, 1863, James G. Baxley to Pilcher, June 7, 1863, Pilcher Papers. Mackey, *Uncivil War*, 123–204, emphasizes this as the principal strategy in Tennessee and Kentucky.

53. *OR*, IV:2:71–72, 82–83, 113, 206–7, 301–4, 359, 639; Crist et al., *Papers of . . . Davis*, 9:197; Delauter, *McNeill's Rangers*, 30ff.; Weaver, *Thurmond's Partisan Rangers*, 27ff.

54. John B. Fontaine to sister, July 8, 1861, Meade Family Papers; T. Campbell, *Fire and Thunder*, 1–19, 248–56; W. H. Roberts, *Now for the Contest*, 72–76, 134–35; Luraghi, *History of the Confederate Navy*, 234–64.

55. John Taylor Wood to wife, August 4, 11, 1862, Wood Papers; L. S. Butler, *Pirates, Privateers, and Rebel Raiders*, 18–24, 171–72, 185–87; Shingleton, *John Taylor Wood*, 61–62.

56. Shingleton, *John Taylor Wood*, 62–69; Crabtree and Patton, *"Journal of a Secesh Lady,"* 396. For another proposal to use waterborne guerrillas, see P. G. Scott to James A. Seddon, January 31, 1863, U.S. War Department, Letters Received by Confederate Secretary of War.

57. Ramage, *Gray Ghost*, 46–57, 73.

58. Ibid., 73; James E. B. Stuart to John S. Mosby, March 25, 1863, Mosby Papers (LC); Wert, *Mosby's Rangers*, 73–76; Noland Cochran Diary, March 23, April 28, 1863; N. C. Baird, *Journals of . . . Edmonds*, 152.

59. Vogtsberger, *Dulanys of Welbourne*, 79, 95, 98–99; Dulaney Diary, May 1, 1863; George T. Rust to Rebecca A. Rust, April 12, 1863, Rust Papers; John S. Mosby to F. W. Powell et al., February 4, 1863, Mosby to James E. B. Stuart, February 4, 1863, Mosby Papers (LC).

60. James Farnadis to Augustus W. Bradford, January 24, 1863, W. H. Thomas et al. to Bradford, August 11, 1863, Letterbook, 1838–96, Maryland Governor Papers; Willie White to Sallie Offutt, August 12, 1862, Elizabeth White to Sallie Offutt, January 9, 1863, Moxley-Offutt Family Papers; Daniel Engel to Augustus W. Bradford, August 15, 1862 (Box 68), William T. Duvall to Bradford, August 12, 1862 (Box 68), Thomas A. Smith to Bradford, November 28, 1862 (Box 69), John Frazier to Bradford, June 30, 1863 (Box 78), W. E. Cole to Bradford, June 23, 1863 (Box 78), Miscellaneous, Maryland Governor Papers; J. A. Wallace to Augustus W. Bradford, October 15, 1862, Civil War Executive Papers, Letters from Officers, Maryland Adjutant General Papers. For at least one successful army expedition against Maryland guerrillas, see William Cogswell to Samuel A. Christie, October 1, 1889, Cogswell Letter.

61. George D. Summers to Augustus W. Bradford, April 3, 1863, W. H. J. McKinley et al. to Bradford, July 24, 1863, Henry C. McCoy to Bradford, July 17, 1863, E. Gerry to Bradford, July 18, 1863, Civil War Executive Papers, Letters to Governor, Maryland Adjutant General Papers; George A. Pearre to Augustus W. Bradford, August 28, 1862 (Box 72), John Q. Correll to Bradford, September 11, 1862 (Box 72), William Ulrich to Bradford, September 16, 1862 (Box 72), John L.

Cost to Bradford, July 1, [1863] (Box 79), Miscellaneous, Maryland Governor Papers; C. L. Graffin to Edwin M. Stanton, May 4, 1863, U.S. War Department, Letters Received by U.S. Secretary of War: Irregular Series.

62. T. M. Downing to David Tod, September 9, 1862 (51:28), S. W. Curtis and M. C. Palmer to Tod, June 23, 1863 (79:23), O. E. Clarke to Tod, June 20, 1863 (79:147), Leonard B. Peck to Tod, August 19, 1862 (48:116), W. E. Richter to Tod, June 19, 1863 (51:149), Series 147, Correspondence to Governor and Adjutant General, Ohio Adjutant General Records; Cheeks, "Border Rangers," 55; A. J. Wright to Thomas W. Ewing Jr., November 20, 1862, Thomas Ewing Family Papers.

63. John C. Bolt to Richard Yates, August 18, 1862, William H. Edison to Yates, April 31, 1863, William H. Cole to Yates, May 8, 1863, W. H. Roosevelt to Yates, May 29, 1863, James Wheatley to Yates, June 22, 1863, Peoples and Ridgeway to Yates, November 20, 1862, Yates Family Collection; John W. Foster to Jacob Ammen, May 5, 1863, Ammen Papers.

64. George E. Sellars to J. C. Underwood, November 16, 1862, U.S. War Department, Letters Received by U.S. Secretary of War: Irregular Series; Ebenezer Hutchinson to Richard Yates, September 4, 1862, Jonathan Richmond to Yates, February 1, 1863, Yates Family Collection; T. D Clark to Richard Yates, June 24, 1863, John W. Foster to Jacob Ammen, May 5, 1863, Ammen Papers.

65. Francis M. Edmonds to Lazarus Noble, November 21, 1862, George MacLeod to Noble, August 18, 1862, Civil War Miscellany (A4017), Indiana Adjutant General Records; R. A. Black to Oliver P. Morton, August 1, 1862, T. J. Lucas to Morton, August 4, 1862, James L. Foley to Morton, August 8, 1862, W. W. Straight to Morton, August 14, 1862, M. H. Blake to Morton, August 14, 1862, Morton Correspondence; Baron P. Stow Diary, September 6, 1862, Baron P. and Viola Stow Diaries; Sallie Hendricks to Abram W. Hendricks, September 12, 1862, Hendricks Correspondence; George Van Pelt to Aurora Koehler, September 25, 1862 (two letters), Hutchings-Koehler Papers; G. W. Crosier to Cousin Grimes, November 7, 1862, Crosier Family Letters; Daniel F. Bates to Lazarus Noble, February 3, 1863, Box 1, Indiana Legion Papers (L504), Indiana Adjutant General Records; F. H. Sellers to H. C. Freeman, November 2, 1862, U.S. War Department, Letters Received by U.S. Secretary of War: Irregular Series.

66. A. W. Flinn to Oliver P. Morton, April 2, 1863, T. P. Anderson to Morton, April 25, 1863, James Guthrie to Morton, May 9, 1863 (L816), J. J. Johnson to Lazarus Noble, April 28, 1863 (A4017), Civil War Miscellany, Indiana Adjutant General Records; John Wiley to Lazarus Noble, June 11, 1863, Box 4, Indiana Legion Papers (L507), Indiana Adjutant General Records; James W. Ellis to mother, June 28, 1863, James W. Ellis Letters; Haskell Diary, June 24, 1863; Charles W. Starr to father, May 3, 1863, Starr Papers; Roller, "Business as Usual," 3–6; John W. Royse to son, June 21, 1863, Royse Papers. Roller also offers an interesting perspective on how politics affected the local defenses of Indiana

before and after the Hines raid. The best contemporary summary of the state's preparations, the perceived guerrilla threat, and the response to internal and external threats is Terrell, *Indiana in the War of the Rebellion.*

67. R. Hamilton to James Hamilton, August 8, 1863, Ruffin, Roulhac, and Hamilton Family Papers; S. R. Ford, *Raids & Romances*; Lucy Jennings to Mrs. Basil Duke, August 3, 1862, Morgan-Duke Family Papers; Hume Diary, February 1, 1863; Ramage, *Rebel Raider*, 3, 62–63. That Morgan's entire command was aware of its status, image, and responsibilities may be seen in the surviving issues of the camp newspaper, *The Vidette.* See Doll, "John Hunt Morgan and the Soldier Printers."

68. Barr Journal, July 16–17, 1863; Ramage, *Rebel Raider*, 147, 157–59; Marszalek, *Diary of . . . Holmes*, 261–62.

69. Ramage, *Rebel Raider*, 159–70; Henry L. Stone to father, July 8, 1863, Stone Papers.

70. Ramage, *Rebel Raider*, 170–79; F. Moore, *Rebellion Record*, 7(2):42, 257–62, 453–56; Daniel R. Larned to sister, July 21, 1863, Larned Papers.

71. Thomas S. Hawley to parents, July 26, 1863, Hawley Papers; George H. Cadman to wife, July 20, 1863, Cadman Papers; Davidson, *Letters of . . . Hartley*, 50; Thomas Prickett to Maltilda Darr, July 12, 1863, Prickett Correspondence.

72. Ramage, *Rebel Raider*, 179–82; Roller, "Business as Usual," 8–25; George W. Thompson to Robert Hume, July 18, 1863 (82:112), Daniel S. Brown to Robert Hume, July 24, 1863 (81:70), Ohio Adjutant General Records; Daniel R. Larned to sister, July 16, 1863, Larned Papers.

73. Sallie Parker to George W. Parker, August 3, 1863, George Washington Parker Papers.

CHAPTER 9

1. A. B. Carter, *Tarnished Cavalier*, 83–88, 127–46; General Orders No. 38 (August 17, 1862), 42 (August 23, 1862), copies in Museum of the Confederacy, Richmond.

2. Castel, *Sterling Price*, 95–96; *OR*, I:17(2):668–69; Agnew Diary, July 15, 1862; *Memphis Daily Appeal*, August 25, 1862; A. Brown, "First Mississippi Partisan Rangers," 378.

3. J. P. Tehul to John J. Pettus, October 26, 1862, Pettus Papers; E. Cort Williams, "Cruise of 'The Black Terror.'"

4. Castel, *Sterling Price*, 128–34; Agnew Diary, March 23–24, April 21, 1863; case of John W. Atkinson (LL719), U.S. War Department, Court Martial-Cases; A. Brown, "First Mississippi Partisan Rangers," 381–88.

5. Crist et al., *Papers of . . . Davis*, 8:377; A. Brown, "Sol Street," 156; Hoar, "Colonel William C. Falkner," 52–53; A. Brown, "First Mississippi Partisan Rangers," 378–81; E. J. Ellis to sister, July 29, 1862, Ellis Family Papers; Agnew Diary, August 1, 6–7, 9, 12–13, 18, 25–27, September 11–12, 22, 24, 27–28, 1862;

Citizens of Green County to John J. Pettus, August 1862, James E. Matthews to T. C. Tuppen, [August 1862], Pettus Papers; Ferguson Diary, October 5, 1862; S. E. Ambrose, *Wisconsin Boy in Dixie*, 32–33; Eliza to mother, October 18, 1862, Howland and Tilton Papers; Gallaher, "Peter Wilson . . . : In Battle and On Parole," 308–9; Ballard, *Vicksburg*, 69–71.

6. Freeman Jones to John J. Pettus, December 24, 1862, William C. Falkner to Col. Thomson, March 15, 1863, Pettus Papers.

7. Annette Koch to C. D. Koch, April 29, [1863], May 13, [1863], Koch Family Papers.

8. Annette Koch to C. D. Koch, April 29, May 13, July 1, 7, 1863, C. D. Koch to Annette, April 14, 15, 1863, C. D. Koch to Elers Koch, August 2, 1863, Koch Family Papers.

9. S. M. Thompson to O. R. Singleton, February 10, 1863, U.S. War Department, Letters Received by Confederate Secretary of War; Louisa Q. Lovell Journal, June 21–August 2, 1863, and Louisa Q. Lovell to Joseph Lovell, August 7, 1863, Quitman Family Papers; Annette Koch to C. D. Koch, July 1, 7, 1863, Koch Family Papers; J. T. Simms to John J. Pettus, February 11, 1863, Howard H. Williamson to Pettus, January 1, [1863], Pettus Papers; Dubay, *John Jones Pettus*, 148–50; Bettersworth, *Confederate Mississippi*, 67–68.

10. Agnew Diary, December 19, 1862, January 2, 14, April 2, 1863; Jason Niles Diary, February 2, 21, 1863, Niles Papers; Crist et al., *Papers of . . . Davis*, 9:34–35; Blain, "'Banner' Unionism in Mississippi," 208–9; Dubay, *John Jones Pettus*, 151–63; A. Brown, "Sol Street," 157–59; Special Order No. 101, April 11, 1863, "Army of Mississippi" folder, Confederate States of America Archives.

11. Ballard, *Vicksburg*, 208–11; John Buie to brother, April 2, 1863, Buie Papers; Newton N. Davis to Bettie, April 27, 1863, Newton N. Davis Papers; James E. Matthews to T. C. Tuppen, [August 1862], M. Horton to John J. Pettus, October 18, 1862, Irwin J. Warren to Pettus, November 8, 1862, James B. Ross to Pettus, January 8, 1863, William T. Landrum to Pettus, January 26, 1863, N. L. Lowery to Pettus, February 10, 1863, A. K. Brantley to Pettus, April 24, 1863, W. A. Armstead et al. to Pettus, April 27, 1863, George H. Moore to Pettus, April 28, 1863, W. C. Turner to Pettus, March 4, 1863, Charles A. Lewers to Pettus, May 9, 1863, Pettus Papers; Agnew Diary, September 27, 1862, February 2, 8, 12, 20, April 10, 13, July 16, 1863; Amanda Worthington Diary, April 29, May 6, 1863, Worthington Family Papers; case of Seth Moore (LL715), U.S. War Department, Court-Martial Cases; Foster Diary, July 4, 1863; W. H. Worthington to Jefferson Davis, February 16, 1863, Howard W. Wilkerson to James S. Seddon, June 24, 1863, U.S. War Department, Letters Received by Confederate Secretary of War.

12. *Memphis Daily Appeal*, September 1, 1862; *OR*, I:17(1):39–40; D. L. Ambrose, *From Shiloh to Savannah*, 89, 93, 104, 107.

13. Feis, *Grant's Secret Service*, 123–30, 166–67; Receipts, and E. D. Coe to

Brother James, April 12, 1863, Box 63, vol. 148, Dodge Papers; Throne, "A Commissary in the Union Army," 64, 70–71. See Cockrell and Ballard, *Chickasaw*, 101ff., for the adventures of one of Dodge's scouts.

14. Agnew Diary, April 27, 1863; A. Brown, "Sol Street," 159–63.

15. Agnew Diary, March 23, 1863; Wiggenton et al., *Tennesseans in the Civil War*, 1:333–36; A. Brown, "Sol Street," 163–66; Graf et al., *Papers of Andrew Johnson*, 6:88–90.

16. A. Brown, "Sol Street," 165–68; Agnew Diary, March 7, April 2, 1863.

17. Rainwater, "Letters of Cordelia Scales," 169, 177–79. See also Lumpkin, *"Dear Darling Loulie."*

18. *Memphis Daily Appeal*, June 29, 1863.

19. Ballard, *Vicksburg*, 180–81; Alexander R. Miller Diary, December 24, 1862, March 8–9, April 30, 1863; John S. Morgan Diary, February 11, 27, March 9–10, 1863, John S. Morgan Papers; Harlan, "Pearson's War Diary" (Pt. 1), 112–17, 123; Thomas S. Hawley to parents, May 10, 1863, Hawley Papers; Popchock, *Soldier Boy*, 32–37; Dimond and Hattaway, *Letters from Forest Place*, 309–11; Corbin, *Star for Patriotism*, 402–5.

20. Ballard, *Vicksburg*, 157, 160, 170; General Orders No. 2 and 4, in "Orders," (Lord Division) Eltinge-Lord Family Papers; Hearn, *David Dixon Porter*, 144–52; "Journal of Occurrences during the War of the Rebellion," 424–25, 433–34, David Dixon Porter Papers; M. J. Bennett, *Union Jacks*, 90–94; *ORN*, I:24:369, 25:4, 136, 195, 209.

21. "Journal of Occurrences during the War of the Rebellion," 409, David Dixon Porter Papers; Hearn, *Ellet's Brigade*, 74–79.

22. Hearn, *Ellet's Brigade*, 143–51; William H. Bradbury to wife, April 7, 1863, Bradbury Papers.

23. Hearn, *Ellet's Brigade*, 151–84; F. Moore, *Rebellion Record*, 7(2):276. For firsthand accounts of some of these expeditions, see Clarke, *Warfare along the Mississippi*. Members of the Marine Brigade always considered themselves an elite group, even forming their own "Society of Survivors," printing a newsletter, and holding annual reunions after the war. See Perry Gregg to Warren D. Crandall, September 1, 1903, Crandall Papers.

24. *OR*, I:24(1):25–27, 501–2, 547–50; M. W. Robbins to Grenville M. Dodge, April 12, 1863, Box 2, vol. 4, f. 6, Dodge Papers; Longacre, *Mounted Raids*, 91–122; Leckie and Leckie, *Unlikely Warriors*, 83, 95.

25. S. E. Ambrose, *Wisconsin Boy in Dixie*, 85, 88–89; Thomas Hawley to parents, May 18, 1863, Hawley Papers; *ORN*, I:25:301–2; *OR*, I:24(2):666–67, 674, 683, 687, (3):571–73, 579, 826, 837, 852–53, 1024–25.

26. Rohr, *Incidents of the War*, 81–90; Solomons Scrapbook, p. 480; Mary Fielding Diary, August 11, 1862; Joshua Burns Moore Diary, August 14, 1862; Joseph W. Keifer to wife, July 29, August 7, 20, 1862, Keifer Papers; N. K. Brown to John Sherman, August 11, 1862, Sherman Papers; Pirtle Journal, August 31,

September 2, 4, 1862, Pirtle Papers; M. C. McMillan, *Disintegration of a Confederate State*, 179.

27. M. C. McMillan, *Disintegration of a Confederate State*, 179–80.

28. Storey, *Loyalty and Loss*, 93–96; *Mobile Advertiser and Register*, January 25, 1863; Nelson Fennell to John G. Shorter, September 17, 1862, Shorter to Fennell, September 24, 1862, Shorter to Jefferson Davis, November 13, 1862, A. B. Moore to Braxton Bragg, November 13, 1862, Shorter to Jonathan A. Averett Jr., March 28, 1863, Alabama Governor Papers: Shorter; J. R. McLendon to wife, September 12, October 1, 1862, Civil War Soldier Letters; 1st Alabama Battalion Partisan Rangers, 12th Alabama Battalion Partisan Rangers, Confederate Cavalry Battalion History File; U.S. War Department, Register of Partisan Rangers, chap. 1, vol. 113, pp. 1–5, 24; Joseph H. Hall to Dear Major, February 27, 1863, Hall Family Papers; Robert A. McClellan to father, August 3, 10, 1863, McClellan Papers.

29. Storey, *Loyalty and Loss*, 96–104, 133–57; M. C. McMillan, *Disintegration of a Confederate State*, 58–60; J. H. Parrish to sister, March 31, 1863, Henry Watson Jr. Papers; Robert A. McClellan to father, August 15, 1863, McClellan Papers; Espy Diary, January 12, May 3, 7, 22, June 20, 1863. For one of the most successful Unionist rebellions, see Sewell, "Dissent," 35–37, and Dodd, "Free State of Winston," 15–17.

30. M. C. McMillan, *Disintegration of a Confederate State*, 60–67; "An Appeal to the People of Alabama," December 22, 1862, Broadsides folder, John G. Shorter to Nelson Fennell, September 24, 1862, Shorter to William J. Swanson, January 8, 1863, Shorter to Jefferson Davis, January 10, 1863, Shorter to Braxton Bragg, July 24, 1863, Shorter to Howell Cobb, August 4, 1863, Alabama Governor Papers: Shorter; William A. Stricklin et al. to James A. Seddon, February 10, 1863, U.S. War Department, Letters Received by Confederate Secretary of War; Martin, *Desertion of Alabama Troops*, 31, 43–47.

31. B. Martin, *Desertion of Alabama Troops*, 49–51; John G. Shorter to William J. Swanson, January 8, 1863, Shorter to James A. Seddon, January 14, 1863, Shorter to Howell Cobb, August 4, 1863, Alabama Governor Papers: Shorter. For the problems with slaves, see Storey, *Loyalty and Loss*, 111–22.

32. Buker, *Blockaders, Refugees, and Contrabands*, 51; Johns, *Florida during the Civil War*, 69–71.

33. Johns, *Florida during the Civil War*, 71; *OR*, I:14:12, 139–40, 227, 229, 234–35, 696–98, 730–31, 53:259–60, IV:2:49–50; Crist et al., *Papers of . . . Davis*, 8:349; William E. Chalmers to George W. Randolph, August 30, 1862, E. G. Clay to Randolph, September 24, 1862, Citizens of Nassau County to Randolph, [October 10, 1862], U.S. War Department, Letters Received by Confederate Secretary of War; John Milton to George W. Randolph, August 5, 1862, Letterbooks, Vol. 6 (Series 32), Florida Governor Papers; William E. Russell to John Milton, September 1, 1862, John Chain to Milton, September 13, 1862, John Mc-

Nulty et al. to Milton, October 3, 1862, Incoming Correspondence (Series 577), Florida Governor Papers.

34. F. Moore, *Rebellion Record*, 6(2):186–87; William H. Boyce to mother, September 28, 1862, William H. Boyce to Jim Boyce, September 29, 1862, Boyce Letters; Hayes, *Du Pont: . . . Letters*, 2:319–21; Dickison, *Dickison and His Men*, xi–xviii; *OR*, I:14:237–40, 661, 739, 825, 861, 53:262. See also Koblas, *J. J. Dickison*.

35. *ORN*, I:13:301–2, 368–69, 406–7, 426–27, 461, 463, 465, 467, 469–70, 17:309, 318, 321, 387–88, 547.

36. Theodore W. Brevard to John Milton, November 9, 1862, Incoming Correspondence, Florida Governor Papers; *OR*, I:14:1055 (notes); U.S. War Department, Register of Partisan Rangers, chap. 1, vol. 113, p. 17.

37. E. A. Miller, *Lincoln's Abolitionist General*, 121–24, 136–38, 141–45; *OR*, I:14:447–48.

38. E. A. Miller, *Lincoln's Abolitionist General*, 145; Cornish, *Sable Arm*, 148–51; K. Wilson, "In the Shadow of John Brown," 309–11, 318–27; Trudeau, *Like Men of War*, 72–73.

39. Oliphant et al., *Letters of . . . Simms*, 6:226; *Southern Literary Messenger* 34 (February–March 1862): 103. The poem was published after the war as "The Mountain Partisan" in Simms, *War Poetry of the South*, 104–6.

40. *Charleston Mercury*, August 8, 1863; Simms, *War Poetry of the South*, 442–44; Wharton, *War Songs and Poems*, 177–78.

41. *OR*, I:14:603, 823–24, 28(2):11–13, 53:257; U.S. War Department, Register of Partisan Rangers, pp. 57–58; proclamation of June 16, 1863, Bonham Papers.

42. R. M. Myers, *Children of Pride*, 967–68, 1057, 1089. For the problem in volatile northern Georgia, see Sarris, "Anatomy of an Atrocity," 688–98, "'Shot for Being Bushwhackers,'" 33–37, and *Separate Civil War*, 65–100.

43. Bohannon, "They Had Determined to Root Us Out," 103–11; Charles G. McAdoo Diary, September 29, October 11, December 31, 1862, Floyd-McAdoo Family Papers; E. M. Galt to Henry C. Wayne, January 24, February 1, 1863, Georgia Adjutant General Records; John Bryson to Joseph E. Brown, October 16, 1862, George W. Lee to Brown, January 27, 1863, E. W. Chastain to Brown, August 11, 1863, Georgia Governor Correspondence: Brown.

44. E. M. Galt to Henry C. Wayne, January 24, February 1, 1863, Fred B. Hodges to Joseph E. Brown, June 8, 1863, Georgia Adjutant General Records; W. A. Campbell to Joseph E. Brown, February 26, 1863, J. H. Worley to Brown, March 4, 1863, Ambrose Woodward to Brown, June 4, 1863, E. W. Chastain to Brown, August 5, 11, 19, 1863, Georgia Governor Correspondence: Brown.

45. Sarris, "Anatomy of an Atrocity," 696–98.

46. Scaife and Bragg, *Joe Brown's Pets*, 3–4; S. M. Sellers to George W. Randolph, August 25, 1862, Elisha C. Coleman to Randolph, September 6, 1862,

U.S. War Department, Letters Received by Confederate Secretary of War; U.S. War Department, Register of Partisan Rangers, pp. 20–26; G. C. Carmichael to Joseph E. Brown, August 3, 1862, Sidney S. Matthews to Brown, December 10, 1862, George W. Lee to Brown, January 27, 1863, T. S. Hopkins to Brown, April 29, 1863, T. N. Brain to Brown, May 29, 1863, W. W. Bonner to Brown, June 22, 1863, Jonathan B. Mallard to Brown, June 29, 1863, Citizens of Whitfield County to Brown, December 2, 1862, Georgia Governor Correspondence: Brown.

47. Barrett, *Civil War in North Carolina*, 131–48, 171–73; Inscoe and Mc-Kinney, *Heart of Confederate Appalachia*, 110–16, 147–53; McKinney, *Zeb Vance*, 110–13; D. A. Norris, "'The Yankees Have Been Here!'" 1–3; Kruman, *Parties and Politics in North Carolina*, 235–49; R. E. Baker, "Class Conflict and Political Upheaval," 164–73; Honey, "War within the Confederacy," 82–86.

48. M. J. McSween to James A. Seddon, March 2, 1863, U.S. War Department, Letters Received by Confederate Secretary of War; U.S. War Department, Register of Partisan Rangers, pp. 50–54; D. M. Buie to Zebulon B. Vance, November 6, 1862, William Lamb to Vance, November 17, 1862, William Gardner to Vance, March 1, 1863, Incoming Correspondence, Vance Papers; Thorpe, *Fifteenth Connecticut Volunteers*, 68–70; Nate Lanpheur to L. C. Newton, June 15, August 9, 1863, Lanpheur Papers; Barrett, *Civil War in North Carolina*, 149–70; *ORN*, I:8:586–87; Wills, *War Hits Home*, 119; Durrill, *War of Another Kind*, 166–77.

49. Current, *Lincoln's Loyalists*, 61–73; Barrett, *Civil War in North Carolina*, 59, 174–76; Durrill, *War of Another Kind*, 166–85; Yearns and Barrett, *North Carolina Civil War Documentary*, 47–49; McKinney, *Zeb Vance*, 155–64; B. A. Myers, "Executing Daniel Bright," chap. 2. For a general view of the state's guerrilla battle—concentrating on the western mountain region—see O'Brien, *Mountain Partisans*, 3–36. For a shootout between state militia and a large band of draft evaders, see Casstevens, *Civil War and Yadkin County*, 85–96.

50. Johnston and Mobley, *Papers of . . . Vance*, 1:48–49; Crabtree and Patton, *"Journal of a Secesh Lady,"* 290–91, 303; Docton Warren Bagley Diary, August 1, 3, September 9, 11–13, 1862, May 29, August 4, 1863, Bagley Papers. "The Guerillas: A Southern War Song," can be found in Simms, *War Poetry of the South*, 146–49, and Wharton, *War Songs and Poems*, 101–3.

51. Williams and Hamilton, *Papers of . . . Graham*, 6:441–43; Crist et al., *Papers of . . . Davis*, 8:298; M. Fain to Zebulon B. Vance, July 18, 1863, W. C. Walker to Vance, July 23, 1863, Vance Papers; Sarah Ann Tillinghast to brother, July 31, 1863, Tillinghast Papers. For the adventures of a husband and wife bushwhacking team, see Stevens, *Rebels in Blue*. For the situation in the central part of the state, see James S. Dunn to E. J. Hale & Sons, January 8, 1863, R. R. Buxton to Zebulon B. Vance, January 21, 1863, William M. Swann to Vance, February 11, 1863, R. Street to Vance, April 10, 1863, T. Monroe to Vance, April 17, 1863, O. S. Hamer to Vance, April 17, 1863, Emily Branson to Vance, April 21, 1863, N. A. Cameron to Vance, July 18, 1863, Vance Papers.

52. Stephen Whitacker to father, August 13, 25, 1863, Whitacker Papers; Inscoe and McKinney, *Heart of Confederate Appalachia*, 110, 125; Thomsen, *Rebel Chief*, 187–98; Crow, *Storm in the Mountains*, 15–17, 26–27; Crabtree and Patton, *"Journal of a Secesh Lady,"* 284; J. G. Martin to Colonel, January 12, 1863, Letterbooks, North Carolina Adjutant General Records; R. F. Armfield to Zebulon B. Vance, February 19, 1863, M. Fain to Vance, July 18, 1863, W. C. Walker to Vance, July 27, 1863, Vance Papers; R. C. E. to Addy, February 26, 1863, Mary A. Gash Papers; Stephen Whitacker to father, August 2, 1863, Stephen Whitacker Papers; James Wilse and Calvin Dial to Quill Hunter, July 29, 1863, Dial Letter.

53. Inscoe and McKinney, *Heart of Confederate Appalachia*, 115–22; A. S. Merrimon to Zebulon B. Vance, February 16, 1863, Mark Nelson to Vance, June 11, 1863, Vance Papers; Zebulon B. Vance to Jefferson Davis, February 27, 1863, Letterbooks, Vance Papers. A detailed study of the Shelton Laurel "massacre" is provided in Paludan, *Victims.*

54. Martin Crawford, *Ashe County's Civil War*, 112–13; McKinney, *Zeb Vance*, 141; Yearns and Barrett, *North Carolina Civil War Documentary*, 100–101; Allen T. Davidson to Jefferson Davis, July 22, 1863, U.S. War Department, Letters Received by Confederate Secretary of War; William M. Swann to Zebulon B. Vance, February 11, 1863, A. F. Armfield to Vance, February 19, 1863, N. A. Cameron et al. to Vance, July 18, 1863, Vance Papers; Inscoe and McKinney, *Heart of Confederate Appalachia*, 114–15, 122; Johnston and Mobley, *Papers of . . . Vance*, 2:5, 27–29, 89–90, 191. For a deserter who regretted his impulsive act and requested a pardon, see R. N. Hager to Vance, July 31, 1863, Vance Papers.

55. Johnston and Mobley, *Papers of . . . Vance*, 2:87–88, 101; McKinney, *Zeb Vance*, 197; Crabtree and Patton, *"Journal of a Secesh Lady,"* 415; Yearns and Barrett, *North Carolina Civil War Documentary*, 101–2.

CHAPTER 10

1. Goodrich, *Bloody Dawn*, is the best account of the Lawrence raid, but also Leslie, *Devil Knows How to Ride*, 157–244, and Castel, *Quantrill*, 118–43. For the broader context of the raid, see J. Neely, *Border between Them*, 96–131.

2. Goodrich, *Bloody Dawn*, 133–49; Samuel Ayres to Lyman Langdon, August 24, 1863, Ayres Correspondence; McLarty, "Letters of . . . Lazear: Part II," 390–91; Malin, "Letters of . . . Lovejoy: . . . Part Five," 195–98; John W. Rogers to Thomas Carney, August 25, 1863, R. B. Taylor et al. to Carney, August 27, 1863, John E. Campbell to Carney, September 8, 1863, J. T. Lane to Carney, September 10, 1863, General Correspondence, 1861–65, Kansas Adjutant General Records; L. Barnes, "An Editor Looks at Early-Day Kansas," 143–45.

3. L. Barnes, "An Editor Looks at Early-Day Kansas," 147–49; Goodrich, *Bloody Dawn*, 156–66; Thomas Carney to John Schofield, August 24, 1863, Carney Letters; A. Comingo to James O. Broadhead, August 20, 1863, Broadhead Papers; Camilla Anne Kensinger to father and brother, August 17, 1863, Kensinger Family

Papers. See Castel, *Civil War Kansas*, 110–23, 166–67, for the political complications.

4. Castel, *Civil War Kansas*, 25–27, 121–22; W. E. Parrish, *History of Missouri*, 54; Thomas Ewing Jr. to wife, November 8, 19, 1862, Ewing to James Lane, December 14, 1862, James S. McDowell to Ewing, June 20, 1863, Ewing to Lane, June 29, 1863, Ewing to Thomas Ewing Sr., July 24, August 15, 1863, Edmund G. Ross to Ewing, August 3, 1863, Alexander H. Baird to J. F. Seary, September 3, 1863, Ewing to D. L. Payne, October 13, 1863, Thomas Ewing Family Papers.

5. Castel, *Civil War Kansas*, 142–45, and *Winning and Losing*, 51–62; Hatley and Ampssler, "Army General Orders Number 11"; Niepman, "General Orders No. 11." For Ewing's perspective on the political maze, see Thomas Ewing Jr. to Thomas Ewing Sr., August 28, November 20, 1863, May 2, December 1, 1864, Ewing to Abraham Ellis, May 28, 1864, Ewing to Hoyt Olathe, May 31, 1864, Ewing to D. L. Payne, October 13, 1864, Thomas Ewing Family Papers. For his line of reasoning in issuing order 11, see F. Moore, *Rebellion Record*, 7(2):513–17.

6. Thomas Carney to John M. Schofield, August 24, 1863, Carney Letters; John M. Schofield Diary, September 6, 1863, Schofield Papers; Thomas Ewing Sr. to Thomas Ewing Jr., September 3, 1863, Thomas Ewing Family Papers; M. E. Neely, "'Unbeknownst' to Lincoln"; Francis F. Audsley to wife, September 3, 1863, Audsley Letters.

7. D. B. Connelly, *John M. Schofield*, 73–83; John M. Schofield to Ulysses S. Grant, July 8, 1863, Schofield to Henry W. Halleck, August 10, 1863, John M. Schofield Diary, August 26, 31, September 1–2, 6, 8, October 1, 1863, Schofield Papers; Castel, *Civil War Kansas*, 145–53; John M. Schofield to Thomas Ewing Jr., September 19, 1863, Thomas Ewing Family Papers; John M. Schofield to Thomas Carney, August 27, 29, September 3, 1863 (two letters), Thomas Ewing Jr. to Thomas Carney, August 27, 1863 (telegram), Thomas C. Stevens Papers; W. E. Parrish, *History of Missouri*, 100–107; John M. Schofield to Stephen Hurlbut, August 8, 1863, Schofield to Henry W. Halleck, September 15, 19, October 6, 1863, Schofield Papers; O'Flaherty, *Jo Shelby*, 189–207; Edward Bates to Hamilton R. Gamble, October 10, 1863, Gamble to Bates, October 17, 1863, Bates Family Papers; Basler, *Works of Abraham Lincoln*, 6:499–504; Boman, *Lincoln's Resolute Unionist*, 218–37.

8. J. T. Lane to Thomas Carney, September 10, 1863, General Correspondence, Kansas Adjutant General Records; Herklotz, "Jayhawkers in Missouri," 97–98; John F. Williams to Oden Guitar, September 29, 1863, Guitar Collection; James H. Mosley to Willard P. Hall, September 27, 1863, Gamble Papers; Castel, *Winning and Losing*, 56–57; McLarty, "Letters of . . . Lazear: Part II," 391–92.

9. Castel, *Civil War Kansas*, 62, 152–53, and *Winning and Losing*, 58–59.

10. People of Wellsville, Mo., to Oden Guitar, September 1, 1863, Sanford Bullock to Guitar, September 9, 1863, People of Columbia, Mo., to Guitar, October 29, 1863, A. Kempinspy to Guitar, December 4, 1863, Guitar Collection; McLarty,

"Letters of . . . Lazear: Part II," 392–93; Hamilton R. Gamble to Basil F. Lazear, November 24, 1863, Lazear Papers; James Fortiner to Emma Squires, October 10, [1863], Fortiner Papers; Sherman Bodwell Diaries, September 8–October 4, 1863, Bodwell Diaries and Notebooks.

11. O'Flaherty, *Jo Shelby*, 4–5, 30–45, 189–207; John M. Schofield to Henry W. Halleck, October 6, 7, 11, 13, 18, 1863, Schofield to Abraham Lincoln, October 25, 1863, Schofield Papers.

12. Alice to aunt and cousin, August 23, 1863, Lizzie to Cousins, August 9, 1864, Gilmore Papers; John M. Farland to James L. Campbell, August 26, 1864, James L. Campbell Papers; Lizzie E. Brannock to brother, January 13, 1864, Lizzie E. Brannock Papers.

13. M. M. Frazier, *Missouri Ordeal*, 4–7, 75, 78–80, 163–64; cases of C. A. Alderman, William D. Coller, Joseph Harris, Louis Vandever (LL777), James R. Hamilton (NN1241), James R. Crosswhite (MM1885), Abraham N. McGuire (NN1461), U.S. War Department, Court-Martial Cases.

14. Castel, *Quantrill*, 148–51; Leslie, *Devil Knows How to Ride*, 268–70.

15. Lindberg and Matthews, "'It Haunts Me Night and Day,'" offers the best account of the Baxter Springs episode. For Union reports, see F. Moore, *Rebellion Record*, 7(2):596–602.

16. Leslie, *Devil Knows How to Ride*, 282–85; Lindberg and Matthews, "'It Haunts Me Night and Day,'" 52; Hardeman, "Bloody Battle That Almost Happened," 251–58; Castel, *Quantrill*, 155–56.

17. Castel, *Quantrill*, 155–68; Leslie, *Devil Knows How to Ride*, 284–301.

18. Leslie, *Devil Knows How to Ride*, 293–95; Thomas C. Reynolds to James Seddon, January 3, February 16, 1863, Reynolds to Edward C. Cabell, June 28, 1863, Reynolds to Sterling Price, October 30, 1863, Reynolds to Waldo P. Johnson, December 24, 1863, Reynolds to C. Franklin, January 14, 1863, Reynolds Papers (LC).

19. Thomas C. Reynolds to Edmund Kirby Smith, March 26, 1864, Reynolds Papers (LC).

20. James O. Broadhead to Edward Bates, July 24, 1864, Broadhead Papers; W. W. Smith, "Experiment in Counterinsurgency," 376–77; Fusz Diary, August 4, 21, 1864; Asa Burlingame to brother, December 31, 1863, Hazen S. Burlingame to Asa Burlingame, June 26, 1864, Sophia H. Burlingame to Asa Burlingame, July 17, 1864, Rodolphus Goodrich to Asa Burlingame, July 15, 1864, Lizzie Goodrich to Asa Burlingame, July 24, 1864, Burlingame Family Papers; M. M. Frazier, *Missouri Ordeal*, 181, 195–96; W. H. Kesterson to Joseph Kesterson, February 24, June 16, July 11, 1864, Kesterson Correspondence; James T. Wheeler to Mrs. Arretta Davidson, August 1, 1864, Davidson Letters; Hardeman, "Bushwhacker Activity on the Missouri Border," 270–72; Thomas Gammon to Odon Guitar, February 6, 1864, Guitar Collection; Boyd Handbill, dated January 18, 1864.

21. K. Ross, *Autobiography of Hildebrand*, xiii–xvi; Daniel Bates to Oden Guitar, February 25, 1864, Guitar Collection; W. H. Kesterson to Joseph Kesterson, July 11, 1864, Kesterson Correspondence; Canan, "Missouri Paw Paw Militia," 438–46; W. E. Parrish, *History of Missouri*, 54; proclamation by Gen. J. B. Douglas, July 23, 1864, Dorsey-Fuqua Family Collection; Abraham Cole to Commander, [September 1864], Abraham Cole Muster Roll; William Crede to brother, June 25, July 28, August 27, 1864, Crede Family Papers; Harwell, *Union Reader*, 263–73; Canan, "Milton Birch," 234–39; McLarty, "Letters of . . . Lazear: Part II," 399–401, and "Letters of . . . Lazear: Part III," 48–51; George Wolz to father, May 30, 1864, Wolz to Mary Wolz, June 6, 21, September 19, 1864, Wolz Papers; Brophy, *In the Devil's Dominion*, February–August 1864; W. J. Dunn to John A. Pigg, June 18, 1864, Dunn Letters; Stith, "At the Heart of Total War," 36–41; Deposition of William Monks, May 12, 1864, U.S. War Department, Union Provost Marshal . . . Two or More Citizens; Bradbury and Wehmer, *History of Southern Missouri and Northern Arkansas*, xviii–xxviii; Geiger, "Missouri's Hidden Civil War"; Sophia H. Burlingame to Asa Burlingame, June 5, 1864, Henry Webster to Asa Burlingame, September 17, 1864, Burlingame Family Papers; Henry C. Crawford to Dear Friends, August 5, 1864, Henry and William Crawford Letters; William C. Crump to M&A Barth, September 5, 7, 1864, John N. Hartman to Moses Barth, September 7, 1864, Barth Family Papers.

22. Leslie, *Devil Knows How to Ride*, 186–90; Eakin, *Little Gods*, 2:35–36, 80–81; McLarty, "Letters of . . . Lazear: Part III," 50; Dougan, *Confederate Arkansas: The People*, 109; F. Moore, *Rebellion Record*, 9(2):6; Bunch, "Confederate Women in Arkansas"; Leonard, *All the Daring of a Soldier*, 88–93; Fellman, *Inside War*, 193–230; case of Mary E. Davis (NN1900), U.S. War Department, Court-Martial Cases. For other instances of female guerrillas being released by their captors, see Marcus Frost to sister, February 21, 1863, Frost Papers; Pena, "F. S. Twitchell's Letter," 89.

23. Eno, "Activities of the Women of Arkansas," 16; Proceedings of Military Commission at St. Louis, Department of Missouri, November 7, 1864, Sarah Jane Smith Papers; case of Sarah Jane Smith (LL2742), U.S. War Department, Court-Martial Cases; Massey, *Bonnet Brigades*, 105; Brophy, *In the Devil's Dominion*, "Found No Bushwhackers," 35, and *Bushwhackers of the Border*, 33–34; Goodrich, *Black Flag*, 43–44; Gerteis, *Civil War St. Louis*, 200–201.

24. Case of Julia Martin, U.S. War Department, Union Provost Marshal Files . . . Two or More Citizens.

25. Castel, *Sterling Price*, 199–201; O'Flaherty, *Jo Shelby*, 214–15; A. W. Doniphan to W. H. Jennings, September 2, 1864, Doniphan Letter; Robinett and Canan, "Military Career of James Craig," 66–69; *OR*, I:34(1):924–30, (3):829, (4):669–70, 41(2):1023–24; Sutherland, "1864," 124–26, 134–38; R. W. Williams and Wooster, "With Wharton's Cavalry," 260.

26. Sutherland, "Guerrillas: Real War," 140; Castel, *Sterling Price*, 202;

Andrews, *Christopher C. Andrews*, 185–86; John F. Benjamin to John Paddock, September 30, 1864, Benjamin Letters.

27. Sheldon S. Eaton to Dear Father, September 26, 1864, Eaton Letter; Robinett and Canan, "Military Career of James Craig," 69; Canan, "Milton Birch," 239–41; A. A. Hess to General Fiske, September 17, 1864, U.S. War Department, Union Provost Marshal Files . . . Two or More Citizens; Lizzie Gilmore to Dear Cousins, December 6, 1864, Gilmore Papers; Castel, *Quantrill*, 183–200, and *Sterling Price*, 226–27.

28. Castel and Goodrich, *Bloody Bill Anderson*, 69–86, 111–24; Watts, *Babe of the Company*, 3–6; Frizzell, "'Killed by Rebels,'" 383–95; Kemper, "Reminiscences of Danville Female Academy"; "Bushwhacking in Chariton," n.d., and "Report of Bushwhackers," 1864–65, in Benecke Family Papers; Stiles, *Jesse James*, 119–22.

29. Castel and Goodrich, *Bloody Bill Anderson*, 87–97; Stiles, *Jesse James*, 123–27; *Confederate Veteran* 17 (January 1909): 30–31; John F. Benjamin to John Paddock, September 30, 1864, Benjamin Letters.

30. Castel, *Quantrill*, 197–98, 202–3; Brophy, *In the Devil's Dominion*, October 31, 1864.

31. J. N. Cornish to N. B. Baker, March 15, 1864, John Whitcomb et al. to Baker, July 26, 1864, John Flick to M. M. Trumball, August 1, 1864, Correspondence of Southern Border Brigade, Box 68, Iowa Adjutant General Records; Joseph Andrews to N. B. Baker, August 13, 1864, Alfred Grange to Baker, August 18, 1864, Isaiah Humphrey to Baker, August 18, 1864, Correspondence: Disloyal Sentiments, 1861–66, Iowa Adjutant General Records; Wubben, *Civil War Iowa*, 162–64; Larimer, *Love and Valor*, 319, 333.

32. Corder, *Confederate Invasion of Iowa*; S. A. Moore, "Hostile Raid"; Samuel P. Glenn to N. B. Baker, October 8, 1864, Correspondence: Disloyal Sentiments, Iowa Adjutant General Records; E. H. Stiles to N. B. Baker, October 17, 1864, David N. Steele to Baker, November 9, 1864, Correspondence: Southern Border Brigade, Box 68, Iowa Adjutant General Records; Wubben, *Civil War Iowa*, 165.

33. Adolphus Meyer to W. P. Ammen, November 21, 1863, Ammen Papers; Murray and Rodney, "Letters of Peter Bryant—Concluded," 479–80.

34. George R. Clark to W. P. Ammen, November 28, 1863, Ammen Papers. A useful but poorly organized compilation of reports and reminiscences of the Illinois troubles can be found in C. L. Stanton, *They Called It Treason*.

35. Reuben C. Hidalgo to Richard Yates, [February 1864], J. W. Noel to Yates, February 22, 1864, William Weer to Yates, February 25, 1864, H. G. McPike to Yates, February 29, 1864, James W. Wills to J. R. Kelso, March 3, 1864, Yates Family Collection.

36. Tingley, "Clingman Raid"; C. L. Stanton, *They Called It Treason*, 19–54; William M. Fry to James Oakes, July 28, 1864, E. S. Condit to Oakes, July 30,

1864, Condit to Richard Yates, July 31, 1864, D. L. Phillips to Yates, July 29, 1864, Yates Family Collection; *OR*, I:41(2):455, 505.

37. Tingley, "Clingman Raid," 358–63; *OR*, I:41(3):477; case of David T. Hampton (NN 3335), U.S. War Department, Court-Martial Cases; Richard F. Adams to Richard Yates, August 8, 1864, N. M. McGurdy et al. to Yates, August 15, 1864, W. R. Miner to Yates, August 17, 1864, J. H. Mott et al. to Yates, August 23, 1864, Yates Family Collection.

38. DeBlack, *With Fire and Sword*, 91–103.

39. Bearss and Gibson, *Fort Smith*, 282–85; W. D. Baird, *Creek Warrior*, 92–93; *Fort Smith New Era*, November 14, December 5, 1863, March 26, April 2, 9, 23, May 14, 28, 1864.

40. See accompanying photograph of McNeil's warning; also, Langsdorf, "Letters of Joseph H. Trego: Part Three," 384; *OR*, IV:2:1047.

41. *OR*, I:34(3):179–80; Huff, *Letters of Albert Demuth*, 42–45, 58; Popchock, *Soldier Boy*, 88, 93, 139; *OR*, I:34(4):231–32; Mackey, "Bushwhackers, Provosts, and Tories," 173.

42. James, "Civil War in Independence County," 260–66; *OR*, I:34(2):23–24, 51–52, 64–67.

43. Feathers, "Military Activities in the Vicinity of Fayetteville"; Schaefer, "Letters of . . . Badger"; Patrick and Price, "Life with the Mountain Feds," 306–7; Beall, "Wildwood Skirmishers," 202–15, 243–44.

44. J. M. Wilson, "Killing of Three Brothers"; Prier, "Under the Black Flag," 88–101; Bellas, "Forgotten Loyalists," 62–64; John M. Schofield to Stephen Hurlbut, August 6, 1863, Schofield Papers; M. A. Hughes, "Wartime Gristmill Destruction," 37, 152.

45. Bearss and Gibson, *Fort Smith*, 287–90; Fortin, "Confederate Military Operations in Arkansas," 107–17; M. A. Hughes, "Wartime Gristmill Destruction," 40–45; Neal and Kremm, "Experiment in Collective Security."

46. Popchock, *Soldier Boy*, 85; Roth, *Well Mary*, 26–27; Sutherland, "Guerrillas: Real War," 149–50; Prier, "Under the Black Flag," 121–50; K. C. Barnes, "Williams Clan," 163–68; John S. Morgan Journal, November 7, 1863, John S. Morgan Papers; Banasik, *Serving with Honor*, 105, 111–12; *ORN*, I:26:408; Moneyhon, *Impact of the Civil War*, 160–68; Bellas, "Forgotten Loyalists," 59–62; John M. Schofield to Edwin Stanton, December 5, 1863, Schofield Papers; *OR*, I:22(2):533, 617–18, 718, 756; George W. Towne to sister, November 2, 1863, Towne Letters.

47. Maddox, *Hard Trials*, 50–52, 82; T. L. Baker, *Confederate Guerrilla*, 52, 56–57; Hallum, *Reminiscences*, 1:95; Sutherland, "Guerrilla Conflict in 1864."

48. B. J. Williams, "Missouri State Depredations in Arkansas"; T. L. Baker, *Confederate Guerrilla*, 45–47, 52; Joe M. Scott, *Four Years' Service*, 31–32, 39–40; Maddox, *Hard Trials*, 81–82; R. H. Powell to Harris Flanagin, May 5, 1863, T. H. Hill to Flanagin, June 1, 1863, F. J. Boston to Flanagin, August 17, 1863, Oldham Collection; Quesenberry Diary, September 13, 1863. For a renegade Union de-

serter, see Samuel T. Wells to Lizzie, December 30, 1863, Samuel T. Wells Papers; Roesch Diary, December 1863. For a summary of the violence created by deserters across the South, see Weitz, *More Damning Than Slaughter*, 183–233.

49. Case of Gideon D. Bruce (LL1938), U.S. War Department, Court-Martial Cases. See also the controversial case presented in M. A. Davis, "Legend of Bill Dark."

50. Prier, "Under the Black Flag," 99–102; Furry, *Preacher's Tale*, 109–30.

51. Sutherland, "Guerrillas: Real War," 143–45; O'Flaherty, *Jo Shelby*, 212–15; *OR*, I:22(2):1058–59, 34(1):924–30, (3):829, (4):669–70; Quesenberry Diary, September 13, 1863.

52. Case of Joseph Harris (LL1881), U.S. War Department, Court-Martial Cases; Vol. 110/360, pp. 2–5, 14–17, 22–23, 28–29, 32–35, 62–63, 72–73, U.S. War Department, Letters Received by Provost Marshal, Department of Arkansas; John Connally to Harris Flanagin, February 29, July 17, 1864, Oldham Collection; James H. Campbell Reminiscences.

53. T. L. Baker, *Confederate Guerrilla*, 58–61.

54. Lemke, "Confederate Soldier Writes to His Wife"; McBrien, "Letters of Arkansas Confederate Soldier: Pt. III," 278, 281.

55. Bradbury, "'Buckwheat Cake Philanthropy'"; Mills Reminiscences; cases of Benjamin Fortenberry (NN1453) and Eldridge M. Ball (NN1800), U.S. War Department, Court-Martial Cases; E. D. Rushing to Isaac Murphy, June 7, 1864, printed in *[Little Rock] Constitutional Union*, June 16, 1864; Jonathan MacLean to Daniel H. Reynolds, March 10, October 16, 1864, Daniel Harris Reynolds Papers.

56. John William Brown Diary, November 13, 16, December 11, 31, 1863, March 21, April 8, May 6, July 22, December 23, 1864. See also People of Sevier County to Harris Flanagin, November 26, 1863, James Abraham to Flanagin, February 8, 1864, John Connally to Flanagin, February 29, July 17, 1864, Oldham Collection; H. H. Reynolds to Daniel H. Reynolds, July 24, 1864, Daniel Harris Reynolds Papers; Sarah Bevens Kellogg to Sister Eva, February 29, April 4, 1864, Kellogg Papers.

57. Sutherland, "1864," 138–39, 142–44; Popchock, *Soldier Boy*, 161–63, 166.

58. Hyde, *Pistols and Politics*, 127–31; LeGayden Batchelor to Albert A. Batchelor, August 30, 1863, Batchelor Papers; Sara Lois Wadley Diary, September 2, 1863, Wadley Papers; Michot, "'War Is Still Raging,'" 169–72; Alexander R. Miller Diary, March 17, 1864; D. S. Frazier, "'Out of Stinking Distance,'" 161–70.

59. Winters, *Civil War in Louisiana*, 301–13; *ORN*, I:25:331, 335, 346–47, 413–15, 424, 432–33, 440–41, 464, 515–17, 520–24, 572–73, 592, 707–10, 736–37; Edwin A. Cutter to Dear Friends, [June 30, 1863], Cutter Papers; Foner, *Reconstruction*, 56–59.

60. Current, *Lincoln's Loyalists*, 89–93, 216; Bergeron, "Dennis Haynes"; Haynes, *Thrilling Narrative*, xv–xxi; Charles H. Richardson to mother, January

27, 1864, Lois (Wright) Richardson Davis Papers; Horace Smith to family, February 28, 1864, Horace Smith Papers; George Putnam to Mary Loines, March 18, 1864, Low-Mills Family Papers; Ephraim Brown to Prusilla and Calphurnia, April 28, 1864, Ephraim Brown Papers.

61. George H. Putnam to Mary H. Loines, August 23, 1863, Low-Mills Family Papers; William H. Whitney to Franklin Whitney, August 30, 1863, William H. Whitney to mother, September 14, 1863, March 8, 14, 1864, Whitney Letters; Edward H. Ingraham to sister, September 26, 1863, Ingraham Letters; William G. Thompson to wife, September 17, 1863, William G. Thompson Correspondence; William F. Patterson to wife, August 30, 1863, William Franklin Patterson Papers; Samuel M. Quincy to Josiah Quincy, December 8, 1863, Quincy-Wendell-Upham-Holmes Family Papers; Alexander R. Miller Diary, September 2, October 7, November 18, December 22, 26, 1863, January 17, 29, February 15–16, 1864; S. S. Marrett to wife, November 8, 17, 1863, Marrett Papers; Charles H. Richardson to mother, December 26, 1863, February 6, 1864, Lois (Wright) Richardson Davis Papers.

62. Bergeron, *Guide to Louisiana Confederate Military Units*, 41–43, 59–61, 64–65, 170–71; Crist et al., *Papers of . . . Davis*, 8:114–15, 191, 10:566; Special Orders No. 126 (September 1, 1863), No. 132 (September 8, 1863), No. 140 (September 17, 1863), No. 145 (September 23, 1863), No. 178 (October 31, 1863), Headquarters, Trans-Mississippi Department, Edmund Kirby Smith Papers.

63. Winters, *Civil War in Louisiana*, 304, 323, 392–94; Edwards, *Noted Guerrillas*, 221–25, 270–80; *OR*, I:34(2):967, 975–76; Hearn, *Ellet's Brigade*, 216–17, 224.

64. William N. Mercer to C. H. Russell, January 24, 1864, Mercer Papers; D. S. Frazier, "'Out of Stinking Distance,'" 165–67; Michot, "'War Is Still Raging,'" 164–69, 172.

65. Winter, *Civil War in Louisiana*, 210–11, 305–8, 322–23; Hyde, *Pistols and Politics*, 126; E. Taylor, "Discontent in . . . Louisiana," 424–25; Sacher, "'A Very Disagreeable Business'"; Edwin A. Cutter to Dear Friends, February 4, 13, 1863, Edwin A. Cutter Diary, Cutter Papers; Shelly Diary, March 20, June 1, 4, 5, 20, 1863; Alexander R. Miller Diary, May 9, 1863; George H. Putnam to Mary H. Loines, March 15, 1863, Low-Mills Family Papers; Charles Brown Tompkins to Mollie, January 29, February 10, 1863, Tompkins Papers; Oren E. Farr to Nellie Farr, April 26, May 21, July 7, 1863, Farr Papers; Edmund Cottle to Hattie, July 5, 1863, Cottle Papers; Seneca B. Thrall to wife, February 14, 1863, Thrall Letters; LeGayden Batchelor to Albert A. Batchelor, August 30, 1863, Batchelor Papers; William H. Whitney to Frank Whitney, January 21, 1864, Whitney Letters; Bergeron, *Guide to Louisiana Confederate Military Units*, 43, 51, 171; Kinard, *Lafayette of the South*, 121–22.

66. *OR* I:34(2):972–77, 53:900–901; N. C. Hughes, *Liddell's Record*, 172–74; Winter, *Civil War in Louisiana*, 387, 392–94; John W. Burruss to Edward Bur-

russ, February 18, 1864, Burruss Papers; E. Taylor, "Discontent in . . . Louisiana," 423–28.

67. *OR*, IV:1:475; E. Taylor, "Discontent in . . . Louisiana," 425–26; Priscilla Munnikhuysen Bond Diary, March 6, April 26, May 3, 1864, Bond Papers; Louis A. Bringier to Stella Bringier, May 17, 1864, Bringier and Family Papers. See also an exchange of letters between Bringier and R. W. Wooley, October 27, November 4, 1864, for the complexity of the jayhawker issue.

68. *Galveston Weekly News*, September 2, 30, 1863; Brasseaux, "Ozème Carrière," 640–42; *OR*, I:34(2):962–66.

69. Goyne, *Lone Star and Double Eagle*, 135–36; Brasseaux, "Ozème Carrière," 642–44; D. S. Frazier, "'Out of Stinking Distance,'" 162–65; *OR*, I:34(2):966–67, 977, 1025.

70. Garig Diary, January 5, 14, February 11, 1864, Garig Family Papers. A few entries are written in code, although for what purpose is unclear. See, e.g., entry for April 14, 1864.

71. Cuccia, "'Gorillas' and White Glove Gents"; Dollar, "Red River Campaign"; *ORN*, I:26:51–52, 61, 74, 89, 92–95, 288, 778–79; Alexander R. Miller Diary, April 10–11, 20, 1864; Newton W. Perkins to parents, April 14, 1864, Montgomery Family Papers; Samuel Zinser to Dear Lizzie, May 18, 1864, Zinser Letters, Cullom Davis Library, Bradley University; Tyson Diary, April 24, 1864; Nathan S. Dye Diary, April 2–3, 1864, Nathan G. Dye to Dear Friends, April 3, 17, 18, 1864, Dye Papers. For the campaign, see L. H. Johnson, *Red River Campaign*; Joiner, *Through the Howling Wilderness*.

72. *ORN*, I:21:360–61; J. B. Cook to James Stewart McGehee, January 6, 1904, Eve Brower to McGehee, February 22, 1904, McGehee Family Papers; A. F. Rightor to Andrew McCollam, December 3, 1864, McCollam Papers; Bearss, *Louisiana Confederate*, 194–201; John W. Burruss to Edward Burruss, June 1, 1864, Burruss Family Papers; Tyson Diary, September 21, 1863, October 12, 1864; T. A. C. Batchelor to Albert A. Batchelor, December 26, 1864, Batchelor Papers; William H. Whitney to brother, June 12, 1864, Whitney Letters; F. W. Mitchell, "Fighting Guerrillas on the La Fourche"; Michot, "'War Is Still Raging,'" 163–64, 173–74; Hyde, *Pistols and Politics*, 132–37; Kiper, *Dear Catharine, Dear Taylor*, 213–14; Horace Smith to family, June 17, 1864, [July 1864], Horace Smith Papers; Kamphoefner and Helbich, *Germans in the Civil War*, 191; Ephraim Brown to parents, July 22, 1864, Brown to wife and daughter, August 22, September 25, 1864, Ephraim Brown Papers.

73. John Hunter to Edmund Kirby Smith, January 28, 1864, Kirby Smith Papers; Anne to Mrs. Honore P. Morancey, May 17, 1864, Morancey Papers; William G. Thompson to wife, November 11, 1863, William G. Thompson Correspondence; Goyne, *Lone Star and Double Eagle*, 134–35; Lincecum et al., *Gideon Lincecum's Sword*, 232, 245, 286; George Putnam to Mary Loines, December 1, 1863, Low-Mills Family Papers.

74. D. P. Smith, *Frontier Defense*, 55–56, 67–74.

75. Ibid., 74–77, 81.

76. Ibid,. 77, 79–86, 106–10.

77. Ibid., 114–28, 144–51, 156–64. See also McCaslin, "Dark Corner of the Confederacy."

CHAPTER 11

1. Elihu Price to John W. Finnell, August 17, 1863, Joel H. Roark to Thomas E. Bramlette, September 4, 17, 1863, Jeff Roark to John Boyle, October 1, 1863, J. C. Eversode to Bramlette, October 12, 1863, G. W. Daniel to Boyle, November 3, 1863, W. W. Tice to D. W. Lindsey, November 19, 1863, February 19, 1864, Kentucky Adjutant General Records; Herberger, *Yankee at Arms*, 178; Smith and Cooper, *Union Woman*, 166–67; John M. Wilson et al. to Thomas E. Bramlette, October 7, 1863, William L. Hurst to Bramlette, October 6, 1863, Military Correspondence, Kentucky Governor Papers: Bramlette; Lyman P. Spencer Diary, January 29, 1864, Spencer Family Papers; Matthew Cook to Martha Winn, October 6, 1863, Robert Winn to Martha Winn, January 3, 1864, Winn-Cook Family Papers; Marshal M. Miller to wife, October 11, 1863, Marshal M. Miller Letters; Coulter, *Civil War . . . in Kentucky*, 231–32; Gallaher, "Peter Wilson . . . , 1863–1865," 397; *OR*, I:31(3):58, 32(3):41.

2. Lyman P. Spencer Diary, April 28–29, May 8, 1864, Spencer Family Papers; Ramage, *Rebel Raider*, 197–207; Marszalek, *Diary of . . . Holmes*, 334–35; *Memphis Daily Appeal*, January 6, 1864; Duke, *History of Morgan's Cavalry*, 530; George A. Elsworth to James A. Seddon, December 10, 1863, J. J. Calhoun to Jefferson Davis, January 17, 1864, U.S. War Department, Letters Received by Confederate Secretary of War. The John Hunt Morgan Papers contain many letters from men hoping to serve in the upcoming campaign. See, e.g., Charles D. Foote to Morgan, December 29, 1863, T. W. Harris to Morgan, January 17, 1864, E. C. Davidson to Morgan, January 17, 1864.

3. Ramage, *Rebel Raider*, 208–38; General Orders No. 2, June 25, 1864, Box 2, f. 25, John Hunt Morgan Papers; Hamilton, *Papers of . . . Ruffin*, 3:416; R. R. Jones to Daniel W. Lindsey, May 13, 1864, R. V. Grinter to Thomas E. Bramlette, May 25, 1864, Kentucky Adjutant General Records; Mark L. Dismukes to brother, July 17, 1864, Donelson Papers; Davis and Swentor, *Bluegrass Confederate*, 464, 472, 477, 493, 521.

4. W. W. Tice to Daniel W. Lindsey, February 19, 1864, H. H. Parker to Thomas E. Bramlette, February 28, 1864, W. H. H. Faris to Bramlette, April 24, 1864, Stephen E. Jones to Bramlette, April 28, 1864, R. L. Wilson to Bramlette, May 5, 1864, Otho Miller to Lindsey, June 4, 1864, James C. Duncan to Lindsey, G. W. Caplinger to Bramlette, June 25, July 2, 1864, J. Stuart to Lindsey, July 6, 1864, J. Smith to Lindsey, July 20, 1864, J. L. Woodward to Bramlette, [August 5, 1864], Kentucky Adjutant General Records; L. H. Harrison, *Civil War in Ken-*

tucky, 70–71; Simpson and Berlin, *Sherman's Civil War*, 584; Wills, *Confederacy's Greatest Cavalryman*, 170–79; Whitesell, "Military Operations in the Jackson Purchase Area . . . Part II," 244–65; *ORN*, I:25:277, 480–81, 484–85, 534, 586, 594–95, 613, 631, 650–51, 681, 26:361, 704–5; Hubert Saunders to mother, February 20, March 5, 15, June 23, 1864, Saunders Papers.

5. R. V. Grinter to Thomas E. Bramlette, May 25, 1864, Benjamin F. Allen to Daniel W. Lindsey, August 22, 1864, George W. Taylor to Lindsey, September 11, 1864, Kentucky Adjutant General Records; Troutman, *Heavens Are Weeping*, 119; Wilberforce Nevin to father, December 13, 1862, Sayre Papers; Smith and Cooper, *Union Woman*, 190–203; *ORN*, I:26:384; Thomas Speed to Will, August 8, 1864, Speed Papers.

6. Ramage, *Rebel Raider*, 212–13, 215–25; Smith and Cooper, *Union Woman*, 193; L. H. Harrison, *Civil War in Kentucky*, 76–78; *OR*, I:32(2):486, 39(2):135–36. For the evolution of Sherman's attitude toward the guerrilla warfare since 1862, see Foster, *Sherman's Mississippi Campaign*, 1–13, 114–15, 130–31.

7. *OR*, I:39(2):146–67, 153–54; L. H. Harrison, *Civil War in Kentucky*, 77–78.

8. Charles Buford to wife, July 28, 1864, Buford Papers; *OR*, I:39(2):174, 248–49; *OR*, I:39(2):198, 208, 212–15, 231; *ORN*, I:26:384; Troutman, *Heavens Are Weeping*, 180.

9. Bradley and Hal, "'Shoot If You Can by Accident,'" 36; Morgan, "Reminiscences of Service with Colored Troops"; Robert Winn to sister, March 5, 1864, Winn-Cook Family Papers; *OR*, I:32(2):103, 268, 39(2):232; Whitesell, "Military Operations in the Jackson Purchase Area . . . Part II," 264–67, and "Military Operations in the Jackson Purchase Area . . . Part III," 323–30; Danforth, "How I Came to Be in the Army," 330–39; L. C. Barton, "Reign of Terror in Graves County"; Robert H. Milroy to Mary Milroy, May 6–19, 1864, Milroy Letters; James M. Brannock to wife, September 12, 26, 1864, James Madison Brannock Papers: George W. Carvill to sister, December 12, 1864, Carvill Letters. Paine's men thought his policies admirable: see Hardie N. Revelle to brother, August 25, September 10, November 29, 1864, Revelle Letters, and Andrew Lucas Hunt Papers for 1864.

10. *OR*, I:39(2):19, (3):457, II:7:18–19; Newburger Diary, May 31, 1864; Coulter, *Civil War . . . in Kentucky*, 232–36.

11. L. H. Harrison, *Civil War in Kentucky*, 77–79; *OR*, I:39(3):321–22, 456, 724–25, 739, 749, 761; Hume Diary, November 11, 1864; Troutman, *Heavens Are Weeping*, 182; Prichard, "General Orders No. 59." There appears to have been an unusually large number of men falsely accused of either being guerrillas or supporting guerrillas in the months before the election. See files for Willis G. Ragan (Box 1), O. B. F. Ritter, Jesse Brand, James Wickes (Box 2), U.S. War Department, Affidavits, and Oaths Relating to Civilians Charged with Illegal or Disloyal Acts, 1863–64, Provost Marshal Correspondence, Department of Kentucky; Charles Buford to wife, August 3, 1864, Buford Papers.

12. Martin, "Black Flag over the Bluegrass," 359–63; *OR*, I:39(2):121, 212–13, (3):355; *ORN*, I:26:272–73, 279, 488, 501; files for Moses Webster, Moore, Bowling, John Grady, Jacob Baker, James Barrett, Charles Hall, Box 1, U.S. War Department, Provost Marshal Correspondence, Department of Kentucky; statement of Marshall Carson, October 3, 1863, Thomas M. Green to Jeremiah T. Boyle, October 1, 1863, U.S. War Department, Union Provost Marshal Files . . . Two or More Citizens; Frances M. Vaughn to [Daniel W. Lindsey], December 30, 1864, Kentucky Adjutant General Records; Whitesell, "Military Operations in the Jackson Purchase Area . . . Part III," 331–38; Sanders, "Confederate Raider's Kentucky Rampage."

13. Amelia Winn to sister, September 6, December 26, 1864, Winn-Cook Family Papers; Thomas Speed to parents, June 29, November 1, 1864, Speed to father, December 14, 1864, Speed Papers; *ORN*, I:26:333, 533, 771–72; Jonathan L. Neal to John Boyle, December 22, 1863, James C. Culton to Daniel W. Lindsey, November 22, 1864, J. S. S. to E. L. Van Winkle, November 26, 1864, David W. McCowan and John N. Crow to Edwin M. Stanton, November 28, 1864, A. Dupuy to Lindsey, December 2, 1864, Kentucky Adjutant General Records; Davis and Swentor, *Bluegrass Confederate*, 356–57; Troutman, *Heavens Are Weeping*, 140–41; H. R. Littell to James T. Robinson, July 2, 1863, Applications for Requisitions of Fugitives from Justice, Box 3, Kentucky Governor Papers: Robinson; Smith and Cooper, *Union Woman*, 167; Whitely, "Civil War Letters," 262; Mary Bell to Darwin Bell, July 13, 31, 1863, Mary Walker Meriwether Bell Letters; *Confederate Veteran* 37 (July 1930): 270–71; John M. Wilson et al. to Thomas E. Bramlette, October 7, 1863, Military Correspondence, Kentucky Governor Papers: Bramlette; Manering Lowery to Thomas E. Bramlette, October 9, 1863, M. L. Treadwell to Bramlette, February 9, 1864, L. Thomas Hauser to Bramlette, October 17, 1863, Apprehension of Fugitives, Box 7, Kentucky Governor Papers: Bramlette. J. B. Martin, "Black Flag over the Bluegrass," identifies the contending groups but restricts himself to Francis Lieber's definitions.

14. *ORN*, I:26:245; Troutman, *Heavens Are Weeping*, 182, 186; George W. Carvill to sister, July 21, 1864, Carvill Letters; Account of Confinement and Release of Prisoners of War, McLean Barracks, Cincinnati, Ohio, April 1863–June 1864, and Register of Civilian Prisoners, Mclean Barracks, Cincinnati, April 1863–July 1865, U.S. War Department, Records Relating to Confederate Prisoners of War; cases of Henry Turner (MM2406), Thomas B. Payne (MM1733), E. L. Hussey, Thomas Ford, and E. A. Street (NN1091), W. F. Ashcroft and Alfred Nichols (MM1733), U.S. War Department, Court-Martial Cases; James C. Howard to Thomas E. Bramlette, September 10, 1864, Richard J. Browne to Bramlette, November 29, 1864, Nat Gaither et al. to Daniel W. Lindsey, December 7, 1864, Kentucky Adjutant General Records; J. W. Cardwell to Daniel W. Lindsey, October 10, 1864, Box 5, Kentucky Quartermaster General Records.

15. Allison, "Sue Mundy," 299–300; Valentine, "Sue Mundy of Kentucky:

Part I," 178–88, 191–92, nn.66–67. For an example of Clark and Magruder's association with Quantrill, see Mangum, "Disaster at Woodburn Farm."

16. Allison, "Sue Mundy," 301–3; Valentine, "Sue Mundy of Kentucky: Part II," 288–91, 301–2, 304; case of Jerome Clark (MM1732), U.S. War Department, Court-Martial Cases.

17. Valentine, "Sue Mundy of Kentucky: Part II," 305; file on Henry C. Magruder, Box 2, U.S. War Department, Provost Marshal Correspondence, Department of Kentucky; James Wood and John A. Terrell to Daniel W. Lindsey, November 16, 1864, J. J. Barrell to Lindsey, November 14, 1864, April 21, 1865, Kentucky Adjutant General Records.

18. *ORN*, I:26:272–73; *OR*, I:39(2):174, 177, 280; John Bishop to Lazarus Noble, August 9, 1864, Civil War Miscellany, Indiana Adjutant General Records; J. Stuart to Oliver P. Morton, June 27, 1864, Thomas W. Gibson to Morton, October 19, 1864, Morton Correspondence.

19. Lazarus Noble to Thomas E. Bramlette, July 2, 3, 1864, Military Correspondence, Kentucky Governor Papers: Bramlette; James H. McNeely to Oliver P. Morton, June 13, 1864, Lewis Jordan and James J. Wright to Morton, June 24, 1864, Morton Correspondence; *OR*, I:39(2):324; Citizens of Harrison County to Oliver P. Morton, [June 1864], Box 2, Henry Jordan to W. H. H. Terrell, November 25, 1864, Box 10 (L508), James Hughes to Lazarus Noble, August 15, 16, 1864, Box 1 (L828), Indiana Legion Papers, Indiana Adjutant General Records; *ORN*, I:26:343–44, 367, 381, 441, 488–89, 512–14, 532–33. For a former Kentucky partisan who volunteered to lead a company of "scouts" against the guerrillas, see H. H. Parker to Thomas E. Bramlette, February 28, 1864, Kentucky Adjutant General Records.

20. Lewis Jordan and James J. Wright to Oliver P. Morton, June 24, 1864, Morton Correspondence; James Hughes to Lazarus Noble, August 15, 1864, Box 2 (L504), Indiana Legion Papers, Indiana Adjutant General Records; A. R. Johnson, *Partisan Rangers*, 161; *OR*, I:39(2):236–38, (3):61–62.

21. Cooling, *Fort Donelson's Legacy*, 292–326; Longacre, *Mounted Raids*, 202–4.

22. *ORN*, I:25:477, 479, 546–47, 631, 648, 650–51, 656; Lysander Wheeler to family, October 29, 1863, Wheeler Letters; Anthony Francis O'Neil Diary, September 1, October 25, December 28, 1863, Charles O'Neil Papers; A. R. Greene, "From Bridgeport to Ringgold," 273–74; "Use of Block-Houses during the Civil War," p. 3, in Box 38, vol. 87, f. 7, Dodge Papers; Harvey W. Wiley Diary, June 2, 1864, Wiley Papers; S. E. Rankin to parents, December 31, 1863, John D. Walker Correspondence; John W. Garriott to brother, September 12, 27, 1863, Garriott to sister, December 29, 1863, Garriott Letters; George W. Healey to family, September 5, 14, 24, 1863, Healey Civil War Letters; George H. Cadman to wife, October 6, November 5, 17, 1863, Cadman Papers; Thomas S. Hawley to [parents], November 4, 1863, Hawley Papers; Eugene Marshall Diaries, September 10, 26,

1863, Eugene Marshall Papers; Rezin W. Kile to Ma, September 20, October 8, 1863, Kile to wife, October 27, November 3, 1863, Kile Papers.

23. Swedberg, *Three Years with the 92nd Illinois*, 143.

24. Edwin A. Van Cise Diary, June 9, 28, July 2, 17, August 3, 14, 1864, Van Cise Papers.

25. Henry P. Andrews to wife and children, February 13, 1864, Henry P. Andrews Papers; Benjamin Morris to Sarah Morris, May 15, 1864, Morris Papers; Charles S. Brown to "Hadassa," [May 20, 1864], Charles S. Brown Papers; Lonn Dun to Friend Doc, June 21, 1864, Beall-Booth Family Papers; Henry Howland to mother, October 23, 1864, Walter M. Howland to mother, August 28, September 25, 1864, Howland and Tilton Papers; Bela T. St. John to father, December 2, 1864, St. John Papers; Marshall M. Miller to wife, December 5, 1864, Marshall M. Miller Letters; J. L. Donaldson to Dear Sir, February 9, 1865, Pinckney L. Powers Papers; Robertson, "'Such Is War,'" 325–28; Nashville Convict Record Books, vol. 87, pp. 21–33, Prison Records, 1831–1922; cases of John W. Jennings (LL3293), William Dunbar (NN1442), Thomas J. Turner and Uruah R. Parchman (NN1487), Oscar Scarborough (NN1452), U.S. War Department, Court-Martial Cases.

26. Ash, *Middle Tennessee Society*, 96–100; Graf et al., *Papers of Andrew Johnson*, 6:399, 625, 7:153–54, 159–60, 173, 200–201, 259–62, 268–69.

27. Ash, *Middle Tennessee Society*, 123, 148, 150; *OR*, I:32(2):268; Gildrie, "Guerrilla Warfare," 169–70; Mays, *Saltville Massacre*, 58–59, 72, and "Battle of Saltville." For racial atrocities, see Urwin, *Black Flag over Dixie*, and for Fort Pillow, see Cimprich, *Fort Pillow*, and Burkhardt, *Confederate Rage, Yankee Wrath*.

28. Ash, *Middle Tennessee Society*, 149–50; Fisher, *War at Every Door*, 79–87; Graf et al., *Papers of Andrew Johnson*, 6:459; Sarah Jane Full Hill Reminiscences, pt. 2, pp. 32, 39; George H. Cadman to wife, March 16, 1864, Cadman Papers; petition of John B. Rodgers (LL3292), U.S. War Department, Court-Martial Cases.

29. Ash, *Middle Tennessee Society*, 155; Nimrod Porter Diary, August 31, September 2, 4, 14, 19, October 20–21, 23, December 6, 1863; French Diaries, July 20, 29, August 5, 12, 16, 30, 1863; William E. Sloan Diary, July 31, August 20–21, 1863, March 16, 1864; James M. Brannock to wife, September 12, 17, 1864, James Madison Brannock Papers.

30. Raab, *With the 3rd Wisconsin Badgers*, 244–45.

31. Graf et al., *Papers of Andrew Johnson*, 6:666–67, 7:262, 306.

32. *OR*, I:30(4):589; Crist et al., *Papers of . . . Davis*, 11:47–49, 148–49; Fisher, *War at Every Door*, 133–35; Davis and Swentor, *Bluegrass Confederate*, 498–505; Amanda McDowell Diary, January 25, 1864, Curtis McDowell Papers. For a detailed look at wartime Knoxville, see McKenzie, *Lincolnites and Rebels*.

33. Sensing, *Champ Ferguson*, 159–88; T. D. Smith, "'Don't You Beg, and Don't You Dodge,'" 46, 72; Sallie E. Broyles Diary, June 6, 1864, in Cocke Papers; Graf et al., *Papers of Andrew Johnson*, 6:538–39, 553, 591, 643, 646, 685, 7:10–20, 86–

87; *OR*, I:32(1):162–63; Siburt, "John M. Hughs"; *Memphis Daily Appeal*, May 3, 1864; Duncan Milner to father, August 27, 1863, Milner Letters; Harvey W. Wiley Diary, June 16, 1864, Wiley Papers; S. E. Rankin to father and mother, December 31, 1863, Frank Walker Correspondence; Reyburn and Wilson, *"Jottings from Dixie,"* 144–46, 150, 152; Herberger, *Yankee at Arms*, 179–80; Robert H. Milroy to Mary Milroy, June 19, 1864, Milroy Letters.

34. Cooling, *Fort Donelson's Legacy*, 326–30; Whitesell, "Military Operations in the Jackson Purchase Area . . . Part II," 240–44; Fisher, *War at Every Door*, 78–81, 92–95, 126–29; Mary Chester to William B. Chester, February 18, 1864, in Robert I. Chester Biographical Sketch; John Johnston Memoir; Amanda McDowell Diary, January 25, 1864, Curtis McDowell Papers; Fisher, *War at Every Door*, 87; Crist et al., *Papers of . . . Davis*, 9:335, 10:342, 344, 345 n.3, 348 n.21; Sarah Broyles Diary, June 1, 6, 18, September 4, December 30, 1864, and Sarah E. J. (Broyles) Dilworth, "Reminiscences of the Sixties" (1924), both in Cocke Papers.

35. Hugh L. White Roberts to [Secretary of War], January 8, 1863, U.S. War Department, Letters Received by Confederate Secretary of War; file of William C. Allen, Box 2, Provost Marshal Correspondence, Department of Kentucky; Fisher, *War at Every Door*, 81; cases of Elijah J. Ford and John Hedgecoth (NN1236), David Martin (MM1340), James M. Fraley (MM1298), U.S. War Department, Court-Martial Cases; J. C. Williamson, "Diary of John Coffee Williamson," 63–67; Murphree, "Autobiography and Civil War Letters of Joel Murphree," 201; John W. Garriott to sister, December 29, 1863, Garriott Letters; Raab, *With the 3rd Wisconsin Badgers*, 239.

36. Graf et al., *Papers of Andrew Johnson*, 7:3–4; Crist et al., *Papers of . . . Davis*, 11:283–84; Ash, *Middle Tennessee Society*, 162–67; Fisher, *War at Every Door*, 87–89; Dunn, *Cades Cove*, 131–38; Nimrod Porter Diary, January 1, 25, February 6, 26, May 26, July 7, November 20, 1864.

37. J. C. Williamson, "Diary of John Coffee Williamson," 65; French Diaries, August 30, 1863; Amanda McDowell Diary, July 27, September 2, 7, 15, 28, December 7, 17, 1863, Curtis McDowell Papers; Ash, *Middle Tennessee Society*, 167–69.

38. Fisher, *War at Every Door*, 89–92, 130–52; Ash, *Middle Tennessee Society*, 152–56; Jane Smith Washington to William L. Washington, December 18, 1864, Jane Smith Washington Letter; Trimble, "Behind the Lines in Middle Tennessee," 64–65; Raab, *With the 3rd Wisconsin Badgers*, 238–40; J. S. White to William B. Campbell, August 23, [1863], Campbell Family Papers; *ORN*, I:25:540–41; Levi A. Ross to parents, August 2, 1863, Ross Papers. For the intensity of the guerrilla war in the vicinity of Sherman's supply base at Chattanooga that summer, see Lyman P. Spencer Diary, June 19, July 10, 13, 15–16, 18, 1864, Spencer Family Papers. For examples of the treachery Sherman abhorred, see R. Bennett, "Ira Van Deusen," 204, and William J. Helsley to wife, August 15, 1863, Helsley Papers.

39. Bradley and Hal, "'Shoot If You Can by Accident,'" 33–38, 42–43; Robert H. Milroy to Mary Milroy, May 6–19, 1864, Milroy Letters.

40. Harvey W. Wiley Diary, June 16, 1864, Wiley Papers; Graf et al., *Papers of Andrew Johnson*, 7:77–79; Bradley and Hal, "'Shoot If You Can by Accident,'" 34–35, 43–46; Trimble, "Behind the Lines in Middle Tennessee," 74–75; Robert H. Milroy to Mary Milroy, July 6, 16, 26, August 8, September 11, 1864, Milroy Letters.

41. Cases of Cyrus Lee Cathy, William Lemmons, Jesse B. Neeren, Thomas R. West, and Benjamin F. West (NN1368), James M. Johnson (MM1345), U.S. War Department, Court-Martial Cases.

42. Henry Solomon White Diary, July 30, August 20, 27, 1863; Edward W. Whitacker to Ada, November 6, 1863, Edward W. Whitacker Letters; Howard M. Smith to D. M., December 2, 14, 18, 1863, Howard Malcolm Smith Papers; William Patterson Diary, January 15, February 12, 1864; Nat Pendleton to mother, April 2, 1864, Kennedy Family Papers; Daniel R. Larned to ———, May 1, 1864, Larned Papers; John Chester White Memoir, 22–23, 39; McLean, *California Sabers*, 52–63, 70–77; Curry and Ham, "Bushwhackers' War," 431–32; Matthew Holt et al. to Francis H. Pierpont, June 1, 1863, Pierpont Papers; West Virginia Historical Records Survey, *Calendar of the . . . Boreman Letters*, 9, 12, 16, 19, 22–23, 26.

43. McKinney, *Civil War in Fayette County*, 187–92; Jonathan S. Wilcher to Kellian V. Whaley, February 22, 1864, Ramsdell to Whaley, February 6, 1864, Whaley Papers; Nancy Hunt to Mr. and Mrs. Hoppings, September 28, 1863, May 29, 1864, Nancy Hunt Letters. For a detailed look at the divisions in one county, see Shaffer, *Clash of Loyalties*.

44. M. P. Morse to Francis H. Pierpont, September 13, 1863, Pierpont to Col. Wells, September 30, 1863, Leopold P. Cowper to Pierpont, November 13, 1863, Pierpont Papers; Weaver, *Civil War in Buchanan and Wise Counties*, 187–214; Noe, "Red String Scare." Ash, *When the Yankees Came*, 76–107, gives a good explanation of the divisions within areas of Union occupation.

45. Mann, "Family Group, Family Migration," 382–89, and "Ezekiel Counts's Sand Lick Company"; S. R. Alexander to William Smith, September 11, 1864, Virginia Governor Papers: Smith; Henry Keel, "Dead Man's Hollow" (Box 12), Isabelle Sutherland to E. J. Sutherland, December 26, 1921, Margaret Yates Hale to E. J. Sutherland, June 14, 1925, Henry Keep to E. J. Sutherland, October 28, 1924, Patsy Keel Bogg to E. J. Sutherland, September 28, 1941, Noah B. Sutherland to E. J. Sutherland, January 27, 1927, Jasper Sutherland to E. J. Sutherland, October 15, 1921 (Box 22), Sutherland Papers.

46. *ORN*, I:5:414–15, 423–25, 452, 454–57, 469–70, 476–77, 480, 482, 9:40–42, 127, 309–11, 526–27.

47. Shingleton, *John Taylor Wood*, 74–89; *ORN*, I:9:306–7, 318; Horan, *Confederate Agent*, 153–65, 255–59; L. S. Butler, *Pirates, Privateers, and Rebel Raiders*, 187–97; Tidwell et al., *Come Retribution*, 199–206.

48. Barrett, *Civil War in North Carolina*, 227–31, 256–57.

49. Ramage, *Gray Ghost*, 134–35; *OR*, I:33:1081–82.

50. Crist et al., *Papers of . . . Davis*, 9:347; Confederate Congress, "Proceedings of the First . . . Congress: First and Second Sessions," 191, 253, "Proceedings of the First . . . Congress: Second Session," 4–8, 48, 184, and "Proceedings of the First . . . Congress: Fourth Session," 401, 427–28, 440, 450; Ramage, *Gray Ghost*, 134–37; *OR*, I:33:1082–83, 1124, 1252–53, IV:3:194. For the B&O episode, see Ackinclose, *Sabres and Pistols*, 82–89; Ruffner, "'More Trouble than a Brigade,'" 399–401; William Patterson Diary, February 12, 1864; Vogtsberger, *Dulanys of Welbourne*, 193.

51. Joseph W. Caldwell to James A. Seddon, March 10, 1864, R. G. Bachand to Seddon, April 15, 1864, U.S. War Department, Letters Received by Confederate Secretary of War; cases of Nicholas W. Dorsey (MM1346), Phillip Trammell and Jack Barnes (MM1271), U.S. War Department, Court-Martial Cases; Bright, "McNeill Rangers," 353. For an example of how one former ranger company continued to operate as an "independent" company, see Weaver, *Thurmond's Partisan Rangers*, 41–71. For a Confederate surgeon who tried to persuade his brother not to join McNeill's battalion, see E. B. Williams, *Rebel Brothers*, 131–32.

52. Francis H. Pierpont to Sampson Snider, February 25, 1864, Muster roll of August 31, 1864, "Personal Sketch," January 9, 1904, all in Snider Papers; R. E. Crouch, "Loudoun Rangers"; Drickamer and Drickamer, *Fort Lyon to Harper's Ferry*, 138–43, 160–63; E. B. Williams, *Rebel Brothers*, 196–97, 203–4, 261 n.13; Ramage, *Gray Ghost*, 125–29; Waugh, "New England Cavalier," 314–20; Stephenson, *Headquarters in the Brush*. For a failed effort to recruit a counterguerrilla unit in Virginia, see 1863–64 correspondence with Francis H. Pierpont, various Union soldiers, and one writer's mother in Hazard Stevens Papers.

53. R. E. Crouch, "Mobberly Mysteries," 32–45; *Confederate Veteran* 28 (August 1920): 288–89; Sacquety, "John W. Mobberly."

54. Sacquety, "John W. Mobberly"; Elias W. Price to sister, November 29, 1864, Elias Winans Price Papers; *Confederate Veteran* 28 (August 1920): 289; R. E. Crouch, "Loudoun Rangers," 24; Current, *Lincoln's Loyalists*, 179–86.

55. McPherson, *Drawn with the Sword*, 66–86; Engle, *Yankee Dutchman*, 178–99. For the Overland campaign's political implications, see Fleche, "Uncivilized War."

56. E. A. Miller, *Lincoln's Abolitionist General*, 167–74; Duncan, *Beleaguered Winchester*, 184–92; Hanchett, *Irish*, 107–13; F. Moore, *Rebellion Record*, 10:172.

57. Mahon, *Shenandoah Valley*, 110–13; Union Soldier Diary, May 24, 26, 30, 1864, Bound Vol. 27, Roy Bird Cook Collection; William Patterson Diary, July 17, 1864; Freda to sister, June 25, 1864, Hite Papers; E. A. Miller, *Lincoln's Abolitionist General*, 174–76, 192–97; Hanchett, *Irish*, 118–29.

58. Ramage, *Gray Ghost*, 178–81; F. Moore, *Rebellion Record*, 10:68–69;

Bright, "McNeill Rangers," 357–58; Delauter, *McNeill's Rangers*, 71–73; E. B. Williams, *Rebel Brothers*, 197–201.

59. Cooling, *Jubal Early's Raid*; E. H. Smith, "Chambersburg."

60. Morris, *Sheridan*, 183–90, 208–9; Simon, *Papers of . . . Grant*, 12:13, 15, 64–65, 139–40, 272, 286. Mahon, *Shenandoah Valley*, 114–27, challenges the belief that Sheridan succeeded in making the valley a "barren waste," but there is no doubting that was Sheridan's or Grant's intent. Heatwole, *The Burning*, believes Sheridan fulfilled Grant's wishes.

61. Morris, *Sheridan*, 205–9; Ramage, *Gray Ghost*, 184–200, 209–12. Commanders in the Virginias were already ordering their men to execute bushwhackers. See John V. Young to Pauline Young, May 20, October 12, 1864, John V. Young Letters; Nathan G. Dye to Dear Friends, April 17–18, October 12, 25, 1864, Dye Papers; Britton and Reed, *To My Beloved Wife and Boy*, 253, 259–60, 281; Stephen W. Thompson Diary, August 28, September 23, 29, October 6, 1864, Stephen W. Thompson Papers. For the controversial killing of Meigs, see Giunta, *Civil War Soldier*, 241–43, 249–51.

62. Duncan, *Beleaguered Winchester*, 207–12, 230–34; W. Thomas, "Nothing Ought to Astonish Us"; Howard Malcolm Smith Diary, October 4, 27, 28, 1864, Howard Malcolm Smith Papers; Marshall, *War of the People*, 264–65.

63. Urwin, *Custer Victorious*, 174–75, 188 n.13; Morris, *Sheridan*, 226–28; Ramage, *Gray Ghost*, 212–15; P. A. Brown, *Take Sides with the Truth*, 37–39; A. H. Mitchell, *Letters of . . . Mosby*, 34–35, 178–79.

64. Simon, *Papers of . . . Grant*, 12:397; Wert, *Mosby's Rangers*, 259–64; *OR*, I:43(2):581, 671–72. Mark E. Neely, *The Civil War and the Limits of Destruction*, 109–39, discounts the destruction caused by the campaign.

65. Wert, *Mosby's Rangers*, 262; Morris, *Sheridan*, 228–31; Ramage, *Gray Ghost*, 228–42; *OR*, I:42(2):679; Stephen W. Thompson Diary, November 28–30, December 1–2, 1864, Stephen W. Thompson Papers; Howard M. Smith to D. M., December 4, 1864, February 20, 1865, Howard Malcolm Smith Papers. Examples of milder punishments dispensed a year earlier in the Virginias are Daniel N. Jones to Col. M. McCaslin, December 9, 1863, deposition of John W. Murser vs. James Patterson, November 13, 1863, George W. Gageby to Jacob M. Campbell, November 13, 1863, S. Porter to Campbell, November 12, 1863, all in Jacob M. Campbell Papers; cases of George E. Shearer (NN1907) and John P. Rotchford (NN1799), U.S. War Department, Court-Martial Cases; cases of William Wallace (#3249), Elijah Kase (#3250), Thomas Brown (#3261), U.S. War Department, Case Files of Investigations by Levi Turner and Lafayette C. Baker. The Turner-Baker files also cover a large number of captured Mosby men. For Grant's views on burning private property see, Simon, *Papers of . . . Grant*, 12:17–18.

66. *OR*, I:43(2):671–72; Cochran Diary, 2:31–32, 51–52; Vogtsberger, *Dulanys of Welbourne*, 244–45; Ramage, *Gray Ghost*, 234–37.

67. Curry and Ham, "Bushwhackers' War," 432–33; M. T. Haderman to Dear

Friend, November 10, December 18, 1864, Haderman Papers; Elias W. Price to sister, November 17, 29, 1864, Elias W. Price Papers.

CHAPTER 12

1. *OR*, I:29(1):913–14; Barrett, *Civil War in North Carolina*, 177–79; Wills, *War Hits Home*, 202–4. See generally Casstevens, *Edward A. Wild*.

2. *OR*, I:29(1):912; Yearns and Barrett, *North Carolina Civil War Documentary*, 53–56; Lowe, *Meade's Army*, 92, 94.

3. *OR*, I:29(1):914–15, (2):596; Nolan, *Benjamin Franklin Butler*, 242–44; B. Butler, *Correspondence*, 3:268–71; Alonzo C. Draper to Hiram W. Allen, December 24, 1862, Edward A. Wild to John T. Elliott (draft), December 17, 1863, Wild to Willis Sanderlin (draft), December 22, 1863, Wild Papers.

4. Johnston and Mobley, *Papers of . . . Vance*, 2:357; Barrett, *Civil War in North Carolina*, 178–79; Nolan, *Benjamin Franklin Butler*, 243–44; B. Butler, *Correspondence*, 3:312–14; Edward A. Wild to James Barnes, June 10, 1864 (draft), Wild Papers; *OR*, I:29(1):915, 917. For an example of how contact with U.S. troops could alienate even Unionists, see Browning, "Removing the Mask of Nationality."

5. *OR*, I:29(1):916, (2):597–98; Barrett, *Civil War in North Carolina*, 180–81. For a detailed account of Wild's raid and its aftermath, see B. A. Myers, "Executing Daniel Bright."

6. Hamilton, *Papers of . . . Ruffin*, 3:348. For the variety of ways North Carolinians may have reacted to this chaos, see McKinney, "Layers of Loyalty."

7. B. M. Edney to James A. Seddon, December 8, 1863, U.S. War Department, Letters Received by Confederate Secretary of War; Barrett, *Civil War in North Carolina*, 192–94; Yearns and Barrett, *North Carolina Civil War Documentary*, 101–2; Stevens, *Rebels in Blue*, 89–145.

8. Barrett, *Civil War in North Carolina*, 182–93; Docton Warren Bagley Diary, September 15, 1863, Bagley Papers; J. C. Kirkman to Vebulon B. Vance, August 27, 1863, Robins Papers; J. V. B. Rogers to Zebulon B. Vance, October 2, 1863, Vance Papers; Inscoe and McKinney, *Heart of Confederate Appalachia*, 122–28 (although for more peaceful Unionist activities, see pp. 139–45).

9. J. A. Little to D. C. Pearson, July 15, 1864, Confederate Conscript Bureau Papers; Joseph C. Norwood to Walter Lenoir, August 13, 1863, Lenoir Family Papers; Inscoe and McKinney, *Heart of Confederate Appalachia*, 129; R. W. Freeman to Zebulon B. Vance, July 5, 1863, J. G. Reynolds to Vance, July 12, 1863, Vance Papers; B. Washington Bell to Alfred W. Bell, March 11, 1864, Alfred W. Bell Papers; Docton Warren Bagley Diary, February 1, August 22, 1864, Bagley Papers; Paul E. Hubbell, "The James Eller Family and the Bushwhackers of Wilkes County, North Carolina, 1864–65," pp. 5–12, manuscript in J. B. Hubbell Papers; Crist et al., *Papers of . . . Davis*, 11:199–201; To My Dear Sir, November 2, 1864, Stephens Papers.

10. Joseph C. Webb to Robina N. Webb, September 19, 1863, Lenoir Family Papers; *OR*, I:51(2):714–16; Special Orders No.2 (August 27, 1863), No. 8 (September 9, 1863), J. W. Mallet to R. C. Gatlin, September 26, 1863, J. H. Foush to Zebulon B. Vance, December 30, 1863, R. C. Gatlin to J. H. Foush, March 14, 1864, Sarah F. Robins to M. S. Robins, September 19, 1864, all in Robins Papers; Barrett, *Civil War in North Carolina*, 194–96; McKinney, *Zeb Vance*, 189–90, 236; Williams and Hamilton, *Papers of . . . Graham*, 5:538–40; W. H. George to Zebulon B. Vance, November 21, 1863, Jane and Martha Bryan to Vance, December 23, 1863, Vance Papers; [Richard C. Gatlin] to C. Dowd, March 16, 1864, Letterbook of Home Guard, 1863–65 (AG52), North Carolina Adjutant General Records.

11. B. F. Rose to James A. Seddon, September 21, November 10, 1863, F. A. Rutherford to Seddon, September 23, 1863, B. M. Edney to Seddon, December 3, 1863, Moses Jordan to Seddon, December 11, 1863, T. D. Crawford to Seddon, February 24, 1864, W. D. Sneed to Seddon, March 9, 1864, U.S. War Department, Letters Received by Confederate Secretary of War; John W. Graham to Zebulon B. Vance, December 6, 1863, Vance Papers; McKinney, *Zeb Vance*, 154–55, 232–33. Somewhat different circumstances surrounded a famous incident at Kinston, where Gen. George E. Pickett hanged twenty-two Confederate deserters who had subsequently joined the Union army. See Gordon, "'In Time of War,'" and Patterson, *Justice or Atrocity*.

12. Inscoe and McKinney, *Heart of Confederate Appalachia*, 129–33; Evans, *To Die Game*, 36–41; Thomas McNaughton to D. C. Pearson, July 9, 14, 1864, Confederate Conscript Bureau Papers; J. H. Foush to Vance, August 29, 1863, Mrs. M. B. Morse to Vance, September 10, 1863, C. Dowd to Vance, November 30, 1863, William Church et al. to Vance, June 9, 1864, William Horton et al. to Vance, June 20, 1864, W. W. Hampton to Vance, August 10, 1864, Vance Papers; J. A. Sugg to husband, September 23, 1863, Mollie Sugg to Lewis O. Sugg, January 22, August 9, 1864, Sugg Papers.

13. McKinney, *Zeb Vance*, 197, 232–33; Richard C. Gatlin to Zebulon Vance, May 16, November 19, 1864, Gatlin to Commanding Officer, 68th N.C. Troops, July 1864, North Carolina Adjutant General Records; Richard C. Gatlin to B. T. Bullock, September 29, 1863, Gatlin to A. S. Merrimac, December 24, 1863, Letterbook of Home Guard, North Carolina Adjutant General Records; J. C. McRae to Zebulon B. Vance, November 3, 1863, Joseph Jones to Vance, January 7, 1865, Vance Papers; Alfred W. Bell to wife, April 8, 1864, Alfred W. Bell Papers; Williams and Hamilton, *Papers of . . . Graham*, 5:539.

14. Barrett, *Civil War in North Carolina*, 233–38; Inscoe and McKinney, *Heart of Confederate Appalachia*, 233–38; Stevens, *Rebels in Blue*, 68–70, 106–45; Graf et al., *Papers of Andrew Johnson*, 7:19–21; O'Brien, *Mountain Partisans*, 18–23; Crow, *Storm in the Mountains*, 104–8; Yearns and Barrett, *North Carolina Civil War Documentary*, 114–16.

15. Thomsen, *Rebel Chief*, 201–15; Crow, *Storm in the Mountains*, 50–63,

99–104, 114–16; Godbold and Russell, *Confederate Colonel*, 115–25; William H. Thomas to Samuel Cooper, August 2, 1864, William Holland Thomas Papers.

16. Inscoe and McKinney, *Heart of Confederate Appalachia*, 136–38; James A. McFerrin to Zebulon B. Vance, October 12, 1864, Vance Papers; Martin Crawford, *Ashe County's Civil War*, 142–44.

17. D. Williams et al., *Plain Folk in a Rich Man's War*, 161–68; O'Brien, *Mountain Partisans*, 127–38; Bohannon, "They Had Determined to Root Us Out," 109–12; R. S. Davis, "Memoir of a Partisan War," 109–13; J. A. Caldwell to Henry C. Wayne, January 4, 1864, Joseph McConnell to Wayne, January 28, 1864, S. C. Dobbs to Wayne, March 8, 24, 1864, F. M. Cowen to Wayne, March 29, 31, 1864, Robert McMillan to Wayne, April 9, 1864, F. M. Cowen to E. M. Galt, May 5, 1864, Georgia Adjutant General Records.

18. Sarris, "Anatomy of an Atrocity," 692–96, 700–705, and "'Shot for Being Bushwhackers,'" 35–42; R. S. Davis, "Forgotten Union Guerrilla Fighters"; Joseph McConnell to Henry C. Wayne, January 28, 1864, Nat Mangum to Wayne, February 15, 1864, S. C. Dobbs to Wayne, March 8, 24, 1864, Robert McMillan to Wayne, March 9, 1864, Georgia Adjutant General Records; W. N. Bilbo to Joseph E. Brown, February 22, 1864, John S. Fair to Brown, September 26, 1864, Georgia Governor Papers: Brown. See generally, Sarris, *Separate Civil War*, 101–43.

19. Sarris, "'Shot for Being Bushwhackers,'" 41–42, and "Anatomy of an Atrocity," 679–80, 698–99; O'Brien, *Mountain Partisans*, 155–63.

20. D. Williams et al., *Plain Folk in a Rich Man's War*, 164, 168–74; Carlson, "Loanly Runagee," 598–615; Elijah C. Morgan to Henry C. Wayne, October 17, 1864, Georgia Adjutant General Records; J. Adams to Mary McAdoo, November 11, 1864, McAdoo Papers.

21. O. P. Finney to Henry C. Wayne, August 8, 1864, B. B. de Graffenried to Wayne, September 23, 1864, General Orders No. 3, August 3, 1864, Georgia Adjutant General Records; Chandler, *Confederate Records of . . . Georgia*, 3:383–84; Carlson, "Loanly Runagee," 610–11; D. Williams et al., *Plain Folk in a Rich Man's War*, 131–32, 140–50. Williams defines anti-Confederate activity in the context of a class war, but that need not have been the case.

22. McMurry, *Atlanta 1864*, 26–30; Castel, *Decision in the West*, 348–49, 469.

23. Swedberg, *Three Years with the 92nd Illinois*, 213–14, 221–22; James S. Thompson Journal, May 17, 26, 31, June 16, July 18–24, 28, August 18, 1864; Athearn, *Soldier in the West*, 195, 199–200; D. L. Ambrose, *From Shiloh to Savannah*, 174; Robert Winn to sister, July 28, 29, 1864, Winn-Cook Family Papers; Edward P. Stanfield to mother, August 14, 1864, Stanfield Correspondence; *OR*, I:38(5):140–41.

24. Robert Winn to sister, July 28, August 1, 1864, Winn-Cook Family Papers; E. P. Brown to Henry C. Wayne, September 1, 1864, Georgia Adjutant General Records; Cash and Howarth, *My Dear Nellie*, 193, 197.

25. James S. Thompson Journal, September 10, October 15, 24, 1864; Samuel W. Pruitt to Bettie Pruitt, September 13, 1864, Pruitt to Martha Pruitt, October 1, 1864, Pruitt Papers; Robert Winn to sister, September 5, 1864, Winn-Cook Family Papers; Chandler, *Confederate Records of . . . Georgia* 3:582, 587, 613–14; Sarris, "Anatomy of an Atrocity," 698; Angle, *Three Years in Army of the Cumberland*, 281, 296; Heath Diary, September 3, 5, November 1–2, 1864; *OR*, I:39(2):480, 503, (3):415; Glatthaar, *March to the Sea and Beyond*, 124, 127–28, 147, 153.

26. Jonathan D. Ashmore to Dear Colonel, August 3, 1863, Ashmore Papers; Burr Wright to James F. Sloan, October 6, 1863, James F. Sloan Papers; Franklin J. Moses Jr. to Robert Quarters, November 12, 1864 (as Circular No. 1), Moses Papers; Proclamation of Milledge L. Bonham, September 5, 1864, Bonham Papers.

27. J. C. Burgess to James A. Seddon, ca. July 15, 1864, U.S. War Department, Letters Received by Confederate Secretary of War; Mother to son, January 6, 1865, Sims Family Papers; Cauthen, *South Carolina Goes to War*, 174–77.

28. Waters, "Florida's Confederate Guerrillas," 145–48; John Milton to John K. Jackson, August 7, 1864, Milton to Sam Jones, August 28, 1864, Milton to Jefferson Davis, September 9, 1864, C. H. Du Pont to Milton, October 7, 1864, Milton to James A. Seddon, October 18, 1864, Letterbooks, Florida Governor Papers; Dickison, *Dickison and His Men*, 211.

29. Waters, "Florida's Confederate Guerrillas," 143–45; Buker, *Blockaders, Refugees, and Contrabands*, 114–41, 148–60; John Milton to Jefferson Davis, September 19, 1864, Letterbooks, Florida Governor Papers.

30. Reiger, "Deprivation, Disaffection, and Desertion," 288–96; John Milton to James A. Seddon, December 6, 1862, Milton to Stephen R. Mallory, May 23, 1864, Milton to Seddon, June 30, 1864, Letterbooks, Florida Governor Papers; Johns, *Florida during the Civil War*, 159–68; *OR*, I:15:947–48; Buker, *Blockaders, Refugees, and Contrabands*, 1–8, 171–74, 181–82. The fluidity of the Florida-Georgia-Alabama border region is illustrated in D. Williams, *Rich Man's War*.

31. Johns, *Florida during the Civil War*, 162, 165–67; Reiger, "Deprivation, Disaffection, and Desertion," 296–98; Buker, *Blockaders, Refugees, and Contrabands*, 88, 98–114, 183–87.

32. W. C. Davis, *Confederate General*, 4:190–91, 5:104–5; O'Brien, *Mountain Partisans*, 97–101; Sifakis, *Compendium of the Confederate Armies: Alabama*, 27–45, 81; Confederate Cavalry Company History File; Confederate Cavalry Battalion History File.

33. Crist et al., *Papers of . . . Davis*, 10:498–99; McMillan, *Disintegration of a Confederate State*, 98–102, 106–8; Sifakis, *Compendium of the Confederate Armies: Alabama*, 45–50.

34. Roth, *Well Mary*, 46–47; John H. Parrish to Henry Watson, November 9, 1863, Henry Watson Jr. Papers; D. P. Lewis to Thomas H. Watts, February 9, [1864], A. C. Bean to Watts, November 30, 1864, Alabama Governor Papers:

Watts; cases of J. J. Tipton, Robert L. Welch, E. Bingham, and Alexander St. Clair (NN1796), K. J. Daniel (NN3831), U.S. War Department, Court-Martial Cases; Mary Fielding Diary, November 25, 1864; Rohr, *Incidents of the War*, 175–77, 182–85; Coleman Diary, February 2, 1864; *Confederate Verteran* 15 (July 1907): 326–27.

35. Levi A. Ross Diary, September 10, 1863, Ross Papers; David Garver to sister, April 9, 1864, Garver Letters; Alonzo A. Van Vlack to father and mother, June 27, 1864, Van Vlack Letters; George H. Cadman to wife, March 12, 19, April 2, 18, 1864, Cadman Papers; Swedberg, *Three Years with the 92nd Illinois*, 147, 152, 175; Charles A. Harper to father, July 4, 20, 27, 1864, Harper to Dear All, September 23 1864, Charles A. Harper Papers.

36. *OR*, I:31(3):39; Eugene Marshall Diary, November 6–8, 22, 1863, Eugene Marshall to sister, November 4–9, 15, 1863, September 20, 1864, Eugene Marshall Papers.

37. Dodd and Dodd, *Winston*, 122, 271–77; Storey, *Loyalty and Loss*, 159–69; O'Brien, *Mountain Partisans*, 89–96; B. Martin, *Desertion of Alabama Troops*, 153–54, 189–98; Bush Jones to John G. Shorter, July 16, 1863, Shorter to Braxton Bragg, July 24, 1863, Alabama Governor Papers: Shorter; McMillan *Disintegration of a Confederate State*, 60–63, 93–94; Charles F. Hinrichs Diary, March 26–27, 1864, Hinrichs Papers; David Hobbard to Thomas H. Watts, December 19, 1863, Watts to W. D. Chadwick, December 12, 1863, Watts to James A. Seddon, December 14, 1863, January 1864, Watts to W. B. Wood, March 29, [1864], Watts to Alabama General Assembly, October 7, 1864, Alabama Governor Papers: Watts; Crist et al., *Papers of . . . Davis*, 10:129, 276.

38. N. C. Hughes, *Memoir of . . . Stephenson*, 260; *OR*, I:32(3):770, 785–86, 824–25; Espy Diary, August 10, 1864; J. W. Harmon Memoir, pp. 40–47.

39. Crist et al., *Papers of . . . Davis*, 10:276; W. S. Robinson to Mary L. Robinson, August 8, 20, 1864, W. S. Robinson Papers; case of Thomas F. Ellen (LL3258), U.S. War Department, Court-Martial Cases; statement by W. M. Banister, October 28, 1864, Whittle Papers.

40. D. Williams, *Rich Man's War*, 144–48; Espy Diary, September 8, 12–18, 1863, July 22, 29–30, August 19, 1864; Thomas B. Cooper to Thomas H. Watts, June 18, 1864, Catherine Powell to Watts, June 13, 1864, Wilson Ashby to Watts, August 15, 1864, C. W. Snowden to Watts, August 12, 1864, Jonathan P. West to Watts, September 9, [1864], B. W. Starke to Watts, September 16, 1864, Alabama Governor Papers: Watts.

41. John Ventress to Charles Clark, February 6, 1864, Charles Clark Papers; Jason Niles Diary, August 22, September 28–29, October 1–3, 7, 14, 30, November 16, 1863, January 21, 1864, Niles Papers; Agnew Diary, August 7, November 12, 1863, July 20, 1864.

42. Joseph Lovell to Mrs. W. Lovell, June 17, 1863, Quitman Family Papers;

Richard T. Archer to J. J. Pettus, June 17, 1863, Pettus Papers; Bettersworth, *Confederate Mississippi*, 223–24; Silver, "Breakdown of Morale," 106–7, 115–15; Captain Hardy to Charles Clark, February 8, 1864, J. M. Wesson to Clark, March 26, 1864, H. S. Van Eaton to Clark, July 26, 1864, Charles Clark Papers.

43. Agnew Diary, August 26, 1863; Bettersworth, *Confederate Mississippi*, 216–26, 236–41; W. H. Quarles to Charles Clark, March 28, 1864, S. J. Gholson to Clark, April 16, 1864, George Bayliss to Clark, August 24, 1864, Charles Clark Papers; Blain, "'Banner' Unionism," 211–13.

44. G. F. Seals to James A. Seddon, June 17, 1864, U.S. War Department, Letters Received by Confederate Secretary of War; Annette Koch to C. D. Koch, August 9, 1863, [April 24], June 19, July 6, 19, 1864, C. D. Koch to Annette Koch, August 14, 1863, February 7, April 27, 1864, Koch Family Papers.

45. Annette Koch to C. D. Koch, September 18, 26, 28, October 3, 1864, Elers Koch to C. D. Koch, October 3, 1864, Koch Family Papers.

46. Annette Koch to C. D. Koch, September 26, October 3, November 14, 1864, Elers Koch to C. D. Koch, October 3, 12, 1864, Koch Family Papers.

47. Bynum, *Free State of Jones*, 94–95, 98–119, 124–29.

48. Crist et al., *Papers of . . . Davis*, 10:32, 42, 61–64; H. Cassidy to Charles Clark, September 12, 1864, Charles Clark Papers.

49. Foner, *Reconstruction*, 56–58; Shoemaker Diary, February 27, March 3, 22, 30, April 23, 24, 28, 30, May 24, 1864.

50. Agnew Diary, July 16, August 2, 9, September 30, October 1, 8, 25–26, November 4, 12, 1863, January 23, February 4, 25, March 14, 19, 22, August 10, 1864; Jason Niles Diary, July 19, 1863, Niles Papers; Mother to Jane Silvey, November 4, 8, 27, 1863, March 4, 30, 1864, Silvey Papers; George E. Spencer to Grenville M. Dodge, September 7, 1863, Box 2, vol. 5, f. 3, Dodge Papers; Bela T. St. John to brother, March 18, 1864, St. John Papers; Samuel Ayres to Lyman Langdon, July 16, 1864, Ayres Correspondence; A. Brown, "Sol Street," 168–72; John N. LeGrand et al. to Charles Clark, November 30, 1863, Clark to LeGrand et al., December 6, 1863, H. B. Bramen et al. to Clark, February 2, 1864, J. D. Burton to Clark, May 12, 1864, W. D. Sneed to Clark, May 27, 1864, J. D. W. Duckworth to Clark, June 15, 1864, M. A. Banks to Clark, June 15, 1864, Goodwyn Nixon to Clark, June 20, 1864, George J. Mortimer to Clark, August 20, 1864, Charles Clark Papers. For a Union soldier who believed that some "bands of desperadoes" exploited the image of Confederate guerrillas as thieves, see George H. Cadman to wife, August 21, 1863, Cadman Papers.

51. W. E. Montgomery to Charles Clark, November 25, 1863, Clark to Montgomery, February 12, March 16, 1864, Charles Clark Papers.

52. G. G. Torrey et al. to Charles Clark, February 20, 1864, W. E. Montgomery to Clark, November 25, 1863, January 24, February 1, August 7, 1864, Charles Clark Papers.

53. Hearn, *Ellet's Brigade*, 189; W. E. Montgomery to Charles Clark, November 25, 1863, January 24, 1864, Charles Clark Papers; Mother to Jane Silvey, February 14, 1864, Silvey Papers.

54. *OR*, I:39(2):731, 887, 45(1):785–86; John C. Burris to Katie Swan, September 27, 1863, John C. Burris Papers; Clarke, *Warfare along the Mississippi*, 101; recruitment handbill dated September 11, 1864, Crandall Papers; Hearn, *Ellet's Brigade*, 150–219, 260–69; *ORN*, I:25:693–98, 701–2, 722–31.

55. *ORN*, I:25:404–5, 437, 513–14, 535–37, 622–23, 682, 26:271, 313–14, 340–51, 376–77, 446–47, 470–71; Hearn, *David Dixon Porter*, 268–71. For illicit trade, see also L. H. Johnson, *Red River Campaign*, 49–78; Hearn, *When the Devil Came Down to Dixie*, 180–97; Ned C. Ellis to mother, October 4, 1864, Edmund Curtis Ellis Papers.

56. Scarborough, *Diary of Edmund Ruffin*, 3:xxiv, 126.

57. Ibid., 3:180, 285, 333, 524, 546–47, 571–72, 591, 595–600, 646, 651.

58. Ibid., 3:99–103, 126, 300–301, 357, 661.

EPILOGUE

1. Lankford, *Richmond Burning*, 62–63, 70–71, 77–79, 91.

2. Ibid., 193; *OR*, I:46(3):1383.

3. *OR*, I:46(3):1390–91, 1395, 47(3):740, 786–87, 810. For the controversy over Davis's intentions, see Kerby, "Why the Confederacy Lost," 332–35; Beringer et al., *Why the South Lost*, 342–47; Feis, "Jefferson Davis and the 'Guerrilla Option'"; Winik, *April 1865*, 146–64; W. C. Davis, *Honorable Defeat*, 80–83.

4. Dowdey and Manarin, *Wartime Papers of R. E. Lee*, 939; *OR*, I:47(3):806–7, 823–24. See also Lee's reported remarks to one of his officers in Gallagher, *Fighting for the Confederacy*, 532–33.

5. *OR*, I:47(3):823–34.

6. William Hollander to Clayton Gray, January 26, 1865, Box 1, f. 1a, Confederate Conscript Bureau Papers; Samuel F. Harper to sister, December 30, 1864, Samuel Finley Harper Papers; Louis A. Bringier to wife, December 7, 1864, Bringier and Family Papers; Edmund Fontaine to Richard H. Meade, April 23, 1865, Meade Family Papers.

7. Scarborough, *Diary of Edmund Ruffin*, 3:843, 850–51; Agnew Diary, April 15, 1865; Docton Warren Bagley Diary, April 19–20, 1865, Bagley Papers; N. C. Baird, *Journals of . . . Edmonds*, 220; Drickamer and Drickamer, *Fort Lyon to Harper's Ferry*, 233.

8. Ash Welch to Basil Duke, January 17, 1865, Duke Papers; Eliza Silvey to Jane Silvey, March 21, 1865, Silvey Papers; Hazard Stevens to mother, April 15, 1865, Hazard Stevens Papers; Charles S. Brown to Etta, April 26, 1865, Charles S. Brown Papers.

9. McMillan, *Alabama Confederate Reader*, 439; Marszalek, *Diary of . . . Holmes*, 438; *Augusta Chronicle and Sentinel*, April 26, 1865; T. L. Baker, *Con-*

federate Guerrilla, 63; Edmund Fontaine to Richard H. Meade, April 23, 1865, Meade Family Papers; William W. Garig Diary, May 3, 9, 1865, Garig Family Papers.

10. Maddox, *Hard Trials*, 75; Towles, *World Turned Upside Down*, 473.

11. Asprey, *War in the Shadows*; J. Ellis, *From the Barrel of a Gun*; Joes, *Guerrilla Conflict* and *America and Guerrilla Warfare*; Birtle, *U.S. Army Counterinsurgency*. For convenient samples of the strategy and philosophy of guerrilla warfare, see Laqueur, *Guerrilla Reader*, and Chaliand, *Art of War*, 653–70.

12. R. H. Nichols, *In Custer's Shadow*, 66–70; Isaac H. Rowland to father, February 26, 1865, Rowland-Shilliday Papers; Hubert Saunders to mother, March 14, 27, 1865, Saunders to brother, March 24, April 24, 1865, Saunders Papers; James S. Thompson Journal, February 22, 1865; McLarty, "Letters of . . . Lazear: Part III," 60–61; J. R. Perkins, *Trails, Rails and War*, 156–69; Alexander Denny to Grenville M. Dodge, January 14, 1865, Thomas Gammon to Thomas R. Reed, January 12, 1865, John Small to W. T. Kittredge, April 25, 1865, Box 63, vol. 148, Report of Scouts, 1865, Box 63, vol. 143, f. 5, Dodge Papers; J. W. Bailey, "McNeill Rangers and the Capture of Crook and Kelley"; Vogtsberger, *Dulanys of Welbourne*, 276–77; Crook, *His Autobiography*, 135–36, 303–5.

13. H. L. Giltner to Basil Duke, January 31, 1865, Duke Papers; Michot, "'War Is Still Raging'" 174–82; Henry W. Griffin to Joseph L. Brent, March 9, 1865, Griffin to D. F. Boyd, March 29, April 4, 11, 1865, Joseph L. Brent Papers, in Civil War Manuscripts, Louisiana Adjutant General Records; Lewis O. Sugg to parents, February 6, 1865, Sugg Papers; Evans, *To Die Game*, 41–53; Nevins and Thomas, *Diary of . . . Strong*, 3:581–82. See also Alexander Jackson to William H. Jackson, February 26, 1865, Jackson Papers; Wyatt Liscomb to Mr. Lenoir, February 4, 1865, Lenoir Family Papers; T. L. Fry to Maraduke S. Robins, February 4, 1865, Micah McMasters to Robins, February 16, 1865, Robins Papers; Agnew Diary, April 11, 1865.

14. Glatthaar, *March to the Sea and Beyond*, 127–28, 140, 153; Charles S. Brown to Etta, April 26, 1865, Charles S. Brown Papers; Robertson, "'Such Is War,'" 349. See generally J. G. Campbell, *When Sherman Marched North*, although the author says little about guerrillas.

15. Cauthen, *South Carolina Goes to War*, 222–25, 228; Andrew G. Magrath to People of South Carolina, February 27, 1865, Orderbook, and Paul F. Hammond to Magrath, January, 23, 1865, Magrath to A. J. Frederick, February 23, 1865, Correspondence, Magrath Papers.

16. J. A. Townsend to Andrew G. Magrath, April 1, 1865, W. A. Hemingway to Magrath, April 6, 1865, Magrath Papers; J. A. Keller to John M. Obey, March 16, 1865, Keller Letter; Schwalm, *Hard Fight for We*, 131–34; Towles, *World Turned Upside Down*, 446, 453–554.

17. Schwalm, *Hard Fight for We*, 134–35, 208; J. G. Campbell, *When Sherman Marched North*, 76–77, 79–82.

18. Wert, *Mosby's Rangers*, 279–90; *OR*, I:46(3):830–31, 839, 897, 910, 1396, 47(3):303, 48(2):249; Monaghan, *Swamp Fox of the Confederacy*, 98–105.

19. *Fort Smith New Era*, March 18, 1865; Prier, "Under the Black Flag," 120, 277; Sacquety, "John Mobberly," 19–21; R. E. Crouch, "Mobberly Mysteries," 35–38; *OR*, I:46(3):444–45, 590, 840–41, 868–70, 49(2):843; case of Champ Ferguson (MM2997), U.S. War Department, Court-Martial Cases. Mays, *Cumberland Blood*, chap. 9, believes even Ferguson might have escaped death had he not continued his criminal ways after Lee's surrender.

20. Beamer, "Gray Ghostbusters," 256–59, 262; Nevins and Thomas, *Diary of . . . Strong*, 3:582–83; *OR*, I:46(3):1091, 1108, 1134, 49(2):418–19.

21. *OR*, I:49(2):557, 691, 711, 737, 885, 911, 1000, 1025–26, 1088–90; Bright, "McNeill Rangers," 385–87; Leslie, *Devil Knows How to Ride*, 363–69; Castel, *Quantrill*, 208–13.

22. Kerby, *Kirby Smith's Confederacy*, 399–429; D. S. Frazier, "'Out of Stinking Distance,'" 168–70; Michot, "'War Is Still Raging,'" 182–84.

23. Cleveland Diary, May 4, 12, 1864; Francis F. Audsley to wife, May 12, 1865, Audsley Letters; *OR*, I:48(2):508–9, 705–6, 822–23; Mat to William E. Hill, May 15, 1865, William and Bettie Hill Letters. For the situation on the Kansas and Missouri border, see J. Neely, *Border between Them*, 132–252.

24. *OR*, I:49(2):963.

25. Storey, *Loyalty and Loss*, 189–91; Fisher, *War at Every Door*, 159–64; Shepherdstown Civil War Diary, July 17, 1865, Roy Bird Cook Collection; cases of Andrew Steerman, Moses Webster, Henry Metcalf (Box 1), James C. Hooker (Box 2), U.S. War Department, Provost Marshal Correspondence, Department of Kentucky; case of James Harvey Wells, U.S. War Department, Union Provost Marshal Files . . . Two or More Citizens; case of Henry Turner (MM2406), U.S. War Department, Court-Martial Cases.

26. Kamphoefner and Helbich, *Germans in the Civil War*, 444–45; Storey, *Loyalty and Loss*, 191–95; Fisher, *War at Every Door*, 156–59; D. Williams et al., *Plain Folk in a Rich Man's War*, 174–75, 185; Stevens, *Rebels in Blue*, 151–87; Groce, *Mountain Rebels*, 127–51; McKenzie, *Lincolnites and Rebels*, 206–23; Lyman P. Spencer Diary, May 1, 1865, Spencer Family Papers.

27. Joe M. Scott, *Four Years' Service*, 48–49; *Confederate Veteran* 1 (May 1893): 132, 13 (June 1905): 250, 33 (May 1925): 165; D. T. Carter, *When the War Was Over*, 10–23; Sutherland, *Very Violent Rebel*, 181.

28. Jason Niles Diary, April 29, May 10, 13, 1865, Niles Papers; Agnew Diary, May 1, 1865; Ellen Cooper Johnson Memoir, pp. 18–27, Ellen Cooper Johnson Papers; *OR*, I:46(3):792–93, 810–11; Espy Diary, July 10–11, 1865; *Confederate Veteran* 27 (April 1919): 132–33, 142; John W. Brown Diary, May 28, 31, 1865.

29. Rable, *But There Was No Peace*, 1–15; Hyde, "Bushwhacking and Barn Burning," 185–86; Bynum, *Free State of Jones*, 131–44; Storey, *Loyalty and Loss*,

196–231; Inscoe and McKinney, *Heart of Confederate Appalachia*, 266–85; K. C. Barnes, *Who Killed John Clayton?*, 7–32.

30. D. T. Carter, *When the War Was Over*, 14–15; Castel, *Quantrill*, 221–23; Stiles, *Jesse James*, 168–87; Monks, *History of Southern Missouri and Northern Arkansas*, 131–40; K. Ross, *Autobiography of Hildebrand*, xiii–xvi.

31. Inscoe, *Race, War, and Remembrance*, 322–49; Sutherland, "Forgotten Soldiers"; Membership Rosters, New York Camp, United Confederate Veterans Collection; Castel, *Quantrill*, 231–32; Wert, *Mosby's Rangers*, 290–95.

32. Maddox, *Hard Trials*, 80–81; M. A. Davis, "Legend of Bill Dark," 428–29; A. H. Mitchell, *Letters of Mosby*, 100, 214–15. For Mosby's postwar opinions on "Quantrill's gang" of "outlaws," see P. A. Brown, *Take Sides with the Truth*, 134.

BIBLIOGRAPHY

MANUSCRIPT ABBREVIATIONS

ADAH	Alabama Department of Archives and History, Montgomery
AHC	Arkansas History Commission, Little Rock
DU	Special Collections, Duke University Libraries, Durham, North Carolina
FC	Filson Club Historical Society, Louisville, Kentucky
FSA	Florida State Archives, Tallahassee
GDAH	Georgia Department of Archives and History, Atlanta
IHLA	Iowa Historical Library and Archives, Iowa City
IHS	Indiana Historical Society, Indianapolis
ISHL	Illinois State Historical Library, Springfield
JCL	Jasper County Library, Rensselaer, Indiana
KDLA	Kentucky Department for Libraries and Archives, Frankfort
KSHS	Kansas State Historical Society, Topeka
LC	Manuscript Division, Library of Congress, Washington, D.C.
LSA	Louisiana State Archives, Baton Rouge
LSU	Special Collections, Louisiana State University Libraries, Baton Rouge
MC	Museum of the Confederacy, Richmond
MDAH	Mississippi Department of Archives and History, Jackson
MHM	Military History Museum, Kentucky Department of Military Affairs, Frankfort
MHS	Missouri Historical Society, St. Louis
MSA	Maryland State Archives, Annapolis
NA	National Archives and Records Administration, Washington, D.C.
NCDAH	North Carolina Department of Archives and History, Raleigh
OHS	Ohio Historical Society, Columbus
PC	Private Collection
SCA	South Carolina Archives and History Center, Columbia
SCL	South Caroliniana Library, University of South Carolina, Columbia
SHC	Southern Historical Collection, University of North Carolina, Chapel Hill
TSLA	Tennessee State Library and Archives, Nashville

UA	Special Collections, University of Arkansas Libraries, Fayetteville
UVW	Special Collections, University of Virginia's College at Wise Library, Wise
VHS	Virginia Historical Society, Richmond
VSL	Virginia State Library, Richmond
WMHC	Western Manuscripts and Historical Collection, University of Missouri, Columbia
WVU	West Virginia Regional History Collection, West Virginia University Libraries, Charleston

MANUSCRIPTS

Adams-Miller Family Letters, AHC

Samuel A. Agnew Diary, SHC

Oliver Perry Aiken Papers, IHS

Alabama Adjutant General Records, 1862–65, ADAH

Alabama Governor Papers: Andrew B. Moore, ADAH

Alabama Governor Papers: John Gill Shorter, ADAH

Alabama Governor Papers: Thomas H. Watts, ADAH

Amasa O. Allen Correspondence, IHLA

Wellington Allen Reminiscences, WMHC

Thomas Allin Papers, MHS

Amanda Letter, TSLA

Jacob Ammen Papers, ISHL

John Emerson Anderson Memoir, LC

Charles W. Andrews Papers, DU

Henry P. Andrews Papers, ISHL

George Angle Papers, DU

Jonathan D. Ashmore Papers, SCL

Francis F. and Harriet E. Audsley Letters, WMHC

Samuel Ayres Correspondence, KSHS

Bennette M. Bagby Papers, DU

Docton Warren Bagley Papers, DU

G. W. Ballow Letter, WMHC

Nathaniel Prentice Banks Papers, DU

Henrietta Fitzhugh Barr Journal, WVU

Barth Family Papers, WMHC

Albert A. Batchelor Papers, LSU

Bates Family Papers, MHS

Charles Edward Bates Papers, VHS

Thomas Baxter Papers, DU

Beall-Booth Family Papers, FC

Alfred W. Bell Papers, DU

Mary Walker Meriwether Bell Letters, TSLA
William R. Bell Papers, LSU
Ansel Bement Letter, FC
Benecke Family Papers, WMHC
John Forbes and Diana Benjamin Letters, WMHC
William Bishop Papers, WMHC
Richard Emerson Blair Letters, IHS
Blow Family Papers, MHS
Sherman Bodwell Diaries and Notebooks, KSHS
Bond and Fentriss Family Papers, SHC
Priscilla Munnikhuysen Bond Papers, LSU
Milledge Luke Bonham Papers, SCA
John A. Boon Papers, ISHL
P. L. Bonny Papers, LSU
Frederick Fillison Bowen Papers, VHS
William Henry Boyce Letters, SHC
John R. Boyd Handbill, WMHC
Boykin Family Papers, SHC
William H. Bradbury Papers, LC
James E. Bradley Family Papers, LSU
Elias Brady Papers, SHC
James Madison Brannock Papers, VHS
Lizzie E. Brannock Papers, MHS
Branscomb Family Letters, ADAH
Louis A. Bringier and Family Papers, LSU
William L. Broaddus Papers, DU
James O. Broadhead Papers, MHS
John McDonald Broadside, MHS
Charles S. Brown Papers, DU
Ephraim Brown Papers, OHS
John William Brown Diary, AHC
Marthe M. Brown Reminiscences, PC
William Brown Memoir, WMHC
Charles Buford Papers, LC
John Buie Papers, DU
Stephen Gano Burbridge Papers, FC
Burlingame Family Papers, MHS
B. Burnham Letters, LSU
John C. Burris Papers, MDAH
James C. Burruss Family Papers, LSU
Lucy Wood Butler Papers, SHC
George Hovey Cadman Papers, SHC

Peter Calhoun Correspondence, OHS
Campbell Family Papers, DU
Andrew Jackson Campbell Diary, TSLA
Jacob M. Campbell Papers, WVU
James H. Campbell Reminiscences, PC
James L. Campbell Papers, DU
Cannon County, Tennessee, Records, 1861–65, TSLA
Milton T. Carey Papers, FC
Thomas Carney Letters, KSHS
Christopher (Kit) Carson Collection, MHS
John H. Carson Papers, LSU
George W. Carvill Letters, WMHC
Mary Jane (Cook) Chadwick Diary, DU
A. B. Chandler Letters, VSL
Robert I. Chester Biographical Sketch, TSLA
Joseph Chew Papers, WMHC
Chisolm Family Papers, SHC
E. A. Christy Letter, WMHC
Civil War Collection: Confederate, TSLA
Civil War Letters, WVU
Civil War Miscellaneous Papers, WVU
Civil War Soldier Letters, ADHA
John Francis Hamtramck Claiborne Papers, SHC
Charles Clark Papers, MDAH
Charles Clark and Family Papers, MDAH
Henry Toole Clark Papers, NCDAH
Joseph Dent Clark Papers, TSLA
Peter F. Clark Papers, MHS
Edmund James Cleveland Diary, SHC
Charles L. Coburn Correspondence, OHS
Mary Catherine Noland Cochran Diary, FC
William Johnston Cocke Papers, DU
Sarah (Horton) Cockrell Papers, DU
Alexander D. Coffee Papers, SHC
William Cogswell Letter, LSU
Abraham Cole Muster Roll, 1864, WMHC
Daniel Coleman Diary, SHC
Confederate Cavalry Battalion History File, ADAH
Confederate Cavalry Company History File, ADAH
Confederate Conscript Bureau Papers, SHC
Confederate Military Records, ADAH
Confederate States of America Archives, Army Units, DU

War Letters of Drury Connally, UA
Holmes Conrad Papers, VHS
Benjamin Franklin Cook Memorandum, LSU
Roy Bird Cook Collection, WVU
Cooper Family Papers, TSLA
Edmund Cottle Papers, DU
Josephine Wells Covington Letter, FC
Craft, Fort, and Thorne Family Papers, SHC
Warren D. Crandall Papers, MHS
Henry Clay and William H. Crawford Letters, WMHC
John D. Crawford Letters, WMHC
Crede Family Papers, WMHC
Joseph Crider Letters, WMHC
M. S. Cromwell Letter, UA
Crosier Family Letters, IHS
W. A. Crouch Letters, UA
M. S. Crowell Letters, UA
Samuella (Hart) Curd Diary, VHS
Edwin A. Cutter Papers, DU
John A. B. Dahlgren Papers, LC
Davenport Family Papers, MDAH
Arretta Davidson Letters, WMHC
Lois (Wright) Richardson Davis Papers, DU
Lowndes Henry Davis Papers, MHS
Newton N. Davis Papers, ADAH
Davis-Vandiver Letters, WMHC
John G. Deatherage Memoir, WMHC
Wilse Dial Letter, SHC
Eugene Digges Company Muster Roll, MC
Harry St. John Dixon Papers, SHC
William Y. Dixon Papers, LSU
Grenville M. Dodge Papers, IHLA
Stockly Donelson Papers, TSLA
A. W. Doniphan Letter, WMHC
Dorsey-Fuqua Family Collection, WMHC
Douglass-Maney Family Papers, TSLA
Draper-McClurg Family Papers, WMHC
Dudley Family Papers, FC
Basil Wilson Duke Papers, SHC
Mary Eliza (Powell) Dulany Diary, VHS
Helium H. Dunn Letters, IHS
W. J. Dunn Letter, WMHC

Charles William Dustan Letters, SHC
Nathan G. Dye Papers, DU
Sheldon S. Eaton Letter, MHS
Edmund Curtis Ellis Papers, MHS
Ezekiel John and Thomas C. W. Ellis Family Papers, LSU
James W. Ellis Letters, IHS
John W. Ellis Papers, NCDAH
Eltinge-Lord Family Papers, DU
Francis Marion Emmons Letters, WMHC
Sarah R. Espy Diary, ADAH
Hugh Boyle Ewing Papers, OHS
Thomas Ewing Family Papers, LC
Oren E. Farr Papers, DU
John Newton Ferguson Diary, LC
Mary Fielding Diary, ADAH
William Eppa Fielding Diary, ADAH
Joseph Wilson Fifer Papers, ISHL
Augustus C. Fink Papers, IHS
E. George Flanders Civil War Letters, KSHS
Florida Governor Papers, FSA
Floyd-McAdoo Family Papers, LC
James Fortiner Papers, FC
Kate D. Foster Diary, DU
John C. Francis Family Papers, ADAH
Lucy Virginia French Diaries, TSLA
Marcus Frost Papers, MHS
Louis Fusz Diary, MHS
Daniel B. Gale, MHS
Hamilton R. Gamble Papers, MHS
William W. Garig Family Papers, LSU
Jill Knight Garrett Collection, TSLA
John W. Garriott Letters, WMHC
David Garver Letters, ADAH
Gash Family Papers, NCDAH
Mary A. Gash Papers, NCDAH
Noah L. Gebbart and Emmanuel Martin Gebbart Papers, DU
Georgia Adjutant General Records, GDAH
Georgia Governor Correspondence: Joseph E. Brown, GDAH
Georgia Governor Papers: Joseph E. Brown, GDAH
George Washington Gift Papers, SHC
Lizzie C. Gilmore Papers, WMHC
Roberta Pollock Gilmour Reminiscences, MC

Charles Austin Goddard Papers, VHS
John W. Grattan Papers, LC
William H. Gregg Memoir, WMHC
Benjamin H. Grierson Papers, ISHL
Odon Guitar Collection, WMHC
Odon Guitar Papers, WMHC
M. T. Haderman Papers, DU
Hall Family Papers, ADAH
Wade Hampton Family Papers, SCL
Hardgrove Family Papers, OHS
J. M. Harmon Memoir, TSLA
Charles A. Harper Papers, IHS
John and Alexander Harper Papers, ISHL
Samuel Finley Harper Papers, NCDAH
Isham G. Harris Papers, TSLA
James Henry Harris Diary, IHS
John W. Harris Letters, TSLA
Oliver C. Haskell Diary, IHS
Thomas S. Hawley Papers, MHS
Samuel Haycroft Jr. Journal, FC
William Casper Haynes Papers, KSHS
Hays Family Papers, MHS
George Healey Civil War Letters, IHLA
William McKindree Heath Diary, OHS
William Jefferson Helsley Papers, FC
Abram W. Hendricks Correspondence, IHS
Henry Letters, FC
John A. Higgins Papers, ISHL
Sarah Jane Full Hill Reminiscences, LC
William E. and Bettie R. Hill Letters, WMHC
William G. Hills Diary, LC
Hines Family Papers, FC
Charles F. Hinrichs Papers, WMHC
Hinsdale Family Papers, DU
Cornelius Baldwin Hite Jr. Papers, DU
Edward Henry Hobson Papers, FC
William Alexander Hoke Papers, SHC
Theophilus Hunter Holmes Papers, DU
Holyoke Family Papers, FC
Thomas C. Honnell Correspondence, OHS
Walter King Hoover Collection, TSLA
Walter M. Howland and George S. Tilton Papers, DU

J. B. Hubbell Papers, DU
Cora Owens Hume Diary, FC
Daniel R. Hundley Diary, ADAH
Mary T. Hunley Diary, SHC
Andrew Lucas Hunt Papers, SHC
Nancy Hunt Letters: War Times in Mountain Cove, WVU
Hunter-Taylor Family Papers, LSU
Andrew Jackson Hunter Papers, KSHS
Robert M. T. Hunter Papers, VHS
Andrew Jackson Huntoon Papers, KSHS
William Davies Hutchings Correspondence, IHS
Hutchings-Koehler Papers, IHS
Cyrus Hutchinson Papers, ISHL
Thomas Smith Hutton Diary, TSLA
Frank M. Imboden Diary, WVU
John D. Imboden Papers, MC
Indiana Adjutant General Records, IHS
Edward H. Ingraham Letters, ISHL
Iowa Adjutant General Records, IHLA
Iowa Governor Papers, IHLA
James Ireland Correspondence, IHS
Sallie Lawing Ivie Scrapbook, TSLA
William Hicks Jackson Papers, TSLA
Robert Edwin Jameson Papers, LC
Milton P. Jarnagin Memoirs, TSLA
Johnson Family Papers, FC
Absalom Y. Johnson Diary, FC
Culp P. Johnson Diary, FC
Ellen Cooper Johnson Papers, DU
John Johnston Memoir, TSLA
Kansas Adjutant General Records, KSHS
Kansas Governor Papers: Thomas Carney, KSHS
Kansas Governor Papers: Charles S. Robinson, KSHS
Joseph Warren Keifer Order Book, DU
Joseph Warren Keifer Papers, LC
J. A. Keller Letter, SCL
Robert R. Kellogg Papers, OHS
John R. Kelso Letter, MHS
Kennedy Family Papers, VHS
Will Kennedy Papers, DU
Kennett Family Papers, MHS
Kensinger Family Papers, WMHC

Kentucky Adjutant General Records, MHM
Kentucky Governor Papers: Thomas E. Bramlette, KDLA
Kentucky Governor Papers: Beriah Magoffin, KDLA
Kentucky Governor Papers: James T. Robinson, KDLA
Kentucky Quartermaster General Records, MHM
W. H. Kesterson Correspondence, MHS
Rezin W. Kile Papers, ISHL
Frank L. King Letters, ADAH
Samuel J. Kirkwood Papers, IHLA
Christian D. Koch Family Papers, LSU
Anna Cameron Kranz Papers, MHS
Nate Lanpheur Papers, DU
John W. Large Letters, IHS
Daniel R. Larned Papers, LC
Henry Champlin Lay Papers, SHC
Bazel F. Lazear Papers, WMHC
Elisha Leaming Letters, IHLA
Robert E. Lee Papers, VHS
Samuel P. Lee Papers, LC
Henry C. Leighton Diary, DU
Lenoir Family Papers, SHC
Francis Lieber Papers, SCL
William C. Long Papers, WMHC
Charles Phineas Lord Papers, DU
Louisiana Adjutant General Records, LSA
James Edwin Love Papers, MHS
Low-Mills Family Papers, LC
William Lowery Diary, ADAH
Charles Macgill Papers, DU
Andrew Gordon Magrath Papers, SCA
John B. Magruder Letters, MHS
Stephen R. Mallory Papers, LC
Edwin R. Manson Papers, DU
Rowland S. H. Mantor Papers, WMHC
S. S. Marrett Papers, DU
Isaac Marsh Papers, DU
Marshall Family Papers, FC
Eugene Marshall Papers, DU
Humphrey Marshall Papers, FC
John Wesley Marshall Papers, OHS
Martin Family Papers, MHS
Maryland Adjutant General Papers, MSA

Maryland Governor Papers, MSA

Philip Neely Matlock Memoir, TSLA

Charles Gibbs McAdoo Papers, LC

William E. McBride and Family Papers, MDAH

McCants Family Papers, SCL

Robert Anderson McClellan Papers, DU

Andrew McCollam Papers, SHC

Ellen Waddle McCoy Papers, MHS

James Bennett McCreary Diary, DU

Curtis McDowell Papers, TSLA

James L. McDowell Papers, KSHS

Sallie Florence McEwen Diary, TSLA

McGee and Charles Family Papers, SCL

James Stewart McGehee Family Papers, LSU

Robert T. McMahan Diary, WMHC

Dandridge McRae Papers, UA

John J. McRae Papers, MDAH

A. J. McRoberts Family Letters, WMHC

Meade Family Papers, VHS

John Rodgers Meigs Papers, TSLA

William Newton Mercer Papers, DU

Solomon Meredith Papers, IHS

Alexander R. Miller Diary, LSU

George Knox Miller Papers, SHC

L. C. Miller Memoir, WMHC

Marshall M. Miller Letters, LC

Minos Miller Papers, UA

Marthe E. Mills Reminiscences, PC

D. C. and J. R. Milner Letters, WMHC

Robert H. Milroy Letters, JCL

Minor Family Papers, VHS

Missouri Volunteer Militia Papers, DU

Montgomery Family Papers, LC

W. E. Montgomery Confederate Papers, MDAH

Joshua Burns Moore Diary, ADAH

Thomas O. Moore Papers, LSU

Honore P. Morancy Family Papers, LSU

John Hunt Morgan Papers, SHC

John S. Morgan Papers, IHLA

John T. Morgan Papers, ADAH

L. J. Morgan Letter, ADAH

Morgan-Duke Family Papers, FC

Sarah Hall Morris Papers, OHS
Oliver P. Morton Correspondence, IHS
John S. Mosby Collection, MC
John S. Mosby Papers, LC
John S. Mosby Papers, VHS
John Singleton Mosby Papers, DU
John Singleton Mosby Papers, VHS
Franklin S. Moses Papers, SCL
Moxley-Offutt Family Papers, FC
Nashville Convict Record Books, Prison Records, 1831–1922,
    Record Group 25, NA
Alexander Newburger Diary, LC
Jason Niles Papers, SHC
Mary Catherine Noland Diary, FC
North Carolina Adjutant General Records, NCDAH
LeRoy Moncure Nutt Papers, SHC
Ohio Adjutant General Records, OHS
Kie Oldham Papers, AHC
Charles O'Neil Papers, LC
John F. O'Neil Papers, DU
Emerson Opdycke Papers, OHS
Martin Oviatt Papers, LC
George Washington Parker Papers, MHS
Oliver Parker Letters, WVU
Mosby Monroe Parsons Papers, DU
Robert D. Patrick Letters, LSU
William Patterson Diary, SHC
William Franklin Patterson Papers, LC
John Patton Memoir, LC
Patton-Scott Family Papers, WMHC
Kelion Franklin Peddicord Papers, MHS
John Wilson Peel Papers, UA
Pendleton Family Papers, VHS
Elisha A. Peterson Papers, DU
John J. Pettus Papers, MDAH
Maria Louise Sumner Phillips Journal, WVU
Francis Wilkinson Pickens Papers, SCA
Francis H. Pierpont Papers, WVU
Francis H. Pierpont Papers: Small Collection, WVU
W. S. Pilcher Papers, MC
Gideon Johnson Pillow Papers, DU
Jacob Pinick Papers, WVU

Ethan A. Pinnell Diary, MHS
Alfred Pirtle Papers, FC
David W. Poak Letters, ISHL
John J. Polsley Papers, WVU
Fletcher Pomeroy Diary, KSHS
David Dixon Porter Papers, LC
John M. Porter Memoirs, TSLA
Lemuel C. Porter Diary, FC
Nimrod Porter Diary, SHC
J. L. Power and Family Papers, Pinckney MDAH
L. Powers Papers, MHS
Joseph Hyde Pratt Papers, NCDAH
Reuben T. Prentiss Correspondence, ISHL
Elias Winans Price Papers, SHC
Robert J. Price Letters, IHS
Thomas Prickett Correspondence, IHS
Prisoner of War Collection, MC
Samuel W. Pruitt Papers, FC
John R. Purvis Papers, SHC
John Wesley Puryear Reminiscences, VSL
John P. Quesenberry Diary, WMHC
Quincy-Wendell-Upham-Holmes Family Papers, LC
Quitman Family Papers, SHC
Isaac Nelson Rainey Memoir, TSLA
Mrs. Charles C. Rainwater Reminiscences, DU
Stephen D. Ramseur Papers, NCDAH
D. M. Ransdell Papers, SHC
George J. Reed Family Papers, LC
Edward Paul Reichhelm Collection, LC
Hardie Norville Revelle Letters, FC
Daniel Harris Reynolds Papers, UA
Thomas C. Reynolds Papers, LC
Thomas C. Reynolds Papers, MHS
Nathan J. Rhodes Letters, IHLA
Richardson Collection, GDAH
Frank Liddell Richardson Papers, SHC
Sue Richardson Diary, GDAH
Ella V. Rinker and Reuben E. Hammon Papers, DU
Maraduke Swain Robins Papers, SHC
Robinson Family Papers, WVU
Charles and Sarah T. Robinson Papers, KSHS
W. S. Robinson Papers, DU

Philip Roesch Diary, TSLA
Levi Adolphus Ross Papers, ISHL
Rowland-Shilliday Papers, IHS
John W. Royse Papers, DU
Edmund Ruffin Papers, SHC
Ruffin, Roulhac, and Hamilton Family Papers, SHC
Daniel Ruggles Papers, DU
George Thomas Rust Papers, VHS
Rutherfoord Family Papers, VHS
Hubert Saunders Papers, DU
Phineas Messenger Savery Papers, DU
Francis Bowes Sayre Papers, LC
John M. Schofield Papers, LC
Elvira A. (Weir) Scott Diary, WMHC
W. W. Scott Papers, DU
Helen L. Shell and Mary Virginia Shell Papers, DU
William Shelly Diary, LSU
Shepherdstown [W. Va.] Civil War Diary, WVU
John Sherman Papers, LC
Stephen V. Shipman Diary, ADAH
Isaac Shoemaker Diary, DU
Silliman Family Letters, WMHC
Jane Silvey Papers, SHC
Sims Family Papers, SCL
William Leslie Skaggs Collection, AHC
James F. Sloan Papers, SCL
William E. Sloan Diary, TSLA
E. Hubard Smith Papers, FC
Edmund Kirby Smith Papers, SHC
Horace Smith Papers, DU
Howard Malcolm Smith Papers, LC
Oscar Smith Diary, LC
Sarah Jane Smith Papers, UA
William Austin Smith Diary, TSLA
Sampson Snider Papers, WVU
M. J. Solomons Scrapbook, DU
South Carolina Adjutant and Inspector General Records, SCA
C. Southworth Eugene Papers, DU
Charles H. Sowle Papers, DU
Spaulding Family Papers, LC
Autobiography of P. H. Spears, PC
Thomas Speed Papers, FC

Spencer Family Papers, LC
Abby E. Stafford Papers, DU
Edward P. Stanfield Correspondence, IHS
William and Anna C. Starr Papers, IHS
David T. Stathem Papers, OHS
George L. and Mary E. Stearns Papers, KSHS
Alexander Hamilton Stephens Papers, DU
Hazard Stevens Papers, LC
Thomas C. Stevens Papers, KSHS
John Dunlop Stevenson Papers, MHS
William H. Stewart Diary, SHC
Stith-Moreman Family Papers, FC
Bela T. St. John Papers, LC
Henry L. Stone Papers, IHS
Baron P. and Viola Stow Diaries, IHS
Oscar J. E. Stuart and Family Papers, MDAH
William R. Stuckey Papers, IHS
E. P. Sturges Papers, OHS
Lewis Osborne Sugg Papers, DU
Elihu J. Sutherland Papers, UVW
Franklin D. Swap Papers, MHS
Augustus B. Tanner Correspondence, OHS
Cabell Tavenner and Alexander Scott Withers Papers, DU
Thomas W. Taylor Letters, LC
James Warey Terrell Papers, DU
David Harrison Thomas Papers, OHS
William Holland Thomas Papers, DU
Gordon Thompson Papers, VHS
James Thompson S. Journal, IHS
M. Jeff Thompson Papers, SHC
Stephen W. Thompson Papers, DU
William G. Thompson Correspondence, IHLA
Seneca B. Thrall Letters, IHLA
W. D. Thurmond's Partisan Rangers Descriptive Roll, WVU
William Norwood Tillinghast Papers, DU
Charles Brown Tompkins Papers, DU
George W. Towne Letters, IHLA
Harrison Toy Correspondence, OHS
Samuel Treat Letters, LC
Joseph Harrington Trego Correspondence, KSHS
Joseph Harrington Trego Diary, KSHS
Samuel C. Trescott Correspondence, OHS

John A. Trimble Family Papers, OHS

D. M. and J. H. Tucker Papers, WMHC

Robert A. Tyson Diary, LSU

John C. Underwood Papers, LC

Union Soldier Diary, WVU

United Confederate Veterans Collection, MC

U.S. War Department, Case Files of Investigations by Levi C. Turner and Lafayette C. Baker, Records of Adjutant General's Office, Record Group 94 (M797), NA

———. Court-Martial Cases, 1809–94, Judge Advocate General Records, Record Group 153, NA

———. Letters Received by Confederate Secretary of War, War Department Collection of Confederate Records, Record Group 109, NA

———. Letters Received by Executive, 1860–63, Records of Louisiana Government, 1850–88, War Department Collection of Confederate Records, Record Group 109, NA

———. Letters Received by Provost Marshal, Department of Arkansas, Records of U.S. Army Continental Commands, 1821–1920, Record Group 393, NA

———. Letters Received by Provost Marshal, Department of the Gulf and Louisiana, Records of U.S. Army Continental Commands, 1821–1920, Record Group 393, NA

———. Letters Received by U.S. Secretary of War: Irregular Series, 1861–66, Records of the Office of the Secretary of War, Record Group 107 (M492), NA

———. Letters Received by U.S. Secretary of War: Main Series, 1801–70, Records of the Office of the Secretary of War, Record Group 107 (M221), NA

———. Letters Sent by Confederate Secretary of War, War Department Collection of Confederate Records, Record Group 109 (M522), NA

———. Letters Sent by Provost Marshal, Department of Arkansas, 1863–64, Records of U.S. Army Continental Commands, Record Group 393, NA

———. Letters Sent by U.S. Secretary of War, Military Affairs, 1800–1889, Records of the Office of the Secretary of War, Record Group 107 (M6), NA

———. List of Bushwhackers, Guerrillas, etc., Department of Arkansas, Records of U.S. Army Continental Commands, Record Group 393, NA

———. Provost Marshal Correspondence, Department of Kentucky, 1862–69, Records of U.S. Army Continental Commands, 1821–1920, Record Group 393, NA

———. Records of Courts-Martial, 1861–65, War Department Collection of Confederate Records, Record Group 109, NA

———. Records Relating to Confederate Prisoners of War, War Department Collection of Confederate Records, Record Group 109, NA

———. Register of Partisan Rangers, War Department Collection of Confederate Records, Record Group 109, NA

———. Rosters of Commissioned Officers of Battalions, War Department Collection of Confederate Records, Record Group 109, NA

———. Two or More Names File, Department of Arkansas, Records of U.S. Army Continental Commands, 1821–1920, Record Group 393, NA

———. Union Provost Marshal Files Relating to Individual Citizens, War Department Collection of Confederate Records, Record Group 109 (M345), NA

———. Union Provost Marshal Files Relating to Two or More Citizens, War Department Collection of Confederate Records, Record Group 109 (M416), NA

Zebulon Baird Vance Papers, NCDAH

Edwin A. Van Cise Papers, LC

Arthur Vanhorn Papers, LC

Alonzo A. Van Vlack Letters, ADAH

Virginia Cavalry Papers: 43rd Battalion, MC

Virginia Governor Executive Letter Books: Francis Harrison Pierpont, VSL

Virginia Governor Executive Papers: John Letcher, VSL

Virginia Governor Executive Papers: Francis Harrison Pierpont, VSL

Virginia Governor Executive Papers: William Smith, VSL

Sarah Lois Wadley Papers, SHC

Frank Walker Correspondence, KSHS

John D. Walker Correspondence, KSHS

James T. Wallace Diary, SHC

Thomas Wallace Diary, FC

Allen T. Ward Family Correspondence, KSHS

Alfred Warner Papers, MHS

Jane Smith Washington Letter, TSLA

Henry Watson Jr. Papers, DU

Martha Dent Watson Diary, WVU

Robert W. Wells Letters, WMHC

Samuel T. Wells Papers, FC

Kellian Van Rensalear Whaley Papers, VHS

Lysander Wheeler Letters, ISHL

Edward W. Whitacker Letters, VSL

Stephen Whitacker Papers, NCDAH

George W. White Reminiscences, VSL

Henry Solomon White Diary, WVU

John Chester White Memoir, LC

William H. Whitney Letters, LSU

Daniel Webster Whittle Papers, LC

Edward Augustus Wild Papers, SHC

Wildman Family Papers, OHS

Harvey W. Wiley Papers, LC
James Harrison Wilson Papers, LC
Joseph Hubbard Wilson Papers, VHS
Thomas B. Wilson Reminiscences, SHC
John Q. Winfield Letters, SHC
James H. Wingfield Papers, DU
Winn-Cook Family Papers, FC
Winston-Jones Family Papers, FC
James H. Wiswell Papers, DU
C. A. Withers Reminiscences, SHC
Wolz George Papers, MHS
John Taylor Wood Papers, SHC
Robert Woodlief Diary, SCL
Samuel Woods Family Papers, WVU
Julius P. Work Diary, OHS
Worthington Family Papers, LSU
Nathaniel Wright Family Papers, LC
Yates Family Collection, ISHL
John V. Young Letters, WVU
Sarah Frances Young Diary, WVU
John F. Youngs Correspondence, MHS

PERIODICALS

Arkansas True Democrat
Augusta Chronicle and Sentinel
Charleston Mercury
Fort Smith New Era
Galveston Weekly News
The Guerilla
Harper's Weekly
Leslie's Illustrated Newspaper
[Little Rock] Constitutional Union
Memphis Daily Appeal
Mobile Advertiser and Register
New York Times
Richmond Dispatch
Southern Literary Messenger
The Vidette

PUBLISHED PRIMARY SOURCES

Agle, Anna B., and Sidney H. Wanzer, eds. "Dearest Braddie: Love and War in

Maryland, 1860–1861, Part 1." *Maryland Historical Magazine* 88 (Spring 1993): 73–88.

Alberts, Don E. *Rebels on the Rio Grande: The Civil War Journal of A. B. Peticolas*. Albuquerque, N.Mex., 1984.

Alderson, William T., ed. "The Civil War Diary of Captain James Litton Cooper, September 30, 1861 to January 1865." *Tennessee Historical Quarterly* 15 (June 1956): 141–73.

Allen, Desmond Walls, ed. *Turnbo's Tales of the Ozarks: War and Guerrilla Stories*. Conway, Ark., 1989.

Allison, Young F. "Sue Mundy: An Account of the Terrible Kentucky Guerrilla of Civil War Times." *Register of Kentucky Historical Society* 57 (October 1959): 295–316.

Ambrose, Daniel Leib. *From Shiloh to Savannah: The Seventh Illinois Infantry in the Civil War*. Edited by Daniel E. Sutherland. DeKalb, Ill., 2003.

Ambrose, Stephen E., ed. *A Wisconsin Boy in Dixie: Civil War Letters of James K. Newton*. Madison, Wisc., 1961.

Anderson, John Q., ed. *Campaigning with Parsons' Texas Cavalry Brigade, C.S.A.: The War Journals and Letters of the Four Orr Brothers, 12th Texas Cavalry Regiment*. Hillsboro, Tex., 1967.

Andrews, Alice E., ed. *Christopher C. Andrews: Recollections, 1829–1922*. Cleveland, 1928.

Angle, Paul M., ed. *Three Years in the Army of the Cumberland: The Letters and Diary of Major James M. Connolly*. Bloomington, Ind., 1959.

Athearn, Robert G., ed. *Soldier in the West: The Civil War Letters of Alfred Lacey Hough*. Philadelphia, 1957.

Axford, Faye Acton, ed. *The Journals of Thomas Hubbard Hobbs*. Tuscaloosa, Ala., 1976.

Badger, David W., ed. "Civil War Letters of Corporal David W. Badger." *Flashback* 47 (February 1997): 24–30.

Baird, Nancy C., ed. *Journals of Amanda Virginia Edmonds: Lass of Mosby's Confederacy, 1859–1867*. Stephens City, Va., 1984.

Baird, W. David, ed. *A Creek Warrior for the Confederacy: The Autobiography of Chief G. W. Grayson*. Norman, Okla., 1988.

Baker, T. Lindsay, ed. *Confederate Guerrilla: The Civil War Memoir of Joseph Bailey*. Fayetteville, Ark., 2007.

Banasik, Michael E., ed. *Missouri in 1861: The Civil War Letters of Franc B. Wilkie, Newspaper Correspondent*. Iowa City, Iowa, 2001.

———, ed. *Serving with Honor: The Diary of Captain Eathan Allen Pinnell of the Eighth Missouri Infantry (Confederate)*. Iowa City, Iowa, 1999.

Bandy, William T., trans. "Civil War Notes of a French Volunteer." *Wisconsin Magazine of History* 45 (Summer 1962): 239–45.

Barnes, Lela, ed. "An Editor Looks at Early-Day Kansas: The Letters of Charles Monroe Chase." *Kansas Historical Quarterly* 26 (Summer 1960): 113–51.

Barr, Alwyn, ed. "Records of the Confederate Military Commission in San Antonio, July 2–October 10, 1862." *Southwestern Historical Quarterly* 73 (October 1969): 243–74.

Barry Louise, ed. "With the First U.S. Cavalry in Indian Country, 1859–1861 Concluded." *Kansas Historical Quarterly* 24 (Winter 1958): 399–425.

Barton, O. S. *Three Years with Quantrill: A True Story Told by His Scout John McCorkle*. 1914. Repr., Norman, Okla., 1992.

Basler, Roy P., ed. *The Collected Works of Abraham Lincoln*. 8 vols. New Brunswick, N.J., 1953.

Baxter, William. *Pea Ridge and Prairie Grove; or, Scenes and Incidents of the War in Arkansas*. 1864. Repr., Fayetteville, Ark., 2000.

Bearss, Edwin C., ed. *The Civil War Letters of Major William G. Thompson of the 20th Iowa Infantry Regiment*. Fayetteville, Ark., 1966.

————, ed. *Louisiana Confederate: Diary of Felix Pierre Poche*. Trans. Eugenie W. Somdal. Natchitoches, La., 1972.

Beatty, John. *The Citizen-Soldier; or, Memoirs of a Volunteer*. Cincinnati, 1879.

Bennett, Lyman G. "Recruiting in Dixie: An Eyewitness Account of a Civil War Guerilla Expedition." *Christian County Historian* 4 (Summer 1990): 14–16, (Fall 1990): 28–30, (Winter 1990): 43–46, (Spring 1991): 57–73.

Bennett, Stewart, and Barbara Tillery, eds. *The Struggle for the Life of the Republic: A Civil War Narrative by Brevet Major Charles Dana Miller, 76th Ohio Volunteer Infantry*. Kent, Ohio, 2004.

Benson, Evelyn A., comp. *With the Army of West Virginia, 1861–1864: Reminiscences and Letters of Lt. James Abraham Lancaster*. Lancaster, Pa., 1974.

Bentley, James R., ed. "The Civil War Memoirs of Captain Thomas Speed." *Filson Club History Quarterly* 44 (July 1970): 235–72.

Bigelow, Martha M., ed. "Plantation Lessee Problems in 1864." *Journal of Southern History* 27 (August 1961): 354–67.

Bishop, A. W. *Loyalty on the Frontier; or, Sketches of Union Men of the South-West; with Incidents and Adventures in Rebellion on the Border*. Edited by Kim Allen Scott. 1863. Repr., Fayetteville, Ark., 2003.

Blackford, L. Minor. "The Great John B. Minor and His Cousin Mary Face the War: Correspondence between the Professor of Law and the Lynchburg Blackfords, 1860–1864." *Virginia Magazine of History and Biography* 61 (October 1953): 439–49.

Blunt, James G. "General Blunt: Account of His Civil War Experiences." *Kansas Historical Quarterly* 1 (May 1932): 211–65.

Bock, H. Riley, ed. "Confederate Col. A. C. Riley: His Reports and Letters: Part I." *Missouri Historical Review* 85 (January 1991): 158–81.

Bramlette, Thomas E. *Message of Governor T. E. Bramlette to the General Assembly of Kentucky.* Frankfort, 1865.

Brewerton, G. Douglas. *The War in Kansas.* New York, 1856.

Brigham, Loriman S., ed. "The Civil War Journal of William B. Fletcher." *Indiana Magazine of History* 57 (March 1961): 41–76.

Britton, Ann Hartwell, and J. Thomas Reed, eds. *To My Beloved Wife and Boy at Home: The Letters and Diaries of Orderly Sergeant John F. L. Hartwell.* London, 1997.

Britton, Wiley. *The Civil War on the Border.* 2 vols. 3rd ed. New York, 1899.

Brook, Dan R., ed. "The Rudolph Collection of Civil War Letters." *West Virginia History* 50 (1991): 129–52.

Brophy, Patrick, ed. *"Found No Bushwhackers": The 1864 Diary of Sgt. James P. Mallery, Company A, Third Wisconsin Cavalry.* Nevada, Mo., 1988.

———, ed. *In the Devil's Dominions: A Union Soldier's Adventures in "Bushwhacker County": The Journal of Charles W. Porter.* Nevada, Mo., 1998.

Brown, George William. *Baltimore and the Nineteenth of April 1861: A Study of the War.* 1887. Repr., Baltimore, 2001.

Brown, Peter A., ed. *Take Sides with the Truth: The Postwar Letters of John Singleton Mosby to Samuel F. Chapman.* Lexington, Ky., 2007.

Brownell, Henry Howard. *War-Lyrics and Other Poems.* Boston, 1866.

Buck, Lucy Rebecca. *Sad Earth, Sweet Heaven: The Diary of Lucy Rebecca Buck during the War between the States.* Edited by William P. Buck. Birmingham, Ala., 1973.

Butler, Benjamin. *Private and Official Correspondence of General Benjamin F. Butler during the Period of the Civil War.* 5 vols. Norwood, Mass., 1917.

Calhoun, H. M. *Twixt North and South.* Edited by Harlan M. Calhoun. Franklin, W.Va., 1974.

Carter, Ruth C., ed. *For Honor, Glory, and Union: The Mexican and Civil War Letters of Brigadier General William Haines Lytle.* Lexington, Ky., 1999.

Carter, William D., ed. *"As It Was": The Story of Douglas John Carter's Life.* N.p., 1981.

Cash, William M., and Lucy Sommerville Howorth, eds. *My Dear Nellie: The Civil War Letters of William L. Nugent to Eleanor Smith Nugent.* Jackson, Miss., 1977.

Chadwick, Mrs. W. D. "Civil War Days in Huntsville: A Diary by Mrs. W. D. Chadwick." *Alabama Historical Quarterly* 9 (Summer 1947): 199–333.

Chaliand, Gerard, ed. *The Art of War in World History: From Antiquity to the Nuclear Age.* Berkeley, Calif., 1994.

Chance, Joseph., ed. *My Life in the Old Army: The Reminiscences of Abner Doubleday, from the Collections of the New York Historical Society.* Fort Worth, Tex., 1998.

———, ed. *Mexico under Fire: Being the Diary of Samuel Ryan Curtis, 3rd Ohio*

Volunteer Regiment, during the American Military Occupation of Northern
Mexico, 1846–1847. Fort Worth, Tex., 1994.

Chandler, Allen D., comp. *The Confederate Records of the State of Georgia:
Official Correspondence of Governor Joseph E. Brown, 1860–1865.* 6 vols.
Atlanta, 1909–10.

Chapman, R. D. "A Georgia Soldier." *Confederate Veteran* 37 (July 1930): 270–
73, (August 1930): 308–11.

Clarke, Norman E., ed. *Warfare along the Mississippi: The Letters of Lieutenant
Colonel George E. Currie.* Mount Pleasant, Mich., 1961.

Cockrell, Thomas D., and Michael B. Ballard, eds. *Chickasaw: a Mississippi
Scout for the Union: The Civil War Memoir of Levi H. Naron as Recounted by
R. W. Surby.* Baton Rouge, La., 2005.

Colton, Kenneth E., ed. "The Irrepressible Conflict of 1861: The Letters of
Samuel Ryan Curtis." *Annals of Iowa* 24 (July 1942): 14–58.

Confederate Congress. "Proceedings of the First Confederate Congress: First
and Second Sessions." *Southern Historical Society Papers* 45 (May 1925).

———. "Proceedings of the First Confederate Congress: Second Session."
Southern Historical Society Papers 46 (January 1928).

———. "Proceedings of the First Confederate Congress: Fourth Session."
Southern Historical Society Papers 50 (December 1953).

Connelley, William E., ed. "The Civil War Diary of John Howard Kitts."
Collections of the Kansas State Historical Society 14 (1918): 318–32.

Conner, Daniel Ellis. *A Confederate in the Colorado Gold Fields.* Edited by
Donald J. Berthrong and Odessa Davenport. Norman, Okla., 1970.

Corsan, W. C. *Two Months in the Confederate States: An Englishman's Travels
through the South.* Edited by Benjamin H. Trask. Baton Rouge, La., 1996.

Cory, Charles E. "The Sixth Kansas Cavalry and Its Commanders." *Collections of
the Kansas State Historical Society* 11 (1910): 217–38.

Courtney, W. J. "Guerrilla Warfare in Missouri." *Confederate Veteran* 29 (March
1921): 104.

Cox, Jacob D. *Military Reminiscences of the Civil War.* 2 vols. New York, 1900.

Cox, William E., ed. "The Civil War Letters of Laban Gwinn: A Union Refugee."
West Virginia History 43 (Spring 1982): 227–45.

Crabtree, Beth Gilbert, and James W. Patton, eds. *"Journal of a Secesh Lady":
The Diary of Catherine Anne Devereux Edmondston, 1860–1866.* Raleigh,
N.C., 1979,

Crist, Lynda L., et al., eds. *The Papers of Jefferson Davis.* 11 vols. to date. Baton
Rouge, La., 1971–.

Crook, George. *General George Crook: His Autobiography.* Edited by Martin F.
Schmitt. 2nd ed. Norman, Okla., 1960.

Cudworth, Darius A. "Memories of Fifty Years Ago." *Military Order of the Loyal
Legion of the United States* 31 (1904): 223–37.

Cunningham, John. "A Night with Guerrillas." *Confederate Veteran* 31 (December 1923): 465.

———. "One Night with Guerrillas." *Confederate Veteran* 18 (December 1910): 557.

Curl, Donald Walter, ed. "A Report from Baltimore." *Maryland Historical Magazine* 64 (Fall 1969): 280–87.

Curtis, Finley Paul, Jr. "The Home Guard." *Confederate Veteran* 27 (March 1919): 86–88.

———. "Typical Guerrillas of the War Period: Representing the Character of the Home Guard Enemy." *Confederate Veteran* 27 (April 1919): 132–36.

Cutrer, Thomas W., ed. *Our Trust Is in the God of Battle: The Civil War Letters of Robert Franklin Bunting, Chaplain, C.S.A.* Knoxville, Tenn., 2006.

Danforth, Willis. "How I Came to Be in the Army, and General E. A. Paine's Plan of Federal Salvation." *Military Order of the Loyal Legion of the United States* 46 (1886): 324–39.

Darrow, Caroline Baldwin. "Recollections of the Twiggs Surrender." In *Battles and Leaders of the Civil War*, edited by Robert Underwood Johnson and Clarence Clough Buel, 1:33–39. New York, 1887–88.

Davidson, Garber A., ed. *The Civil War Letters of the Late 1st Lieutenant James J. Hartley, 122nd Ohio Infantry Regiment.* Jefferson, N.C., 1998.

Davis, Kathleen., ed. *Such Are the Trials: The Civil War Diaries of Jacob Gantz.* Ames, Iowa, 1991.

Davis, Robert S., Jr., ed. "Memoir of a Partisan War: Sion Darnell Remembers North Georgia, 1861–1865." *Georgia Historical Quarterly* 80 (Spring 1996): 93–116.

Davis, William C., and Meredith L. Swentor, eds. *Bluegrass Confederate: The Headquarters Diary of Edward O. Guerrant.* Baton Rouge, La., 1999.

Dickison, Mary Elizabeth. *Dickison and His Men: Reminiscences of the War in Florida.* 1890. Repr., Jacksonville, Fla., 1984.

Dimond, E. Grey, and Herman Hattaway, eds. *Letters from Forest Place: A Plantation Family's Correspondence, 1846–1881.* Jackson, Miss., 1993.

Doerschuk, Albert N., ed. "Extracts from War-Time Letters, 1861–1864." *Missouri Historical Review* 23 (October 1928): 99–110.

Doran, Thomas F. "Kansas Sixty Years Ago." *Collections of the Kansas State Historical Society* 15 (1919–22): 482–501.

Dougan, Michael B., ed. *Confederate Women of Arkansas in the Civil War, 1861–1865: Memorial Reminiscences.* 1907. Repr., Fayetteville, Ark., 1993.

Dowdey, Clifford, and Louis H. Manarin, eds. *The Wartime Papers of R. E. Lee.* New York, 1961.

Drickamer, Lee C., and Karen D. Drickamer, eds. *Fort Lyon to Harper's Ferry: On the Border of North and South with "Rambling Jour."* Shippensburg, Pa., 1987.

Duke, Basil W. *A History of Morgan's Cavalry.* Edited by Fletcher Holland. Bloomington, Ind., 1960.

Dumond, Dwight Lowell., ed. *Southern Editorials on Secession.* New York, 1931.

Du Pont, Samuel Francis. *Official Dispatches and Letters of Rear Admiral Du Pont, U.S. Navy: 1846–48, 1861–63.* Wilmington, Del., 1883.

Dyer, Gustavus W., and John Trotwood Moore, comps. *The Tennessee Civil War Veterans Questionnaires.* 5 vols. Easley, S.C., 1985.

Eakin, Joanne Chiles, ed. *A Civil War Guerrilla Goes on Trial: The Case of G. Byron Jones in 1864.* Independence, Mo., 1997.

———, ed. *The Little Gods: Union Provost Marshals in Missouri, 1861–1865.* 2 vols. Independence, Mo., 1996.

———, ed. *Recollections of Quantrill's Guerrillas, as Told by A. J. Walker.* Independence, Mo., 1996.

———, ed. *Warren Welch Remembers: A Guerrilla Fighter from Jackson County, Missouri.* Independence, Mo., 1997.

Easley, Virginia, ed. "Journal of the Civil War in Missouri: 1861, Henry Martyn Cheavens." *Missouri Historical Review* 56 (October 1961): 12–25.

Editors. "The Civil War Diary of John Howard Kitts." *Collections of the Kansas State Historical Society* 14 (1915–16): 318–27.

———. "Civilized (?) Warfare." *Confederate Veteran* 25 (August 1917): 349–51.

———. "An Interesting Letter." *Pennsylvania Magazine of History and Biography* 25 (1901): 77–79.

———. "The Letters of Samuel James Reader, 1861–1863." *Kansas Historical Quarterly* 9 (February 1940): 26–57.

———. "Roll of Quirk's Scouts, C.S.A." *Register of Kentucky State Historical Society* 2 (January 1904): 35–36.

———. "A Warrensburg Family during the Civil War." *Missouri Historical Review* 38 (July 1944): 452–58.

Edwards, John N. *Noted Guerrillas; or, Warfare of the Border.* St. Louis, 1877.

———. *Shelby and His Men; or, The War in the West.* Cincinnati, 1867.

Elder, Donald C., III, ed. *Love amid the Turmoil: Civil War Letters of William and Mary Vermilion.* Iowa City, Iowa, 2003.

Ellis, Daniel. *Thrilling Adventures of Daniel Ellis.* New York, 1867.

Estes, Thomas Jerome. *Early Days and War Times in Northern Arkansas.* Yellville, Ark., n.d.

Evans, Clarence., ed. and trans. "Memoirs, Letters, and Diary Entries of German Settlers in Northwest Arkansas, 1853–1863." *Arkansas Historical Quarterly* 6 (Fall 1947): 225–49.

Fitzhugh, George. "The Times and the War." *DeBow's Review.* 31 (July): 2–4.

Ford, John Salmon. *Rip Ford's Texas.* Edited by Stephen B. Oates. Austin, Tex., 1963.

Ford, Sally R. *Raids & Romances of Morgan and His Men.* Mobile, Ala., 1863.

Fox, S. M. "The Early History of the Seventh Kansas Cavalry." *Collections of the Kansas State Historical Society, 1909–1910* 11 (1910): 238–53.

Frazier, Margaret Mendenhall, trans. *Missouri Ordeal, 1862–1864: Diaries of Willard Hall Mendenhall*. Newhall, Calif., 1985.

Furry, William, ed. *The Preacher's Tale: The Civil War Journal of Rev. Francis Springer, Chaplain, U.S. Army of the Frontier*. Fayetteville, Ark., 2001.

Galbraith, Loretta, and William Galbraith, eds. *A Lost Heroine of the Confederacy: The Diaries and Letters of Belle Edmondson*. Jackson, Miss., 1990.

Gallagher, Gary W., ed. *Fighting for the Confederacy: The Personal Recollections of General Edward Porter Alexander*. Chapel Hill, N.C., 1989.

Gallaher, Ruth A., ed. "Peter Wilson in the Civil War: "In Battle and on Parole." *Iowa Journal of History and Politics* 40 (July 1942): 261–320.

———, ed. "Peter Wilson in the Civil War: The Training Period." *Iowa Journal of History and Politics* 40 (April 1942): 153–203.

———, ed. "Peter Wilson in the Civil War, 1863–1865." *Iowa Journal of History and Politics*. 40 (October 1942): 339–414.

Garrett, Jill Knight, ed. *The Civil War Diary of Andrew Jackson Campbell*. Columbia, Tenn., 1965.

Giunta, Mary A., ed. *A Civil War Soldier of Christ and Country: The Selected Correspondence of John Rodgers Meigs, 1859–1864*. Urbana, Ill., 2006.

Glover, Robert W., ed. "The War Letters of a Texas Conscript in Arkansas." *Arkansas Historical Quarterly* 20 (Winter 1961): 355–87.

Goyne, Minetta Altgelt, ed. *Lone Star and Double Eagle: Civil War Letters of a German-Texas Family*. Fort Worth, Tex., 1982.

Graf, Leroy P., et al., eds. *Papers of Andrew Johnson*. 16 vols. Knoxville, Tenn., 1967–2000.

Greene, Albert Robinson. "From Bridgeport to Ringgold by Way of Lookout Mountain." *Military Order of the Loyal Legion of the United States* 37 (1890): 271–312.

———. "Campaigning in the Army of the Frontier." *Collections of the Kansas State Historical Society* 14 (1915–18): 283–310.

Greene, John T., ed. *The Ewing Family Civil War Letters*. East Lansing, Mich., 1994.

Guyer, Max Hendricks, ed. "The Journal and Letters of Corporal William O. Gulick." *Iowa Journal of Politics and History* 28 (April 1930): 194–267.

———, ed. "The Journal and Letters of Corporal William O. Gulick." *Iowa Journal of Politics and History* 28 (July 1930): 390–455.

———, ed. "The Journal and Letters of Corporal William O. Gulick." *Iowa Journal of Politics and History* 28 (October 1930): 543–603.

Gwin, Minrose C., ed. *A Woman's Civil War: A Diary with Reminiscences of the War*. Madison, Wisc., 1992.

Hallum, John. *Reminiscences of the Civil War*. 2 vols. Little Rock, Ark., 1903.

Hamilton, J. G. de Roulhac, ed. *The Papers of Thomas Ruffin*. 4 vols. Raleigh, N.C., 1918–20.

Hardeman, Nicholas P. "Bushwhacker Activity on the Missouri Border: Letters to Dr. Glen O. Hardeman, 1862–1865." *Missouri Historical Review* 58 (April 1964): 265–77.

Harlan, Edgar R., ed. "Benjamin F. Pearson's War Diary" (Pt. 1). *Annals of Iowa* 15 (October 1925): 83–129.

————, ed. "Benjamin F. Pearson's War Diary" (Pt. 2). *Annals of Iowa* 15 (January 1926): 194–222.

Harris, Robert F., and John Niflot, comps. *Dear Sister: The Civil War Letters of the Brothers Gould*. Westport, Conn., 1998.

Hayes, John D., ed. *Samuel Francis Du Pont: A Selection from His Civil War Letters*. 3 vols. Ithaca, N.Y., 1969.

Haynes, Dennis E. *A Thrilling Narrative of the Sufferings of Union Refugees*. Edited by Arthur W. Bergeron Jr. 1866. Repr., Fayetteville, Ark., 2006.

Heartsill, W. W. *Fourteen Hundred and 91 Days in the Confederate Army*. Edited by Bell Irvin Wiley. Wilmington, N.C., 1992.

Herberger, Charles F., ed. *A Yankee at Arms: The Diary of Lieutenant Augustus D. Ayling, 29th Massachusetts Volunteers*. Knoxville, Tenn., 1999.

Herr, Pamela, and Mary Jane Spence, eds. *The Letters of Jessie Benton Frémont*. Urbana, Ill., 1993.

Hinkley, J. W. "Some Experiences of a Veteran in the Rear." *Military Order of the Loyal Legion of the United States* 29 (1893): 112–23.

Hinton, Richard J. *Rebel Invasion of Missouri and Kansas and the Campaign of the Army of the Border against General Sterling Price in October and November 1864*. 1865. Repr., Ottowa, Kans., 1994.

Huff, Leo E., ed. *The Civil War Letters of Albert Demuth and the Roster Eighth Missouri Cavalry [U.S.]*. Springfield, Mo., 1997.

Hughes, Nathaniel Cheairs, ed. *The Civil War Memoir of Philip Daingerfield Stephenson, D.D.* Conway, Ark., 1995.

————, ed. *Liddell's Record: St. John Richardson Liddell*. Baton Rouge, La., 1997.

Hutch, Ronald K., ed. "The Civil War Letters of Herbert Saunders." *Register of the Kentucky Historical Society* 69 (January 1971): 17–29.

Johnson, Adam Rankin. *Partisan Rangers of the Confederate Army*. 1904. Repr., Austin, Tex., 1995.

Johnson, Robert Underwood, and Clarence Clough Buel, eds. *Battles and Leaders of the Civil War*. 4 vols. New York, 1887–88.

Johnston, Frontis W., and Joe A. Mobley, eds. *The Papers of Zebulon Baird Vance*. 2 vols. Raleigh, N.C., 1963–95.

Johnston, James J., ed. "The Summer of 1863." *White River Valley Historical Quarterly* 38 (Spring 1999): 3–14.

Jomini, Baron de. *The Art of War*. Philadelphia, 1862.

Jones, John B. *A Rebel War Clerk's Diary at the Confederate State Capital*. 2 vols. Philadelphia, 1866.

Kamphoefner, Walter D., and Wolfgang Helbich, eds. *Germans in the Civil War: The Letters They Wrote Home*. Translated by Susan Carter Vogel. Chapel Hill, N.C., 2006.

Keifer, Joseph Warren. *Slavery and Four Years of War: A Political History of Slavery in the United States* 2 vols. New York, 1900.

Kemper, Mary Lee. "Civil War Reminiscences of Danville Female Academy." *Missouri Historical Review* 62 (April 1968): 314–20.

Kendall, George Wilkins. *Dispatches from the Mexican War*. Edited by Lawrence Delbert Cress. Norman, Okla., 1999.

Kentucky Adjutant General. *Report of the Adjutant General of the State of Kentucky*. 2 vols. Frankfort, Ky., 1866.

Kiper, Richard L., Jr. *Dear Catharine, Dear Taylor: The Civil War Letters of a Union Soldier and His Wife*. Lawrence, Kans., 2002.

Kronenberg, Kenneth, trans. *Lives and Letters of an Immigrant Family: The von Dreveldt's Experiences along the Missouri, 1844–1866*. Lincoln, Neb., 1998.

Lafferty, W. T., ed. "Civil War Reminiscences of John Aker Lafferty." *Register of the Kentucky Historical Society* 59 (January 1961): 1–28.

Langsdorf, Edgar, ed. "The Letters of Joseph H. Trego, 1857–1864—Linn County Pioneer: Part Two, 1861, 1862." *Kansas Historical Quarterly* 19 (August 1951): 287–309.

———, ed. "The Letters of Joseph H. Trego, 1857–1864—Linn County Pioneer: Part Three, 1863, 1864." *Kansas Historical Quarterly* 19 (November 1951): 381–400.

Langsdorf, Edgar, and R. W. Richmond, eds. "Letters of Daniel R. Anthony, 1857–1862—Continued." *Kansas Historical Quarterly* 24 (Autumn 1958): 351–70.

———, eds. "Letters of Daniel R. Anthony, 1857–1862—Concluded." *Kansas Historical Quarterly* 24 (Winter 1958): 458–75.

Laqueur, Walter, ed. *The Guerrilla Reader: A Historical Anthology*. Philadelphia, 1977.

Larimer, Charles E., ed. *Love and Valor: Intimate Civil War Letters between Captain Jacob and Emiline Ritner*. Western Springs, Ill., 2000.

Leib, Charles. *Nine Months in the Quartermaster's Department; or, The Chances of Making a Million*. Cincinnati, 1862.

Lemke, Walter J., ed. "A Confederate Soldier Writes to His Wife in Washington County." *Flashback* 2 (October 1952): 5–6.

————, ed. *The War-Time Letters of Albert O. McCollom, Confederate Soldier.* Fayetteville, Ark., 1961.

Lewis, A. B. "Chasing Guerrillas in Arkansas." *Confederate Veteran* 29 (June 1921): 220–22.

Lieber, Francis. *The Miscellaneous Writings of Francis Lieber.* 2 vols. Philadelphia, 1880.

Lincecum, Jerry B., et al., eds. *Gideon Lincecum's Sword: Civil War Letters from the Texas Home Front.* Denton, Tex., 2001.

Lowe, David W., ed. *Meade's Army: The Private Notebooks of Lt. Col. Theodore Lyman.* Kent, Ohio, 2007.

Lumpkin, Martha N., ed. *"Dear Darling Loulie": Letters of Cordelia Lewis Scales to Loulie W. Irby during and after the War between the States.* Boulder, Colo., 1955.

Lupold, Harry Forrest, ed. "An Ohio Doctor Views Campaigning on the White River, 1864." *Arkansas Historical Quarterly* 34 (Winter 1975): 333–51.

Maddox, George T. *Hard Trials and Tribulations of an Old Confederate Soldier.* Edited by Richard T. Norton and J. Troy Massey. 1897. Repr., Springfield, Mo., 1997.

Malin, James C., ed. "Letters of Julia Louisa Lovejoy, 1856–1864: Part Five, 1860–1864." *Kansas Historical Quarterly* 16 (May 1948): 175–211.

Marcotte, Frank B., ed. *Private Osborne, Massachusetts 23rd Volunteers: Burnside's Expedition, Roanoke Island, Second Front Against Richmond.* Jefferson, N.C., 1999.

Marshall, Jeffrey D., ed. *A War of the People: Vermont Civil War Letters.* Hanover, N.H., 1999.

Marszalek, John F., ed. *The Diary of Miss Emma Holmes, 1861–1866.* Baton Rouge, La., 1979.

Martin, George W. "War Incidents at Kansas City." *Collection of Kansas State Historical Society* 11 (1910): 282–91.

Mathews, Alfred E. *Interesting Narrative: Being a Journal of the Flight of Alfred E. Mathews.* N.p., 1861.

Mathias, Frank Furlong, ed. *Incidents and Experiences in the Life of Thomas W. Parsons from 1826 to 1900.* Lexington, Ky., 1975.

McBrien, D. D., ed. "Letters of an Arkansas Confederate Soldier: Pt. I." *Arkansas Historical Quarterly* 2 (March 1943): 58–70.

————, ed. "Letters of an Arkansas Confederate Soldier: Pt. II." *Arkansas Historical Quarterly* 2 (June 1943): 171–84.

————, ed. "Letters of an Arkansas Confederate Soldier: Pt. III." *Arkansas Historical Quarterly* 2 (September 1943): 268–86.

McCutchan, Kenneth P., ed. *Dearest Lizzie: The Civil War as Seen through the Eyes of Lt. Colonel James Maynard Shanklin.* Evansville, Ind., 1988.

McDonald, Cornelia Peak. *A Woman's Civil War: A Diary with Reminiscences of the War from 1862*. Edited by Minrose C. Gwen. Madison, Wisc., 1992.

McDonald, William N. *A History of the Laurel Brigade*. Edited by Bushrod C. Washington. Baltimore, 1907.

McGhee, James E., ed. and comp. *Voices of the Swamp Fox Brigade: Supplemental Letters, Orders and Documents of General M. Jeff Thompson's Command, 1861–1862*. Independence, Mo. 1999.

McLarty, Vivian Kirkpatrick, ed. "The Civil War Letters of Colonel Bazel F. Lazear: Part I." *Missouri Historical Review* 44 (April 1950): 254–73.

————, ed. "The Civil War Letters of Colonel Bazel F. Lazear: Part II." *Missouri Historical Review* 44 (July 1950): 387–401.

————, ed. "The Civil War Letters of Colonel Bazel F. Lazear: Part III." *Missouri Historical Review* 45 (October 1950): 47–63.

McMillan, Malcolm C., ed. *The Alabama Confederate Reader*. Tuscaloosa, Ala., 1963.

Merrill, W. E. "Block-houses for Railroad Defense in the Department of the Cumberland." *Military Order of the Loyal Legion of the United States* 3 (1888): 416–21.

Miller, Robert Ryal, ed. *The Mexican War Journal and Letters of Ralph W. Kirkham*. College Station, Tex., 1991.

Mills, George, ed. "The Sharp Family Civil War Letters." *Annals of Iowa* 34 (January 1959): 481–532.

Missouri State Guard. *Letter and Order Book Missouri State Guard, 1861–1862*. Edited by James E. McGhee. Independence, Mo., 2001.

Mitchell, Adele H., ed. *The Letters of John S. Mosby* 2nd ed. Clarksburg, Va., 1986.

Mitchell, Frederick W. "Fighting Guerrillas on the La Fourche, La." *Military Order of the Loyal Legion of the United States* 44 (1904): 163–76.

Moneyhon, Carl, ed. "Life in Confederate Arkansas: The Diary of Virginia Gray Davis, 1863–1865, Part I." *Arkansas Historical Quarterly* 42 (Spring 1983): 47–85.

————, ed. "Life in Confederate Arkansas: The Diary of Virginia Gray Davis, 1863–1866, Part II." *Arkansas Historical Quarterly* 42 (Summer 1983): 134–69.

Monks, William. *A History of Southern Missouri and Northern Arkansas*. Edited by John F. Bradbury Jr., and Lou Wehmer. 1907. Repr., Fayetteville, Ark., 2003.

Montgomery, Asbe. *An Account of R. R. Blazer and His Scouts*. Marietta, Ohio, 1865.

Moore, Frank, ed. *The Rebellion Record: A Diary of Events with Documents, Narratives*. 12 vols. New York, 1861–68.

Morgan, Thomas J. "Reminiscences of Service with Colored Troops in the Army of the Cumberland, 1863–65." *Military Order of the Loyal Legion of the United States* 36 (1885): 77–78.

Morrison, James L., Jr., ed. *The Memoirs of Henry Heth*. Westport, Conn., 1974.

Morrison, Marion A. *A History of the Ninth Regiment Illinois Volunteer Infantry*. Monmouth, Ill., 1864.

Morse, Loren J., ed. *Civil War Diaries and Letters of Bliss Morse*. Tahlequah, Okla., 1985.

Mosgrove, George Dallas. *Kentucky Cavaliers in Dixie: Reminiscences of a Confederate Cavalryman*. Edited by Bell Irwin Wiley. Wilmington, N.C., 1991.

Moss, James E., ed. "A Missouri Confederate in the Civil War: The Journal of Henry Martyn Cheavens, 1862–1863." *Missouri Historical Review* 57 (October 1962): 16–52.

Munson, John W. *Reminiscences of a Mosby Guerrilla*. New York, 1906.

Murphree, Joel. "Autobiography and Civil War Letters of Joel Murphree of Troy, Alabama, 1864–1865." *Alabama Historical Quarterly* 19 (Spring 1957): 170–208.

Murray, Donald M., and Robert M. Rodney, eds. "The Letters of Peter Bryant, Jackson County Pioneer." *Kansas Historical Quarterly* 27 (Autumn 1961): 320–52.

———, eds. "The Letters of Peter Bryant, Jackson County Pioneer, Concluded." *Kansas Historical Quarterly* 27 (Winter 1961): 469–96.

Myers, Robert Manson, ed. *The Children of Pride: A True Story of Georgia and the Civil War*. New Haven, Conn., 1972.

Neely, Mark E., Jr. "'Unbeknownst' to Lincoln: A Note on Radical Pacification in Missouri during the Civil War." *Civil War History* 44 (September 1998): 212–16.

Nevins, Allan, ed. *Diary of Battle: The Personal Journals of Colonel Charles S. Wainwright, 1861–1865*. New York, 1962.

Nevins, Allan, and Milton Halsey Thomas, eds. *The Diary of George Templeton Strong*. 4 vols. New York, 1952.

Nichols, William E. "Fighting Guerrillas in West Virginia." *Civil War Times Illustrated* 6 (April 1967): 20–25.

Nolte, Eugene A. "Downeasters in Arkansas: Letters of Roscoe G. Jennings to His Brother." *Arkansas Historical Quarterly* 18 (Spring 1959): 3–25.

Norton, Richard L., ed. *Behind Enemy Lines: The Memoirs and Writings of Brigadier General Sidney Drake Jackman*. Springfield, Mo., 1997.

Oliphant, Mary C. Simms, ed. *The Letters of William Gilmore Simms*. 6 vols. Columbia, S.C., 1952–82.

Park, Ruie Ann Smith, ed. *"Dear Parents": The Civil War Letters of the Shibley Brothers of Van Buren, Arkansas*. Fayetteville, Ark., 1963.

Patrick, Jeffrey L., ed. "This Regiment Will Make a Mark: Letters from a

Member of Jennison's Jayhawkers, 1861–1862." *Kansas History* 20 (Spring 1997): 50–58.

Patrick, Jeffrey L., and Michael L. Price, eds. "Life with the Mountain Feds: The Civil War Reminiscences of William McDowell, 1st Arkansas Cavalry." *Arkansas Historical Quarterly* 64 (Autumn 2005): 287–313.

Pena, Chris, ed. "F. S. Twitchell's Letter Describing a Female Guerrilla." *Louisiana History* 39 (Winter 1998): 85–90.

Perkins, Allen, ed. *Volunteers: The Mexican War Journals of Private Richard Coulter and Sergeant Thomas Barclay, Company E, Second Pennsylvania Infantry.* Kent, Ohio, 1991.

Phillips, David L., and Rebecca L. Hill, eds. *War Stories: Civil War in West Virginia.* Leesburg, Va., 1991.

Phillips, Ulrich B., ed. *Correspondence of Robert Toombs, Alexander H. Stephens, and Howell Cobb.* Washington, D.C., 1913.

Popchock, Barry, ed. *Soldier Boy: The Civil War Letters of Charles O. Musser, 29th Iowa.* Iowa City, Iowa, 1995.

Pratt, Harry E., ed. "Civil War Letters of Brigadier-General William Ward Orne, 1862–1866." *Journal of the Illinois State Historical Society* 23 (July 1930): 246–315.

———, ed. "Civil War Letters of Winthrop S. G. Allen." *Journal of the Illinois State Historical Society* 24 (October 1931): 553–77.

Raab, Steven S., ed. *With the 3rd Wisconsin Badgers: The Living Experience of the Civil War through the Journals of Van R. Willard.* Mechanicsburg, Pa., 1999.

Raines, C. W., ed. *Six Decades in Texas: A Memoir of Francis Richard Lubbock.* Austin, Tex., 1900.

Rainwater, Percy L., ed. "The Civil War Letters of Cordelia Scales." *Journal of Mississippi History* 1 (July 1939): 169–81.

Rea, Ralph R., ed. "Diary of Private John P. Wright, U.S.A., 1864–1865 [1863–64]." *Arkansas Historical Quarterly* 16 (Autumn 1957): 304–18.

Reed, Thomas J., ed. *To My Beloved Wife and Boy at Home: The Letters and Diaries of Orderly Sergeant John F. L. Hartwell.* London, 1997.

Reyburn, Philip J., and Terry L. Wilson, eds. *"Jottings from Dixie": The Civil War Dispatches of Sergeant Major Stephen F. Fleharty, U.S.A.* Baton Rouge, La., 1999.

Rich, A. M. "Remarkable Scouting in Arkansas." *Confederate Veteran* 14 (April 1906): 182–83.

Ridley, Bromfield L., ed. *Battles and Sketches of the Army of Tennessee.* Mexico, Mo., 1906.

Robertson, James I., Jr., ed. *Soldier of Southwestern Virginia: The Civil War Letters of Captain John Preston Sheffey.* Baton Rouge, La., 2004.

————, ed. "'Such Is War': The Letters of an Orderly in the 7th Iowa Infantry." *Iowa Journal of History* 58 (October 1960): 321–56.

Rohr, Nancy M., ed. *Incidents of the War: The Civil War Journal of Mary Jane Chadick*. Huntsville, Ala., 2005.

Romeyn, Henry. "Scouting in Tennessee." *Military Order of the Loyal Legion of the United States* 44 (1905): 241–65.

Ross, FitzGerald. *Cities and Camps of the Confederate States*. Edited by Richard Barksdale Harwell. 1865. Repr., Urbana, Ill., 1997.

Ross, Kirby, ed. *Autobiography of Samuel S. Hildebrand: The Renowned Missouri Bushwhacker*. 1870. Repr., Fayetteville, Ark., 2005.

Roth, Margaret Brobst, ed. *Well Mary: Civil War Letters of a Wisconsin Volunteer*. Madison, Wisc., 1960.

Rowland, Dunbar, ed. *Jefferson Davis, Constitutionalist: His Letters, Papers and Speeches*. 10 vols. Jackson, Miss., 1923.

Ruggles, C. L. *Perils of Scout-life; or, Exploits and Adventures of a Government Scout and Spy in the Great Rebellion*. New York, 1875.

Russell, Charles Wells, ed. *The Memoirs of Colonel John S. Mosby*. Boston, 1917.

Russell, William Howard. *My Diary North and South*. Edited by Eugene H. Berwanger. 1863. Repr., New York, 1988.

Saltador, The. "The Guerrilla." *Fraser's Magazine* 36 (November 1847): 546–57, (December 1847): 719–27.

————. "The Guerrilla." *Fraser's Magazine* 37 (February 1848): 224–31.

Scarborough, William K., ed. *The Diary of Edmund Ruffin*. 3 vols. Baton Rouge, La., 1972–89.

Schaefer, Don, ed. "Civil War Letters of Corporal David W. Badger." *Flashback* 47 (February 1997): 26–28.

Scott, Joe M. *Four Years' Service in the Southern Army*. 1897. Repr., Fayetteville, Ark., 1958.

Scott, John. *Partisan Life with Colonel John S. Mosby*. New York, 1867.

Scott, Paul, ed. "With Tears in Their Eyes." *Civil War Times Illustrated* 21 (January 1983): 26–29.

Sedinger, James D. "War-Time Reminiscences of James D. Sedinger, Company E, 8th Virginia Cavalry (Border Rangers)." *West Virginia History* 51 (1992): 55–78.

Shaw, John, ed. *Crete and James: Personal Letters of Lucretia and James Garfield*. East Lansing, Mich., 1994.

Silver, James W., ed. "The Breakdown of Morale in Central Mississippi in 1864: Letters of Judge Robert S. Hudson." *Journal of Mississippi History* 16 (April 1954): 99–120.

Simms, W. Gilmore. *The Life of Francis Marion*. New York, 1856.

————. *The Partisan: A Romance of the Revolution*. New York, 1864.

————. *War Poetry of the South*. New York, 1867.

Simon, John Y., ed. *The Papers of Ulysses S. Grant*. 26 vols. to date. Carbondale, Ill., 1967–.

Simpson, Brooks D., and Jean V. Berlin, eds. *Sherman's Civil War: Selected Correspondence of William T. Sherman, 1860–1865*. Chapel Hill, N.C., 1999.

Skinner, James L., III., ed. *The Autobiography of Henry Merrell, Industrial Missionary*. Athens, Ga., 1991.

Smith, John David, and William Cooper Jr., eds. *A Union Woman in Civil War Kentucky: The Diary of Frances Peter*. Lexington, Ky., 2000.

Smith, Thomas C. *Here's Yer Mule: The Diary of Thomas C. Smith, 3rd Sergeant, Company G, Wood's Regiment, 32nd Texas Cavalry, CSA*. Waco, Tex., 1958.

The Soldier in Our Civil War. Abridged ed. New York, 1894.

Soman, Jean Powers, and Frank L. Byrne, eds. *A Jewish Colonel in the Civil War: Marcus M. Spiegel of the Ohio Volunteers*. Lincoln, Neb., 1995.

Stanton, Carl L., comp. *They Called It Treason: An Account of Renegades, Copperheads, Guerrillas, Bushwhackers and Outlaw Gangs That Terrorized Illinois during the Civil War*. Bunker Hill, Ill., 2002.

Stewart, Norman, ed. "Eight Months in Missouri: The Civil War Letters of Philander H. Nesbit." *Missouri Historical Review* 75 (April 1981): 261–84.

Stone, Henry Lane. *Morgan's Men: A Narrative of Personal Experience*. Louisville, Ky., 1919.

Stone, Lewis P. "I Was Completely Surrounded by a Band of Guerrillas." *Civil War Times Illustrated* 10 (December 1971): 26–33.

Sullins, D. *Recollections of an Old Man: Seventy Years in Dixie, 1827–1897*. Bristol, Tenn., 1910.

Summers, Festus P., ed. *Borderland Confederate*. Pittsburgh, 1962.

Sutherland, Daniel E., ed. *A Very Violent Rebel: The Civil War Diary of Ellen Renshaw House*. Knoxville, Tenn., 1996.

Swedberg, Claire E. ed. *Three Years with the 92nd Illinois: The Civil War Diary of John M. King*. Mechanicsburg, Pa., 1999.

Swift, Lester L., ed. "Letters from a Sailor on a Tinclad." *Civil War History* 7 (March 1961): 48–62.

Sylvester, Lorna Lutes, ed. "'Gone for a Soldier': The Civil War Letters of Charles Haring Cox." *Indiana Magazine of History* 68 (March 1972): 24–78.

Terrell, W. H. H. *Indiana Adjutant General Report: Statistics and Documents*. Indianapolis, 1869.

———. *Indiana in the War of the Rebellion: Official Report of W. H. H. Terrell, Adjutant General*. Indianapolis, 1869.

Tharin, R. S. *Arbitrary Arrests in the South; or, Scenes from the Experience of an Alabama Unionist*. 1863. Repr., New York, 1969.

Thomas, Clarence. *General Turner Ashby: The Centaur of the South: A Military Sketch*. Winchester, Va., 1907.

Thornwell, James H. "Our Danger and Our Duty." *DeBow's Review* 33 (May–August 1862): 45–48.

Thorpe, Sheldon B. *History of the Fifteenth Connecticut Volunteers in the War for the Defense of the Union, 1861–1865*. New Haven, Conn., 1893.

Throne, Mildred, ed. *The Civil War Diary of Cyrus F. Boyd, Fifteenth Iowa Infantry, 1861–1863*. Baton Rouge, La., 1998.

———, ed. "The Civil War Diary of John Mackley." *Iowa Journal of History and Politics* 48 (April 1950): 141–68.

———, ed. "A Commissary in the Union Army: Letters of C. C. Carpenter." *Iowa Journal of History and Politics* 53 (January 1955): 59–88.

———, ed. "Diary of W. H. Turner, M.D., 1863." *Iowa Journal of History* 48 (July 1950): 267–82.

———, ed. "An Iowa Doctor in Blue: The Letters of Seneca B. Thrall, 1862–1864." *Iowa Journal of History* 58 (April 1960): 97–188.

———, ed. "Iowa Farm Letters, 1856–1865." *Iowa Journal of History* 58 (January 1960): 37–88.

Tilley, Nannie M., ed. *Federals on the Frontier: The Diary of Benjamin F. McIntyre, 1862–1864*. Austin, Tex., 1963.

Towles, Louis P., ed. *A World Turned Upside Down: The Palmers of South Santee, 1818–1881*. Columbia, S.C., 1996.

Trimble, Sarah Ridley, ed. "Behind the Lines in Middle Tennessee, 1863–65: The Journal of Bettie Ridely Blackmore." *Tennessee Historical Quarterly* 12 (March 1953): 48–80.

Troutman, Richard L., ed. *The Heavens Are Weeping: The Diaries of George Richard Browder, 1852–1886*. Grand Rapids, Mich., 1987.

Tucker, Nathaniel Beverley. *The Partisan Leader: A Tale of the Future*. Edited by C. Hugh Holman. 1836. Repr., Chapel Hill, N.C., 1971.

United Daughters of the Confederacy, Missouri Division. *Reminiscences of the Women of Missouri during the Sixties*. Jefferson City, Mo., 192?.

U.S. Adjutant General. *General Orders Affecting the Volunteer Force: 1863*. Washington, D.C., 1864.

U.S. Navy Department. *Official Records of the Union and Confederate Navies in the War of the Rebellion*. 35 vols. Washington, D.C., 1894–1927.

U.S. War Department. *War of the Rebellion: A Compilation of the Official Records of the Union and Confederate Armies*. 128 vols. Washington, D.C., 1880–1901.

Vaught, Elsa, ed. "Diary of an Unknown Soldier." *Arkansas Historical Quarterly* 18 (Spring 1959): 50–89.

Viles, Jonas, ed. "Documents Illustrating the Troubles on the Border, 1858." *Missouri Historical Review* 1 (October 1907–July 1908): 198–215.

———, ed. "Documents Illustrating the Troubles on the Border, 1860." *Missouri Historical Review* 2 (October 1907–July 1908): 61–77.

Virginia Assembly. *Acts of the General Assembly of the State of Virginia, Passed in 1861–62*. Richmond, 1862.

Vogtsberger, Margaret Ann. *The Dulanys of Welbourne: A Family in Mosby's Confederacy*. Berryville, Va., 1995.

Wagandt, Charles L., ed. "The Civil War Journal of Dr. Samuel A. Harrison." *Civil War History* 13 (June 1967): 131–46.

Walton, Buck. *An Epitome of My Life: Civil War Reminiscences*. Austin, Tex., 1965.

Waterman, Robert E., and Thomas Rothrock, eds. "The Earle-Buchanan Letters of 1861–1876." *Arkansas Historical Quarterly* 33 (Summer 1974): 99–174.

Watson, Ronald G., ed. *From Ashby to Andersonville: The Civil War Reminiscences of George A. Hitchcock*. Campbell, Calif., 1997.

Watson, William. *Life in the Confederate Army*. New York, 1888.

Watts, Hamp B. *The Babe of the Company*. 1913. Repr., Springfield, Mo., 1996.

West Virginia Historical Records Survey. *Calendar of the Arthur I. Boreman Letters*. Charleston, W.Va., 1939.

———. *Calendar of the Francis Harrison Pierpont Letters and Papers in West Virginia Depositories*. Charleston, W.Va., 1940.

Wharton, Henry M., comp. *War Songs and Poems of the Southern Confederacy, 1861–1865*. Philadelphia, 1904.

Whitely, Mrs. W. H., comp. "Civil War Letters." *Register of the Kentucky Historical Society* 72 (July 1974): 263–75.

Williams, Charles Richard, ed. *Diary and Letters of Rutherford Birchard Hayes*. 5 vols. Columbus, Ohio, 1922–26.

Williams, E. Cort. "The Cruise of 'The Black Terror.'" *Military Order of the Loyal Legion of the United States* 3 (1888): 155–57

Williams, Edward B., ed. *Rebel Brothers: The Civil War Letters of the Truehearts*. College Station, Tex., 1995.

Williams, Frederick D., ed. *The Wild Life of the Army: Civil War Letters of James A. Garfield*. East Lansing, Mich., 1964.

Williams, G. Mott, ed. "Letters of General Thomas Williams, 1862." *American Historical Review* 14 (January 1909): 304–28.

Williams, Max, and J. G. de Roulhac Hamilton, eds. *The Papers of William Alexander Graham*. 6 vols. Raleigh, N.C., 1967–76.

Williams, R. H. *With the Border Ruffians: Memories of the Far West, 1852–1868*. Edited by E. W. Williams. London, 1907.

Williams, Robert W., Jr., ed. "With Terry's Texas Rangers: The Letters of Dunbar Affleck." *Civil War History* 9 (September 1963): 299–319.

Williams, Robert W., Jr., and Ralph A. Wooster, eds. "With the Confederate Cavalry in East Texas: The Civil War Letters of Private Isaac Dunbar Affleck." 1 *East Texas Historical Journal* (1963): 17–28.

———, eds. "With Wharton's Cavalry in Arkansas: The Civil War Letters of

Private Isaac Dunbar Affleck." *Arkansas Historical Quarterly* 21 (Autumn 1962): 247–68.

Williams, Walter. "Battle at Centralia, Mo." *Confederate Veteran* 17 (January 1909): 30–31.

Williamson, J. C., ed. "The Civil War Diary of John Coffee Williamson." *Tennessee Historical Quarterly* 15 (March 1956): 61–74.

Williamson, James J. *Mosby's Rangers: A Record of the Operations of the Forty-third Battalion Virginia Cavalry*. New York, 1896.

Wilson, J. Mont. "Killing of Three Brothers: Something of Warfare in Arkansas in 1863." *Confederate Veteran* 5 (April 1897): 155–56.

Wooster, Ralph A., ed. "With the Confederate Cavalry in the West: The Civil War Experiences of Isaac Dunbar Affleck." *Southwestern Historical Quarterly* 88 (July 1979): 1–28.

Worley, Ted R., ed. "Documents Relating to the Arkansas Peace Society of 1861." *Arkansas Historical Quarterly* 17 (November 1958): 82–111.

Wyth, John Allan. *With Sabre and Scalpel: The Autobiography of a Soldier and Surgeon*. New York, 1914.

Yearns, W. Buck, and John G. Barrett, eds. *North Carolina Civil War Documentary*. Chapel Hill, N.C., 1980.

Yeary, Miss Mamie, ed. *Reminiscences of the Boys in Gray, 1861–1865*. Dallas, 1912.

Younger, Cole. *The Story of Cole Younger by Himself*. 1903. Repr., Houston, 1955.

PUBLISHED SECONDARY SOURCES

Abel, Christopher A. "Marines under Fire." *Civil War Times Illustrated* 35 (May 1996): 54–61.

Able, James A., Jr. "The Gray Fox of Dixie." *America Civil War* 8 (November 1995): 38–44.

Ackinclose, Timothy R. *Sabres and Pistols: The Civil War Career of Colonel Harry Gilmor, C.S.A.* Gettysburg, Pa., 1997.

Adams, George R. *General William S. Harney: Prince of Dragoons*. Lincoln, Neb., 2001.

Allmon, William B. "Sneak Attack at Lone Jack." *Civil War Times Illustrated* 35 (April 1996): 62–71.

Anderson, Paul Christopher. *Blood Image: Turner Ashby in the Civil War and the Southern Mind*. Baton Rouge, La., 2002.

Ash, Stephen, V. *Middle Tennessee Society Transformed, 1860–1870: War and Peace in the Upper South*. Baton Rouge, La., 1988.

———. "Sharks in an Angry Sea: Civilian Resistance and Guerilla Warfare in Occupied Middle Tennessee, 1862–1865." *Tennessee Historical Quarterly* 45 (Fall 1986): 217–29.

————. *When the Yankees Came: Conflict and Chaos in the Occupied South, 1861–1865*. Chapel Hill, N.C., 1995.

Ashdown, Paul, and Edward Caudill. *The Mosby Myth: A Confederate Hero in Life and Legend*. Wilmington, Del., 2002.

Ashley, Robert P. "The St. Albans Raid." *Civil War Times Illustrated* 6 (November 1967): 18–27.

Asprey, Robert B. *War in the Shadows: The Guerrilla in History*. 2 vols. Garden City, N.Y., 1975.

Athey, Lou. "Loyalty and Civil War Liberty in Fayette County during the Civil War." *West Virginia History* 55 (1996): 1–24.

Aumnan, William T. "Neighbor against Neighbor: The Inner Civil War in the Randolph County Area of Confederate North Carolina." *North Carolina Historical Review* 61 (January 1984): 59–92.

Bailey, Anne J. *Between the Enemy and Texas: Parsons's Texas Cavalry in the Civil War*. Fort Worth, Tex., 1989.

————. *The Chessboard of War: Sherman and Hood in the Autumn Campaigns of 1864*. Lincoln, Neb., 2000.

————. "Defiant Unionists: Militant Germans in Confederate Texas." In John C. Inscoe and Robert C. Kenzer, *Enemies of the Country*, 208–28.

————. "Texans Invade Missouri: The Cape Girardeau Raid, 1863." *Missouri Historical Review* 84 (January 1990): 166–87.

Bailey, Anne J., and Daniel E. Sutherland, eds. *Civil War Arkansas: Beyond Battles and Leaders*. Fayetteville, Ark., 2000.

Bailey, John W., Jr. "The McNeill Rangers and the Capture of Generals Crook and Kelley." *Maryland Historical Magazine* 62 (March 1967): 47–63.

Bakeless, John. "Catching Harry Gilmor." *Civil War Times Illustrated* 10 (April 1971): 34–40.

Baker, Jean H. *The Politics of Continuity: Maryland Political Parties from 1858 to 1870*. Baltimore, 1973.

Baker, Robin E. "Class Conflict and Political Upheaval: The Transformation of North Carolina Politics during the Civil War." *North Carolina Historical Review* 69 (April 1992): 148–78.

Baldwin, Leo T. "First Blood in Baltimore." *America's Civil War* 8 (November 1995): 30–36.

Ball, Alan R. "Night of the Burning Bridges." *America's Civil War* 9 (January 1997): 50–56.

Ballard, Michael B. *Vicksburg: The Campaign That Opened the Mississippi*. Chapel Hill, N.C., 2004.

Barnes, Kenneth C. *Who Killed John Clayton? Political Violence and the Emergence of the New South, 1861–1893*. Durham, N.C., 1998.

————. "The Williams Clan: Mountain Farmers and Union Fighters in North

Central Arkansas." In *Civil War Arkansas*, edited by Anne J. Bailey and Daniel E. Sutherland, 155–75.

Barnett, Cornelli. "Guerilla Warfare." *Horizon* 11 (Winter 1969): 4–11.

Barney, William L. *Flawed Victory: A New Perspective on the Civil War.* New York, 1975.

Barrett, John G. *The Civil War in North Carolina.* Chapel Hill, N.C., 1963.

Barton, Lon Carter. "The Reign of Terror in Graves County." *Register of the Kentucky State Historical Society* 46 (April 1948): 484–95.

Beals, Carleton. *War within a War: The Confederacy against Itself.* Philadelphia, 1965.

Bearss, Edwin C. "Calendar of Events in Mississippi, 1861–1865." *Journal of Mississippi History* 21 (April 1959): 85–112.

———. "General Bussey Takes Over at Fort Smith." *Arkansas Historical Quarterly* 24 (Autumn 1965): 220–38.

———. "The White River Expedition, June 10–July 15, 1862." *Arkansas Historical Quarterly* 21 (Winter 1962): 305–62.

Bearss, Edwin C., and Arrell M. Gibson. *Fort Smith: Little Gibraltar on the Arkansas.* Norman, Okla., 1969.

Beckett, Ian F. W. *Modern Insurgencies and Counter-Insurgencies: Guerrillas and Their Opponents since 1750.* London, 2001.

Bennett, Michael J. *Union Jacks: Yankee Sailors in the Civil War.* Chapel Hill, N.C., 2004.

Bennett, Ron. "Ira Van Deusen: A Federal Volunteer in North Alabama." *Alabama Historical Quarterly* 27 (Fall and Winter 1965): 199–211.

Bergeron, Arthur W., Jr. "Dennis Haynes and His Thrilling Narrative of the Sufferings of the Martyrs of Liberty of Western Louisiana." *Louisiana History* 38 (Winter 1997): 29–42.

———. *Guide to Louisiana Confederate Military Units, 1861–1865.* Baton Rouge, La. 1989.

———. "The Jackson Barracks Civil War Document Collection." *Louisiana History* 36 (Summer 1995): 325–34.

Beringer, Richard E., et al. *Why the South Lost the Civil War.* Athens, Ga., 1986.

Berkey, Jonathan M. "Fighting the Devil with Fire: David Hunter Strother's Private Civil War." In *Enemies of the Country*, edited by John C. Inscoe and Robert C. Kenzer, 18–36.

Bettersworth, John K. *Confederate Mississippi: The People and Policies of a Cotton State in Wartime.* Baton Rouge, La., 1943.

Bible, Donahue. "Shattered Like Earthen Vessels." *Civil War Times Illustrated* 36 (December 1997): 48–54, 86–87.

Birtle, Andrew J. *U.S. Army Counterinsurgency and Contingency Operations and Doctrine, 1861–1941.* Washington, D.C., 2003.

Bittle, George C. "Florida Prepares for War, 1860–61." *Florida Historical Quarterly* 51 (October 1972): 143–52.

Blain, William T. "'Banner' Unionism in Mississippi: Choctaw County, 1861–1869." *Mississippi Quarterly* 29 (Spring 1976): 207–20.

Boehm, Robert B. "Battle of Rich Mountain." *Civil War Times Illustrated* 8 (February 1970): 4–9.

Bohannon, Keith S. "They Had Determined to Root Us Out: Dual Memoirs by a Unionist Couple in Blue Ridge Georgia." In *Enemies of the Country*, edited by John C. Inscoe and Robert C. Kenzer, 97–120.

Boman, Dennis K. *Lincoln's Resolute Unionist: Hamilton Gamble, Dred Scott Dissenter and Missouri's Civil War Governor*. Baton Rouge, La., 2006.

Boone, Jennifer K. "'Mingling Freely': Tennessee Society on the Eve of the Civil War." *Tennessee Historical Quarterly* 51 (Summer 1996): 137–45.

Bowen, Don R. "Counterrevolutionary Guerilla War: Missouri, 1861–1865." *Conflict* 8 (1988): 69–78.

———. "Guerilla War in Western Missouri, 1862–1865: Historical Extensions of the Relative Deprivation Hypothesis." *Comparative Studies in Society and History* 19 (January 1977): 30–51.

———. "Quantrill, James, Younger, et al.: Leadership in a Guerilla Movement, Missouri, 1861–1865." *Military Affairs* 41 (February 1977): 42–48.

Bradbury, John F., Jr. "'Buckwheat Cake Philanthropy': Refugees and the Union Army in the Ozarks." *Arkansas Historical Quarterly* 57 (Autumn 1998): 233–54.

———. "'This War Is Managed Mighty Strange': The Army of Southeastern Missouri, 1862–1863." *Missouri Historical Review* 89 (October 1995): 28–47.

Bradley, George C., and Richard L. Dahlen. *From Conciliation to Conquest: The Sack of Athens and the Court-Martial of Colonel John B. Turchin*. Tuscaloosa, Ala., 2006.

Bradley, Michael. "In the Crosshairs: Southern Civilians Targeted by the U.S. Army." *North & South* 10 (March 2008): 46–61.

Bradley, Michael, and Milan Hal. "'Shoot If You Can by Accident.'" *North & South* 3 (November 1999): 33–46.

Brant, Marley. *The Outlaw Youngers: A Confederate Brotherhood*. Lanham, Md., 1992.

Brasseaux, Carl. "Ozème Carrière and the St. Landry Jayhawkers." In *The Civil War in Louisiana*, edited by Arthur W. Bergeron Jr., 640–46. Lafayette. La., 2002.

Breeden, James O. "Oscar Lieber: Southern Scientist, Southern Patriot." *Civil War History* 36 (September 1990): 226–49.

Brewer, James D. *The Raiders of 1862*. Westport, Conn., 1997.

Bright, Simeon Miller. "The McNeill Rangers: A Study in Confederate Guerrilla Warfare." *West Virginia History* 12 (July 1951): 338–94.

Britton, Wiley. *The Aftermath of the Civil War*. Kansas City, Mo., 1924.

Brophy, Patrick. *Bushwhackers of the Border: The Civil War Period in Western Missouri*. Nevada, Mo., 1980.

Brown, Andrew. "The First Mississippi Partisan Rangers, C.S.A." *Civil War History* 1 (December 1955): 371–99.

———. "Sol Street: Confederate Partisan Leader." *Journal of Mississippi History* 21 (July 1959): 155–73.

Brown, Richard Maxwell. *No Duty to Retreat: Violence and Values in American History and Society*. New York, 1991.

———. *Strain of Violence: Historical Studies of American Violence and Vigilantism*. New York, 1975.

———. "Western Violence: Structure, Values, Myth." *Western Historical Quarterly* 24 (February 1993): 5–20.

Browning, Judkin. "Removing the Mask of Nationality: Unionism, Racism, and Federal Military Occupation in North Carolina, 1862–1865." *Journal of Southern History* 71 (August 2005): 589–620.

Brownlee, Richard S. *Gray Ghosts of the Confederacy: Guerrilla Warfare in the West, 1861–1865*. Baton Rouge, La., 1958.

Bruce, Dickson D. *Violence and Culture in the Antebellum South*. Austin, Tex., 1979.

Brugioni, Dino A. "The Meanest Bushwhacker: Bloody Bill Anderson." *Blue & Gray* 8 (June 1991): 32–36.

Bryant, Thomas Julian. "A War Time Militia Company." *Iowa Journal of History and Politics* 10 (July 1912): 403–14.

Buker, George E. *Blockaders, Refugees, and Contrabands: Civil War on Florida's Gulf Coast, 1861–1865*. Tuscaloosa, Ala., 1993.

Bunch, Clea Lutz. "Confederate Women in Arkansas Face 'the Fiends in Human Shape.'" *Military History of the West* 27 (Fall 1997): 173–87.

Burkhardt, George S. *Confederate Rage, Yankee Wrath: No Quarter in the Civil War*. Carbondale, Ill., 2007.

Bushong, Millard K. *General Turner Ashby and Stonewall: Valley Campaign*. Verona, Va., 1980.

Busick, Sean R. *A Sober Desire for History: William Gilmore Simms as Historian*. Columbia, S.C., 2005.

Butler, Lindley S. *Pirates, Privateers, and Rebel Raiders of the Carolina Coast*. Chapel Hill, N.C., 2000.

Bynum, Victoria E. *The Free State of Jones: Mississippi's Longest Civil War*. Chapel Hill, N.C., 2001.

Cain, Marvin, and John F. Bradbury Jr. "Union Troops and the Civil War in Southwestern Missouri and Northwestern Arkansas." *Missouri Historical Review* 88 (July 1994): 29–47.

Campbell, Jacqueline Glass. *When Sherman Marched North from the Sea: Resistance on the Confederate Home Front.* Chapel Hill, N.C., 2003.

Campbell, Thomas. *Fire and Thunder: Exploits of the Confederate States Navy.* Shippensburg, Pa., 1997.

Canan, Howard V. "Milton Burch: Anti-Guerrilla Fighter." *Missouri Historical Review* 59 (January 1965): 223–42.

———. "The Missouri Paw Paw Militia of 1863–1864." *Missouri Historical Review* 62 (July 1968): 431–48.

Carlson, David. "The Loanly Runagee: Draft Evaders in Confederate South Georgia." *Georgia Historical Quarterly* 84 (Winter 2000): 589–615.

Carnahan, Burrus M. "Lincoln, Lieber and the Laws of War: The Origins and Limits of the Principle of Military Necessity." *American Journal of International Law* 92 (April 1998): 213–31.

Carroll, George. "Lewis Wetzel: Warfare Tactics on the Frontier." *West Virginia History* 50 (1991): 79–90.

Carter, Arthur B. *The Tarnished Cavalier: Major General Earl Van Dorn, C.S.A.* Knoxville, Tenn., 1999.

Carter, Dan T. *When the War Was Over: The Failure of Self-Reconstruction in the South, 1865–1867.* Baton Rouge, La., 1985.

Casstevens, Frances H. *The Civil War and Yadkin County, North Carolina.* Jefferson, N.C., 1997.

———. *Edward A. Wild and the African Brigade in the Civil War.* Jefferson, N.C., 2003.

Castel, Albert E. "The Bloodiest Man in American History." *American Heritage* 11 (October 1960): 22–24, 97–99.

———. *Civil War Kansas: Reaping the Whirlwind.* 1958. Repr., Lawrence, Kans., 1997.

———. *Decision in the West: The Atlanta Campaign of 1864.* Lawrence, Kans., 1992.

———. *General Sterling Price and the Civil War in the West.* Baton Rouge, La., 1968.

———. "The Guerilla War, 1861–1865." *Civil War Times Illustrated.* Special Issue (October 1974).

———. "The Jayhawkers and Copperheads of Kansas." *Civil War History* 5 (September 1959): 283–93.

———. "Kansas Jayhawking Raids into Western Missouri in 1861." *Missouri Historical Review* 54 (October 1959): 1–11.

———. "Order No. 11 and the Civil War on the Border." *Missouri Historical Review* 47 (July 1963): 357–68.

———. "Quantrill's Bushwhackers: A Case Study in Partisan Warfare." *Civil War History* 13 (March 1967): 40–50.

———. *Tom Taylor's Civil War.* Lawrence, Kans., 2000.

———. *William Clarke Quantrill: His Life and Times*. 1962. Repr., Norman, Okla., 1999.

———. *Winning and Losing in the Civil War: Essay and Stories*. Columbia, S.C., 1996.

Castel, Albert, and Thomas Goodrich. *Bloody Bill Anderson: The Short, Savage Life of a Civil War Guerrilla*. Mechanicsburg, Pa., 1998.

Cauthen, Charles E. *South Carolina Goes to War, 1860–1865*. Chapel Hill, N.C., 1950.

Cheatham, Gary L. "'Desperate Characters': The Development and Impact of the Confederate Guerrillas in Kansas." *Kansas History* 14 (Autumn 1991): 144–61.

———. "Divided Loyalties in Civil War Kansas." *Kansas History* 11 (Summer 1988): 93–107.

Cheeks, Robert C. "Border Rangers' Daring Raid." *America's Civil War* 6 (January 2000): 50–56.

Chicoine, Stephen. *John Basil Turchin and the Fight to Free the Slaves*. Westport, Conn., 2003.

Christ, Mark K., ed. *Rugged and Sublime: The Civil War in Arkansas*. Fayetteville, Ark., 1994.

Cimprich, John. *Fort Pillow, a Civil War Massacre, and Public Memory*. Baton Rouge, La., 2005.

Cisco, Walter Brian. *War Crimes against Southern Civilians*. Gretna, La., 2007.

Clark, Charles B. "Baltimore and the Attack on the Sixth Massachusetts Regiment, April 19, 1861." *Maryland Historical Magazine* 56 (March 1961): 39–71.

Cochran, Darrell. "Confederates' Brilliant Exploit." *America's Civil War* 4 (September 1991): 40–45.

Confer, Clarissa W. *The Cherokee Nation in the Civil War*. Norman, Okla., 2007.

Connelley, William Elsey. *Quantrill and the Border Wars*. Cedar Rapids, Iowa, 1910.

Connelly, Donald B. *John M. Schofield and the Politics of Generalship*. Chapel Hill, N.C., 2006.

Cooling, Benjamin Franklin. *Fort Donelson's Legacy: War and Society in Kentucky and Tennessee, 1862–1863*. Knoxville, Tenn., 1997.

———. *Jubal Early's Raid on Washington, 1864*. Baltimore, 1989.

———. "A People's War: Partisan Conflict in Tennessee and Kentucky." In *Guerrillas, Unionists, and Violence*, edited by Daniel E. Sutherland, 113–32.

Corbin, William E. *A Star for Patriotism: Iowa's Outstanding Civil War College*. Monticello, Iowa, 1972.

Corder, Russell. *The Confederate Invasion of Iowa*. Unionville, Iowa, 1997.

Cornish, Dudley T. *The Sable Arm: Negro Troops in the Union Army, 1861–1865*. New York: W. W. Norton, 1966.

Cornish, Dudley T., and Virginia J. Laas. *Lincoln's Lee: The Life of Samuel Phillips Lee, United States Navy, 1812–1897.* Lawrence. Kans., 1986.

Coulter, E. Merton. *The Civil War and Readjustments in Kentucky.* Chapel Hill, N.C., 1926.

Courtwright, David T. *Violent Land: Single Men and Social Disorder from the Frontier to the Inner City.* Cambridge, Mass., 1996.

Covington, James W. "The Camp Jackson Affair, 1861." *Missouri Historical Review* 55 (April 1961): 197–212.

Cozzens, Peter. *General John Pope: A Life for the Nation.* Urbana, Ill., 2000.

Crawford, Mark J. "An Eye for an Eye." *Columbiad* 2 (Fall 1998): 118–36.

Crawford, Martin. *Ashe County's Civil War: Community and Society in the Appalachian South.* Charlottesville, Va., 2001.

Crawford, Samuel J. *Kansas in the Sixties.* Chicago, 1911.

Crosby, David F. "The Wrong Side of the River." *Civil War Times Illustrated* 36 (February 1998): 48–54.

Crouch, Barry A. "A 'Fiend in Human Shape'?: William Clarke Quantrill and His Biographers." *Kansas History* 22 (Summer 1999): 143–56.

Crouch, Barry A., and Donaly E. Bruce. *Cullen Montgomery Baker: Reconstruction Desperado.* Baton Rouge, La., 1997.

Crouch, Richard E. "Loudoun Rangers." *America's Civil War* 11 (March 1998): 18–24, 64.

———. "The Mobberly Mysteries: The Strange Life and Death of Loudoun County's Exceedingly Romantic Bastard(?)/Hero(?)." *Civil War Quarterly* 7 (December 1986): 32–45.

Crow, Vernon H. *Storm in the Mountains: Thomas' Confederate Legion of Cherokee Indians and Mountaineers.* Cherokee, N.C., 1982.

———. "The Thomas Legion." *Civil War Times Illustrated.* 10 (June 1971): 40–45.

Cuccia, Phillip. "'Gorillas' and White Glove Gents: Union Soldiers in the Red River Campaign." *Louisiana History* 36 (Fall 1995): 413–30.

Cunningham, Frank. *Knight of the Confederacy: General Turner Ashby.* San Antonio, Tex., 1960.

Current, Richard Nelson. *Lincoln's Loyalists: Union Soldiers from the Confederacy.* Boston, 1992.

Curry, Richard O., and F. Gerald Ham, eds. "The Bushwhackers' War: Insurgency and Counter-Insurgency in West Virginia." *Civil War History* 10 (December 1964): 416–33.

Cutrer, Thomas W. *Ben McCulloch and the Frontier Military Tradition.* Chapel Hill, N.C., 1993.

Davis, Michael A. "The Legend of Bill Dark: Guerrilla Warfare, Oral History, and the Unmaking of an Arkansas Bushwhacker." *Arkansas Historical Quarterly* 58 (Winter 1999): 414–29.

Davis, Robert S., Jr. "Forgotten Union Guerrilla Fighters from the North Georgia Mountains." *North Georgia Journal* 5 (Summer 1988): 30–40.

Davis, Stephen. "Jeff Thompson's Unsuccessful Quest for a Confederate Generalship." *Missouri Historical Review* 85 (October 1990): 53–65.

Davis, William C. *"A Government of Our Own": The Making of the Confederacy.* New York, 1994.

———. *An Honorable Defeat: The Last Days of the Confederate Government.* New York, 2001.

———, ed. *The Confederate General.* 6 vols. Mechanicsburg, Pa., 1991.

DeBlack, Thomas A. *With Fire and Sword: Arkansas, 1861–1874.* Fayetteville, Ark., 2003.

Delauter, Roger U., Jr. *McNeill's Rangers.* Lynchburg, Va., 1986.

Demuth, David O. "The Burning of Hopefield." *Arkansas Historical Quarterly* 36 (Summer 1977): 123–28.

Dirck, Brian R. "By the Hand of God: James Montgomery and Redemptive Violence." *Kansas History* 27 (Spring–Summer 2004): 100–115.

Dodd, Donald B. "The Free State of Winston." *Alabama Heritage* 28 (Spring 1993): 8–19.

Dodd, Donald B., and Wynelle S. Dodd. *Winston: An Antebellum and Civil War History of a Hill Country County of North Alabama.* Birmingham, Ala., 1972.

Doll, Howard D. "John Hunt Morgan and the Soldier Printers." *Filson Club History Quarterly* 47 (January 1973): 29–55.

Dollar, Susan E. "The Red River Campaign, Natchitoches Parish, Louisiana: A Case of Equal Opportunity Destruction." *Louisiana History* 43 (Fall 2002): 411–32.

Dougan, Michael B. *Confederate Arkansas: The People and Politics of a Frontier State in Wartime.* Tuscaloosa, Ala., 1976.

Dubay, Robert W. *John Jones Pettus, Mississippi's Fire-Eater: His Life and Times, 1813–1867.* Jackson, Miss., 1975.

Duncan, Richard R. *Beleaguered Winchester: A Virginia Community at War.* Baton Rouge, La., 2007.

———. "The Raid on Piedmont and the Crippling of Franz Sigel in the Shenandoah Valley." *West Virginia History* 55 (1996): 25–40.

Dunn, Durwood. *Cades Cove: The Life and Death of a Southern Appalachian Community, 1818–1937.* Knoxville, Tenn., 1988.

Durden, Robert F. "The American Revolution as Seen by Southerners in 1861." *Louisiana History* 19 (Winter 1978): 33–42.

Durrill, Wayne K. *War of Another Kind: A Southern Community in the Great Rebellion.* New York, 1990.

Eckstein, Harry. "On the Etiology of Internal Wars." *History and Theory* 4 (1965): 134–63.

Edgar, Walter. *Partisans and Redcoats: The Southern Conflict That Turned the Tide of the American Revolution.* New York, 2001.

Editors. "A German Partisan Ranger." *Civil War Times Illustrated* 38 (March 1998): 80

Ellenberger, Matthew. "Whigs in the Streets?: Baltimore Republicanism in the Spring of 1861." *Maryland Historical Magazine* 86 (Spring 1991): 23–38.

Ellington, Ter. *The Myth of the Noble Savage.* Berkeley, Calif., 2001.

Ellis, John. *From the Barrel of a Gun: A History of Guerrilla, Revolutionary and Counter-Insurgency Warfare, from the Romans to the Present.* 1975. Repr., London, 1995.

Engle, Stephen D. *Don Carlos Buell: Most Promising of All.* Chapel Hill, N.C., 1999.

———. *Yankee Dutchman: The Life of Franz Sigel.* Fayetteville, Ark., 1993.

Eno, Clara B. "Activities of the Women of Arkansas during the War between the States." *Arkansas Historical Quarterly* 3 (Spring 1944): 5–27.

Esdaile, Charles J. *Fighting Napoleon: Guerrillas, Bandits and Adventurers in Spain, 1808–1814.* New Haven, Conn., 2004.

Etcheson, Nicole. *Bleeding Kansas: Contested Liberty in the Civil War Era.* Lawrence, Kans., 2004.

Evans, William McKee. *To Die Game: The Story of the Lowry Band, Indian Guerrillas of Reconstruction.* Syracuse, N.Y., 1995.

Evitts, William J. *A Matter of Allegiance: Maryland from 1850 to 1861.* Baltimore, 1974.

Fachs, Alice. *The Imagined Civil War: Popular Literature of the North and South, 1861–1865.* Chapel Hill, N.C., 2001.

Feathers, Tom. "The History of Military Activities in the Vicinity of Fayetteville, Arkansas." *Flashback* 3 (April 1953): 19–27.

Feis, William B. *Grant's Secret Service: The Intelligence War from Belmont to Appomattox.* Lincoln, Neb., 2002.

———. "Jefferson Davis and the 'Guerrilla Option': A Reexamination." In *The Collapse of the Confederacy*, edited by Mark Grimsley and Brooks D. Simpson, 104–28.

Fellman, Michael. "At the Nihilist Edge: Reflections on Guerrilla Warfare during the American Civil War." In *On the Road to Total War*, edited by Stig Forster and Jorg Nagler, 519–40.

———. *Citizen Sherman.* New York, 1995.

———. *Inside War: The Guerrilla Conflict in Missouri during the American Civil War.* New York, 1989.

Ferguson, Clyde R. "Functions of the Partisan Militia in the South during the American Revolution: An Interpretation." In *The Revolutionary War in the South: Power, Conflict, and Leadership: Essays in Honor of John Richarch Olden*, edited by W. Robert Higgins, 239–58. Durham, N.C., 1979.

Fischer, LeRoy H. "A Civil War Experience of Some Arkansas Women in Indian Territory." *Chronicles of Oklahoma* 57 (Summer 1979): 137–63.

Fisher, Noel C. "Definitions of Loyalty: Unionist Histories of the Civil War in East Tennessee." *Journal of East Tennessee History* 67 (1995): 58–88.

———. "'Prepare Them for My Coming': General William T. Sherman, Total War, and the Pacification in West Tennessee." *Tennessee Historical Quarterly* 51 (Summer 1992): 75–86.

———. *War at Every Door: Partisan Politics and Guerrilla Violence in East Tennessee, 1860–1869.* Chapel Hill, N.C., 1997.

Fleche, Andre. "Uncivilized War: The Shenandoah Valley Campaign, the Northern Democratic Press, and the Election of 1862." In *Shenandoah Valley Campaign of 1864*, edited by Gary W. Gallagher, 200–21.

Foner, Eric. *Reconstruction: America's Unfinished Revolution, 1863–1877.* New York, 1988.

Foos, Paul. *A Short, Offhand, Killing Affair: Soldiers and Social Conflict during the Mexican-American War.* Chapel Hill, N.C., 2002.

Forster, Stig, and Nagler Jorg., eds. *On the Road to Total War: The American Civil War and the German Wars of Unification, 1861–1871.* Cambridge, England, 1997.

Foster, Buck T. *Sherman's Mississippi Campaign.* Tuscaloosa, Ala., 2006.

Frank, Joseph Allan. *With Ballot and Bayonet: The Political Socialization of American Civil War Soldiers.* Athens, Ga., 1998.

Frazier, Donald S. "'Out of Stinking Distance': The Guerrilla War in Louisiana." In *Guerrillas, Unionists, and Violence*, edited by Daniel E. Sutherland, 151–70.

Fredrickson, George M. *Why the Confederacy Did Not Fight a Guerrilla War after the Fall of Richmond: A Comparative View.* Gettysburg, Pa., 1996.

Freehling, William W. *The South vs. the South: How Anti-Confederate Southerners Shaped the Course of the Civil War.* New York, 2001.

Friedel, Frank. *Francis Lieber: Nineteenth-Century Liberal.* Baton Rouge, La., 1947.

———. "General Orders 100 and Military Government." *Mississippi Valley Historical Review* 32 (March 1946): 541–56.

Frizzell, Robert W. "'Killed by Rebels': A Civil War Massacre and Its Aftermath." *Missouri Historical Review* 71 (July 1977): 369–95.

Gallagher, Gary W., ed. *The Shenandoah Valley Campaign of 1864.* Chapel Hill, N.C., 2006.

———, ed. "'We Are Our Own Trumpeters': Robert E. Lee Describes Winfield Scott's Campaign to Mexico City." *Virginia Magazine of History and Biography* 95 (July 1987): 363–75.

Gates, John M. "Indians and Insurrectos: The U.S. Army's Experience with Insurgency." *Parameters* 13 (March 1983): 59–68.

———. "People's War in Vietnam." *Journal of Military History* 54 (July 1990): 325–44.

George, Joseph, Jr. "'Black Flag Warfare': Lincoln and the Raids against Richmond and Jefferson Davis." *Pennsylvania Magazine of History and Biography* 115 (July 1991): 291–318.

Gerteis, Louis S. *Civil War St. Louis*. Lawrence, Kans., 2001.

Gildrie, Richard P. "Guerrilla Warfare in the Lower Cumberland River Valley, 1862–1865." *Tennessee Historical Quarterly* 49 (Fall 1990): 161–75.

Gilmore, Donald L. "Total War on the Missouri Border." *Journal of the West* 35 (July 1996): 70–80.

Glatthaar, Joseph T. *March to the Sea and Beyond: Sherman's Troops in the Savannah and Carolina Campaigns*. New York, 1985.

Godbold, E. Stanley, and Mattie V. Russell. *Confederate Colonel and Cherokee Chief: The Life of William Holland Thomas*. Knoxville, 1990.

Goodrich, Thomas. *Black Flag: Guerrilla Warfare on the Western Border, 1861–1865*. Bloomington, Ind., 1995.

———. *Bloody Dawn: The Story of the Lawrence Massacre*. Kent, Ohio, 1991.

———. *War to the Knife: Bleeding Kansas, 1854–1861*. Mechanicsburg, Pa., 1998.

Gordon, Lesley Jill. "'In Time of War': Unionists Hanged in Kinston, North Carolina, February 1864." In *Guerrillas, Unionists, and Violence*, edited by Daniel E. Sutherland, 45–58.

Graham, Adele. "And Strike Again Tomorrow." *Civil War* 8 (November–December 1990): 58–64.

Grant, Carl E. "Partisan Warfare, Model 1861–65." *Military Review* 38 (November 1958): 42–56.

Grimsley, Mark. *The Hard Hand of War: Union Military Policy toward Southern Civilians, 1861–1865*. Cambridge, England, 1995.

Grimsley, Mark, and Brooks D. Simpson, eds. *The Collapse of the Confederacy*. Lincoln, Neb., 2001.

Grimsted, David. *American Mobbing, 1828–1861: Toward Civil War*. New York, 1998.

Groce, W. Todd. *Mountain Rebels: East Tennessee Confederates and the Civil War, 1860–1870*. Knoxville, Tenn., 1999.

Hammond, Michael D. "Arkansas Atlantis: The Lost Town of Napoleon." *Arkansas Historical Quarterly* 65 (Autumn 2006): 201–23.

Hanchett, William. *Irish: Charles G. Halpine in Civil War America*. Syracuse, N.Y., 1970.

Hardeman, Nicholas P. "The Bloody Battle That Almost Happened: William Clarke Quantrill and Pete Hardeman on the Western Border." *Civil War History* 23 (September 1977): 251–58.

Harris, William C. "The Southern Unionist Critique of the Civil War." *Civil War History* 31 (March 1985): 39–56.

Harrison, Lowell H. *The Civil War in Kentucky*. Lexington, Ky., 1975.

Harrison, Noel G. "'Atop an Anvil': The Civilians' War in Fairfax and Alexandria Counties, April 1861–April 1862." *Virginia Magazine of History and Biography* 106 (Spring 1998): 133–64.

Harwell, Richard B. "The Richmond Stage." *Civil War History* 1 (September 1955): 295–304.

———, ed. *The Union Reader*. New York, 1958.

Hatley, Paul B., and Noor Ampssler. "Army General Orders Number 11: Final Valid Option or Wanton Act of Brutality? The Missouri Question in the American Civil War." *Journal of the West* 33 (July 1994): 77–87.

Hauptman, Laurence M. *Between Two Fires: American Indians in the Civil War*. New York, 1995.

Hearn, Chester G. *Admiral David Dixon Porter: The Civil War Years*. Annapolis, Md., 1996.

———. *Ellet's Brigade: The Strangest Outfit of All*. Baton Rouge, La., 2000.

———. *When the Devil Came Down to Dixie: Ben Butler in New Orleans*. Baton Rouge, La., 1997.

Heatwole, John L. *The Burning: Sheridan in the Shenandoah Valley*. Charlottesville, Va., 1998.

Heilbrun, Otto. "Guerrillas in the 19th Century." *Journal of the Royal United Service Institution* 108 (May 1963): 153–58.

Heiman, Leo. "Organized Looting: The Basis of Partisan Warfare." *Military Review* 45 (February 1965): 61–68.

Henry, J. Milton. "The Revolution in Tennessee, February 1861, to June 1861." *Tennessee Historical Quarterly* 18 (June 1959): 99–119.

Herklotz, Hildegarde Rose. "Jayhawkers in Missouri, 1858–1863." *Missouri Historical Review* 18 (October 1923): 64–101.

Herrera, Ricardo A. "Self-Governance and the American Citizen as Soldier, 1775–1861." *Journal of Military History* 65 (January 2001): 21–52.

Hewett, Janet B., ed. *Roster of Confederate Soldiers, 1861–1865*. 16 vols. Wilmington, N.C., 1995.

Hicken, Victor. *Illinois in the Civil War*. Urbana, Ill., 1966.

Higginbotham, Don. *War and Society in Revolutionary America: The Wider Dimensions of Conflict*. Columbia, S.C., 1988.

Hoar, Victor. "Colonel William C. Falkner in the Civil War." *Journal of Mississippi History* 27 (February 1965): 42–62.

Hobsbawm, E. J. *Bandits*. Revised ed. New York, 1989.

———. *Primitive Rebels: Studies in Archaic Forms of Social Movement in the 19th and 20th Centuries*. New York, 1963.

Hoffman, Ronald, and Peter J. Albert, eds. *Arms and Independence: The Military Character of the American Revolution.* Charlottesville, Va., 1984.

Honey, Michael K. "The War within the Confederacy: White Unionists of North Carolina." *Prologue* 18 (Summer 1986): 75–93.

Horan, James D. *Confederate Agent: A Discovery in History.* New York, 1954.

Hornbeck, Betty. *Upshur Brothers of the Blue and the Gray.* Parsons, W.Va., 1967.

House, Thomas L. "James R. Vanderpool: Civil War Union Leader from Newton County." *Newton County Homestead* 1 (Summer 1979): 2–6.

Howard, Nathan. "A Two-Front Dilemma: The Texas Rangers in the Civil War." *Southern Historian* 23 (Spring 2002): 43–55.

Huff, Leo E. "Guerrillas, Jayhawkers and Bushwhackers in Northern Arkansas during the Civil War." *Arkansas Historical Quarterly* 24 (Summer 1965): 127–48.

Hughes, Michael A. "Wartime Gristmill Destruction in Northwest Arkansas and Military Farm Colonies." In *Civil War Arkansas*, edited by Anne J. Bailey and Daniel E. Sutherland, 31–45.

Hulston, John K., and John W. Goodrich. "John Trousdale Coffee: Lawyer, Politician, Confederate." *Missouri Historical Review* 77 (April 1983): 272–95.

Hunsicker, Nova Ingram. "Rayburn the Raider." *Arkansas Historical Quarterly* 7 (September 1948): 87–91.

Hunter, Alexander. *Women of the Debatable Land.* Washington, D.C., 1912.

Hyde, Samuel C., Jr. "Bushwhacking and Barn Burning: Civil War Operations and the Florida Parishes' Tradition of Violence." *Louisiana History* 36 (Spring 1995): 171–86.

———. *Pistols and Politics: The Dilemma of Democracy in Louisiana's Florida Parishes, 1810–1899.* Baton Rouge, La., 1996.

Hyman, Harold M. "Deceit in Dixie." *Civil War History* 3 (March 1957): 65–82.

Inscoe, John C. "Coping in Confederate Appalachia: Portrait of a Mountain Woman and Her Community at War." *North Carolina Historical Review* 69 (October 1992): 388–413.

———. "'Moving through Deserter Country': Fugitive Accounts of the Inner Civil War in Southern Appalachia." In *Civil War in Appalachia*, edited by Kenneth W. Noe and Shannon H. Wilson, 158–86.

———. *Race, War, and Remembrance in the Appalachian South.* Lexington, Ky., 2008.

Inscoe, John C., and Robert C. Kenzer, eds. *Enemies of the Country: New Perspectives on Unionists in the Civil War South.* Athens, Ga., 2001.

Inscoe, John C., and Gordon B. McKinney. *The Heart of Confederate Appalachia: Western North Carolina in the Civil War.* Chapel Hill, N.C., 2000.

James, Nola A. "The Civil War in Independence County, Arkansas." *Independence County Chronicles* 26 (October 1984–July 1985): 1–43.

Janda, Lance. "Shutting the Gates of Mercy: The American Origins of Total War, 1860–1880." *Journal of Military History* 59 (January 1995): 7–26.

Jewett, Clayton E. *Texas in the Confederacy: An Experiment in Nation Building.* Columbia, Mo., 2002.

Joes, Anthony James. *Guerrilla Conflict before the Cold War.* Westport, Conn., 1996.

Johns, John E. *Florida during the Civil War.* Gainesville, Fla., 1963.

Johnson, Ludwell H. *The Red River Campaign: Politics and Cotton in the Civil War.* 1958. Repr., Kent, Ohio, 1996.

Johnson, Timothy D. *Winfield Scott: The Quest for Military Glory.* Lawrence, Kans., 1998.

Johnston, James J. "Jayhawker Stories: Historical Lore in the Arkansas Ozarks." *Mid-South Folklore* 4 (Spring 1976): 3–9.

Joiner, Gary D. *Through the Howling Wilderness: The 1864 Red River Campaign and Failure in the West.* Nashville, Tenn., 2006.

Jones, Allen W. "Military Events in Louisiana during the Civil War, 1861–1865." *Louisiana History* 2 (Summer 1961): 301–21.

———. "Military Events in West Virginia during the Civil War, 1861–1865." *West Virginia History* 47 (1988): 39–52.

Jones, Virgil C. *Gray Ghosts and Rebel Raiders: The Daring Exploits of the Confederate Guerillas.* 1956. Repr., New York, 1995.

———. "The Problem of Writing about the Guerrillas." *Military Affairs* 21 (Summer 1958): 21–25.

Jordan, Thomas E. "Captain Martin Hart's Date with Death." *Civil War Times Illustrated* 36 (May 1997): 40–46.

Josephy, Alvin M., Jr. *The Civil War in the West.* New York, 1991.

Kerby, Robert L. *Kirby Smith's Confederacy: The Trans-Mississippi South, 1863–1865.* Tuscaloosa, Ala., 1972.

———. "Why the Confederacy Lost." *Review of Politics* 35 (July 1973): 326–45.

Kerrihard, Bowen. "Bitter Bushwhackers and Jayhawkers." *America's Civil War* 5 (January 1993): 26–33.

Kibby, Leo P. "Some Aspects of California's Military Problems during the Civil War." *Civil War History* 5 (September 1959): 251–62.

Kinard, Jeff. *Lafayette of the South: Prince Camille de Polignac and the American Civil War.* College Station, Tex., 2001.

Kincaid, Mary Elizabeth. "Fayetteville, West Virginia, during the Civil War." *West Virginia History* 14 (July 1953): 339–64.

Kirkpatrick, Arthur Roy. "Missouri in the Early Months of the Civil War." *Missouri Historical Review* 55 (April 1966): 235–66.

Koblas, John J. *J. J. Dickison: Swamp Fox of the Confederacy.* St. Cloud, Minn., 2000.

Kohl, Rhonda M. "'This Godforsaken Town': Death and Disease at Helena, Arkansas, 1862–63." *Civil War History* 50 (June 2004): 109–44.

Kruman, Marc W. *Parties and Politics in North Carolina, 1836–1865.* Baton Rouge, La., 1983.

Kutger, Joseph P. "Irregular Warfare in Transition." *Military Affairs* 24 (Fall 1960): 113–23.

Kwasny, Mark V. *Washington's Partisan War, 1775–1783.* Kent, Ohio, 1996.

Lady, Claudia Lynn. "Five Tri-State Women during the Civil War: Views on the War." *West Virginia History* 43 (Summer 1982): 303–21.

Langsdorf, Edgar. "Jim Lane and the Frontier Guard." *Kansas Historical Quarterly* 9 (February 1940): 13–25.

Lankford, Nelson. *Richmond Burning: The Last Days of the Confederate Capital.* New York, 2002.

Laqueur, Walter. "The Origins of Guerrilla Doctrine." *Journal of Contemporary History* 10 (July 1975): 341–82.

Lash, Jeffrey N. "'The Federal Tyrant at Memphis': General Stephen A. Hurlbut and the Union Occupation of West Tennessee, 1862–64." *Tennessee Historical Quarterly* 48 (Spring 1989): 15–28.

———. *A Politician Turned General: The Civil War Career of Stephen Augustus Hurlbut.* Kent, Ohio, 2003.

Lathrop, Barnes F. "The Lafourche District in 1861–1862: A Problem in Local Defense." *Louisiana History* 1 (Spring 1960): 99–129.

———. "The Lafourche District in 1862: Militia and Partisan Rangers." *Louisiana History* 1 (Summer 1960): 230–44.

———. "The Lafourche District in 1862: Confederate Revival." *Louisiana History* 1 (Fall 1960): 300–19.

———. "The Lafourche District in 1862: Invasion." *Louisiana History* 2 (Spring 1961): 175–201.

Leckie, William H., and Shirley A. Leckie. *Unlikely Warriors: General Benjamin Grierson and His Family.* Norman, Okla., 1984.

Lenin, V. I. "Partisan Warfare." *Orbis* 2 (Summer 1958): 194–208.

Leonard, Elizabeth D. *All the Daring of a Soldier: Women of the Civil War Armies.* New York, 1999.

Leslie, Edward E. *The Devil Knows How to Ride: The True Story of William Clarke Quantrill and His Confederate Raiders.* New York, 1996.

Levinson, Irving W. *War within War: Mexican Guerrillas, Domestic Elites, and the United States of America, 1846–1848.* Fort Worth, Tex., 2005.

Lindberg, Kip, and Matt Matthews. "'It Haunts Me Night and Day': The Baxter Springs Massacre." *North & South* 4 (June 2001): 42–53.

Linn, Brian McAllister. *The U.S. Army and Counterinsurgency in the Philippines War, 1899–1902.* Chapel Hill, N.C., 1989.

Longacre, Edward G. *Mounted Raids of the Civil War.* New Brunswick, N.J., 1975.

Lonn, Ella. *Desertion during the Civil War.* 1928. Repr., Lincoln, Neb., 1998.

Luraghi, Raimondo. *History of the Confederate Navy.* Annapolis, Md., 1996.

Lyman, William A. "Origins of the Name 'Jayhawker,' and How It Came to Be Applied to the People of Kansas." *Collections of the Kansas State Historical Society* 14 (1918): 203–7.

Mackey, Robert R. "Bushwhackers, Provosts, and Tories: The Guerrilla War in Arkansas." In *Guerrillas, Unionists, and Violence.* edited by Daniel E. Sutherland, 171–85.

———. *The Uncivil War: Irregular Warfare in the Upper South, 1861–1865.* Norman, Okla., 2004.

Madden, David. "Unionist Resistance to Confederate Occupation: The Bridge Burners of East Tennessee." *East Tennessee Historical Society Publications* No. 53 (1981): 22–39.

Mahan, Bruce E. "Home Guards." *Palimpsest* 5 (June 1924): 189–203.

———. "A July Alarm." *Palimpsest* 5 (June 1924): 214–25.

———. "Marching as to War." *Palimpsest* 5 (June 1924): 226–33.

———. "Over the Border." *Palimpsest* 5 (June 1924): 204–13.

Mahon, Michael G. *The Shenandoah Valley, 1861–1865: The Destruction of the Granary of the Confederacy.* Mechanicsburg, Pa., 1999.

Manarin, Louis H., et al., comps. *North Carolina Troops, 1861–1865: A Roster.* 14 vols. Raleigh, N.C., 1966–98.

Mangrum, Robert G. *Route Step March: Edwin M. Stanton's Special Military Units and the Prosecution of the War, 1862–1865.* Manhattan, Kans., 1978.

Mangum, William Preston, III. "Disaster at Woodburn Farm: R. A. Alexander and the Confederate Guerrilla Raids of 1864–1865." *Filson Club History Quarterly* 70 (April 1996): 143–85.

Mann, Ralph. "Ezekiel Counts's Sand Lick Company: Civil War and Localism in the Mountain South." In *Civil War in Appalachia,* edited by Kenneth W. Noe and Shannon H. Wilson, 78–103.

———. "Family Group, Family Migration, and the Civil War in the Sandy Basin of Virginia." *Appalachian Journal* 19 (Summer 1992): 374–93.

———. "Guerrilla Warfare and Gender Roles: Sandy Basin, Virginia, as a Test Case." *Journal of the Appalachian Studies Association* 5 (1993): 59–66.

Marszalek, John F. *Commander of All Lincoln's Armies: A Life of General Henry W. Halleck.* Cambridge, Mass., 2004.

———. *Sherman: A Soldier's Passion for Order.* New York, 1993.

Martin, Bessie. *Desertion of Alabama Troops from the Confederate Army: A Study in Sectionalism.* New York, 1932.

Martin, James B. "Black Flag over the Bluegrass: Guerrilla Warfare in Kentucky, 1863–1865." *Register of the Kentucky Historical Society* 86 (Autumn 1988): 352–75.

Martin, Michael J. "A Match for Mosby?" *America's Civil War* 7 (July 1994): 26–33.

Martin, Richard A. "Defeat in Victory: Yankee Experience in Early Civil War Jacksonville." *Florida Historical Quarterly* 53 (July 1974): 1–32.

Massey, Mary Elizabeth. *Bonnet Brigades*. New York, 1966.

Matheny, H. E. *Wood County, West Virginia, in Civil War Times: With an Account of the Guerrilla Warfare in the Little Kanawha Valley*. Parkersburg, W.Va., 1987.

Matthews, Gary Robert. *Basil Wilson Duke, CSA: The Right Man in the Right Place*. Lexington, Ky., 2005.

Matthews, Matt, and Kip Lindberg. "'Better Off in Hell': The Evolution of the Kansas Red Legs." *North & South* 5 (May 2002): 20–31.

Mays, Thomas D. "The Battle of Saltville." In *Black Soldiers in Blue*, edited by John David Smith, 200–26.

———. *Cumberland Blood: Champ Ferguson's Civil War*. Carbondale, Ill., 2008.

———. *The Saltville Massacre*. Abilene, Tex., 1998.

McCaslin, Richard B. "Dark Corner of the Confederacy: James G. Bourland and the Border Regiment." *Military History of the West* 24 (Spring 1994): 62–70.

———. *Tainted Breeze: The Great Hanging at Gainesville, Texas, 1862*. Baton Rouge, La., 1994.

McClelland, Russ. "'We Were Enemies': Pennsylvanian and Virginia Guerrillas." *Civil War Times Illustrated* 22 (December 1983): 40–45.

McDonnell, Michael A. "Popular Mobilization and Political Culture in Revolutionary Virginia: The Failure of the Minutemen and the Revolution from Below." *Journal of American History* 85 (December 1998): 946–81.

McDonough, James L. *Schofield: Union General in the Civil War and Reconstruction*. Tallahassee, Fla., 1972.

———. *War in Kentucky: From Shiloh to Perryville*. Knoxville, Tenn., 1994.

McGee, Val L. "The Confederate Who Switched Sides—The Saga of Captain Joseph G Sanders." *Alabama Review* 47 (January 1994): 20–28.

McKenzie, Robert Tracy. "Contesting Secession: Parson Brownlow and the Rhetoric of Proslavery Unionism, 1860–61." *Civil War History* 48 (December 2002): 294–312.

———. *Lincolnites and Rebels: A Divided Town in the American Civil War*. New York, 2006.

McKinney, Gordon B. "Layers of Loyalty: Confederate Nationalism and Amnesty Letters from Western North Carolina." *Civil War History* 51 (March 2005): 5–22.

———. "Women's Role in Civil War Western North Carolina." *North Carolina Historical Review* 69 (January 1992): 37–56.

———. *Zeb Vance: North Carolina's Governor and Gilded Age Political Leader.* Chapel Hill, N.C., 2004.

McKivigan, John R., and Stanley Harrold, eds. *Antislavery Violence: Section, Racial, and Cultural Conflict in Antebellum America.* Knoxville, Tenn., 1999.

McKnight, Brian D. *Contested Borderland: The Civil War in Appalachian Kentucky and Virginia.* Lexington, Ky., 2006.

McLean, James. *California Sabers: The 2nd Massachusetts Cavalry in the Civil War.* Bloomington, Ind., 2000.

McMillan, Malcolm C. *The Disintegration of a Confederate State: Three Governors and Alabama's Western Home Front, 1861–1865.* Macon, Ga., 1986.

McMurry, Richard M. *Atlanta 1864: Last Chance for the Confederacy.* Lincoln, Neb., 26–30.

McPherson, James M. *Drawn with the Sword: Reflections on the American Civil War.* New York, 1996.

McWhiney, Grady. *Cracker Culture: Celtic Ways in the Old South.* Tuscaloosa, Ala., 1988.

———. "Jefferson Davis and the Art of War." *Civil War History* 21 June 1975): 101–12.

Meriwether, James B., ed. *South Carolina Women Writers.* Spartanburg, S.C., 1979.

Michot, Stephen S. "'War Is Still Raging in This Part of the Country: Oath-Taking, Conscription, and Guerrilla War in Louisiana's Lafourche Region." *Louisiana History* 38 (Spring 1997): 157–84.

Miller, Edward A., Jr. *Lincoln's Abolitionist General: The Biography of David Hunter.* Columbia, S.C., 1997.

Miller, Robert E. "Daniel Marsh Frost, C.S.A." *Missouri Historical Review* 85 (July 1991): 381–401.

Mobley, Joe A. *"War Governor of the South": North Carolina's Veb Vance in the Confederacy.* Gainesville, Fla., 2005.

Monachello, Anthony. "Struggle for St. Louis." *America's Civil War* 11 (March 1998): 44–49, 74.

Monaghan, Jay. *Swamp Fox of the Confederacy: The Life and Military Services of M. Jeff Thompson.* Tuscaloosa, Ala., 1956.

Moneyhon, Carl H. *The Impact of the Civil War and Reconstruction on Arkansas: Persistence in the Midst of Ruin.* Baton Rouge, La., 1994.

Moore, George Ellis. *A Banner in the Hills: West Virginia's Statehood.* New York, 1963.

Moore, Samuel A. "Hostile Raid into Davis County, Iowa." *Annals of Iowa* 13 (July 1922): 362–74.

Morris, Roy, Jr. *Sheridan: The Life and Wars of General Phil Sheridan*. New York, 1992.

Mullis, Tony. *Peacekeeping on the Plains: Army Operations in Bleeding Kansas*. Columbia, Mo., 2004.

Neal, Diane, and Thomas W. Kremm. "An Experiment in Collective Security: The Union Army's Use of Armed Colonies in Arkansas." *Military History of the Southwest* 20 (Fall 1990): 169–81.

———. *Lion of the South: General Thomas C. Hindman*. Macon, Ga., 1993.

Neely, Jeremy. *The Border between Them: Violence and Reconciliation on the Kansas-Missouri Line*. Columbia, Mo., 2007.

Neely, Mark E., Jr. *The Civil War and the Limits of Destruction*. Cambridge, Mass., 1993.

Newton, Steven H. "The Confederate Home Guard: Forgotten Soldiers of the Lost Cause." *North & South* 6 (December 2002): 40–50.

———. "Evaders, Resisters, and Predators: Patterns of Anti-Confederate Behavior." *North & South* 7 (August 2004): 24–35.

Ney, Virgil. "Guerrilla War and Modern Strategy." *Orbis* 2 (Spring 1958): 66–82.

Nichols, Ronald H. *In Custer's Shadow: Major Marcus Reno*. Norman, Okla., 2000.

Niepman, Ann Davis. "General Orders No. 11 and Border Warfare during the Civil War." *Missouri Historical Review* 66 (January 1972): 185–210.

Noe, Kenneth W. "Exterminating Savages: The Union Army and Mountain Guerrillas in Southern West Virginia, 1861–1862." In *Civil War in Appalachia*, edited by Kenneth W. Noe and Shannon H. Wilson, 104–30.

———. "Red String Scare: Civil War in Southwest Virginia and the Heroes of America." *North Carolina Historical Review* 69 (July 1992): 301–22.

———. *Southwest Virginia's Railroad: Modernization and the Sectional Crisis*. Urbana, Ill., 1994.

———. "Who Were the Bushwhackers?: Age, Class, Kin, and Western Virginia's Confederate Guerrillas, 1861–1862." *Civil War History* 49 (March 2003): 5–31.

Noe, Kenneth W., and Shannon H. Wilson, eds. *The Civil War in Appalachia: Collected Essays*. Knoxville, Tenn., 1997.

Nolan, Dick. *Benjamin Franklin Butler: The Damnedest Yankee*. Novato, Calif., 1991.

Norris, David A. "'The Yankees Have Been Here!': The Story of Brigadier General Edward E. Porter's Raid on Greenville, Tarboro, and Rocky Mount, July 19–23, 1863." *North Carolina Historical Review* 73 (January 1996): 1–27

Norris, Gary D. *Tinker Dave Beaty's Independent Scouts*. Albany, N.Y., 2001.

Noyalas, Jonathan A. "The Most Hated Man in Winchester." *America's Civil War* 17 (March 2004): 30–36.

Oates, Dan, ed. *Hanging Rock Rebel: Lt. John Blue's War in West Virginia and the Shenandoah Valley*. Shippensburg, Pa., 1994.

Oates, Stephen B. "Texas under the Secessionists." *Southwestern Historical Quarterly* 67 (October 1963): 167–212.

O'Brien, Sean. *Mountain Partisans: Guerrilla Warfare in the Southern Appalachians, 1861–1865*. Westport, Conn., 1999.

O'Flaherty, Daniel. *General Jo Shelby: Undefeated Rebel*. 1954. Repr., Chapel Hill, N.C., 2000.

Olpin, Larry. "Missouri and the American Civil War Novel." *Missouri Historical Review* 85 (October 1990): 1–20.

Osborne, Randall, and Jeffrey C. Weaver. *Virginia State Rangers and State Line*. Lynchburg, Va., 1994.

Paludan, Phillip Shaw. "The American Civil War Considered as a Crisis in Law and Order." *American Historical Review* 77 (October 1972): 1013–34.

———. *Victims: A True Story of the Civil War*. Knoxville, Tenn., 1981.

Parrish, T. Michael. *Richard Taylor: Soldier Prince of Dixie*. Chapel Hill, N.C., 1992.

Parrish, William E. *History of Missouri, 1860–1875*. Columbia, Mo., 1973.

Parsons, Joseph A. "Indiana and the Call for Volunteers, April, 1861." *Indiana Magazine of History* 54 (March 1958): 1–23.

Patterson, Gerald A. *Justice or Atrocity: General George E. Pickett and the Kinston, N.C., Hangings*. Gettysburg, Pa., 1998.

Perkins, J. R. *Trails, Rails, and War: The Life of General G. M. Dodge*. Indianapolis, 1929.

Perret, Geoffrey. *Lincoln's War: The Untold Story of America's Greatest President as Commander in Chief*. New York, 2004.

Perry, Robert. *Jack May's War: Colonel Andrew Jackson May and the Civil War in Eastern Kentucky, Eastern Tennessee, and Southwestern Virginia*. Johnson City, Tenn., 1998.

Phillips, Christopher. *Missouri's Confederate: Claiborne Fox Jackson and the Creation of the Southern Identity in the Border West*. Columbia, Mo., 2000.

Pickering, David, and Judy Falls. *Brush Men and Vigilantes: Civil War Dissent in Texas*. College Station, Tex., 2000.

Pope, Thomas E. *The Weary Boys: Colonel J. Warren Keifer and the 110th Ohio Volunteer Infantry*. Kent, Ohio, 2002.

Prichard, James M. "General Orders No. 59: Kentucky's Reign of Terror." *Civil War Quarterly* 10 (September 1987): 32–34.

———. "'A Grim Warning to Others of Their Kind': The Cumberland Ford Tragedy." *North & South* 1 (September 1998): 22–24.

Pruitt, Wade, ed. *Bugger Saga: The Civil War Story of Guerrilla and Bushwhacker Warfare in Lauderdale County, Alabama*. Columbia, Tenn., 1978.

Quisenberry, A. C. "The First Kentucky Cavalry, USA." *Register of the Kentucky State Historical Society* 18 (1921): 15–20.

Rable, George C. *But There Was No Peace: The Role of Violence in the Politics of Reconstruction*. Athens, Ga., 1984.

———. *The Confederate Republic: A Revolution against Politics*. Chapel Hill, N.C., 1994.

Rafuse, Ethan S. *McClellan's War: The Failure of Moderation in the Struggle for the Union*. Bloomington, Ind., 2005.

Ramage, James A. *Gray Ghost: The Life of Col. John Singleton Mosby*. Lexington, Ky., 1999.

———. *Rebel Raider: The Life of General John Hunt Morgan*. Lexington, Ky., 1986.

———. "Recent Historiography of Guerrilla Warfare in the Civil War—A Review Essay." *Register of the Kentucky Historical Society* 103 (Summer 2005): 517–41.

Reid, Brian Holder, and Bruce Collins. "Why the Confederacy Lost." *History Today* 38 (November 1988): 32–41.

Reiger, John E. "Deprivation, Disaffection, and Desertion in Confederate Florida." *Florida Historical Quarterly* 48 (January 1970): 279–98.

Richardson, Hila Appleton. "Raleigh County, West Virginia, in the Civil War." *West Virginia History* 10 (April 1949): 213–98.

Robbins, Peggy. "By Land and by Sea." *Civil War Times Illustrated* 37 (March 1998): 42–45, 53–59.

Roberts, Bobby L. "General T. C. Hindman and the Trans-Mississippi District." *Arkansas Historical Quarterly* 32 (Winter 1973): 297–311.

Roberts, William H. *Now for the Contest: Coastal and Oceanic Naval Operations in the Civil War*. Lincoln, Neb., 2004.

Robertson, James I., Jr. *Stonewall Jackson: The Man, the Soldier, the Legend*. New York, 1997.

Robinett, Paul M., and Howard V. Canan. "The Military Career of James Craig." *Missouri Historical Review* 66 (October 1971): 49–75.

Robinson, Armstead L. *Bitter Fruits of Bondage: The Demise of Slavery and the Collapse of the Confederacy, 1861–1865*. Charlottesville, Va., 2005.

———. "In the Shadow of Old John Brown: Insurrection Anxiety and Confederate Mobilization, 1861–1863." *Journal of Negro History* 65 (Fall 1980): 279–97.

Roller, Scott. "Business as Usual: Indiana's Response to the Confederate Invasions of the Summer of 1863." *Indiana Magazine of History* 88 (March 1992): 1–25.

Royster, Charles. *The Destructive War: William Tecumseh Sherman, Stonewall Jackson, and the Americans*. New York, 1991.

Rubin, Anne Sarah. *A Shattered Nation: The Rise and Fall of the Confederacy, 1861–1868.* Chapel Hill, N.C., 2005.

Ruffner, Kevin Conley. "'More Trouble Than a Brigade': Harry Gilmor's 2nd Maryland Cavalry in the Shenandoah Valley." *Maryland Historical Magazine* 89 (Winter 1994): 389–411.

Sacher, John M. "'A Very Disagreeable Business': Confederate Conscription in Louisiana." *Civil War History* 53 (June 2007): 141–69.

Sanborn, Franklin B., ed. "Some Notes on the Territorial History of Kansas." *Collections fo the Kansas State Historical Society* 13 (1913–14): 249–65.

Sanders, Stuart W. "Bloody Bill's Centralia Massacre." *America's Civil War* 12 (March 2000): 34–40, 82.

———. "Confederate Raider's Kentucky Rampage." *America's Civil War* 12 (July 1999): 30–36.

Sarris, Jonathan D. "Anatomy of an Atrocity: The Madden Branch Massacre and Guerrilla Warfare in North Georgia, 1861–1865." *Georgia Historical Quarterly* 78 (Winter 1993): 679–710.

———. "An Execution in Lumpkin County: Localized Loyalties in North Georgia's Civil War." In *Civil War in Appalachia,* edited by Kenneth W. Noe and Shannon H. Wilson, 131–57.

———. *A Separate Civil War: Communities in Conflict in the Mountain South.* Charlottesville, Va., 2006.

———. "'Shot for Being Bushwhackers': Guerrilla War and Extralegal Violence in a North Georgia Community, 1862–1865." In *Guerrillas, Unionists, and Violence,* edited by Daniel E. Sutherland, 31–44.

Sawyer, William E. "Martin Hart: Civil War Guerrilla." *Texas Military History* 3 (Fall 1963): 146–53.

———. "The Martin Hart Conspiracy." *Arkansas Historical Quarterly* 23 (Summer 1964): 154–65.

Scaife, William R., and William Harris Bragg. *Joe Brown's Pets: The Georgia Militia, 1861–1865.* Macon, Ga., 2004.

Schultz, Duane. *Quantrill's War: The Life and Times of William Clarke Quantrill, 1837–1865.* New York, 1996.

Schutz, Wallace J., and Walter N. Trenerry. *Abandoned by Lincoln: A Military Biography of General John Pope.* Urbana, Ill., 1990.

Schwalm, Leslie A. *A Hard Fight for We: Women's Transition from Slavery to Freedom in South Carolina.* Urbana, Ill., 1997.

Scott, Kim Allen. "The Preacher, the Lawyer, and the Spoils of War." In *Civil War Arkansas,* edited by Anne J. Bailey and Daniel E. Sutherland, 101–5.

Sensing, Thurman. *Champ Ferguson: Confederate Guerilla.* Nashville, Tenn., 1942.

Sewell, Alan. "Dissent: The Free State of Winston." *Civil War Times Illustrated* 20 (December 1981): 30–37.

Shaffer, John W. *Clash of Loyalties: A Border County in the Civil War.* Morgantown, W.Va., 2003.

Sharp, Arthur G. "Battle at Lake Chicot." *Civil War Times Illustrated* 21 (October 1982): 18–23.

Shea, William L. "1862: 'A Continual Thunder.'" In *Rugged and Sublime*, edited by Mark K. Christ, 21–58.

———. "A Semi-Savage State: The Image of Arkansas in the Civil War." In *Civil War Arkansas*, edited by Anne J. Bailey and Daniel E. Sutherland, 85–99.

Sheads, Scott Sumpter, and Daniel Carroll Tooney. *Baltimore during the Civil War.* Linthicum, Md., 1997.

Sheridan, Richard B. "From Slavery in Missouri to Freedom in Kansas: The Influx of Black Fugitives and Contrabands in Kansas, 1854–65." *Kansas History* 12 (Spring 1989): 28–47.

Shillingsburg, Miriam J. "The Influence of Sectionalism on the Revisions in Simms's Revolutionary Romances." *Mississippi Quarterly* 29 (Fall 1976): 526–38.

Shingleton, Royce. "Confederate Commando: John Taylor Wood's Raid on New Berne." *Civil War* 8 (November–December 1990): 12–17, 74–75.

———. *John Taylor Wood: Sea Ghost of the Confederacy.* Athens, Ga., 1979.

Siburt, James T. "Colonel John M. Hughs: Brigade Commander and Confederate Guerrilla." *Tennessee Historical Quarterly* 51 (Summer 1992): 87–95.

Sifakis, Stewart. *Compendium of the Confederate Armies: Alabama.* New York, 1992.

Skelton, William B. *An American Profession of Arms: The Army Officer Corps, 1784–1861.* Lawrence, Kans., 1992.

Slatta, Richard W., ed. *Bandidos: The Varieties of Latin American Banditry.* New York, 1987.

Smith, David Paul. *Frontier Defense in the Civil War: Texas' Rangers and Rebels.* College Station, Tex., 1992.

Smith, Duane Allan. "The Confederate Cause in the Colorado Territory, 1861–1865." *Civil War History* 7 (March 1961): 71–80.

Smith, Edward Conrad. *The Borderland in the Civil War.* New York, 1927.

———. *A History of Lewis County, West Virginia.* Weston, W.Va., 1920.

Smith, Everard H. "Chambersburg: Anatomy of a Confederate Reprisal." *American Historical Review* 96 (April 1991): 432–55.

Smith, G. Wayne. "Nathan Goff Jr. in the Civil War." *West Virginia History* 14 (January 1953): 108–35.

Smith, John David, ed. *Black Soldiers in Blue: African American Troops in the Civil War Era.* Chapel Hill, N.C., 2002.

Smith, Myron J. *Le Roy Fitch: The Civil War Career of a Union River Gunboat Commander.* Jefferson, N.C., 2007.

Smith, Robert F. "The Confederate Attempt to Counteract Reunion Propaganda in Arkansas: 1863–1865." *Arkansas Historical Quarterly* 16 (Summer 1957): 54–62.

Smith, Troy D. "'Don't You Beg, and Don't You Dodge.'" *Civil War Times Illustrated* 40 (December 2001): 40–46, 72–73.

Smith, W. Wayne. "An Experiment in Counterinsurgency: The Assessment of Confederate Sympathizers in Missouri." *Journal of Southern History* 35 (August 1969): 361–80.

Speer, Lonnie R. *War of Vengeance: Acts of Retaliation against Civil War POWs.* Mechanicsburg, Pa., 2002.

Stanton, Donald J., et al. "General M. Jeff Thompson: Soldier-Rhetorician." *Missouri Historical Review* 71 (October 1976): 44–58.

Starr, Stephen Z. *Jennison's Jayhawkers: A Civil War Cavalry Regiment and Its Commander.* Baton Rouge, La., 1973.

Stauffer, John. "Advent among the Indians: The Revolutionary Ethos of Gerrit Smith, James McCune Smith, Frederick Douglass, and John Brown." In *Antislavery Violence*, edited by John R. McKivigan and Stanley Harrold, 236–73.

Steenburn, Donald H. "Wanted for Murder." *Civil War Times Illustrated* 40 (August 2001): 56–62.

Stevens, Peter F. *Rebels in Blue: The Story of Keith and Malinda Blalock.* Dallas, 2000.

Stiles, T. J. *Jesse James: Last Rebel of the Civil War.* New York, 2002.

Stone, Jayme Lynne. "Brother against Brother: The Winter Skirmishes along the Arkansas River, 1864–1865." In *Civil War Arkansas*, edited by Anne J. Bailey and Daniel E. Sutherland, 195–211.

Storey, Margaret M. "Civil War Unionists and the Political Culture of Loyalty in Alabama, 1860–61." *Journal of Southern History* 69 (February 2003): 71–106.

———. *Loyalty and Loss: Alabama's Unionists in the Civil War and Reconstruction.* Baton Rouge, La., 2004.

Stout, Harry S. *Upon the Altar of the Nation: A Moral History of the American Civil War.* New York, 2006.

Stutler, Boyd B. *West Virginia in the Civil War.* 2nd ed. Charleston, W.Va., 1966.

Summers, Festus P. *The Baltimore and Ohio in the Civil War.* New York, 1939.

Summers, Mark W. "'Freedom and Law Must Die Ere They Sever': The North and the Coming of the Civil War." In *Why the Civil War Came*, edited by Gabor S. Boritt, 179–200. New York, 1996.

Sutherland, Daniel E. "Abraham Lincoln, John Pope, and the Origins of Total War." *Journal of Military History* 56 (October 1992): 567–86.

———. "1864: 'A Strange, Wild Time.'" In *Rugged and Sublime*, edited by Mark K. Christ, 105–44.

———. "Forgotten Soldiers: Civil War Guerrillas." *Hallowed Ground* 2 (Summer 2001): 20–24.

———. "Guerrilla Conflict in 1864: Day of the Outlaw." In *"The Earth Reeled and Trees Trembled": Civil War Arkansas, 1863–1864*, edited by Mark K. Christ, 150–59. Little Rock, Ark., 2007.

———. "Guerrillas: The Real War in Arkansas." In *Civil War Arkansas*, edited by Anne J. Bailey and Daniel E. Sutherland, 133–53.

———. "Guerrilla Warfare, Democracy, and the Fate of the Confederacy." *Journal of Southern History* 68 (May 2002): 259–92.

———. "Mansfield Lovells's Quest for Justice: Another Look at the Fall of New Orleans." *Louisiana History* 24 (Summer 1983): 233–59.

———. *Seasons of War: The Ordeal of a Confederate Community, 1861–1865.* New York, 1995.

———. "Sideshow No Longer: A Historiographical Review of the Guerrilla War." *Civil War History* 46 (March 2000): 5–23.

———. "Without Mercy, and Without the Blessing of God." *North & South* 1 (September 1998): 12–21.

———, ed. *Guerrillas, Unionists, and Violence on the Confederate Home Front.* Fayetteville, Ark., 1999.

Tatum, Georgia Lee. *Disloyalty in the Confederacy.* Chapel Hill, N.C., 1934.

Taylor, Ethel. "Discontent in Confederate Louisiana." *Louisiana History* 2 (Fall 1961): 410–28.

Taylor, Morris F. "Confederate Guerrillas in Southern Colorado." *Colorado Magazine* 46 (Fall 1969): 304–23.

Tegtmeier, Kristen A. "The Ladies of Lawrence Are Arming!: The Gendered Nature of Sectional Violence in Early Kansas." In *Antislavery Violence*, edited by John R. McKivigan and Stanley Harrold, 215–35.

Thomas, David Y. *Arkansas in War and Reconstruction, 1861–1874.* Little Rock, 1926.

Thomas, Emory. *The Confederacy as a Revolutionary Experience.* Englewood Cliffs, N.J., 1971.

Thomas, William. "Nothing Ought to Astonish Us: Confederate Civilians in the 1864 Shenandoah Valley Campaign." In *Shenandoah Valley Campaign of 1864*, edited by Gary W. Gallagher, 222–56.

Thomsen, Paul A. *Rebel Chief: The Motley Life of Colonel William Holland Thomas, C.S.A.* New York, 2004.

Tidwell, William A., et al. *Come Retribution: The Confederate Secret Service and the Assassination of Lincoln.* Jackson, Miss., 1988.

Tingley, Donald F. "The Clingman Raid." *Journal of the Illinois State Historical Society* 56 (Summer 1963): 350–63.

Towers, Frank. *The Urban South and the Coming of the Civil War.* Charlottesville, Va., 2004.

————. "'A Vociferous Army of Howling Wolves': Baltimore's Civil War Riot of April 19, 1861." *Maryland Historian* 23 (1992): 1–27.

————, ed. "Military Waif: A Sidelight on the Baltimore Riot of 19 April 1861." *Maryland Historical Magazine* 89 (Winter 1994): 427–46.

Trotter, William R. *Bushwhackers: The Civil War in North Carolina: The Mountains*. Winston-Salem, N.C., 1988.

Trudeau, Noah Andre. *Like Men of War: Black Troops in the Civil War, 1862–1865*. Boston, 1998.

Tucker, Spencer C. *Brigadier General John D. Imboden: Confederate Commander in the Shenandoah*. Lexington, Ky., 2003.

Unnerstall, Jay. "Unprovoked Tragicomedy in St. Louis." *America's Civil War* 4 (May 1991): 30–36.

Urwin, Gregory J. W. *Custer Victorious: The Civil War Battles of General George Armstrong Custer*. East Brunswick, N.J., 1983.

————, ed. *Black Flag over Dixie: Racial Atrocities and Reciprocals in the Civil War*. Carbondale, Ill., 2004.

Utley, Robert M. *Lone Star Justice: The First Century of the Texas Rangers*. New York, 2002.

Valentine, L. L. "Sue Mundy of Kentucky: Part I." *Register of the Kentucky Historical Society* 62 (July 1964): 175–205.

————. "Sue Mundy of Kentucky: Part II." *Register of the Kentucky Historical Society* 62 (October 1964): 278–306.

Vandiver, W. D. "Two Forgotten Heroes—John Hanson McNeill and His Son Jesse." *Missouri Historical Review* 21 (April 1927): 404–19.

Voorhis, Jerry. *The Life and Times of Aurelius Lyman Voorhis*. New York, 1976.

Waal, Carla. "The First Original Confederate Drama: *The Guerrillas*." *Virginia Magazine of History and Biography* 70 (October 1962): 459–67.

Wakelyn, Jon, ed. *Southern Pamphlets on Secession, November 1860–April 1861*. Chapel Hill, N.C., 1996.

Ward, Harry W. *Between the Lines: Banditti of the American Revolution*. Westport, Conn., 2002.

Waters, Zack C. "Florida's Confederate Guerrillas: John W. Pearson and the Oklawaha Rangers." *Florida Historical Quarterly* 70 (October 1991): 133–49.

Waugh, Joan. "New England Cavalier: Charles Russell Lowell and the Shenandoah Valley Campaign of 1864." In *Shenandoah Valley Campaign of 1864*, edited by Gary W. Gallagher, 299–340.

Weaver, Jeffrey C. *The Civil War in Buchanan and Wise Counties: Bushwhackers' Paradise*. Lynchburg, Va., 1994.

————. *Thurmond's Partisan Rangers and Swann's Battalion of Virginia Cavalry*. Lynchburg, Va., 1993.

Weigley, Russell F. *The Partisan War: The South Carolina Campaign of 1780–1782*. Columbia, S.C., 1970.

Weinwert, Richard P. "Dickison: The Swamp Fox of Florida." *Civil War Times Illustrated* 5 (December 1966): 4–11, 48–50.

Weitz, Mark A. *The Confederacy on Trial: The Piracy and Sequestration Cases of 1861.* Lawrence, Kans., 2005.

————. *A Higher Duty: Desertion among Georgia Troops during the Civil War.* Lincoln, Neb., 2000.

————. *More Damning Than Slaughter: Desertion in the Confederate Army.* Lincoln, Neb., 2005.

Weller, Jac. "Nathan Bedford Forrest: An Analysis of Untutored Military Genius." *Tennessee Historical Quarterly* 18 (September 1959): 213–51.

————. "Wellington's Use of Guerrillas." *Royal United Service Institution Journal* 108 (May 1963): 153–58.

Wert, Jeffry D. *Mosby's Rangers.* New York, 1990.

West, Stephen A. "Minute Men, Yeomen, and the Mobilization for Secession in the South Carolina Upcountry." *Journal of Southern History* 71 (February 2005): 75–104.

Whitesell, Hunter B. "Military Operations in the Jackson Purchase Area of Kentucky, 1862–1865, Part I." *Register of Kentucky Historical Society* 63 (April 1965): 141–67.

————. "Military Operations in the Jackson Purchase Area of Kentucky, 1862–1865, Part II." *Register of Kentucky Historical Society* 63 (July 1965): 240–67.

————. "Military Operations in the Jackson Purchase Area of Kentucky, 1862–1865, Part III." *Register of Kentucky Historical Society* 63 (October 1965): 323–48.

Wiggenton, Thomas A., et al. *Tennesseans in the Civil War.* 2 vols. Nashville, Tenn., 1964.

Willet, Robert L. "We Rushed with a Yell." *Civil War Times Illustrated* 8 (February 1970): 16–21.

Williams, Burton J. "Missouri State Depredations in Arkansas: A Case of Restitution." *Arkansas Historical Quarterly* 23 (Winter 1964): 343–52.

Williams, David. *Rich Man's War: Class, Caste, and Confederate Defeat in the Lower Chattahoochie Valley.* Athens, Ga., 1998.

————. "'Rich Man's War': Class, Caste, and Confederate Defeat in Southwest Georgia." *Journal of Southwest Georgia History* 11 (Fall 1996): 1–42.

————, et al. *Plain Folk in a Rich Man's War: Class and Dissent in Confederate Georgia.* Gainesville, Fla., 2002.

Williams, Glenn F. "Under the Despot's Heel." *America's Civil War* 13 (May 2000): 22–28.

Wills, Brian Steel. *The Confederacy's Greatest Cavalryman: Nathan Bedford Forrest.* 1992. Repr., Lawrence, Kans., 1998.

———. *The War Hits Home: The Civil War in Southeastern Virginia*. Charlottesville, Va., 2001.

Wilson, Keith. "In the Shadow of John Brown: The Military Service of Colonels Thomas Higginson, James Montgomery, and Robert Gould Shaw in the Department of the South." In *Black Soldiers in Blue*, edited by John David Smith, 306–35.

Windham, William T. "The Problem of Supply in the Trans-Mississippi Confederacy:" *Journal of Southern History* 27 (May 1961): 149–68.

Winik, Jay. *April 1865: The Month That Saved America*. New York, 2001.

Winters, John D. *The Civil War in Louisiana*. Baton Rouge, La., 1963.

Woodward, Harold R., Jr. *Defender of the Valley: Brigadier General John Daniel Imboden, CSA*. Berryville, Va., 1995.

Worley, Ted R. "The Arkansas Peace Society of 1861: A Study in Mountain Unionism." *Journal of Southern History* 24 (November 1958): 445–56.

Wubben, Hubert H. *Civil War Iowa and the Copperhead Movement*. Ames, Iowa. 1980.

———. "The Maintenance of Internal Security in Iowa, 1861–1865." *Civil War History* 10 (December 1964): 401–15.

UNPUBLISHED SECONDARY SOURCES

Barkesdale, Ethelbert Courtland. "Semi-Regular and Irregular Warfare in the Civil War." Ph.D. dissertation, University of Texas, 1941.

Beall, Wendell P. "Wildwood Skirmishers: The First Federal Arkansas Cavalry." M.A. thesis, University of Arkansas, 1988.

Beamer, Carl B. "Gray Ghostbusters: Eastern Theatre Union Counterguerrilla Operations in the American Civil War, 1861–1865." Ph.D. dissertation, Ohio State University, 1988.

Beckenbaugh, Terry L. "The War of Politics: Samuel Ryan Curtis, Race, and the Political/Military Establishment." Ph.D. dissertation, University of Arkansas, 2001.

Bellas, Joseph R. "The Forgotten Loyalists: Unionism in Arkansas, 1861–1865." M.A. thesis, Ohio State University, 1991.

Belser, Thomas A., Jr. "Military Operations in Missouri and Arkansas, 1861–1865." Ph.D. dissertation, Vanderbilt University, 1958.

Boulden, Benjamin. "'So Long as Strangers Are the Rulers': General Frederick Steele and the Politics of Wartime Reconstruction in Arkansas." M.A. thesis, University of Arkansas, 1986.

Cox, Larry. "Hawkeye Heroes: The Iowa Southern Border Militia and the Civil War." Seminar paper, Northwest Missouri State College, June 1972. Copy in IHLA.

Daniel, John S., Jr. "Special Warfare in Middle Tennessee and Surrounding Areas, 1861–62." M.A. thesis, University of Tennessee, 1971.

Fortin, Maurice G., Jr. "Confederate Military Operations in Arkansas, 1861–1865." M.A. thesis, North Texas State University, 1978.

Geiger, Mark W. "Financial Conspiracy and the Guerrilla War in Missouri, 1861–1865." Ph.D. dissertation, University of Missouri, 2005.

Martin, James B. "The Third War: Irregular Warfare on the Western Border, 1861–1865." Ph.D. dissertation, University of Texas, 1997.

Mountcastle, John C. "The Guerrilla Problem and the Union Response: Punitive War in America, 1861–1865." Ph.D. dissertation, Duke University, 2006.

Myers, Barton A. "Executing Daniel Bright: Power, Political Loyalty, and Guerrilla Violence in a North Carolina Community, 1861–1865." M.A. thesis, University of Georgia, 2005.

Prier, Jay A. "Under the Black Flag: The Real War in Washington County, Arkansas, 1861–1865." M.A. thesis, University of Arkansas, 1998.

Ross, E. M. "Irregular Warfare during the Civil War." M.A. thesis, University of Texas, 1934.

Smith, Robert F. "Confederate Attempts to Influence Public Opinion in Arkansas, 1861–1865." M.A. thesis, University of Arkansas, 1952.

Stith, Matthew M. "At the Heart of Total War: Guerrillas, Civilians, and the Union Response in Jasper County, Missouri, 1861–1865." M.A. thesis, University of Arkansas, 2005.

Suite, Barry R. "Federal Military Policy and Strategy in Missouri and Arkansas, 1861–1863: A Study of Command Level Conflict." Ph.D. dissertation, Temple University, 1987.

Abolitionists, 11, 12, 15–16, 24–25, 28, 47

Alabama: Athens, 103, 104; Bridgeport, 104; Decatur, 103, 104; defense of, 42, 103, 181, 257–58; Greensboro, 258; guerrillas from, 51; guerrillas in, 103–6, 180–82, 257–60; Huntsville, 103, 104, 180–81, 258; Jackson County, 158; Limestone County, 45–46; militia, 103, 181–82, 260; Mobile, 42, 103, 257; Paint Rock, 104; Selma, 247; Stevenson, 181; Talladega, 275; Tuscumbia, 103; Unionists, 45–46, 106–9, 116, 175, 181, 259–60, 275; Winston County, 259

Alabama soldiers
—Confederate, 181
—Union, 181; 1st Cavalry, 259

Allen, Henry W., 216

Allen, Jack, 224

Aloe Indians, 49

American Revolution: and Civil War, 9–10, 19–20, 31, 51, 74–75, 99, 114, 117, 189, 245, 271; guerrillas in, 9–10, 19–20, 51, 74–75, 99, 114, 117

Anderson, William "Bloody Bill," 65, 199, 203, 211

Anti-Confederates, 136, 138, 186, 189, 215, 217–18, 251

Antietam campaign, 166, 246

Arizona Territory, 49

Arkansas: Batesville, 133, 211; Clarksville, 208, 210; Conway County, 209–10; Dardanelle, 136, 210; defense of, 44, 65–67; Fayetteville, 138, 206, 208–9; guerrillas from, 44; guerrillas in, 44, 65–70, 134–39, 202, 206–13; Helena, 44, 67–68, 71, 133–34, 178; Hopefield, 134–35; Little Rock, 67–68, 133, 136, 206, 208, 209–10, 213, 275; Napoleon, 134; Pine Bluff, 206, 208; politics in, 209–10; Russellville, 209–10; Searcy, 66, 138–39; Unionists, 44, 135–38, 209–10; Washington County, 212

Arkansas Peace Society, 135–36

Arkansas soldiers, Union, 138; 1st Cavalry, 138, 208–9; 1st Infantry, 138

Ashby, Turner, 29–30, 54, 77–78, 93, 94, 166, 188, 237, 239

Assessments, monetary, 20–21, 60, 123, 124, 149, 162, 220, 240, 307–8 (n. 7)

Baggs, John P., 31–32, 161

Bailey, Joe, 212

Bails, Captain, 80–81

Baltimore and Ohio Railroad, 89, 161, 238, 242

Baltimore riots, 2–6, 9, 93, 166. See also Maryland

Banks, Nathaniel P., 142, 217

Baskett, Wilford, 211

Bates, Edward, 14, 24, 122–23

Bates, Julian, 14

Baxter, George L., 171

Beall, John Y., 237

Beatty, John, 104, 105

Beaty, David "Tinker Dave," 83, 232, 273

Beauregard, Pierre G. T., 110, 185

Benjamin, Judah P., 82, 268

Bennett, Jacob, 224

Berry, Captain, 158–59

Berry, Samuel O., 224

Biffle, Jacob, 78

Bingham, George Caleb, 196–97

Bishop, Albert W., 138

Black flag (no quarter), 90, 110, 181, 203, 273–74

Black market. *See* Illicit trade

Blair, Frank, 13–14

Blazer, Richard S., 238–39

Bledsoe, Scott Willis, 82, 83, 101

Blockhouses, 146–48, 227–28

Blunt, James G., 130–31, 198–99

Blythe, Green L., 179–80

Boland, Alfred (*or* Bowline, Bolin), 122, 307 (n. 4)

Bonham, Milledge L., 185, 254

Border Rangers, 32

"Border Rangers, The" (poem), 184–85

Boreman, Arthur I., 235–36, 244–45

Boren, Henry, 219

Boudreaux, Omer, 274–75

Bounties/rewards, 74, 122, 218, 225, 273

Boykin, Alexander H., 53, 300 (n. 36)

Bradford, Augustus, 166–67

Bradford, Jefferson Davis, 215

Bragg, Braxton, 158, 168, 267

Bramlette, Thomas E., 220, 221, 222, 224, 225, 226–27

Breckinridge, John C., 268

Brevard, Theodore W., 183

Brixey, Captain, 230–31

Brown, Buck, 138, 208–9, 212, 273

Brown, Egbert B., 197

Brown, George W., 2, 4–5

Brown, H. U. M. C., 274–75

Brown, John, Jr., 58

Brown, Joseph E., 45, 113–14, 186–87, 272

Brownlow, William G. "Parson," 35

Bruce, Gideon D., 211

Brush men, 144, 219. *See also* Texas

Buchanan, Pleasant W., 209

Buckner, Simon, 37–38

Buell, Don Carlos, 81, 83–84, 95, 106

Buffaloes, xi–xii, 188, 248. *See also* North Carolina

Burbridge, Stephen G., 222–24, 225, 226, 253, 266

Bushwhackers, defined, xi–xii, 160, 166, 188–89, 232, 234, 236, 248, 249–50, 251–52

Butler, Benjamin, 72–73, 74–75, 140–41, 142, 206–8, 246–47, 266

Cajuns, 41

Camden Chasseurs, 41–42

Cameron, Simon, 41–42

Camp Jackson (Missouri), 12–13

Capers, Henry D., 257

Carney, Thomas, 193–94

Carrick's Ford, battle of, 30

Carrière, Ozème, 217

Chalmers, James R., 174, 179–80

Charleston Mercury, 185

Cheat River, 32

Cherokee Indians, 47–49, 117–18, 189, 206

Cherokee Rangers, 43

Chesapeake Bay, 237

Chewning, Jack, 93

Chickasaw Indians, 48

Choctaw Indians, 48–49, 206

Chrisman, Jack, 67

Church, Andy, 258

Civilians, treatment by military of:

Confederate, 35–36, 242, 257; Union, 4, 13, 20–21, 23, 59, 68, 72–73, 103–4, 113, 124–25, 131, 133, 134–35, 140, 145–46, 149, 151–52, 154–55, 177, 179, 184, 196–97, 206–8, 222–23, 227–28, 236, 240, 246–47, 253–55, 258, 264

Clark, Charles, 261, 263–64

Clark, Henry T., 116–17

Clark, Jerome, 225–26, 273

Cleveland, Marshall, 16

Clingman, Thomas L., 205–6

Coastal defense, 41–42, 47, 103, 113–14, 116–17

Cocker, James, 256–57

Cockrell, Jeremiah V., 133

Coffee, John T., 133

Coldwater River, 178

Cole, Henry A., 238–39

Comanche Indians, 48, 99, 142

"Comanches," 164, 238–39

Confederate Congress, 54, 67, 93–94, 101, 163–64, 238

Confederate nationalism, 53, 102, 139, 154–55, 260–61, 312 (n. 51)

Confederate soldiers, response to guerrillas, 155–56, 211–13

Confederate view of northerners, 28, 29–30, 42–43

Confederate War Department, 53–54, 71–72, 74, 93, 100–101, 163–64

Connolly, Perry (or Conley), 31–32, 87, 89

Conscription: avoiding, 106–7, 136, 142, 143, 174, 181, 189–90, 215–16, 248–50, 303 (n. 5); and guerrillas, 101, 170, 181–82, 185–86, 188, 215–16, 218–19, 221

Cool, Wat, 97

Cooper, Duncan, 94

Copperheads, 129, 130, 131, 205

Corinth, battle of, 172

Cotton: confiscated or destroyed, 73, 134–35, 151, 154, 174–75, 215, 217, 263–64; smuggled, 151, 157, 263–64. See also Illicit trade

Coulter, Isiah, 225

Cox, Mr., 276

Creek Indians, 49, 206

Creoles, 41, 217

Crook, George, 259, 270–71

Crossland, Obed C., 158

Cumberland River, 149–51, 221, 228–29

Currie, George E., 264

Curry clan, 86–87

Curtis, Henry Z., 198–99

Curtis, Samuel R., 65–66, 67–68, 133–34, 196

Cushing, William B., 237

Cushman, Albert W., 156

Custer, George A., 243–44

Cutting out, 165

Davis, Jefferson, 1, 14, 27, 66–67, 71, 94, 99, 100, 163, 206–8, 211–12, 215, 238, 262–63, 271; and military policy, 52, 53–54, 102, 178, 247–48, 250–51, 266–69

Davis, Robert W., 4

DeBow's Review, 26, 28, 93

Deserters: Confederate, 100–101, 135, 173, 174, 186, 187, 205, 210, 217, 225, 248–50, 251–52, 254, 256–57, 259–60, 260–62, 270; as guerrillas, 100–101, 138–39, 174, 181–82, 185–86, 188–90, 205, 210, 217–19, 225, 232, 238, 248–50, 251–52, 256–57, 259–62, 270, 272–73, 333–34 (n. 48); Union, 205, 210, 225, 33–34 (n. 48). See also Outliers

Detectives, 124–25, 130. See also Secret service; Spies

Dickison, John D., 183, 256
Dixie Boys, 87–89
Dodge, Grenville M., 146, 157, 175, 179, 270
Douglas, Arthur, 162–63
Downs, George, 91, 92–93
Dunbar gang, 228–29
Du Pont, Samuel F., 115–16
Dusky, Daniel (or Duskey), 31, 86–87, 89
Dusky, George (or Duskey), 91

Early, Jubal, 237–38, 240, 242, 243, 244
Ellet, Alfred W., 178–79, 215, 264–65
Ewing, Thomas, Jr., 194–97

Fairless, John A. "Jack," 188
Falkner, William C., 110–11, 171, 172–73, 174, 177, 179–80, 263
Family divisions, 35, 37, 86, 106, 236
Farm colonies, 209
Farragut, David G., 72, 140
Fennell, Nelson, 181
Fenton (Unionist), 209–10
Ferguson, Champ, 82–83, 224, 229–30, 232–33, 234, 273
Fitch, Graham N., 68–70
Fitch, LeRoy, 149–50, 169, 179, 221, 227
Fitzhugh, George, 26
Flanagan, Harris, 139
Florida: Apalachicola, 42, 114; defense of, 42, 43, 114, 182–83; Fernandina, 114; guerrillas in, 42, 114–16, 182–83, 256–57; Jacksonville, 114; Key West, 114; Pensacola, 114, 183; St. Augustine, 114; Tampa, 114, 115; Unionists, 114, 115–16, 182, 183, 256–57
Florida Rangers, 256
Florida Royals, 256–57

Florida soldiers
—Confederate: 2nd Cavalry, 183
—Union: 2nd Cavalry, 256
Folsom, Sampson N., 206
Ford, John S. "Rip," 50
Forrest, Nathan Bedford, 78, 114, 221, 224, 227, 233
Fort Jefferson (Florida), 114
Fort Leavenworth (Kansas), 130
Fort Morgan (Alabama), 42
Fort Myers (Florida), 256
Fort Pickens (Florida), 114
Fort Scott (Kansas), 198, 206
Forts Henry and Donelson campaign, 70, 77
Fort Smith (Arkansas), 136, 198, 206–8, 211
Fort Taylor (Florida), 114
Foster, Mr., 276
Fox Indians, 49
Fowler, Jacob, 125
Frémont, Jessie, 24–25, 96
Frémont, John C., 23–25, 57, 96–97, 162–63, 175, 184
French Revolution, 59, 159, 248
Frontier Guard, 11–12

Gamble, Hamilton R., 14, 15, 17–18, 19–20, 21, 23–24, 60, 64, 122, 129, 196
Garfield, John A., 81
Gatewood, John P., 186–87, 252, 260
Garig, William H., 141–42, 217–18
Garvey, Bartholomew, 161
General Orders (Union): No. 10, 194; No. 11, 194–97; No. 100, 128
Georgia: Atlanta, 42–43, 51, 253; Brooks County, 252–53; Camden, 41–42; Cassville, 254; Dahlongea, 186; defense of, 41–42, 42–43, 113–14, 185–86; Gilmor County, 252; guerrillas from, 42–43, 51,

113; guerrillas in, 116, 186–87, 251–54; Lumpkin County, 252; militia, 187, 252; Okefenokee Swamp, 252; Savannah, 113, 254; Unionists, 45, 116, 175, 185–86, 251–53, 254; West Point, 116

Germans: in Missouri, 13, 15, 23; in Texas, 142–43; prejudice against, 15

Gettysburg, battle of, 153, 166, 169, 193, 234

Gilmor, Harry W., 238, 240

Gossett, Robert, 158

Granger, Gordon, 174–75

Grant, Ulysses S., 19, 80, 97, 134–35, 146, 149, 154, 171, 175, 178, 220, 240, 242–43, 270, 274

Green, Mary Jane, 90, 96

Grierson, Benjamin H., 156, 180

Gristmills, 124, 209

Guerilla, The (newspaper), 161

"Guerilla Martyrs, The" (poem), 185

"Guerillas, The" (poem), 188

Guerrillas, 9–11, 19–20, 127–28, 165–66, 278–79; definitions of, xi–xii; in history, xii–xiii, 9–11, 26–27, 50, 60, 74–75, 80, 99–100, 117, 270; as law enforcement problem, 45–46, 225; legacy, 276–79; in literature, 10, 20, 26–27; naval, 164–65, 236–37; numbers, xi–xii

—Confederate: decline in popular support, 121, 153–55, 163, 166, 171–72, 199–200, 213, 234, 247–48, 269; effectiveness, 25, 33, 61, 73–74, 84, 106, 107, 118, 146, 173, 174–75, 206, 209, 214, 229, 258–59, 262, 264–65; efforts to control, 52–54, 74, 91, 93–94, 99–102, 157, 163–64, 237–38, 267–68; and election of 1864, 202, 224, 229, 242–43, 338 (n. 11); execution of,

33–34, 62–63, 81, 96, 123–24, 156, 213, 223–24, 234–35, 237, 243, 258–59, 273, 275–76; as outlaws, 14–15, 16, 38–39, 82, 86–87, 125–26, 157–58, 181–82, 186, 193, 195, 198–200, 203, 210–12, 220–21, 224–26, 236, 238, 248–49, 274 (*see also* Outlawry); personal traits, 65, 86–87, 199, 200–202, 211; in poetry, 162, 184–85, 188, 220; self–justification, 203, 212, 278–79; urban, 2–6, 13

Guerrillas, The (play), 162–63

Guerrilla service, attractions of: Confederate, 26–29, 34–35, 50, 51–52, 53, 76–77, 100–101, 109–10, 138–39, 167–68, 186–87, 210, 239, 268–69; Union, 14–16, 17, 30, 31–32, 83, 87–89, 136–37, 158–59, 161, 166–67, 181

Guerrilla war: as community defense, 14–15, 30, 34–35, 39–40, 43, 53, 87, 102, 109–10, 139, 186; economic impact, 73, 121, 130, 135, 199–200, 225; legality of, 33, 59–61, 63–64, 68, 74–75, 99, 126–29; as paradox, 51–54, 99–100; promotion of, 14, 26–27, 28–29, 93, 109–10, 177–78; psychological stress on enemy, 34, 59, 146; as social war, 14–15, 33, 37, 41, 90–91

Guess, Ben, 211

Guitar, Odon, 129

Gunter, William, 158

Halleck, Henry Wager, 58–61, 63–64, 97–98, 106, 111–13, 123–24, 126–28, 133, 196, 240, 254, 266

Haller, Ab, 197

Hamilton, Oliver P., 83

Harmony Rangers, 39

Harper, Ellis, 94

Harper's Weekly, 3, 22, 36, 77, 79, 84–85, 137, 148, 176, 195, 241

Harris, Isham G., 35–37

Harris, Joseph, 212

Harrison, Marcus LaRue, 208–9

Hart, Joseph, 63

Hart, Martin D., 136

Hart, Nancy, 31, 89

Harvey's Scouts, 262–63

Hawkins Battalion, 258

Hawkins gang, 228–29

Hayes, Rutherford B., 34, 83, 90

Haymond, Ben, 91

Hayne, Paul Hamilton, 188

Hays, Perregrine G. "Perry," 86–87

Hays, Upton, 133

Henry, Tom, 244

Herndon Rangers, 264–65

Heroes of America, 236

Heth, Henry, 92–93, 155

Hicks, James E., 63

Hicks, Thomas H., 2, 5, 45

Hildebrand, Sam, 200

Hindman, Thomas C., 66–67, 68–70, 139

Hines, Thomas H., 168

Hinson, Jack, 153

Holt, Joseph, 222–23, 224, 275

Holtzclaw, Clifton, 204

Home guards, 12, 19–20, 27, 30–31, 35–36, 41, 43–44, 46, 60, 64, 89, 112, 116, 130–31, 138, 143–44, 159, 174, 186, 187, 202–3, 205, 230, 234–35, 244–45, 249–50, 283 (n. 16)

Home Guards (Missouri), 12–13, 15

Hood, John Bell, 234, 266

Horton (guerrilla), 153

Howard, James, 63

Hoyt, George H., 130, 193–94

Hunter, David, 57–58, 116, 183–84, 240–42, 254

Hurlbut, Stephen A., 21, 134–35, 179

Hurst, Fielding, 175–77, 232–33

Huston, George, 115–16

Hyre, Minerva, 97

Illicit trade, 151, 157, 171, 263–64, 265

Illinois, 20; Adams County, 132; Brown County, 132; Cairo, 38; Carbondale, 39; Chicago, 37, 94; Clinton, 167; Fayette County, 205; guerrilla defense, 17, 35, 38–39, 132, 167–68, 205–6; guerrilla threat, 35, 38–39, 167–68, 204–5, 226; guerrillas in, 205–6; Little Egypt, 38–39, 132; Montgomery County, 205; Pike County, 132; pro-Confederates in, 38–39, 132, 204–5; Quincy, 132; Schyler County, 132; Scott County, 205; Shawnee-town, 167; Wayne County, 167

Illinois soldiers, 19, 59, 66, 174–75, 228, 253, 258; 7th Infantry, 153; 83rd Infantry, 154–55; 113th Infantry, 205; 129th Infantry, 147

Imboden, John D., 94, 162, 164, 238, 240

Independent Union Rangers, 256–57

Indiana: Cannelton, 168; Evansville, 227; guerrilla defense, 17, 94–95, 168, 169–70, 226–27; guerrilla threat, 17, 35, 39, 51, 94–95, 168, 226–27; guerrillas in, 168–70, 227; home guards, 168, 169; Indianapolis, 37, 168; Madison, 39; pro-Confederates in, 39, 227; Terre Haute, 227; Washington County, 227

Indiana Legion, 168

Indiana soldiers, 80, 151–52, 169, 258; 21st Infantry, 73; 46th Infantry, 68–70

Indians, 189; in Arkansas, 47–48,

206; in Florida, 47; as guerrillas, 48–49, 117–18; image of, 28–29, 47, 99; in North Carolina, 47–48, 117–18, 189; style of fighting, 28–29, 99, 206; in Texas, 47–49, 142, 144, 218–19. *See also individual tribes*

Indian Territory, 48–49, 75, 143–44

Ingrun, James, 138

Iowa: Border Brigade, 131–32; Davis County, 204; Fremont County, 61; guerrilla defense, 17, 131–32; guerrillas in, 17, 131–32, 204; guerrilla threat, 16–17, 61, 131–32, 204; pro-Confederates in, 131–32; refugees in, 17, 132

Iowa soldiers, 59, 66, 213, 228; 5th Cavalry, 152–53, 154–55

Iuka, battle of, 172

Jackman, Sidney, 133

Jackson, Claiborne, 12, 13–14, 25

Jackson, Jim, 204

James, Frank, 203, 277, 279

James, Jesse, 203, 277

Jayhawkers, defined, xi–xii, 97, 130, 133, 134, 151, 173, 210, 212, 215–16, 262, 271

Jenkins, Albert G., 32, 76, 161, 167

Jennison, Charles R., 11, 15–16, 58, 60, 193–94, 265–60

Jessee, George M., 224

Jessie Scouts, 96

Johnson, Adam R., 94, 168, 224, 227

Johnson, Alf, 134

Johnson, Andrew, 81–82, 83, 159–60, 229, 232

Johnson, James, 235

Johnston, Albert Sidney, 77

Johnston, Joseph E., 33, 92, 267, 268, 273

Jones, Charles C., Jr., 114

Kanawha River, 30

Kansas: Baxter Springs, 198–99; Council Grove, 130; jayhawkers, 11, 15–16, 48–49, 50, 58, 61, 193–94, 196; Lawrence, 193–96, 199, 210, 236, 242, 265–66; Leavenworth, 193; and Missouri, 11, 15–16, 43, 129–31, 193–94, 196–97, 239; Paola, 193–94; politics in, 23–24, 194–96

Kansas soldiers, 97, 196–97; 7th Cavalry, 58, 113, 153; 11th Cavalry, 58, 113, 153; 9th Infantry, 131

Kaw Indians, 49

Keary, Patrick F., 215

Keifer, Joseph W., 83–84, 89, 101–2, 104, 107, 109

Kelley, Benjamin F., 89, 270–71

Kentucky: Alexandria, 80; Bowling Green, 149; Brandenburg, 318 (n. 41); Caseyville, 149; Clinton County, 82; Columbus, 38; Cynthiana, 94–95; defense of, 51; Frankfort, 37, 157–58; guerrillas in, 38, 51, 78–84, 94–95, 152, 155–56, 157–60, 220–26; Harrodsburg, 225; Henderson, 167; Henry County, 226; Louisville, 225, 274, 275; Marion County, 226; militia, 220; Nelson County, 225–26; Paducah, 38; politics in, 36–38, 221, 223, 224; Simpson County, 225–26; State Guards, 37–38, 77; strategic importance, 37; Unionists, 37–38, 80–81, 157–60, 221–22; Woodford County, 226

Kentucky soldiers, Union, 170; 14th Cavalry, 159–60

King, Sarah "Kate," 201

Kiowa Indians, 48, 99

Kirk, George W., 232–33, 250–51, 277

Kirk, Lewis, 94

Kirkwood, Samuel J., 16–17, 61, 131
Knights of the White Camelia, 277
Knoxville Whig, 35
Koch, Elers, and family, 173, 261–62
Ku Klux Klan, 277

Lake Erie, 169, 237
Lane, James H., 11–12, 16, 23–24, 58, 97, 193–94, 253, 265–66
Laurel Hill, battle of, 30
Lazear, Bazel F., 196
Leased plantations, 214, 215, 263–64
Lee, Fitzhugh, 237–38
Lee, Robert E., 92–93, 94, 95–96, 99–100, 102, 164, 165, 168, 237–38, 266–68
Leslie's Illustrated Magazine, 62, 112, 150
Letcher, John, 27, 33, 91–93, 95, 242
Lexington Rifles, 77
Lieber, Francis, 126–29
Liddell, St. John Richardson, 216
Lincoln, Abraham, 1–2, 11–12, 23, 64, 105–6, 122–23, 159–60, 184, 196, 202, 209–10, 213–14, 269, 273–74; and military policy, 24–25, 57–58, 95–96, 97–98, 104–5, 109, 133, 178, 222, 242
Livingston, Robert R., 208
Loan, Benjamin, 125
Longstreet, James, 227
Loudoun Rangers, 238–40
Louisiana: Alexandria, 216; Baton Rouge, 71, 72, 73, 140, 217; Bayou Sarah, 142; defense of, 41, 70–71, 139; Donaldsonville, 140, 141; guerrillas from, 51; guerrillas in, 70–75, 139–42, 213–18, 274–75; Houma, 73; jayhawkers in, 215–16; New Orleans, 41, 70, 72, 77, 139, 142; Opelousas, 71; Port Hudson, 71, 139; St. Landry's Parish, 217;
Shreveport, 217; Simmsport, 179; Unionists, 72, 213–14, 215–17
Louisiana soldiers, Confederate, 268; 1st Cavalry, 78; 3rd Cavalry, 215; 4th Cavalry, 216–17; 9th Partisan Rangers, 215
Louisville and Nashville Railroad, 223
Louisville Daily Journal, 225
Love, James H., 138–39
Lovell, Mansfield, 70–71, 72–73
Lowry, W. W., 174, 177
Lyon, Hylon B., 224
Lyon, Nathaniel, 12, 13–14

Maddox, George T., 138–39
Magoffin, Beriah, 37–38
Magrath, Andrew C., 272
Magruder, Henry C., 225–26, 273
Magruder, John B., 143
Mallory, Stephen, 165
Mankins, Peter, 138
Marion, Francis, 10, 20, 26, 29, 43, 76, 78, 245, 271
Marmaduke, John, 133
Marshall, Eugene, 152–53, 158, 259
Marshall, Humphrey, 155–56
Martin, Julia, 201–2
Martin, R. C., 141
Martin, William, 138
Maryland: Annapolis, 5–6; Cumberland, 270–71; guerrillas in, 5–6, 166–67; Lebanon, 166–67; Unionists, 2, 4–5, 166–67. *See also* Baltimore riots
Maryland Avengers, 166–67
Maryland soldiers
—Confederate: 2nd Cavalry Battalion, 238
—Union: Home Brigade of Maryland Cavalry, 238–39
Massachusetts soldiers, 6th Infantry, 1–5

Mayfield, Ella, 201
Mayfield, Jennie, 201
Mayfield, Sallie, 201
McCabe, James Dabney, 162–63
McCallum, Charlotte, 235
McCallum, Cynthia, 235
McClellan, George B., 32, 33, 95–96, 202
McCook, Robert L., 84–85
McCulloch, Ben, 50, 51
McCulloch, Henry, 199, 219
McKean, Thomas J., 132
McNeil, John, 123–24, 206–9
McNeill, John Hanson, 164, 238–39, 242, 250–51
McNeill's Rangers, 238–39, 240, 270–71, 274, 344 (n. 51)
McRae, Dandridge, 139
McWaters, James A., 140, 141
Means, Samuel C., 239–40
Meigs, John R., 243, 266
Memphis and Little Rock Railroad, 208
Mendenhall, Willard, 198, 200
Merrill, Lewis, 123
Mexican War: guerrillas in, 99–100; military commissions, 63, 125, 211, 235, 275
Mill Spring, battle of, 77
Milroy, Robert H., 161–62, 164, 234–35, 266, 274
Milton, John, 42, 114–15, 182–83, 256, 257
Minnesota, guerrilla defense, 17
Minnesota troops, 7th Infantry, 205
Minutemen (Missouri), 12
Mississippi: Austin, 179, 265; Biloxi, 42; Bolivar County, 264; Choctaw County, 174, 261; Corinth, 109, 172, 175; defense of, 42, 43, 109, 171, 260–61; Eastport, 179; guerrillas from, 27, 51; guerrillas in, 109–13, 260–65; Hancock County, 262; Hinds County, 180; Holly Springs, 171; Jackson, 174, 180, 260, 261; Jones County, 262; militia, 110; Mississippi City, 42; Natchez, 263; Pass Christian, 42; Pearlington, 173–74; Reinzi, 174; Tippah County, 110–11, 175; Unionists, 111, 174, 175, 261–62; Vicksburg, 71, 133, 171, 174, 260
Mississippi Marine Brigade, 178–79, 215, 264–65, 324 (n. 23)
Mississippi River, 20, 70–71, 111, 133–35, 140, 145, 177–79, 214, 217, 228, 264
Mississippi soldiers, Union, 1st Battalion Mounted Rifles, 261
Missouri: Centralia, 203, 279; Enrolled Missouri Militia, 64; Forsyth, 122; guerrillas in, 14–15, 18–25, 58–65, 121–26, 129–31, 200–204, 275; Hannibal, 18; Independence, 131; Ironton, 19; Jackson County, 64–65; Jefferson City, 14; Johnson County, 196; and Kansas, 11, 15–16, 58, 129–31; Kansas City, 131; Lafayette County, 196; Lexington, 129–30; Marion County, 21; Mexico, 126; militia, 12–13, 15, 64, 123, 202–4, 275; Palmyra, 121–22; politics in, 23–24, 129, 196, 202; Rolla, 68, 200; St. Joseph, 129; St. Louis, 12–14, 60, 202; Shelbyville, 15; Springfield, 23; State Guard, 13, 14, 19–20; Unionists, 12–13, 18, 23, 60–61, 126, 196, 275; Warrensburg, 121
Missouri soldiers, Union: 1st Cavalry (Militia), 196; 9th Cavalry (Militia), 129; 11th Cavalry, 122
Mitchel, Ormsby M., 103–6, 107, 180

Mobberly, John W., 239, 273

Mobile and Ohio Railroad, 113, 146, 156–57

Moccasin Rangers, 31–32, 86–89, 91, 92, 161

Montgomery, James, 11, 15–16, 184

Montgomery, William E., 263–65

Mooney, Funderburk, 174, 263

Moore, Andrew B., 45–46

Moore, James M., 212

Moore, Thomas O., 70–72, 74, 139–40, 141

Morgan, John Hunt, 76–80, 81, 83, 93, 105–6, 113, 114, 117, 155–56, 157–58, 166, 188, 204, 220–21, 224, 225, 269, 305–6 (n. 39); raids by, 94–95, 168–70, 220–21, 222, 226, 227

Morgan, John T., 105, 257

Morrow, Tom, 224

Morton, Oliver P., 39

Mosby, John Singleton, 165–66, 225–26, 236, 238–39, 240–45, 265–66, 269, 273, 278–79, 305–6 (n. 39)

"Mountain Federals," 136

Mountain Forest Rangers, 43, 45

Mountain Marksmen, 90

Munday, Sue, 225. *See also* Clark, Jerome

Napier, T. Alonzo, 94

Napoleonic warfare, 78, 99

Nebraska: guerrilla defense, 17, 49; guerrilla threats, 49

Nebraska soldiers, 1st Cavalry, 208

New England: response to guerrilla war, 5; soldiers from, 243

New York City, 1, 170, 245

New York Times, 123–24

Noncombatants. *See* Civilians

North Carolina: Beaufort, 41; Cape Fear, 237; defense of, 41, 116–17, 185–86; Elizabeth City, 187; Guard for Home Defense, 190, 249; guerrillas in, 41, 116–18, 187–90, 237, 246–51, 275; Hertford County, 188; Kinston, 347 (n. 11); Madison County, 189; militia, 117, 189, 190, 249–50; New Bern, 116–17, 187; Plymouth, 116–17, 187–88, 237; Roanoke Island, 116–17; Shelton Laurel, 189; Unionism, 44–45, 116–18, 185–86, 187–90, 248–51, 275; Washington, 116–17

North Carolina soldiers
—Confederate, 268; 64th Infantry, 189
—Union: 2nd Mounted Infantry, 250–51; 3rd Mounted Infantry, 250–51

North Missouri Railroad, 20–21

Nueces River, 143

Ohio: Cincinnati, 37, 94–95, 170; guerrilla defense, 94–95, 167; guerrillas in, 161, 169; guerrilla threat, 30–31, 32, 35, 39–40, 51, 94–95, 167; home guards, 30–31, 169; pro-Confederates in, 30–31; West Point, 169

Ohio River, 30, 32, 37, 39, 94–95, 149–50, 167, 226–27

Ohio soldiers, 59, 61, 95, 103–4, 105, 145, 152, 214

Oklawaha Rangers, 115

Outlawry, 125–26, 135, 181–82, 188, 197–98, 210, 215–17, 218–19, 224–25, 232–33, 236, 248–49, 251–52, 254–56, 259, 260–62, 276–77

Outliers, 181–82, 186, 248–49. *See also* Conscription; Deserters

Overland campaign, 228–29, 240, 242–43

Owens, Bill, 232

Paine, Eleazor A., 223, 234–35, 266
Partisan Leader, The (novel), 10, 26,
    162–63
Partisan Ranger Act, 67, 70–71, 93–
    94, 100–101, 109, 113, 117, 139–40,
    185, 256, 263; as paradox, 100–101
Partisan Rangers, 71–72, 74, 93–94,
    109–11, 136, 140–42, 156–57, 163,
    165–66, 172, 177, 178, 181–82, 183,
    187–88, 215, 250, 257; criticism of,
    74, 93–94, 171–72, 187, 190, 237–
    38, 247; reduction of, 141, 163–64,
    171–72, 183, 215, 238, 256, 263
Partisans: in American Revolution,
    9–10; defined, xi–xii, 9–10
Partizans. *See* Partisans
Pea Ridge, battle of, 65
Pearson, John W., 115
Pemberton, John C., 174, 178, 185
Peninsula campaign, 92, 105–6
Pennsylvania: Chambersburg, 242,
    266; Philadelphia, 47, 94; Pitts-
    burgh, 161
Pennsylvania soldiers, 33–34, 97, 124;
    militia, 2
Perkins band, 158
Pettus, John J., 109–10, 111, 172–73,
    177
Phillippi, battle of, 30
Pierpont, Francis H., 30–31, 91, 162,
    235–36
Pike, Albert, 49
Piney Woods Rangers, 42
Polk, Leonidas, 38, 259–60
Pool, John, 190
Pope, John, 20–21, 23, 97–98, 105–6
Porter, David D., 149–51, 178–79, 214,
    265
Porter, Joseph C., 121–22
Prairie Grove, battle of, 133, 138–39
Prairie Rangers, 140
Prentice, George D., 225

Price, Sterling, 13–14, 19–20, 25, 57,
    60–61, 63–64, 65–66, 171, 172,
    202–3, 266, 295 (n. 24)
Provost marshal, 107, 123, 124–25,
    135, 156, 202, 205

Quantrill, William C., 64–65, 125,
    130–31, 193–96, 198–200, 202–4,
    215, 225, 265–66, 274, 278, 355
    (n. 32)

Railroads: as guerrilla targets, 20, 22,
    32, 39, 59–60, 61, 77, 78, 146–47,
    175, 205, 242; protection of, 20–
    21, 30, 32, 61, 72, 89, 113, 146–48,
    227–28, 253. *See also railroads by
    name*
Rains, James, 133
Randolph, George W., 74, 93–94,
    95–96, 155, 163
Rappahannock River, 237
Reconstruction, 276–77
Rector, Henry M., 66–67
Red Legs, xi–xii, 130–31
Red River, 48, 49; campaign, 217
Red Strings, 236
Refugees: banishment, 125, 145–46,
    194–97, 212–13; black, 133–34,
    157, 180, 182, 214, 263; white, 11,
    17, 35, 44, 49, 50–51, 61–62, 96,
    131–32, 135, 138, 182, 213, 214, 227
"Revanche, En," (poem), 188
Reynolds, Thomas C., 14, 23, 199–200
Richardson, Robert V., 156–57, 179–
    80, 263
Rich Mountain, battle of, 30
Rightor, John, 91
Rightor, Peter B., 86–87, 91
River traffic: as guerrilla targets, 20,
    68–70, 77, 111, 134–35, 140, 145,
    147–51, 177–79, 206, 227, 228–29,
    264; protection of, 133–35, 140,

145–46, 147–51, 177–79, 227–28.
  See also rivers by name
Robinson, Charles, 16, 23–24, 58
Roddey, Philip D., 227, 257, 258
Rodgers, John B., 234
Rosecrans, William S., 32, 33, 147,
  175, 205–6
Rosser, Thomas, 237–38, 268–69
Rousseau, Lovell H., 107
Ruffin, Edmund, 27, 29–30, 37, 40,
  76, 221, 247–48, 265–66, 269
Ruffin, Thomas, 247–48
Ruggles, Daniel, 27, 74–75
Rules of war, disputed, 59, 60–61,
  63–64, 68–70, 74–75, 76, 81, 95–
  96, 126–29, 178
Rutherford, George W., 67, 209

Sac Indians, 49
St. Johns River, 115, 183, 256–57
Savage war, defined, 28–29, 102
Scales, Cordelia, 177
Scarborough, Oscar, 229
Schofield, John M., 64, 123–24, 193–
  96, 197, 250, 275
Scott, John S., 78, 215, 217
Scott, Winfield, 11–12
Scottish Chiefs, 187
Scouters, 236
Secret service (Union), 39, 175. *See
  also* Detectives
Secret societies, 135–36, 236. *See also
  by name*
Seddon, James A., 128, 163–64, 238,
  268
Seminole Indians, 28, 47–48, 99
Sexton, Green, 224
Shaw, Robert Gould, 184
Shelby, Joseph O., 133, 196, 197
Shenandoah Valley, 87, 93, 94, 237–
  38, 240–44, 254
Sheridan, Philip H., 242–44, 266

Sherman, William T., 13, 180, 194,
  213, 240, 251–52, 253–54, 266,
  271–72; and guerrillas, 145–46,
  149, 154, 175, 200, 202, 222, 223–
  24, 234, 253–54
Shiloh, battle of, 78, 109
Shoemaker, Isaac, 263
Shorter, John Gill, 103, 104, 105, 181–
  82, 257–58, 259
Sigel, Franz, 240
Simms, William Gilmore, 10, 26, 28–
  29, 184–85, 271
Sioux Indians, 168, 259
Slaves: assist Union army, 74, 107–9,
  157–58; and Confederate guerrillas, 46–47, 107, 111–12, 114–15,
  180, 181–82, 229–30, 246–47,
  262–63, 272–73; emancipation
  of, 15–16, 24–25, 74, 109, 129,
  132, 161, 180–81, 183–84, 246; as
  political issue, 24–25, 109, 221,
  223; rebellion by, 46–47, 108–9,
  111, 129–30, 173–74, 187, 188, 232,
  250, 252–53, 262–64, 272–73;
  and Unionists, 46–47, 107–9
Smith, Edmund Kirby, 48–49, 199–
  200, 215
Smith, Mary Jane, 201
Smith, William Tucker "Tuck," 209
Snake Hunters, 31–32, 161
Social classes, 35, 45, 106, 159, 172–73
South Carolina: Bluffton, 184; Columbia, 272; Darien, 184; defense of,
  43, 183–84, 254–56, 271–72; guerrillas from, 27, 53, 113, 271; guerrillas in, 185, 271–73; militia, 272;
  Pickens County, 256; Pineville, 272
Southern Kansas Jay-Hawkers, 16
Southern Literary Messenger, 185
Southern perceptions of northerners,
  27–28, 29–30, 76, 94
Spies, 175. *See also* Detectives

Spriggs, John S., 91, 93, 95–96
Springer, Francis, 211
Stanton, Edwin D., 95–96, 97–98, 104–6, 111–13, 196, 239–40
Starnes, James W., 78
Steed's Rangers, 173–74
Stevenson, Carter L., 178
Stewart, John, 16
Stockades. *See* Blockhouses
Stokes, William B., 160, 232–33
Strachan, William R., 123–24
Street, Sol, 147, 156, 174, 175–77, 179–80, 224, 263
Strickland, William W., 256–57
Stuart, James E. B., 165–66, 238
Sumter, Thomas, 271
Survival lying, 80
Sutherland, Edwin W., 178
Swamp Dragoons, 87–89, 238–39

Taliaferro, Bob, 216
Tallahatchie River, 178
Taylor, Richard, 139–40, 141, 216, 269
Taylor, W. A., 140
Telegraph lines, as guerrilla target, 32, 59–60, 72, 77, 78, 81, 90, 201–2, 206, 208
Tennessee: Betsy Town, 149; Chattanooga, 106, 227, 253, 257; Clarksville, 154–55; Covington, 156; Dechard, 84; Fentress County, 83, 232; Gallatin, 147, 223; Greenville, 82; guerrillas from, 38; guerrillas in, 34–35, 78–84, 95, 106, 147, 152–60, 223, 227–35, 250–51, 274; Hickman County, 229; Humphreys County, 229; Knoxville, 35, 227–28, 232, 276; La Grange, 147; McMinnville, 159; Memphis, 71, 77, 81, 111, 134–35, 145–46, 178, 227–28, 260; Murfreesboro, 151–52; Nashville, 77, 81, 146, 234, 253; Palmyra, 149; politics in, 35–37; Randolph, 145; Robertson County, 158; Tullahoma, 230–31, 234–35; Unionists, 34–37, 44–45, 80–81, 117–18, 157–60, 175, 188–89, 228–29, 230–34, 250–51; Warren County, 234; Waverly, 152–53; White County, 82; Winchester, 84
Tennessee River, 149–51
Tennessee soldiers
—Confederate: 3rd Cavalry, 78; 5th Cavalry, 160; 19th Cavalry, 78
—Union: 5th Cavalry, 160; 6th Cavalry, 175–77
Terry, Benjamin F., 50
Texas: Austin, 218; Collins County, 219; Cooke County, 144; Dallas, 143; defense of, 50, 142; Fredericksburg, 143, 219; Frontier Regiment, 144; Gainsville, 143–44, 218; Galveston, 47; guerrillas from, 50, 66, 73–74, 78, 134; guerrillas in, 53, 142–44, 199–200, 218–19; San Antonio, 50–51; Unionists, 50–51, 142–44, 218–19
Texas Rangers, 50–51, 78, 144, 259–60
Thomas, William Holland, 117–18, 189, 250–51
Thomison, E. D., 87
Thompson, Gideon, 133
Thompson, Meriwether Jefferson, 14, 20, 23, 25, 59, 93, 111, 273, 274
Thurmond, William, 164, 344 (n. 51)
Todd, George, 65, 203–4
Todd, Samuel M., 140
Tories, defined, 31
Tough, William S., 130
Trevor, Douglas, 10, 162–63
Triplett, Marshall, 93, 95–96
Tucker, John, 87

Tucker, Nathaniel Beverley, 10, 26, 162–63
Turchin, John B., 104, 105–6, 206–8
Twiggs, David E., 50

Union League, 142–43
U.S. loyalty oath, 72, 77, 90, 135, 154–55, 157, 215, 234. *See also* Survival lying
U.S. military policy: conciliatory, 18–19, 24–25, 75, 80, 95, 106, 293 (n. 9); retaliatory, 20–21, 24, 33, 58–60, 72, 96–98, 103–6, 121–23, 145–46, 153, 157, 174–75, 194–96, 234, 240–44, 246–47, 254
U.S. Navy: blockade by, 114, 115–16, 164, 182, 256–57; counterguerrilla operations, 73, 115–16, 124–25, 140, 149–51, 178–79, 182, 183, 237
U.S. soldiers: African American, 183–84, 221, 229–30, 246–47, 256; attitudes toward guerrillas, 18–20, 23, 33–34, 58–59, 105, 214–15, 258; attitudes toward white southerners, 18–25, 33, 80–81, 89–90, 124; counterguerrilla operations, 89–90, 113, 159, 161–62, 175–77, 265; demoralized, 21, 34, 59, 109, 146, 151–53, 259; experiences with guerrillas, 18–20, 33–34, 58–59, 66, 134, 146, 152–53, 227–28; guerrilla "hunters," 89, 138, 153, 159–60, 175–77, 178–79, 232–33, 234–35, 238–40, 250–51, 256–57; raids by, 133–34, 139–40, 171, 173, 174, 177, 181, 187, 213–14, 222–24, 246–47, 258, 260–61; retaliation against guerrillas, 20–25, 59, 61, 66, 84, 105, 208–9, 240–42, 253–54; as "scouts," 113, 124–25, 130, 175; and Unionists, 80–81, 87, 158

Vance, Zebulon, 164, 186, 189–90, 247, 249–51, 272
Van Dorn, Earl, 65–66, 110, 171
Varner, Jacob, 89
Vaughn, Richard C., 129–30
Vickery, John, 252–53
Vicksburg campaign, 153, 169, 180, 193, 194, 257, 259, 261
Vidette, The (newspaper), 322 (n. 67)
Vigilance committees, 43–44, 45, 46–47, 106–7, 111, 135–36, 142–44, 190, 244–45
Virginia: Alexandria, 29; Danville, 267; Fairfax County, 166; Fauquier County, 166; guerrillas in, 27–30, 165–66, 236–37, 238–45; Hampton, 29; Hanover County, 27–28; Lexington, 242; Loudoun County, 166, 239, 244, 247; Newtown, 240; Norfolk, 246; Petersburg, 267; Prince William County, 166; Richmond, 267, 269; Saltville, 229–30; Staunton, 86; Unionists, 236, 244; Winchester, 242
Virginia Military Institute, 242
Virginia and North Carolina Irrepressibles, 27–28
Virginia soldiers
—Confederate: 7th Cavalry, 29; 8th Cavalry, 32; 35th Cavalry Battalion ("Comanches"), 238–39
—Union: Loudoun Rangers, 238–40
Virginia State Line, 93
Virginia State Rangers, 91–93

Walker, Leroy Pope, 27
Wallace, Lew, 39
Wallis, S. Treacle, 188
War weariness, 121, 154, 234, 236, 269–70
Washington, D.C., 1–5, 11–12, 242

Watie, Carlos, 50–51
Watie, Stand, 49, 65–66, 206, 274
Watts, Thomas H., 257–58, 259–60
Webster, Moses, 224
Welles, Gideon, 149, 214
Westcott, John, 183
West Virginia: Beverly, 33–34; Charleston, 30, 31, 161; Clarksburg, 32; Fayette County, 87; Gilmer County, 235–36; Grafton, 161; guerrillas in, 30–34, 84–96, 160–62, 235–36, 242, 244–45; Hardy County, 87; Harpers Ferry, 30, 33; Huntersville, 161; Parkersburg, 89, 161; Pendleton County, 87–89; Putnam County, 161; Unionists, 30–32, 86–91, 96–97, 161, 235–36; Weston, 34; Wheeling, 30, 96, 161
West Virginia soldiers, Union: 1st Infantry, 89; 11th Infantry, 89
Wheeler, Joseph, 227
White, Elijah V., 164, 237–39, 240
White, William, 256–57
White River (Arkansas), 68–70, 208
Wide-Awakes (Missouri), 12
Wild, Edward R., 246–47, 266
Williams, Thomas, 72

Williams, Thomas Jefferson, 209–10, 277
Wilson, White, 174
Wilson's Creek, battle of, 14, 23, 25
Wingfield, James H., 215
Wisconsin, guerrilla defense, 17
Wisconsin soldiers, 204, 232; 30th Infantry, 226
Women: aiding guerrillas, 201–2, 253–54; as guerrillas, 27, 31–32, 35, 201–2, 331 (n. 22); rape of, 216–17, 226, 274; treatment by guerrillas, 23, 97, 202, 210, 212, 226, 230, 255–56, 274; treatment by soldiers, 68, 131, 151–52, 177, 221, 222, 234–35, 246–47, 253–54, 257, 258; as "war widows," 201. *See also personal names*
Wood, John J., 105
Wood, John Taylor, 165, 237
Worming expeditions, 178

Yates, Richard, 38–39, 167, 205–6
Yazoo River, 178
Young, John V., 161
Younger brothers, 277

Zollicoffer, Felix K., 35–37